CORPORATE PRACTICE HANDBOOK

CORPORATE PRACTICE HANDBOOK

Sponsored by
The Committee on Continuing Legal Education
of the
New York State Bar Association

Copyright 1992
by
New York State Bar Association
All rights reserved
Library of Congress Catalog Card Number: 92-61676
ISBN Number: 0-942954-55-6

to D.J.E. and C.A.M.

CORPORATE PRACTICE HANDBOOK

Prepared by
THE NEW YORK STATE BAR ASSOCIATION

EDITORS
Raymond W. Merritt
Clifford R. Ennico

AUTHORS

Leona Beane	Elisabeth Tavss Ohman
Michael A. Buxbaum	William A. Perrone
Henry M. Cohn	Stuart B. Ratner
Clifford R. Ennico	Alexander W. Samor
Elizabeth A. Hartnett	Orrin E. Tilevitz
Idelle A. Howitt	Cornelius S. Van Rees
Raymond W. Merritt	Joanne M. White

ABOUT THE EDITORS

CLIFFORD R. ENNICO practices corporate, commercial, securities and international law in the Southport, Connecticut law firm of Kleban & Samor, P.C., where he is a specialist in the legal problems of the emerging growth business. He received his A.B. degree from Dartmouth College in 1975 and his J.D. degree in 1980 from Vanderbilt University School of Law, where he was articles editor of the *Vanderbilt Law Review* and law clerk to the late New York State Comptroller, Arthur Levitt Sr. Mr. Ennico was editor of *The New York Corporate Handbook*, published by NYSBA in 1983, and *Corporate Counseling*, published by NYSBA in 1988, and authored the Corporate and Partnership Law sections of *Pitfalls of Practice*, to be published by NYSBA in 1993. He is also the author of *The Business Lawyer's Handbook*, a guide to the business lawyer's life and work published by Clark Boardman Callaghan (375 Hudson Street, New York, New York 10014, $39.95 softcover), and *The Legal Job Interview: Winning the Law-Related Job in Today's Market*, which is published by Biennix Corporation (2490 Black Rock Turnpike, Suite 407, Fairfield, Connecticut 06430-2404, $25.00 softcover). Mr. Ennico is a frequent speaker at programs on corporate law and practice sponsored by the New York State Bar Association, including "Drafting Documents for the Closely Held Corporation," "Buying and Selling the Small Business," and "Forming and Advising Businesses."

RAYMOND W. MERRITT practices general corporate, securities and partnership law as a senior member of the New York City firm of Willkie Farr & Gallagher. He received his undergraduate degree from The College of the Holy Cross in 1960 and his law degree from Columbia University Law School in 1963, where he was an editor of the *Columbia Law Review*. Actively involved in various bar association matters, Mr. Merritt served as the editor-in-chief of *The New York Corporate Handbook*, which was published in 1983 by the New York State Bar Association, and was a co-author of *The Partnership Hand-*

book, which was published in 1986 by the New York State Bar Association and the New York State Society of Certified Public Accountants. Mr. Merritt was co-editor of the two volumes of *Corporate Counseling*, published by the New York State Bar Association in 1988. Along with Clifford R. Ennico, Mr. Merritt serves as editor-in-chief of the *Corporate Counseling Monograph Series*, a continuing series of monographs on subjects relating to corporate practice. Mr. Merritt also serves as a trustee of the Loyola Foundation, the Murray and Isabella Rayburn Foundation, Inc., and The Buhl Family Foundation.

ABOUT THE AUTHORS

LEONA BEANE is a Full Professor of Law at Baruch College (City University) in New York City. She has been a practicing attorney involved in the closely held business, estates, and conservatorships, and is an active member of several bar associations. The past few years, she has chaired and lectured at several programs for the New York State Bar Association, particularly "Drafting Corporate Documents for the Close Corporation" and "Forming and Advising Businesses." She has also chaired and lectured at programs for the American Bar Association, the New York County Lawyers' Association, and other bar associations. She is a past president of both the National Association of Women Lawyers and the Association of Small Claims Arbitrators. Professor Beane has published several articles on partnership law, contracts and the Uniform Commercial Code, and is the author of *The Essentials of Partnership Law* (Kendall Hunt, 1982) and *The Essentials of Corporation Law* (Kendall Hunt, 2d ed. 1987).

MICHAEL A. BUXBAUM is a partner in the New York City law firm of Kreindler & Relkin, P.C., where he specializes in corporate and tax law. He is a graduate of Yale University and the University of California School of Law (Berkeley-Boalt Hall), and holds an LL.M. degree in taxation from the New York University School of Law. Mr. Buxbaum is currently Adjunct Professor of Law at the Bridgeport (Connecticut) School of Law of Quinnipiac College, where he teaches courses in federal income taxation, corporate reorganizations and income tax accounting.

HENRY M. COHN is a partner in the New York City law firm of Willkie Farr & Gallagher, where he specializes in tax law. He received his A.B. degree from Princeton University in 1977, his J.D. degree from St. John's University School of Law in 1980, and his LL.M. (taxation) degree from New York University School of Law in 1981.

CLIFFORD R. ENNICO practices corporate, commercial, securities and international law in the Southport, Connecticut law firm of Kleban & Samor, P.C., where he is a specialist in the legal problems of the emerging growth business. He received his A.B. degree from Dartmouth College in 1975 and his J.D. degree in 1980 from Vanderbilt University School of Law, where he was articles editor of the *Vanderbilt Law Review* and law clerk to the late New York State Comptroller, Arthur Levitt Sr. Mr. Ennico was editor of *The New York Corporate Handbook*, published by NYSBA in 1983, and *Corporate Counseling*, published by NYSBA in 1988, and authored the Corporate and Partnership Law sections of *Pitfalls of Practice*, to be published by NYSBA in 1993. He is also the author of *The Business Lawyer's Handbook*, a guide to the business lawyer's life and work published by Clark Boardman Callaghan (375 Hudson Street, New York, New York 10014, $39.95 softcover), and *The Legal Job Interview: Winning the Law-Related Job in Today's Market*, which is published by Biennix Corporation (2490 Black Rock Turnpike, Suite 407, Fairfield, Connecticut 06430-2404, $25.00 softcover). Mr. Ennico is a frequent speaker at programs on corporate law and practice sponsored by the New York State Bar Association, including "Drafting Documents for the Closely Held Corporation," "Buying and Selling the Small Business," and "Forming and Advising Businesses."

ELIZABETH A. HARTNETT is a partner in the Syracuse, New York law firm of Hunter & Hartnett, where she specializes in taxation, estate planning, corporate law and employee benefit plans. She received her B.S. degree in accounting from the Syracuse University College of Business Administration in 1971, and her J.D. degree from the Syracuse University College of Law in 1974. A certified public accountant and adjunct lecturer at Syracuse University's College of Law and School of Management, Ms. Hartnett is a frequent speaker at programs sponsored by the New York State Bar Association and the New York State Society of Certified Public Accountants, among others.

IDELLE A. HOWITT is the founder of Howitt & Associates, a securities valuation firm based in Manhattan. She received her B.A. degree from Boston University, her J.D. degree from the Temple University School of Law and her M.B.A. degree from the New York University Graduate School of Business Administration. Ms. Howitt is co-editor of the *Federal Tax Valuation Digest*, published by Warren,

Gorham & Lamont, Boston, Mass. She has testified before the United States Senate Finance Committee, the Department of Labor and the Internal Revenue Service on the valuation of closely held securities for estate and gift tax purposes, employee benefit plans and corporate financial planning. Ms. Howitt is a nationally recognized expert in her field, and she is a frequent speaker before bar associations and other organizations throughout the country.

RAYMOND W. MERRITT practices general corporate, securities and partnership law as a senior member of the New York City firm of Willkie Farr & Gallagher. He received his undergraduate degree from The College of the Holy Cross in 1960 and his law degree from Columbia University Law School in 1963, where he was an editor of the *Columbia Law Review*. Actively involved in various bar association matters, Mr. Merritt served as the editor-in-chief of *The New York Corporate Handbook*, which was published in 1983 by the New York State Bar Association, and was a co-author of *The Partnership Handbook*, which was published in 1986 by the New York State Bar Association and the New York State Society of Certified Public Accountants. Mr. Merritt was co-editor of the two volumes of *Corporate Counseling*, published by the New York State Bar Association in 1988. Along with Clifford R. Ennico, Mr. Merritt serves as editor-in-chief of the *Corporate Counseling Monograph Series*, a continuing series of monographs on subjects relating to corporate practice. Mr. Merritt also serves as a trustee of the Loyola Foundation, the Murray and Isabella Rayburn Foundation, Inc., and The Buhl Family Foundation.

ELISABETH TAVSS OHMAN is the Head Librarian at the New York City law firm of Thacher Proffitt & Wood. She received her B.A. degree from the University of Virginia and her M.L.S. degree from Columbia University School of Library Service. She is currently a part-time student at New York University's Stern Graduate School of Business.

WILLIAM A. PERRONE practices corporation, securities and computer law as a partner of the Southport, Connecticut law firm of Kleban & Samor, P.C. A native of New York City, Mr. Perrone received his B.A. degree, *cum laude*, in 1974 from the Brooklyn College of the City University of New York, and his J.D. degree, *cum laude*, in 1979 from the Western New England College School of Law. A member of the Connecticut and American Bar Associations, Mr. Perrone is a frequent lecturer on business law and related topics.

STUART B. RATNER is a tax partner at Kleban & Samor, P.C. in Southport, Connecticut. Mr. Ratner concentrates in the practice of federal and state tax matters such as tax collection problems, penalty abatements, employment tax and 100 percent penalty liability cases, tax lien and levy relief, property discharges, offers-in-compromise, payout agreements, technical advice requests, audits, tax protests and appeal hearings, tax court litigation, refund claims, state sales tax appeals, and in structuring corporate, partnership and individual transactions to minimize tax and business exposure. A graduate of the University of Connecticut, Syracuse University College of Law and New York University (LL.M. in Taxation), Mr. Ratner is a member of the American Bar Association and the Connecticut Bar Association and is admitted to practice in both New York and Connecticut. Mr. Ratner also holds a CPA certificate and is a member of both the American Institute of Certified Public Accountants and the Connecticut Society of Certified Public Accountants.

ALEXANDER W. SAMOR is a member of the corporate practice group of Kleban & Samor, P.C., specializing in corporate and securities matters. A native of Bridgeport, Connecticut, Mr. Samor is a graduate of Fairfield University (A.B. Economics) and the University of Connecticut School of Law (J.D.). Upon graduation from law school, Mr. Samor spent one year as a law clerk to Associate Justice Howard W. Alcorn of the Connecticut Supreme Court. Mr. Samor is a member of the American, Connecticut and Greater Bridgeport Bar Associations and is admitted to practice before the Connecticut state courts, the Supreme Court of the United States and the U.S. Court of Appeals for the Second Circuit.

ORRIN E. TILEVITZ practices tax law in the Brooklyn, New York law firm of Cullen and Dykman. He received his B.A. degree from Harvard College in 1975, his J.D. degree from Columbia University Law School in 1979, and his LL.M. in Taxation from the New York University School of Law in 1983. Mr. Tilevitz has written and lectured on tax planning for small businesses and several other tax subjects.

CORNELIUS S. VAN REES is a partner in the New York City law firm of Thacher Proffitt & Wood. He received his B.A. degree from

Denison University in 1951 and his LL.B. degree from the Columbia University School of Law. A former president of the Alumni Federation of Columbia University, Inc., Mr. Van Rees is a member of the Committee on Developments in Business Financing of the American Bar Association and the Committee on Recreational Boating and International Law of the Sea of the Maritime Law Association, and has lectured extensively on corporate law and practice for the New York State Bar Association.

JOANNE M. WHITE is a general practitioner in Albany, New York, with an interest in the areas of corporate, bankruptcy, real property, labor and matrimonial law. She received an A.B., *cum laude*, in English literature from Smith College and a J.D. from Boston College Law School in 1988 and has also attended graduate school in English at Middlebury College in Vermont and Lincoln College, Oxford. Ms. White, the Third District Representative to the Executive Committee of the New York State Bar Association's Young Lawyers' Section, is currently editing *Pitfalls of Practice*, a Young Lawyers' Section publication prepared by attorneys statewide and intended to point out the pitfalls in 22 areas of modern legal practice.

EDITORS' FOREWORD

The roots of the *Corporate Practice Handbook* go back to 1977, when the Continuing Legal Education Department of the New York State Bar Association began publishing legal texts, treatises and handbooks to supplement the continuing education seminars the Department offers throughout New York State. In that year, the Department published one of its first efforts, entitled *The New York Business Association System*, which was a complete, step-by-step layout of the birth, life and termination of a New York corporation. This "System Series" book utilized checklists, forms, information lists, worksheets and written instructions on how to use and interrelate these items in a way suitable for use in a combined effort by lawyers, legal assistants and word processor operators with a minimum of accompanying "hornbook-type" text. As originally conceived, *The New York Business Association System* was designed to synthesize the best features of a "hornbook," a formbook, a bar review outline and a law office manual.

In 1981, the Department sought to update and expand *The New York Business Association System* into a practical handbook for the practitioner who does not have access to the more sophisticated (and expensive) materials available in the library of a large law firm. To edit this project, the Association tapped Raymond W. Merritt, a senior partner at the law firm of Willkie Farr & Gallagher in New York City, who in turn enlisted the aid of Clifford R. Ennico, a former newspaper reporter and editor who was then an associate at Willkie Farr & Gallagher. The result of this collaboration was *The New York Corporate Handbook*, which the Association published in early 1983.

In the beginning, the *Handbook* was intended to be a corporate practice manual, with chapters roughly tracking the articles of New York's Business Corporation Law, in the style of the Practising Law Institute's *Israels on Corporate Practice* or the ALI-ABA's *Basic Corporate Practice*. Early on, however, the editors realized that what the general practitioner needed was not a rehashing of New York's corporation statute, but rather a practical handbook that would enable him/her to address the many and varied questions—most having little or nothing to do with corporate law—which corporate clients raise. The editors then spent several weeks searching for books that could be used as models and were astonished to discover that in the wide world of legal publications, no useful guide to corporate "counseling," as opposed to corporate "practice," existed.

The editors set out to fill this gap and furnish the general practitioner with a "first reference" in solving his/her corporate clients' problems. When your corporate client approached you with a novel problem, or if an individual client approached you with a question requiring you to enter the realm of corporate practice for the first time, it was hoped that the *Handbook* would be the first book you reached for. In simple, easy-to-read English, with a minimum of detail, the *Handbook* collected and outlined in one place the problems raised by your client's question, pointed out other problems "below the surface," and pointed you to other, more comprehensive, sources of information that may have been helpful.

More important than its style, however, the *Handbook* took an interdisciplinary approach to corporate counseling, with chapters by prominent practicing attorneys on corporate taxation, estate planning considerations for shareholders of closely held New York corporations, and the treatment of corporations under New York's equitable distribution statute when shareholders are divorced or separated, in addition to the more traditional discussion of the Business Corporation Law.

The *Handbook* expanded to two volumes in 1988, with the Association's publication of *Corporate Counseling*. In addition to a solid discussion of the Business Corporation Law and updates of the original *Handbook* chapters, *Corporate Counseling* sought to become a "desktop encyclopedia" for business lawyers, with new chapters in the fields of labor relations law, compensation and benefits for corporate executives, environmental law, patent and trademark law, business franchises, trade regulation, bankruptcy/creditors' rights, federal immigration law, ethics for the corporate counselor, and corporate finance. No fewer than eleven chapters focused on the federal, New York State and local taxation of small business corporations, while three chapters were devoted to corporate mergers and acquisitions. A "Forms and Materials" section contained 36 valuable and useful legal forms for the practitioner to use in addressing some of the problems covered in the text.

The publication of *Corporate Counseling* and its success in the legal community led the editors to wonder what they could possibly do for an encore. Readers suggested a number of additional chapters which would have expanded *Corporate Counseling* even further into a multivolume (and quite expensive) treatise. Accordingly, the decision was made in 1990 to begin reprinting and adding individual chapters in the form of stand-alone monographs. The first of these "little lawbooks," entitled "New York Securities Law: Practice and Policy," appeared in paperback that year, and was quickly followed by monographs on corporate sentencing guidelines and doing business in Europe. As of this writing, monographs in the *Corporate Counseling* series on estate planning, marital dissolution and taxation, financing the small business corporation, social legislation affecting corporations, and corporate criminal practice and procedure are in various stages of development.

Each monograph in the *Corporate Counseling* series is a combination of text, forms and materials designed to help the practitioner become a "quick study" in a new or different field of practice, without having to spend his or her life's savings in the process. All monographs are written by prominent New York State attorneys who have contributed their time and efforts to the Association and to this project in exchange for the chance to "strut their stuff" in a format that is much more flexible than a book chapter.

As the *Corporate Counseling* monographs began to take shape, it soon became clear that a number of chapters in the original *Corporate Counseling* volumes—particularly the "core" chapters on the Business Corporation Law and corporate taxation—would not lend themselves to the monograph format because they were highly interrelated. Accordingly, the decision was made in 1991 to keep these chapters together in a single volume which would be updated or reissued every two years on average, depending on the number of significant new cases, statutes and regulations each year in this field.

Thus the New York State Bar Association celebrates 15 years of publications for the business bar by publishing the *Corporate Practice Handbook*, a working, accessible and affordable introduction to the federal and New York laws affecting business corporations. Like its predecessors, the *Corporate Practice Handbook* is designed to be a "first reference" to the corporate counselor who is faced with a new problem, or who wishes to refresh his or her memory in an area of corporate practice that was once familiar. By focusing on the core provisions of the Business Corporation Law ("BCL") and related provisions of the federal and New York tax laws, the *Corporate Practice Handbook* is intended to complement the *Corporate Counseling Monograph Series,* thereby preserving the interdisciplinary approach to corporate practice that has distinguished this project from the very beginning.

The reader is reminded that, despite the comprehensive scope of the *Corporate Practice Handbook* and the *Corporate Counseling Monograph Series,* no book or set of books can be all-encompassing in its coverage, especially these days when new areas of practice sprout like mushrooms on a damp summer evening and changes in the demand for legal services can occur as quickly as a segue in a music video. Attorneys practicing in the '90s must learn to adapt their practice and style quickly and frequently to avoid becoming obsolete or surplus. No matter how much or how often the editors of the *Corporate Practice Handbook* and the *Corporate Counseling Monograph Series* update and expand these works, there will always be more to learn.

If an area of particular concern is not covered at all in this volume, or is not covered in sufficient depth, it may be a warning to the practitioner that what he/she needs is not a book, but another lawyer. As New York lawyer J. Robert LaPann, a member of the Committee on Professional Standards of the Third Judicial Department, puts it in his tongue-in-cheek article entitled "Twelve Surefire Ways to Get in Trouble," which appeared in the June 1982 issue of *The New York State Bar Journal*:

> In your day to day practice, there are some types of work which you encounter frequently and which you handle very skillfully. You know the statutes, the case law and the practical factors and you have developed a body of forms which enable you to handle these matters promptly, efficiently and profitably. Unfortunately, you'll never get into trouble limiting yourself to these matters. You should widen your horizons and accept personal injury cases, labor disputes, corporate mergers, tax planning and all those interesting matters

which you have been reading about but have never tried. Since these cases are complicated, you will have to put them aside from time to time in order to take care of your other work. Your law library may not contain any books on these new fields you are exploring. As a result, you will probably take a great deal of time to start or complete work in unaccustomed areas. You will probably make a number of mistakes in the process. The average client will get upset about the delay and the mistakes and undoubtedly file a complaint with the Committee on Professional Standards. If you should complete your unaccustomed work promptly and successfully, don't be discouraged. Just keep an eye out for work that is even more complicated and further from your usual type of practice.

In reading the *Corporate Practice Handbook*, please keep in mind that commandment of the Lord Chancellor in Gilbert and Sullivan's lawyerly operetta *Iolanthe* and "never take work you're unable to do."

The *Corporate Practice Handbook* could not have been completed without the assistance of many people, but particular thanks are in order to the following persons: to the attorneys throughout New York State who have contributed to the course materials books for the New York State Bar Association's seminars on "Forming and Advising Businesses" and "Drafting Documents for the Closely Held Corporation," from which some of the forms appearing in the "Forms and Materials" section of the *Corporate Practice Handbook* were adapted; to the corporate and tax departments of Willkie Farr & Gallagher (particularly Henry Cohn) in New York City and Kleban & Samor, P.C. in Southport, Connecticut, members of which reviewed several of the manuscript chapters of this book and offered invaluable comment on the current state of the "real world" of corporate practice; a special thanks is due to Ralph Gibson, the renowned art photographer, for his continued help in the design and layout of the *Corporate Practice Handbook* and the continuing *Corporate Counseling Monograph Series*. He has made our work pleasing to the eye; we hope we have made it pleasing to the mind. Thanks are also in order to the staff of the New York State Bar Association's Department of Continuing Legal Education, in particular Jean E. Nelson, Daniel McMahon, and Melody VanAlstyne, who collectively were the "unseen hands" behind the *Corporate Practice Handbook*, for their invaluable assistance and patience in coordinating the publication of this volume. The laboring oar on this volume was in the hands of Cliff Ennico. Without his steadfast efforts, the volume would have remained in the limbo of revisions where many such works unfortunately find their final repose.

We especially acknowledge our indebtedness to the individuals who took time out from their busy law practices (to say nothing of their free time) to contribute chapters and forms to this project. Without them and people like them, not only this book but much of the Association's work would be impossible.

Finally, this book is dedicated to Carol Merritt and Dolores Ennico.

RAYMOND W. MERRITT
CLIFFORD R. ENNICO

New York, New York
September 1, 1992

TABLE OF CONTENTS

Chapter   **Page**

About the Editors ix
About the Authors xi
Editors' Foreword xvii

1. Selection of the Corporate Structure -
   Leona Beane 1
2. Federal Income Tax Aspects of Corporations and Alternative Ways of Doing Business -
   Henry M. Cohn 29
3. The Subchapter S Alternative - Stuart B. Ratner .. 47
4. Incorporation and Recordkeeping -
   Alexander W. Samor and Clifford R. Ennico 85
5. Federal Income Tax Aspects of Incorporation -
   Henry M. Cohn 105
6. The Financial Structure of a Corporation -
   Joanne M. White 115
7. Federal Income Tax Aspects of Corporate Capital Structure - Orrin E. Tilevitz 143
8. Directors and Officers of the New York Corporation - Clifford R. Ennico and William A. Perrone 155
9. Obligations of the Corporation to Shareholders; Obligations of Shareholders to Each Other -
   Leona Beane 187
10. Federal Income Tax Aspects of Corporate-Shareholder Relations - Michael A. Buxbaum 215
11. Buying and Selling the Small Business Corporation - Cornelius S. Van Rees 235

12. Tax Aspects of Buying and Selling
    the Small Business - Henry M. Cohn............ 281
13. The Effectuation of a Corporate Event: A
    Practitioner's Overview - Raymond W. Merritt... 309
14. Corporate Operations I: Some Corporate Law
    Aspects of Day-to-Day Management -
    Clifford R. Ennico........................ 381
15. Corporate Operations II: Federal Income Tax
    Pitfalls - Orrin E. Tilevitz 399
16. Dissolution, "Winding Up" and Liquidation of the
    Closely Held Corporation - Clifford R. Ennico... 421
17. Federal Income Tax Aspects of Corporate
    Liquidation - Elizabeth A. Hartnett 445
18. A Corporate Tax Checklist for the Lawyer
    Representing the Small Business -
    Orrin E. Tilevitz.......................... 463
19. Valuation of Closely Held Corporations -
    Idelle A. Howitt........................... 485
20. Some Ethical Considerations for the Corporate
    Lawyer - Clifford R. Ennico 507
21. One Hundred Basic Books for the Lawyer
    Representing the Small Business -
    Elisabeth Tavss Ohman 529

Forms and Materials
(See specific table of contents on page 543).............. 541

Table of Authorities 957

DETAILED TABLE OF CONTENTS

CHAPTER 1: SELECTION OF THE CORPORATE STRUCTURE
By Leona Beane

I.	Introduction	3
II.	Different Forms of Doing Business	3
	A. The Sole Proprietorship	3
	B. The General Partnership	4
	C. The Limited Partnership	6
	D. The Revised Limited Partnership Act	8
	E. The Joint Venture	14
	F. The Joint Stock Association	14
	G. The Corporation	15
III.	Selection of Jurisdiction	17
	A. In General	17
	B. Delaware vs. New York	19
	1. Delaware Advantages	19
	2. New York Advantages	21
IV.	Anatomy of a Corporation	21
	A. The Corporation as a "Person"	21
	1. Statutory Rules	21
	2. Constitutional Provisions	22
	B. The Corporation as an Entity	23
	C. Purposes and Powers of a Corporation—Some Problems	25

| | 1. | *Ultra Vires* and Charitable Contributions | 25 |
| | 2. | Political Contributions .... | 26 |

CHAPTER 2: FEDERAL INCOME TAX ASPECTS OF CORPORATIONS AND ALTERNATIVE WAYS OF DOING BUSINESS
By Henry M. Cohn

I. Introduction and Overview 31
II. Determining the Form of a Business Entity for Tax Purposes 32
III. Certain Tax Attributes of Corporations, Partnerships and Proprietorships 35
    A. Tax Rates 36
    B. Alternative Minimum Tax 36
    C. Computation of Taxable Income and Deductions 37
    D. Deductions Which Only a Corporation May Take 37
    E. Net Operating Losses and Capital Losses ... 38
    F. Charitable Contributions 39
    G. Depreciation Recapture 40
    H. Characterization of Income 40
    I. Availability of Tax-Advantaged Fringe Benefits 40
IV. Some Tentative Guidelines in Selecting the Structure of a Small Business Entity 41
    A. If Form is Legally Unavailable, Do Not Consider It 41
    B. S Corporation vs. C Corporation 41
    C. Partnership vs. C Corporation 42
    D. Partnership vs. S Corporation 43
    E. Proprietorship vs. Partnership/Corporation.. 44

	F.	General vs. Limited Partnership	44
	G.	Limited Partnership with Corporate General Partner	44
	H.	State Tax Considerations	45

CHAPTER 3: THE SUBCHAPTER S ALTERNATIVE
By Stuart B. Ratner

I.	Introduction		49
II.	Advantages of an S Corporation		49
	A.	Tax Considerations	49
	B.	Nontax Considerations	51
III.	Criteria Defining a Small Business Corporation		52
	A.	Ineligible Corporations	53
		1. Affiliated Groups	53
		2. Banks	54
		3. Insurance Companies	54
		4. Corporation Claiming U.S. Possession Tax Credits	54
		5. DISC	55
	B.	Domestic Corporation	55
	C.	Number of Shareholders	55
	D.	Character of the Shareholders	56
	E.	Nonresident Aliens	59
	F.	One Class of Stock	60
IV.	Electing S Corporation Treatment		61
	A.	Manner of Election	61
	B.	Timing of the Election	64
V.	Operation of an S Corporation		64
	A.	Corporate-Level Taxation	64
		1. Built-in Gains	64

xxvii

		2.	Passive Investment Income	66
		3.	Recapture of Investment Tax Credit....	68
	B.	Taxable Income		68
	C.	Elections............................		71
	D.	Taxable Year.........................		71
VI.	Effect of the Election on Shareholders..........			73
	A.	Taxation of Shareholders		73
	B.	Distributions to Shareholders.............		76
	C.	Adjustments to Basis		78
VII.	Termination of S Corporation Status			79
	A.	Voluntary Revocation of the S Corporation Election		79
	B.	Involuntary Termination of the S Corporation Election		80
	C.	Safeguarding Against Termination.........		81
	D.	Tax Treatment of a Year in Which a Termination Occurs		82
VIII.	Concluding Observations....................			83

CHAPTER 4:   INCORPORATION AND RECORDKEEPING

By Alexander W. Samor and Clifford R. Ennico

I.	Incorporation	87
	A. Selecting the Name	87
	B. Reserving the Name....................	90
	C. The Certificate of Incorporation...........	92
	D. Fees and Expenses	95
II.	By-laws	96
III.	Organizational Meetings	98
	A. Incorporators	98
	B. Directors	99

		C.	Shareholders	100
		D.	Subscription for Shares	100
	IV.	Recordkeeping and Other Post-Incorporation Issues		100
		A.	Records	100
		B.	Corporate Seal	101
		C.	Tax Forms	102
		D.	Corporate Minute Book	102
		E.	Qualification in Other States	103
	V.	Professional Assistance		103

CHAPTER 5: FEDERAL INCOME TAX ASPECTS OF INCORPORATION

By Henry M. Cohn

	I.	Introduction and Overview		107
	II.	Tax-Free Incorporation under Section 351		107
		A.	In General	107
		B.	What Constitutes "Property" for Purposes of Section 351?	108
		C.	What Does "Solely in Exchange for Stock or Securities" Mean?	109
		D.	What Does it Mean to Say that the Shareholders Must Be in "Control" of the Corporation "Immediately after the Exchange"?	110
	III.	Transfers to a Corporation of Property Subject to Liabilities under Section 357 of the Code		111
		A.	In General	111
		B.	Tax Avoidance/No Bona Fide Business Purpose Exception	112
		C.	Liabilities in Excess of Basis Exception	112
		D.	Determination of Basis in Transferred Assets	113

IV. Recapture Considerations 113

CHAPTER 6: THE FINANCIAL STRUCTURE OF A CORPORATION

By Joanne M. White

I. Introduction 117
II. Authority to Issue Shares 117
III. Share Subscriptions 120
    A. Definition and Requirements for Validity.... 120
    B. Revocability 120
    C. Acceptance............................ 120
    D. Time and Manner of Payment 121
    E. Penalties.............................. 121
IV. Consideration and Payment for Shares 121
    A. Nature of Consideration................. 122
    B. Amount of Consideration................ 123
    C. Valuation 123
    D. Treasury Shares 124
V. Rights and Options to Purchase Shares 124
    A. Poison Pill Defense 126
VI. Stated Capital............................. 126
VII. Compensation for Formation, Reorganization and Financing 127
VIII. Share Certificates.......................... 127
IX. Fractional Shares and Scrip 129
X. Dividends and Distributions.................. 130
    A. Dividends............................. 130
    B. Share Distributions and Changes 131
XI. Redeemable Shares 133
XII. Purchase or Redemption of Shares............ 134

	A.	Greenmail Defense........................	135
XIII.		Contracts for Corporation's Purchase of Its Own Shares.........	136
XIV.		Reacquired Shares	136
XV.		Reduction of Stated Capital under Section 516 ...	137
XVI.		Surplus and Reserves.......................	138
XVII.		Corporate Bonds	139
XVIII.		Convertible Shares and Bonds	139

CHAPTER 7: FEDERAL INCOME TAX ASPECTS OF CORPORATE CAPITAL STRUCTURE

By Orrin E. Tilevitz

I.		Introduction	145
II.		The Stakes	146
	A.	The Investor...........................	146
		1. Basic Tax Rules	146
		2. Original Issue Discount	147
		3. Accrual Basis Investor	147
		4. Losses from Worthless Securities and Bad Debts.....	148
	B.	Section 1244 Stock.....................	149
	C.	The Issuing Corporation	151
	D.	The Bottom Line	152
III.		Classifying Debt and Stock	152

CHAPTER 8: DIRECTORS AND OFFICERS OF THE NEW YORK CORPORATION

By Clifford R. Ennico and William A. Perrone

- I. Introduction and Overview 157
- II. The Board of Directors 157
    - A. Authority of the Board 157
    - B. Establishing the Board; Qualifications and Size 158
    - C. Election of Directors; Term of Office 159
    - D. Changes in Number of Directors 160
    - E. Removal of Directors.................... 161
    - F. Action by the Board; Quorum and Voting ... 161
    - G. Committees of the Board 163
- III. Officers of the Corporation 164
    - A. Authority of Officers 164
        - 1. Express Authority 164
        - 2. Implied Authority................. 165
        - 3. Apparent Authority 165
        - 4. Authority by Virtue of Ratification 166
    - B. Selection of Officers and Term of Office 166
- IV. Executive Officer Employment Agreements 167
- V. Duties and Liabilities of Directors and Officers... 169
    - A. In General 169
    - B. Duty of Care 169
    - C. Duty of Loyalty 170
    - D. Other Prohibited Actions 172
- VI. Duties and Liabilities of Directors and Officers of Publicly Traded Companies 172
    - A. Stock Ownership Reporting Requirements .. 173

		1.	Initial Reports on Form 3	173
		2.	Changes in Ownership Reports on Form 4	173
		3.	Exemption for Small Transactions	174
		4.	Annual Report on Form 5	175
		5.	Filing of Reports	175
		6.	Beneficial Ownership	175
		7.	New SEC Enforcement Provisions	177
	B.	Liability for Short-Swing Profits		177
	C.	Prohibition Against Short Sales		178
	D.	Insider Trading—Federal Law		178
	E.	Common Law Insider Trading		179
	F.	Suggestions Regarding Insider Trading and Disclosing Information		180
VII.	Indemnification of Directors and Officers and Limitation of Directors' Liability			180
	A.	Indemnification		181
		1.	Nonexclusivity of Statutory Provisions	181
		2.	Statutory Indemnification Rights	182
	B.	Limitation of Directors' Liability		185

CHAPTER 9: OBLIGATIONS OF THE CORPORATION TO SHAREHOLDERS; OBLIGATIONS OF SHAREHOLDERS TO EACH OTHER

By Leona Beane

I.	Introduction			189
II.	Shareholder Rights			189
	A.	Shareholders' Meetings		189
		1.	Call of Meetings	189
		2.	Notice of Meetings	190
		3.	Waiver of Notice	190

xxxiii

		4.	Quorum of Shareholders	190
		5.	Proxies	191
		6.	Record Date of Shareholders	192
		7.	Conduct of the Shareholders' Meeting	192
		8.	Inspector of Elections	193
		9.	Voting of the Shareholders	194
		10.	Cumulative Voting for Directors	194
		11.	Powers of the Supreme Court Respecting Elections	195
		12.	Unanimous Written Consent of Shareholders in Lieu of Meeting	195
	B.	Additional Rights of Shareholders		196
		1.	Removal of Directors	196
		2.	Voting on Amendment of the By-laws	196
		3.	Voting on Amendment to Certificate of Incorporation	196
		4.	Voting for Mergers and Consolidations	197
		5.	Inspection of Books and Records of the Corporation	197
		6.	Dividends	197
		7.	Preemptive Rights of the Shareholder	198
		8.	Right of Appraisal	199
	C.	Proceeding by Shareholders—The Shareholders' Derivative Suit		201
III.	Obligations to Minority Shareholders			203
IV.	Arrangements among Shareholders in the Closely Held Corporation			205
	A.	Shareholders' Agreement		205
	B.	Voting Agreements		207
	C.	Buy-Sell Agreements		209
	D.	The Irrevocable Proxy		211

	E.	The Voting Trust.................... 211
V.	Minority Shareholders Who Are Employees..... 213

CHAPTER 10: FEDERAL INCOME TAX ASPECTS OF CORPORATE-SHAREHOLDER RELATIONS

By Michael A. Buxbaum

I.	Introduction and Overview 217
II.	Tax Treatment of Dividends.................. 218
	A.	General Rule 218
	B.	"Earnings and Profits" 219
	C.	Earnings and Profits "Accumulated Since February 28, 1913"..................... 220
	D.	Property Dividends 221
	E.	Stock Dividends....................... 222
	F.	Constructive Dividends 223
III.	Corporate Redemptions of Stock 224
	A.	General Rule 224
	B.	Distributions "Not Essentially Equivalent to a Dividend" 225
	C.	"Substantially Disproportionate" Redemptions 226
	D.	"Complete Termination" Redemptions 226
	E.	"Partial Liquidation" Redemptions 227
	F.	"Death Tax" Redemptions............... 228
	G.	"Earnings and Profits" Adjustments for Stock Redemptions..................... 229
IV.	Two Special Situations: Sections 304 and 306 230
	A.	Introduction 230
	B.	"Preferred Stock Bailouts" under Section 306 230

		C.	Redemptions through Related Corporations under Section 304 of the Code	232

CHAPTER 11: BUYING AND SELLING THE SMALL BUSINESS CORPORATION
By Cornelius S. Van Rees

I.	Introduction and Overview			237
II.	Background Considerations			238
		A.	Many Fields	238
		B.	Many Players	238
		C.	The Lawyer and the "Team"	239
		D.	Why?	240
		E.	Valuation Considerations	240
		F.	Brokerage Agreement	242
		G.	Timetable	243
		H.	"Purchase" and "Pooling of Interest" Accounting for Business Combinations	244
		I.	Employee Benefits and Relations	244
		J.	Assignability of Contracts and Rights	245
		K.	Forms and Checklists	245
		L.	Bulk Transfer Considerations	246
III.	Initial Legal Considerations			247
		A.	General	247
		B.	Unintended Assumption of Liabilities	247
		C.	Antitrust Considerations	249
		D.	Securities and Exchange Commission and Stock Exchange Acts, Rules and Regulations	249
		E.	State Law Requirements	249
			1. In General	249
			2. Mergers and Consolidations	250

xxxvi

		3. Short-Form Mergers	253
		4. Mergers and Consolidations of Foreign and Domestic Corporations	254
		5. Sales of Assets	255
		6. Exchanges of Shares	256
		7. Appraisal Rights of Dissenting Shareholders	257
	F.	Insider Information, Minority Stockholder Rights (Selling Control)	258
	G.	Fraudulent Conveyances	259
	H.	Binding the Deal	259
IV.	Investigation		261
	A.	Business Investigation	262
	B.	Legal Investigation	262
	C.	Accounting Investigation	263
V.	Sale of Assets or Sale of Stock		265
VI.	Drafting the Agreement: Some Practical Suggestions		265
	A.	Drafting Responsibility	265
	B.	Desired Length	266
	C.	Closing Date	266
	D.	Terms of Purchase and Sale	266
	E.	Some Basic Agreement Provisions	267
	F.	Other Documents	269
	G.	Forms	270
	H.	Practice and Drafting Techniques and Hints	270
		1. Preparation	270
		2. Fairness	270
		3. Negotiating	270
		4. Liabilities	271

5.	Representations and Warranties Generally	271
6.	Financial Statements	272
7.	Assets.	272
8.	Accounts Receivable	272
9.	Inventory	272
10.	Liabilities.	273
11.	Taxes	273
12.	Commitments and Agreements	273
13.	Sales Warranties.	274
14.	Other Representations	274
15.	Waiver	274
16.	Affirmative and Negative Covenants . . .	275
17.	Special Conditions to Closing	275
18.	Survival of Representations	275
19.	Limitation of Representations	275
20.	Materiality	276
21.	Indemnification	276
22.	Escrow or Setoff	277
23.	Covenant not to Compete.	277
24.	Installment Sales	277
25.	Security	277
26.	Bulk Transfers	278
27.	Union Pension Withdrawal Liability . . .	278
28.	Opinion Letters Delivered at Closing. . .	278
29.	Employment Agreement	279

CHAPTER 12: TAX ASPECTS OF BUYING AND SELLING THE SMALL BUSINESS

By Henry M. Cohn

I.	Introduction and Overview	283
II.	Determining the Tax Objectives of Buyer and Seller	284
III.	Tax-Free Reorganizations	285
	A. Tax-Free Reorganizations: In General	285
	B. Acquisitive Reorganizations	287
	1. Type A: Merger or Consolidation under State Law	287
	2. Type B: Stock for Voting Stock Exchange	289
	3. Type C: Acquisition of Assets for Stock	291
	C. Divisive Reorganizations	293
	1. Type D: General Considerations	293
	2. Type D: Asset Transfer Downward	294
	3. Type D: Spin-Offs	295
	4. Type D: Split-Offs	295
	5. Type D: Split-Ups	295
	6. Tax Consequences of Divisive Reorganizations	296
	D. "Neutral" Acquisitions	296
	1. Type E: Recapitalization	296
	2. Type F: A "Mere Change"	296
	3. Type G: Insolvent Corporations	296
IV.	Taxable Reorganizations	297
	A. Taxable Asset Purchases	297
	B. Taxable Stock Purchase if no Section 338 Election is Made	298

- C. Taxable Stock Purchase with Section 338 Election by Buyer.................. 299
- D. Taxable Stock Purchase with Section 338(h)(10) Election by Buyer and Seller 299
- E. Taxable Asset Purchase Followed by Liquidation of the Selling Corporation...... 300

V. "Hybrid" Reorganizations.................... 301
- A. The "Cash-or-Stock" Merger 301
- B. The "Preferred Stock Forward Triangular Merger"............................. 301
- C. Recapitalization Followed by Cash Purchase of Shares 303
- D. The Two-Tiered "Freeze Out" Cash Merger. 303

VI. Carryover of Tax Attributes in Corporate Reorganizations and Acquisitions 305
- A. Net Operating Loss Carryovers 305
- B. Earnings and Profits.................... 307
- C. Capital Losses 307
- D. Method of Accounting; Depreciation....... 307
- E. Limitation on Excess Credit.............. 307
- F. Built-in Gains and Losses................ 308

CHAPTER 13: THE EFFECTUATION OF A CORPORATE EVENT: A PRACTITIONER'S OVERVIEW

By Raymond W. Merritt

I. Introduction: The Three Phases of a Corporate Transaction................................ 311
II. Getting Background Information 313
- A. In General: Where to Look 313
  1. Review of Consultants' Reports........ 313
  2. Review of SEC Filings and Offering Circulars 313

		3.	Review of Corporate Minutes	314
		4.	Review of Filings with Other Regulatory Agencies........................	314
		5.	Review Data Bases.................	314
	B.	Formation and Good Standing		315
		1.	Articles of Incorporation	315
		2.	Franchise Taxes	316
		3.	Qualification in Other States	316
	C.	Capital Stock		316
		1.	Authorized Capital Structure	316
		2.	Stockholder Restrictions	317
		3.	Voting Control	317
		4.	Issuance of Stock	318
		5.	Dividends........................	319
		6.	Repurchase of Stock...............	319
		7.	Trading Market	319
	D.	Indebtedness and Obligations............		320
		1.	Borrowings from Banks and Other Outsiders	320
		2.	Borrowings from Insiders	320
		3.	Loans to Insiders	321
	E.	Property............................		321
		1.	Leases	321
		2.	Fee Title........................	322
		3.	Easements and Licenses............	322
		4.	Patents, Trademarks, Copyrights and Other Intangibles	322
		5.	Use of Properties	323
		6.	Condition and Adequacy of Buildings and Equipment	324

		7.	Insurance	324
	F.	Business Operations		324
		1.	Financial Statements	324
		2.	Budgets and Sales Data	325
		3.	Purchases and Inventory	326
		4.	Accounts and Notes Receivable	326
		5.	Liability Insurance	326
		6.	Business Licenses and Permits	327
		7.	Joint Ventures and Partnerships	327
		8.	Competition and Marketing Policies	327
		9.	Pending Negotiations	328
	G.	Management and Employees		329
		1.	Management	329
		2.	Employee Relations	330
	H.	Litigation		331
		1.	Review of Pending and Threatened Litigation and Administrative Proceedings	331
		2.	Review of Unasserted Claims	331
		3.	Review Data Bases	331
III.	Drafting an Acquisition Agreement			331
IV.	Agreement for Purchase of Assets (Annotated)			333
	A.	Definitions		333
	B.	Balance Sheet		337
	C.	Purchase and Sale of the Purchased Property		337
	D.	Payment of Purchase Price		343
	E.	Closing		344
	F.	Representations and Warranties of Seller and the Parent		345
	G.	Representations and Warranties of Buyer		355

	H.	Covenants of Seller and the Parent.........	357
	I.	Covenants of Buyer	360
	J.	Conditions Precedent of Buyer	361
	K.	Conditions Precedent of Seller...........	365
	L.	Indemnification	367
	M.	Guaranty	372
	N.	Brokerage................................	373
	O.	Notices..................................	373
	P.	Entire Agreement; Modification	374
	Q.	Nature and Survival of Representations...	374
	R.	Bulk Sales Law	375
	S.	Specific Performance....................	375
	T.	Compliance with Closing Conditions.......	376
	U.	Termination	376
	V.	Parties	376
	W.	New York Law to Govern	377
	X.	Assignment	377
	Y.	Counterparts.............................	377
	Z.	Paragraph Headings.......................	378
	AA.	Taxes	378
V.	Conclusion..................................	379

CHAPTER 14: CORPORATE OPERATIONS I: SOME CORPORATE LAW ASPECTS OF DAY-TO-DAY MANAGEMENT

By Clifford R. Ennico

I.	Introduction and Overview		383
II.	Counsel as Corporate Manager: The Secretary's Function.......................................		384
	A.	Counsel as Shareholder	384

	B.	Counsel as Director	385
	C.	Counsel as Officer	385
	D.	The Corporate Secretary's Function	386
		1. The Recordkeeping Function	386
		2. Communicating with Shareholders	389
		3. Meetings and Minutes	391
III.	Determining the Level of Management at Which a Decision Should be Made: Amending the Certificate of Incorporation		393
	A.	In General	393
	B.	Decisions Requiring a Meeting of Directors	393
	C.	Decisions Requiring a Meeting of Shareholders	394
	D.	Decisions Requiring Amendment to the Certificate of Incorporation	395
	E.	Procedure to Amend or Change the Certificate of Incorporation	397

CHAPTER 15: CORPORATE OPERATIONS II: FEDERAL INCOME TAX PITFALLS

By Orrin E. Tilevitz

I.	Scope of the Chapter		401
II.	Personal Holding Company Tax		401
	A.	Earnings Test	402
	B.	Ownership Test	403
	C.	Exemptions	404
	D.	Computation of Tax	404
	E.	Avoiding the Tax	404
III.	Accumulated Earnings Tax		405
IV.	Section 269A		407
V.	At-Risk Rules		409

VI.	Passive Activity Losses	411
	A. Coverage	412
	B. Loss Limitation	412
	1. Personal Service Corporations	412
	2. Closely Held C Corporations	414
VII.	Collapsible Corporations	415
	A. Introduction and Overview	415
	B. Definition of "Collapsible Corporation"	417
	C. Exceptions	417
	1. Inventory	417
	2. Minority Shareholders	417
	3. 70-30 Rule	417
	4. Three-Year Rule	418
	5. Section 341(e)	418
	6. The Section 341(f) Consent	418
VIII.	Denial of Graduated Rates	418
IX.	Alternative Minimum Tax	419

CHAPTER 16: DISSOLUTION, "WINDING UP" AND LIQUIDATION OF THE CLOSELY HELD CORPORATION

By Clifford R. Ennico

I.	Introduction and Overview	423
II.	Expiration of Term	424
III.	Voluntary Dissolution under Article 10 of the BCL	425
IV.	Involuntary Dissolution under Article 11 of the BCL	427
	A. In General	427
	B. By the Attorney General	428
	C. By the Shareholders: the "10% Majority Rule" of Section 1103	431

	D.	By the Shareholders: Deadlocks	432
	E.	By Minority Shareholders: the "20% Rule" of Section 1104-a	433
	F.	By the Directors	436
	G.	Procedure	436
	H.	The Problem of Assessable "Nonassessable" Stock	438
V.		The "Winding Up" Process	439
VI.		Liquidation	440

CHAPTER 17: FEDERAL INCOME TAX ASPECTS OF CORPORATE LIQUIDATION

By Elizabeth A. Hartnett

I.	Introduction		447
	A.	Internal Revenue Code Section 336	447
	B.	Internal Revenue Code Section 331	447
	C.	Internal Revenue Code Sections 332, 334 and 338	447
II.	Tax Reasons for Liquidation		448
	A.	Lowering Tax Rates	448
	B.	Reducing Double Taxation	448
	C.	Avoiding Constructive Dividends	449
	D.	Avoiding Accumulated Earnings Tax	449
	E.	Avoiding Personal Holding Company Tax	450
III.	Alternatives to Liquidation		451
	A.	Stock Sale	451
	B.	Tax-Free Exchange of Stock	451
	C.	Tax-Free Divisive Reorganizations	451
	D.	Election of S Corporation Status	451
	E.	Tax Planning to Avoid Penalty Taxes	452
	F.	Qualified Stock Purchase Election	452

IV.	Tax Consequences to the Corporation	452
	A. The General Rule	452
	B. Corporate Liabilities	453
	C. Related Parties—Loss Limitation under Section 336.	453
	D. S Corporation Liquidation and New "Built-in Gain" Rules of Section 1374	455
	E. Liquidation-Reincorporation	456
V.	Tax Consequences to the Shareholder	457
	A. General Rule	457
	B. Installment Obligations	458
	C. Collapsible Corporations	458
	D. Tax Basis Rules	458
VI.	Liquidation of a Subsidiary	459
	A. General Rule	459
	B. Indebtedness of Subsidiary to Parent	460
	C. Minority Interests	460
	D. Tax Basis Rules	460
VII.	Procedure	461
	A. Federal Income Tax Return	461
	B. New York State Requirements	462

CHAPTER 18: A CORPORATE TAX CHECKLIST FOR THE LAWYER REPRESENTING THE SMALL BUSINESS

By Orrin E. Tilevitz

I.	Scope of the Chapter	465
II.	What This Chapter Does Not Cover	465
III.	An Introduction to Federal Excise Taxes	466
	A. Penalty Taxes	466

		1.	Employee Benefit Plans	467
		2.	Golden Parachutes	467
	B.	Excise Taxes on Specific Business Activities		468
IV.	Payroll Taxes			468
	A.	Income Tax Withholding		469
	B.	FICA		469
	C.	Unemployment Taxes		469
V.	New York State Business Taxes			469
	A.	Corporate Franchise Tax		469
		1.	Scope	469
		2.	Rate	470
			a. C Corporations	470
			b. S Corporations	470
		3.	Bases of State Franchise Tax	470
		4.	Small Business Corporations	471
		5.	MTA Surcharge	472
		6.	Additional Surcharge	472
		7.	Further Information	472
	B.	Sales and Use Taxes		472
		1.	Scope	472
		2.	Rate	473
		3.	Basis	473
		4.	Exempt Purchasers	473
		5.	Exempt Transactions	473
		6.	Collection	474
		7.	Further Information	474
	C.	Real Property Transfer Gains Tax		474
		1.	Scope	474
		2.	Basis and Rate	474

		3.	Examples of Taxable Transactions	474
		4.	Exempt Transactions	475
		5.	Filing Requirements	475
		6.	Further Information	475
	D.	Stock Transfer Tax		476
		1.	Scope	476
		2.	Basis and Rate	476
		3.	Examples of Taxable Transactions	476
		4.	Rebate	476
		5.	Exempt Transfers	476
		6.	Further Information	476
	E.	Mortgage Recording Tax		476
		1.	Scope	476
		2.	Basis and Rate	477
		3.	Payment	477
		4.	Further Information	477
	F.	Real Estate Transfer Tax		477
		1.	Scope	477
		2.	Basis and Rate	477
		3.	Examples of Taxable Transfers	477
		4.	Exempt Transfers	478
		5.	Payment	478
		6.	Further Information	478
	G.	Utility Vendor's Tax		478
		1.	Scope	478
		2.	Basis and Rate	478
		3.	Further Information	479
VI.	New York City Business Taxes			479
	A.	General Corporation Tax		479

		1.	Scope	479
		2.	Basis and Rate	479
		3.	Further Information	480
	B.	Sales and Use Taxes		480
	C.	Commercial Rent or Occupancy Tax		480
		1.	Scope	480
		2.	Basis and Rate	480
		3.	Examples of Taxable Transactions	481
		4.	Exempt Transactions	481
		5.	Further Information	481
	D.	Real Property Transfer Tax		481
		1.	Scope	481
		2.	Basis and Rate	481
		3.	Examples of Taxable Transfers	481
		4.	Exempt Transfers...................	482
		5.	Administration	482
		6.	Further Information	482
	E.	Utility Vendor's Tax		482
	F.	Mortgage Recording Tax		482
VII.	Forms			482
VIII.	Calling for Assistance			483

CHAPTER 19: VALUATION OF CLOSELY HELD CORPORATIONS

By Idelle A. Howitt

I.	Introduction	487
II.	Distinctive Features of a Closely Held Corporation	487
III.	Appraisals Required by Recent Federal Laws	488
IV.	Recommended Appraisals	488
V.	Common Corporate Valuation Situations	489

	A.	Buy-Sell Agreements	489
	B.	Estate Taxes	489
	C.	Employee Stock Ownership Plans ("ESOPs")	490
	D.	Charitable Contributions	491
VI.	Valuation Methods		492
	A.	The Cost Approach/Net Asset Value Analysis	492
	B.	The Income Approach	493
	C.	The Market Approach	493
	D.	Comparison of the Three Approaches	494
VII.	Revenue Ruling 59-60: The Industry Guideline		495
	A.	The Nature of the Business and the History of the Enterprise from its Inception	495
	B.	The Economic Outlook in General and the Condition and Outlook of the Specific Industry	495
	C.	The Book Value of the Stock and the Financial Condition of the Business	496
	D.	The Earning Capacity of the Company	496
	E.	Dividend-Paying Capacity	496
	F.	Whether the Enterprise has Goodwill or Other Intangible Value	497
	G.	Sales of the Stock and the Size of the Block to be Valued	497
	H.	The Market Price of Stocks of Corporations Engaged in the Same or a Similar Line of Business Having Their Stocks Actively Traded in a Free and Open Market, Either on an Exchange or Over-the-Counter	497
VIII.	Premiums and Discounts		497
	A.	Premium for Control	497
	B.	Discounts for Minority Interests	498

	C.	Discounts for Lack of Marketability	499
IX.	Valuation Penalties	499
	A.	Penalties for Valuation Overstatement	499
	B.	Penalties for Valuation Understatement	499
	C.	Section 6662	499
	D.	Exceptions	501
	E.	Section 170 of the Internal Revenue Code	501
	F.	Appraiser Penalties	502
X.	The Valuation Engagement	502
	A.	Define What is to be Valued	502
	B.	Define the Purpose of the Valuation	503
	C.	Select the Date of the Valuation Carefully	503
	D.	Decide on the Standard of Value	504
	E.	Define the Terms and Conditions of the Engagement	504
		1. The Valuation Report	504
		2. The Schedule	505
		3. The Fee	505
XI.	Summary	505

CHAPTER 20: SOME ETHICAL CONSIDERATIONS FOR THE CORPORATE LAWYER

By Clifford R. Ennico

I.	Introduction: The Legal Limits on what Business Lawyers Can Do	509
II.	The Sources of Ethical Rules Governing the Business Lawyer's Conduct	509
III.	The Lawyer's Basic Duties to the Client	510
IV.	Conflicts of Interest within the Client Organization	512
	A. Who is the Business Lawyer's Client?	512

		B.	The Organization vs. the Human Beings who Make Up the Organization...............	513
		C.	When the Human Beings Fail to Follow the Business Lawyer's Instructions	514
V.	Conflicts of Interest Between the Business Lawyer and the Organization Client			515
		A.	The Lawyer-Director and the Lawyer-Executive	515
		B.	Investing in Stock or Securities of a Client Organization..........................	517
VI.	Ethical Aspects of the Client Monitoring Function			518
		A.	The Ethical Duties of Diligence and to Keep the Client Informed Do Not Apply.........	518
		B.	The Prohibition on Soliciting Legal Business.	518
VII.	Ethical Aspects of the Client Counseling Function			519
		A.	The Business Lawyer as Advisor	519
		B.	The Business Lawyer's Evaluation of a Client for Use by Third Parties.................	519
		C.	The Business Lawyer's Association with Specialists............................	520
VIII.	Ethical Aspects of the Transaction Management Process.....................................			520
		A.	The Duty of Fairness to the Opposing Party and its Counsel.......................	520
		B.	Communication with Persons Represented by Counsel; Dealing with Unrepresented Persons.............................	521
		C.	Dealing with Other Professionals; Preventing the Unauthorized Practice of Law	522
IX.	Cross-Border Problems			523
X.	Some Ethical Aspects of In-house Lawyering			523

CHAPTER 21: ONE HUNDRED BASIC BOOKS FOR THE LAWYER REPRESENTING THE SMALL BUSINESS
By Elisabeth Tavss Ohman........... 529

CHAPTER ONE

SELECTION OF THE CORPORATE STRUCTURE

Leona Beane

SELECTION OF THE CORPORATE STRUCTURE

I. INTRODUCTION

The basic forms of business organization in New York are the sole proprietorship, the general partnership, the limited partnership, the joint venture, the joint-stock association, and the corporation. Although this volume deals primarily with the formation and operation of a corporation under New York law, a brief comparison of the several forms of enterprise is presented in order to facilitate selection of the most advantageous form for a particular business.

II. DIFFERENT FORMS OF DOING BUSINESS

A. The Sole Proprietorship

The sole proprietorship is the simplest and most common form of business enterprise. An individual trading in his/her own name may operate in New York as a sole proprietor without any formality or expense of organization. If, however, the proprietor wishes to do business under an assumed or fictitious name, he/she must file in the county clerk's office in each county in which such business is conducted a certificate containing the business name and address and his/her own full name and address. *See* N.Y. Gen. Bus. Law § 130. Failure to file constitutes a misdemeanor but does not affect the proprietor's liability to third persons. In addition, if the sole proprietor wishes to open a bank account under an assumed or fictitious name, a certified copy of the certificate must be produced to the bank. Use of the name "and Company" or "& Co." for a sole proprietorship is expressly prohibited in New York, N.Y. Gen. Bus. Law § 132; also, a fictitious name cannot be used if it would be misleading or if it would otherwise constitute unfair competition, trademark infringement or invasion of privacy. The person affected by the name could go to court to seek an injunction.

A sole proprietor retains all profits and is subject to unlimited personal liability for acts committed by employees within the scope of their employment. The proprietorship ends on the proprietor's death or retirement, and the business is an asset of the estate.

PRACTICE GUIDE

The sole proprietorship is initially the simplest and cheapest form of business formation but fraught with the danger of unlimited personal liability. If you permit, or your client insists on, its use, stress the need for substantial liability insurance coverage for tort claims to protect the client's other assets from such risks.

B. The General Partnership

A partnership is an association of two or more persons to carry on as co-owners a business for profit. For this purpose, a "person" may be a corporation, and thus a corporation may be a member of a partnership.

In a general partnership, each partner has unlimited personal liability and a voice in management. General partnership law in New York has been codified based largely on the Uniform Partnership Act ("UPA"), most of which New York has adopted in the Partnership Law. As with the sole proprietorship, a general partnership may be formed without any formality or expense, and may arise by an express or implied agreement among the partners to associate themselves in business for purposes of a profit.

New York, however, requires that a general partnership file, in every county in which it does business, a certificate indicating the name and address of the partnership and the full name and address of each partner. N.Y. Gen. Bus. Law § 130. The partnership name may consist simply of the names of the partners themselves or may be assumed or fictitious, but may not include the name of one not a member of the partnership. *See id.*; N.Y. Part. Law § 82.

If the membership of the partnership or the address of any of the partners changes, an amended certificate must also be filed. N.Y. Gen. Bus. Law § 130(3). Failure to comply with these filing provisions constitutes a misdemeanor and precludes the partnership from maintaining any action or proceeding in the courts of New York State, but does not affect the contractual rights, duties and liabilities of the partners. N.Y. Gen. Bus. Law § 130(8) and (9).

SELECTION OF THE CORPORATE STRUCTURE

Although no written agreement is necessary to form a partnership, it is most advisable to have a written partnership agreement, often called "Articles of Partnership." It will usually spell out the rights and duties of the partners as among themselves, and the respective investments, profit-sharing rights, management and voting powers of the partners, as well as the consequences of the death or withdrawal of a partner from the partnership, and the methods by which the partnership may be voluntarily dissolved.

The major disadvantages of a general partnership are unlimited personal liability, lack of management flexibility, and lack of continuity of existence. With respect to liability, each of the general partners stands not only to lose the capital contribution invested in the partnership, but personal assets as well. Each partner is jointly liable for all partnership contracts, debts and obligations, and is jointly and severally liable for any torts or other wrongful acts of the copartners, employees and agents of the partnership committed within the scope of the partnership business. Since each partner is an agent for the others in connection with partnership business, a partner's lack of consent to partnership obligations incurred by the copartners is irrelevant. Partners are entitled to contribution and indemnity from the copartners for partnership losses, and the partnership agreement may provide additional contribution and indemnity provisions for specific transactions. However, even though a partner may obtain indemnification and contribution for losses from one or more of the copartners, a partner could still be held personally responsible by partnership creditors for the entire obligation.

Since each general partner has an equal voice in the management and control of the enterprise (absent an express agreement to the contrary), the general partnership is a relatively inflexible form of running a business. Important actions such as admission of new members or amendment of the partnership agreement require unanimous consent; ordinary matters within the scope of the business require a majority vote. The partnership agreement may, of course, alter these rules. It should be noted that there is a very strong fiduciary duty among partners.

As with the sole proprietorship, the general partnership does not have perpetual life. The partnership is legally dissolved upon the death, bankruptcy, or withdrawal of any partner, followed by "winding up" and termination of the partnership.

To provide some measure of continuity, the partnership agreement should give the remaining partners the right to buy out the interest of the withdrawing or deceased partner.

PRACTICE GUIDES

- *A general partnership, without a detailed, written agreement governing its operation, is unworkable.*

- *Avoid the general partnership in most instances unless necessary because of special circumstances such as tax considerations (e.g., holding real estate).*

- *Provide clearly in the agreement for firm governance and consider imposing arbitration for dispute resolution.*

- *Stress the need for adequate partnership and individual liability insurance against tort claims to insulate nonbusiness assets better.*

- *Stress the need for life insurance on the lives of the partners, payable to the partnership, so that there will be sufficient proceeds to buy out the deceased partner's interest.*

C. The Limited Partnership Formed Prior to July 1, 1991

A limited partnership consists of one or more general partners with unlimited liability for all obligations incurred by the partnership and one or more limited partners whose liability is limited to the extent of his/her capital contribution. Unlike the general partnership, which may arise solely by conduct, a limited partnership can be formed only by a writing pursuant to the New York Partnership Law, a requirement derived from the Uniform Limited Partnership Act ("ULPA"). *See* N.Y. Part. Law § 90 *et seq.* The New York statute requires the filing of a certificate detailing the names and addresses of all partners, their respective contri-

SELECTION OF THE CORPORATE STRUCTURE

butions and profit shares, the duration of the partnership and other information on the partners' respective rights and duties. *See* N.Y. Part. Law § 91. The certificate together with any amendments must be filed in the clerk's office in the county where the partnership has its principal place of business and a copy published once a week for six weeks in two newspapers of general circulation in the county where the partnership has its principal place of business. N.Y. Part. Law § 91(b).

The limited partnership offers the principal advantages of a general partnership with the significant added advantage of limited liability for the limited partners. A limited partner retains limited liability so long as he/she does not take an active part in managing the business and does not allow his/her surname to appear in the partnership name. *See* N.Y. Part. Law § 94. In addition, a limited partner will be liable for damages sustained by anyone who relies on statements in the partnership certificate which the limited partner knows to be false. *See* N.Y. Part. Law § 95.

The position of limited partners in a limited partnership corresponds somewhat to that of shareholders in a corporation. Both enjoy limited liability while lacking managerial power, except that shareholders in a corporation elect directors on a regular basis. Like corporate shareholders, limited partners enjoy rights of inspection of records, N.Y. Part. Law § 99, and in New York, may sue derivatively in the right of the limited partnership to procure a judgment in its favor. N.Y. Part. Law § 115-a *et seq*. Moreover, limited partnership interests are considered "securities" and as such must be registered with the Securities and Exchange Commission or otherwise comply with the federal securities laws if offered for sale to the public.

In theory, a limited partner's freedom to assign his/her interest is nearly as great as that of a corporate shareholder. A limited partner may assign the right to receive profits, and may sell his/her interest in the partnership, and substitute another limited partner if the certificate so provides. N.Y. Part. Law § 108. As a practical matter, however, there normally is no ready market for a partner's interest in a limited partnership.

The continuity of a limited partnership is more easily maintained than in a general partnership, but nevertheless is not perpetual as in the case of a corporation. Death or withdrawal of a general partner may not automatically dissolve the partnership if the certificate so provides, or if unanimous consent of the remaining partners is obtained to continue the business. N.Y. Part. Law § 109. By definition, the partnership will be dissolved upon the death of the sole or all general partners or at the expiration of the term stated in the certificate.

PRACTICE GUIDES

- *The limited partnership is a useful and effective vehicle for many businesses, especially where the parties' contribution to the venture differs in nature or amount.*

- *Great care must be taken literally to comply with all of the statutory requirements. A defectively formed limited partnership could well be characterized by the Internal Revenue Service (the "IRS") as an unincorporated association and lead to disastrous tax consequences; a defective limited partnership also could make the limited partners liable to creditors.*

- *Do not use a corporate general partner unless (1) it has an appropriate independent net worth (e.g., 15 percent of the total amount invested in the partnership) or (2) there is also an individual general partner.*

D. The Revised Limited Partnership Act

In 1976, the Commissioners on Uniform State Laws promulgated a Revised Uniform Limited Partnership Act ("RULPA"). Subsequently, the Commissioners promulgated a 1985 version of RULPA; approximately 40 states have so far adopted some form of RULPA.

This author is happy to report that as of July 1, 1991, New York has amended its limited partnership statute, being one of the last states to adopt a version of RULPA. A committee of the New York State Bar Association, of which this author was a member, had been actively working on and completed a draft for submission to the legislature as far back as 1984. Since that date the committee has still continued to strive

SELECTION OF THE CORPORATE STRUCTURE 9

for its adoption by the New York State legislature; various modifications were included so that the statute could finally be passed. A great deal of credit should be given to Bruce Rich, Chair of the Partnership Subcommittee of the Corporation Committee's Business Law Section of the New York State Bar Association, for his consistent devoted attention in seeing that the Limited Partnership Act was in fact finally amended.

The new Limited Partnership Law is contained in Article 8-A and is referred to as the "Revised Limited Partnership Act." This has been added to the Partnership Law pursuant to Chapters 950, 951, and 952 of the Laws of 1990, and Chapter 33 of the Laws of 1991.

The new law applies to all domestic limited partnerships formed on or after July 1, 1991, and to all foreign limited partnerships whenever they were formed. As part of the statutory amendment, the Legislature repealed the original Article 8-A on Foreign Limited Partnerships. §§ 120 - 120-1. The Revised Limited Partnership Act, contained in Article 8-A of the Partnership Law, has section numbers from 121-101 to 121-1300.

The new law can be available to any existing domestic limited partnership previously formed, provided it elects to be governed by the new law's provisions. If an existing limited partnership amends its certificate of limited partnership at any time after the effective date of July 1, 1991, it will automatically be covered and will then be applicable to the Revised Limited Partnership Law.

The Revised Limited Partnership Act ("RLPA") provides various improvements and modernization to the Limited Partnership Act, initially based upon the original Uniform Limited Partnership Act, passed in New York in the year 1916.

Included herein is a summary of some of the RLPA provisions.

There will be centralized filing of the limited partnership certificate with the Secretary of State. There will be a centralized place for filing and for checking limited partnership names, thus making it similar to the corporate filing system. This system is in lieu of that under the prior law where filing was countywide. The limited partnership shall contain the words "Limited Partnership" or "L.P." RLPA § 121-102. Also, a limited partnership name can be reserved.

RLPA provides a more streamlined certificate of limited partnership (the "Certificate"), requiring only 6 to 7 enumerated items, which is much less than the prior requirement of 14. The required items include the name of the partnership; the county in which the office of the limited partnership is to be located; designation of the Secretary of State as agent for service of process and designation of an address to which copies of process will be sent; the listing of a registered agent, if any; the names and addresses of all general partners; the term of the limited partnership; and any additional items that the general partners decide to include. You may note that some of these requirements are similar to the filing requirements for a corporation.

There is no longer a requirement for describing the capital structure and for listing the names, addresses and capital contributions of limited partners. The Certificate has to be filed by the general partners, and any amendments can be signed by one general partner and any new general partner. A certificate of cancellation, however, must be signed by all general partners. The limited partnership is formed upon filing the Certificate with the Department of State or on a later date specified in the Certificate (not to exceed 60 days thereafter). RLPA § 121-201.

However, there must thereafter be compliance with the notice provisions; to wit, the Certificate or a notice containing the substance thereof must be published in two newspapers (to be designated by the county clerk) once a week for six successive weeks. Proof of publication must be filed within 120 days after the Certificate is filed; the failure to file such proof shall prohibit the limited partnership from maintaining any action or proceeding in this state. This applies to new limited partnerships formed after July 1, 1991, and to all foreign limited partnerships. *See* §§ 121-201(c) and 121-902(d). Thus, RLPA still retains some of the antiquated features of the New York statute (e.g., the publication requirement), and in addition provides for publication of all foreign limited partnerships.

SELECTION OF THE CORPORATE STRUCTURE

The partnership agreement sets forth the basic relationship between the partners. RLPA § 121-110. The partnership agreement shall be signed by all general partners, but need not be signed by the limited partners.

All existing domestic limited partnerships formed prior to July 1, 1991, continue to be subject to the provisions of the existing Article 8 of the Partnership Law. N.Y. Part. Law § 90-115-c. However, if any existing domestic limited partnership wishes to be covered pursuant to the provisions of RLPA, it must comply with all of the new provisions.

An existing limited partnership may elect to be governed by RLPA by filing with the Department of State a "Certificate of Adoption of Revised Limited Partnership Act." RLPA § 121-1202. Such filing is basically a certificate of limited partnership and must include the required items for certificates of limited partnership under the new law, and the notice of such filing must be filed with the county clerk of the county. If a limited partnership elects to be governed under RLPA, the general partners of the limited partnership may make the election at any time. Once a certificate of adoption has been filed, the limited partnership will then be subject to RLPA Article 8-A.

There are specific provisions included in RLPA to allow an existing limited partnership to keep its name, notwithstanding restrictions on names in the new law.

If an existing limited partnership does not elect to be subject to RLPA and does not file any amended certificate, the provisions of the existing law would continue to be applicable to such partnership. RLPA § 121-1201.

New York will continue to have limited partnerships formed pursuant to the prior act, which will be in full force and effect, as well as limited partnerships formed pursuant to RLPA. The legal community will continue to be familiar with the previously existing Limited Partnership Law, Part. Law § 90-115-c, and also the Revised Limited Partnership Law, RLPA Article 8-A.

If an existing limited partnership seeks to file an amendment after July 1, 1991, the amendment must be filed with the Department of State and must include certain prescribed information. After the amendment is filed, all filing requirements under RLPA are then applicable to the limited partnership. In addition, a notice of the filing with the Department of State must also be made with the county clerk of the county in which the prior Certificate was filed, indicating that an amendment has been filed with the Department of State. Thereafter, no further county notifications are required.

The capitalization requirements of a limited partnership have been greatly expanded to include cash, property, services rendered, or a promissory note or other obligation to contribute cash or property or to render services. RLPA § 121-501.

The limited partner is not liable for obligations and liabilities of the limited partnership, unless he/she participates in the control of the partnership business. RLPA provides for an increased role of the limited partners in certain partnership decisions, while still protecting their limited liability, and provides a safe harbor of various activities in which a limited partner may engage without incurring full unlimited liability. RLPA creates an extensive list of activities which do not cause a limited partner to lose its limited liability status. This extensive list of permitted activities for a limited partner include some of the following: transacting business with, including being a contractor for, or an agent or employee of the limited partnership or of a general partner or an officer, director or shareholder of a corporate general partner, or a partner of a partnership that is a general partner of the limited partnership; holding positions on behalf of the general partner, such as being an officer, director, shareholder, trustee, fiduciary or executor of such entity; and approving or disapproving amendments of the partnership agreement or calling for or participating in meetings of the partners. The limited partners may also propose, approve or disapprove and vote for amendment of the agreement, dissolution and winding up of the limited partnership, sale, exchange, lease, mortgage or other transfer, or grant of security interest in any assets of the limited partnership, as well as any other matters as are stated in the partnership agreement for such pur-

SELECTION OF THE CORPORATE STRUCTURE 13

poses. All of these can be performed by a limited partner without losing status as a limited partner with limited liability. *See* RLPA § 121-303 for an extensive list of permitted activities.

If a limited partner does actually participate in the control of the business, the limited partner may be liable, but only to the person who transacted business with the limited partnership, reasonably believing, based upon the limited partner's conduct, that such limited partner is a general partner. RLPA § 121-303(a).

A limited partner who consents in writing to the use of his name in the name of the limited partnership also will be liable to creditors who extend credit unaware that such person is not a general partner. RLPA § 121-303(d).

RLPA provides for mergers and consolidations of limited partnerships. RLPA §§ 121-1101 - 1104.

There is provision for a limited partner to commence a derivative action. RLPA §§ 121-1002 - 1003).

As stated previously, all foreign limited partnerships, no matter when they were formed, are governed by RLPA, as the previously existing sections of Article 8-A regarding foreign limited partnerships have been repealed.

The above are several of the provisions in summary form pursuant to the Revised Limited Partnership Act. There may be various technical and other amendments proposed after attorneys start using the new law. Certainly the new statute has numerous benefits for a business, even though the publication requirement is still present.

The author wishes to caution any attorneys undertaking the formation of new limited partnerships to be cautious of the new law and how it works, and the attorney should check periodically for any recent or new amendments. Any attorney representing an existing limited partnership who elects to be covered under the new statute should discuss this carefully with the client as to whether the client wishes to be covered, considering the costs involved. This enactment is finally modernizing

New York's Limited Partnership Law, but, as noted previously, there may be many other amendments over the months and several years to come.

E. The Joint Venture

A joint venture (sometimes called joint adventure) is very similar to a general partnership but differs in that a joint venture is more limited in its purpose, scope and duration. Very often a joint venture is formed for a single undertaking.

The arrangement is also generally more informal than that of a partnership; often a joint venture will have no group name. The joint venture is so similar in most respects to a general partnership that the rules governing partnerships will also be applied by courts to it. Thus the joint venture is characterized by unlimited liability and equality of control and is generally taxed as a partnership.

The term "joint venture" is often used in agreements between two parties to give effect to a common purpose. Such agreements normally are not intended to set up a true partnership. Consequently, the draftsman should take great care specifically to deny that the agreement creates a partnership or enables one party to bind the other.

F. The Joint Stock Association

A joint stock company or association is an unincorporated business enterprise with ownership interests represented by shares of stock pooled in a common fund. As used in the New York General Associations Law, the term "joint stock association" includes every unincorporated joint stock enterprise having written articles of association and capital stock divided into shares, other than a corporation or business trust. N.Y. Gen. Assn's Law § 2.

The joint stock association is very often referred to as an unincorporated association. It is not an artificial person and has no existence independent of its members. The New York statutes specifically recognize joint stock associations as legal entities, impose certain regulations

SELECTION OF THE CORPORATE STRUCTURE 15

and grant them the privilege of operating as a corporation in virtually every respect except that shareholders are personally liable for the debts of the company.

The unincorporated association may sue or be sued in the name of its president or treasurer and is a form commonly used by labor unions. New York law specifically sets out procedures to facilitate incorporation of a joint stock association. *See* N.Y. Gen. Assn's Law § 7-a.

PRACTICE GUIDES

- *The joint venture and joint stock association, in their pure forms, are rarely used business entities.*

G. The Corporation

A corporation is a legal entity created by statute that exists as a legal person, separate and distinct from its individual owners or shareholders. A corporation may be formed by one or more natural persons, 18 years of age or older. It is the only form of business enterprise which combines the elements of limited liability, perpetual existence, and free transferability of interests. In addition, it offers a reliable form for raising capital from outside investors and flexible operation for those interested primarily in profits rather than day-to-day control. The corporate form may pose certain tax disadvantages in comparison with the partnership form, particularly for small businesses, but the necessity for one or more of the distinct corporate elements frequently dictates the decision to incorporate. Moreover, a small business may elect to incorporate and be taxed in much the same way as a partnership under Subchapter S of the Internal Revenue Code, which is discussed in detail in Chapter 3.

The Business Corporation Law (the "BCL"), the general statutory plan governing stock corporations for profit in New York, requires filing for approval with the Secretary of State a certificate of incorporation detailing the corporate name, corporate purpose or purposes, place of office, duration (if other than perpetual), number of shares authorized to be issued (including a description of classes and series of shares, if any), and name and address of the registered agent, if any, for service of process. BCL § 402. In addition, the certificate must state the aggregate number of shares the corporation is authorized to issue, the classes of stock, if more than one, with their relative rights, preferences and limitations, and must designate the Secretary of State as agent for service of process against the corporation. The certificate may also contain any other provisions governing operation of the corporation which are not inconsistent with law.

Incorporation also requires payment of organization taxes and filing fees, the drafting of by-laws and the recording of minutes of the organization meeting of the incorporators and of the board of directors. Although corporations face more pervasive and continuing governmental regulation than other forms of business, they remain clearly the most proper form of business organization, even for small enterprises looking for simple operation.

In many states, corporations are required to have a minimum amount of capital paid in as a condition of doing business. New York, however, has no such requirement. The initial capitalization of a New York corporation is discussed more fully in Chapter 4.

Management of a corporation is vested in the board of directors, elected by the shareholders. Shareholders, as the ultimate beneficial owners of the corporation, retain the power to approve or disapprove certain major policy decisions such as merger, dissolution or sale of substantially all of the corporate assets. Shareholders do not, however, hold actual title to corporate assets; title is in the name of the corporation, a separate entity.

Probably the most attractive advantage of a corporation from an investor standpoint is that a shareholder has liability limited only to the extent of his/her capital contribution. The advantage, however, is more theoretical than real in many closely held corporate situations.

Realizing the problem of limited liability, creditors, particularly the more experienced ones, will frequently demand a personal guarantee of the corporate debt by the shareholders and/or officers of the corporation before credit will be extended to the corporation. In that way, the creditor is protected: If the corporation does not pay, the creditor will still be

SELECTION OF THE CORPORATE STRUCTURE 17

able to sue the person(s) who have personally guaranteed the corporate obligation. The shareholder, even though he/she has limited liability for corporate debts, will find that as a practical matter, most creditors (particularly banks and other lenders) will request a personal guarantee, and thus the shareholder will lose its limited liability to that creditor.

In New York, the ten largest shareholders of a corporation (whose shares are not traded on a national exchange) are personally responsible for unpaid wage claims. BCL § 630. If the corporation does not pay its employees, they may have the right under certain circumstances to sue the ten largest shareholders personally for this claim. In addition, counsel should read Section 630 carefully, as salary and unpaid wages also include vacation pay, union benefits to be paid by the employer, and payments to the union welfare fund, etc. It is believed that New York is the only state with such a provision. The New York Court of Appeals has upheld the constitutionality of Section 630 in *Sasso v. Vachris*, 66 N.Y.2d 28, 494 N.Y.S.2d 856 (1985).

Shareholders are not fiduciaries for each other, as are partners, and provided they are not majority or controlling owners, shareholders may act in their own best interest, even to the detriment of the corporation. They may freely transfer their shares, absent agreement to the contrary, thus making possible perpetual succession of the corporate entity, notwithstanding change in ownership.

III. SELECTION OF JURISDICTION

A. In General

Deciding where to incorporate is important because the law of the state of incorporation ordinarily governs the internal affairs of a corporation. Internal affairs encompass the relationships among the shareholders, directors and officers, between shareholders and corporate creditors, and among the shareholders themselves. For example, the shareholders' rights to vote, to compel distribution of dividends and to inspect corporate records are all matters of internal operation governed by the law of the state of incorporation—in New York, the Business Corporation Law.

In choosing a state in which to incorporate, one should also consider each state's external rules such as tax or pollution control laws imposed by states on domestic corporations and on foreign corporations (i.e., those incorporated in another state) "doing business" within the state's borders. If a corporation incorporated elsewhere transacts local business within New York, it is required to file and qualify as a foreign corporation, which subjects it to New York regulation and enables it to sue and be sued in the New York courts. *See* BCL §§ 1301, 1312.

Occasionally, a state will even apply its own corporation law governing internal affairs to a "nominal" or "pseudo" foreign corporation that is incorporated elsewhere but which in fact does most of its business in the local state. The Business Corporation Law, for example, specifically subjects foreign corporations doing business in New York to various provisions of the BCL, particularly with regard to director or officer misconduct, but exempts such firms from certain of those provisions if they are listed on a national securities exchange or if less than one-half of their total business income is allocable to New York for franchise tax purposes. *See* BCL §§ 1317-1320.

Consequently, an enterprise doing business only in New York should ordinarily be incorporated in New York; otherwise, it may be subjected to regulation and taxation not only in its own state of incorporation but also in New York as a "foreign corporation." If, however, a corporation anticipates doing substantial local business outside New York (as opposed to purely interstate business), or if it wishes to avoid a particularly onerous BCL provision, or wishes to obtain the benefit of a particular provision of another state's corporation law, incorporation in another jurisdiction may be advantageous despite the additional expense. In most cases, if not all, the alternative state to which one would turn would be Delaware, which has traditionally been the most accommodating state toward corporations, and, in particular, corporate management. Of the 1,565 corporations listed on the New York Stock Exchange, over 40 percent are incorporated in the state of Delaware. Of the 500 largest corporations, more than one-third are likewise incorporated in Delaware.

SELECTION OF THE CORPORATE STRUCTURE

The following section lists some of the major advantages and disadvantages of incorporation in Delaware and in New York.

B. Delaware vs. New York

1. Delaware Advantages

a. Organization tax rates in Delaware are significantly lower than in New York; both, however, are relatively nominal (see discussion in Chapter 18).

b. New York requires one or more natural persons to act as incorporators (one is sufficient). BCL § 401. Delaware permits any partnership, association or corporation, as well as any natural person, to act as incorporator.

c. A Delaware corporation may be organized for any lawful purpose; a New York corporation must specify its authorized purpose or purposes in its certificate of incorporation, BCL § 402, although New York now does permit an all-purpose clause.

d. Delaware permits a corporation to issue any class of stock in series, with varying voting and preference rights if the articles so provide. New York permits issuance in series only within the class of preferred stock. BCL § 402.

e. A Delaware corporation may issue stock options upon approval of the board of directors. New York requires majority shareholder approval if options are to be issued to officers, directors or employees of the corporation. BCL § 505(d).

f. Delaware permits dividends to be paid out of surplus or if there is no accumulated surplus, out of the net profits for the fiscal year for which the dividend is declared (provided capital represented by preferred stock is not impaired). New York limits the available funds for dividends to "surplus," provided the corporation is not insolvent and will not be rendered insolvent. BCL § 510.

g. In Delaware, a majority vote of shareholders is sufficient to approve a merger, a dissolution or a sale or lease of all or substantially all of the corporation's assets. In New York, a two-thirds vote of the shareholders is required to approve these actions. BCL §§ 903, 909, 1001.

h. Delaware permits shareholder action by written consent if signed by the requisite number of shareholders necessary to authorize or take such action. New York permits written consent in lieu of a meeting, but such shareholder consent must be unanimous. BCL § 615.

i. Under Delaware law, a shareholder's proxy is valid for three years or for such longer time as the proxy states. Under New York law, a proxy ceases to be valid after eleven months, unless it expressly provides otherwise. BCL § 609(b).

j. Under Delaware law, committees may consist of one or more directors. New York requires a committee to consist of a minimum of three directors. BCL § 712.

k. Under New York law, the ten largest shareholders of a New York corporation, whose shares are not traded on a national exchange, are personally responsible (and jointly and severally liable) for unpaid wages and other salary claims due and owing to the employees of the corporation. BCL § 630. Delaware has no such provisions.

l. Both New York and Delaware law contain liberal provisions for indemnification of directors and officers for litigation expenses by the corporation. Both states amended their indemnification statutes recently (for a detailed discussion, see Chapter 8). New York and Delaware both declare that the indemnification statutes are not exclusive of any other rights to which directors and officers may be entitled under any by-law or other agreement of stockholders or disinterested directors. *See* BCL §§ 721-726.

m. New York grants to shareholders much more extensive appraisal rights than are available under Delaware law. *See* BCL § 623.

n. The Delaware corporation statute has benefited from drafting and construction by corporate specialists, and traditionally Delaware corporations have enjoyed favorable treatment by a sympathetic legislature. The result is a body of well-settled law offering greater predictability and accommodation to corporations than any to be found elsewhere.

SELECTION OF THE CORPORATE STRUCTURE   21

2. New York Advantages

a. By statute, nonresident directors of Delaware corporations are deemed to have appointed either the registered agent of the corporation or the Secretary of State as their agent for service of process. New York has no similar provision. The constitutionality of the Delaware provision is unclear, however. For example, see *Shaffer v. Heitner*, 433 U.S. 186 (1977), which struck down on due process grounds a predecessor Delaware statute subjecting any nonresident stockholder of a Delaware corporation to suit in Delaware regardless of the stockholder's other contacts with the state.

b. New York makes express provision for reservation of a corporate name. BCL § 303. In Delaware, reservation of name is by administrative courtesy.

c. In New York, filing of the certificate of incorporation is conclusive evidence of the proper formation of the corporation as against anyone but the Attorney General in a special proceeding. BCL § 403. In Delaware, the filing is *prima facie* evidence only.

It can be seen that the disadvantages of incorporating in Delaware are relatively minor compared with the advantages. Nevertheless, most of the advantages of the Delaware law are not of great consequence to small, closely held corporations. Unless a corporation plans to operate with little or no surplus, or unless it will have a large number of inaccessible shareholders making it difficult to obtain their consent when needed, there is little need for the added flexibility offered by the Delaware statute. The attraction of Delaware law is greatest for large, Fortune 500-type companies, the majority of which are in fact incorporated there.

IV. ANATOMY OF A CORPORATION

A. The Corporation as a "Person"

1. Statutory Rules

As already noted, a corporation is considered a legal person, separate and distinct from its shareholder-owners. It differs principally in that it enjoys perpetual existence. The Business Corporation Law also specifically grants to corporations, in furtherance of their corporate purposes, the power to sue and be sued, to own and convey property, to make contracts and to become a partner or member of other business enterprises. BCL § 202. Generally, unless it appears by express provision or context that the intention is otherwise, the word "persons," when used in a statute, includes a corporation. Thus a corporation has been held to be a "client" for purposes of the attorney-client privilege and may be held to have committed a crime or tort. A corporation may sue for defamation, but not for invasion of privacy. For purposes of federal diversity jurisdiction, a corporation is a "citizen" of every state in which it is incorporated, and of the one state where it is deemed to have its principal place of business. For purposes of federal court venue, a corporation may be sued in any district where it is incorporated, or does business, or is licensed to do business. In New York, a corporation, for venue purposes, is deemed a resident of the county in which its principal office (as stated in the certificate of incorporation) is located. N.Y. C.P.L.R. § 503(c); BCL § 102(a)(10).

2. Constitutional Provisions

Under the federal Constitution, a corporation enjoys the fourth amendment right against unreasonable searches and seizures, the fourteenth amendment rights not to be deprived of liberty or property without due process and the right not to be denied by any state the equal protection of the laws. A corporation does not, however, enjoy the fifth amendment privilege against self-incrimination. This is of some significance since it precludes virtually any constitutional objection a corporation might enter against an administrative subpoena ordering production of documents for investigatory purposes.

The United States Supreme Court has significantly expanded the first amendment rights of corporations in recent years, particularly in the areas of political and so-called commercial "speech." *See, e.g., First National Bank of Boston v. Bellotti*, 435 U.S. 765 (1978) (political speech); *Virginia State Board of Pharmacy v. Virginia Citizens Con-*

sumer Council, Inc., 425 U.S. 748 (1976) (commercial speech). The state of the law in these areas is still somewhat uncertain.

B. The Corporation as an Entity

Generally, the corporate entity remains distinct even though all of its shares are owned by a single individual or by another corporation. Nevertheless, on occasion, courts will ignore the corporate entity in instances where fraudulent incorporation and/or fraudulent operation can be proven. In such situations, courts may "pierce the corporate veil" by imposing personal liability upon the controlling shareholder(s) for the benefit of corporate creditors. As a result, the creditors are allowed to look beyond the corporate assets (which are often deliberately minimal) and can reach into the shareholders' personal assets for recovery. Where the veil pierced is that of a subsidiary corporation, thereby exposing the parent corporation to liability as the sole shareholder, the liability of the parent's shareholders will still be limited to their investment in the parent. The law permits incorporation of a business for the very purpose of enabling its owners to escape personal liability and therefore, unless two entities are represented to creditors as one unit to the point of fraud, disregard of the corporate entity is extremely unlikely. Indeed, the leading New York cases indicate a strong antipathy toward veil-piercing. See *Walkovszky v. Carlton*, 18 N.Y.2d 414, 223 N.E.2d 6, 276 N.Y.S.2d 585 (1966); *Bartle v. Home Owners Co-op., Inc.*, 309 N.Y. 103, 127 N.E.2d 832 (1955). More common are cases in which putative loans to the corporation by corporate insiders are treated as contributions to capital rather than loans, enabling creditor claims by controlling shareholders to be subordinated to the claims of outside creditors. *See, e.g., Pepper v. Litton*, 308 U.S. 295 (1939); *SEC v. Liberty Banking Corp.*, 240 F.2d 511 (2d Cir.), *cert. denied*, 353 U.S. 930 (1957).

Thus it can be seen that instances of corporate veil-piercing are relatively rare. Ordinarily, courts will respect the corporate entity so long as shareholders segregate the corporate assets from their individual assets, maintain separate corporate records, hold separate shareholders' and directors' meetings for affiliated entities, and observe the legal formalities of the corporation's existence and operation. *See Walter E. Heller & Co. v. Video Innovations, Inc.*, 730 F.2d 50, 53 (2d Cir. 1984) and *In Establishment Tomis v. Shearson Hayden Stone*, 459 F. Supp. 1355 (S.D.N.Y. 1978) for a list of criteria courts examine in this area.

Some courts also look at the question of whether the corporation has adequate capitalization. Although this may be a strong factor in favor of piercing the corporate veil in other states, it is not a major deciding factor in the New York courts and is merely one factor to be considered. Theoretically, in New York, if a corporation is formed with a limited amount of capital, even as little as $1, that would not be grounds in and of itself to pierce the corporate veil. *See Gardner v. Snyder*, 607 F.2d 582 (2d Cir. 1979).

Courts will pierce the corporate veil only in extreme situations of fraud; it is a remedy that is not very often granted. However, courts may use other methods to reach shareholders' assets in particularly egregious cases. For example, in *Farm Stores Inc. v. School Feeding Corp.*, 102 A.D.2d 249, 477 N.Y.S.2d 374 (1984), *aff'd*, 64 N.Y.2d 1065, 489 N.Y.S. 2d 877 (1985), the court set aside a transfer of funds from the corporation to its shareholders as a fraudulent conveyance, and entered judgment against the shareholders individually for the sums each of the shareholders wrongfully received.

Shareholders of a professional corporation likewise have limited liability, except for malpractice claims. By statute, any shareholder of a professional corporation who commits malpractice while performing professional services is personally liable for the damage caused; in addition, the professional person is personally liable for the negligent or wrongful professional acts performed by employees and other professionals under his/her supervision and control. *See* BCL § 1505. However, shareholders in a professional corporation have the benefit of limited liability as to all other types of claims, the same as shareholders in other corporations. *See We're Associates Co. v. Cohen, Stracher & Bloom P.D.*, 65 N.Y.2d 148, 490 N.Y.S.2d 743 (1985).

SELECTION OF THE CORPORATE STRUCTURE

C. Purposes and Powers of a Corporation—Some Problems

1. *Ultra Vires* and Charitable Contributions

Although New York law permits a corporation to be formed for "any lawful business purpose or purposes," BCL § 201(a), the certificate of incorporation must be reasonably specific with regard to what that business will be. BCL § 402. However, New York now permits an "all-purpose" clause. BCL § 402(a)(2). The certificate might specify that the corporation is organized to "manufacture, produce . . . and sell or otherwise dispose of" a certain product or products. Careful counsel will draft the "purposes" clause in as broad language as possible so as to encompass every possible corporate activity envisioned by the founders. The corporation must then confine its activities to those stated in the certificate of incorporation and those which are in furtherance of its stated purposes, so as to expose investors only to business risks specifically assumed, and not to exceed the authority granted by the state. Since a corporation is formed pursuant to statute, the corporation obtains its express authority and corporate powers from the state upon approval of the powers contained in the certificate of incorporation. Although under Section 402(a)(2) of the BCL it is no longer necessary to include a specific purpose clause, most attorneys will still include one or more specific purposes in addition to a general purpose clause.

The corporation has no permission from the state and thus no authority to perform acts that exceed the express stated corporate purposes. Nor may a corporation act outside its implied powers. Actions which exceed the scope of the stated or implied corporate powers are considered to be *ultra vires*.

The doctrine of *ultra vires*, once prevalent, has less force under modern statutes and decisions. In New York today, remedies for *ultra vires* activities are expressly limited to actions (a) by a shareholder to enjoin unauthorized acts of the corporation; (b) by the corporation (or by a shareholder on its behalf) against its officers or directors for damages to the corporation caused by unauthorized acts; and (c) by the Attorney General to dissolve the corporation or to enjoin it from performing unauthorized acts. BCL § 203. Thus, *ultra vires* is no longer a defense in claims between the corporation and third parties. Even where it may be asserted, the doctrine rarely serves as an effective control on corporate action, since the modern view of the permissible scope of corporate activities is considerably expanded. For example, corporate contributions to charity are generally upheld today as incidental to their stated purposes, though they were once viewed as suspect on the theory that the purpose of a business is to make profits. New York specifically empowers corporations to make donations for the public welfare or for charitable, scientific, civic or educational purposes, regardless of corporate benefit. BCL § 202(a)(12). To the extent, however, that corporate managers implement their own notions of social responsibility, or advance their own political ambitions by excessive gifts of corporate property, they may be found to have wasted corporate assets.

2. Political Contributions

State and federal restrictions on corporate political activity illustrate the distinction between *ultra vires* and illegality, which are sometimes confused. Ordinarily, political contributions by corporations in furtherance of their own interest would seem safely within a permissible corporate purpose, and thus not *ultra vires*. *See, e.g., Schwartz v. Romnes*, 495 F.2d 844, 854 (2d Cir. 1974), where a telephone company's expenditures to publicize its views on a proposed state transportation bond issue were held not to be *ultra vires* since they were within the traditional New York corporate benefit rule. Indeed, the New York State Election Commission does not require reporting by committees formed to support issue adoption. Furthermore, with respect to campaigns in support of statewide propositions or constitutional amendments, there are no effective limits on the dollar amount of corporate support.

Nevertheless, a political expenditure by a New York corporation that is not *ultra vires* may still be illegal under either Section 14-116 of the New York Election Law (prohibiting corporate expenditures above $5,000 in the aggregate per calendar year for any political candidate or party or for any political purpose) or illegal under the Federal Elections Campaign Act, 2 U.S.C. § 441(b) (prohibiting any corporate political contribution in federal elections). Within the federal framework, corpo-

SELECTION OF THE CORPORATE STRUCTURE 27

rations may form political action committees, not supported by corporate funds except for basic organization and administration, in order to have a repository for employee contributions, the sole purpose of which is to make political contributions. In light of recent United States Supreme Court Decisions, however, both the New York and federal statutes may yet be subject to constitutional challenge. *See Buckley v. Valeo*, 424 U.S. 1 (1976) (first amendment prohibits restrictions on campaign expenditure by individuals); *cf. First National Bank of Boston v. Bellotti*, 435 U.S. 765 (1978) (corporation is a person for first amendment purposes). *See also Consolidated Edison Co. v. Public Service Commission*, 447 U.S. 530 (1980) (state prohibition on utility's inclusion in monthly bills of inserts discussing controversial public issues was held to be unconstitutional).

CHAPTER TWO

FEDERAL INCOME TAX ASPECTS OF CORPORATIONS AND ALTERNATIVE WAYS OF DOING BUSINESS

Henry M. Cohn

FEDERAL INCOME TAX ASPECTS OF CORPORATIONS

I. INTRODUCTION AND OVERVIEW

Probably the biggest dilemma facing the lawyer with small business clients is the extent to which he/she needs to become a "tax expert." The resolution of this dilemma is not an easy one. Tax considerations permeate the entire field of corporate practice, and despite recent efforts by Congress to reduce the need for tax planning when making business decisions, counsel still needs to be familiar with basic tax principles and must keep abreast of changes in this highly volatile field. While most small business clients will (or should) have retained an accountant or accounting firm to assist them in preparing and filing tax returns and to advise them on the tax consequences of corporate transactions, it is difficult in practice to isolate the tax and nontax consequences of a particular business decision—the two tend to impact on each other, and often a tradeoff must be made whereby the client accepts a less-than-optimal tax consequence in order to reap a nontax benefit, or vice versa. To the extent the client can go to one professional to assist in assessing both the tax and nontax consequences of a decision, so much the better.

It is not necessary that the small business lawyer become a "tax expert," but it is necessary that he/she have sufficient knowledge to recognize tax issues as they arise and determine when a tax specialist needs to be consulted. This volume contains two resources to assist counsel in this effort: Several chapters—containing in their titles the words "Federal Income Tax Aspects"—summarize the Internal Revenue Code provisions relating to the subject matter of these chapters, while Chapter 18 summarizes the federal (other than the federal corporate income tax) and New York State tax statutes with which counsel to a small business in New York State must be familiar. Several textbooks and publications in the tax field which counsel may find useful are discussed in Chapter 21.

When reading these materials, however, counsel should keep in mind that business decisions should never be made solely for tax reasons, but should take into account all relevant business, financial, legal, regulatory and personal factors as well. To the extent the general practitioner can work with the client's tax professionals to make sure that the client's goals do not become lost in tax analysis, he/she will have performed a great service.

This section discusses the tax implications of selecting a form for the small business entity. Generally, there are five forms a small business can take: sole proprietorship, partnership (whether general or limited), S corporation, regular corporation (or "C corporation," after the subchapter of the Internal Revenue Code under which it is taxed), or trust (including a Massachusetts-type business trust). For purposes of the federal corporate income tax, however, there are only two relevant questions: (1) whether the form of a particular business is an "association," which is taxed separately from the individual human beings that make up the business; and (2) if the business is incorporated for purposes of state law, whether the corporation is an "S corporation" or a "C corporation." Because the rules governing S corporations are quite complicated, the distinctions between S and C corporations are reserved for discussion in Chapter 3.

II. DETERMINING THE FORM OF A BUSINESS ENTITY FOR TAX PURPOSES

The basic tax question confronting the lawyer in forming a small business is whether it will be deemed an "association" or a "conduit" for tax purposes. An "association" will be taxed separately from the individuals who comprise the business and act as its shareholders, employees, etc. This gives rise to the "double taxation" of corporate income, because an association's earnings will be taxed once to the "association," and taxed a second time if distributed to the members or shareholders that make up the "association." This is true both for operating income and for income realized upon liquidation of a corporation. Although a corporation could distribute or sell its assets in liquidation and generally not recognize income or loss (the "*General Utilities* doctrine") prior to the Tax Reform Act of 1986, since that Act a liquidating corporation cannot avoid recognition of gain. If the business is deemed to be a "conduit," on the other hand, it will not be taxed separately from

FEDERAL INCOME TAX ASPECTS OF CORPORATIONS

the individuals who make up the business. All income, profits, losses, etc., of the "conduit" will pass through to the individuals and be taxed only at the individual level.

In general, proprietorships and partnerships are "conduits" for tax purposes, while corporations and some types of trusts (because they are quite rare, this section does not discuss business trusts in detail) are "associations" for tax purposes. Making this determination, however, whether the business was formed as a partnership or a corporation for state law purposes, or even whether the business was properly formed under the partnership or corporation statute of a particular state, is not dispositive. Rather, Treasury Regulations require an examination of six factors: associates, business objective, centralized management, limited liability, continuity of life, and free transferability of interests. *See* I.R.C. § 7701; 26 C.F.R. § 301.7701. Under this six-factor test, a partnership properly formed under state law may be an "association" for tax purposes. It is extremely unlikely, however, that a corporation properly formed under state law will be treated as a partnership for tax purposes.

Because business entities generally have partners or shareholders ("associates") and are usually formed for the objective of carrying on a business and dividing the gains among the "associates," the "associates" and "business objective" prongs of the six-factor test tend to be disregarded by the Internal Revenue Service (the "IRS") and the courts in determining the tax status of the entity. The inquiry thus focuses on the four remaining prongs of the test: whether the entity terminates upon the withdrawal or death of an "associate" (i.e., whether or not there is "continuity of life"); whether all or only some of the "associates" participate in management decisions (i.e., whether or not there is "centralized management" on behalf of others); whether all "associates" are individually liable for the obligations of the entity or whether such liability is limited only to the amount of their investment in the entity (i.e., whether or not there is "limited liability"); and whether an "associate" may freely transfer his/her interest in the entity without the consent of the other "associates" (i.e., whether or not there is "free transferability of interest"). Under Treasury Regulations and several well-established court decisions, an entity will be deemed an "association" if it has at least three of these four characteristics, and will be deemed a partnership if it lacks two or more of these characteristics. *See, e.g., Zuckman v. United States*, 524 F.2d 729 (Ct. Cl. 1975).

Centralized Management. If the limited partners of a limited partnership own substantially all of the partnership interests and those partners do not participate in management decisions, that partnership will generally have centralized management, because the general partner or partners would manage the partnership on behalf of the limited partners. A general partnership, or a limited partnership where the general partners own a substantial portion of the partnership interests, lacks centralized management because the general partners are considered to be managing the partnership on their own behalf.

Limited Liability. A general or limited partnership where at least one general partner is an individual or well-capitalized corporation will generally lack limited liability; limited liability is lacking where at least one member (e.g., a general partner) is personally liable for the debts of the entity. A limited partnership with a single general partner that is a thinly capitalized corporation, however, may possess limited liability under the Treasury Regulations if the corporation lacks "substantial assets" other than its interest in the partnership and if the corporation is a "dummy acting as the agent of the limited partners." Revenue Procedure 89-12, 1989-1 C.B. 319 (setting forth the conditions under which the IRS will rule on the tax classification of a particular organization) provides a safe harbor for capitalizing corporate general partners: The net worth of the corporate general partner should be at least 10 percent of total partnership contributions throughout the life of the partnership to satisfy the safe harbor. It is quite common to not satisfy the 10 percent safe harbor, however, particularly where at least two other corporate characteristics are clearly lacking (such as "continuity of life" and "free transferability") or where the capital contributions to the partnership are very large (in which case counsel may feel comfortable that a lesser percentage of the capital contributions constitutes "substantial assets").

FEDERAL INCOME TAX ASPECTS OF CORPORATIONS   35

Both general and limited partnerships generally lack "continuity of life" since the death of the general partner under most state partnership statutes automatically terminates the life of the partnership, and also do not usually have "free transferability of interest" since limited partners usually cannot sell their interests without the consent of the general partner or a stated percentage of the limited partners. Accordingly, most partnerships organized under the law of a state that corresponds to the Uniform or Revised Uniform Partnership or Limited Partnership Act will be classified as partnerships for tax purposes and will therefore be deemed "conduits" such that partnership income would be taxed only at the partners' level. In general, counsel need examine this issue only for a limited partnership with a single, inadequately capitalized general partner or for a limited partnership when the same individual or entity owns substantially all of the partnership interests.

While C corporations will almost always be deemed "associations" for tax purposes, and there is little counsel can do to change that result, in certain rare instances where a corporation does not engage in a trade or business, the IRS and the courts may disregard its separate corporate existence and treat it as a nominee or agent for shareholders such that all corporate income will be taxed directly to the shareholders. For example, a corporation formed for the sole purpose of holding title to unimproved real estate, which does not lease the property, collect rents, or pay the property taxes thereon, may be treated as a nominee. It is very dangerous, however, to rely on "nominee" status for planning purposes, and taxpayers often lose such cases with disastrous results.

III. CERTAIN TAX ATTRIBUTES OF CORPORATIONS, PARTNERSHIPS AND PROPRIETORSHIPS

A number of the tax publications described briefly in Chapter 21 contain charts which show the different treatment of certain tax items for proprietorships, partnerships, S corporations and C corporations. The most important tax considerations are briefly summarized below.

A. Tax Rates

For proprietorships and for individual partners in a partnership, there are three progressive rates (15%, 28% and 31%). I.R.C. § 1. However, net long-term capital gains are subject to a maximum tax rate of 28%, and there are proposals to reinstitute an even larger preference for capital gains. For corporations, there are three progressive rates: 15% on taxable income up to $50,000; 25% on taxable income of more than $50,000 but less than (or equal to) $75,000; and 34% on taxable income of more than $75,000. I.R.C. § 11. Thus, a calendar-year corporation with taxable income of $90,000 in 1992 will compute its tax liability as follows: $7,500 (15% x $50,000) plus $6,250 (25% x $25,000) plus $5,100 (34% x $15,000) for a total tax liability of $18,850. The benefit of the lower rates will be phased out for corporations whose taxable income exceeds $100,000 in any taxable year; the tax payable by a corporation will be increased by the lesser of 5 percent of such excess or $11,750. For example, a calendar-year corporation with taxable income of $300,000 in 1988 will compute its tax liability as follows: $7,500 (15% x $50,000) plus $6,250 (25% x $25,000) plus $76,500 (34% x $225,000) plus $10,000 (5% x $200,000—the excess of taxable income over $100,000) for a total of $100,250. Because the top tax rate for corporations is higher than the top tax rate for individuals, there is an added incentive for doing business in noncorporate form, i.e., as a partnership or sole proprietorship.

B. Alternative Minimum Tax

Both corporations and individuals are subject to an alternative minimum tax (or "AMT"), which is generally calculated in much the same way for both. For corporations, the AMT is 20% (as opposed to 24% for individual partners in a partnership and for proprietorships) of "alternative minimum taxable income" in excess of $40,000, but if "alternative minimum taxable income" exceeds $150,000, the $40,000 exemption is reduced by 25% of such excess. I.R.C. §§ 55-59. For example, a corporation with "alternative minimum taxable income" of $200,000 in a given year would compute its AMT liability as follows:

FEDERAL INCOME TAX ASPECTS OF CORPORATIONS 37

because its "alternative minimum taxable income" exceeds $150,000 by $50,000, it would first reduce its $40,000 minimum by $12,500 (25% x $50,000) to $28,500; it would then subtract the $28,500 exemption from its "alternative minimum taxable income" of $200,000 for a result of $171,500; it then would calculate 20% of $171,500 for a result of $34,300. If the $34,300 is greater than the corporation's tax liability for that year calculated in the normal fashion, the corporation will be obligated to pay back up to the amount of the AMT; otherwise the standard calculation is used. (Note that the corporation would not be obligated to pay both the regular tax and the AMT.)

Generally, "alternative minimum taxable income" is the taxable income of the corporation plus certain "tax preference items" which are basically the same for proprietorships, partnerships and corporations. A major exception for corporations is that 75 percent of the excess of adjusted earnings and profits over alternative minimum taxable income is considered a tax preference item (see Chapter 10 for a discussion of the "earnings and profits" concept).

C. Computation of Taxable Income and Deductions

Generally, because a corporation by definition cannot take personal deductions as an individual can, there is no computation of "adjusted gross income" for a corporation. *See* I.R.C. § 63(a). While corporations may avail themselves of the "trade or business" deductions of Section 162 of the Internal Revenue Code, they need not be concerned about itemized deductions, the standard deduction or the $100 floor on personal casualty and theft losses, as a partner or proprietor would. Thus, taxable income for a corporation is computed simply by subtracting from gross income all Section 162 deductions and losses.

D. Deductions Which Only a Corporation May Take

In addition to Section 162 deductions, a corporation may take two deductions which are not available to partnerships or proprietorships. Under Section 243(a) of the Code, a corporation is entitled to deduct an amount equal to 70, 80 or 100 percent of the amount of dividends received from United States corporations. The 100 percent rate applies to dividends received from corporations that are members of a group affiliated with the corporation receiving the dividend, the 80 percent rate to dividends received from 20-percent-owned corporations, and the 70 percent rate to other cases. The dividends-received deduction is not available for dividends paid on stock held for 45 days or less (90 days in the case of preferred stock). Also, under Section 1059, the nontaxed portion of "extraordinary dividends" reduces the recipient corporation's basis in the stock with respect to which the dividend was paid. (An "extraordinary dividend" is one in which the dividend amount equals or exceeds 10 percent of the taxpayer's tax basis in such stock (5 percent for preferred stock).)

Under Section 248 of the Code, a corporation may deduct certain expenses in connection with its organization, including legal services in drafting organizational documents, accounting services, expenses of organizational meetings, and fees payable to the state of incorporation, provided the expenses are incurred prior to the end of the tax year in which the corporation begins business. For example, a calendar-year corporation which begins business on July 1, 1992, may deduct all qualifying organizational expenses incurred by it on or prior to December 31, 1992, but may not deduct such expenses if they are incurred on or after January 1, 1993. Expenses incurred in connection with issuing or selling shares of stock or other securities, or with the transfer of assets to the corporation, do not qualify for the deduction. A corporation may deduct qualifying organizational expenses either (1) in whole when the corporation dissolves and liquidates (*see* Chapter 16) or (2) over a period of at least 60 months, beginning the month it commences business, provided it makes an election to do so in a statement attached to the corporation's tax return for its first taxable year. *See* 26 C.F.R. § 1.248-1.

E. Net Operating Losses and Capital Losses

Under Section 172 of the Code, the net operating loss of a corporation may be carried back three years and forward fifteen years to offset taxable income for those years, in much the same fashion as a partnership or proprietorship. In addition, a corporation's calculation of net operating losses need not be adjusted for nonbusiness deductions or personal exemptions, as is required of a partnership or proprietorship, and may include the amount of a dividends-received deduction to which it is entitled under Section 243 of the Code. A corporation, however, may only use a net operating loss to offset its own corporate income from other years. A proprietor or a partner, on the other hand, may use a proprietorship's or partnership's net operating losses to offset other income of the proprietor or partner (subject to a variety of potential limitations such as the at-risk rules and the passive activity loss limitation).

Under Section 1211 of the Code, a proprietor or partner can deduct up to $3,000 of net capital losses and may carry them forward (not backward) indefinitely until absorbed by capital gains or by the $3,000 deduction in future years. I.R.C. § 1212. A corporation, on the other hand, is not allowed to deduct net capital losses from ordinary income—capital losses of a corporation can be used only as an offset against capital gains. Corporations may carry back net capital losses to the three immediately preceding years, applying them first to the earliest year and working forward in time, and may carry them forward for a period of five years. While a capital loss which is carried forward by a proprietor or partner retains its character as either a short-term or long-term capital loss, a capital loss which is carried back or forward by a corporation is converted to a short-term capital loss, whatever its initial characterization.

F. Charitable Contributions

Under Section 170 of the Code, a proprietor or partner may deduct a charitable contribution only for the year in which the contribution is made. A corporation reporting its income on the accrual method, on the other hand, may deduct a charitable contribution in the year preceding payment if the contribution was authorized by the corporation's board of directors before the last day of the year and the contribution is paid on or before the 15th day of the third month of the next year. I.R.C. § 170(a)(2). The amount of a deductible charitable contribution by a corporation is limited to 10 percent of its taxable income, computed without regard to the charitable deduction, any net operating loss or capital loss carryback, and the dividends-received deduction. A proprietor or partner, however, may deduct charitable contributions up to 50 percent of his/her adjusted gross income. I.R.C. § 170(b). Finally, Sections 170(e)(3) and 170(e)(4) of the Code set forth two special benefits for corporations that contribute to charity certain types of inventory and scientific property.

G. Depreciation Recapture

Depreciation recapture for property subject to Section 1245 of the Code is determined in the same manner for corporations, partners and proprietors. Under Section 291(a)(1) of the Code, however, corporations realize more recapture of depreciation upon sales of depreciable real property that is subject to Section 1250 of the Code.

H. Characterization of Income

In a partnership or a proprietorship, tax-advantaged items of income "pass through" to the partners or proprietor. For example, if a partnership invests in municipal bonds, the interest on which is exempt from taxation (at least at the federal level), each partner will be able to avail himself/herself of the exemption to the extent of his/her pro rata share of such investment. However, if a corporation invests in municipal bonds and distributes the interest to shareholders, the interest will be exempt from taxation at the corporate level but will be fully taxable to the shareholders as a dividend.

I. Availability of Tax-Advantaged Fringe Benefits

In general, there is parallel tax treatment of fringe benefits for C corporations, S corporations and partnerships. However, some differences do exist. For example, employees may be able to borrow from a profit-sharing plan set up by a C corporation; that is generally not so for S corporations and partnerships. For this reason, counsel may wish to consult a specialist in this area.

IV. SOME TENTATIVE GUIDELINES IN SELECTING THE STRUCTURE OF A SMALL BUSINESS ENTITY

Definitive advice in this area cannot be given without reviewing the particular client's goals and objectives and the "tradeoffs" that the particular client is willing to make. A few basic observations may, however, be made in light of the above discussion.

A. If Form Is Legally Unavailable, Do Not Consider It

It goes without saying that if a particular form of doing business is legally unavailable to a client, counsel should not even consider such a form in giving advice in this area. For example, under the laws of most states, certain professionals (e.g., doctors) may not do business as a limited partnership or C corporation, and these should automatically be ruled out in favor of a general partnership or S corporation. Similarly, any small business with more than 35 investors, or with a single corporate or partnership investor, will be automatically disqualified for S corporation status, as discussed in Chapter 3.

B. S Corporation vs. C Corporation

As a practical matter there are few situations in which a client, especially a business organizing from scratch, should opt for C corporation status over S corporation status. In a few limited situations, however, C corporation status will be preferable. If S corporation status is legally unavailable because there are more than 35 investors or one of the investors is something other than a human being, or because the capital structure of the business requires more than one class of stock (e.g., preferred and common), and partnership or proprietorship status has been ruled out, obviously the business will have to incorporate as a C corporation. In addition, if the business plans to grow aggressively via acquisitions, S corporation status may constrain the principals' business plans more than is desirable. A C corporation with earnings and profits that conducts a business that will generate substantial passive investment income should be wary of changing to an S corporation. Any business that has substantial net operating loss or capital loss carryforwards from prior or current tax years should avoid S corporation status, because under Section 1371(b) of the Code an S corporation cannot use carryforwards which were generated in a taxable year when it was not an S corporation. Finally, the availability in a C corporation of certain types of fringe benefits and employee benefit programs which are unavailable to partnerships and proprietorships may be a strong incentive to organize in that form.

An S corporation may have advantages over a C corporation even where the business to be conducted is capital intensive. A C corporation must pay taxes on its income at a top rate of 34 percent. An S corporation, however, that only distributed cash to its shareholders in an amount sufficient to enable them to pay their federal taxes needs to make distributions only at a top rate of 31 percent. (Shareholders of an S corporation must pay tax on their share of the income of the S corporation whether or not the income is distributed.)

C. Partnership vs. C Corporation

Generally, new small businesses generate more losses than profits in their first few years of operation. It will usually be more advantageous to have these "pass through" to the individuals forming the business via a partnership or proprietorship structure. Once the partnership or proprietorship begins making profits, it can always incorporate in a tax-free exchange under Section 351 of the Code (discussed in Chapter 5). Moreover, the partnership statutes of most states allow for more flexibility in drafting basic organizational documents, such as partnership agreements, than do corporation statutes, thereby reducing the overall costs of forming the business. Finally, most small businesspeople, especially those who are entering into business for the first time, will prefer to act informally, without a great deal of protocol. Many small businesses are formed by people who are personal friends and who, when push comes to shove, may not wish to threaten their friendship over business disputes. (The wisdom of forming a business with one's friends is beyond the scope of this volume.) A partnership or proprietorship is the least formal of all available forms of business organization and entails the least amount of paperwork on an ongoing basis.

D. Partnership vs. S Corporation

The decision to form a small business as an S corporation rather than as a partnership, particularly a limited partnership, is more difficult. Obviously, a partnership is unencumbered by some of the Subchapter S restrictions. Thus a partnership can have an unlimited number of partners (although as a practical matter a point is reached where the number of partners having input into management decisions will be unwieldy), and may have several "tiers" of partners, each having different rights and responsibilities, while an S corporation must not have more than 35 investors and a single class of stock. Moreover, in a partnership it is possible (although not easy) to allocate certain tax items to partners in a manner different from their partnership "shares" in profits and losses, provided that there is a "substantial economic effect" for so doing. I.R.C. § 704(b). This is not possible in an S corporation.

A final distinction worthy of note is that in a partnership, unlike an S corporation, obligations of the partnership to persons other than partners (e.g., a loan from a bank) are added to each partner's tax basis pro rata in accordance with his/her share. I.R.C. § 752. In an S corporation, by contrast, a shareholder's tax basis is the sum of his/her contributions to capital, his/her share of profits distributed to him/her, and loans by the shareholder to the corporation only. Thus, if A and B form an S corporation to which they contribute $50,000 each and make loans totalling $100,000 each, and the S corporation borrows an additional $500,000 from a bank, the tax basis of each will be $150,000, whereas in a partnership it would have been $400,000 (assuming A and B share equally in profits and losses). This may be important because losses may only be deducted to the extent of a partner's basis in a partnership or a shareholder's basis in his/her stock in an S corporation plus the shareholder's basis in any indebtedness owed by the S corporation to the shareholder. The shareholder's or partner's ability to use losses may also be limited by the "at-risk limits" contained in Section 465 of the Code and by the "passive loss limits" contained in Section 469 of the Code.

E. Proprietorship vs. Partnership/Corporation

For tax purposes, a partnership is simply a proprietorship with several owners. Accordingly, wherever for tax reasons the partnership form is preferable to the corporate form, the proprietorship form will be preferable to the corporate form.

F. General vs. Limited Partnership

Because the tax consequences of general and limited partnerships are substantially the same, the choice between these two forms will depend mostly upon nontax factors (e.g., the willingness of all partners to assume liability for partnership obligations, or the desire of the partners to centralize management in one or two partners). There are some tax distinctions between general and limited partnerships. For example, the rules governing the allocation of income and loss and a partner's share of partnership debt (relevant in computing a partner's basis in the partnership) distinguish in certain circumstances between general and limited partners.

G. Limited Partnership with Corporate General Partner

A structure that combines the benefits of a partnership (primarily flexibility in capital structure and allocations) with the advantages of a corporation (limited liability), but that achieves "conduit" treatment, is a limited partnership with a corporate general partner. The corporate general partner can be an S corporation or a C corporation (if the latter, conduit treatment is lost to the extent income is allocable to the general partner). Conservative counsel will recommend that the corporate general partner have a net worth meeting the IRS guidelines set forth in Revenue Procedure 89-12. Also, counsel must carefully analyze the structure if the same interests own the partnership interests and control the general partner before concluding that the partnership will be treated as a partnership for tax purposes.

FEDERAL INCOME TAX ASPECTS OF CORPORATIONS

H. State Tax Considerations

While a discussion of state taxes is beyond the scope of this chapter, counsel must be aware that the state tax treatment of an entity may differ from the federal tax treatment. Some states and local jurisdictions do not, for example, respect S corporation treatment. For example, New York City subjects S corporations to its regular corporate franchise tax. New York State generally respects the conduit treatment of S corporations, but it also imposes a tax on the S corporation based on the difference between the highest marginal corporate franchise tax rate and the highest marginal individual tax rate imposed by New York State for the year. New York City also imposes a rather unusual tax on "unincorporated businesses" such as partnerships at the rate of 2 percent of net income.

CHAPTER THREE

THE SUBCHAPTER S ALTERNATIVE

Stuart B. Ratner

THE SUBCHAPTER S ALTERNATIVE 49

I. INTRODUCTION

In 1958 Congress enacted Subchapter S of the Internal Revenue Code of 1954 as a means to aid small business corporations. The provisions of Subchapter S essentially permit a corporation to avoid double taxation at the corporate and shareholder levels by taxing each shareholder directly on its pro rata share of income that the corporation generates. The Subchapter S Revision Act of 1982, the Deficit Reduction Act of 1984, the Tax Reform Act of 1986 and the Revenue Act of 1987 each wrought substantial changes to Subchapter S that have enhanced the attractiveness of S corporation status for small businesses.

This chapter identifies some of the salient factors for a business in deciding whether to opt for Subchapter S treatment. The analysis bears primary relevance for those ventures that have not yet selected a particular business structure as well as for established C corporations that could adapt to and benefit from the S corporation provisions; it does not purport to provide a comprehensive outline for the operation of an S corporation. Consequently, the discussion focuses on the tax laws in effect for corporations electing to apply Subchapter S after January 1, 1987, and specifically eschews any extended treatment of the transition rules that affect existing S corporations. Because C corporation tax rules generally apply to S corporations also, this chapter does not address the full range of corporate tax issues, except where specific provisions have a disproportionate impact on S corporations. The considerations summarized herein should enable either a company in the process of formation or a small C corporation to ascertain if the Subchapter S alternative merits further, more detailed investigation.

II. ADVANTAGES OF AN S CORPORATION

A. Tax Considerations

The tax consequences of S corporation treatment constitute the core of any decision to elect Subchapter S treatment. Instead of taxing a corporation's income once at the corporate level and again at the shareholder level upon distribution, Subchapter S generally transforms the corporation into a conduit to pass income through to its shareholders for inclusion in their respective individual tax returns. Moreover, the maximum tax rate imposed on corporations compares unfavorably with the lower tax rates currently applicable to individuals. Although Subchapter S still taxes the corporation on such items as built-in gains and passive investment income, an S corporation more closely resembles a partnership for tax purposes. Thus, there is no great benefit from an "S" election if the purpose of the corporation is to accumulate wealth; however, if that wealth is ever distributed to shareholders (other than as compensation), without an "S" election in place, a second level of tax is imposed at the individual level.

Although Parts V and VI of this chapter address the federal tax implications of the S corporation election for the corporation and the shareholder, respectively, state and local taxes also constitute an element in the tax calculations. These concerns may become acute where the S corporation engages in multistate income-producing activities or has shareholders from different states. For example, the State of New York recognizes the federal S corporation election and exempts such corporations from imposition of the corporation franchise (income) tax (*see* discussion in Chapter 18), provided that every shareholder consents to application of the New York State personal income tax on its pro rata share of the S corporation's income. N.Y. Tax. Law §§ 209(8), 612, 660. The law taxes nonresident shareholders only on that portion of the S corporation's income attributable to sources within the state of New York. N.Y. Tax. Law § 632(a)(2). Conversely, the City of New York does not recognize the S corporation election and subjects all corporations doing business therein to its general corporation tax. N.Y.C. Admin. Code § 11-601, *et seq.*

Ascertaining the desirability of an S corporation election for a particular business necessitates a precise calculation of the tax liability of an S corporation structure, a C corporation structure and a partnership structure under the Internal Revenue Code of 1986 (the "Code"). Any meaningful tax computation also requires some projection of the revenues that the business will generate at various stages in its development. For example, shareholders may favor an S corporation election if it enables

THE SUBCHAPTER S ALTERNATIVE   51

them to utilize the losses frequently associated with a new business to offset their personal income from other sources. Similarly, factors relating to the operation of the corporation, such as the anticipated policies of the corporation regarding the distribution of earnings as dividends (*see* discussion in Chapter 10), will impact on the decision to make the election. However, individual shareholders may benefit disproportionately from S corporation treatment. Notwithstanding the fact that Subchapter S may prove advantageous for the shareholders in the aggregate, the tax analysis for each shareholder could produce conflicting conclusions regarding the desirability of the S corporation election.

B. Nontax Considerations

Although Subchapter S constrains the structure of the corporation and the composition of its shareholders relative to a C corporation, as described in Part III of this chapter, a corporation possesses certain nontax advantages in comparison to a Partnership. The primary benefit of the corporate form of organization—limited liability for the shareholders—may constitute a paramount concern if the business involves speculative or hazardous activities. Although a limited partnership could achieve a similar result, the Uniform Limited Partnership Act requires a general partner with unlimited liability, and the limited partners cannot engage in the active management of the business (*see* discussion in Chapter 1). The active management restriction as limited partners can be minimized by forming the limited partnership under Texas or Delaware law, both of which specifically permit a limited partner to act as an officer of the corporate general partner. To the extent that such passive investors exist, an S corporation can accommodate any desire to retain corporate control, through the vehicle of voting power, in those who actively manage the business by the issuance of nonvoting stock to the passive investors.

The corporate structure also maintains a certain continuity of life not inherent in partnerships, which dissolve upon the withdrawal or death of a partner, for instance. The relatively free transferability of ownership interests in the business through the exchange of shares provides one example of this characteristic. Although Subchapter S does limit transferability by imposing certain restrictions on the number and character of the shareholders, the issues that pervade the transfer of a partnership interest do not burden an S corporation, except in the case of shareholder agreements restricting the transfer of shares. Indeed, the formation of a corporation might actually pose fewer substantive and procedural problems than the preparation of a partnership agreement, which often requires substantial negotiation. Although this chapter does not discuss federal and state securities laws, restrictions on the number of shareholders in an S corporation enhance the likelihood that limited offering exemptions will apply to the issuance and distribution of the stock.

There are several specific disadvantages to electing S corporation status. In today's recessionary economy, many taxpayers, especially real estate developers and owners, are experiencing economic difficulties which lead to situations where debt is forgiven. Each shareholder of an S corporation that experiences forgiveness of indebtedness income will recognize his or her pro rata share of the forgiveness of indebtedness income without receiving any cash to pay the tax incurred. Many S corporations in this situation are terminating S status to prevent the phantom forgiveness of indebtedness income from being distributed to shareholders. Additionally, if a major shareholder of an S corporation is audited, the S corporation and all of its other shareholders are also usually audited. Thus, a shareholder may not wish to elect S status simply to minimize the chance of audit if other shareholders are audit risks.

III. CRITERIA DEFINING A SMALL BUSINESS CORPORATION

The provisions of Subchapter S enable any "small business corporation" to elect S corporation treatment in accordance with Section 1362(a) of the Code. I.R.C. § 1361(a). In order to qualify as a "small business corporation," a corporation must satisfy the requirements of Section 1361(b) of the Code regarding the nature of the business, its shareholders and its structure.

A. Ineligible Corporations

The Code defines five types of "ineligible corporations" that will not qualify as a small business corporation. I.R.C. 1361(b)(1)(2).

1. Affiliated Groups

A corporation that is a member of an "affiliated group" cannot constitute a small business corporation. I.R.C. § 1361(b)(2)(A). From a practical perspective, the corporation cannot be a parent corporation that owns stock in a subsidiary aggregating both 80 percent or more of the total voting power of such stock and 80 percent or more of the total value of such stock. The stock subject to this requirement does not include certain preferred, nonvoting, nonconvertible stock that is limited both as to dividends and as to liquidation and redemption rights and that does not participate in corporate growth to a significant extent. I.R.C. § 1504(a)(1)-(2), (4). No subsidiary with a corporate parent will qualify as a small business corporation because this arrangement would violate the separate requirement that a small business corporation have no corporations as shareholders. The fact that the affiliated group has never filed a consolidated return will not affect the analysis. Prop. Reg. § 1.1361-1A(d)(1)(i)(A).

The affiliated group prohibition excepts an inactive subsidiary. To constitute an "inactive corporation," the subsidiary must not have "begun business" at any time on or before the close of the relevant taxable year and must not have gross income for such period. I.R.C. § 1361(c)(6). Although the facts and circumstances of each individual situation will determine if a subsidiary has "begun business," merely being "in existence" will not suffice; the subsidiary must have commenced the business operations for which it was organized. Although organizational activities such as obtaining a corporate charter or even incorporating to reserve a corporate name will not deny the availability of the "inactive corporation" exception, the acquisition of operating assets or other activities that establish the nature of the business indicate that the corporation has "begun business." Prop. Reg. § 1.1361-1A(d)(2)(ii).

Pursuant to another exception, the temporary acquisition of stock in a corporation might not contravene the prohibition against stock ownership in excess of the permitted levels. The Internal Revenue Service ("IRS") has suggested that the acquisition of the assets of a corporation through the acquisition of its stock would be acceptable where the acquiring small business corporation holds the stock of the target for a brief period not exceeding 30 days before liquidating the target. Rev. Rul. 73-496, 1973-2 C.B. 312; *but see Haley Bros. Constr. Corp. v. Comm'r*, 87 T.C. 498 (1986) (intention to liquidate is insufficient where the acquired corporation conducted business for almost two years after acquisition of stock, but court also states *in dicta* that same result would apply even if the corporation was liquidated within 30 days).

2. Banks

A small business corporation cannot be a financial institution that constitutes a bank under Section 585(a)(2) of the Code or that is subject to Section 593 of the Code. I.R.C. § 1361(b)(2)(B). For purposes of Section 585(a)(2), a bank includes any bank or trust company that accepts deposits and makes loans or that exercises fiduciary powers. I.R.C. § 581. Certain building and loan associations, mutual savings banks, and cooperative banks without capital stock organized and operated for mutual purposes and without profit will also fall within this category of ineligible corporations. I.R.C. § 593(a)(1)-(2).

3. Insurance Companies

The Code also excludes insurance companies subject to taxation under Subchapter L from the purview of small business corporations. I.R.C. § 1361(b)(2)(C). Although certain stock casualty insurance companies taxable under Section 831(a) may qualify under certain conditions, a newly formed corporation may not avail itself of this exception. Prop. Reg. § 1.1361-1A(d)(1)(ii).

4. Corporation Claiming U.S. Possession Tax Credits

A corporation claiming tax credits based upon income derived from trade or business in any United States possession will be an "ineligible

THE SUBCHAPTER S ALTERNATIVE 55

corporation." I.R.C. §§ 1361(b)(2)(D), 936(a)(1)-(2). United States possessions include the Commonwealth of Puerto Rico and the Virgin Islands. I.R.C. § 936(d)(1).

5. DISC

A former Domestic International Sales Corporation also constitutes an "ineligible corporation." I.R.C. §§ 1361(b)(2)(E), 992(a)(1), (3).

B. Domestic Corporation

The Code limits the definition of a "small business corporation" to domestic corporations. I.R.C. § 1361(b)(1). A domestic corporation includes any association or joint stock company that is organized in the United States or under the laws of the United States, the District of Columbia or any state. I.R.C. § 7701(a)(3)-(4), (9). Thus, foreign corporations cannot claim Subchapter S treatment even if they operate in the United States.

C. Number of Shareholders

The Code requires that the S corporation be closely held by restricting the number of shareholders in a small business corporation to 35. I.R.C. § 1361(b)(1)(A). Proposed regulations state that any entity that includes in its gross income dividends distributed with respect to the stock of the corporation will constitute a shareholder of the corporation. As a result, each joint tenant in a joint tenancy and each tenant-in-common in a tenancy-in-common will constitute a separate shareholder. Prop. Reg. § 1.1361-1A(e)(1). Similarly, a custodian holding stock for one or more minors pursuant to the Uniform Gifts to Minors Act or the Gifts of Securities to Minors Act does not constitute the shareholder; each minor counts as a separate shareholder. T.I.R. No. 113 (Nov. 26, 1958). Conversely, a husband and wife, and their respective estates, count as a single shareholder for purposes of determining the number of shareholders, but this special characterization ceases upon dissolution of the marriage for any reason other than death. I.R.C. § 1361(c)(1); Prop. Reg. § 1.1361-1A(e)(2). The IRS will not recognize attempts to satisfy this requirement by splitting a single business with more than 35 shareholders into multiple corporations with less than 35 shareholders each when such corporations engage in joint business ventures. *See* Rev. Rul. 77-220, 1977-1 C.B. 263.

The 35-shareholder limit constrains the ability of shareholders to transfer stock as a gift or to use the stock as a vehicle for estate planning without jeopardizing the small business corporation status. Indeed, the shareholders may well enter into agreements that restrict the alienability of the stock in order to maintain compliance with this provision. Similarly, the corporation cannot freely distribute stock to employees as part of a compensation package without running afoul of this basic prerequisite for an S corporation. More importantly, the corporation cannot engage in extensive public stock offerings to raise additional capital.

Limitations on "top-heavy" employee benefit plans also impact disproportionately on S corporations in their structuring of retirement benefit packages because S corporations will likely have one or more "key employees" in the form of shareholders, each owning 5 percent or more of the stock of the S corporation. I.R.C. § 416(i)(1). Moreover, cumulative accrued benefits or aggregate accounts for such key employees may well exceed the permitted threshold of 60 percent of all cumulative benefits in a benefit plan or aggregate accounts in a contribution plan. I.R.C. § 416(g)(1). Remaining a qualified plan under such circumstances requires compliance with the vesting and minimum benefit provisions of the Code, further restricting the flexibility of the S corporation. I.R.C. § 416(a)-(e).

D. Character of the Shareholders

Only individuals, estates or certain defined trusts may hold stock in a qualifying small business corporation. I.R.C. § 1361(b)(1)(B). Corporations, partnerships and nonqualifying trusts cannot be shareholders in a small business corporation, nor can any shareholder's interest in such stock be a legal life estate, a usufruct interest or an interest for a term of years. Prop. Reg. § 1.1361-1A(f)(1). However, a split interest such as a legal life estate or a usufruct interest that existed prior to January 1, 1983, or a split interest that was created on or after that date that is

THE SUBCHAPTER S ALTERNATIVE 57

owned by one individual, that has not been transferred and that must terminate on the death of the individual for whom the interest was created, will qualify. Prop. Reg. § 1.1361-1A(f)(2)-(3). The Code specifically provides that the estate of a bankrupt individual may be a shareholder. I.R.C. § 1361(c)(3). In a recent Private Letter Ruling (9010042, 12/11/89), the IRS held that a partnership could be an S corporation shareholder momentarily after all of the partnership's assets were contributed to the S corporation in exchange for all of the S corporation's stock, which stock was immediately distributed to each partner in liquidation of the partnership.

If a trust holds stock, then the trust will usually constitute the shareholder, and the corporation cannot qualify as a small business corporation. Prop. Reg. § 1.1361-1A(h)(1). Four basic exceptions exist, but in no case can a foreign trust hold stock in a small business corporation. First, a trust will qualify if an individual owns the corpus and the income, if the individual is a United States citizen or resident, and if the trust is taxed under Subpart E of Part I of Subchapter J of the Code. I.R.C. § 1361(c)(2)(A)(i). Trusts subject to taxation under Subpart E include grantor trusts and Section 678 trusts in which an entity has a power exercisable solely by itself to vest the corpus and income in itself. The deemed owner of the trust constitutes the shareholder. I.R.C. § 1361(c)(2)(B)(i). A husband and wife who are each a deemed owner but who file a joint return will qualify as a single shareholder. Prop. Reg. § 1.1361-1A(h)(3)(i).

Second, a trust of the type described in the preceding paragraph that continues in existence after the deemed owner's death will not run afoul of the shareholder restrictions for a period of 60 days after the deemed owner's death or, if the entire corpus of the trust is includable in the decedent's gross estate, for a period of two years. I.R.C. § 1361(c)(2)(A)(ii). The Code disregards the spouse's community property interest under the law of the applicable state for such purposes. Prop. Reg. § 1.1361-1A(h)(1)(i). The estate will be the deemed owner of the trust and the shareholder. I.R.C. § 1361(c)(2)(B)(ii).

Third, a trust with respect to which stock is transferred pursuant to a will qualifies for a period of 60 days after such transfer. I.R.C.

§ 1361(c)(2)(A)(iii). In such testamentary trusts, the estate of the testator is the shareholder. I.R.C. § 1361(c)(2)(B)(ii).

Finally, a voting trust is permissible, and each beneficiary of the trust, meaning each beneficial owner of the stock, will be a shareholder. I.R.C. § 1361(c)(2)(A)(iv), (B)(iv); Prop. Reg. § 1.1361-1A(h)(1)(ii). Thus, each beneficiary of a voting trust must independently qualify as a shareholder. The proposed regulations set forth the following parameters for a "voting trust": (1) it must be memorialized in a written agreement or document, such as a will; (2) it must delegate the right to vote the stock to one or more trustees; (3) it must make distributions to the beneficial owners of the stock; (4) it must vest title and possession of the stock in the beneficial owners upon termination of the trust; and (5) it must terminate on or before a specific date or event. Prop. Reg. § 1.163-1A(h)(3)(ii). In each of the following IRS Private Letter Rulings, the trust qualified as an S shareholder: 9009010 (11/29/89) (beneficiaries' annual withdrawal rights greater than amount of grantor's annual contribution causes beneficiaries to be the deemed owner of entire corpus); IRS Private Letter Ruling 9015024 (4/13/90) (grantor entitled to all trust income during initial ten-year term and all principal if grantor dies during initial ten-year term); IRS Private Letter Ruling 9017025 (1/26/91) (revocable trust created by husband and wife).

The Code also defines a specific "Qualified Subchapter S Trust" that merits treatment as a Section 1361(c)(2)(A)(i) trust. I.R.C. § 1361(d)(1)(A). Initially, a Qualified Subchapter S Trust must meet five requirements: (1) it must permit only one income beneficiary during the life of the current income beneficiary; (2) the corpus of the trust must be distributable only to the current income beneficiary during such life; (3) the income interest must terminate upon the earlier of the death of the current income beneficiary or the termination of the trust; (4) upon termination during the life of the current income beneficiary, the trust must distribute all assets to such beneficiary; and (5) all income must be distributable to one individual who is a United States citizen or resident. I.R.C. § 1361(d)(3)(A)-(B). The terms of the trust instrument and the local law governing the trust instrument control this analysis. Prop. Reg. § 1.1361-1A(i)(2). The Qualified Subchapter S Trust re-

THE SUBCHAPTER S ALTERNATIVE 59

quirements are strictly interpreted, as demonstrated by Rev. Rul. 89-55 in which the IRS determined that a trust did not qualify as a Qualified Subchapter S Trust where the trust document provided that the trust could be terminated during the income beneficiary's life in the event the trust did not hold shares of an S corporation.

The beneficiary of the Qualified Subchapter S Trust or its legal representative may elect to have Section 1361(d) of the Code apply to the trust, which results in the characterization of the trust as a Section 1361(c)(2)(A)(i) trust. I.R.C. § 1361(d)(2)(A). The beneficiary or its legal representative will file this Qualified Subchapter S Trust election with the IRS after the corporation has filed its Section 1362(a) election as an S corporation, but in no event shall the Qualified Subchapter S Trust file its election later than two and one-half months after the beginning of the taxable year for which the S corporation election is effective. I.R.C. § 1361(d)(2)(D); Prop. Reg. § 1.1361-1A(i)(3). If the Qualified Subchapter S Trust owns stock in more than one S corporation, it must make a separate election with respect to each corporation. I.R.C. § 1361(d)(2)(B)(i). Moreover, the Code deems each successive income beneficiary to have consented to the election unless it affirmatively refuses to consent by filing such objection within two and one-half months after becoming the income beneficiary. I.R.C. § 1361(d)(2)(B)(ii); Prop. Reg. § 1.1361-1A(i)(5).

The requirements for an eligible trust automatically exclude Employee Stock Ownership Plans, denying to the S corporation a frequently used method to compensate employees. Although the provisions for Qualified Subchapter S Trusts permit a variety of forms, the essential limitations on the nature of such a trust complicate estate planning for the shareholder by eliminating from consideration certain traditional types of trusts.

E. Nonresident Aliens

No nonresident alien may be a shareholder of a small business corporation for Subchapter S purposes. I.R.C. § 1361(b)(1)(C). The IRS has interpreted this to mean that the shareholder must be a resident of one of the 50 states or the District of Columbia; this section specifically excludes residents of Puerto Rico. Rev. Rul. 73-478, 1973-2 C.B. 310. Nonetheless, a recent IRS Private Letter Ruling allowed nonresident aliens to act as custodian for a minor shareholder (*see* Pvt. Ltr. Rul. 9044003, 7/29/90) and that a shareholder holding a valid green card would not be considered a nonresident alien for S corporation purposes, even if the shareholder intends to return to his home country (*see* Pvt. Ltr. Rul. 9018045, 2/5/90). *See* further Prop. Treas. Reg. § 1.1361-1A(e)(1).

F. One Class of Stock

On August 13, 1991, the Internal Revenue Service issued proposed regulations relating to the requirement that a small business corporation (hereinafter an "S corporation") have only one class of stock. The proposed regulations generally provide rules relating to the one-class-of-stock requirement. Generally, a second class of stock will not exist if all outstanding shares of stock of the S corporation confer identical rights to distribution and liquidation proceeds under the S corporation governing provisions, and the S corporation has not entered into any of a list of specified arrangements which are deemed to create a second class of stock.

The determination of whether all outstanding shares of stock confer identical rights to distribution and liquidation proceeds is based on the corporate charter, articles of incorporation, by-laws, applicable state law, and any binding agreements relating to distribution or liquidation proceeds. A routine commercial contractual arrangement such as a lease, employment agreement, or loan agreement is not generally considered a governing provision. Agreements to redeem or purchase stock at the time of death, disability or termination are disregarded.

The proposed regulations also provide that instruments, obligations or arrangements may be treated as a separate class of stock under certain circumstances. However, the proposed regulations also provide a number of safe harbors or exceptions for certain ordinary business arrangements entered into by S corporations and their shareholders.

THE SUBCHAPTER S ALTERNATIVE

A safe harbor also exists for "straight debt" of the corporation. "Straight debt" consists of any written, unconditional promise to pay on demand or on a specified date a sum certain in money where (1) the interest rate and payment dates are not contingent on factors such as the corporation's profits or its discretion, (2) the debt is not convertible into stock and (3) the creditor is an individual (other than a nonresident alien), an estate or a trust specified in Section 1361(c)(2) of the Code. A debt instrument meeting this definition will not constitute a second class of stock, whatever the economic realities of the corporation's capitalization. I.R.C. § 1361(c)(5).

The prohibition against multiple classes of stock certainly inhibits complex corporate structuring and estate-planning techniques by removing the flexibility of having different classes of stock with varying rights to the profits and assets of the S corporation. The ability to issue voting and nonvoting stock mitigates these problems to some degree.

IV. ELECTING S CORPORATION TREATMENT

A. Manner of Election

A corporation that meets the definition of a "small business corporation" may elect to be treated as an S corporation by filing IRS Form 2553. I.R.C. § 1362(a)(1); Temp. Reg. § 18.1362-1(a). The IRS will not recognize verbal elections. *Hooper v. Comm'r*, 33 T.C.M. 759 (1974). All shareholders of the corporation on the day of the election must consent to such election on IRS Form 2553 or in a separate statement, and such consents are binding and may not be withdrawn after a valid election by the corporation. I.R.C. § 1362(a)(2); Temp. Reg. § 18.1362-2(a). If the corporation makes an S corporation election during the first taxable year for which the election will be effective, then all shareholders who held stock during that portion of the year before the election must also consent. Temp. Reg. § 18.1362-2(b)(1). Although the effect of nonacquiescence by a former shareholder will only delay the effectiveness of the election until the following taxable year, this provision prevents potentially prejudicial tax consequences to a shareholder that transfers its interest in the stock of a C corporation that subsequently elects S corporation status. An election will be valid for the effective taxable year and for all succeeding taxable years until terminated. I.R.C. § 1362(c).

When ascertaining the shareholders who must properly consent to the election, both a husband and wife holding stock, all tenants-in-common holding stock, and all joint tenants holding stock must consent. If a custodian holds stock for a minor, then the minor, or the minor's legal representative or natural or adoptive parent, must consent. Similarly, the executor or administrator of an estate, the deemed owner of a trust, the estate of the testator of a testamentary trust, and each beneficiary of a voting trust must consent. Temp. Reg. § 18.1362-2(b)(2). However, a party holding stock for another as a mere nominee with no beneficial interest therein need not consent. *See, e.g.*, Rev. Rul. 75-261, 1975-2 C.B. 350 (a taxpayer holding stock under an acknowledgment of trust with no beneficial interest therein is a nominee and not a trustee).

Although all consents should be timely filed, the IRS has adopted a flexible approach that will not invalidate an election based solely upon the failure of a shareholder to file within the required period. The IRS will apply the following standards in deciding whether to grant such an extension: (1) the IRS must be satisfied that reasonable cause existed for such delay and that the interests of the government are not prejudiced thereby, (2) the shareholder must file the consent within the extended time that the IRS has granted, and (3) all shareholders who held stock during the taxable year and those shareholders who held stock after such taxable year but before the end of the extension period must file new consents. Temp. Reg. § 18.1362-2(c). Similarly, the failure of the corporation to complete fully IRS Form 2553 might not adversely affect the purported election if the form contains sufficient information to confirm that a timely filing occurred. *See, e.g., Leve v. Comm'r*, 49 T.C.M. 1575 (1985).

According to the Instructions to IRS Form 2553, the IRS will notify the corporation of acceptance of the election within 60 days after the filing of IRS Form 2553. Where the IRS has denied receipt of IRS Form 2553 and challenged the validity of the election, courts have accepted

THE SUBCHAPTER S ALTERNATIVE 63

elections if independent evidence exists that the proper forms were signed and mailed to the IRS. *See Zaretsky v. Comm'r*, 26 T.C.M. 1283 (1967); *but cf. Ober v. Comm'r*, 41 T.C.M. 379 (1980) (mere preparation and execution of the forms does not constitute the filing of a valid election). When assessing the timeliness of a disputed election, the date of the postmark, if ascertainable, will be dispositive. *Feldman v. Comm'r*, 47 T.C. 329 (1966).

The Code imposes an additional statutory prerequisite for election as an S corporation in order to prevent a corporation from manipulating its S corporation status to gain beneficial tax treatment based upon transient factors, such as yearly variations in income and losses resulting from changes in the corporation's business cycle. In general, a corporation that held S corporation status which subsequently terminated, either voluntarily or involuntarily, cannot elect S corporation treatment for a period of five years after such termination without the consent of the IRS. I.R.C. § 1362(g). The S corporation has the burden of persuading the IRS to grant such consent, but the IRS has indicated that a change in the ownership of a majority of the stock since the first taxable year after the termination will militate in favor of such consent. Absent such a factor, the IRS will usually withhold its consent unless the termination "was not reasonably within the control of the corporation or shareholders having a substantial interest in the corporation and was not part of a plan to terminate the election in which plan such shareholders participated." 26 C.F.R. § 1.1372-5.

Nonstatutory considerations also affect the availability of the S corporation election. Courts have held that the corporation must validly exist under applicable state law in order for a corporation to opt for Subchapter S treatment. *Frentz v. Comm'r*, 375 F.2d 662 (6th Cir. 1967). Conversely, the fact that the corporation faces an impending bankruptcy or liquidation does not affect the ability of the corporation to make such an election. *Hauptman v. Director of Internal Revenue*, 309 F.2d 62 (2d Cir. 1962).

B. Timing of the Election

The S corporation should file the election in the taxable year preceding the taxable year for which the S corporation desires the election to be effective or within two and one-half months of the commencement of such effective taxable year. I.R.C. § 1362(b)(1). Filing the election after the first two and one-half months of a taxable year results in the election being effective for the following taxable year. I.R.C. § 1362(b)(3). An election filed within two and one-half months after the first day of the taxable year is timely, even if the relevant taxable year is less than two and one-half months in duration. I.R.C. § 1362(b)(4). Thus, a corporation formed on November 1 has until January 15 to elect S corporation status for the preceding two-month taxable year. If the corporation files the election within the two and one-half month window but either (1) the corporation did not qualify as a "small business corporation" for one or more days during such period or (2) one or more shareholders during such taxable year did not consent to the election, then the election will be effective beginning the following taxable year. I.R.C. § 1362(b)(2).

V. OPERATION OF AN S CORPORATION

A. Corporate-Level Taxation

An S corporation is generally not subject to the taxes normally imposed on a C corporation, but the Code does levy a tax on S corporations in three circumstances. I.R.C. § 1363(a).

1. Built-in Gains

The Code imposes a tax on the taxable income of the S corporation for a taxable year in which it has "recognized built-in gain," meaning any gain recognized upon the disposition of any asset during the first ten years after the corporation attains S corporation status (*see* discussion in Chapter 17). I.R.C. § 1374(a), (d)(2)-(3). This tax does not apply to a corporation for which a Subchapter S election has been in effect for each taxable year of the corporation and any predecessor corporation. I.R.C. § 1374(c)(1). For certain small, closely held C corporations electing S corporation status, liquidating distributions prior to January 1, 1989, will not result in the imposition of the tax if, at all times after August 1, 1986, no more than ten qualified S corporation shareholders will have owned a majority of the value of the stock of the corporation. This benefit applies to corporations valued at less than $5,000,000, but corporations valued at an amount between $5,000,000 and $10,000,000 will merit partial relief from the tax. Rev. Rul. 86-141, 1986-2 C.B. 151.

The legislative history indicates that Congress sought to eliminate the Code's unintentional preferences for the distribution of assets of the corporation in the context of a liquidation, which Congress felt encouraged liquidations and acquisitions for artificial reasons. Congress specifically intended to repeal the *General Utilities* doctrine, which ameliorated the impact of the two-tier taxation of corporate distributions of appreciated assets. A corporation that acquires the assets of an S corporation in a liquidation or a shareholder who obtains assets from the S corporation in a liquidation no longer can claim a stepped-up basis in those assets equal to their fair market value and escape the imposition of a corporate-level tax on the theory that the transferor has not recognized any gain on the sale.

The tax on built-in gains does not apply to a disposition of assets that the corporation acquired after electing S corporation status or to gains based upon appreciation of the property after the first day of the corporation's first taxable year as an S corporation. The excess of the fair market value of such assets on the first day of the S corporation's first taxable year over its adjusted basis at such time determines the amount of gain, and a valuation of the assets upon conversion to S corporation status seems prudent to establish and document such values. I.R.C. § 1374(d)(2). To the extent that such gain derives from passive investment income, that portion of excess net passive income attributable to such gain reduces the amount subject to the built-in gains tax. I.R.C. § 1375(c)(2). Similarly, this provision does not impose a tax on the excess of (1) net unrealized built-in gain, which equals the excess of (a) the fair market value of the corporation's assets at the beginning of its first taxable year as an S corporation over (b) the aggregate adjusted bases of such assets at such time, over (2) the recognized built-in gains of the corporation since the beginning of the first year of its S corporation election. I.R.C. § 1374(c)(2), (d)(1).

In the case of inventory, the IRS has indicated that it will respect the accounting method of the corporation in ascertaining whether the property existed at the time of the conversion into an S corporation. For example, no built-in gains tax will apply to an S corporation using a last-in, first-out method until the date of sale of inventory existing prior to the conversion. Announcement 86-128, 1986-51 I.R.B. 22. However, Congress subsequently enacted a provision for the recapture of any benefits accruing from the use of a last-in, first-out ("LIFO") method as opposed to a first-in, first-out ("FIFO") method. Essentially, if a C corporation employs the LIFO method and it elects S corporation status, then it may be subject to an additional tax, payable in four equal, annual installments, on the excess of the inventory amount of the inventory assets under a FIFO method over the inventory amount of such assets under the LIFO method. The basis of the inventory will be adjusted accordingly. I.R.C. § 1363(d)(f).

The corporation confronts taxation at the highest corporate rate on the lesser of the recognized built-in gains or its taxable income were it a C corporation. The corporation may deduct from the applicable amount of income any net operating loss carryforwards from its years as a C corporation, but it may only claim as a credit against the tax any business credit carryforwards arising from its years as a C corporation. I.R.C. § 1374(b)(1)-(3).

2. Passive Investment Income

If a corporation has Subchapter C earnings and profits and if passive investment income constitutes more than 25 percent of its gross receipts, then the corporation is subject to a tax at the highest corporate rate on its excess net passive income. The Code defines "Subchapter C earnings and profits" as earnings and profits of the corporation for years in which no S corporation election was in effect. I.R.C. § 1362(d)(3)(B). Thus, an S corporation cannot itself generate Subchapter C earnings and profits, but it can have accumulated earnings and

THE SUBCHAPTER S ALTERNATIVE

profits from two primary sources: (1) its years, if any, as a C corporation prior to the S corporation election, and (2) the acquisition pursuant to Section 381 of the Code of a C corporation with earnings and profits. Regulations in effect under prior incarnations of Subchapter S indicate that "gross receipts" is broader than "gross income" and includes all amounts received or accrued in accordance with the accounting method that the corporation employs to calculate its taxable income. 26 C.F.R. § 1.1372-4(b)(5)(iv). However, gross receipts from the disposition of a capital asset, other than the sale of stock or securities, are limited to capital gain net income. I.R.C. § 1362(d)(3)(C). "Passive investment income" includes gross receipts from royalties, rent, dividends, interest, annuities and, to the extent of gain only, sales or exchanges of stock or securities. I.R.C. § 1362(d)(3)(D). The definition of "passive investment income" excludes income from four sources: (1) interest on obligations from the sale of inventory in the ordinary course of the corporation's business, (2) amounts received from the active and regular conduct of a lending or finance business that is not a personal holding company, (3) gross receipts from the sale or exchange of stock or securities as payment in exchange for stock in a Section 331 liquidation where the corporation owned a majority of each class of stock, and (4) certain amounts where the corporation is an options or commodities dealer. I.R.C. § 1362(d)(3)(D).

"Excess net passive income" equals net passive income multiplied by a fraction, the numerator of which is the amount by which the passive investment income exceeds 25 percent of gross receipts of the S corporation and the denominator of which is the amount of passive investment income. "Net passive income" equals passive investment income less any allowable deductions that are directly connected with the production of such income, excluding deductions for net operating losses pursuant to Section 172 of the Code. These deductions must have a "proximate and primary relationship to the income" and include "expenses, depreciation, and similar items attributable solely to such income." In the case of deductions allocable to other types of income as well, the corporation may apply the portion of such deductions reasonably attributable to passive investment income. 26 C.F.R. § 1.1375-1A(b)(3).

Excess net passive income cannot exceed the taxable income of the S corporation, defined as income less certain deductions, such as organizational expenses, but specifically excluding net operating losses. I.R.C. §§ 1375(b)(1)(B), 1374(d)(4). Other than certain fuel credits, no credits are available to offset this tax. I.R.C. § 1375(c)(1).

The corporation can avoid the imposition of this tax in either of two ways. First, the corporation can distribute its Subchapter C earnings and profits, if any, to its shareholders as a dividend. I.R.C. § 1368(e)(3). Second, if the S corporation discovers that it inadvertently retained Subchapter C earnings and profits, then it may petition the IRS to waive the tax. I.R.C. § 1375(d). The regulations provide that the IRS may waive the tax if the S corporation satisfies its burden to demonstrate (1) that the S corporation determined in good faith that it had no Subchapter C earnings and profits at the close of the relevant taxable year and (2) that it distributed such earnings and profits within a "reasonable" period of time after their discovery. 26 C.F.R. § 1.1375(d).

3. Recapture of Investment Tax Credit

Electing S corporation status constitutes a "mere change in the form of conducting a trade or business" so as not to trigger the recapture of investment tax credits claimed by the predecessor C corporation with respect to Section 38 property. However, the S corporation remains liable for any increase in tax occasioned by such acts as the early disposition of the Section 38 property. I.R.C. §§ 1371(d)(1)-(2), 47(a)-(b). This recapture will reduce the earnings and profits of the S corporation. I.R.C. § 1371(d)(3).

B. Taxable Income

Although the S corporation is not subject to a general corporate tax, the computation of its taxable income is relevant for determining the tax treatment of items passed through to the shareholders. The taxable income of an S corporation is computed in the same manner as for an individual, with four exceptions. First, items of income (including tax-exempt income), loss, deduction or credit will be separately stated, if the separate treatment of such items will affect the tax liability of any

THE SUBCHAPTER S ALTERNATIVE 69

shareholder. Second, deductions not allowable to a partnership will not be allowable to an S corporation. Such deductions include deductions for personal exemptions, foreign taxes, charitable contributions, net operating losses, certain individual deductions and oil and gas depletion deductions. Third, organizational expenses may be amortized and deducted as deferred expenses. Finally, if the S corporation was a C corporation for any of the three immediately preceding taxable years, corporate tax preference rules will apply, effectively denying a C corporation the ability to avoid such rules by electing S corporation status. I.R.C. §§ 1363(b), 291. Losses will be deductible only if the S corporation engages in a trade or business as opposed to a hobby. *DuPont v. United States*, 234 F. Supp. 681 (D.C. Del. 1964).

Except for the corporate liquidation context, the Code specifically disallows deductions from losses incurred in the sale or exchange of property between related taxpayers. I.R.C. § 267(a). Related parties exist in the following situations: (1) an S corporation and a partnership, if the same persons own a majority in value of the stock of the S corporation and a majority of the capital interest or profits interest in the partnership; (2) two S corporations, if the same persons own a majority in value of the stock of each S corporation; and (3) an S corporation and a C corporation, if the same persons own a majority in value of the stock in both the S corporation and the C corporation. I.R.C. § 267(b)(10)-(12). Thus, a shareholder or group of shareholders having an interest in multiple entities engaged in the same business transaction may lose the benefit of certain deductions at the corporate level.

In determining the availability of deductions for employee fringe benefits, the S corporation will be treated as a partnership. Any shareholder owning more than 2 percent of the total outstanding stock or stock possessing more than 2 percent of the total combined voting power of all the stock of the S corporation, including stock deemed owned pursuant to the attribution rules of Section 318 of the Code, will be treated in the same manner as a partner of a partnership. As a result, the S corporation cannot deduct as business expenses fringe benefits paid to such employee-shareholders, although fringe benefits payable to employee-shareholders who own 2 percent or less of the total outstanding voting stock will be eligible for deduction. The obvious intent of the rule is to preclude distributions to shareholders in the guise of fringe benefits that would be tax-deductible business expenses for the S corporation, such as corporate contributions to a medical plan. I.R.C. § 1372.

The discharge of indebtedness owed by the S corporation to a shareholder will result in income to the S corporation. I.R.C. § 61(a)(12). Exceptions exist for discharge of debt in connection with a bankruptcy proceeding involving the S corporation or while it is insolvent, but the amount excluded from gross income reduces any net operating loss, certain business credits, capital loss carryovers, the shareholder's basis in its property and foreign tax credit carryovers. I.R.C. § 108(a)-(b). These adjustments will be made at the corporate level. I.R.C. § 108(d)(7)(A). For purposes of computing income, if an S corporation acquires its indebtedness from a shareholder as a contribution to capital, such corporation will be deemed to have satisfied the indebtedness with an amount of money equal to the shareholder's adjusted basis in the indebtedness. I.R.C. § 108(e)(6).

The S corporation recognizes gain from the distribution of property of the corporation (other than obligations of the corporation) with respect to its stock if the market value of such property exceeds its adjusted basis in the hands of the corporation. Such gain is recognized as if the corporation had sold such appreciated property to the distributee at fair market value. I.R.C. § 1363(d). However, the corporation does not recognize gain on a distribution of certain property in connection with a reorganization qualifying under either Section 354, 355 or 356 of the Code (*see* discussion in Chapter 12). I.R.C. § 1363(e).

The S corporation will be treated as a partnership and its shareholders as partners for purposes of foreign income. The making or termination of an S corporation election constitutes a disposition of a business in determining the applicability of rules concerning recapture of foreign losses under Section 904(f) of the Code. I.R.C. § 1373.

THE SUBCHAPTER S ALTERNATIVE 71

C. Elections

The S corporation itself makes most elections affecting the computation of income, loss and other tax items derived from the S corporation. I.R.C. § 1363(c)(1). The tax treatment of an item "more appropriately determined at the corporate level than at the shareholder level" (a "Subchapter S Item") will be determined at the corporate level. I.R.C. §§ 6241, 6245; cf. I.R.C. § 1366(g). Subchapter S Items determined at the corporate level include the corporation's income (including tax-exempt income), losses, deductions (including expenditures not deductible in computing taxable income), credits, tax preference items, liabilities, recapture of investment tax credits and amounts at risk. Similarly, the accounting methods and legal and factual determinations regarding such items also constitute Subchapter S Items. Temp. Reg. § 301.6245-1T. An exception permits an S corporation to elect "Small S corporation" status and thereby avoid corporate level determinations on items otherwise falling within the parameters of Subchapter S Items. To qualify as a "Small S corporation," the S corporation must not have more than five shareholders at any one time during the taxable year, all of which are natural persons or estates and none of which are pass-through entities such as trusts. Temp. Reg. § 301.6241-1T.

The Code permits shareholders to make certain elections analogous to those that the partners in a partnership may make separately. Accordingly, shareholders may separately elect to have the deduction and recapture provisions for mining exploration expenditures and the foreign and possession tax rules apply. I.R.C. § 1363(c)(2).

D. Taxable Year

The Code seeks to conform the taxable year of an S corporation to the taxable year of its shareholders. As a result, an S corporation must adopt a taxable year ending December 31, unless either (1) the corporation can establish a "business purpose" justifying the use of another accounting period or (2) the corporation elects a different taxable year in accordance with Section 444 of the Code. I.R.C. § 1378. Adoption of a fiscal year as opposed to a calendar year results in the deferral of income to a shareholder, but such a motive will not constitute a valid business purpose. The legislative history further indicates that even certain business-related reasons will not suffice. For example, accounting or regulatory requirements, seasonal hiring patterns, administrative considerations (e.g., promotions), and the existence of price lists or model years will not justify the choice of a fiscal year.

However, Congress explicitly endorsed the adoption of a different taxable year when the corporation has certain peak periods that establish a natural business year that does not coincide with the calendar year. The IRS has adopted procedures for the "expeditious approval" of a fiscal year. If an S corporation, or its predecessor C corporation, has incurred more than 25 percent of its gross receipts from sales or services in the last two months of the proposed fiscal year for each of the last three consecutive years, then a "natural business year" will exist, provided that such fiscal year results in less deferral of income to shareholders than its current taxable year. As an alternate test, if shareholders owning a majority of the issued and outstanding shares adopt such a fiscal year, then the S corporation may also select such a fiscal year. Rev. Proc. 87-32, 1987-28 I.R.B. 14. Adoption of a fiscal year may be disadvantageous for an S corporation that is expected to generate losses because it results in the deferral of losses to be passed through to the shareholders.

As an alternative means to avoid the imposition of a taxable year ending December 31, Section 444 permits an S corporation that is not part of a tiered structure of partnerships or S corporations with different taxable years to elect a taxable year ending on a date other than December 31, provided that the deferral does not exceed the shorter of three months or the deferral period of the taxable year being changed. I.R.C. § 444(a)-(b), (d); Temp. Reg. § 1.444-1T. The S corporation must also remit certain "required payments" that offset the tax otherwise due on the income resulting from the application of a fiscal year. I.R.C. §§ 444(c), 7519. An S corporation may only make a Section 444 election once. I.R.C. § 444(d)(2)(B).

THE SUBCHAPTER S ALTERNATIVE   73

No carrybacks or carryforwards are allowed for years in which the corporation was a C corporation to or from years in which the corporation was an S corporation. However, the years in which a corporation claims S corporation status still count as taxable years for carryforward and carryback purposes. I.R.C. § 1371(b)(1)-(3). The year in which an S corporation terminates its election and resumes C corporation status counts as a single year, despite the fact that it might have two short tax years for purposes of allocation of income and the imposition of taxes for that year, as outlined in Part VII of this chapter.

VI. EFFECT OF THE ELECTION ON SHAREHOLDERS

A. Taxation of Shareholders

The S corporation constitutes a mere conduit to channel income to the shareholders for tax purposes. The S corporation passes income through to its shareholders as if the shareholders realized the income directly from the source and incurred it in the same manner as the S corporation. I.R.C. § 1366(b). However, the treatment of Subchapter S Items at the corporate level affects such income, and the shareholder's tax return must comport with the tax return of the S corporation. I.R.C. §§ 6241, 6242.

Each shareholder is allocated its pro rata share of income (including tax-exempt income), losses, deductions and credits of the S corporation, if separate treatment could affect the tax liability of any shareholder. This includes such items as charitable contributions and foreign tax credits that are excluded from consideration at the corporate level, but it excludes fuel credits accounted for at the corporate level. I.R.C. § 1366(a)(1)(A). Each shareholder also receives its pro rata share of non-separately computed income and loss, meaning gross income less deductions allowed to the S corporation on all amounts not falling within the parameters of Section 1366(a)(1)(A) of the Code. I.R.C. § 1366(a)(1)(B), (2).

Each shareholder's pro rata share of any item consists of the sum of the daily, per-share portion of such item multiplied by the number of shares that the shareholder owns on each such day. To calculate the daily, per-share amount, an equal portion of each item is allocated to each day of the year, and for each day that amount is divided by the number of shares outstanding on such day. I.R.C. § 1377(a)(1). If a shareholder terminates completely its interest in the stock of the S corporation, then the taxable year may be treated as two separate taxable years for purposes of application of the Section 1377(a)(1) proration formula, provided that all shareholders during such taxable year so elect. The first taxable year will end on the date of such termination. I.R.C. § 1377(a)(2); Temp. Reg. § 18.1377-1. As a result of these proration rules, a former shareholder may suffer adverse tax consequences from S corporation activities subsequent to the termination of its interest if no Section 1377(a)(2) election occurs, and the remaining shareholders may incur greater tax liabilities if they make a Section 1377(a)(2) election and the S corporation generates substantially more income in the "second year" than in the "first year."

Subject to certain limitations, the gross income of each shareholder includes its pro rata share of the gross income of the S corporation. I.R.C. § 1366(c). Losses and deductions passed through to the shareholder to compute the shareholder's gross income cannot exceed the sum of the adjusted basis of the shareholder's stock in the S corporation and the adjusted basis of any indebtedness owed by the S corporation to the shareholder. Income of the S corporation increases the shareholder's basis in such stock, but distributions, losses and deductions do not decrease the shareholder's basis in any indebtedness. I.R.C. §§ 1366(d)(1), 1367(a)-(b). If an insufficient basis exists to offset losses and deductions, such losses and deductions may be carried over indefinitely to subsequent taxable years of the S corporation. I.R.C. § 1366(d)(2).

A variety of special rules affect the calculation of the shareholder's taxable income. For example, a shareholder may not be able to deduct all S corporation losses passed through if the shareholder is not "at risk" for such amounts. Such a determination occurs at the shareholder level and depends upon the amount of money and the adjusted basis of other property that each shareholder has contributed to the S corpora-

THE SUBCHAPTER S ALTERNATIVE 75

tion, as well as amounts borrowed for use by the S corporation to the extent that such shareholder is personally liable for such amounts or has pledged its property as security for such borrowings. I.R.C. § 465.

Similarly, S corporation shareholders who do not "materially participate" in the conduct of the trade or business may not claim passive activity losses or passive activity credits to offset income from other sources or taxes on such income. I.R.C. § 469(a), (c)(1). Passive activities include rental activities regardless of any material participation by shareholders. I.R.C. § 469(c)(2). Conversely, the Code excludes income from certain passive sources such as interest, dividends, annuities or royalties not derived in the ordinary course of trade or business. I.R.C. § 469(e)(1). Material participation by shareholders means a regular, continuous and substantial involvement in the operation of the activity; simply approving decisions, managing in name only or providing legal, tax or accounting services will be insufficient. I.R.C. § 469(h)(1).

If the S corporation issued its stock in exchange for money or other property (excluding stock or other securities) not totalling more than $1,000,000 and if the majority of the corporation's aggregate receipts in the prior five years did not derive from passive sources, then the shareholder may account for losses from the sale or exchange of such "Section 1244 Stock" as an ordinary loss up to $50,000, or $100,000 for a husband and wife filing a joint return. However, additional contributions to capital that increase the basis of the shareholder's stock by operation of Section 1367(a) of the Code are allocated to non-Section 1244 Stock, so a shareholder disposing of its stock may only treat a portion of any such loss as an ordinary loss. I.R.C. § 1244.

To the extent that built-in gains are passed through to the shareholders, each shareholder's pro rata share of any taxes payable by the S corporation pursuant to Section 1374 of the Code on such built-in gains reduces that portion of such gain allocated to such shareholder. I.R.C. § 1366(f)(2). Similarly, each shareholder's portion of any tax imposed under Section 1375 of the Code with respect to each item of passive investment income reduces any passive investment income passed through to the shareholder. I.R.C. § 1366(f)(3).

If a family member of a shareholder renders services or contributes capital to the S corporation without receiving "reasonable compensation" therefor, the IRS may adjust income to reflect the value of such services or capital. I.R.C. § 1366(e). This section effectively prevents the allocation of income to a family member in a lower tax bracket, such as a child, when a family member in a higher tax bracket renders the value to the S corporation. Indeed, the transfer of ownership of stock to a child when the economic benefit and corporate control remain in the hands of the parent may result in a tax to the parents on the income attributable to the transferred shares. *Speca v. Comm'r*, 38 T.C.M. 544 (1979).

B. Distributions to Shareholders

Distributions of property of the S corporation to its shareholders with respect to stock receive variable treatment in the hands of the shareholders depending upon the financial status of the corporation. For this purpose, property includes money, securities (other than stock of the S corporation or warrants or options to purchase such stock) and other property. I.R.C. § 317(a). In cases where the S corporation distributes property to the shareholders with a contemporaneous extension of loans from the shareholders to the S corporation, only the excess constitutes a distribution by the S corporation. *Roesel v. Comm'r*, 56 T.C. 14 (1971). (The IRS has not acquiesced in this decision, 1978-1 C.B.2.)

The tax implications for the shareholder of a distribution of property are contingent initially upon the existence of accumulated earnings and profits of the S corporation. If the S corporation has no accumulated earnings and profits, then only amounts in excess of the shareholder's basis in stock of the S corporation are included in gross income as a gain from the sale or exchange of property. I.R.C. § 1368(b). If the S corporation has accumulated earnings and profits, then that portion of the distribution in excess of the amount in the Accumulated Adjustments Account, discussed below, is treated as a nontaxable return of capital. Such decreases that exhaust the Accumulated Adjustments Account result in its allocation among the distributions in accordance with their relative sizes. The Code specifically acknowledges that forthcoming

THE SUBCHAPTER S ALTERNATIVE 77

regulations may vary this pattern of allocation, and the legislative history implies that different rules may be appropriate where a "substantial" portion of the stock has been transferred during the year. Additional amounts attributable to the distribution are treated as a dividend to the extent of the S corporation's earnings and profits. Any remainder will be considered a nontaxable return of capital to the extent of the shareholder's basis in the stock of the S corporation, with any additional amounts includable in the gross income of the shareholder as gain from the sale or exchange of property. I.R.C. § 1368(c).

The Accumulated Adjustments Account represents income of the S corporation that has been taxed but not distributed to shareholders. For each year that the corporation has been an S corporation in the most recent continuous period (the "S Period"), the Accumulated Adjustments Account is adjusted in the same manner as adjustments to basis in stock under Section 1367 of the Code, except that no adjustments are made for tax-exempt income, expenses related to tax-exempt income and federal taxes paid by a predecessor C corporation. I.R.C. § 1368(e)(1)-(2). The Accumulated Adjustments Account starts at zero on the first day of the S corporation's first taxable year and is increased for separately stated and passed-through income and for non-separately stated income. The Accumulated Adjustments Account is decreased for distributions that constitute nontaxable returns of capital by the corporation, losses separately stated and passed through to the shareholders, non-separately computed losses, and nondeductible amounts not related to the production of tax-exempt income.

If there is a redemption that constitutes an exchange under either Section 302(a) or Section 303(a) of the Code (*see* discussion in Chapter 10), then the Accumulated Adjustments Account is further adjusted by an amount equal to the percentage of the total shares of the S corporation so redeemed. Adjustments to the Accumulated Adjustments Account may result in a negative balance that will only become positive by subsequent additions to the Accumulated Adjustments Account. Upon termination of the S corporation election, any amounts in the Accumulated Adjustments Account are irretrievably lost.

If all shareholders receiving a distribution in any taxable year so elect, the corporation may distribute earnings and profits first. I.R.C. § 1368(e)(3). Such an election could permit the S corporation to avoid tax on any excess net passive income by distributing accumulated Subchapter C earnings and profits. Similarly, a shareholder could utilize a net operating loss or avoid the imposition of the alternative minimum tax by exhausting earnings and profits.

C. Adjustments to Basis

The basis of stock of an S corporation held by a shareholder is increased for income (including tax-exempt income), separately computed income, and the excess of deductions for depletion over the basis of such property. I.R.C. § 1367(a)(1). These items also must be included in the gross income of the shareholder on its return or such items will not increase the shareholder's basis. I.R.C. § 1367(b). Cancellation of indebtedness will result in an increase in basis. *Haber v. Comm'r*, 52 T.C. 255 (1969), *aff'd*, 422 F.2d 198 (5th Cir. 1970). Distributions not includable in the income of a corporation under Section 1368 of the Code, separately computed losses and deductions, non-separately computed losses, expenses of the corporation deductible and not chargeable to the capital account, and deductions for oil and gas depletion each result in decreases in the basis of stock. I.R.C. § 1367(a)(2).

Sham contributions that do not result in any economic outlay have no effect on basis. *Pike v. Comm'r*, 78 T.C. 822 (1982); *see also Perry v. Comm'r*, 54 T.C. 1293 (1970) (exchange of notes does not create any indebtedness). When nonrecourse notes are issued to obtain cash used to purchase stock of an S corporation and the notes are secured by such stock, the cash proceeds from the loan do not augment the basis of the stock because no money was advanced. Rev. Rul. 80-236, 1980-2 C.B. 240. When a nonshareholder contributes capital in the name of a shareholder and such contribution is evidenced by a nonrecourse note from the shareholder to the nonshareholder secured by stock, the amount of the contribution is properly includable in the basis of the stock. *Millar v. Comm'r*, 34 T.C.M. 554, *vacated and rem'd on other grounds*, 540 F.2d 184 (3d Cir. 1976). A shareholder's guarantee of a loan to the S corporation does not increase the shareholder's basis; the shareholder must actually advance funds on behalf of the S corporation pursuant to the guarantee. *Brown v. Comm'r*, 706 F.2d 755 (6th Cir. 1983); *but cf. Selfe v. United States*, 778 F.2d 769 (11th Cir. 1985) (shareholder's guarantee of loan to an S corporation may increase basis in stock "where the facts demonstrate that, in substance, the shareholder has borrowed funds and subsequently advanced them to [the S corporation]").

Upon reduction of the shareholder's basis in stock to zero, subsequent decreases reduce the shareholder's basis in any indebtedness that the corporation owes to such shareholder. I.R.C. § 1367(b)(2)(A). Any subsequent increases in basis will first restore the shareholder's basis in any indebtedness before any amount increases its basis in stock. I.R.C. § 1367(b)(2)(B).

If the stock or indebtedness becomes worthless, the adjustments for distributions stated in Sections 1366 and 1367 of the Code are taken into account before the application of the loss of capital asset or debt provisions in Sections 165(g) and 166(d) of the Code, respectively. I.R.C. § 1367(b)(3). Thus, part of the loss from stock or indebtedness is converted into ordinary loss. To the extent that the stock constitutes Section 1244 Stock, the loss may also qualify as an ordinary loss under that section.

VII. TERMINATION OF S CORPORATION STATUS

A. Voluntary Revocation of the S Corporation Election

The Code permits an S corporation to revoke its S corporation status and to resume treatment as a normal C corporation. I.R.C. § 1362(d)(1)(A). Shareholders holding a majority of the issued and outstanding shares of stock in the S corporation, including nonvoting shares, must consent to the revocation, which consents should be submitted with the revocation. I.R.C. § 1362(d)(1)(B); Temp. Reg. § 18.1362-3. The revocation may specify a prospective date for effectiveness. I.R.C. § 1362(d)(1)(D). If the revocation specifies no particular effective date, then a revocation within the first two and one-half months of the taxable year will be effective as of the first day of such taxable year, whereas a revocation after that date will be effective as of the first day of the following taxable year. I.R.C. § 1362(d)(1)(C).

Prior versions of Subchapter S permitted a new shareholder to affirmatively refuse to consent to the S corporation election within 60 days of acquiring the stock, thereby terminating the election. Although the current version of the law has eliminated this provision, a single shareholder may still cause the termination of the S corporation election. An income beneficiary of a Qualified Subchapter S Trust may revoke its Qualified Subchapter S Trust election with the consent of the IRS, causing a termination of the S corporation by having a nonqualifying trust as a shareholder. I.R.C. § 1361(d)(2)(C). Moreover, a successive income beneficiary may affirmatively refuse to consent to the Qualified Subchapter S Trust election by filing such objection within two and one-half months of becoming the income beneficiary, again triggering a termination of the S corporation election. I.R.C. § 1361(d)(2)(B)(ii); Prop. Reg. § 1.1361-1A(i)(5).

B. Involuntary Termination of the S Corporation Election

If the corporation ceases to qualify as a "small business corporation" at any time after the first of its first taxable year as an S corporation, then its election terminates effective on the date of such failure to meet the requirements for a "small business corporation." I.R.C. § 1362(d)(2)(A). If the termination results from the failure of a trust to fall within the parameters of a Qualified Subchapter S Trust because it does not distribute income to only one individual who is a United States citizen or resident alien, then the Qualified Subchapter S Trust election will terminate as of the first day of the next taxable year, the corporation will cease to qualify as a "small business corporation" as of that date, and the S corporation election will likewise terminate on that date. I.R.C. § 1361(d)(4).

The S corporation election also terminates involuntarily if the corporation has Subchapter C earnings and profits for three consecutive years during which it has been an S corporation and has gross receipts in each

THE SUBCHAPTER S ALTERNATIVE 81

such year more than 25 percent of which derive from passive investment income. Such termination will be effective on the first day of the following taxable year. I.R.C. § 1362(d)(3)(A)(i)-(iii). An S corporation that never existed as a C corporation or that had previously distributed all such earnings and profits as a dividend to its shareholders would not confront this problem.

C. Safeguarding Against Termination

The shareholders of an S corporation should consider steps to minimize the possibility that a dissident shareholder could cause the termination of the election by such acts as transferring its shares to an ineligible shareholder or selling them to multiple entities that will raise the total number of shareholders over the limit of 35. Because all of the shareholders on the date of the election must consent thereto, a shareholder agreement that restricts the ability of a shareholder to transfer its shares in such a manner as to terminate the election should not be difficult to obtain. Such an agreement should state that any attempted transfer is void and not merely a violation of the agreement. *See* IRS Private Letter Ruling 7748034 (transfer void and S corporation election did not terminate); *but cf.* IRS Private Letter Ruling 7716014 (transfer merely violated shareholder agreement and S corporation election terminated). The agreement could even permit other shareholders to purchase shares tendered for sale or allow the corporation to redeem such shares.

Applicable state and federal laws impose limitations on the enforcement of such agreements. Certain states may restrict the inclusion of stock transfer restrictions in the charter or by-laws of corporations organized under its laws. Attempts to enforce even a separate written shareholder agreement may also confront opposition in some jurisdictions. To bind subsequent transferees of initial stockholders, the stock certificate itself should note the transfer restrictions. U.C.C. § 8-204. Despite such limitations, transfer restrictions in some form constitute a viable means (1) to minimize the possibility that one shareholder can trigger the termination of the election, and (2) to lay the foundation for an action for damages against any shareholder causing a termination that results in adverse tax consequences for other shareholders. Transfer restrictions are discussed in greater detail in Chapter 9.

If an involuntary termination nonetheless occurs, the Code expressly provides for a degree of flexibility in maintaining S corporation status if remedial actions follow. The IRS may deem the termination inadvertent and disregard it if the corporation takes steps to reestablish itself as a "small business corporation" within a "reasonable period of time after discovery of the event resulting in such termination" and the corporation and each shareholder during such period agree to such adjustments as the IRS may require. I.R.C. § 1362(f).

D. Tax Treatment of a Year in Which a Termination Occurs

Upon termination of an S corporation election, the corporation enters into a Post-Termination Transition Period extending to the later of one year after the day after the final day of the last taxable year of the S corporation or the due date for filing the return of the corporation for such final year. In the event of a controversy regarding whether or not a termination has occurred, the Post-Termination Transition Period will be extended to 120 days after any final court decision, closing agreement or agreement with the IRS confirming the termination of the S corporation election. I.R.C. § 1377(b). Upon termination of the S corporation election, any remaining disallowed losses and deductions are treated as incurred by the shareholder on the last day of the Post-Termination Transition Period. These losses and deductions permit a tax-free distribution to the extent of each shareholder's basis in its stock of the corporation, as reduced by such deductions. I.R.C. § 1366(d)(3). The shareholder may not apply any additional losses or deductions to a reduction in the basis of any indebtedness owed by the corporation to the shareholder.

The distribution of money with respect to stock during the Post-Termination Transition Period results in a decrease in the adjusted basis of the stock to the extent of any amounts in the Accumulated Adjustments Account. Distributions of other forms of property do not qualify for such treatment. However, if all shareholders consent, the S corporation may elect to treat such a distribution as a dividend paid out of earnings and profits in order to avoid the imposition of an accumulated earnings tax or a personal holding company tax (*see* discussion in Chapter 15). I.R.C. § 1371(e).

The termination of an S corporation election on any day other than the first day of a taxable year results in two short years for calculation of income and tax. I.R.C. § 1362(e)(1). The Code refers to the year in which such termination occurs as the "S Termination Year." For the portion of the S Termination Year that the election was in effect (the "S Short Year"), the corporation prorates the amount of income, losses, deductions and credits and the amount of non-separately computed income and loss. I.R.C. § 1362(e)(2). This section does not apply to asset acquisitions that result from Section 338 stock purchases. I.R.C. § 1362(e)(6)(C). The taxable income of the C corporation is "annualized" by multiplying the taxable income for the short year for which no election was in effect (the "C Short Year") by the quotient of the number of days in the S Termination Year divided by the number of days in the C Short Year. I.R.C. § 1362(e)(5)(D). For carryover purposes, the two short years will count as a single year. I.R.C. § 1362(e)(6)(A).

If all of the shareholders during the S Year and all of the shareholders on the first day of the C Short Year consent, the corporation may elect not to prorate. I.R.C. § 1362(e)(3). The legislative history indicates that Congress intended to permit the shareholder of a corporation to attribute gain or losses to each short year based upon the time when such gain or loss was incurred or recognized, as reflected in the corporation's records. Moreover, if there is a sale or exchange of more than one-half of the stock of the corporation during the S Termination Year, then the proration rule automatically does not apply. I.R.C. § 1362(e)(6)(D).

VIII. CONCLUDING OBSERVATIONS

A detailed evaluation of the Subchapter S alternative should constitute an integral part of the process of forming any small business. Although this chapter outlines some of the major considerations in any decision regarding a Subchapter S election, the complexities of Subchapter S certainly exceed the scope of this analysis, and their resolution depends upon the particular circumstances of each situation. Moreover, Subchapter S continues to evolve, and forthcoming regulations will undoubtedly clarify, and could even alter, the interpretation and application of the statute. Similarly, subsequent Congressional modifications of the Code, such as the possible reinstatement of capital gains treatment, would have profound consequences for the operation of Subchapter S. Whatever form Subchapter S may assume, it will nonetheless provide significant tax benefits for many small business corporations and their shareholders.

CHAPTER FOUR

INCORPORATION AND RECORDKEEPING

Alexander W. Samor
Clifford R. Ennico

I. INCORPORATION

Corporations are "creatures of statute." The act of incorporating and matters relating thereto, including the selection and reservation of the corporation name and the filing of the certificate of incorporation, are governed by various sections of the New York Business Corporation Law ("BCL") and the New York Code of Rules and Regulations ("NYCRR"). New York filing clerks are notorious for requiring strict compliance with the applicable statutory provisions and as a general rule of practice, strict adherence to the statutory requirements of the BCL and NYCRR will help avoid delay in the filing and processing of the documents which are part of the incorporating process.

A. Selecting the Name

Except for the requirement of Section 104 of the BCL that the corporation's name be written in English letters or characters, a person forming a corporation has wide latitude in choosing its name. Section 301 of the BCL, however, requires that the name (1) contain the word "incorporated," "corporation" or "limited" or an abbreviation thereof; (2) shall be such as to distinguish it from the names of other domestic corporations, foreign corporations authorized to do business in New York and names previously reserved; (3) not contain any word, phrase or abbreviation thereof prohibited by statute; (4) not contain any word, phrase or abbreviation thereof which indicates or implies that the corporation possesses powers or purposes which it does not or may not possess; (5) not contain any of the following phrases or abbreviations thereof: board of trade, chamber of commerce, community renewal, state police, state trooper, tenant relocation, urban development, or urban relocation; (6) not contain any of a specified list of words which imply that the corporation is engaged in banking or insurance (those words are: acceptance, annuity, assurance, bank, benefit, bond, casualty, endowment, fidelity, finance, guaranty, indemnity, insurance, investment, loan, mortgage, savings, surety, title, trust, and underwriter), unless the approval of the Superintendent of Insurance or the Superintendent of Banks is attached to the certificate of incorporation; (7) not contain the words "doctor" or "lawyer" or abbreviations thereof unless the corporation is a professional corporation (formed pursuant to Article 15 of the BCL) or unless the words are used in a context which clearly denotes a purpose other than the practice of law or medicine; (8) not contain words implying that the corporation is a labor organization, unless the approval of the New York State Board of Standards and Appeals is attached to the certificate of incorporation; (9) not contain the words "blind" or "handicapped," unless the approval of the New York State Board of Social Welfare is attached to the certificate of incorporation; (10) not contain words that imply a relationship to government; (11) not contain words which are indecent, obscene or which ridicule a person, group or agency of government or indicate unlawful activity; or (12) not contain the word "exchange" unless the approval of the New York State Attorney General is attached to the certificate of incorporation.

Section 302, however, carves out certain exceptions to the above prohibitions, relating to foreign corporations or corporations formed as a result of extraordinary corporate transactions (i.e., merger or consolidation). Additionally, Section 302 permits the use of certain words in a corporate name (such as "broker," "investment company," "bank" and other terms relating to the securities or finance industry) if the corporation is organized in compliance with the various federal statutes (such as the Securities Exchange Act of 1934) governing such industries. Careful scrutiny of Section 302 is advised in order to determine its applicability.

The most troublesome of these requirements is probably (2) above. At the time a certificate of incorporation is filed, the Secretary of State decides whether to approve or reject a corporation name. This process is at least partly subjective with the result that some disapprovals by the Secretary may seem unwarranted. For instance, a name consisting of just initials or numbers with no obvious meaning will probably be disapproved unless the corporation is involved in real estate or shipping and the numbers correspond to addresses or ship identification numbers. Additionally, a corporation name which is too similar (in the discretion of the Secretary of State) to an existing or reserved name will be rejected. Although the Secretary's decision can be attacked by writ of

INCORPORATION AND RECORDKEEPING

mandamus, the costs and time involved in litigating probably outweigh the possibility that the Secretary's decision will be overturned.

If a name is similar to that of an existing corporation, the Secretary may approve it if a consent is obtained from the existing corporation. Although a consent does not assure approval, it will probably be honored if the existing corporation and the proposed one will be affiliated (e.g., parent and subsidiary). Even the use of one's own given name may be disapproved if someone or something else has used it first. In some instances in which a given name is similar to that of another corporation, the Secretary of State will allow its use only if the person named signs as incorporator. Presumably, this assures the Secretary that the choice of the corporation's name is motivated by bona fide business reasons and is not an attempt to engage in unfair competition by using an established corporation's name.

A common practice used by lawyers when their chosen corporate names are deemed too close to an existing corporation's name is to add the words "of New York" or "in New York" to the otherwise forbidden name, and then file a "doing business" certificate (discussed in Chapter 1) in the county where the corporation will be doing business using the forbidden corporate name without the words "of New York" or "in New York." The rules and regulations of the New York Secretary of State (copies of which are included in the "Forms and Materials" section of this volume) expressly authorize this procedure. Using a corporate name that is virtually identical to that of another corporation, however, carries the risk of a lawsuit by the other corporation, which will claim that the "usurper" is infringing upon a trade name or trademark. Counsel should use some judgment in deciding whether his/her corporate client should adopt a new corporate name (which may entail amendments to filings in other states) or accept the risk of an infringement lawsuit. If, for example, one is incorporating a corporation for a client named McDonald, one should be wary of using the client's name in the corporation's name if the corporation is to have anything to do with the restaurant business.

B. Reserving the Name

Section 303 of the BCL provides a mechanism whereby the availability of a particular name or names can be ascertained by way of a record search and, if available, "reserved" for use. Because the Secretary of State will reject a certificate of incorporation containing a name which has already been used, or which does not sufficiently distinguish itself from the names of other domestic corporations, foreign corporations authorized to do business in New York or previously reserved names, reserving a name pursuant to Section 303 of the BCL may save valuable time and avoid the expense of resubmitting a certificate of incorporation.

The first step in reserving a name is to draw up a list of names, ranking them in order of preference. An application for the reservation of a name (a form of which appears in the "Forms and Materials" section of this volume) must be completed for each such name and must set forth the name and address of the applicant, the reason for the making of the application (e.g., that the applicant intends to form a domestic corporation or that a foreign corporation intends to apply for authority to do business) and must be signed by the applicant, his/her attorney or his/her agent. Section 303 states that the Secretary may require the application to include a statement regarding the nature of the business to be conducted. Therefore, to reduce the possibility that the application will be returned for lack of such statement, it should contain a short but accurate description of the nature of the business in which the corporation will engage.

At this point it should be ascertained whether the corporation anticipates doing substantial business in another state or states. If so, the corporation will have to qualify to do business in those states which in turn will require that the name not conflict with names already in use in those states. Therefore, a name search and reservation should be performed for each of those states at the same time a name search and reservation is performed in New York State.

If the application complies with Section 303, the Corporation and Records division of the Department of State will reserve the first name

INCORPORATION AND RECORDKEEPING

on the list not previously used or reserved, and the Department of State will issue a "certificate of reservation." The reservation lasts for a period of 60 days, during which time no one else may use the reserved name, and may be extended for up to two additional 60-day periods upon written application to the Department of State by the applicant, or his/her attorney or agent. The certificate of reservation should be maintained for safekeeping because it must be included when the certificate of incorporation is filed.

However, if it is necessary to incorporate very quickly, it may be wise not to reserve an approved name. It takes several days for the Secretary to issue a certificate of reservation, but once the application for the reservation of a particular name or names is filed, a certificate of incorporation using one of those names cannot be filed without the certificate of reservation. Thus, there may be a delay before the certificate of incorporation can be filed. Therefore, if the certificate of incorporation is prepared and a name approved but not reserved, the certificate of incorporation may be filed immediately. This presents two problems. First, between approval of the name and filing of the certificate of incorporation someone else may file an application for reservation or a certificate of incorporation for the same or a similar name. Second, an approval is not binding without name reservation. Therefore, the name will be reviewed again when the certificate of incorporation is filed and it might be rejected. This result is unlikely, but possible.

PRACTICE GUIDES

- *Check Section 301 of the BCL for a list of prohibited words and phrases.*
- *Select three names in order of preference.*
- *Consider obtaining approval for and reservation of the name from the New York Department of State.*
- *If the corporation will do business in other states, check to make sure the name has not been used in those states.*
- *If the name is similar to that of a parent or affiliated corporation, obtain written consent to use it.*

- *If the name is reserved, be sure to include the certificate of reservation when filing the certificate of incorporation.*

C. The Certificate of Incorporation

Section 401 of the BCL states that one or more natural persons 18 years of age or over may act as incorporators of a corporation. Section 402 of the BCL requires the certificate to be entitled "Certificate of Incorporation of [name of corporation] under Section 402 of the Business Corporation Law." The certificate must be signed by each incorporator with his/her name, address and the word "incorporator" beneath or opposite the signature. The certificate must be signed under penalties of perjury and notarized (a form of notarization appears in the "Forms and Materials" section of this volume), and the certificate becomes effective upon its filing by the New York Department of State.

Section 402 of the BCL requires that the certificate include the following nine items: (1) the name of the corporation; (2) the purpose(s) for which the corporation is formed; (3) the county (but do not include the address) in New York where the office of the corporation is to be located (Section 102(a)(10) of the BCL states that the office need not be the place where the business of the corporation is or will be conducted); (4) the total number of shares authorized, the par value of those shares or, if the shares have no par value, a statement to that effect; (5) if there is more than one class of shares, the number of shares of each class and the par value of those shares (or, if the shares have no par value, a statement to that effect), the designation of each class and a statement describing the rights, preferences and limitations of each class; (6) if preferred shares are to be authorized in series, a designation of each series and a statement of the variations in the relative rights, preferences and limitations as between series; (7) a designation of the New York Secretary of State as agent for service of process and a post office address (in-state or out-of-state) to which a copy of process may be sent; (8) if the corporation is to have a registered agent, the name and address of the registered agent within the state; and (9) the duration of the corporation if other than perpetual. In addition, Section 104 of the BCL requires the certificate to be in English.

INCORPORATION AND RECORDKEEPING

Both Sections 402 and 304 require that the certificate designate the Secretary of State as agent for service of process and list the address to which a copy of any process served on the Secretary will be mailed. In addition, Sections 402 and 305 permit the certificate to name a registered agent (including the agent's address) and a statement that the registered agent is to be the agent of the corporation upon whom process against it may be served. The primary benefit of a registered agent is that the corporation will stand a better chance of receiving process papers promptly.

While the certificate of incorporation may set forth the purpose or purposes for which the corporation is being formed, Section 402 permits the certificate to state that the purpose of the corporation (either alone or with other specific purposes) is to engage in any lawful act or activity for which corporations may be organized under the BCL provided that it also sets forth that the corporation is not engaged in any act or activity requiring the consent or approval of any state official, department, board, agency or other body without such consent or approval first being obtained. The inclusion of this statement places all lawful acts and activities within the scope of the corporation's purpose unless otherwise limited by the certificate, the by-laws or other statutory provisions. Consequently, inclusion of this language by itself or in addition to any other purpose will provide the corporation maximum flexibility with which to conduct its affairs. (Sections 405-407 of the BCL require that if the corporation's purposes include the establishment and/or operation of a day-care center or alcohol or substance abuse program, the approval of the appropriate state regulatory agency must be filed with the certificate of incorporation.)

Nevertheless, consideration should be given as to whether the certificate should limit the corporation to specific purposes. For instance, certain shareholders may not be active in the management of the corporation and may wish to limit the corporation's activities. The inclusion of a specific purpose clause and omission of the general purpose language forces a corporation to amend its certificate of incorporation in order to change or broaden its allowable activities. In this way, a corporation's expansion into different areas of business is put to shareholder vote. Additionally, Section 203 of the BCL limits the use of the *ultra vires* defense to actions by shareholders of a corporation to enjoin its acts; the inclusion of a general purpose clause may effectively negate the ability of a shareholder to assert that the corporation acted outside its stated purposes.

While Section 202 enumerates the powers of a corporation, Section 402 does not require the certificate of incorporation to list them. Section 202 is comprehensive, encompassing nearly every conceivable corporate power, and the powers of a corporation are limited only by (1) the requirement that the powers exercised further a stated corporate purpose, and (2) the express limitations, if any, contained in the certificate, the by-laws or by the limits of statutory or common law. Nevertheless, inserting specific corporate powers in the certificate limits the corporation to specific activities and it may be advisable for those reasons set forth in the above discussion of corporate purposes.

Should there be a need to limit either the purposes or the powers of the corporation, care should be taken that the language in the certificate be broad enough to include all activities which are necessarily concomitant to the desired business or activity.

The certificate may also include other provisions relating to the business, organization or operation of the corporation so long as those provisions do not violate any sections of the BCL or other statutes. Of particular concern, however, are those provisions which are effective only if included in the certificate. These include provisions altering or limiting the one-vote-per-one-share concept granted by the BCL (Section 612); altering or eliminating preemptive rights (Section 622); altering or limiting the right of holders of different classes of shares to vote (Section 613); altering the percentage of votes necessary to elect directors or take other corporate action (Sections 614 and 708); altering the quorum requirement (i.e., simple majority) for shareholder meetings or the votes necessary to amend the certificate of incorporation (Sections 616 and 709); providing for class voting (Section 617); providing for cumulative voting for the election of directors (Section 618); and other provisions regulating shareholder participation in the corporation's af-

INCORPORATION AND RECORDKEEPING 95

fairs (Section 620(b)). The relevant sections of the BCL should be carefully examined to determine their applicability.

The decision as to whether provisions should be set forth in the certificate or the by-laws must also take into consideration the possibility that shareholders may later wish to alter these provisions. Amending the by-laws can be accomplished without the time and expense involved in amending the certificate (which requires filing an amended certificate with the Department of State—see discussion in Chapter 15). Moreover, if so provided for in the certificate, the by-laws can be amended by vote of the board, while in all but a few limited circumstances the certificate can be amended only by board and shareholder vote. Additionally, while a certificate of incorporation is a public document available for inspection by the public, the by-laws are not, and there may be circumstances in which the affairs and governance of a corporation should be kept confidential.

D. Fees and Expenses

The State of New York charges $5 to check the availability of a corporate name and $20 to reserve the name. The filing fee for a certificate of incorporation is $110 plus a tax on the authorized shares of capital stock (for par value shares: 1/20 of 1% of the total par value; for no-par shares: $.05 per share). The minimum tax is $10. For a fee of $120 the filing will be done on an expedited basis. Under Section 150.4 of the Rules and Regulations of the Department of State, all fees paid to the Department must be payable in cash, by money order or by certified check, except that uncertified checks under $250 will be accepted from attorneys admitted to the bar in any of the United States. These numbers may change and the practitioner is urged to call one of the services listed in Part V of this chapter to confirm the filing and reservation fees.

PRACTICE GUIDES

- *One or more natural persons over 18 may act as incorporator; a corporation may not act as incorporator.*
- *Only one incorporator is required.*

- *The certificate of incorporation must be written in English and must be notarized.*

- *The information required by Section 402 of the BCL must be provided.*

- *The certificate must state the county but not the address where the corporation's office is to be located.*

- *Although corporate powers need not be stated specifically, listing certain powers or purposes should be considered.*

- *The certificate should be on 8-1/2 x 11 size paper with a backing attached setting forth the incorporator's name and address.*

- *The filing receipt is official evidence of incorporation, not the certified copy of the certificate.*

II. BY-LAWS

By-laws are the rules and regulations adopted by a corporation to govern its affairs and its shareholders, directors and officers. By-laws need not be filed with or approved by any New York State office. Section 601(c) of the BCL provides that the by-laws of a corporation "may contain any provision relating to the business of the corporation, the conduct of its affairs, its rights or powers or the rights or powers of its shareholders, directors or officers" so long as each provision is consistent with the BCL, the certificate of incorporation or other statutory law. Pursuant to Section 601(a), the initial by-laws must be adopted by the incorporators.

Normally, by-laws are adopted, amended or repealed by a vote of the shareholders. However, pursuant to Section 601(a), the power to adopt, amend or repeal by-laws may be given to the board if so provided in the certificate of incorporation or provided in a by-law adopted by the shareholders. Any by-law adopted by the board may be amended or repealed by the shareholders entitled to vote.

As indicated in the sample by-laws included in the "Forms and Materials" section of this volume, the by-laws should contain provisions

INCORPORATION AND RECORDKEEPING

concerning meetings of and voting by shareholders; number, election and responsibilities of directors; and number, election and responsibilities of officers.

Additionally, the by-laws should provide for the date of the annual meeting of shareholders. It is preferable to select a day of the week of a month, rather than a particular date (for example, the first Tuesday in June rather than June 4). This provision will avoid a meeting scheduled on a weekend. The date selected should be sufficiently after the end of the fiscal year to allow accountants to prepare financial data for the year (usually 90 days is sufficient). If a place for the meeting is not indicated in the by-laws, Section 602 of the BCL requires that it be held at the office of the corporation. The by-laws should indicate the voting rights of each shareholder at the annual meeting. The by-laws may include provisions for calling special meetings of the shareholders. If it is desired to permit shareholders or specific persons other than the directors to call special meetings, this permission must be in the certificate or the by-laws. In the absence of such permission, shareholders may demand special meetings only to elect directors as set forth in Section 603 of the BCL.

The by-law provisions concerning directors should include their number, responsibilities, method of election, term of office, method of removal, method of filling vacancies, regular time and place of meetings and provision for notice of meetings. The by-laws (or the certificate of incorporation) must provide for telephonic meetings and for formation of committees of directors if desired. Although some of the provisions listed above will merely repeat provisions of the BCL, it is a good idea to include them in the by-laws to assure knowledge of and compliance with the statute and ease of reference for directors, officers and shareholders.

The by-law provisions concerning officers should indicate their number, qualifications, method of election, term of office, method of removal and duties.

The fiscal year of the corporation may be fixed by the by-laws, the certificate of incorporation or by resolution of the board of directors.

The latter option may be preferable since it gives the board the flexibility to change the fiscal year without the necessity of amending the by-laws or the certificate. In any case, the fiscal year should be fixed in light of the particular nature of the corporation's business cycle and based on the needs of the corporation's accountants rather than the calendar year.

The by-laws may include any other governing provisions permitted by law including the manner of transfer of shares, distribution of dividends, safekeeping of funds and indemnification of directors and officers. The location of a principal office for the corporation may be set forth and provisions may be made for the directors to select other offices within or without the state of New York.

PRACTICE GUIDES

- *Initial by-laws must be adopted by the incorporator(s).*
- *Select a day of the week and of the month rather than a particular day for the annual meeting of shareholders.*
- *Provide for number, term of office, method of removal and method of filling vacancies on the board of directors.*
- *Consider providing for telephonic meetings of the board of directors.*

III. ORGANIZATIONAL MEETINGS

A. Incorporators

After the certificate of incorporation has been filed and the by-laws drafted, the incorporator or incorporators must hold an organizational meeting pursuant to Section 404 of the BCL. This meeting must be held on five days' written notice to incorporators unless all the incorporators attend the meeting or sign a waiver of notice before or after the meeting. At the meeting, directors must be elected to hold office until the first annual meeting of shareholders and by-laws must be adopted. No corporate action may be taken until the organizational meeting is held and directors are elected. If classes of directors are authorized by the certificate or by-laws, then the terms of the directors elected are governed by

INCORPORATION AND RECORDKEEPING

Section 704 of the BCL. Other business may, but need not, be transacted. Other actions typically taken by the incorporators include adoption of a form of stock certificate and a form of corporate seal.

Section 404 permits the actions required to be taken at the organizational meeting to be taken without a meeting if each incorporator or his/her attorney-in-fact signs a statement which sets forth the actions so taken. A statement of the incorporators should indicate the signatories' status as incorporators and state that the certificate of incorporation was filed with the New York Secretary of State. A sample Statement of Sole Incorporator is included in the "Forms and Materials" section of this volume.

B. Directors

The BCL does not require an organization meeting of directors, but such a meeting is desirable in order to complete the corporate organization. At this meeting, the following actions should be taken: (1) acceptance of share subscriptions; (2) fixing consideration for shares; (3) authorization of the issuance of shares; (4) authorization of the payment of incorporation expenses; (5) approval and ratification of the actions of the incorporator(s); (6) election of officers; (7) fixing compensation for directors, officers or employees; (8) designation of a depository and authorization to open and maintain a corporate bank account; (9) authorization of applications of admission or qualification to do business in other jurisdictions; and (10) adoption of a form of share certificate. If a corporate seal is desired, a form of seal should be adopted by the directors at this time.

The actions described above may be taken without a meeting pursuant to Section 708 of the BCL (unless otherwise restricted in the certificate of incorporation). The written consents of all of the directors are required, and such consents should be filed in the minute book. A sample Action by Unanimous Written Consent of the Board of Directors is included in the "Forms and Materials" section of this volume.

C. Shareholders

If the certificate of incorporation empowers the shareholders to act in managerial capacities or requires shareholder approval for particular actions of the directors, then a shareholders' meeting should be held in addition to the directors' meeting.

D. Subscription for Shares

Once the directors fix the consideration to be received for each share, Section 504 requires that money, property, labor or services be "actually received" before shares can be issued. Directors must be cognizant of the fact that Section 504 does not allow the corporation's stock to be given away for free. However, in the absence of fraud, the judgment of the directors or shareholders as to the value of consideration received for shares is conclusive.

IV. RECORDKEEPING AND OTHER POST-INCORPORATION ISSUES

A. Records

Section 624 of the BCL requires each corporation to keep correct and complete financial records and minutes of the meetings of its shareholders, board of directors and executive committee(s), if any. Additionally, the corporation must maintain a record of the names and addresses of its shareholders, their shareholdings and the date they became owners of record. This record must be kept in New York State, either in the corporation's office, in the offices of a registrar or transfer agent or in the offices of the corporation's attorney.

Care should be taken that all records required to be maintained by the BCL be kept accurate and current because Section 624(g) of the BCL states that such records are *prima facie* evidence of the facts stated therein in favor of a plaintiff in actions against the corporation or any of its officers, directors or shareholders.

While not required by the BCL, corporate resolutions should also be prepared and kept together with the minutes. A corporate resolution is the mechanism whereby a board of directors ratifies the actions of the

INCORPORATION AND RECORDKEEPING 101

corporation. Examples of corporate action which should be ratified by resolution are leasing office space, opening a bank account, corporate borrowings, issuing share subscriptions and extraordinary corporate transactions such as merger or consolidation. Resolutions may be separate documents or may be incorporated within the minutes for the meeting at which the action was ratified.

Special care should be taken to ensure that the minutes and resolutions correctly and adequately summarize shareholder, board and executive committee meetings and the actions ratified therein. The maintenance of accurate minutes and resolutions is particularly important in the context of a sale of corporate stock or assets or the borrowing of money by the corporation: counsel for the buyer or lender will almost certainly examine the minutes and resolutions to ensure that corporate actions have been properly executed.

B. Corporate Seal

Section 202(a)(3) of the BCL empowers a New York corporation to have a corporate seal, to alter the corporate seal at its pleasure and to use the corporate seal by causing it or a facsimile to be affixed, impressed or reproduced in any other manner. Traditionally, the corporate seal is a metal stamp containing the name of the corporation and is embossed on share certificates and other corporate documents. Section 202(a)(3), however, permits a facsimile of the seal to be used. Section 107 of the BCL provides that the presence of the seal on a document executed on behalf of a corporation is *prima facie* evidence that the document was so executed.

The BCL no longer requires that a corporation have or use a corporate seal. However, a corporate acknowledgment must either refer to the seal or to the fact that the corporation has no seal. Such reference may be made to a freehand drawing of the seal. While seals are not required and have very limited effect, banks often require corporations to use their seals when executing documents, and most corporations have and use them.

C. Tax Forms

The final steps in the incorporation process are to file required forms with the Internal Revenue Service and the New York State Tax Commission. Section 275-a of the New York Tax Law requires a corporation to file, within ten days of establishing a principal office or place of business in New York, a stock transfer certificate that designates a place for sale, transfer or delivery of the corporation's stock. The form (MT610.1) is usually provided in commercially available minute books or may be requested from the Tax Commission.

The Internal Revenue Service requires that a corporation file an Application for Employer Identification Number regardless of whether the corporation will have any employees. The form (SS-4) is relatively straightforward and simple to complete and is available from the Internal Revenue Service.

Chapter 18 of this volume discusses other tax forms a corporation must periodically file with the IRS and the State Tax Commission.

D. Corporate Minute Book

The corporate minute book is a useful device for keeping the corporation's records in one place. Generally, corporate books come in the form of three-ring binder notebooks, or "kits," in which are placed minutes, stock certificates, the certificate of incorporation, other official documents, a stock ledger indicating transfers of shares, board and shareholder resolutions and any other document pertaining to the existence or governance of the corporation. Corporate book kits may be ordered for a particular corporation and usually include (1) a corporate seal containing the corporation's name; (2) stock certificates on which the corporation's name is printed; and (3) a stock transfer ledger. Most corporate book kits also include sample forms of by-laws and minutes. Corporate books may be obtained at costs ranging between approximately $42 and $65 from the companies listed below or from local corporate stationers.

Hasbrouck, Thistle & Co., Inc.
100 Avenue of the Americas
New York, New York 10013
(212) 966-3001

Julius Blumberg, Inc.
62 White Street
New York, New York 10013
(212) 431-5000

E. Qualification in Other States

If a corporation intends to do business in states other than New York, the corporation must qualify to do business in those states. How much business must be done in a state in order to require qualification varies from state to state. As a general rule, however, if a corporation intends to transact a substantial part of its business activities in a foreign jurisdiction, it should apply for qualification in that state. In many states, the following activities do not require qualification: holding directors' or shareholders' meetings; maintaining bank accounts; effecting sales through independent contractors; soliciting orders to be accepted outside the state; or conducting isolated business transactions. If a corporation intends to operate outside New York, the applicable law of the foreign jurisdiction must be consulted to ascertain whether it is necessary to qualify to do business in that state.

V. PROFESSIONAL ASSISTANCE

The companies listed below provide assistance to attorneys in connection with incorporations. In addition to obtaining approval and reserving corporate names and filing required documents with the New York Department of State, these services will provide model certificates of incorporation, by-laws and organizational minutes and/or will prepare such documents to the attorney's specifications. These companies will also act as or provide a statutory agent for service of process. These services are generally well versed in the often complicated details regarding the filing of official documents, and their representatives can and will answer most practical questions regarding incorporation and qualifying to do business in New York and other states.

CT Corporation System
1633 Broadway
New York, New York 10019
(212) 664-1666

Prentice-Hall Corporate Services
1 Gulf & Western Plaza
New York, New York 10023-7773
(212) 373-7500 or (800) 223-1727 (out-of-state)

Servico
283 Washington Avenue
Albany, New York 12206
(518) 463-4179

XL Corporate Services Inc.
33 Rensselaer Street
Albany, New York 12202
(518) 463-8842
(212) 732-7661 (in New York City)

CHAPTER FIVE

FEDERAL INCOME TAX ASPECTS OF INCORPORATION

Henry M. Cohn

FEDERAL INCOME TAX ASPECTS OF INCORPORATION

I. INTRODUCTION AND OVERVIEW

Generally, the documents drafted by counsel in forming a corporation are not tax-sensitive. The tax consequences of incorporation arise when the incorporators or initial shareholders transfer cash, property or other assets to the corporation to enable it to conduct business.

This section discusses three problems that counsel should address when determining how a new corporation should be capitalized: (1) whether the transfer of assets from the shareholders to the corporation is tax-free under Section 351 of the Internal Revenue Code; (2) whether the transfer to a corporation of assets that are subject to liabilities (e.g., real property subject to a first mortgage lien) will trigger gain under Section 357 of the Code; and (3) the extent to which the transfer to a corporation of assets that have generated tax benefits to the shareholders will trigger a recapture of such benefits.

Other tax problems counsel will encounter in establishing the capital structure of a new corporation are addressed in Chapter 7.

II. TAX-FREE INCORPORATION UNDER SECTION 351

A. In General

Absent Section 351 of the Code, the transfer by an individual (say, a sole proprietor) of business assets to a newly formed corporation would trigger a recognition of gain or loss—an undesirable result to say the least, since no new assets have been created and since the assets have not been liquidated (e.g., sold for cash). The owner of the assets has merely exchanged those assets for shares of stock in a newly formed corporation, in essence merely changing the identity or form under which he/she does business. Therefore, Congress enacted Section 351(a), which provides that gain or loss is not recognized upon the transfer by one or more persons of property to a corporation solely in exchange for stock in that corporation if, immediately after the exchange, such person or persons are in control of the corporation to which the property was transferred. Under Section 351(b) of the Code, if money or property other than stock is delivered by a corporation in exchange for property, gain (but not loss) will be recognized by the transferor to the extent of (i) the gain realized by the transferor (i.e., the excess, if any, of the fair market value of the stock) and other property (commonly referred to as "boot") received by the transferor over the adjusted basis of the assets transferred by the transferor and (ii) the fair market value of the "boot" received by the transferor. Note that as a consequence of amendments to Section 351 made in 1989, "boot" includes debt securities of the transferee corporation. The Internal Revenue Service (the "IRS") takes the position that for purposes of Section 351, gain realized upon a transfer of one asset to a corporation cannot be offset by loss realized upon a transfer of another asset to the corporation, so that if "boot" is received, the transferor must determine its gain realized on an aggregate basis, but must determine gain realized with respect to each asset transferred to the corporation. *See* Rev. Rul. 68-55, 1968-1 C.B. 140. The shareholder's basis in the stock of the newly formed corporation is a "carryover" basis—in other words, it is the same as his/her basis in the property transferred to the corporation, increased by the amount, if any, of gain recognized on the transfer and decreased by the fair market value of any "boot" received. I.R.C. §§ 358(a) and 362(a).

B. What Constitutes "Property" for Purposes of Section 351?

Generally, except for services rendered, virtually all types of tangible and intangible property will qualify for purposes of Section 351. Past or future services do not constitute property; therefore, the exchange of the stock of a corporation as payment for past or future services rendered to the corporation will not qualify as a tax-free exchange under Section 351 and gain will be recognized with respect to such stock. I.R.C. § 351(d)(1). Moreover, in such a case the value of the stock delivered to the shareholder will be taxed under Section 83 of the Code. If the stock received by the shareholder is subject to a substantial risk of forfeiture (e.g., forfeiture upon voluntary termination of employment) and is not transferable (and usually, in the case of a closely held corporation, it will be so restricted) and if the shareholder fails to file promptly an election under Section 83(b) of the Code to include the excess of the fair market value of the stock over the amount, if any, paid for the stock in his/her gross income in the year the stock is received, the increase in value of the stock between the date of the exchange and the time the restrictions on transfer elapse (i.e., the expiration of any holding period under SEC Rule 144) will be taxed as under Section 83(a) of the Code.

Even if a shareholder elects to bear the unfavorable tax consequences of contributing only his/her services in exchange for stock of a newly formed corporation, he/she cannot be counted toward the 80 percent "control" requirement—only those persons contributing *property* can be counted in the control group. Therefore, if more than 20 percent of the stock is distributed to a shareholder contributing only services, the entire transaction will not qualify under Section 351 and accordingly will be taxable to all stockholders. Only if such a stockholder contributes some property and some services in exchange for stock will this risk be removed, but only if the property contributed is not such as to be "of relatively small value in comparison to the value of the stock and securities . . . to be received for services." 26 C.F.R. § 1.351-1(a)(1)(ii). The Internal Revenue Service has taken the position that a transfer by a shareholder of property having a fair market value at least equal to 10 percent of the value of the stock to be received for services rendered will satisfy this requirement. *See* Rev. Proc. 76-22, 1976-1 C.B. 562.

C. What Does "Solely in Exchange for Stock" Mean?

In order to qualify as a tax-free (or more precisely, tax-deferred) exchange under Section 351, a transfer of property to a corporation must be "solely in exchange for stock." The term "stock" includes both common and preferred stock but does not include stock rights or warrants. 26 C.F.R. § 1.351-1(a)(1)(ii).

It bears repeating that if property other than "stock" is exchanged by a corporation for property, it does not disqualify the entire transaction for Section 351 purposes. The shareholders will merely recognize gain to the extent of the lesser of the gain realized on the entire exchange or the fair market value of the "boot" received.

D. What Does it Mean to Say that the Shareholders Must Be in "Control" of the Corporation "Immediately after the Exchange"?

In order for a transfer of property to a corporation to qualify under Section 351, the transferors must have "control" of the corporation "immediately after the exchange." "Control" is defined in Section 368(c) of the Code to mean at least 80 percent of the total combined voting power of all classes of stock entitled to vote and at least 80 percent of the total number of stock of all other classes of stock of the corporation. If transfers by more than one shareholder do not occur simultaneously, counsel should draft either a subscription agreement or a provision in a pre-incorporation agreement providing for the exchange and have it executed by all shareholders before the exchange occurs; otherwise the IRS may look only to the first exchange to determine if control was acquired "immediately after the exchange." *See* 26 C.F.R. § 1.351-1(a)(1). For example, assume a two-step stock purchase without a written agreement, with A purchasing 30 percent of the stock in year 1 and B purchasing the remaining 70 percent of the stock in year 2. The first purchase will certainly qualify under Section 351, since immediately after the exchange A owns 100 percent of the outstanding stock of the corporation. The purchase by B, however, will probably not qualify under Section 351, since he/she did not acquire 80 percent of the corporation's voting stock "immediately after the exchange."

Another frequently litigated question in this area is the extent to which Section 351 treatment may be lost if a shareholder resells some of his/her stock to a person who was not a party to the exchange within a short time after the exchange takes place. For example, assume a father transfers property to a corporation in exchange for 100 percent of its outstanding voting stock, and on the same day transfers 21 percent of the stock to a child, thereby ending up with less than 80 percent of the stock in the corporation. In the case of such a father-child transfer, courts have divided on the question of whether Section 351 treatment is lost, although the majority rule is that such a transfer will not disqualify the exchange for Section 351 purposes. *Compare Wilgard Realty Co. v.*

FEDERAL INCOME TAX ASPECTS OF INCORPORATION 111

Commissioner, 127 F.2d 514 (2d Cir. 1942) with *Florida Machinery & Foundry Co. v. Fahs*, 168 F.2d 957 (5th Cir. 1948). In the case of stock transfers to unrelated third parties within a short time after the Section 351 exchange, courts are more willing to apply the step-transaction doctrine to "integrate" the two transfers (by shareholder to corporation and by shareholder to third party) to determine if the "control" requirement is met. See *American Bantam Car Co. v. Commissioner*, 11 T.C. 397 (1948).

Finally, if shareholders transfer property to a corporation and receive stock in amounts that are disproportionate to their respective interests in the property transferred, Section 351 treatment is not lost. 26 C.F.R. § 1.351-1(b)(1). Such a transaction may, however, trigger a gift tax liability.

III. TRANSFERS TO A CORPORATION OF PROPERTY SUBJECT TO LIABILITIES UNDER SECTION 357 OF THE CODE

A. In General

Section 357 of the Code provides that when a shareholder transfers property subject to a liability to a corporation, the liability will not be considered as "boot" if the exchange otherwise qualifies under Section 351, except in two situations: (1) if the principal purpose of the assumption of the liability by the corporation is to avoid tax or if the exchange has no bona fide business purpose, I.R.C. § 357(b); or (2) if the sum of the liabilities of all property transferred to the corporation by a shareholder exceeds the adjusted basis of all properties transferred. I.R.C. § 357(c).

To simplify the discussion which follows, the term "mortgaged property" will be used instead of "property subject to a liability." The reader should, however, keep in mind that a liability may take any form—that of a lien, unsecured claim, charge, encumbrance or security interest as well as a mortgage.

B. Tax Avoidance/No Bona Fide Business Purpose Exception

If the liability on mortgaged property which is transferred to a corporation was incurred in the ordinary course of the shareholder's trade or business, this exception should pose no problem. If, however, the shareholder incurred the liability within a reasonably short period prior to the exchange and used the proceeds of the liability (e.g., a bank loan) for personal purposes, he/she would have to prove by a "clear preponderance of the evidence" that the principal purpose of the entire transaction (i.e., the incurring of the liability and the subsequent transfer of the mortgaged property to the corporation) was not to avoid taxes and had a bona fide business purpose. *See* I.R.C. § 357(b)(2).

C. Liabilities in Excess of Basis Exception

Under Section 357(c) of the Code, if the total amount of liabilities on mortgaged property transferred by a shareholder to a corporation exceeds the total adjusted bases of the properties transferred, the excess is taxable gain. Because the *tax basis* rather than the accounting basis of mortgaged property is used for Section 357 purposes, this provision has created numerous problems for cash-basis taxpayers who transfer mortgaged property upon the incorporation of their businesses. For example, assume a proprietor who uses the cash basis accounting method incorporates his/her business and transfers to the corporation $10,000 cash, $100,000 of accounts receivable, and $50,000 of inventory and that the only liabilities on his/her balance sheet at that time are $60,000 of accounts payable. If the accounting basis were used, his/her assets would exceed his/her liabilities by $100,000 ($160,000 assets minus $60,000 liabilities). Under Section 357, however, the $60,000 liabilities would exactly equal the assets because the accounts receivable have a zero tax basis. *Peter Raich*, 46 T.C. 604 (1966). In the same example, if the inventory had been $40,000 instead of $50,000, the proprietor would have tax basis assets of only $50,000 such that liabilities would actually exceed assets by $10,000, and which Section 357(c) would treat as taxable gain. If the $60,000 accounts payable constituted liabilities, the payment of which "would give rise to a deduction," they would

FEDERAL INCOME TAX ASPECTS OF INCORPORATION 113

not be counted as liabilities for purposes of Section 357 and this harsh result would be offset. I.R.C. § 357(c)(3). This saving clause would not, however, be available in the case of liabilities which were not deductible business expenses, thus counsel should review Section 357(c) whenever his/her client wishes to transfer to a corporation assets whose fair market value significantly exceeds their basis. If any such assets are subject to a lien based on their fair market value, a Section 357(c) problem may lurk in the background.

D. Determination of Basis in Transferred Assets

Even if a transfer of mortgaged property to a corporation satisfies the Section 357 requirements so that the transfer will not produce "boot" to the shareholder in a Section 351 exchange, if the corporation "assumes" or "takes subject to" the liability, the shareholder will be required to reduce his/her basis in the stock received from the corporation by the amount of the assumed liability. I.R.C. § 358(d). For example, if a shareholder transfers mortgaged property with an adjusted basis of $50,000, a fair market value of $80,000, subject to a liability of $30,000, to a corporation in a Section 351 exchange, and the corporation assumes the $30,000 liability, the exchange is tax-free to the shareholder, who does not recognize gain or loss as a result thereof; however, under Section 358(d) the shareholder's basis in the stock received from the corporation is $20,000 (the $50,000 adjusted basis in the property transferred minus the $30,000 liability assumed by the corporation) rather than $50,000. On the other hand, the corporation's basis in the mortgaged property is $50,000.

IV. RECAPTURE CONSIDERATIONS

There is no recapture of depreciation previously claimed by the shareholder upon a Section 351 transfer. If, however, the corporation subsequently disposes of the depreciated property in a taxable transaction, it will be subject to recapture to the same extent as the shareholder would have been. In other words, with respect to depreciation recapture, the corporation steps into the shoes of the transferring shareholder. I.R.C. §§ 1245(b)(3) and 1250(d)(3).

Counsel should also be aware that items previously expensed by his/her client may be subject to recapture under the so-called "tax benefit rule." Perhaps the most common application of the "tax benefit rule" in a Section 351 context is the deduction for bad debt reserves when a shareholder transfers accounts receivable to a corporation. For example, assume a proprietor incorporates his/her business and transfers to the corporation accounts receivable in the face amount of $50,000 and a reserve for bad debts of $5,000. If the shareholder had previously deducted the reserve and thereby reaped a tax benefit of $5,000, the "tax benefit rule" would not apply and the shareholder will not be required to recapture any of the $5,000 benefit if the shareholder recognizes no gain on the transfer. *Nash v. United States*, 398 U.S. 1 (1970). The law is not clear if the shareholder recognizes gain on the transfer (e.g., receives property other than stock from the corporation).

CHAPTER SIX

THE FINANCIAL STRUCTURE OF A CORPORATION*

Joanne M. White

---

* Portions of this chapter were written by Denise R. Hamer and appeared in Chapter 4 of *Corporate Counseling*, which was published in 1988 by the New York State Bar Association.

THE FINANCIAL STRUCTURE OF A CORPORATION

I. INTRODUCTION

This chapter outlines the provisions of Article V of the Business Corporation Law concerning the financing of both closely held and public corporations. Specifically, the chapter discusses share issuance pursuant to the certificate of incorporation, subscriptions, consideration and payment for shares, rights and options to purchase shares, share certificates, fractional shares and scrip, dividends and distributions, share redemption and reacquisition, corporate bonds, and convertible bonds or shares.

The statute permits a degree of flexibility in structuring the finances of a corporation so long as certain rules are obeyed, such as avoidance of impairment of capital, payment of dividends from surplus, and appropriate disclosure to shareholders in the event that their equity interests are affected. On other issues the statute is silent and the creative practitioner should consult relevant provisions of the tax law or common law principles. For example, where shareholders contribute money to the corporation, it may be preferable to characterize repayments to shareholders as loans rather than dividends, thereby avoiding double taxation. Practitioners caution that, where payments are intended to serve as loans, careful documentation characterizing such payments as loans, such as promissory notes, is essential. A contribution to capital should be evidenced by a certificate. Similarly, where a corporation issues money to shareholders, the intent to treat this as a loan should be clear from the existence of a note and additional documentation.

II. AUTHORITY TO ISSUE SHARES

Section 501 of the BCL grants a corporation the power to create and issue the number of shares stated in its certificate of incorporation.

BCL § 501 provides that shares may be either all of one class or divided into two or more classes. Each class may consist of shares with or without par value, having those designations, voting, dividend, liquidation and other rights, preferences and limitations which are enumerated in the certificate of incorporation and are consistent with the BCL.

Although the certificate of incorporation may deny, limit or otherwise define voting rights of any class, no denial, limitation or definition is deemed effective unless full voting rights are retained by one class or divided among two or more classes of outstanding shares or bonds (secured and unsecured bonds, debentures, and notes as defined in Section 102(a)(1) of the BCL). For example, the certificate of incorporation may give Class A and Class B full voting rights, or it may give Class A the exclusive right to vote in the election of directors, and Class B the exclusive right to vote on all other matters.

Similarly, the certificate of incorporation may limit or otherwise define dividend or liquidation rights, provided that unlimited dividend and liquidation rights are retained in their entirety, either by one class of outstanding shares (not bonds) or by division among one or more classes of shares. Unlike voting rights, the statute, by implication, precludes the denial of dividend or liquidation rights.

Where shares are divided into two or more classes, the statute requires that each class be designated to distinguish it from other classes. Shares entitled to preference in the distribution of dividends or assets may not be designated as "common" shares and, correlatively, shares not entitled to preference may not be designated as "preferred" shares. Where only one class of shares exists, such shares are effectively "common" shares, regardless of their identification or designation.

Section 501 of the BCL permits a corporation to create two classes of capital stock, designated as "Class A" and "Class B." These designations are typically used to identify such differences as voting rights, dividend payments, or the number of directors specified in the certificate of incorporation.

Within a single class, each share is expressly equal to each other share, subject to differences in designation, rights, preferences, and limitations of separate series. The sole exception to this rule is in the case of cooperative apartment corporations. Section 501(c) provides that, so long as maintenance charges, general assessments, and voting, liquidation or other distribution rights are substantially equal per share,

THE FINANCIAL STRUCTURE OF A CORPORATION   119

shares of the same class will not be deemed unequal due to variations in fees or charges payable to such corporations upon the sale or transfer of shares.

Section 502 of the BCL allows a corporation to issue any class of preferred shares in a series, provided that this is authorized by the certificate of incorporation. The certificate of incorporation may fix the number, designation, relative rights, preferences or limitations of shares included in any series of any class of preferred shares. This is subject to the restriction that, if the stated dividends and amounts payable on liquidation are not paid in full, the shares of all series of the same class shall share ratably in the payment of dividends and distribution of assets.

Conversely, if the certificate of incorporation authorizes the issuance, but does not fix the number, designation, relative rights, preferences, or limitations of such shares, these terms may be fixed by the corporation's board of directors. Such action constitutes an amendment of the certificate of incorporation and necessitates the filing of a certificate of amendment with the New York Department of State pursuant to Section 502(d). (*See* Chapter 15 for a more detailed discussion of the certificate of amendment.) The certificate of amendment must state the number, designation, relative rights, preferences, and limitations of the created shares. Upon filing, the certificate of amendment is incorporated into the certificate of incorporation. The corporation's shareholders are not required to vote on or to receive notice of the amendment.

Section 502 of the BCL affords a corporation substantial flexibility. By eliminating the need for prior shareholder approval, the statute enables the board of directors to issue a series of preferred shares in a commercial context where time is of the essence, such as a stock market fluctuation or an acquisition by the corporation of another business in exchange for shares of the corporation's preferred stock. Moreover, the board may tailor the terms of each preferred share issuance to fit the particular conditions of each transaction.

III. SHARE SUBSCRIPTIONS

A. Definition and Requirements for Validity

One method of obtaining shares and thereby infusing the corporation with sufficient capital to carry on its business purposes is through the purchase of subscriptions. Share subscriptions are agreements for the purchase of original unissued shares which may be executed both before and after incorporation. A subscription which is entered into before incorporation (a "pre-incorporation subscription") constitutes an offer, which must be accepted by the corporation after its formation. A subscription entered into after the corporation is formed is a post-incorporation subscription. A shareholders' agreement may be characterized as a written share subscription for each participating investor.

To be enforceable, a subscription must be in writing and signed by the subscriber. BCL § 503(b). Thus, a subscription which is either oral or unsigned is unenforceable.

B. Revocability

A subscription for shares of a corporation to be formed is generally irrevocable for three months. BCL § 503(a). In reality, however, the statute provides a much more flexible approach to revocation. First, the subscription agreement itself may provide for a different period of revocability. Second, subscribers may revoke their subscriptions during the period of irrevocability if they obtain the consent of all other subscribers or the corporation. Moreover, a subscription is not enforceable until the corporation is formed and may be revoked anytime up until formation or until it is accepted by the corporation.

C. Acceptance

While no statutory provision governs acceptance of a post-incorporation subscription by the corporation, since a post-incorporation subscription is merely an offer, some act of acceptance by the corporation after formation is essential. The filing of the certificate of incorporation does not constitute acceptance unless the subscription is listed in the

THE FINANCIAL STRUCTURE OF A CORPORATION 121

certificate. A subscriber is not bound by the subscription where there is a variance from the corporation as contemplated in the subscription, since an individual may not be compelled to invest in a corporation in which he never contracted to participate.

D. Time and Manner of Payment

Unless the subscription states the time and manner of payment, pre- and post-incorporation subscriptions are payable in full or in installments as the board of directors prescribes, except that all calls for payment must be uniform as to all shares of the same class or series. Except for partly paid shares issued to directors, officers, and employees under BCL §§ 505(e) and (f), subscribers are not entitled to all of the rights and privileges of shareholders until their shares are paid in full. BCL § 504(i).

E. Penalties

Section 503(d) of the BCL details penalties for defaults in the payment of subscriptions. The board may utilize its standard debt collection procedures or declare a forfeiture, provided that 30 days have elapsed after written demand for payment. The shareholders' agreement or other form of subscription may prescribe other penalties less severe than forfeiture. Once forfeiture is declared, if at least 50 percent of the subscription price has been paid, the subscribed-for share must be offered for sale at a cash price sufficient to pay the balance owed plus expenses, with excess proceeds returned to the defaulting subscriber or his legal representative. If less than 50 percent of the subscription price has been paid, the subscribed-for shares are cancelled and restored to the status of authorized but unissued shares. Payments previously made by the subscriber are then forfeited to the corporation and transferred to capital surplus.

IV. CONSIDERATION AND PAYMENT FOR SHARES

BCL § 504 enumerates the type and amount of consideration required for an original issue of shares.

A. Nature of Consideration

Sections 504(a) and (b) detail the nature of consideration which may be exchanged for shares. Consideration may consist of money or other property, tangible or intangible, or labor or services actually received by or performed for the corporation or for its benefit or in its formation or reorganization. Services rendered prior to incorporation, including promoters' services and services rendered in organizing or reorganizing the corporation, constitute valid consideration for shares. The issuance of shares to a creditor in cancellation of corporate indebtedness is equivalent to payment in cash and constitutes adequate consideration so long as the aggregate par value of the shares issued does not exceed the value of the debt. Legal services and good will, if capable of valuation, may constitute valid consideration for the issuance of shares.

Under Section 504(b) of the BCL, promises to make payments or perform services in the future constitute neither full or partial payment for shares, although they may constitute valid consideration at common law. Thus, shares cannot be issued in contemplation of an individual becoming employed by the corporation, for the purchase of an executory contract, or in exchange for a promissory note or subscription contract. Moreover, property or services incapable of valuation, such as purely speculative patents, copyrights, trademarks, secret processes, or know-how, do not constitute good consideration.

Shares issued in contravention of Section 504(b) are subject to cancellation and are voidable, albeit not void. Thus, where shares are partially paid for with a promise to pay and the remaining shareholders do not move to declare the shares void, they are estopped to deny their validity at a later date.

Section 504(f) of the BCL provides that, upon distribution of authorized but unissued shares to shareholders, that portion of the surplus which is transferred to stated capital pursuant to Section 511(a) constitutes the consideration for the issue of such shares. Section 511(a) requires a corporation, upon distribution of authorized but unissued shares, to transfer to stated capital an amount of surplus equal to the

THE FINANCIAL STRUCTURE OF A CORPORATION

aggregate par value of the distributed par value shares or the aggregate stated capital of distributed shares without par value.

B. Amount of Consideration

The amount of consideration required for original issue shares depends upon whether they have a stated par value. Under Sections 504(c) and (d) of the BCL, shares with par value may not be issued at less than par. There is no corresponding restriction on shares without par value, which may be issued for such consideration as is fixed by the board of directors, unless the certificate of incorporation reserves this right to the shareholders. If the certificate reserves this right to the shareholders, they must either vote to fix the consideration or authorize the board to fix the consideration. Shares exchanged for less than full monetary consideration are "discount" shares and shares exchanged for no consideration are "bonus" shares.

Under Sections 504(h) and (i) of the BCL, when consideration for shares has been paid in full, a subscriber is entitled to all the rights and privileges of a shareholder and to a certificate representing that the shares are fully paid and nonassessable.

C. Valuation

If the consideration received for shares is in the form of property or services instead of money, valuation may present a problem. Shares exchanged for overvalued property or services, which constitute less than full consideration, may be treated as "watered" shares. New York adheres to the "Good Faith Rule" with respect to "watered" shares. In the absence of fraud, the good-faith judgment of the board of directors or shareholders as to the value of consideration received is presumed conclusive.

Under Section 628(a) of the BCL, an original shareholder or subscriber who has obtained shares in exchange for less than full consideration may be liable for the unpaid portion. If "watered" shares are deemed void, the shareholder or subscriber may escape liability for the unpaid portion of consideration, but may not enjoy any rights with respect to the stock. Under Section 628(b), this liability does not extend to an assignee or transferee of the shares or subscription who takes in good faith and without knowledge or notice that full consideration has not been paid. The transferor remains liable.

D. Treasury Shares

Treasury shares are defined in BCL § 102(a)(14) as shares which have been issued and subsequently acquired and which are retained uncancelled by the corporation. Treasury shares are issued but not outstanding shares and are not assets of the corporation. Unlike other corporate shares, treasury shares may be issued for future payment or services. Under Section 504(e) of the BCL, treasury shares may be disposed of by a corporation on such terms and conditions as are fixed from time to time by the board. A corporation may thereby keep a number of its shares in the corporate treasury at all times.

Under Section 504(e) of the BCL, a corporation may issue treasury shares for less than their stated par value or for no consideration at all, provided that such shares were originally issued for valid consideration in an amount at least equal to their stated par value. Treasury shares may be disposed of for any consideration fixed by the board or distributed to shareholders as part of a share dividend or other distribution because they are issued shares and are already represented in stated capital.

V. RIGHTS AND OPTIONS TO PURCHASE SHARES

Section 505(a) of the BCL empowers a corporation to create and issue rights or options to purchase shares of any class or series, including authorized but unissued shares, treasury shares, shares to be purchased or acquired, or assets from the corporation. The conditions and terms of a purchase may be fixed by the board of directors but must comply with the consideration requirements of Section 504.

Under Section 505(d) of the BCL, majority shareholder approval is required for the issuance of rights or options which are granted as an incentive to service or continued service to the directors, officers or

THE FINANCIAL STRUCTURE OF A CORPORATION 125

employees of the corporation or its subsidiaries or affiliates, although shareholder approval is not required for rights or options granted to others.

If the certificate of incorporation provides that option shares are subject to preemptive rights, the approval of the employee option or option plan by a majority of preemptive shareholders is binding on the minority and releases the preemptive rights of all shareholders having such rights.

As an alternative to recurring shareholder votes on the issuance of rights and options to management and employees, shareholders may adopt a general plan of approval. Section 505(e) of the BCL requires the plan to include the material terms and conditions upon which rights or options are to be issued, such as (1) restrictions on the number of shares that may be purchased, (2) the method of administering the plan, (3) the terms and conditions of payment for shares in full or by installment, (4) the issue of certificates for shares to be paid for by installment, (5) any limitations upon the transferability of such shares, and (6) the voting and dividend rights to which such holders may be entitled, though the full amount of the consideration for such shares has not been paid.

As an exception to the general rule of Section 504(i) that certificates may not be issued until full consideration is paid, Section 505(e) permits the issuance of a certificate for partly paid shares issued in connection with a stock option or right. While partly paid shares cannot be delivered directly to directors, officers, and employees, Section 505 can be employed to achieve almost immediate direct issue of such shares through the use of short-term options. The fact that the shares are partly paid must be noted conspicuously on the face or back of the certificate.

The holder of a right or option is not a shareholder. Section 505(e) provides that grantees of rights or options pursuant to a plan may have voting and dividend rights even though shares are not fully paid. Conversely, under Section 505(f), grantees of rights or options not pursuant to a plan do not have such rights until shares are fully paid.

Sections 505(g) and (h) of the BCL afford the board of directors considerable discretion regarding the issuance of rights and options.

Section 505(g) provides that if prior shareholder approval for the issuance of rights and options is obtained, the board may be authorized, by amendment to the certificate of incorporation, to increase the authorized number of shares of any class or series to an amount sufficient to satisfy the outstanding rights and options. There is no requirement that shareholders approve or receive notice of the amendment. Moreover, the judgment of the board of directors is conclusive as to the adequacy of consideration received for rights or options in the absence of fraud.

A. Poison Pill Defense

BCL § 505(a)(2), which has been extended until July 1, 1993, permits New York corporations to raise "poison pill" defenses to hostile takeover attempts. The "poison pill" permits a corporation to distribute to its shareholders the right to purchase additional shares at below-market prices upon the occurrence of a specified event, typically occurring when a hostile tender offeror obtains a specified percentage of the corporation's shares. Specifically, the statute provides that the terms and conditions of rights or options to purchase shares may include, without limitation, restrictions or conditions that preclude or limit the exercise, transfer, or receipt of such rights or options by an interested shareholder or a transferee of an interested shareholder or that invalidate or void rights or options held by an interested shareholder or transferee. In recognition of the potential for abuse, in addition to the temporary measures, the statute provides for judicial review of board determinations.

VI. STATED CAPITAL

Consideration received for par value original issue shares constitutes the corporation's stated capital. The excess, if any, constitutes capital surplus, to be held for distribution as dividends or for other corporate purposes.

The entire consideration received for original issue shares without par value constitutes stated capital, unless within 60 days after issuance the board allocates a portion of such consideration to capital surplus. If the board decides to make the allocation after the 60-day period, it may be able to do so without shareholder consent by means of a reduction in stated capital pursuant to BCL § 516.

The board is precluded from allocating all consideration received for original issue shares to capital surplus. Section 506(b) of the BCL precludes allocation of any portion of the consideration received for shares without par value having a preference in the assets of the corporation upon involuntary liquidation, except the amount of consideration which exceeds the preference. The point of this provision is to prevent the impairment of a corporation's capital by restricting the board's discretion to allocate excess funds to capital surplus.

Under Section 506(c), the board may increase stated capital by transferring all or part of the surplus (both capital surplus and earned surplus) to stated capital.

VII. COMPENSATION FOR FORMATION, REORGANIZATION, AND FINANCING

Section 507 of the BCL addresses those situations in which a corporation sells shares at a discount to an underwriter or deducts a portion of consideration to pay the expenses of selling or underwriting the sale of shares. The statute authorizes the corporation to pay the expenses and compensation for the sale or underwriting of its shares out of consideration received for shares without impairing the fully paid and nonassessable status of the shares. Similarly, the statute authorizes the corporation to pay reasonable expenses of formation and reorganization, such as attorneys' or accountants' fees, out of the consideration for shares, without impairing their fully paid and nonassessable status. The reasonableness of such payments is to be determined by the board of directors.

VIII. SHARE CERTIFICATES

Section 508(a) of the BCL provides that the shares of a corporation may be certificated or, unless otherwise precluded by the certificate of incorporation or by-laws, uncertificated. The certificate evidences the holder's ownership of the shares and facilitates the transfer of such interest, although this interest may exist without a certificate. Under Section 508(f), the rights and obligations of holders of certificated and uncertificated shares are identical. Under Section 504(h), certificates may no longer be issued for partly paid shares, except in connection with rights and options issued to directors, officers and employees with shareholder approval.

Under Section 508(a) of the BCL, each certificate must be signed by two officers (1) the chairman or vice-chairman of the board of directors or the president or a vice-president and (2) the secretary or an assistant secretary or the treasurer or an assistant treasurer. The certificate may, but is not required to, be sealed with the corporate seal or a facsimile thereof. Facsimile signatures are permissible if the certificate is countersigned by a transfer agent or registered by a registrar other than the corporation itself or its employee, or if the shares are listed on a registered national securities exchange.

In the event that an officer whose signature or facsimile signature appears on the certificate is no longer an officer when the certificate is issued, the corporation may still issue the certificate with the same force and effect as if the officer still held its position.

Where a corporation is authorized to issue more than one class of shares, each certificate of each class must set forth on its face or back either a full statement of the designation, relative rights, preferences and limitations of each class or series of shares authorized to be issued, or a statement that such information shall be furnished upon request and without charge to the shareholder. Note that only a shareholder of the corporation may have access to such information.

If the corporation is authorized to issue any class of preferred shares in a series, the certificate must state the designation, relative rights, preferences, and limitations of each series and the authority of the board to designate the rights, preferences, and limitations of other series. Under Section 508(c), each certificate must state: (1) that the corporation is formed under the laws of New York, (2) the name of the person(s) to whom the certificate is issued, and (3) the number and class of shares and the designation of the series, if any, which the certificate represents. In practice the certificate is also numbered and states the name of the corporation and the date of issuance.

For a certificate to be valid and enforceable, certain other provisions must also be noted on the certificate, including (1) that the certificate of incorporation contains supermajority provisions with respect to quorums and voting by shareholders and directors; (2) a provision controlling the board's discretion to manage corporate affairs, or a provision for dissolution upon the occurrence of a specified event; (3) that the shares are subject to transfer restrictions, a lien, or a shareholders' voting agreement; (4) that the certificate is issued under a right or option to a director, officer or employee before fully paid; or (5) the existence of a proxy and its revocability.

If the shares are uncertificated, the corporation must send the owner written notice of the information required on the certificates within a reasonable time after their issuance. In addition, UCC 8-408 requires that transaction statements be sent to owners of noncertificated securities and should be consulted for specific requirements.

Because a certificated share is a "negotiable instrument," a transferee of the certificate acquires the rights of a transferor, and if the transferee is a bona fide purchaser, the transferee acquires such shares free of adverse claims.

Certificates may be typewritten or engraved, as required by the New York Stock Exchange. A corporation may replace a lost or destroyed certificate; however, Section 508(e) of the BCL permits the board to require a shareholder to indemnify the corporation against claims arising from the original certificate.

IX. FRACTIONAL SHARES AND SCRIP

Under Section 509(a) of the BCL, a corporation, at its option, may issue certificated or uncertificated fractions of a share. Fractional shares may be substituted for partly paid shares, which are generally not permitted, and are typically issued to effect share transfers, share distributions, reclassifications, mergers, consolidations or reorganizations.

They are particularly useful where the number of shares might otherwise require authorization of a large number of shares in order for each shareholder's proportionate interest to be represented by full shares. A fractional shareholder is entitled to exercise voting rights, receive dividends and participate in distributions upon liquidation to the extent of his/her proportional holding.

As alternatives to the issuance of fractional shares, Section 509(b) of the BCL permits a corporation to pay the value of the fractional share in cash and Section 509(c) permits a corporation to issue scrip. Scrip is a certificate exchangeable for cash or shares which does not entitle a holder to the rights of a shareholder. Scrip may be issued subject to the condition that it will be void if not exchanged by a specified date or that the shares for which it is exchangeable may be sold by the corporation and the proceeds distributed to the holder. Section 509(d) allows a holder to sell or purchase fractional shares or scrip as necessary in order to acquire a full share.

X. DIVIDENDS AND DISTRIBUTIONS

A. Dividends

Section 510 of the BCL permits a corporation to declare and pay dividends or make other distributions in cash, bonds, or property, including the shares or bonds of other corporations, subject to certain restrictions. First, dividends may only be declared and paid on outstanding shares. Thus, holders of treasury shares are not entitled to dividends. Second, a corporation may not pay dividends or distributions if it is currently insolvent or such action would render it insolvent. For purposes of the BCL, insolvency is defined as the inability to pay debts as they become due in the usual course of business. Third, there must not be any restrictions on the payment or distribution in the certificate of incorporation. Fourth, the dividend or distribution may only be paid from surplus, leaving the remaining net assets at least equal to the amount of the corporation's stated capital as a protection for creditors of the corporation.

THE FINANCIAL STRUCTURE OF A CORPORATION

Where a dividend or distribution is paid from sources other than earned surplus, it must be accompanied by written notice disclosing the amounts or approximate amounts by which the dividend or distribution affects stated capital, capital surplus and earned surplus. Under Section 520, the corporation is liable to the shareholder for failure to comply with notice and disclosure provisions.

The question of whether a dividend or distribution should be paid is a matter of business judgment for the directors of the corporation, so long as their decision is not the result of bad faith or a clear abuse of discretion. Directors who vote for or concur in the declaration of an unlawful dividend or distribution are personally liable to the corporation unless when acting in good faith and with due care they rely, and are entitled to so rely, upon information or opinions prepared by officers and employees, counsel, accountants, or others, or a board committee on which they do not serve.

An exception to the rule that no dividends or distributions to shareholders in excess of the corporation's surplus may be made exists in the case of a corporation engaged in the exploitation of natural resources or other wasting assets, including patents, or formed primarily for the liquidation of specific assets.

B. Share Distributions and Changes

Section 511 of the BCL governs pro rata distributions of authorized but unissued shares to holders of any class or series of outstanding shares, subject to enumerated conditions. Unlike cash and property dividends, share distributions do not involve distributions of corporate assets to shareholders and have no effect on corporate solvency, but because they do affect stated capital and surplus accounts, they may require disclosure to shareholders.

If a corporation distributes shares with par value, they must be issued for at least par value, and an amount of surplus equal to the aggregate par value of the shares must be transferred to stated capital. If a distribution of shares without par value is made, the amount of stated capital they represent must be fixed by the board of directors, unless the certificate of incorporation reserves this right to the shareholders, and an amount of surplus equal to the aggregate stated capital represented by the shares must be transferred to surplus.

Distributions of shares of any class or series must be made to holders of the same class or series, unless the certificate of incorporation permits distribution to holders of another class or series or such distribution is approved by the holders of a majority of the outstanding shares to be distributed. Note that this is one of the few instances where shareholders may act without a meeting by less than unanimous written consent.

Like cash and property dividends, share distributions are declared and distributed to shareholders pursuant to resolutions by the board of directors. A split-up, change or reclassification requires an amendment, authorized by the shareholders, to the certificate of incorporation.

When making a pro rata distribution of authorized but unissued shares to holders of any class or series of outstanding shares, a corporation may make an equivalent distribution of treasury shares of the same class or series. Share distributions on treasury shares are permitted to enable the corporation to comply with antidilution provisions in outstanding share options and conversion privileges.

A corporation may change issued shares into a different number of shares of the same class or into the same or a different number of shares of a different class or series. Under Section 511(c), a change of issued shares which increases stated capital may be made only if the corporation has sufficient surplus and a transfer from surplus to stated capital is made of an equivalent amount of the increase.

Distribution of treasury shares to holders of any class of outstanding shares does not require a transfer from surplus to stated capital because treasury shares remain a part of stated capital and may therefore be distributed as share dividends. Similarly, a stock split (two shares for one) or reverse split (one share for two) does not require a transfer to surplus from stated capital unless there is an increase in the aggregate stated capital represented by the shares.

Sections 511(f) and (g) require disclosure of distributions or changes in issued shares in order to keep shareholders apprised of any changes

THE FINANCIAL STRUCTURE OF A CORPORATION

affecting their equity interest in the corporation or of share distributions which represent a capitalization of earnings. Section 511(f) provides that every distribution to shareholders of certificates representing a share distribution or change of shares affecting stated capital, capital surplus, or earned surplus must be accompanied by written notice disclosing the amounts or approximate amounts of stated capital or surplus which are affected. Section 511(g) provides that where a change in issued shares affects stated capital or capital or earned surplus and no distribution of certificates representing such shares is made, disclosure of the effect on stated capital or surplus must be made in the next financial statement covering the period in which the change is made or in the first notice of dividend, share distribution or change furnished to the shareholders between the date of the change and the next financial statement, within six months of the date of the change.

XI. REDEEMABLE SHARES

The BCL specifically provides for the redemption or "call" of shares by a corporation, as, for example, where senior securities in the form of preferred shares are replaceable at a lower interest or preferred dividend rate. In limited instances, the statute also provides for compulsory redemption by shareholders.

Under Section 512 of the BCL, a corporation may provide in its certificate of incorporation for redemption of preferred or common shares at the option of the corporation. Section 512(c) provides, with three exceptions, that redeemable common shares may only be redeemed as long as a corporation has outstanding a nonredeemable class of common shares. The exceptions to this rule are (1) shares of an investment company, (2) shares of a member corporation of a national securities exchange registered under a New York statute, and (3) common shares of a corporation which directly or through a subsidiary has a license or franchise from a governmental agency to conduct its business, which license or franchise is conditioned upon some or all of the holders of the corporation's common shares possessing prescribed qualifications, and which may be made subject to redemption by the corporation to the extent necessary to prevent the loss of, or to reinstate, the license or franchise.

Compulsory redemption of common shares by shareholders is permitted in the case of an open-end investment company ("mutual funds") subject to federal regulation where the certificate of incorporation so provides. One reason for this restriction is that, where the shareholder has the right to compel redemption, the shares appear more akin to debt than equity securities. Where it is desirable that shareholders have these rights, they can be inserted by contract under Section 514.

The BCL readily permits the creation of redeemable preferred shares, while restricting the creation of redeemable common shares as a matter of policy. By making preferred shares redeemable, the corporation is able to permit senior security holders to participate in the growth of the corporation. Conversely, common shares are typically made non-redeemable, thereby preserving capital for the benefit of creditors and preferred shareholders.

In close corporations, it is sometimes useful to create redeemable common shares. For example, they might be included in an employment agreement, creating an incentive for the employee to participate in corporate growth, while permitting recall of the shares upon termination and thereby avoiding a situation where an ex-employee continues to have a stake in the assets of the corporation.

XII. PURCHASE OR REDEMPTION OF SHARES

Because a corporation's purchase or redemption of shares involves distribution of corporate assets, the BCL imposes restrictions, as in the case of dividends, to prevent impairment of capital.

Section 513(a) permits a corporation, subject to restrictions in the certificate of incorporation, to purchase its own shares or redeem its redeemable shares out of surplus, except when the corporation is insolvent or would thereby become insolvent.

A corporation may purchase shares out of stated capital, except when it is insolvent or would thereby become insolvent, for the following

THE FINANCIAL STRUCTURE OF A CORPORATION 135

purposes: (1) eliminating share fractions, (2) collecting or compromising indebtedness, or (3) paying dissenting shareholders as required by BCL § 623.

When a corporation redeems its shares within the period of redeemability (i.e., no "call" is necessary), the purchase price may not exceed the applicable redemption price stated in the certificate of incorporation. When shares are called for redemption, the statute permits the corporation to include the redemption price plus accrued dividends following the next dividend date after the date of redemption.

Subject to restrictions in the certificate of incorporation, a corporation may redeem or purchase its shares out of stated capital except when the corporation is insolvent or would thereby become insolvent. To preserve stated capital for the benefit of creditors, the redemption or purchase may not be made when it would reduce net assets below stated capital.

A. Greenmail Defense

Section 513(e) prohibits a resident corporation from purchasing more than 10 percent of the stock of the corporation from a shareholder for more than market value unless both director and shareholder approval are obtained. Shareholder approval consists of a majority of the outstanding shares entitled to vote at a meeting, unless the certificate of incorporation requires a greater percentage for approval.

The provision is designed to prevent the "greenmail" defense to hostile takeovers, whereby corporations purchase at above-market value the stock of a shareholder who would otherwise vote to accomplish the takeover. The provision does not apply where a corporation offers to purchase the shares of all shareholders or of a shareholder who has held the stock for more than two years. Nor does it preclude purchase of shares at market value or the purchase of less than 10 percent of such shares.

XIII. CONTRACTS FOR CORPORATION'S PURCHASE OF ITS OWN SHARES

Section 514 of the BCL permits a corporation to enter into an agreement for the purchase of its own shares. These contracts are often employed by close corporations in connection with shareholder buy-out agreements or employment agreements.

Both directors and shareholders may enforce these contracts to the extent that purchase is permitted by Section 513 of the BCL. Consistent with Section 513(a), these contracts are specifically enforceable to the extent that the corporation is solvent and has sufficient surplus to complete the purchase without impairing stated capital. Conversely, where the corporation is insolvent or would become so as a result of the purchase, or where there is insufficient surplus, the contract may not be specifically enforced. If under Section 513 the corporation is only able to purchase a portion of the shares, then the contract is enforceable only to that extent. Agreements may provide for shareholder vote to reduce stated capital or to dissolve in order to accomplish performance.

XIV. REACQUIRED SHARES

Under Section 515 of the BCL, shares that have been issued and purchased, redeemed, or otherwise reacquired by a corporation must be cancelled if they are reacquired out of stated capital, if they are converted shares, or if the certificate of incorporation so provides.

Reacquired shares not subject to automatic cancellation, either because they were reacquired from surplus or because the certificate of incorporation does not require cancellation, may be retained as treasury shares or cancelled by the board at the time of reacquisition or any time thereafter. Whether reacquired shares are retained as treasury shares, distributed to shareholders, or disposed of for consideration, the stated capital of the corporation remains unchanged. Conversely, because treasury shares are reacquired out of surplus, surplus is reduced by the cost of the reacquisition.

Thus, when treasury shares are disposed of for consideration, the entire consideration received becomes capital surplus pursuant to Sec-

THE FINANCIAL STRUCTURE OF A CORPORATION

tion 515(c), unless the corporation reacquired such shares with earned surplus. Where earned surplus was used for the reacquisition, the corporation, pursuant to Section 517(a)(5), may exercise its option to use the consideration received to restore all earned surplus reduced at the time of acquisition. Where the reacquisition price of the treasury shares was less than the cost of resale, the corporation may restore the amount of the original reduction to earned surplus and apply the excess to capital surplus.

Where reacquired shares other than converted shares are cancelled, stated capital is reduced by the amount represented by the shares, and notice to shareholders is required in the next financial statement or first notice of dividend or distribution and no later than six months after the date of reduction of capital. Under Section 520, failure to disclose subjects the corporation, and possibly the directors, to liability for resultant damage to shareholders.

Cancelled shares are typically restored to the status of authorized but unissued shares. If, however, the certificate of incorporation prohibits reissuance, then the board of directors, without the need for shareholder approval, must reduce the number of authorized shares by a certificate of amendment.

XV. REDUCTION OF STATED CAPITAL UNDER SECTION 516

The BCL enumerates three primary situations in which stated capital may be reduced. Under Section 515, as previously noted, stated capital may be reduced when reacquired shares are cancelled. Under Section 802, stated capital may be reduced by a certificate of amendment authorized by shareholder vote. Under Section 516, the board of directors may reduce stated capital where not prohibited by the certificate of incorporation (1) by eliminating stated capital amounts previously transferred from surplus and not allocated to a designated class or series of shares, (2) by eliminating an amount represented by issued shares with a par value which exceeds the aggregate par value of such shares, or (3) by reducing the amount of stated capital represented by issued shares without par value. Note that this provision does not require an amendment of the certificate of incorporation or shareholder approval, since the board is merely undoing action previously taken and the corporation's financial condition remains unchanged. Since such action increases capital surplus, shareholders actually may benefit through dividends and distributions. Section 516(b) prohibits reduction where it would result in an impairment of the rights of a holder of a class or series with preferential liquidation rights.

XVI. SURPLUS AND RESERVES

Since dividends and distributions derive from either corporate earnings or capital surplus resulting from consideration received for low or no-par shares in excess of stated capital attributable to those shares, it is necessary, for purposes of disclosure, to establish mechanisms for determining the amount of earned surplus. Section 102(a)(6) defines earned surplus as that portion of surplus representing the net earnings, gains, or profits of a corporation, after losses are deducted, that have neither been distributed as dividends or applied to stated capital or capital surplus, nor to other legally permissible purposes.

The value or availability of earned surplus may be determined under the rules of Section 517 of the BCL. Section 517(a) provides that the amount or availability of earned surplus may be computed either from the date of incorporation or from the latest date when a deficit in the corporation's earned surplus was eliminated by an application of capital surplus. Section 517(a)(2) permits the board at any time to transfer all or part of the corporation's earned surplus to capital surplus or stated capital. Section 517(a)(4) permits the board to use any portion of the corporation's capital surplus to eliminate any earned surplus deficit upon approval by shareholder vote, and requires that it notify shareholders within six months of such action. Section 517(a)(5) states that when a corporation has acquired treasury shares with earned surplus and such shares are subsequently disposed of for consideration, the corporation, at its option, may apply all or part of the consideration received to restore the earned surplus account to the level it was at prior to acquisition of the treasury shares, with excess consideration becoming capital surplus.

XVII. CORPORATE BONDS

Section 518 of the BCL governs the issuance by a corporation of its bonds. For purposes of the BCL, "bonds" are defined in Section 102(a)(1) to include "secured and unsecured bonds, debentures, and notes."

Under Section 518(a), the consideration received for the issuance of bonds must be money or other property, tangible or intangible, labor or services actually received by or performed for the corporation or for its benefit or in its formation or reorganization, or a combination thereof, including pre-incorporation services. (The tax consequences of each possible form of consideration are discussed in Chapter 5.) These provisions are identical to those pertaining to issuance of shares in Section 504(a), except that in the absence of fraud, the judgment of the board as to the value of consideration received shall be conclusive, whereas Section 504 also permits determination by shareholders. Unlike shares, bonds may be issued for less than their par value and in consideration for future payments or future services.

If a corporation distributes bonds to its shareholders, it must concurrently transfer to the liability accounts on the balance sheet an amount of surplus equal to the principal amount of and accrued interest on the bonds distributed. The amount of surplus transferred is deemed the consideration for the issuance of the bonds. Section 518(c) specifically permits the certificate of incorporation to confer upon bondholders the right to inspect corporate books and records and vote in the election of directors and on any other matters on which shareholders of the corporation may vote.

XVIII. CONVERTIBLE SHARES AND BONDS

Under Section 519 of the BCL, a corporation may issue convertible bonds or shares which are typically more marketable and permit the corporation to generate funds at lower dividend or interest rates. The certificate of incorporation may permit the corporation to issue shares convertible at the option of the holder only into shares of any other class or series, except those having dividends or liquidation rights senior to the rights of the shares being converted. The corporation may not issue shares convertible into rights senior to those of the shares being converted because this would be incompatible with the purpose of conversion, which is to permit senior security holders to participate in the equity of the corporation. Where it is desirable to convert junior securities into senior securities, this may be accomplished by a contract whereby the corporation repurchases the junior security and issues the holder a senior security.

In the case of a member corporation of a national securities exchange registered under a U.S. statute, convertible shares may be issued at the option of the corporation or upon a specified occurrence into shares of any class or series or into any other corporate security. Moreover, authorized nonconvertible shares, whether issued or unissued, may be made convertible within such period and upon such terms and conditions as are stated in the certificate of incorporation.

A corporation may also issue bonds convertible into other bonds or shares within such period and upon such terms and conditions as are fixed by the board. No issue of convertible bonds or shares may be made unless (1) the board has reserved a sufficient number of authorized but unissued shares of the appropriate class or series, to be issued only in satisfaction of the conversion privileges of the bonds or shares, or (2) the aggregate of the conversion privileges of the convertible bonds or shares when issued does not exceed the aggregate of the reserved shares and any additional authorized shares.

Section 519(e) provides that no conversion of shares shall result in a reduction of stated capital, nor may shares or bonds be converted if less than the minimum required consideration would be received upon the issuance of new shares. Consideration for shares issued upon conversion, pursuant to Section 504(g), consists of the sum of (1) either the principal sum of, and accrued interest on, the bonds so exchanged or converted, plus (2) any additional consideration paid to the corporation for the new shares, plus (3) any stated capital not previously allocated to a designated class or series which is allocated to the new shares, and (4) any surplus transferred to stated capital and allocated to the new shares.

When shares have been converted, they must be cancelled and disclosure of the effect of conversion on stated capital must be made in the next financial statement or first notice of dividend thereafter, within six months of the date of conversion. When bonds have been converted, they must be cancelled and not reissued, except upon compliance with the provisions governing the issue of convertible bonds.

CHAPTER SEVEN

FEDERAL INCOME TAX ASPECTS OF CORPORATE CAPITAL STRUCTURE

Orrin E. Tilevitz

I. INTRODUCTION

For tax purposes, a corporation's capital structure consists of debt and stock. Of course, debt and stock may be in various forms, such as zero-coupon bonds, subordinated debentures, common stock, preferred stock, convertible preferred stock, and nearly anything else a creative lawyer can dream up. Moreover, some tax consequences, largely beyond the scope of this chapter, depend on such matters as the number of classes of stock (e.g., the ability to make an S election, discussed in Chapter 3); whether stock is preferred or common (e.g., the taxability of stock dividends, discussed in Chapter 10); and whether stock is voting or nonvoting (e.g., the tax-free status of corporate reorganizations, discussed in Chapter 12). Also, in addition to debt and stock, the basic capital structure may have attached to it such cornices and gargoyles as warrants, options, stock appreciation rights and the like, the taxation of which can be complex and is best handled by a specialist. Still, the principal tax issues concerning a corporation's capital structure center on the fundamental question of whether an instrument should be characterized for tax purposes as debt or stock. The tax characterization of an instrument will not necessarily be the same as the characterization for state corporate law purposes or that adopted by the parties.

This chapter discusses (1) some of the stakes involved for both the investor and the corporate issuer (the "issuer") in characterizing an instrument as debt or stock for tax purposes; (2) a peculiar tax construct called "Section 1244 Stock"—stock with some aspects of debt—which was designed to help investors in small corporations; and (3) in general, how to tell debt from stock for tax purposes. For a more extensive discussion, see Chapter 4 of B. Bittker and J. Eustice, *Federal Income Taxation of Corporations and Shareholders* (5th ed., 1987, with current supplements). It is assumed in the following discussion that the investor in the corporation is a United States resident individual, partnership or taxable corporation, and that any corporate investor owns less than 80 percent of the issuer's stock. Radically different consequences may ensue for an investor who is a foreigner, pension plan, or tax-exempt entity or for an issuer which is an 80-percent-or-more subsidiary of a corporate investor.

Unless the context indicates otherwise, references in this chapter to "debt" or "stock" are to instruments characterized as such for tax purposes.

II. THE STAKES

Whether an instrument is debt or stock for tax purposes can affect both the investor and the issuer.

A. The Investor

1. Basic Tax Rules

Interest on debt is fully taxable to an investor. By contrast, under Sections 301(c)(1) and 316(a) of the Internal Revenue Code of 1986, as amended (the "Code"), cash dividends on stock are taxable only up to the corporation's earnings and profits (*see* Chapter 10); additional amounts are taxable (as capital gain) only if they exceed the investor's stock basis. I.R.C. § 301(c)(3). (Both the earnings and profits limitation and the distinction between debt and equity arise where a housing co-op has excess cash which it wishes to distribute to its members. Section 216(b)(1)(C) of the Code generally prohibits any co-op "stockholder" from being "entitled . . . to receive any distribution not out of earnings and profits of the corporation except on a complete or partial liquidation of the corporation." The strange ramifications of this obscure provision are explored in O. Tilevitz, " 'Condopping' a Co-op," 69 *Taxes* 558 (September 1991). However, once all interest due currently is received, principal is returned tax-free, while dividends continue to be taxable, no matter what the rate of return, up to the corporation's earnings and profits. When a debt is redeemed, the principal is returned tax-free, but when stock is redeemed, if the corporation has sufficient earnings and profits and the investor (or a related person) continues to own stock in the corporation, in many cases the entire redemption proceeds will be taxed as a dividend. A corporate investor, though, may deduct 80 percent of the amount of dividends received, 70 percent if the corporate investor owns less than 20 percent of the issuer's stock.

TAX ASPECTS OF CORPORATE CAPITAL STRUCTURE 147

2. Original Issue Discount

When a debt instrument bears interest at a below-market interest rate, the Internal Revenue Service (the "IRS") may treat the issuer as having paid interest at a market rate and the investor as having returned the imputed interest to the issuer as (depending on the relationship between the investor and the issuer) a contribution to capital or a gift to the issuer's shareholder(s). I.R.C. § 7872; Prop. Regs. § 1.7872-4(d)(1), (g)(1). Also, for a debt instrument with a maturity of over one year, if some or all interest is deferred (e.g., a zero-coupon bond) or the amount payable at maturity otherwise exceeds the issue price, deferred interest (called "original issue discount" or "OID") at a market rate will generally be treated as having been paid over the term of the debt, resulting in premature income for the investor. I.R.C. § 1272 *et seq.* (As discussed below, the issuer may receive a corresponding deduction for interest it has not yet paid. However, even if an issuer is losing money and is thus relatively indifferent to the availability of a deduction, the issuer must determine the amount of OID on debt held by individual investors and, under Sections 6041 and 6049 of the Code, report the amount to the investor and the IRS.)

The complexities of the below-market loan and OID rules are beyond the scope of this chapter. Note, however, that for both below-market loans and loans with OID, the notion of a market interest rate is not subjective: interest will generally be "below market" for purposes of this discussion unless it is payable currently at a rate which equals or exceeds the "Applicable Federal Rate" for debt of comparable maturity, tables of which the IRS issues monthly. I.R.C. § 1274. Of course, the below-market loan and OID rules are basically irrelevant for an instrument which is stock rather than debt because stock pays dividends, not interest.

3. Accrual-Basis Investor

Interest is taxable to an accrual-basis investor when the investor becomes legally entitled to it, even if the issuer does not have the funds to pay the interest. 26 C.F.R. § 1.446-1(c)(1)(ii). By contrast, a dividend is taxable when it is "unqualifiedly made subject" to the shareholder's demand. 26 C.F.R. § 1.301-1(b); *Beneficial Corporation v. Commissioner*, 18 T.C. 396 (1952), *aff'd*, 202 F.2d 150 (3d Cir. 1953). Therefore, if an issuer eliminates a dividend, even a preferred dividend to which an investor may be entitled by contract, the investor will not be taxed on it. Note, though, that if the dividend is really payable in all events, regardless of earnings, the underlying instrument may (as discussed below) be debt rather than stock.

4. Losses from Worthless Securities and Bad Debts

Section 165(g) of the Code permits an investor to recognize a loss in the year a "security" becomes completely worthless. No deduction is allowed if the security becomes partially worthless, although the investor could recognize the loss by selling the security. (The loss will be disallowed, however, if the sale is to a related party. I.R.C. § 267(a)(1).) A "security" for this purpose includes a share of stock and includes debt issued in registered form. Any debt with a maturity of more than one year must generally be issued in registered form because if it is not, various sanctions discussed below may apply to the issuer and/or the investor.

If an investor holds such a security as a *capital* asset (as will almost always be the case, with the possible exceptions discussed below), any loss on the worthlessness of that security will be a capital loss, except if the security is "Section 1244 Stock," discussed below. Capital losses are much less valuable than ordinary losses because they are deductible only against capital gain plus (for an individual investor only) taxable income of up to $3,000.

If an investor holds such a security as a *noncapital* asset, any loss on that security (through worthlessness or when the security is sold) will be ordinary. (So will gain, a fact that matters little now that ordinary income and capital gain are taxed at the same rate.) A security in the hands of a dealer in securities is a noncapital asset. I.R.C. § 1221(1). Also, it is possible in very limited cases that if an investor buys stock or makes a long-term loan to protect the investor's business, e.g., a manufacturer invests in a supplier of raw materials to assure a source of supply, the security would be a noncapital asset and any loss would be ordinary. In

TAX ASPECTS OF CORPORATE CAPITAL STRUCTURE

Corn Products Refining Co. v. Commissioner, 350 U.S. 46 (1955), the United States Supreme Court held that corn futures, which met the statutory definition of a "capital asset," were not capital assets in the hands of a manufacturer of products from corn because the company's commodity transactions were an integral part of its business. However, in *Arkansas Best Corp. and Subsidiaries v. Commissioner*, 108 S. Ct. 971 (1988), the Court held that the *Corn Products* doctrine was inapplicable to the ownership of capital stock.

By contrast, an investor may take a deduction for a bad-debt loss if a "business" debt which is not a security (generally, debt with a maturity of one year or less is not a security unless it was issued in registered form) becomes totally or partially worthless. I.R.C. § 166(a)(2). A "nonbusiness" bad debt is deductible only if it is totally worthless, and any loss is treated as a short-term capital loss. If a "business" debt becomes worthless, the loss is ordinary, not capital, and, absent a limitation on the deductibility of losses generally (*see, e.g.*, the passive activity loss rules discussed in Chapter 18), may be used to offset ordinary income without limit. A "business" debt is one arising from the operation or conduct of the investor's trade or business. Loans made or acquired by a corporate investor are always treated as "business" debts. In the case of a noncorporate investor, the issue of whether a debt is "business" or "nonbusiness" has engendered considerable litigation. While a loan made by a person in the business of lending money is generally a "business" debt, in other cases, particularly when the investor is both a lender and a stockholder, whether a debt is "business" or "nonbusiness" generally turns on whether the dominant motivation for making the loan is personal or to protect the investor's interest in the corporation (a nonbusiness debt), or some other position such as an employee or service provider (a business debt). *See, e.g., Bart v. Commissioner*, 21 T.C. 880 (1954); *Grauman v. Commissioner*, 357 F.2d 504 (9th Cir. 1966).

B. Section 1244 Stock

To mitigate the harshness of the general rule that losses from worthless or devalued securities are capital losses, and thereby to encourage equity investment in small businesses, in the case of an individual investor (but not an investor which is a corporation, trust or estate) Section 1244 of the Code permits ordinary loss treatment up to a maximum of $50,000 ($100,000 if a joint return is filed) for losses on the sale or worthlessness of "Section 1244 Stock" issued by a so-called "small business corporation." (New York State also taxes such "small business corporations" at a favorable rate—*see* Chapter 18.) Gain on the sale of Section 1244 Stock (to the extent it matters these days) is still capital.

A corporation is a "small business corporation" if the amount of money and adjusted basis (to the corporation) of property contributed to the corporation for stock or as a capital contribution is $1 million or less. Special rules apply to stock issued during the year in which a corporation's equity capitalization first exceeds $1 million. 26 C.F.R. § 1.1244(c)-2(b)(2). The limitation applies as of the time the money and property are contributed; subsequent appreciation or depreciation in the value of the company is irrelevant. I.R.C. § 1244(c)(3). Generally, stock is Section 1244 Stock if (1) the corporation is a small business corporation (as defined above) when the stock is issued; (2) the stock is issued in exchange for money or property (other than stock and securities); and (3) less than half of the corporation's aggregate gross receipts during the five previous taxable years (or, if less, the entire time the corporation was in existence) were from such investment-type sources as interest, dividends, rent, and gains from sales of securities.

This last condition applies only if the corporation's total gross income for the entire period exceeded its deductions other than the dividends-received deduction (*see* Chapter 2) and any net operating loss deduction. However, even if the condition is met or does not apply, ordinary loss treatment is unavailable if the corporation was not largely an operating company during the period. 26 C.F.R. § 1.1244(c)-1(e)(2). Also, in addition to possibly being ineligible to issue Section 1244 Stock, a corporation with predominantly investment income may be a personal holding company, discussed in Chapter 18.

The corporation need not make an election or adopt a formal plan to issue Section 1244 Stock, and any such action serves no purpose: if the conditions are met, stock is automatically Section 1244 Stock. Counsel may come across written Section 1244 Stock plans. The statutory requirement to adopt such plans was repealed in 1978, effective for stock issued after November 6, 1978. (Note also that stock issued on or before July 18, 1984, had to be common stock, not preferred stock, in order to qualify as Section 1244 Stock.)

C. The Issuing Corporation

Interest on debt is generally deductible to the paying corporation, while dividends paid on stock almost never are. For this purpose, the interest deduction extends to original issue discount discussed above. I.R.C. § 163(e). Therefore, by issuing debt on which interest payments are deferred, an issuer may receive an interest deduction even if the interest is not currently payable. Even if the issuer is currently losing money and so gets no current benefit from an interest deduction, the issuer would generate a net operating loss which is deductible (within limits) against income in future (or previous) years. I.R.C. § 172.

There are limitations on the issuer's ability to deduct interest. For example, a corporate issuer may deduct interest on a debt with a maturity exceeding one year only if the debt is issued in "registered form," which means it is registered on the corporation's books both as to principal and interest. I.R.C. § 163(f)(1). Under Section 163(f)(2)(A)(ii) of the Code, the registration requirement does not apply to a debt obligation which "is not of a type offered to the public," but this exception has yet to be defined in IRS regulations. Failure to register a "registration-required obligation" may lead to other sanctions being imposed on the issuer under Sections 312(m) and 4701 of the Code and/or on the investor under Section 165(j) of the Code. Thus a corporation is effectively barred from issuing, for example, bearer bonds and coupon bonds. Also, an issuer using the accrual basis of accounting (*see* Chapter 2) may not deduct interest paid to a related cash-basis investor until the interest is includable in the investor's income. I.R.C. § 267(a)(2). In addition, under Section 279 of the Code, in some cases an issuer may not deduct interest on debt incurred to acquire the stock or assets of another corporation. Finally, under Section 265(a)(2) of the Code, the interest deduction may be limited to the extent the indebtedness was incurred to "purchase or carry" tax-exempt bonds.

D. The Bottom Line

Given the interest deduction, an issuing corporation is almost invariably better off, and almost never worse off, characterizing an instrument as "debt" for tax purposes. In the long run, for tax purposes, an individual investor is generally better off owning debt (although a corporate investor will generally prefer to own stock). Particularly since corporate tax rates now exceed individual rates, the total corporate and shareholder tax liability of a closely held corporation generally is the least if the corporation's debt-equity ratio is as high as possible. The limits on this type of planning are discussed in the next section.

III. CLASSIFYING DEBT AND STOCK

Because of the sharply varying tax treatment of debt and stock and the incentive which most corporations have to maximize debt and minimize equity, the question of whether an instrument is debt or stock for tax purposes is the subject of frequent litigation. The classic analysis of the subject is W.T. Plumb, Jr., *The Federal Income Tax Significance of Corporate Debt: A Critical Analysis and a Proposal*, 26 Tax L. Rev. 369 (1971). In brief, case law permits the IRS to look through the form of an instrument to the economic reality behind it and classify purported "debt" as stock—and, for that matter, purported "stock" as debt, although reported instances of the latter are rare. In some cases, even a taxpayer (the issuer or the investor) may also argue that an instrument labeled "debt" was really stock or vice versa. *See, e.g., LDS, Inc. v. Commissioner*, 51 T.C.M. (CCH) 1433 (1986); *Segel v. Commissioner*, 89 T.C. 816 (1987).

Courts have identified various factors which distinguish debt from stock. For example, the factors enumerated in *Hardman v. United States*, 827 F.2d 1409 (9th Cir. 1987) include (a) the presence (debt) or absence (stock) of a fixed maturity date; (b) whether the obligation to repay is unconditional (debt) or dependent on earnings (stock); (c)

TAX ASPECTS OF CORPORATE CAPITAL STRUCTURE 153

whether the instrument is subordinate to the issuer's other debt (stock); (d) whether the corporation's overall capitalization is adequate (debt) or thin (stock), *compare Murphy Logging Co. v. United States*, 378 F.2d 222 (9th Cir. 1967) (adequate capitalization) *with Plantation Patterns, Inc. v. Commissioner*, 462 F.2d 712 (5th Cir. 1972), *cert. denied*, 409 U.S. 1076 (1972) (thin capitalization); (e) whether the investors hold the purported "debt" and stock in the same proportion (stock); (f) whether the issuer can obtain loans from outside lenders (debt) or not (stock); (g) whether the investor may vote or participate in management (stock) or not (debt); (h) the subjective intent of the parties; and (i) the labels attached to the instrument by the parties.

Under Section 385 of the Code, the IRS has the authority to issue regulations classifying debt and stock for tax purposes. However, after several attempts at writing workable regulations, the IRS withdrew the most recent version in 1983, and it appears unlikely that further regulations will be promulgated in the near future, if ever.

Generally speaking, an instrument which the issuing corporation books as debt has a fixed maturity (or is payable on demand), is represented by a physical document, requires repayment without regard to the corporation's earnings, and bears (and actually pays) a market rate of interest, will be classified as debt for tax purposes, at least so long as the corporation has some reasonable amount of equity. Conversely, generally speaking, an instrument which the corporation books as common stock will be classified as equity for tax purposes. Problems typically arise where a shareholder advances money to the corporation without any documentation, the corporation does not bother to pay interest, or the corporation's debt-equity ratio wildly exceeds the industry norm. Most of these problems are avoidable if counsel is vigilant.

CHAPTER EIGHT

DIRECTORS AND OFFICERS OF THE NEW YORK CORPORATION*

Clifford R. Ennico
William A. Perrone

---

* Portions of this chapter were written by William A. Smith, Jr., and appeared in Chapter 5 of *Corporate Counseling*, which was published in 1988 by the New York State Bar Association.

I. INTRODUCTION AND OVERVIEW

The duties of managing the New York corporation fall to the corporation's directors and officers. Directors are elected by the shareholders and establish general policies for the corporation's guidance. The board of directors has the ultimate authority for corporate management under New York law. Its authority includes the power to do whatever is permitted by the certificate of incorporation in the ordinary course of business. The officers are elected by the board of directors and execute and administer the policies set by the board. The officers may be granted, and for practical reasons usually are granted, broad authority in the performance of their duties, although the president or chief executive officer has broad inherent authority even absent a specific delegation of powers by the board. Unlike directors, who are vested with their broad power to set corporate policy only when acting collectively as a board, officers have authority individually to pursue their respective duties.

This chapter considers the director and officer provisions of the New York Business Corporation Law, specifically those governing the establishment of a corporation's first board of directors, the term and qualifications for holding office as a director or officer, and the authority and responsibilities of directors and officers. After discussing officers' employment contracts, this chapter considers liabilities which directors and officers face in the discharge of their duties and methods of protecting directors and officers from liability such as indemnification rights and (for directors) limitation of liability. These methods of protecting directors and officers other than by insurance have become increasingly important, and New York law in this area has changed rapidly in the course of a few years. Those changes and their ramifications are discussed in the final section of this chapter.

II. THE BOARD OF DIRECTORS

A. Authority of the Board

As noted above, the board of directors is vested with the broad power to determine corporate policy. The certificate of incorporation may vest the board with certain powers to take action which otherwise would fall within the province of the shareholders. Instances where the BCL permits this are noted in the following material. Conversely, the by-laws may place certain limitations on the broad authority of the board, but no such limitation or attempt to define more precisely the powers of the board may contradict the certificate of incorporation or interfere with the duty of the directors to use their best judgment in making decisions for the corporation.

With one exception, the certificate of incorporation cannot limit the authority of the board to manage the business of the corporation. The exception is for corporations whose stock is neither listed on a national securities exchange nor regularly quoted in an over-the-counter market by any member of a national or affiliated securities association. Such a corporation may restrict board authority or transfer all or part of the board's authority to another person or corporation, if all incorporators or all shareholders have authorized such a provision in the original certificate of incorporation, or in an amendment to it, and if all shareholders acquiring stock after such authorization are given notice of the provision (i.e., by a notation on the face or back of each stock certificate) or consent to it. BCL § 620. Such transfer of the board's authority also transfers, to the shareholders authorizing the provision or consenting to it, the directors' liability for those managerial acts which have been taken from the authority of the board. Thus the shareholders do not enjoy limited liability with respect to such actions, and to the extent that powers of the board are taken from it, the fundamental purpose of organizing an enterprise in the form of a corporation is obviated.

B. Establishing the Board; Qualifications and Size

The first board of directors of a New York corporation is elected by the incorporators at their organizational meeting. BCL § 404(a). If there is only one incorporator, the first board may be named in a signed statement of the sole incorporator. A director must be at least 18 years of age, BCL § 701, although the certificate of incorporation may specify a higher age. The BCL does not require that a director of a New York corporation be a resident of the state of New York. However, the certifi-

DIRECTORS AND OFFICERS OF THE NY CORPORATION

cate of incorporation or by-laws may prescribe this or other qualifications for holding office as a director. BCL § 701.

The minimum number of directors constituting the board of a New York corporation is either three or, if there are fewer than three shareholders, no fewer directors than there are shareholders. BCL § 702. Beyond this provision, however, it is up to the corporation to specify the size of its board in the by-laws. Typically such by-law provisions do not state a fixed number but provide instead that the board shall consist of "not fewer than" a specified minimum "and not more than" a specified maximum. This type of provision allows for future changes in number without requiring amendment of the by-laws.

C. Election of Directors; Term of Office

The initial board chosen by the incorporators serves until the first annual meeting of shareholders. BCL § 404(a). Thereafter the shareholders elect directors at each annual meeting. BCL § 703(a). The certificate of incorporation may specify that all or part of the board will be elected by one or more classes of the shareholders.

The term of office is one year unless the certificate of incorporation states otherwise. BCL § 703(a). However, the certificate of incorporation may provide for election of directors by classes. This is often referred to as "staggering" the board and is employed as an anti-takeover technique, especially by larger or publicly held corporations. Classification of directors is governed by Section 704 of the BCL. There may be as many as four classes of directors, each class being as nearly equal in number as possible and no class including fewer than three directors. The classes are ranked first, second, third and fourth, and the initial term of each class in the ranking is for one year longer than the previous class. After such initial terms, all classes have terms of equal length. For example, a nine-member staggered board would have three directors coming up for reelection in one year, another three members the next year, and another three members the year after that. Thus only one class of directors, rather than the entire board, comes up for reelection each year, making it more difficult for a party attempting a takeover to replace the entire board at once.

Whether or not a board is classified, the term of office of directors is for the term elected and until a successor is elected and has qualified. BCL § 703(b). Thus, until a new election takes place, a person elected as director remains a director notwithstanding expiration of the term for which he or she was elected.

D. Changes in Number of Directors

From time to time it may be necessary or desirable to change the number of directors on the board. The BCL contemplates such changes and Section 702(b) provides that the number of directors may be changed by amending the by-laws of the corporation, or by a vote of shareholders if a shareholder-approved by-law allows the shareholders to increase or decrease the size of the board. Section 702 also permits such a change by vote of the directors, provided that a shareholder-approved by-law permits the directors to change the composition of the board. If the change is made by action of the board, then the vote required to change the number of directors must be a majority of the total number of directors which the corporation would have if there were no vacancies. BCL § 702(b)(1).

Irrespective of the method used to change the composition of the board, no decrease in the number of directors may shorten the term of any incumbent director. BCL § 702(b)(2). When a vacancy on the board occurs due to removal of a director without cause, only the shareholders can fill the vacancy, unless the certificate of incorporation or by-laws allows the directors to fill such vacancies. All vacancies occurring for any other reason, including vacancies occurring due to removal of a director for cause or because of an increase in the number of directors on the board, may be filled by a vote of the directors. A simple majority of directors present and voting is sufficient for this purpose. If so many seats on the board are vacant that the number of remaining directors does not comprise a quorum, the vacancies may be filled by a vote of a majority of the directors then in office. A director elected by the board to fill a vacancy serves until the next meeting of shareholders at which directors are elected. BCL § 705(c). Remember that the provisions discussed in this paragraph represent the statutory scheme; the certificate of incorporation or by-laws may impose stricter requirements, providing that only the shareholders can fill vacancies on the board, or mandating a greater quorum requirement if vacancies are filled by a vote of the board.

E. Removal of Directors

The shareholders of a New York corporation have the power to remove any director for cause. The directors may also have such power if it is granted to them in the certificate of incorporation or in a by-law adopted by the shareholders; however, the board may not remove a director elected by cumulative voting or by a class of shares or bonds. BCL § 706(a). Misconduct or acting in a manner inimical to the interests of the corporation constitutes "cause" for removal. *Abberger v. Kulp*, 156 Misc. 210, 281 N.Y.S. 373 (1935). In extreme cases, usually involving criminal wrongdoing, a director may be removed by judicial proceeding initiated either by the state attorney general or by the holders of 10 percent of the outstanding shares of the corporation.

Directors may be removed without cause if the certificate of incorporation or by-laws so provide, but only by a vote of the shareholders.

The BCL also provides two further limitations on removal of directors, whether for cause or without cause. First, for a corporation having cumulative voting, no director may be removed if the number of votes cast against removal would be sufficient to elect the director if voted cumulatively at an election where the same number of votes were cast and the entire board, or entire class of directors of which the director is a member, were then being elected. BCL § 706(c)(1). Second, where the certificate of incorporation entitles holders of a certain class of shares, or holders of bonds, to elect directors, any director so elected may be removed only upon a vote of holders of the shares of that class or the holders of such bonds, voting as a class. BCL § 706(c)(2).

F. Action by the Board; Quorum and Voting

A quorum of directors is required for the board to take any formal action at a meeting. Unless the certificate of incorporation or by-laws provides otherwise, a majority of the entire board constitutes a quorum.

BCL § 707. The certificate or by-laws may provide for a smaller number of directors to be a quorum, but no quorum constituting fewer than one-third of the members of the entire board is permitted. BCL § 707. Alternatively, the certificate of incorporation (not the by-laws) may provide for a quorum greater than a majority. The certificate may also provide for a greater number of votes than a majority for transacting business or particular items of business. BCL § 709(a). Any New York corporation with a greater-than-majority quorum requirement or greater-than-majority voting requirement must note any such provisions on the face or back of each certificate of the corporation's stock, unless the corporation has any class of equity security registered under Section 12 of the Securities Exchange Act of 1934, as amended. BCL § 709(c).

The time and place of board meetings may be set by the by-laws, BCL § 710, although in most cases it is more convenient to have the by-laws authorize the board to determine its own meeting times and places. If the time and place of meetings are fixed by the by-laws or by the board, regular meetings of the board may be held without notice to directors unless the by-laws provide otherwise. Regular meetings of the board, unless fixed as to time and place in the by-laws, and special meetings of the board require that notice be given to the directors, and the by-laws may prescribe what constitutes adequate notice. Notice of a meeting need not specify the purpose of the meeting unless the by-laws so require. Notwithstanding the notice requirement, notice of a meeting does not need to be given to any director who submits a signed waiver of notice either before or after the meeting, or who attends the meeting without protesting the lack of notice. BCL § 711(c). If a board meeting is held without due notice to all directors, actions taken at the meeting are invalid, unless each director waives notice or, if present at the meeting, fails to protest lack of notice. Such actions may, however, be ratified at a later time by formal action of the board. A form of waiver of notice is included in the "Forms and Materials" section of this volume.

Unless the certificate or by-laws provide otherwise, the board may take action without a formal meeting if all members of the board consent in writing to the adoption of a resolution authorizing the action to be taken. BCL § 709(b). Moreover, if the certificate of incorporation or

DIRECTORS AND OFFICERS OF THE NY CORPORATION

the by-laws authorize action to be taken by a telephone meeting of the board of directors, the board may meet by way of a telephone conference call that enables all participants to hear each other at the same time. BCL § 708(c).

Directors must be present at meetings, or on the conference call in the case of a meeting by telephone, in order to vote. No director may cast a vote by proxy. Note that a unanimous written consent is not a proxy, but rather an alternative to meeting as a way for the board to take action. Thus there is no conflict between the prohibition on proxy voting by directors and the permissibility of board action by unanimous written consent.

At each meeting of the board of directors the secretary of the corporation, or in the absence of the secretary, a member of the board appointed to act as secretary for the meeting, should keep notes of the meeting and afterwards prepare minutes for inclusion in the minute book of the company. Where action of the board is taken by unanimous written consent of the directors, the signed consent should be included in the minute book with the minutes of meetings. When a consent of the directors is to be obtained, it is often easier for the corporation's counsel or for the corporate official handling the matter to send a counterpart execution copy of the consent to each director; when all such counterparts have been returned, they may be placed in the minute book and together they are deemed to constitute a single instrument signed by the directors. Usually this is more convenient than asking directors to forward a single instrument to one another and then back to the company or its counsel.

G. Committees of the Board

The certificate of incorporation or by-laws may empower the board to appoint an executive committee and such other committees as it deems necessary or desirable. Each committee must have at least three directors. BCL § 712(a). Subject to limitations on its authority contained in the certificate, the by-laws, or the resolution creating it, a committee has all the powers of the full board, except that no committee may submit to the shareholders any action that requires shareholder approval, fill a vacancy in the board or any committee, fix compensation of directors, amend or repeal by-laws or adopt new by-laws, or amend or repeal any resolution of the full board which, by its terms, is not amendable or repealable by a committee. BCL § 712.

Committees of the board may be an unimportant issue for many small closely held corporations. However, many large corporations and especially those that are publicly held find that they can facilitate corporate governance by creating appropriate committees. One of the more useful committees is an executive committee having responsibility for general matters of corporate management. Beyond this, other useful committees are an audit committee, a compensation committee, an employee benefits committee, and where appropriate, a stock option committee. These are only examples; an appropriate committee of the board can be helpful in dealing with any aspect of the business of a corporation requiring particularized attention by the board.

III. OFFICERS OF THE CORPORATION

A. Authority of Officers

Unlike directors, who are empowered to do all acts within the corporate purposes stated in the certificate of incorporation, the officers of a New York corporation have more limited power. Specifically, in order for an officer of a New York corporation to bind the corporation by his or her action, the act must fall within one of the four categories of officers' authority: express authority, implied authority, apparent authority, or authority by virtue of ratification of his or her action by the board.

1. Express Authority

Express authority to perform certain acts may be conferred upon an officer by the certificate, the by-laws, or resolutions of the board. In most cases the by-laws and board resolutions set forth the authority of a corporation's officers. Generally these provisions are broad, for the very practical purpose of permitting the officers, and especially the president or chief executive officer, to manage the corporation's busi-

DIRECTORS AND OFFICERS OF THE NY CORPORATION 165

ness with minimal interference. Typical by-law provisions appear in the form of by-laws included in the "Forms and Materials" section of this volume.

2. Implied Authority

In addition to powers expressly delegated, corporate officers have authority to act by virtue of their office. The officers have the power to do the necessary acts within the scope of their usual duties. In this context it is important to know that generally only the president or chief executive officer (or general manager if the corporation has one) has implied authority to bind the corporation by acting in its behalf. The president's implied power in this regard extends to the ordinary business transactions of the corporation. Other officers do not have similar implied authority to bind the corporation, but have only such implied authority as is necessary for the performance of their respective duties.

The implied authority of the president to initiate litigation has received the attention of the New York Court of Appeals on several occasions. The president has no authority to institute litigation if he has sought permission of the board and if the board has refused. Thus submission of a motion to institute litigation and failure of the board to approve the motion vitiates any implied authority of the president to sue on behalf of the company. *Sterling Industries, Inc. v. Ball Bearing Pen Corp.*, 298 N.Y. 483 (1949). However, where the board has neither prohibited litigation or declined to authorize the president to commence litigation, the president has the implied authority to defend and prosecute suits in the name of the corporation. *Westview Hills, Inc. v. Lizau Realty Corp.*, 6 N.Y.2d 344, 189 N.Y.S.2d 863 (1959).

3. Apparent Authority

The officer of a New York corporation has power, deriving from apparent authority, in situations where the corporation causes a third party to believe that the officer has authority to act in behalf of the corporation and such third party has no notice or knowledge of the real limits on the officer's authority. If the third party relies upon the apparent authority of an officer, then the corporation and the officer may be estopped from denying the existence of such authority. However, third parties must exercise due diligence. If circumstances would cause a reasonably prudent person to inquire as to an officer's actual authority and if a third party fails to inquire, then the corporation is not bound by the unauthorized act of its officer acting under color of apparent authority.

A corporation cannot so limit the power of its executive officers as to render the corporation not liable for ordinary commitments made by officers in transacting the company's business with third parties having no knowledge of such limitation. *Powers v. Schlicht Heat Co.*, 23 A.D. 380, 48 N.Y.S. 237 (1st Dep't 1897), *aff'd*, 165 N.Y. 662 (1901).

It has been held that the presence of a corporation's seal on a document does not create a rebuttable presumption of the signing officer's authority to execute the document. *Goldenberg v. Bartell Broadcasting Corp.*, 47 Misc. 2d 105, 262 N.Y.S.2d 274 (1965).

4. Authority by Virtue of Ratification

Any act of an officer, regardless of the absence of any other basis of authority, is authorized if the board of directors subsequently ratifies the action. Such ratification is deemed to relate back to the time of the action and is equivalent to prior authority having been given.

B. Selection of Officers and Term of Office

The board of directors, or the shareholders if the certificate of incorporation so provides, may elect or appoint a president, one or more vice-presidents, a secretary, a treasurer, and such other officers as the board or the by-laws may provide. BCL § 715. The same person may not be both president and secretary unless all of the issued and outstanding stock of the corporation is owned by only one person, in which case that person may hold both offices. BCL § 715(e). Otherwise there are no restrictions in the BCL or New York law on the same person holding multiple offices.

The certificate of incorporation or by-laws may specify the term for which officers shall serve. If neither document specifies terms of office, then an officer's term continues until the meeting of the board following

DIRECTORS AND OFFICERS OF THE NY CORPORATION

the next annual meeting of shareholders or, if officers are elected by the shareholders, until the next annual meeting of shareholders. BCL § 715(c). However, an officer's term does not end until his or her successor takes office. BCL § 715(d).

The board of directors is empowered under the BCL to remove any officer elected by the board from office at any time, with or without cause. An officer elected by the shareholders may be removed, with or without cause, only by vote of the shareholders; however, if the board has cause, it may suspend the authority of a shareholder-elected officer to perform the duties of office. Removal of an officer without cause does not prejudice the officer's contract rights. Thus, if an officer has a contract of employment with the corporation for a particular term and is removed without cause, he or she may have a claim against the corporation for wrongful discharge. This would not be the case if the officer had no contract with the corporation; mere election to office, whether by the board or by the shareholders, without a contract of employment creates no contractual rights. BCL § 716(b). This provision of the BCL, therefore, does not operate to limit the corporation's powers to make binding contracts of employment; rather, it provides that a corporation has the same power to revoke an agency as has an individual principal. *In re Paramount Publix Corporation*, 90 F.2d 441 (2d Cir. 1937).

Since the board of directors has plenary power in managing corporate affairs, it has broad discretion in determining what constitutes "cause" for removal. Since the board and shareholders have the authority to remove officers with or without cause, the question of discretion in determining the existence of cause is not an issue unless an independent factor, such as a shareholder agreement, prevents the removal of officers except for cause.

IV. EXECUTIVE OFFICER EMPLOYMENT AGREEMENTS

It will usually be the case that the key officers of a corporation, typically the president and chief financial officer, will require employment contracts as a condition of their employment. The subject of executive employment contracts merits analysis in much greater detail than is appropriate in a general introductory chapter. This section will touch only on the broad outline of basic points. The "Forms and Materials" section of this volume contains examples of a sample executive employment agreement, a "golden parachute" agreement, and a confidentiality agreement appropriate for employees at all levels as well as executive officers.

As with any contract, certain basic requirements are necessary in order to render an employment contract enforceable: offer, acceptance, consideration, and certainty of contractual terms. The term of the contract, renewal options if any, compensation, nature of services, bonus provisions, benefits and provisions for termination should be set forth with particular detail. These provisions are illustrated in the sample employment contract appearing in the "Forms and Materials" section of this volume.

Often employers will wish to include provisions in a contract of employment restricting the employee from competing for a certain period of time after leaving the service of the employer. These provisions are frequently challenged by ex-employees and such challenges often prevail where the restrictive language is deemed to be unreasonable. In New York the reasonableness requirement is narrowly construed. Restrictive covenants in employment contracts are found "reasonable" only where they are necessary to shield an employer from "unfair competition" that would arise by an ex-employee disclosing or employing trade secrets of the former employer or confidential lists of customers. New York cases have also held that the threat of unfair competition to the ex-employer may exist, even where use of customer lists or trade secrets is not an issue, if the ex-employee performed services for the employer which were "special, unique or extraordinary." Restrictions on competition can also be deemed unreasonable, and therefore unenforceable, if they are found to be oppressive to the employee. Generally, "oppression" relates to the length of time for which the restrictive covenant operates; the longer the period, the more likely a finding of oppression.

As a general proposition, the higher the rank of the employee and the more discretionary the employee's duties, the greater the probability of enforcing a restrictive covenant not to compete.

Frequently, contracts of employment for executive officers will provide for termination of employment prior to the expiration of the term both for cause and without cause. Under New York law, contractual provisions permitting termination without cause in a contract for a fixed term are unenforceable unless they provide that the employer pay a severance amount. *Rothenberg v. Lincoln Farm Camp, Inc.*, 755 F.2d 1017, 1021 (1985). Severance pay is not required, however, where termination is for cause. Provisions following these guidelines appear in Section 8 of the sample employment agreement appearing in the "Forms and Materials" section of this volume.

V. DUTIES AND LIABILITIES OF DIRECTORS AND OFFICERS

A. In General

Directors and officers owe the corporation a duty of care and a duty of loyalty. Provided that they meet the standards of conduct imposed by these duties, which are discussed in detail below, they are protected by the "business judgment rule" from liability for decisions that are within the corporation's powers and within the scope of their own authority, which they have made in good faith and for which there is a reasonable basis. Such good-faith decisions, made in the independent discretion of the directors or officers, as the case may be, will not be set aside by a court, enjoined, or cause directors or officers to be charged for any loss in consequence of their decisions. *Greenbaum v. American Metal Climax, Inc.*, 27 A.D.2d 225, 278 N.Y.S.2d 123 (1st Dep't 1967); *Mayerson v. 3701 Tenants Corp.*, 123 Misc. 2d 235, 473 N.Y.S.2d 123 (Sup. Ct. 1984).

B. Duty of Care

Directors and officers must perform their respective duties in good faith and with the degree of care which an ordinarily prudent person would use under similar circumstances. BCL §§ 715, 717. Directors and officers are entitled to rely on information, opinions, reports and statements, including financial information, of legal counsel, independent accountants or anyone else, as to matters which the director or officer believes to be within the competence of the person on whom he or she relies. Directors and officers may also rely on such information presented by other officers and directors or employees of the corporation or of any of the corporation's subsidiaries in which the corporation owns at least a 50 percent interest. Directors may rely upon information prepared or presented by a duly constituted committee of the board as to matters within the committee's authority, provided that the director's reliance is in good faith and the director so relying has no knowledge that would cause such reliance to be unwarranted. Similarly, the reliance by officers on information prepared or presented by counsel, accountants or others, must be in good faith and the officer must have no knowledge that would cause such reliance to be unwarranted. Such reliance by directors and officers shields them from liability. BCL §§ 715(h), 717.

C. Duty of Loyalty

There are two components of the duty of loyalty to the corporation. The first component is the "undivided loyalty" rule which imposes upon directors and officers a duty not to have personal interests which conflict with the interests of the corporation. There are two principal conflict scenarios: (1) the director or officer sits on the board of one corporation which is considering a transaction with another corporation of which he or she is a director; and (2) the corporation is considering a transaction with any entity in which one of its own officers or directors has an interest. Because of the risk of breach of the duty of loyalty in such circumstances, directors and officers may wish to refrain from participating in discussion or voting on matters which concern them personally. At the very least they should disclose to the board any conflict of interest in connection with a pending or contemplated transaction. The board must consider the fairness to the corporation of any transaction in which a director or officer has a personal interest. Where the corporation approves such a transaction with an interested director, the interested director has the burden of proving that the transaction is fair to the corporation.

When the board of directors approves a transaction with interested directors, there arises a presumption that the transaction is fraudulent and in bad faith. *Kreitner v. Burgweger*, 174 A.D. 48, 160 N.Y.S. 256 (4th Dep't 1916); *Marian v. Mariani*, 84 N.Y.S.2d 335 (Sup. Ct. 1948), *modified on other grounds*, 276 A.D. 205, 93 N.Y.S.2d 370 (1st Dep't 1948). The transaction may then be void or voidable. However, no such transaction will be void or voidable because of a director's personal interest, and the presumption of fraudulence or unfairness can be overcome in one of the following ways:

(a) If the interested director discloses the material facts regarding his or her interest or common directorship and a majority of the disinterested directors approves the transaction. Although interested directors may not vote, they may be counted in determining the presence of a quorum for the meeting at which the vote occurs. BCL § 713(c); BCL § 713(a)(1).

(b) If the interested director discloses the material facts regarding his or her interest or common directorship to the shareholders, or if such material facts are known by the shareholders, and the shareholders approve the transaction. BCL § 713(a)(2).

Unless one of these procedures is followed, a transaction involving an interested director may be avoided by the corporation unless the interested director or officer proves that the transaction was fair. The interested parties have the burden of proof in establishing the fairness of the transaction. BCL § 713(b); *Lewis v. S.L. & E., Inc.*, 629 F.2d 764 (2d Cir. 1980).

The second component of the duty of loyalty involves the abuse of corporate opportunities. Specifically, a director or officer may not take personal advantage of a business opportunity to which the corporation would be entitled. Where the corporation has the right or expectancy to profit from a "corporate opportunity," the directors have a mandate to act for the corporation rather than themselves. *Litwin v. Allen*, 25

N.Y.S.2d 667 (Sup. Ct. 1940). This doctrine of corporate opportunity does not apply where the corporation has refused or is unable to take advantage of the opportunity. If a reasonable expectancy of corporate opportunity exists, then before the director can personally take advantage of it, the opportunity must be disclosed to the board and the disinterested directors must refuse it. If a director or officer takes advantage of a corporate opportunity without having disclosed it and without the board having refused it, then the corporation is entitled to the benefit of the transaction under a constructive trust theory.

D. Other Prohibited Actions

It is a breach of duty for directors of the corporation to approve a loan to any director unless the loan is authorized by a vote of the shareholders. BCL § 714. Shareholder approval must be by a majority of shares entitled to vote, excluding any shares held by the director who would be the borrower. Although the directors violate their duty by authorizing a loan other than as required by this section, violation of the section does not impair the obligation of the borrowing director to the corporation.

Directors may be held jointly and severally liable for approving a dividend in violation of law or of provisions of the certificate of incorporation, for distributing assets after dissolution of a corporation without providing for liabilities of the corporation that are known to the directors, or for repurchasing shares of the corporation in violation of state law or of the certificate of incorporation. BCL § 719(a). There is a presumption that any director who is present at a meeting of the board which approves any of these actions concurred in such approval, unless the director's dissent is noted in the minutes of the meeting, or in another writing in the case of directors who were absent from the meeting. If a director who votes to approve one of the prohibited actions later dissents, such dissent is ineffective to relieve him or her of liability.

VI. DUTIES AND LIABILITIES OF DIRECTORS AND OFFICERS OF PUBLICLY TRADED COMPANIES

Directors of a corporation whose stock is registered under the Securities Exchange Act of 1934, 15 U.S.C. § 78 *et seq.* (the "Exchange

Act"), and officers of such a corporation who have a major policy-making role, are deemed to be "Reporting Persons" under the Exchange Act. As Reporting Persons, their transactions in the stock of the corporation are subject to certain provisions of the federal securities law governing the reporting of stock ownership and the trading of the issuer's stock. Other provisions of federal securities law restrict their transactions in the issuer's stock by reason of their status as insiders or Reporting Persons. The obligations of directors and officers under the Exchange Act are enforced by the Securities and Exchange Commission. Anyone, whether or not a director or officer, is deemed to be a Reporting Person if his or her beneficial ownership of any class of an issuer's stock exceeds 10 percent of such class. The reader should note, however, that persons who are directors or policy-making officers of an issuer's subsidiaries are not deemed to be Reporting Persons of the issuer.

A. Stock Ownership Reporting Requirements

1. Initial Reports on Form 3

Section 16(a) of the Exchange Act requires each Reporting Person of an issuer to file an initial report on SEC Form 3, within ten days after (a) the effective date of registration of any class of equity securities of the issuer, or (b) the person's first election as a director or officer, stating his or her beneficial ownership, indirect as well as direct, of the issuer's stock, including puts, calls, options or other rights or obligations to buy or sell. The Form 3 must be filed whether or not the Reporting Person owns any of the company's securities at the time the report is required.

2. Changes in Ownership Reports on Form 4

Section 16(a) also requires each Reporting Person to report any subsequent change in beneficial ownership by filing a report on SEC Form 4 within ten days after the end of the month in which any such change occurs.

Every change in beneficial ownership, except for small transactions as discussed later in this section, must be reported on Form 4, whether the change occurs due to purchase or acquisition by means of a stock dividend, gift or inheritance, sale, gift or other disposition, or if the change involves only a change in the form of ownership such as a distribution of shares from a trust to the beneficiary.

For reporting purposes, stock acquired pursuant to a stock dividend is deemed to be acquired on the record date of such dividend. Accordingly, a Reporting Person who holds shares on the record date of a stock dividend should complete and file a report on Form 4 reflecting this increase in beneficial ownership by the tenth day of the month following the month in which the reportable transaction took place.

The acquisition, exercise or disposition of a transferable option, put, call, spread or straddle with respect to the issuer's stock is deemed a change in ownership of the underlying stock so as to require the filing of a report. A report must be filed to show all transactions even where the net balance of shares owned is the same at the end of the month as it was at the beginning.

If there is a change in a Reporting Person's beneficial ownership of the issuer's stock within six months after the person's election as a director or officer, he or she must include in the first Form 4 filed not only information with respect to that change, but also information with respect to any other transaction in the stock that took place within six months prior to the date of the change, even though such transactions occurred before the person became a director or officer. When a Reporting Person ceases to be such, the person is required to continue to file Form 4 reports with respect to changes in beneficial ownership of stock that occur within six months after his or her last transaction in the stock prior to the date he or she ceased to be a director or an officer.

3. Exemption for Small Transactions

A Reporting Person need not report on Form 4 either (a) an acquisition of stock if the person makes no subsequent disposition of stock in the six months following the acquisition and the aggregate market value of all his or her transactions in the issuer's stock for any six-month period during which the acquisition occurs does not exceed $10,000; or (b) an acquisition or disposition of the stock by way of gift if the aggregate market value of such gifts of stock made for any six-month period

DIRECTORS AND OFFICERS OF THE NY CORPORATION

does not exceed $10,000. For purposes of computing the aggregate market value of transactions under (a) above, amounts of any such exempt gifts are excluded.

However, it must be noted that when a Reporting Person files his or her first report after an exempt transaction, the person must disclose all acquisitions and dispositions which have occurred since his or her last filing. Accordingly, the exemption for small transactions merely postpones the time of reporting.

4. Annual Report on Form 5

Form 5 is an annual report that must be filed within 45 days after the end of a corporation's fiscal year (for a corporation which has adopted a calendar year, Form 5 would be due on February 14), by every person who was a Reporting Person at any time during the fiscal year, even if they are no longer a Reporting Person at the end of the fiscal year (or indeed are no longer affiliated with the corporation). Although no Form 5 need be filed for a Reporting Person if that Reporting Person had no reportable transactions during the year (a Reporting Person should certify to this effect in writing to the corporation's secretary), all transactions which are exempt from the Form 3 and Form 4 reporting requirements must be reported on Form 5 (this would include acquisitions of stock that are too small to be reported on Form 4).

5. Filing of Reports

Three copies of the Forms 3, 4 and 5 (at least one of which is manually signed) must be filed with the Securities and Exchange Commission, 450 5th Street, N.W., Washington, D.C. 20549. The reports are not deemed filed until they are actually received by the SEC in Washington; therefore, the requirement is not satisfied by mailing on the due date.

6. Beneficial Ownership

For the purpose of Form 3, 4 and 5 reports (as well as for registration statements, proxy statements and certain other SEC reports), securities considered by the SEC to be beneficially owned by a Reporting Person include the following:

(a) Stock held of record for his or her own benefit. However, stock owned of record by a Reporting Person but with benefits therefrom payable to someone else through any contract, agreement, understanding or other arrangement is not beneficially owned by the Reporting Person.

(b) Stock held in the name of a broker or other nominee for the Reporting Person's benefit.

(c) Stock with respect to which the Reporting Person obtains benefits substantially equivalent to those of ownership, such as dividends and voting rights pursuant to any agreement, understanding or arrangement.

(d) Stock as to which the Reporting Person can vest or revest title in himself/herself at once or in the future even though he/she does not have the benefits of ownership.

(e) Stock held by any partnership, estate or trust, or by a holding company used solely as an investment medium, in which the Reporting Person has a proprietary or beneficial interest. If the Reporting Person is not the sole partner, shareholder, or trust beneficiary, he or she is regarded as an indirect beneficial owner of his or her proportionate share of the stock; in that case the person must set forth in the Form 3, 4 and 5 reports the total stock held by the direct owner (i.e., the partnership, trust, estate or holding company) and may, but is not required to, indicate in a footnote the extent of his or her interest in the holding of the direct owner.

(f) Stock held in the name of the Reporting Person's spouse or minor children, or by any relative who lives with the Reporting Person, if the Reporting Person obtains benefits from stock held by any of such persons which are substantially equivalent to ownership by the Reporting Person, e.g., application of the income derived from such stock to maintain a common home, to meet expenses which he or she would otherwise meet from other sources, or the ability to exercise a controlling influence over the purchase or sale of such stock. While the SEC regards such securities as beneficially owned by the person and requires that they be included in his or her Forms 3, 4 and 5 and in proxy

DIRECTORS AND OFFICERS OF THE NY CORPORATION 177

statements and other SEC filings, the person may nevertheless disclaim beneficial ownership of the shares by including the information concerning them in a footnote and making an express disclaimer of beneficial ownership.

Forms 3, 4 and 5 require the Reporting Person to indicate on the form if his or her ownership is "direct" or "indirect." For that purpose, "indirect" ownership includes securities held in the manner indicated in paragraphs (c), (d), (e), and (f) above.

7. New SEC Enforcement Provisions

The SEC has adopted a rule that requires all publicly traded companies to disclose, in their 10-Q quarterly reports and 10-K annual report, the names of all officers and directors who failed to file Forms 3, 4 or 5, or who filed them late. Public companies are required to adopt a compliance program for reports by directors and officers on Forms 3, 4 and 5.

B. Liability for Short-Swing Profits

The Form 3, 4 and 5 reporting requirements of Section 16(a) are intended to permit enforcement of Section 16(b), which provides that any profit realized by a Reporting Person from any purchase and sale, or sale and purchase, of the corporation's stock within a six-month period must be paid to the issuer. Transactions in an issuer's stock other than by purchase and sale are not subject to Section 16(b). "Purchase" and "sale" are defined terms under the Exchange Act and include the exchange of stock for other securities or property.

Although there is some question as to whether a Reporting Person is actually the beneficial owner of stock held by his or her spouse, minor children or any relative who lives with him or her, it would be advisable for a Reporting Person to avoid stock transactions that might be matched with purchases or sales within a six-month period by his spouse or other persons whose shares are included in his or her report, whether or not he or she has disclaimed beneficial ownership of such shares.

Under Section 16(b) the Reporting Person's good faith, lack of intention, or ignorance of inside information are irrelevant. Thus it is no defense that the Reporting Person did not realize the transaction would be deemed a "purchase" or "sale," or did not realize that a transaction by another person would be attributed to him or her. An issuer may not waive the violation or settle for less than the entire profit realized, unless recovery on the merits is in serious doubt. Any shareholder may sue on behalf of an issuer to recover the "short-swing" profit if the issuer fails to do so.

Liability under Section 16(b) cannot be avoided by holding one certificate and selling another, or by any other approach designed to establish that particular securities were held for the requisite six-month period. Each sale and purchase within any period of six months is matched in such a manner as to permit maximum recovery by the issuer, regardless of the order in which the transactions occurred or whether a net profit was realized on all transactions in the relevant six-month period. Profit is determined by matching the lowest purchase price with the highest sale price within the relevant six-month period.

C. Prohibition Against Short Sales

Under Section 16(c) of the Exchange Act it is unlawful for a Reporting Person to sell any of an issuer's stock if (i) he or she does not own the stock or (ii) if he or she has not delivered the stock within 20 days after a sale, or has not deposited the stock in the mails within 5 days after the date of sale. Exceptions to these rules exist in situations where, notwithstanding the exercise of good faith, the seller was unable to make the delivery or mailing or could not have done so without undue inconvenience or expense.

D. Insider Trading—Federal Law

Persons who are "insiders" with respect to an issuer may not disclose material information about the issuer, or trade or recommend trading in the issuer's stock based upon such information, until a reasonable time after the information has been publicly released by the issuer. A reasonable time is sufficient time for the market to absorb and reflect the impact of rumors which the issuer has not publicly confirmed or denied. Twenty-four to forty-eight hours is generally considered a "reasonable

DIRECTORS AND OFFICERS OF THE NY CORPORATION 179

time." For purposes of the law in this area, the term "insider" includes not only Reporting Persons, but also officers who are not Reporting Persons and all other employees of the corporation.

Material information is considered to be information which might have an effect on an investor's decision to buy, sell, or hold the issuer's securities. Examples of information which will usually be material are dividend increases or decreases, major contract awards, significant earnings increases and decreases, acquisitions and other significant developments affecting the issuer.

Trading by a director, officer or other person on the basis of inside information and tipping or otherwise selectively disclosing such information to others who trade on it constitute violations of Rule 10b-5 of the SEC and may subject such director, officer or other person to liability for his or her transactions and for the transactions of his or her tippees. The liability may arise in SEC proceedings as well as in civil suits brought by individual shareholders.

Possessors of inside information about an issuer owe a duty to all purchasers of an issuer's stock. The rule formulated to ensure that this duty is followed is that those in possession of material undisclosed information must either disclose such information or abstain from trading. *S.E.C. v. Texas Gulf Sulphur Co.*, 401 F.2d 833 (2d Cir. 1968), *cert. denied*, 394 U.S. 976 (1969).

Criminal sanctions may also be imposed for violation of Rule 10b-5. As some celebrated cases involving arbitrageurs have demonstrated, when the SEC discovers instances of insider trading, it is today making recourse to criminal sanctions with considerably greater alacrity than in the past.

E. Common Law Insider Trading

A director, officer or other person may be liable for insider trading under New York law as well as under the Exchange Act. Under the common law theory of insider trading, a director or officer is liable if he or she has breached his or her fiduciary duty to the corporation by trading in its stock on the basis of information that has not been disclosed to the corporation's shareholders. In such instances the corporation may sue to recover profits from the transaction, or a shareholder may bring a derivative suit for such purpose on behalf of the corporation. *Diamond v. Oreamuno*, 24 N.Y.2d 494, 301 N.Y.S.2d 78 (1969). Common law liability for insider trading exists in connection with trading in the securities of any corporation, whether or not publicly traded.

F. Suggestions Regarding Insider Trading and Disclosing Information

In connection with the "disclose or abstain" rule, the New York Stock Exchange has made suggestions that may be helpful to directors and officers of any publicly traded corporation, whether or not traded on that exchange. It suggests that purchases by Reporting Persons are most appropriate when made pursuant to an established periodic investment program that is not under the control of the purchaser, or alternatively, when made during a 30-day period commencing a week after the annual report has been mailed to shareholders. Other appropriate times for transactions by Reporting Persons are following the release of quarterly results or other wide dissemination of important information, or during periods of relative stability in company operations, provided that prior to making a purchase or sale an officer or director contacts the appropriate designated officer of the company to determine if there are any important pending developments which need to be made public before he or she can engage in transactions in the issuer's stock. The NYSE also recommends that families and close associates of Reporting Persons be guided by these suggestions in connection with their securities transactions.

VII. INDEMNIFICATION OF DIRECTORS AND OFFICERS AND LIMITATION OF DIRECTORS' LIABILITY

Fewer topics have been of greater interest to corporate directors and officers in recent years than indemnification rights and limitation of liability for actions taken in an official capacity. Directors' and officers'

DIRECTORS AND OFFICERS OF THE NY CORPORATION 181

liability insurance has become extremely expensive, at least in comparison with its costs prior to the mid-1980s. Many companies have found difficulty in obtaining such insurance at all. The celebrated decision in *Smith v. Van Gorkom*, 488 A.2d 858 (Del. 1985), put insurers as well as directors and officers around the country on notice of some substantial holes in the veil of protection afforded by the business judgment rule. In response to the liability insurance crisis, many states, including New York, amended their respective business corporation statutes in 1986 and 1987 to improve protection against liability for officers and directors.

A. Indemnification

1. Nonexclusivity of Statutory Provisions

Until 1986 the indemnification rights of directors and officers of New York corporations were limited to the provisions appearing in the BCL. However, a major change occurred in 1986. Statutory indemnification provisions under the BCL are now nonexclusive of any other indemnification rights to which a director or officer of a New York corporation may be entitled. BCL § 721. This change in the law permits a New York corporation to grant broader indemnification rights than those contained in the BCL, provided that such provisions are contained in the certificate of incorporation or by-laws, or pursuant to (a) a resolution of the shareholders; (b) a resolution of the board of directors; or (c) indemnification agreements between the corporation and individual officers and directors. The reader should note that Section 721 of the BCL does not require shareholder approval of by-laws that provide for nonstatutory indemnification, or that provide for nonstatutory indemnification subject to directors' or shareholders' resolutions or by way of indemnification agreements. However, if indemnification is authorized in any manner not involving shareholder approval, then the corporation is required to notify the shareholders in writing no later than the next annual meeting of shareholders, or 15 months after the action is taken, whichever is sooner. If such action providing for indemnification occurs within 3 months of an annual meeting of shareholders, however, then notice need not be given before the earlier of the next subsequent meeting of shareholders or 15 months after the action is taken. BCL § 725(d).

There is one limitation on the extent to which a corporation may provide for indemnification rights broader than the statutory provisions: there may be no indemnification of a director or officer if a judgment or adjudication adverse to a director or officer establishes that he or she acted in bad faith or dishonestly and that such acts were material to the proceeding so adjudicated, or that the director or officer acted so as to personally gain enrichment or other advantage to which he or she was not legally entitled. BCL § 721.

2. Statutory Indemnification Rights

In addition to allowing nonstatutory indemnification rights for the first time, the 1986 amendments to the BCL also changed statutory indemnification considerably. The new statutory indemnification provisions create a single standard of conduct, regardless of the type of action or proceeding for which indemnification is sought, that directors and officers must meet in order to be entitled to statutory indemnification rights. Previously there had been one standard for derivative suits and another for third-party actions. A New York corporation may indemnify an officer or director provided that the person seeking indemnification acted in good faith for a purpose he or she reasonably believed to be in the best interests of the corporation, or, in the case of a criminal proceeding, if he or she had no reasonable grounds for believing that the conduct was unlawful. BCL § 722(a).

If this standard of conduct is met, then in the case of third-party actions, the corporation may indemnify the director or officer against judgments, fines, amounts paid in settlement and reasonable expenses and attorneys' fees. BCL § 722(a). The reader should note that termination of a third-party action, whether by judgment, settlement, conviction or plea of *nolo contendere,* creates no presumption that the indemnified party failed to meet the good-faith standard described above. BCL § 722(b).

In the case of derivative actions, the corporation may indemnify an officer or director who has met the requisite standard of conduct against

DIRECTORS AND OFFICERS OF THE NY CORPORATION

amounts paid in settlement and reasonable expenses and attorneys' fees. BCL § 722(c). However, there can be no indemnification for a threatened or pending action that is settled or otherwise disposed of, nor in respect of any matter as to which the officer or director is judged liable to the corporation, unless the relevant judicial forum determines, in view of all the circumstances, that the person is reasonably entitled to indemnification for the settlement amount or expenses. In contrast to the Section 722(a) provision governing third-party suits, the Section 722(c) provision governing derivative suits does not provide for indemnification of judgments or fines.

Payment of indemnification is mandatory to a director or officer who has been successful, on the merits or otherwise, in the defense of a civil or criminal action or proceeding, BCL § 723(a); this differs from the previous statutory provision which required that indemnification be mandatory only for a "wholly" successful defendant. Unless payment of indemnification is mandatory, any indemnification under Section 722 of the BCL, or under nonstatutory provisions as allowed by Section 721 of the BCL, shall be made only as follows:

(a) If approved by the board of directors acting by a quorum of directors who are not party to the action or proceeding for which indemnification is sought, upon a finding that the proposed indemnitee has met the requisite standard of conduct (either the good-faith standard of Section 722 or the standard set forth in the corporation's nonstatutory indemnification provisions). BCL § 723(b)(1).

(b) If a quorum is unavailable or a quorum of disinterested directors so directs, payment shall be made if approved by either (i) the board, upon a written opinion of counsel that the director or officer has met the applicable standard of conduct, or (ii) the shareholders, upon a finding that the director or officer has met the applicable standard of conduct.

In another departure from the previous statutory indemnification provisions, Section 723(c) of the BCL now provides that expenses in defending a civil or criminal action may be advanced provided that the party seeking indemnification undertakes to repay the amount advanced if he or she is ultimately found not entitled to indemnification, or to the extent that any expenses advanced exceed the indemnification to which he or she is entitled. Previous provisions required a finding that the relevant standard of conduct had been met. Because Section 721 of the BCL now provides that the statutory provisions for indemnification and advancement of expenses are not exclusive of any other rights, a corporation could permit the advancement of expenses without requiring the undertaking of repayment described in Section 723. That, at least, is the plain meaning of the language; it is, however, reasonable to expect that this interpretation could be challenged. It may therefore be the better practice for directors and officers receiving expense advances to deliver a repayment undertaking even if the corporation permits advancement of expenses without a commitment to repay.

If a corporation fails to pay indemnification, or even if it affirmatively denies indemnification to a director or officer, the party seeking indemnification is entitled, pursuant to Section 724 of the BCL, to apply to the court in which the liability was incurred, or alternatively to the New York State Supreme Court in a separate proceeding, to obtain an order for payment of indemnification. Where such an order is sought the court may allow the party seeking indemnification reasonable expenses, including attorneys' fees, while the litigation is pending, provided that the court determines that the defendant raises genuine issues of fact or law.

No statutory indemnification is payable if payment would be inconsistent with a provision in the certificate of incorporation, by-laws, resolution of the board or of the shareholders, or other proper corporate document (such as a shareholders' agreement). In other words, a corporation may choose to provide narrower indemnification rights than the BCL provides.

A form of indemnification agreement appears in the "Forms and Materials" section of this volume. Its provisions could appropriately be included in a by-law or certificate of incorporation section providing for indemnification rights.

DIRECTORS AND OFFICERS OF THE NY CORPORATION 185

B. Limitation of Directors' Liability

Notwithstanding the expansion of indemnification rights which occurred in 1986, New York declined to take the step which some other states, most notably Delaware, took that year in providing for limitation of liability of directors of a corporation. However, in 1987 the New York legislature concluded that the continuing problem of reduced availability and coverage of liability insurance and its increased cost warranted further action. The BCL was further amended to provide for limitation of liability of directors of a New York corporation. This change in New York law limits liability of directors only and not officers.

The new law provides that the certificate of incorporation may contain a provision eliminating or limiting the personal liability of directors to the corporation or shareholders for damages for any breach of duty while serving in the capacity of director. BCL § 402(b). The provision contains two restrictions. First, no limitation of liability provision may limit liability of a director if any judgment or other final adjudication adverse to the director establishes that his or her behavior was in bad faith or involved intentional misconduct or a knowing violation of law, or establishes that the director personally gained a profit or other advantage to which he or she was not legally entitled or that the director's acts violated any of the proscribed actions enumerated in Section 719 of the BCL. BCL § 402(b)(1). Secondly, no liability limitation provision may have retroactive effect: directors remain fully liable for acts or omissions that occurred prior to the adoption of an amendment of the certificate of incorporation limiting directors' liability. BCL § 402(b)(2).

The BCL's limitation of liability provision has the effect of making any suit under Section 720 of the BCL, for a director's misconduct, subject to provisions in the certificate of incorporation limiting the liability of directors.

In addition to permitting limitation of directors' liability, the 1987 amendment to the BCL amended Section 717 relating to the standard of care owed by directors to the corporation. This amendment provides that in taking action, including any action which may relate to a change in control of the corporation, the director is entitled to consider both the long-term and short-term interests of the corporation and its shareholders. By this amendment the legislature has sought to avoid the outcome in New York of the Delaware case of *Smith v. Van Gorkom* in which directors who believed they were working within the protection of the business judgment rule were held liable, in approving a takeover offer, for not considering both the long- and short-term interests of the corporation. In light of the change in New York law permitting limitation of directors' liability, New York counsel should add such a provision to his or her standard form of certificate of incorporation. Counsel should also include limitation of directors' liability on pre-incorporation checklists and questionnaires.

The form of certificate of incorporation appearing in the "Forms and Materials" section of this volume contains appropriate language regarding both limitation of directors' liability and indemnification of directors and officers.

CHAPTER NINE

OBLIGATIONS OF THE CORPORATION TO SHAREHOLDERS; OBLIGATIONS OF SHAREHOLDERS TO EACH OTHER

Leona Beane

OBLIGATIONS OF CORPORATION TO SHAREHOLDERS

I. INTRODUCTION

This chapter deals with the rights of shareholders within the corporation—essentially the right to elect directors and vote on various other matters, the mechanics of such voting, and the obligations of majority shareholders to act in good faith and fairness toward the minority. The chapter also discusses the special nature of shareholder relationships in the closely held corporation—the problems that may be encountered, as well as the various arrangements that can be made to avoid such problems.

II. SHAREHOLDER RIGHTS

Generally speaking, a corporation is owned by its shareholders but managed by its board of directors. Nevertheless, shareholders exert ultimate control over management in the sense that the shareholders elect the directors, adopt and repeal by-laws, and approve or veto major policy decisions. Shareholder action on these matters takes the form of voting, either at meetings or by proxy, or giving written consent in lieu of a meeting. The mechanics of these procedures are discussed in the following sections.

A. Shareholders' Meetings

Meetings of shareholders may be held at any place within or without the state of New York as is provided in the by-laws. If there is no specific provision in the by-laws, all meetings must be held at the office of the corporation in New York. BCL § 602(a).

1. Call of Meetings

An annual shareholders' meeting must be held for the election of directors and for the transaction of other business on a date fixed by the by-laws. BCL § 602(b). If, for a period of one month after the date fixed by the by-laws for the annual meeting of shareholders, there is a failure to elect a sufficient number of directors to conduct the business of the corporation, or if no date has been fixed to elect the directors after a period of 13 months after formation of the corporation or the last annual meeting, the board is required to call a special meeting for the election of directors. BCL § 603. In addition, special meetings may be called by the board or by such other person(s) as are authorized by the certificate of incorporation or the by-laws. BCL § 602(c).

2. Notice of Meetings

Shareholders must be given written notice of the place, date and hour of the annual meeting, as well as the purpose of any special meeting. Notice of meetings must be given personally or by mail to each shareholder entitled to vote at the meeting no less than 10 nor more than 50 days before the date of the meeting. BCL § 605.

3. Waiver of Notice

A shareholder may waive the notice requirement by submitting a signed waiver of notice before or after the meeting, or by attending the meeting in person or by proxy without protesting the lack of notice. BCL § 606.

4. Quorum of Shareholders

A quorum consisting of a majority of shareholders entitled to vote must be present to transact business at any meeting. BCL § 608. *See Rye Psychiatric Hospital Center v. Schoenholtz*, 66 N.Y.2d 333, 497 N.Y.S.2d 317 (1985) for a clarification of the BCL's quorum requirements for a special meeting.

The certificate of incorporation or the by-laws may allow for a quorum smaller than a majority, but not less than one-third of the holders of shares entitled to vote. In addition, the certificate of incorporation may provide for a quorum greater than a majority. BCL § 616.

Greater-than-majority quorum requirements, sometimes as high as 80 percent or 100 percent, are frequently used in closely held corporations. This device is designed to protect minority interests by ensuring that no shareholder action can be taken without the presence of most or all members. To ensure veto power, minority shareholders in a closely

OBLIGATIONS OF CORPORATION TO SHAREHOLDERS

held corporation should seek to include a high voting requirement and a high quorum requirement, which must be indicated in its certificate of incorporation.

There is no bar to greater-than-majority quorum requirements in New York provided the requirement appears in the certificate of incorporation and is noted conspicuously on the face or back of each share certificate issued. BCL § 616. Shareholders should be aware, however, that high voting and/or quorum requirements create a significant risk of deadlock.

5. Proxies

Rather than attend a meeting and vote in person, a shareholder may vote by proxy. A proxy is essentially a written power of attorney granted by a shareholder enabling another to exercise the shareholder's voting rights at the meeting. Unless the proxy states that it must be voted in a particular manner, the proxy holder has discretion to vote as he/she pleases.

In New York, no proxy is valid 11 months after its issue unless it provides otherwise. Every proxy must be in writing and signed by the shareholder or its attorney-in-fact, and is revocable at the pleasure of the shareholder unless stated to be "irrevocable." BCL § 609.

In earlier times, courts often refused to enforce irrevocable proxies against shareholders on the grounds that arrangements "disenfranchising" the beneficial owners of a corporation were against public policy. Irrevocable proxies were upheld only when "coupled with an interest"—that is, when the proxy holder gained an interest in the stock itself, such as an option to purchase the shares, or when the holder received the proxy as partial inducement to lend money or provide services to the corporation. This rule created problems in the context of the closely held corporation, where shareholders would often grant each other irrevocable proxies as a means of binding themselves to a specified course of action in the future.

The New York statute addresses this problem by allowing a proxy to be made irrevocable if coupled with any of the traditionally sufficient "interests" or if given pursuant to a written agreement between two or more shareholders specifying that each is to vote his/her shares in a stated manner. BCL §§ 609, 620(a). In effect, the statute deems the mutual promises of the shareholders a sufficient "interest" to support their mutual irrevocable proxies.

Without the use of proxies, large public corporations would find it all but impossible to conduct their shareholder meetings. By soliciting proxies for elections, management is able to gather a sufficient number of shareholders to satisfy quorum and voting requirements. Solicitation of proxies is carefully regulated by the Securities and Exchange Commission, which basically requires full disclosure of the purposes and circumstances surrounding the solicitation, in order that shareholders are not misled in deciding how to vote.

6. Record Date of Shareholders

Because thousands of shares in a large public corporation are traded on a daily basis, it is difficult to determine on any given day the exact identity of the shareholders of the corporation who are entitled to vote in elections. For that reason, the corporation is authorized to accept votes cast only by persons who are shareholders of record on a date fixed by the by-laws or by the board of directors as the determinative date. The record date cannot be more than 50 nor less than 10 days before the date of the meeting, nor more than 50 days before any other action. BCL § 604. A list of the shareholders as of the record date is open to inspection upon request at any shareholders' meeting. BCL § 607.

7. Conduct of the Shareholders' Meeting

A shareholders' meeting is called to order and presided over by a chairman, who is usually designated in the by-laws. The presiding officer is usually the chairman of the board of directors or the president of the corporation. The secretary of the corporation makes a statement concerning notice or waiver of notice of the meeting, and reads the minutes of the last previous meeting—a measure which is almost invariably dispensed with. Then the presiding officer usually states that the list of shareholders of record is available for inspection, pursuant to Section 607 of the BCL which requires production of the list at the request of any shareholder. The chairman announces that any share-

OBLIGATIONS OF CORPORATION TO SHAREHOLDERS 193

holder present may vote in person whether or not he/she has previously given a proxy (assuming the proxy was revocable).

The chairman next identifies the inspector(s) of elections, if any, who must take and sign an oath to act with strict impartiality. BCL § 610. The inspectors specify the number of shares present at the meeting in person and by proxy and indicate the presence or lack of a quorum. If a quorum exists, nomination and election of directors proceeds.

The meeting probably will include voting on other matters, as well as presentation of the president's or management's report on corporate affairs.

8. Inspector of Elections

Elections at shareholders' meetings in New York must be supervised by inspectors if the by-laws so require and if compliance with the by-laws is requested by a shareholder who is present in person or by proxy and entitled to vote at the meeting. BCL § 610. If factions are expected to oppose management, inspectors of elections should be appointed prior to the meeting since their report will constitute *prima facie* evidence of the facts and of the votes certified by them. If inspectors are not named prior to the meeting, they may be named by the presiding officer at the meeting and must be named upon the request of any shareholder entitled to vote. There are no statutory requirements for the position of inspector of elections. Usually the inspector is an assistant secretary or assistant treasurer of the corporation, counsel, an independent accountant or auditor, or bank or service company.

The inspectors verify the number of shares represented at the meeting, the existence of a quorum, and the validity and effect of proxies. They hear and determine all challenges and questions on voting rights, count and tabulate the votes, and certify the results. BCL § 611. The inspectors fulfill the important role of determining the validity of contested proxies and certifying the election results. In effect, the inspectors act as a court of first instance, and are sworn to an oath of impartiality.

9. Voting of the Shareholders

Unless otherwise specified in the certificate of incorporation, each shareholder of record is entitled to one vote per share. BCL § 612(a). Frequently, corporations limit or deny voting rights to preferred shareholders, and it is usually the common shareholders who have voting rights. Directors are elected by a plurality of the votes cast at the meeting, unless a different provision is contained in the certificate of incorporation.

Corporate action requiring shareholder approval ordinarily requires a majority vote. Major transactions such as a merger, consolidation, sale of all or substantially all of the corporate assets not in the ordinary course of business, or dissolution require approval by two-thirds of the shareholders.

As with quorum requirements, the certificate of incorporation may specify a higher proportion of votes necessary for any action than would otherwise be required, as long as such provision in conspicuously noted on the face or back of every share certificate issued by the corporation. BCL § 616(c).

10. Cumulative Voting for Directors

As an alternative to the one share/one vote method of electing directors, the certificate of incorporation may provide for voting by a method known as cumulative voting for directors. *See* BCL § 618. Its purpose is to enable an organized minority of shareholders to elect one or more representatives to the board of directors by cumulating its votes for these candidates rather than spreading the votes. If straight voting were the rule, the holders of a bare majority of shares would be in a position practically always to control the election of the entire board, thereby precluding any voice in the corporation's management by a substantial minority group.

The minimum number of shares that will elect a given number of directors out of a total number of directors to be elected under cumulative voting can be calculated by the following formula:

OBLIGATIONS OF CORPORATION TO SHAREHOLDERS

$$X = [(S \times N)(D + 1)] + 1$$

where:

X = minimum number of shares required to elect directors;

S = number of shares represented at meeting;

N = number of directors desired to be elected; and

D = total number of directors to be elected.

For example, if the minority group desires to guarantee the election of one representative to a nine-person board, and 1000 shares will be voted at the meeting, the minority will need 101 shares, since under our formula:

$$[(1000 \times 1)(9 + 1)] + 1 = 101$$

Although some states make cumulative voting mandatory, in New York it is optional and must be specifically provided for in the certificate of incorporation. When a corporation does provide for cumulative voting, no director may be removed by shareholder vote if the votes cast against his/her removal would be sufficient to elect him/her in the first instance if voted cumulatively—a measure necessary to prevent the majority from simply undoing the original purpose behind the cumulative vote. BCL § 706(a).

11. Powers of the Supreme Court Respecting Elections

Pursuant to Section 619 of the BCL, any shareholder aggrieved by an election may petition the New York State Supreme Court for relief in the judicial district where the office of the corporation is located, and, upon notice to the opposing party, the court may hold a hearing on the allegations of the parties to confirm the election or order a new election or to take such other action as justice may require.

12. Unanimous Written Consent of Shareholders in Lieu of Meeting

Whenever, under New York law, shareholders are required or permitted to take action by a vote, the action may be taken without a meeting upon the unanimous written consent of each shareholder who would have been entitled to vote at the meeting. BCL § 615. This is a particularly useful device in the closely held corporation, where the consent necessary to dispense with a formal meeting may easily be obtained.

It is often difficult for shareholders who are employed to attend and vote at a formal shareholders' meeting. Proper shareholder action can be had without the necessity of a formal meeting since written consent of all shareholders has the same effect as a unanimous decision by them. The unanimous written consent of all shareholders to the shareholder action should be kept in the corporate minute book where it has the same effect as the minutes of a shareholders' meeting. If there is less than unanimous consent among the shareholders, then a formal shareholders' meeting must be scheduled.

B. Additional Rights of Shareholders

1. Removal of Directors

Shareholders have the right to remove for cause any or all of the directors during their terms of office. If the certificate of incorporation or the by-laws so provide, any or all of the directors may also be removed without cause by shareholder vote. The certificate of incorporation or by-laws may also give the board of directors the power to remove one or more of its own members but only for cause. BCL § 706.

2. Voting on Amendment of the By-Laws

Unless the certificate of incorporation provides otherwise, shareholders may adopt, amend or repeal any by-law. The certificate of incorporation may give the board of directors the same power, but any by-law adopted by the board may be amended or repealed by the shareholders. BCL § 601.

3. Voting on Amendment to Certificate of Incorporation

The certificate of incorporation may be amended by a vote of the holders of a majority of all outstanding shares entitled to vote (unless a greater percentage is therein specified). BCL § 803. The "certificate of

OBLIGATIONS OF CORPORATION TO SHAREHOLDERS

amendment or change" must be filed with the New York Department of State indicating the manner and nature of the change. This topic is discussed more fully in Chapter 15.

4. Voting for Mergers and Consolidations

In order to effectuate a merger or consolidation, approval must be obtained at a meeting of the shareholders. The holders of two-thirds of all outstanding shares entitled to vote must approve the proposed action. BCL § 903. In addition, any sale, lease, exchange or other disposition of all or substantially all of the assets of the corporation not made in the usual or regular course of business must also be authorized by a vote of two-thirds of all outstanding shares entitled to vote thereon. BCL § 909. This topic is discussed more fully in Chapter 11.

5. Inspection of Books and Records of the Corporation

Any shareholder of record for more than six months or any shareholder who holds at least 5 percent of any class of the outstanding shares may, on five days' written notice to the corporation, have the right to examine the shareholders' minutes, shareholders' lists, and other reccords of the corporation. BCL § 624. In addition, a shareholder will be allowed to make copies of the above-mentioned records. A shareholder may also send his/her attorney or other authorized agent to examine the books and records.

6. Dividends

A corporation may declare and pay dividends to its shareholders in cash, property, or additional shares of the corporation's stock. There is no absolute right, however, for a shareholder to receive dividends. This is within the discretion of the board of directors. Under Section 510 of the BCL, dividends may be paid only out of surplus (*see* discussion in Chapters 6 and 10); if any dividend is paid or any other distribution made from a source other than earned surplus, the dividend shall be accompanied by a written notice disclosing the amount by which the dividend or distribution affects stated capital, capital surplus, and earned surplus. BCL § 510.

The corporation may declare and pay cash dividends or property dividends, unless the corporation is currently insolvent or will thereby be made insolvent. BCL § 510.

The distribution of a stock dividend may be by use of treasury shares or by distribution of unissued shares.

7. Preemptive Rights of the Shareholder

The preemptive right of a shareholder, in effect, permits a shareholder to maintain its same percentage interest in the corporation. Unless the certificate of incorporation provides otherwise, shareholders are entitled to preemptive rights, which give the shareholder the right to purchase any additional shares which are being issued for cash in order to protect his/her existing voting power or claims to dividends. BCL § 622. The right may be excluded or limited by specific provision in the certificate of incorporation. In New York, this right applies both to voting shares and equity shares, which are defined as those having unlimited dividend rights. This is generally the common shareholder. Holders of these shares must be given the opportunity to purchase newly authorized or unissued shares up to an amount which would maintain their percentage of ownership in the corporation. This preemptive right is usually held by shareholders of common stock and ordinarily excludes preferred shareholders. *See* BCL § 622. Specifically exempted from preemptive rights are issuance of treasury shares; issuance of shares to effectuate a merger or consolidation; issuance during the first two years of the corporation's existence of part of the shares authorized in its original certificate of incorporation; issuance of shares to satisfy conversion of option rights; issuance for consideration other than cash. *See* BCL § 622(e). In addition, there may be such other restrictions on the preemptive right as are stated in the certificate of incorporation.

Preemptive rights can be particularly important in closely held corporations where the majority attempts to freeze out the minority by issuing a large number of additional shares with the intention of purchasing all

OBLIGATIONS OF CORPORATION TO SHAREHOLDERS

of them, thereby diluting the minority's proportionate interest to an insignificant level. Preemptive rights allow the minority to protect its pro rata interest in such instances.

8. Right of Appraisal

Pursuant to Section 623 of the BCL, dissenting shareholders can, under certain specific circumstances, require the corporation to buy back their shares of stock at their fair value. These rights may arise in favor of an objecting shareholder if, for example, a proposed amendment to the certificate of incorporation creates, alters or abolishes any provision or right in respect of redemption of any sinking fund, or alters or abolishes any preemptive right or excludes or limits the right to vote or alters or abolishes any preferential right. In addition, if a merger or consolidation is being voted upon, the dissenting shareholders of the nonsurviving constituent corporation generally have appraisal rights. This also applies to any sale, lease or exchange or other disposition of all or substantially all of the corporation's assets (not in the ordinary course of business) under Section 909 of the BCL, where the transaction is for consideration other than cash.

Prior to the adoption of Section 623 of the BCL, a dissenting stockholder did not have a right of appraisal and could not require that the corporation buy back his/her shares of stock and pay the fair value of the shares. Now, however, a dissenting shareholder does have this right under certain circumstances, but the shareholder must proceed with the detailed procedures for enforcement of this right as set forth in Section 623.

The dissenting shareholder must file with the corporation a written objection to the proposed action before the shareholder vote is actually taken. The shareholder must state in the objection that (s)he intends to demand payment for his/her shares if the specified action is taken. The shareholder who does object must file with the corporation a written notice of election to dissent covering all shares beneficially owned by the shareholder and submit the shares to the corporation for notation on the face of the shares that such election was made. The corporation is then given an opportunity to agree on a price to pay to the objecting shareholder for his/her shares.

The corporation subsequently is required to make a uniform written offer to all dissenting shareholders to pay the specified price for their shares which the corporation considers to be their actual value. This offer must be accompanied by the latest available balance sheet and a corporate profit and loss statement for the 12-month period ended on the balance sheet date. In the event the corporation fails to make an offer or there is no agreement on the price, the shareholder or the corporation may institute a judicial proceeding to fix the fair value of the shares. If the corporation does not commence the proceeding, then any objecting shareholder has the right to do so within 20 days. The court determines the fair value of the shares, and interest may be awarded or may be withheld. Each party to the proceeding shall bear its own costs and expenses including counsel fees and expert witness fees, and such costs and expenses may be apportioned or assessed against the corporation or the dissenting shareholder in the court's discretion. The procedure for the appraisal proceeding set forth in Section 623 is quite detailed and should be reviewed carefully.

Recognizing that the shareholder's right to dissent from such actions and to receive payment of the fair market value for his/her shares are basic rights of share ownership, Section 623 provides that the right to dissent is exclusive in the absence of unlawful or fraudulent corporate action. BCL § 623(k).

A shareholder may withdraw his/her notice of election to dissent regarding his/her shares at any time prior to his/her written acceptance of an offer made by the corporation in accordance with Section 623(g) of the BCL, but in no case later than 60 days from the date the corporate action is consummated, unless the corporation fails to make a timely offer under Section 623(g), in which case the shareholder may withdraw his/her notice of election within 60 days of the date the offer is made; also, a corporation's offer to purchase a dissenting shareholder's shares must be accompanied by a statement setting forth the aggregate

OBLIGATIONS OF CORPORATION TO SHAREHOLDERS

number of shares with respect to which notices of election to dissent have been received and the aggregate number of holders of such shares.

If the corporate action has been consummated, such offer must be accompanied by (1) advance payment, to each shareholder who has submitted the certificates representing his/her shares to the corporation as provided in Section 623, of an amount equal to 80 percent of the amount of such offer, or (2) as to each such shareholder who has not yet submitted his/her certificates, a statement that advance payment to him/her of an amount equal to 80 percent of the amount of such offer will be made by the corporation promptly upon submission of the certificates. If the corporate action has not been consummated at the time of the making of an offer, such advance payment or statement as to advance payment shall be sent to each shareholder entitled thereto forthwith upon consummation of the corporate action. Every such advance payment to the shareholder will be accompanied by a statement to the effect that acceptance of such payment does not constitute a waiver of such dissenting shareholder's rights.

If the corporation is insolvent or payment will make it insolvent, the corporation is not permitted to make the payment. BCL § 623(j). In such instance, the dissenting shareholder may withdraw the notice of election or retain his/her status as a claimant against the corporation. The enforcement by a shareholder of his/her right to receive payment for the shares under Section 623 shall exclude the enforcement by the shareholder of any other right to which such shareholder might otherwise be entitled by virtue of share ownership. However, the shareholder will still have the right to bring or maintain an appropriate action to obtain relief on the ground that the corporate action will be or is unlawful or fraudulent as to him/her. BCL § 623(k). Upon consummation of the corporate action, a shareholder who maintains such an action ceases to have any rights of a shareholder other than the right to be paid the fair value of the shares.

C. Proceeding by Shareholders—The Shareholders' Derivative Suit

One of the most powerful remedies of shareholders is the right to commence a derivative suit on behalf of the corporation against its officers and directors for damages. Shareholders are also able to commence an action against the officers and directors to compel an accounting for official conduct or to set aside or enjoin illegal conveyances. Such an action may be maintained by the corporation itself, a receiver, a trustee in bankruptcy, an officer, a director, or a judgment creditor of the corporation, or it may be brought on behalf of the corporation derivatively by a shareholder. BCL § 626. In a shareholders' derivative action, which is brought to procure a judgment in favor of the corporation, the shareholder(s) instituting the suit must have held their shares both at the time the action was instituted and at the time the act complained of was committed. In addition the person instituting the action must show either that he/she has made a reasonable effort to have the board of directors begin the action itself on behalf of the corporation, or must state the reason for not making such effort (e.g., if the current board of directors is still in control and they were the persons against whom the complaint was made, there would be no purpose in making an initial demand, and thus this provision would be satisfied). The corporation must be a party to the action, and if not as a plaintiff, then it must be listed as a defendant. The recovery belongs to the corporation. Any judgment will be rendered in favor of the corporation.

Once the action is commenced, it may not be discontinued, compromised or settled without the approval of the court. Section 626 of the BCL contains detailed provisions for instituting a shareholders' derivative action. In addition, Section 627 of the BCL provides certain safeguards for the corporation, e.g., the right to demand security for costs (including defendant's attorneys' fees and investigation expenses) unless the plaintiff initiating the action holds 5 percent or more of the outstanding shares of any class of stock or whose outstanding shares have a fair value of at least $50,000. Shareholders may combine so that, collectively, the plaintiffs initiating the action own at least 5 percent of the shares of stock in which case they would not be required to post security for costs. BCL § 627. The court may award the plaintiff(s) reasonable expenses including attorneys' fees. BCL § 626(e).

Shareholders' derivative suits have become a very powerful weapon in the shareholders' arsenal of defenses against erring officers and directors, and such suits have been used extensively in recent years.

III. OBLIGATIONS TO MINORITY SHAREHOLDERS

Generally, any shareholder is free to vote in his/her own interest in any matter, regardless of whether that interest conflicts with what is best for the corporation. Nevertheless, majority or controlling shareholders are subject to certain fiduciary duties which prevent them from visiting fraud, oppression or unfairness upon the minority. Perhaps the classic statement of this is contained in *Pepper v. Litton*, 308 U.S. 295, 306 (1939), in which the United States Supreme Court stated that when the self-interested actions of controlling shareholders are challenged, the burden is on such shareholders "not only to prove the good faith of the transaction but also to show its inherent fairness from the viewpoint of the corporation and those interested therein."

The fiduciary duties of dominant shareholders are most frequently brought into question when the dominant shareholders attempt to rearrange the structure of the corporation solely to enhance their own power to the detriment of the minority. For example, the majority issues and acquires new shares in the corporation (without violating preemptive rights), and thus dilutes the voting power of the minority. Issuance of shares solely to "freeze out" the minority may constitute a breach of fiduciary duty. *See Alpert v. 28 William Street Corp.*, 63 N.Y.2d 557, 483 N.Y.S.2d 667 (1984). Similarly, a parent corporation, as dominant shareholder of its subsidiary, might vote to merge the latter into itself or into a third corporation and again "freeze out" the minority shareholders of the subsidiary by paying them off with cash. The dominant corporation, as a majority shareholder standing on both sides of the transaction, has the burden of proving that the merger was fair and has served some valid business purpose beyond elimination of the minority shareholder(s). The same burden may arise in other "going private" transactions where the majority seeks to buy out the minority—with the ultimate question being whether the price forced upon the minority is "fair." A majority shareholder is subject to a fiduciary duty when selling his/her shares—and thereby transferring control of the corporation—to an outside purchaser. The seller must take reasonable care to ensure that the remaining minority shareholders do not become saddled with new ownership whose only intention is to "loot" the corporation by disposing of its assets.

Minority shareholders in New York also enjoy several statutory rights beyond the right of fair treatment. Probably the most significant statutory right, as previously discussed, is that of appraisal. For example, the shareholder of a subsidiary corporation who dissents from a merger is entitled to cash payment of the fair value of his/her shares prior to the merger. BCL § 910(a). Similar appraisal rights are available for shareholders who object to majority approval of the sale of all or substantially all the corporate assets other than for cash, and for shareholders who object to amendments to the certificate of incorporation which may have the effect of diluting their voting or dividend rights. BCL § 806(b)(6). Exercise of appraisal rights does not preclude a shareholder from bringing an action against the majority for breach of its fiduciary duty on the ground that the corporate action is fraudulent or unlawful. *See* BCL § 623(k).

As indicated earlier, preemptive rights allow shareholders to maintain their same percentage interest in the corporation. The right may not be viable, however, if, in order to exercise it, a minority shareholder must utilize large amounts of cash in order to purchase. If the shareholder cannot raise the necessary funds, (s)he may still be able to complain that the majority action is unfair or is acting in bad faith.

It should also be noted that even if preemptive rights are excluded from the certificate of incorporation, the majority still is subject to a duty not to dilute fraudulently or unfairly the minority's proportionate interest through issuance of new shares or reacquisition of outstanding shares.

IV. ARRANGEMENTS AMONG SHAREHOLDERS IN THE CLOSELY HELD CORPORATION

The Business Corporation Law does not expressly distinguish between publicly held and closely held corporations. The statute speaks only in general terms of "corporations." Thus, there are various problems in operating the closely held corporation, which functions far differently from the typical public corporation. Whereas ownership and management of public corporations are divided among shareholders, and directors and officers, the shareholders of a small, private corporation are usually active themselves in the conduct and management of the business; often, the shareholders are also officers and/or directors. Indeed, the shareholders of a closely held corporation usually regard themselves more as general partners who have chosen the corporate form of business in order to limit their liability. Thus they may wish to implement certain procedures that preserve for each of them the normal rights of general partners, e.g., the right to veto admission of new shareholders and other major actions. Minority shareholders, fearful of being frozen out in the future, may also want devices locking in some or all the other shareholders to a united course of action. Finally, since no ready market exists for shares in a closely held corporation, the shareholders may want to provide some method of liquidating their shares should they desire to leave the business.

Cumulative voting, to assure minority representation, and high voting and quorum requirements, to provide minority shareholders a form of veto power, are two devices available for use in the closely held corporation, which have already been discussed. Other more comprehensive devices are (1) the shareholder agreement, spelling out corporate policy and containing a voting agreement (in the form of a voting trust, voting pool or irrevocable proxy), and (2) the buy-sell agreement.

A. Shareholders' Agreement

Just as every partnership should have a partnership agreement, the shareholders of a closely held corporation should have a shareholders' agreement. Usually such an agreement is entered into by the prospective shareholders prior to incorporation, and then ratified by the corporation once it is formed.

One purpose of the shareholders' agreement is to have the participants bind themselves, either as shareholders or as directors, or both, to follow certain specified corporate policies. For example, the agreement may designate certain persons as officers, employ shareholders for various services and salaries, fix dividends and the issuance of shares, and place restrictions on the transfer of shares to limit the admission of new shareholders. The agreement may also contain covenants among some or all of the shareholders to vote for certain directors, pool their votes for directors, or grant each other irrevocable proxies for the election of specified directors. The agreement will generally contain the proposed capital structure of the corporation and the respective shareholder investments and security interests.

It is important also to provide for purchase rights or an option to purchase a shareholder's interest upon his/her death, extended disability, or withdrawal from the corporation. Shareholders' agreements might also contain provisions providing for arbitration of disputes between the shareholders should corporate decisions become deadlocked.

To the extent that the shareholders' agreement binds the parties to pursue a specified course of action, there is no problem with its validity since shareholders are always free to cast their votes as they wish, absent fraud or oppression by the majority. Indeed, as discussed below, New York law specifically validates such agreements.

Agreements which purport to bind the parties as directors, however, may run afoul of the general rule that directors may not delegate away the discretion to manage the corporation which is vested in them by statute. *See* BCL § 701, which provides that the business of a corporation shall be managed by its board of directors. Agreements which tie the hands or otherwise fetter the authority of present and future directors in advance in such fundamental matters as the selection of officers, payment of salaries or the issuance of dividends may be held to be void as against public policy. This may occur despite the fact that such agreements are normally entered into by the parties as shareholders. Case law in New York is not clear with respect to shareholders' agreements which bind the directors. Older cases stand for the general proposition that shareholder agreements that do not unduly restrict board powers are valid if signed by all the shareholders, while less than unanimous agreements are void. *Compare Clark v. Dodge*, 269 N.Y. 410, 199 N.E. 641 (1936) (upholding unanimous shareholders' agreement to retain a party as an officer at a salary based on one-quarter of firm's net income) *with Manson v. Curtis*, 223 N.Y. 313, 119 N.E. 559 (1918) (invalidating a less-than-unanimous agreement) *and McQuade v. Stoneham*, 263 N.Y 232, 189 N.E. 234 (1934) (also invalidating a less-than-unanimous agreement). More recently, the New York Court of Appeals indicated that less-than-unanimous agreements are of questionable legality. *See Triggs v. Triggs*, 46 N.Y.2d 305, 385 N.E.2d 1254, 413 N.Y.S.2d 352 (1978). Often the test of validity is the degree of intrusion upon director discretion. For example, agreements to employ certain persons as officers for life may be void as overly restrictive upon future boards, whereas shorter-term employment contracts may be permissible.

A shareholders' agreement in a closely held corporation may provide for unanimous consent of the shareholders for all action. Such provision is enforceable only if provided for in the certificate of incorporation. BCL § 616. However, it has been held that such a provision (even though not in the certificate of incorporation) may still be valid and binding upon the parties signing the agreement. *See Adler v. Svingos*, 80 A.D.2d 764, 436 N.Y.S.2d 719 (1981) and *Zion v. Kurtz*, 50 N.Y.2d 92, 428 N.Y.S.2d 199 (1980) (involving a Delaware corporation).

PRACTICE GUIDE

- *Shareholders' agreements are imperative for closely held corporations. A sample agreement is contained in the "Forms and Materials" section of this volume and practitioners are urged to review it.*

B. Voting Agreements

Fortunately for the closely held corporation planner, some of the uncertainty discussed previously can be avoided by resorting to Section

620(b) of the BCL. The statute states that "a provision in the certificate of incorporation otherwise prohibited by law as improperly restrictive of the discretion or powers of the board in its management of the corporate affairs shall nevertheless be valid" if authorized by all of the shareholders of a closely held corporation. Shares of such a corporation may subsequently be transferred only to persons who have received notice of the restrictive provisions, so that investors are aware they are buying into a corporation whose board has circumscribed powers. In effect, Section 620 permits shareholders in a closely held corporation to treat themselves as directors of the company and eliminate the traditional separation of powers between owners and managers. As a corollary, the shareholders in such a corporation must assume the same liability for managerial acts and omissions imposed on directors. BCL § 620(f).

The important aspect to note about Section 620(b) is that the passive-board provisions of such shareholders' agreements must be unanimously agreed to by all the shareholders. Since the New York Court of Appeals has not definitively interpreted Section 620(b), it is unclear to what extent the provisions affect less-than-unanimous shareholders' agreements. Unanimous agreements almost certainly remain valid even if not included in the certificate, since such agreements are not "otherwise prohibited" for purposes of Section 620(b).

While Section 620(b) of the BCL provides only an intracorporate device for shareholder management, Section 620(a) expressly validates outside agreements between two or more shareholders to vote their shares in a specified manner. Additionally, Section 620(a) validates the so-called "voting pool" arrangement whereby shareholders agree to pool their votes on certain matters such as the election of named directors. Although identical in substance to the irrevocable proxy, the voting pool device differs in that it is not self-executing. Its effectiveness depends upon a court's willingness to order specific performance when one of the parties refuses to vote as promised. Thus a pooling agreement should include as an enforcement mechanism an irrevocable proxy to a specified individual.

C. Buy-Sell Agreements

Like members of a partnership, the shareholders in a closely held corporation generally desire veto power over admission of new members to the firm. They may also wish to provide for a continuation of the firm's control structure in the event one of the shareholders dies or decides to sell his/her interest. Moreover, the individual shareholder would welcome an arrangement guaranteeing that there will be a willing buyer should (s)he die or decide to sell his/her shares, since the marketability of shares in a closely held corporation is usually limited and often difficult to value fairly. An appropriate means of meeting all these goals is through a buy-sell agreement between shareholders.

Buy-sell agreements usually provide that a shareholder must offer his/her shares to the corporation and/or the other shareholders before selling to an outsider, and that shares so offered must be purchased by the corporation or other shareholders at an agreed-upon price.

Buy-sell agreements alter the normal rule that shareholder interests in a corporation are freely transferable. The typical buy-sell arrangement is usually considered by New York courts to be a "reasonable" restraint or alienation and is therefore enforceable. "Consent" restrictions giving the corporation an absolute veto power over share transfers are normally void unless for limited duration. *See Rafe v. Hindin*, 29 A.D.2d 481, 288 N.Y.S.2d 662 (2d Dep't 1968), *aff'd*, 23 N.Y.2d 759, 296 N.Y.S.2d 955 (1968). Any restriction on the transfer of shares should be definite, clear and reasonable to ensure its enforceability by the courts. *See Allen v. Biltmore Tissue Corp.*, 2 N.Y.2d 534, 161 N.Y.S.2d 418 (1957).

Restrictions on transfer of a security are effective only if "noted conspicuously on the security." N.Y. U.C.C. § 8-204. The restriction need not be set forth in full but may simply be incorporated by reference. Therefore, reference to such provision must be noted conspicuously on the certificate, and the following form would be considered sufficient: "Transfer of this certificate is restricted pursuant to an agreement dated ____, a copy of which may be examined at the office of the corporation."

Determination of the price would be based upon the value of the shares, as determined in advance by agreement, which may be based upon the book value (as per the latest balance sheet) or in the shareholders' agreement itself. Other valuation methods are capitalization of earnings, fixed price, formulas relating to principles of sales or revenues, appraisal or arbitration (*see* discussion in Chapter 19). In any event, the valuation method should consist of more than a simple "agreement to agree."

The agreed price at which the estate of a deceased shareholder is obligated to offer the shares to the corporation may also be useful in establishing a basis for estate and inheritance tax purposes, since the Internal Revenue Service often will accept that price as the proper value of the shares—a subject dealt with more fully in Chapter 19.

In addition, the buy-sell agreement ordinarily provides for the manner of payment of the shares, and may provide in advance for a specific payment plan. Such plans may be funded by life insurance or may stretch over several years, so there is no immediate drain on the corporation's liquid assets.

When the buy-sell agreement is conditioned on the death of a shareholder, it is advisable for the parties to insure the shareholders' lives so that the corporation will have sufficient funds with which to purchase the shares from the estate. Insurance is considered extremely important because a purchase pursuant to a buy-sell agreement constitutes a repurchase of a corporation's own stock, which may only be made out of "surplus" as defined in Section 513 of the BCL. Without available insurance proceeds, the corporation might not have sufficient resources to make the purchase possible.

PRACTICE GUIDE

- *Intrashareholder voting agreements and buy-out provisions require careful analysis. A sample agreement containing both is included in the "Forms and Materials" section of this volume. Its terms must be carefully reviewed before its use.*

- *The method of determining an appropriate formula to satisfy the parties is also difficult to select. Several approaches are suggested in the sample agreement provided in the "Forms and Materials" section of this volume.*

D. The Irrevocable Proxy

A voting arrangement among the shareholders can provide further protection by the use of an irrevocable proxy issued to a person designated by or under an agreement pursuant to Section 620(a) of the BCL. Such an irrevocable proxy would be effective for the duration of the agreement. BCL § 609(f)(5). Section 620(a) makes possible the granting of mutually irrevocable proxies even without the coupling of any "interest" in the shares to be voted. *See* BCL § 609(f)(5).

E. The Voting Trust

A voting trust may also be employed as a control device. Section 621 of the BCL sanctions the use of voting trusts by which shareholders convey legal title to their shares to a trustee, while retaining equitable ownership and the right to receive dividends. In a manner similar to that of the proxy holder, the trustee may be given discretion to vote as he/she pleases, or may be instructed to vote in a certain way. Like the irrevocable proxy, the voting trust originally was subject to the judicial objection that it disenfranchised the owners of the corporation by "separating the vote from the stock."

Under Section 621 of the BCL, a voting trust is valid for up to ten years if the parties comply with the rather intricate registration and recordkeeping requirements contained in the statute. Section 621(a) validates voting trust agreements through which one or more shareholders transfer their shares to one or more voting trustees to confer upon the trustees the right to vote. The shares must be registered in the names of the voting trustees and a duplicate of the agreement must be filed in the office of the corporation. The trustees must keep proper books and records and must also keep a register containing the names of the holders of any outstanding voting trust certificates which must be open to inspection by the holders. Within six months prior to the date when the voting trust agreement expires, any shareholder who becomes a party to the extension agreement may renew it for additional periods, each period not to exceed ten years. BCL § 621(d).

Sometimes a voting trust agreement is drawn to give the trustees effective voting power only as to certain matters such as the election of directors. Such an agreement should then provide that when the trustees, as shareholders of record, receive notice of a meeting for any purpose other than for the election of directors, they should either give notice to the holders of voting trust certificates, call a meeting and vote the shares as directed by a majority vote of such holders, or vote individual shares in accordance with instructions received from the holders of the voting trust certificates. The trustees may be given or may be denied discretion to vote the shares for which they received no instructions. If matters such as these are not adequately covered by the agreement, the trustees may find themselves in a difficult legal position when action is necessary but they lack the authorization to take it. Provision should be made for a method of designation of successor trustees, the mechanics of the issue and transfer of voting trust certificates, the distribution of dividends as received and the distribution of the share certificates on termination of the trust.

The voting trust is a relatively cumbersome device. Unless it is relied upon as a means of implementing temporary creditor control, its real usefulness is probably limited to situations in which the shareholders are widely scattered and no large interest is willing to take the responsibility of providing the enterprise with management. In organizing a small corporation, efforts should be made to work out problems without resort to voting trust devices. It should be noted that if a voting trust is used, the corporation would not be able to elect Subchapter S status since ownership of shares by a trust would preclude Subchapter S tax treatment (*see* discussion in Chapter 3). There is little reason to use this device, since the same effect can be achieved with much less paperwork under a pooling agreement containing irrevocable proxies.

V. MINORITY SHAREHOLDERS WHO ARE EMPLOYEES

Even though a shareholder may also be an employee, the employment is at will (unless agreed to for a contractual term). Two recent Court of Appeals cases have held that there is no fiduciary duty owed to the at-will employee (even though also a minority shareholder); the duty a corporation owes to a minority shareholder is distinct from the duty it might owe the employee (who may also be a shareholder). *See Ingle v. Glamore Motor Sales*, 73 N.Y.2d 183, 538 N.Y.S.2d 771 (1989) (minority shareholder who contractually agrees to the repurchase of his shares upon termination of employment acquires no right against at-will discharge); *Gallagher v. Lambert*, 74 N.Y.2d 562, 549 N.Y.S.2d 945 (1989) (corporation prematurely terminated employment for sole purpose of acquiring employee's stock at a low price).

CHAPTER TEN

FEDERAL INCOME TAX ASPECTS OF CORPORATE-SHAREHOLDER RELATIONS

Michael A. Buxbaum

CORPORATE-SHAREHOLDER RELATIONS

I. INTRODUCTION AND OVERVIEW

By far the majority of tax problems counsel will encounter in representing a regular, or "C," corporation concern the ability of shareholders to "get money out" of the enterprise. Unlike an S corporation (or even a partnership), whose earnings are deemed taxable to the shareholders (or partners) regardless of whether they are distributed, a C corporation may retain earnings (once tax at the corporate level has been paid) without additional taxation, provided it does not run afoul of the accumulated earnings tax or the personal holding company tax. *See* discussion in Chapter 18. Any distribution by a C corporation to its shareholders may take any one of three basic forms: if the shareholder is an employee or independent contractor of the corporation, it may take the form of compensation for services rendered (e.g., salary, bonuses, incentive compensation); if the shareholder has loaned money or leased property to the corporation, it may take the form of interest or rental payments; any other distribution by a C corporation, whether of cash, property, stock or securities, is a distribution taxable under the "dividend" rules of Sections 301 and 316 of the Internal Revenue Code (the "Code"), which determine whether the distribution will generate ordinary income, capital gains, or will be treated merely as a return of the shareholder's capital.

If a payment of cash, property, stock or securities by a corporation to one or more shareholders is in exchange for a surrender by the shareholder of all or part of his/her stock in the corporation, such payment is referred to as a "redemption" and is taxable under Sections 302 and 317 of the Code. Generally, a "redemption" is taxable to the shareholder only to the extent that the amount of cash or the fair market value of property received by the shareholder in exchange for his/her stock exceeds his/her basis in the stock surrendered. The excess (i.e., the amount of consideration received by the shareholder allocable to basis) will be deemed as a return of his/her investment and accordingly not taxed.

This section summarizes briefly the rules governing the tax treatment of dividends and redemptions, and is divided into three parts: taxation of dividends under Sections 301 and 316; taxation of redemptions under Sections 302 and 317; and the tax treatment of two special transactions described in Sections 304 and 306 of the Code. Although much of the following material may be of decreased significance during the immediate future due to the elimination of the differential tax rates for capital gains and ordinary income, there are still important effects associated with the characterization of dividends, redemptions and other corporate payments as either capital gains or ordinary income (e.g., limited use of capital losses by individual and corporate distributees); and it is important to emphasize that, while the tax rates for ordinary income and capital gains may be the same after 1987, the distinction between the two for all other tax purposes has been preserved. In addition, it would be myopic not to foresee the possibility of an eventual restoration of some rate "spread" between capital gains and ordinary income.

II. TAX TREATMENT OF DIVIDENDS

A. General Rule

Under Section 316 of the Code, distributions by a corporation to its shareholders are presumed to be dividends unless it can be proved otherwise. Dividends are deemed to be ordinary income to the shareholders to the extent of a corporation's "earnings and profits" (this concept is a creature of the tax laws and is discussed below) accumulated since February 28, 1913 (the date on which the federal income tax became effective) and are taxed accordingly. If a dividend is paid out which is in excess of a corporation's "earnings and profits," the excess is deemed to be a return of the shareholder's basis in his/her stock and is not taxed up to the amount of his/her basis in his/her stock. If a dividend is paid out which is in excess of both a corporation's "earnings and profits" and a shareholder's basis in his/her stock, the excess is deemed a capital gain to the stockholder and is treated accordingly (i.e., taxed at the same rate as ordinary income but otherwise characterized as capital gains under the Code). I.R.C. § 301(c). Note, however, that while permitted by the tax laws, a dividend in excess of a corporation's "earn-

CORPORATE-SHAREHOLDER RELATIONS

ings and profits" may violate state corporate laws prohibiting the payment of dividends in excess of a corporation's earned surplus or capital surplus accounts. *See* discussion in Chapter 6.

B. "Earnings and Profits"

The concept of "earnings and profits" is a creature of the tax law and should not be confused with the accounting concepts of retained earnings, capital surplus, or earned surplus (although it bears some resemblance to these). "Earnings and profits" is the measure of the earnings of a corporation that are deemed available for distribution as taxable dividends to shareholders, and, unfortunately, is not given a more specific definition in the Code. Although Section 312 of the Code and regulations thereunder list several computations that must be made in determining a corporation's "earnings and profits," the Code section is far from exhaustive; and in determining a corporation's "earnings and profits," counsel (and the corporation's accountants) must make numerous judgments on the impact of specific transactions on the "earnings and profits" account. As a general rule, however, it may be said that if a transaction increases or decreases a corporation's capacity to pay a dividend, it should be added to or subtracted from "earnings and profits" accordingly.

Under Section 312 of the Code, in computing "earnings and profits," one begins with a corporation's taxable income for the year and makes numerous additions and subtractions. Among the additions required by Section 312 are tax-exempt income (such as interest on municipal bonds held by the corporation); proceeds of key-man life insurance policies; carryovers of charitable contributions deductions (i.e., deductions in excess of the 10 percent limitation of Section 170 of the Code which are carried forward to succeeding taxable years); percentage depletion; certain accelerated depreciation; deferred gain on installment sales; long-term contracts reported on the completed contract method (e.g., construction contracts); intangible drilling costs deducted currently under Section 263(c) of the Code; and mining exploration and development costs under Section 616(a) or 617 of the Code. Among the subtractions required by Section 312 are federal income taxes; losses on sales between related parties under Section 267 of the Code; payment of premiums on key-man life insurance policies; charitable contributions in excess of the 10 percent limitation under Section 170 of the Code; cost depletion; and depreciation calculated under the straight-line, units-of-production or machine-hours method. The rules of Section 312 and accompanying regulations are extremely complicated and should be reviewed by counsel in detail when determining a corporation's "earnings and profits" or reviewing an accountant's determination of "earnings and profits."

C. Earnings and Profits "Accumulated Since February 28, 1913"

"Earnings and profits" is an account that runs from year to year, such that if the "earnings and profits" accumulated in a given taxable year are insufficient to make a particular distribution, the corporation may look to any accumulated, i.e., unused, "earnings and profits" from prior years. For example, if a corporation has zero earnings in a particular tax year but has accumulated "earnings and profits" of $25,000 from prior years (going back to February 28, 1913, or the date of incorporation, if later), a distribution of up to $25,000 to its stockholders that year will be taxable as a dividend. If distributions are made out of both current "earnings and profits" and accumulated "earnings and profits" from prior years, the amount of the distribution allocated to each will be prorated. Take, for example, a corporation that has two equal shareholders. If in year 1 the corporation has $100,000 of current "earnings and profits" (assume there are no accumulated "earnings and profits" from prior years available for distribution) and distributes $50,000 in dividends during the year, the $50,000 excess carries over into the next taxable year. If in year 2 the same corporation has $100,000 in current "earnings and profits" (i.e., "earnings and profits" accruing in year 2) and distributes $150,000 during the year, the first $100,000 will be applied to reduce the $100,000 "earnings and profits" in year 2 to zero, and the balance ($50,000) will be applied to reduce the unused "earnings and profits" in year 1 from $50,000 to zero. Each shareholder will be deemed to have received two-thirds

CORPORATE-SHAREHOLDER RELATIONS 221

(i.e., 100,000/150,000) of his/her dividend from current "earnings and profits" and one-third (i.e., 50,000/150,000) from accumulated "earnings and profits."

What if there is a deficit in accumulated "earnings and profits" and a positive current "earnings and profits," or vice versa? If a corporation has a current "earnings and profits" balance of $50,000 and a deficit in accumulated "earnings and profits" of $10,000, a distribution to shareholders of up to $50,000 will still be taxable as a dividend. If, however, a corporation has a current "earnings and profits" deficit balance of $10,000, and a positive accumulated "earnings and profits" balance of $50,000, the two must be netted such that only $40,000 of the distribution will be taxable as a dividend. Because current "earnings and profits" must usually be estimated during a tax year, it is difficult to know precisely the amount which may be distributed. For this reason the Code and the Treasury Regulations provide that unless and until the parties can show otherwise, it is presumed that any distribution is covered by current "earnings and profits" and is therefore fully taxable. Should the facts prove otherwise after a shareholder files his/her individual return, an amendment will be allowed to make the appropriate adjustments. For example, a calendar-year taxpayer receives a dividend of $10,000 on December 31 from a corporation that uses a tax year ending July 31. The taxpayer reports the $10,000 as taxable income on his/her Form 1040 by April 15 the following year. If on July 31 of the following year the corporation determines that it could only have paid a $5,000 dividend to the taxpayer on December 31 the previous year because of an unanticipated business downturn in the first half of the following year (the last half of the corporation's tax year) that threw off the corporation's "earnings and profits" projections, the taxpayer will be permitted to file an amended return reporting the December 31 distribution as a $5,000 dividend and a $5,000 return of capital (assuming his/her basis in the stock exceeds $5,000).

D. Property Dividends

If a corporation distributes property, rather than cash, to a shareholder who is an individual, the amount of the dividend is equal to the fair market value of the property on the date of distribution, less the amount of any liability to which the property is subject immediately before and after the distribution, less any liability of the corporation assumed by the shareholder. The shareholder's basis in the distributed property is the fair market value of the property on the date of distribution. I.R.C. §§ 301(b)(2) and 301(c). If the distributed property has appreciated in value since its acquisition by the corporation, the corporation will recognize gain on the distribution in an amount equal to the difference between the corporation's basis in the property and the fair market value of the property on the date of distribution, as though the corporation had sold the property and distributed the proceeds instead. In contrast, if the distributed property at the time of distribution has a fair market value less than its adjusted basis in the hands of the corporation (e.g., due to obsolescence), the corporation will not recognize a loss upon distribution. If the distributed property is subject to a liability in excess of basis, the corporation recognizes gain in the amount of the difference. I.R.C. § 311. When making a property distribution, the corporation must increase its "earnings and profits" account by the amount of any gain recognized, and simultaneously reduce its "earnings and profits" account by the greater of the property's fair market value or adjusted basis less the amount of any liability on the property. I.R.C. § 312(b).

E. Stock Dividends

Generally, under Section 305 of the Code, a stock dividend paid out to stockholders in proportion to their current holdings of stock (i.e., pro rata) is not taxable, because the stockholder's ownership position has not changed by reason of the distribution. Conversely, dividends which are paid partly in stock and partly in cash or property, dividends which are payable either in stock or in property, stock dividends which "discriminate" between or among stockholders by increasing the proportionate interest of some at the expense of others (e.g., a distribution of preferred stock to some stockholders and common stock to others, a two-to-one-share distribution to some stockholders and a one-to-one-share distribution to others) are taxable to the stockholders under the rules discussed earlier. Distributions of convertible securities are generally taxable to stockholders unless the corporation can show that a disproportionate distribution will not result (not an easy task since conversions are not usually predictable). If a corporation has issued convertible securities and subsequently pays a stock dividend to the holders of the underlying common stock, it must make a corresponding adjustment in the conversion ratio of the convertible securities to avoid a disproportionate distribution. 26 C.F.R. § 1.305-3(d).

If a stock dividend is taxable, the corporation must reduce its current and accumulated "earnings and profits" accounts accordingly but does not do so if the stock dividend is not taxable. I.R.C. § 312(d)(1). If a stock dividend is not taxable, the stockholders' basis in their respective shares must be reallocated in accordance with the rules set forth in Section 307 of the Code. Otherwise their basis in the stock will be the fair market value of the property they are deemed to have received. To summarize, if a stock dividend is taxable, the required basis and "earnings and profits" adjustments will be the same as in a distribution of property.

F. Constructive Dividends

Generally, any payment by a corporation to one or more of its shareholders that conveys a measurable economic benefit to such shareholder(s) may be deemed a "constructive dividend" by the Internal Revenue Service regardless of the parties' intent. As the reader may imagine, there are numerous cases in this area, most of which involve attempts by shareholders of closely held corporations to withdraw or use money or property from the corporation in a manner that will be either deductible to the corporation or result in the nonrecognition of gain to the shareholders. The most common examples of situations that will give rise to "constructive dividend" determinations by the IRS are a sale of property by the corporation to shareholders at a price significantly less than fair market value; a rental of property by the corporation to shareholders at a rental significantly less than fair market rental value; a loan of money by a corporation to a shareholder at an interest rate significantly less than prevailing rates; payments of interest by a corporation to shareholders on debt that is reclassified as equity by the IRS (*see* discussion in Chapter 7); compensation paid to shareholder employees of the corporation that is deemed unreasonable by the IRS; and the payment by a corporation of an obligation owed by one of its shareholders to a third party. *See generally* 26 C.F.R. § 1.301-1 and examples cited therein. The consequences to a corporation or shareholder of receiving a constructive dividend are exactly the same as in a "regular" dividend: the required basis and "earnings and profits" adjustments must be made; and if the dividend exceeds current and accumulated "earnings and profits" of the corporation, the excess will constitute capital gain to the shareholder up to the amount of his/her basis in his/her stock in the corporation.

III. CORPORATE REDEMPTIONS OF STOCK

A. General Rule

Under Sections 302 and 317 of the Code, a redemption of stock is deemed an exchange of stock by a shareholder for cash or property delivered to the shareholder by the issuing corporation—a repurchase by a corporation of its own outstanding stock (a purchase by a corporation from a shareholder of stock in a corporation other than itself is emphatically not a redemption). Generally, a redemption is not taxable to the shareholder to the extent of the shareholder's basis in the stock surrendered to the corporation; this is deemed a return of the shareholder's capital. Any difference between the redemption price and the shareholder's basis is viewed as gain which the shareholder must recognize as such. If, however, the transaction fails to qualify as a "redemption" under Section 302 or 303 of the Code, the entire redemption price will be treated as a taxable dividend and taxed to the shareholder according to the dividend rules discussed in Parts I and II of this chapter.

Under Section 318 of the Code, in determining whether a corporate repurchase of stock qualifies as a "redemption" under Section 302 (but not Section 303), a shareholder must consider not only the stock held in his/her name but also stock held in the name(s) of any "related parties," including immediate family members (spouses, children, grandchildren and parents) and any entity (partnership, corporation, estate or trust) in which the shareholder or any "related party" has 50 percent or more ownership.

The Code recognizes five distinct types of redemptions: distributions which are "not essentially equivalent to a dividend" under Section 302(b)(1); distributions which are "substantially disproportionate" in terms of their effect on shareholders under Section 302(b)(2); distributions "in complete termination" of a shareholder's interest under Section 302(b)(3); distributions "in partial liquidation" of a corporation under Section 302(b)(4); and distributions to pay a shareholder's estate taxes under Section 303. The following paragraphs summarize the rules applicable to each type of redemption.

B. Distributions "Not Essentially Equivalent to a Dividend"

Generally, a distribution is "not essentially equivalent to a dividend" if, immediately after the distribution, there is a "meaningful reduction" of the shareholder's proportionate interest in the corporation. Although the facts and circumstances of each transaction may be expected to vary widely, courts have identified decreases in the redeeming shareholder's voting control under the corporate charter or governing law, or in the redeeming shareholder's rights to share in corporate earnings or assets upon liquidation, as significant "indicators" of a "meaningful reduction" for purposes of Section 302(b)(1). *See, e.g., Jack Paparo*, 71 T.C. 692 (1979) and *Grabowski Trust*, 58 T.C. 650 (1972). Counsel should keep in mind that the attribution rules of Section 318 apply to redemptions under Section 302(b)(1). Thus, if a husband and wife collectively own 100 percent of the stock of a corporation on an equal basis (i.e., the husband owns 50 percent and the wife owns 50 percent), and the corporation redeems 10 percent of the husband's shares (or 5 percent of the corporation), the wife's stock will be attributed to the husband, such that no "meaningful reduction" in the husband's ownership will be found (i.e., both before and after the "redemption" the husband constructively owns 100 percent of the corporation), and the transaction will consequently be taxed as a dividend.

If an alleged "redemption" is treated by the IRS as a dividend, the "redeeming" shareholder's basis in the stock surrendered to the corporation is attached to his/her remaining stock (including stock which he/she owns constructively under the attribution rules). For example, if in the preceding example the husband had owned 5 percent of the corporation's stock, the wife had owned 95 percent, and the corporation had "redeemed" all of the husband's 5 percent interest but none of the wife's, the wife's basis in her remaining shares would increase by her husband's basis in the 5 percent surrendered to the corporation.

C. "Substantially Disproportionate" Redemptions

To qualify as a redemption under Section 302(b)(2) of the Code, a transaction must satisfy two requirements: immediately after the distribution, the redeeming shareholder must own less than 80 percent of his/her interest in the corporation immediately prior to the distribution; and immediately after the distribution, the redeeming shareholder must own, in the aggregate, less than 50 percent of the total combined voting power of all classes of the corporation's stock which are entitled to vote. Again, counsel should keep in mind the application of the attribution rules of Section 318.

D. "Complete Termination" Redemptions

Since the termination of all of a shareholder's interest in a corporation clearly satisfies the requirements of a "substantially disproportionate" redemption under Section 302(b)(2), counsel may wonder why the Code contains a separate provision for complete terminations. The reason is that, unlike a Section 302(b)(2) redemption, the attribution rules of Section 318 do not apply to a "complete termination" under Section 302(b)(3) if (1) immediately after the redemption and for a period of ten years thereafter, the redeeming shareholder has no interest in the corporation as shareholder, officer, director or employee (a shareholder may remain as a creditor to the corporation and may reacquire an interest in the corporation during the ten-year period by bequest or inheritance but not otherwise); and (2) the redeeming shareholder files with the IRS, attached to his/her tax return for the year in which the redemption occurred, an agreement to notify the IRS of any reacquisition of an interest in the corporation during the ten-year period. As will be discussed further below, to the extent that a shareholder's estate is not able to redeem all of the deceased shareholder's shares under Section 303 of the Code, the excess may be redeemable if the estate complies with the two-prong requirements of Section 302(b)(3).

E. "Partial Liquidation" Redemptions

Under Section 302(b)(4) of the Code, redemption treatment is available if a noncorporate shareholder redeems shares, whether either (1) the distribution is "not essentially equivalent to a dividend" or (2) the distribution is "pursuant to the termination of an active business" (i.e., the dissolution and liquidation of a closely held corporation). I.R.C. § 302(e). In the latter case, the distribution must be made within the taxable year in which the plan of liquidation is adopted (*see* discussion in Chapter 17) or within the immediately following year. In the former case, however, lies a true trap for the unwary, in that the meaning of "not essentially equivalent to a dividend" is completely different under Section 302(e) than it is for purposes of Section 302(b)(1), because Section 302(e) has been engrafted into Section 302 from a completely different part of the Code (former Section 346). Under Section 302(e), a transaction is "not essentially equivalent to a dividend" only if it constitutes a genuine contraction of the redeeming corporation's business. *See Joseph W. Imler*, 11 T.C. 836 (1948).

Determining whether a redemption entails a genuine contraction of the redeeming corporation's business is difficult, to say the least, is a matter of substantial case law, and should not be undertaken by counsel without the assistance of sophisticated tax counsel. If, however, a corporation maintains two or more clearly distinguishable and separately identifiable businesses, each of which has been in existence for more than five years, and terminates one while continuing the others, the proceeds from the sale of the one business may be distributed to shareholders in a Section 302(b)(4) redemption as long as the sold business was not acquired by the redeeming corporation in a taxable transaction (*see* discussion in Chapter 12) within the five-year period preceding the redemption. For example, if a corporation has two factories, one in Albany (manufacturing steel girders) and the other in Syracuse (weaving wool sweaters), has operated each business for a period of at least five years and did not acquire either of them in a taxable acquisition during that five-year period, and if the corporation after such five-year period sells the Syracuse plant to third parties in a taxable or tax-free transaction (*see* discussion in Chapter 12), the corporation may distribute the proceeds of the sale to shareholders in a Section 302(b)(4) redemption.

F. "Death Tax" Redemptions

Section 303 of the Code is a special provision which enables estates of deceased shareholders to more easily liquidate shares that comprise a significant portion of the estate's assets. Under this section, a corporation may repurchase shares of a deceased shareholder from his/her estate in a redemption, regardless of whether any of the conditions and qualifications set forth in Section 302(b) would apply, where the value of the stock to be redeemed is in excess of 35 percent of the decedent's "adjusted gross estate" for federal estate tax purposes. If a decedent owned stock in two or more corporations, none of which, in and of itself, was a sufficiently large holding itself to meet the 35 percent requirement, the several holdings may be aggregated to meet the 35 percent requirement, but only if 20 percent or more of the value of the stock in each corporation held by the decedent at death is includable in the estate's "gross income" for tax purposes. I.R.C. § 303(b)(2)(B). The executor of an estate may redeem under Section 303 only so much stock as may be used to pay all estate, inheritance, legacy and succession taxes imposed on the estate plus the amount of any and all funeral and administration expenses which are deductible by the estate. I.R.C. § 303(a). Because capital assets held by a decedent at death are accorded a "step-up" in basis by operation of Section 1014 of the Code, the estate will not recognize gain or loss on the assets transferred to it by the corporation in a Section 303 redemption. In order to qualify under

Section 303, however, the redemption must be made within 90 days after the expiration of the statute of limitations for the assessment of the federal estate tax. I.R.C. § 303(b)(1).

Thus, for example, assume a decedent shareholder has an adjusted gross estate of $800,000, with death taxes and deductible estate expenses totalling $200,000, and that at the time of death the decedent owned $400,000 worth of stock in a closely held corporation, which he acquired for $50,000 upon incorporation many years ago. Because the value of the decedent's stock ($400,000) is greater than 35 percent of the adjusted gross estate of the decedent ($800,000), Section 303 treatment is available and the executor of the estate will be able to redeem $200,000 worth of the stock tax-free under Section 303. The estate will not recognize any gain or loss upon this redemption. Should the executor wish to redeem the remaining $200,000 worth of the decedent's stock, however, he/she will not be able to do so under Section 303 but will instead have to resort to one of the other redemption provisions of Section 302(b) (most likely the "complete termination" provisions of Section 302(b)(3) in this case). This latter redemption will be tax-free to the extent of the decedent's basis in the stock (in this case $50,000), and the estate will recognize gain in the amount of $150,000 ($200,000 minus $50,000); and as part of the latter redemption, both the estate and all of the estate's beneficiaries will have to execute the agreement required by Section 302(b)(3) (i.e., that they will not reacquire an interest in the corporation for ten years).

Unfortunately, as a result of the Tax Reform Act of 1986, if as part of a Section 303 redemption the corporation transfers appreciated property to the decedent shareholder's estate, the corporation must recognize gain in an amount equal to the difference between the fair market value of the property at the time of transfer and the adjusted basis of the property.

G. "Earnings and Profits" Adjustments for Stock Redemptions

Under Section 312(n)(7) of the Code, a corporation which redeems its stock must reduce its current and accumulated "earnings and profits" accounts in an amount not in excess of that portion of "earnings and profits" equal to the percentage of the corporation's outstanding stock being redeemed. For example, assume a corporation has 1,000 shares of stock outstanding and redeems 500 shares for $100,000 at a time when it has a capital account balance of $80,000 and current "earnings and profits" of $100,000. "Earnings and profits" would be reduced by $50,000 ($100,000 times 500/1000, or 50 percent), and the balance of the redemption price ($50,000) would be deducted from the capital account.

IV. TWO SPECIAL SITUATIONS: SECTIONS 304 AND 306

A. Introduction

Generally, if a purported redemption of corporate stock does not fall within one of the situations described in Section 302(b) or 303 of the Code, it will be treated as a dividend to the extent of current and accumulated "earnings and profits." Two sections of the Code—Sections 304 and 306—address two specific instances whereby shareholders attempt to "disguise" dividend distributions as qualifying redemptions, and provide that, notwithstanding technical compliance with the redemption provisions, such transactions will be deemed to be dividend distributions. It is unlikely, however, that counsel will encounter problems under these sections, since by eliminating the favorable tax rates on capital gains that had prevailed prior to the Tax Reform Act of 1986, Congress has eliminated the principal economic incentive for these maneuvers.

B. "Preferred Stock Bailouts" under Section 306

A "preferred stock bailout" generally works as follows: a corporation pays out a nontaxable stock dividend consisting of nonvoting preferred stock; then the shareholder(s) assigns to the preferred stock a portion of the basis of the common stock as required under Section 307(a) of the Code; then the shareholder sells the preferred stock to a third party at fair market value, reaping a capital gain (either short-term or long-term depending on the length of time the original shareholder

CORPORATE-SHAREHOLDER RELATIONS

held the preferred stock) in the process; and then the third party (preferably someone who is unrelated to the corporation or any of the shareholders but who is "in on the action"), after holding the preferred stock for a significant amount of time (at least six months), redeems the preferred stock at a premium under circumstances that would fit one of the Section 302(b) criteria. The original shareholder(s) by this mechanism was (prior to the adoption of Section 306) able to receive a distribution of corporate earnings at capital gain rates, while the third party was compensated for its efforts by the premium paid upon the redemption of the preferred stock. The underlying common stock is unaffected by these transactions.

Section 306 undoes the favorable tax consequences of the "preferred stock bailout" maneuver by providing that upon the sale of the preferred stock to a third party, a shareholder will reap ordinary income to the extent that the fair market value of the preferred stock on the date of the stock dividend would have been a taxable dividend if the corporation had distributed cash instead of preferred stock. The ordinary income to the shareholder would not, however, be deemed a dividend, such that the corporation's "earnings and profits" account would not be adjusted by reason thereof. I.R.C. § 306(a)(1); 26 C.F.R. § 1.306-1(b)(1). If the shareholder redeems the preferred stock rather than transferring it to a third party, he/she will reap dividend income to the extent of the corporation's "earnings and profits" on the date of the redemption. I.R.C. § 306(a)(2).

Section 306 is not merely of historical interest, however. By defining broadly the type of stock to which the above unfavorable tax consequences may apply as "Section 306 Stock," this section must be closely watched in any transaction involving preferred stock whose holders also hold common stock (i.e., a taxable or tax-free reorganization described in Chapter 12). Section 306 applies to preferred stock that (1) is received in a nontaxable stock dividend (but only if the corporation has "earnings and profits" on the date of distribution), (2) is received in a tax-free reorganization under Section 355 or 368 of the Code if the effect of the transaction is substantially the same as the receipt of a stock dividend, (3) is received in a tax-free reorganization under Section 355 or 368 of the Code in exchange for Section 306 Stock, or (4) has a basis determined by reference to the basis of Section 306 Stock (e.g., a "substitute basis" upon a tax-free exchange for Section 306 Stock in a transaction other than a tax-free reorganization). In any of the following situations, preferred stock is deemed not to constitute "Section 306 Stock": if a shareholder sells his/her entire interest (i.e., both common and preferred) to an unrelated third party (i.e., someone other than immediate family members or others described in Section 318); if a shareholder redeems his/her entire interest (i.e., both common and preferred) under Section 302(b)(3) (complete termination) or 302(b)(4) (qualified partial liquidation) of the Code; if a shareholder sells or otherwise disposes of stock in a manner that does not cause recognition of gain or loss; or if the transfer was not in furtherance of a plan "having as one of its principal purposes the avoidance of the Federal income tax." I.R.C. § 306(b); 26 C.F.R. § 1.306-2(b)(3).

C. Redemptions through Related Corporations under Section 304 of the Code

Section 304 requires that a transfer to corporation A of stock in corporation B by a shareholder who owns a controlling interest in both corporations (or who owns a controlling interest in a corporation which controls both corporations), and who receives in return cash or property (but not stock) of corporation A, must comply with one of the redemption provisions in Sections 302(b) and 303 of the Code or else it will be deemed a taxable dividend. Control is defined for purposes of Section 304 as the ownership of at least 50 percent of the total combined voting power of all classes of stock entitled to vote, or at least 50 percent in value of all classes of stock outstanding. Finally, in determining whether a shareholder "controls" both corporations, the attribution rules of Section 318 of the Code must be taken into account. I.R.C. § 304(c)(2). For example, a shareholder (S) owns 30 percent of corporation X, which in turn owns 100 percent of the stock of each of corporations Y and Z. S's wife owns 50 percent of corporation X, while S's son and daughter each own 10 percent of corporation X. Even though S owns less than 50 percent of corporation X, by application of the attribution

CORPORATE-SHAREHOLDER RELATIONS

rules of Section 318 of the Code he would be deemed to constructively own 100 percent of corporation X. Consequently, a transfer by S to corporation Y of 100 shares of corporation Z would have to comply with one of the provisions of Section 302(b) or 303 of the Code or else it will be deemed a taxable dividend to S.

CHAPTER ELEVEN

BUYING AND SELLING THE SMALL BUSINESS CORPORATION

Cornelius S. Van Rees

I. INTRODUCTION AND OVERVIEW

The reader who wishes to learn the subtleties of buying and selling a small business corporation should read Chapter 13 of this volume, which stresses the importance of learning why the buyer wants to buy and the seller wants to sell. The points are basic and should not be forgotten in any small, or for that matter large, transaction. These include special concerns relating to a closely held corporation and particularly a lack of accurate records, informality, inventory cushions or other hidden assets, special attention to "perks" and executive salary levels, environmental liabilities, the extent of warranties, the necessity for a purchase price holdback or escrow account, the importance of personal relationships, and generally the search for overvalued assets and hidden expenses and liabilities.

The frequent need to obtain the help of others, such as tax experts, accountants and bankers, should be recognized from the beginning because completing most acquisitions or sales requires knowledge of many legal disciplines. Chapter 13's emphasis on the need to achieve the expected for your client, to protect against the unexpected through indemnification, covenants and warranties, escrows, deferred purchase price, verification of net worth and constant checking of facts, and the need for counsel to spend time and energy to equip himself/herself responsibly are worth repeating.

In the end, experience is the best teacher, and it is hoped that what follows will provide background to enhance that experience.

The purchase and sale of a business has many of the elements of an adventure: there are unknown roads and very often uncertainty, complexity and loss of faith in the intentions of the other side. On many points no final "truth" may be found. Questioning everything as it is presented by the client and others is a good idea. The enterprise is fragile, and courtship and divorce are analogies not lacking in reality. As in real life there is no necessary order of events flowing seriatim to the goal. Investigation, negotiation and drafting will continue at the same time.

II. BACKGROUND CONSIDERATIONS

A. Many Fields

A list of the fields of law often encountered in the purchase and sale of a business looks somewhat like parts of a law school catalog and includes corporate, tax, finance, litigation, real estate, environmental, bankruptcy, personal property, employment, ERISA, labor, trust and estate, security, Uniform Commercial Code, patent, trademark, insurance, contract, agency, distributorship, antitrust, administrative and regulatory law, accounting and more. Many of these will occur in even a small and apparently simple transaction. Although such a list seems intimidating, its purpose here is to paint a picture and heighten awareness of what to look for and expect.

B. Many Players

Another aspect of the purchase and sale of a business is that there are often many people involved, including not only buyers, sellers and lawyers, but also accountants, business brokers, insurance brokers, actuaries, engineers, appraisers, marketing and public relations firms, employees, bankers, investment bankers, creditors, landlords, union officials, and always tax experts who may be either lawyers or accountants. An early and confidential meeting with bankers or some other source of funds to finance part of the purchase may be not only necessary but helpful in structuring the transaction and sometimes in promoting a harder, realistic view of the acquisition proposal. The requirements of the finance source may be paramount in setting terms and conditions of sale. While this chapter does not attempt to cover aspects of acquisitions involving publicly owned companies and the SEC, it is often the case that even small privately held businesses have relationships with various state and federal tax departments, license bureaus, city agencies, the patent office, the agencies concerned with Equal Employment Opportunity ("EEO"), the Occupational Safety and Health Act ("OSHA") and others. Although found more often in the public company situation, antitrust laws, the Justice Department, the Federal Reserve Bank and the Federal Trade Commission ("FTC") are sometimes involved.

C. The Lawyer and the "Team"

The Code of Professional Responsibility in the state of New York dictates that a lawyer should represent his client competently, that he should strive to become and remain proficient in his practice, and that he should accept employment only in matters which he is or intends to become competent to handle. Recognizing this, and that any given acquisition or sale requires knowledge of many legal disciplines, the first thing the lawyer should do is create a "team." The lawyer may frequently be the "team" captain, in the sense that he deploys his troops and allocates jobs. A frequently used starting point is to prepare and distribute a working group list with names, addresses, telephone and facsimile numbers and possibly job allocations for your "team," including people within both the buyer and the seller. On this list will be accountants, businesspeople, bankers, tax experts, lawyers and others.

It is often said that you should volunteer to draft first, and this is true. Also, you should avoid dual capacity, such as being lawyer and a finder. The lawyer should remember to observe the corporate niceties, obtaining board and shareholder approval, proper legal opinions and backup certificates. The client may often appear not to want to be involved in the nitty-gritty details, but the lawyer should try to involve the client to the maximum extent possible and not be intimidated by client insensibility to the amount or complexity of the work involved. Giving in to arbitrary and impossible time limits with resulting loss of protection to the client will not be beneficial in the long run. The interplay of disciplines dictates expenditure of significant time and energy for counsel to equip himself/herself responsibly. To do this a lawyer must do more than draft. Within the craft of buying and selling a business there are interrelated business and legal issues not within the everyday experience of the client. Ways and means exist for handling most of these problems, but time is a necessary ingredient.

D. Why?

Why the sale, why the purchase? The lawyer should keep this question in his/her mind to the very end. The truth is often elusive and may never be known for sure. In any case, the answer pervades all investigation and negotiation and will help the lawyer do his job, i.e., get the client the deal he thinks he wants. A buyer is often looking for diversification, a strategic fit, augmentation of markets or personnel, the purchase of earnings or just a bargain. A seller's reasons are normally retirement, realization of profit at a point when the business is peaking, financing needs, tax problems, diversification, development costs, concern about competitive disadvantage, internal strife or avoidance of future because of the perception of dark clouds on a business horizon. Sometimes there are hidden liabilities. Ideas about synergy may not be well grounded. Two plus two may not exceed four. The vast majority of business acquisitions that do not work out are not the result of legal problems but of wishful thinking, failure to give the facts a hard look, miscalculations about markets, customers, personnel, efficiencies of combination, costs and similar business factors. While the lawyer is not and should not wear a business hat to decide these things, he may be able to get his client to think more about them. This may occur near the beginning of the transaction, or often during the deal the lawyer may hear various things which he should immediately relate to the client. The more realistic the perceptions are, the better is the documentation and the substance of the closed deal.

E. Valuation Considerations

There is no single rule for negotiation of price, but the lawyer may be able to help a client think. The IRS provides some guidance as to how it values corporations or stock for tax purposes. Reference here should be made to Rev. Rul. 59-60 (Valuation of Stocks and Bonds), Rev. Rule 83-120, Rev. Proc. 79-24, and CCH Master Tax Guide 1695 and 1697, which all concern valuation rules and fair market value; a short summary of basic valuation procedures appears in Chapter 12. The IRS factors are basically the nature and history of the business, the economic outlook in general and particularly the value and financial condition of the business, earning capacity, dividend-paying capacity, goodwill and other intangible values, sales of similar stock or assets, size of block to be valued, and market price for "comparable" publicly held companies engaged in the same or similar lines of business.

Paying too much for a business may come back to haunt a purchaser, i.e., too high a cost cannot be sustained by the business income as witnessed by the rash of leveraged takeover failures. Book value is a favorite in the sale of a small business, but the lawyer must be careful. Depreciation may not reflect actual wear and tear, while intangibles such as favorable leases and patents may not be reflected at all. Actual fair market values of property should be considered, including in particular the real value of inventory and the value of accounts receivable and reserves. The buyer should consider eliminating intangibles such as goodwill and revaluing investments in subsidiaries.

Earning power may be important, especially in the case of an operating company (as opposed to one that primarily invests passively in assets), and capitalization of earnings is an exercise that should be gone through. How many dollars of capital must be invested in order to earn one dollar? Return on investment should be calculated for the past five years. Calculation of current and past earnings should include adjustment for creative or aggressive accounting and fringe benefits and should remove extraordinary and nonrecurring items. Projections may be more important than historical results when future earning capacity has to be adjusted for such factors as new management and consolidation of facilities, but these should be reviewed and reviewed again for realism. If the lawyer can make his client and the client's accountant do these things realistically, a major service will have been performed. Pro forma earnings and expense statements for the next few years should be prepared including the cost of purchasing the business, brokerage fees, covenants not to compete and the cost of new equipment and programs. The buyer should remember that the value of a small business may be substantially depressed by the loss of a principal manager. Negotiation of mutually satisfactory employment, consulting and other similar contracts may appear to take an undue amount of time in the acquisition process but is vital in the end. Liquidation value of the seller's assets is often another worthwhile facet to the valuation question. Subjective considerations, such as the buyer's desire to enter a new or expanded market and the seller's desire to get out of a business, can be major factors but hard to quantify. Valuation opinions of accountants, appraisers, bankers and others, such as American Appraisal Associates, Inc., or Standard Research Consultants, may be useful. Future capital needs are an often neglected subject, and these should be projected along with cash flows and the establishment of other long-range plans. Not infrequently it will be useful to establish a price to be adjusted on the basis of future performance.

F. Brokerage Agreement

The lawyer should be alert to broker-finder problems, since the time to settle them is at the beginning. The lawyer should look into this and remember the statute of frauds, N.Y. Gen. Oblig. Law § 5-701(10), which provides that a contract to pay compensation for negotiating the purchase or sale of a business is void if not in writing, unless it applies to a lawyer or licensed real estate or salesperson.

A broker may approach a buyer and say, "I know that XYZ is for sale. Are you interested?" The buyer might be. If counsel is consulted by the buyer, he should ask whether the broker has authority to offer XYZ. If the broker says yes, counsel should ask for a copy of written authority, which may say seller will pay the broker upon completion or that the broker must collect from buyer. Even if the broker has no written evidence, the buyer may want to use the broker. To avoid uncertainty, counsel should reduce the arrangement to a writing covering the major terms and avoid implied contracts.

Questions for discussion are: Whose agent is the broker, i.e., who pays him? What are the terms and conditions to be fulfilled? What will the amount of the commission be? When will the commission be earned? How long will the broker's contract remain in effect?

The broker may produce a letter from seller saying that the broker is employed to sell the seller in a "tax-free" reorganization at a price

BUYING AND SELLING THE SMALL BUSINESS

satisfactory to the seller, $30,000 commission due on sale payable by seller, no commission payable if transaction not consummated for any reason, broker warrants no other arrangements, broker agreement not to seek commission from buyer and termination in 180 days.

A potential buyer might ask a broker to sign a standard "Conditions of Submission" document saying buyer will only accept submissions conforming to the following conditions: Buyer must see a true and correct copy of the agreement between broker and seller containing certain standard provisions as to responsibility for payment, conditions on which due, term and exclusivity; buyer to assume no obligation to do more than consider submission (if warranted in buyer's sole discretion) and evidence of seller's interest or lack thereof; buyer not to return financials unless otherwise agreed; buyer agrees to treat submission with care but does not warrant to hold submission in confidence; no submissions to be accepted without an asking price and buyer to be provided with complete detailed operating statements, balance sheets, sales and product data, reasons for selling and other reasonable information.

G. Timetable

As soon as possible after an acquisition appears likely, in addition to a working group list, it is a good idea to prepare a timetable. Certain conditions will require varying time allowances, such as:

1. stockholder and board of director meetings and state law notice requirements;
2. administrative rulings (IRS, FTC, license requirements under state or local law);
3. completion of review of seller's financials and other due diligence checks by buyer and accountants;
4. review of seller's patents;
5. real estate titles, abstracts, title opinions, title insurance, etc;
6. appraisals;
7. financing of the purchase price;

8. other.

Such a timetable may be inaccurate and incomplete in the beginning, but it is often worthwhile nonetheless to prepare one and distribute it to the working group or "team" if for no other reason than to instill some sense of order in the process. As facts become known, the timetable can always be modified and redistributed.

H. "Purchase" and "Pooling of Interest" Accounting for Business Combinations

The purchase and sale of a business are normally accounted for either by the "purchase" method or the "pooling of interest" method. Although this is an accounting concept and has no effect on cash position, it may have a substantial effect on future book earnings of a buyer. It is not the place of this chapter to describe these, except to alert the lawyer to the two methods and comment that qualified accounting advice should be sought promptly. Generally speaking, in most cases an acquisition is accounted for as a "purchase," and if the purchase price exceeds book value, the excess is set up as goodwill and amortized. If "pooling of interest" accounting is used, respective book values of the buyer and seller, liabilities and surpluses, etc., are added together (pooled) and net earnings are not reduced by any goodwill amortization. The rules allowing pooling of interest accounting are very strictly construed. Generally there can only be a pooling of interest if there is a business combination of two or more corporations in which the holders of substantially all of the ownership interests of the constituent corporations become the owners of a single corporation. Accordingly, pooling is primarily limited to a case where the buyer pays with stock. There must also be a continuation of the buyer's and seller's business and continuity of management.

I. Employee Benefits and Relations

This chapter is not the place for details on employee benefits and relations problems, which are discussed in detail in Chapters 6 and 18, respectively, but as soon as possible the pension, profit-sharing, stock option, health insurance, and other fringe benefit plans of both the buyer and the seller should be carefully reviewed. These plans can involve grave business, legal and financial problems, substantial assets and liabilities, and always involve human elements. Workmen's compensation can be a factor if backward assessment of premiums is possible. There are minimum IRS requirements for transfers in acquisitions. IRC § 414(a)(1). "Underfunding" of past service credit liabilities is an obvious problem, but there are many more. This is the land of actuaries and ERISA experts: termination pay; announcements to employees, customers, creditors and others; withdrawal of the seller from a multi-employer pension fund and numerous similar factors may all be present.

J. Assignability of Contracts and Rights

Franchises, licenses, favorable leases, loan agreements, new order contracts, supply contracts, patents, trademarks and numerous other key documents must all be reviewed to see how they will be affected by the proposed purchase and sale of the business. Most often this will be more relevant where the seller is selling assets rather than stock; however, transferability of stock may be limited by some arrangements, such as negative covenants in a loan agreement or by the "buy-sell" provisions in a shareholder agreement (these are discussed in Chapter 9).

K. Forms and Checklists

There are numerous sources for forms and checklists. An early walk through both will do much to alert the lawyer to problems and solutions. A list of books on corporate law and practice, many of which include forms and checklists for business combinations, appears as Chapter 21. A sample checklist is also included in the "Forms and Materials" section of this volume.

Early on the lawyer should talk with the client about as many of these points as is possible and despite any impatience encountered. In random order, subjects might include confidentiality agreements; adequacy of seller's source of supply; seller's relationship with employees; seller's relationship with principal customers; adequacy of seller's insurance;

seller's business operation; laws and regulations applicable to the particular type of business involved; description of property to be purchased; noncompetition agreements; escrow and indemnity needs; security for purchase price; access to information and cooperation; products; competition; ability and need to combine functions with existing business (personnel, accounting and facilities); unwanted assets; unwanted liabilities; role of key personnel; retention of employees; employment contracts; patents; franchises; trademarks and trade names; title to assets and identity of all encumbrances; disclosure of existing contracts; disclosure of all claims, suits and other litigation; contingent liabilities under ERISA; accuracy and completeness of audited and unaudited financial statements; adverse changes since last balance sheet date; payment of taxes and filing of tax returns; absence of conflicts with existing agreements; collectibility of accounts; shareholders' agreements; deeds and other documents of title; leases; license agreements; franchise agreements; mortgages; security agreements; UCC filings; creditor agreements and restrictive covenants; union contracts; labor disputes; retirement plans; brokers' agreements; stock ownership and much more.

It sometimes seems as though the client thinks his lawyer will know about all of these things almost by osmosis and they can all be discovered one way or another, but the best source is often your own client who is probably thoroughly familiar with the particular business and knowledgeable about the problems. It is, after all, the client's business.

L. Bulk Transfer Considerations

Section 6-104(1) of the New York Uniform Commercial Code is aimed at preventing fraud on the seller's creditors and calls for a list of existing creditors, a schedule of property transferred, preservation of the list and notice to creditors. Compliance is frequently handled by indemnity from the seller. Under the New York Tax Law relating to bulk sales, the purchaser should notify the Tax Commission ten days prior to the sale. N.Y. Tax Law § 1141(c). Failure to do this renders the buyer liable for any sales taxes the seller owes the State of New York and applies whether the buyer knows that the seller owes the taxes or not.

Failure to notify the Tax Commission results in a statutory lien in favor of the state. The Tax Commission must notify the buyer of taxes owing within 90 days of receipt of notice or the buyer is discharged. Section 6901 of the Internal Revenue Code regarding bulk sales is not unlike Section 1141 of the New York Tax Law and should be carefully heeded.

III. INITIAL LEGAL CONSIDERATIONS

A. General

A brief mental review of the effect which the proposed transaction may have upon various groups, such as creditors, customers, employees, shareholders, directors and government regulatory agencies will serve to focus the lawyer's thinking on the relevant legal problems and facilitate their solution.

B. Unintended Assumption of Liabilities

The buyer in an asset acquisition is generally thought to be protected from preacquisition business liabilities of the seller which are not expressly assumed, if the parties comply with bulk sales laws. Caution about the sedative effect of this thought is in order, because liabilities other than those covered by this general rule of corporate law are possible, such as transferee tax liability, the rights of secured creditors to liens on property purchased, fraudulent conveyances, unmatured warranty and product liability claims, service commitments, liabilities for discharge of hazardous waste into the environment and other contingent liabilities.

Payment of cash to the seller corporation (as opposed to payment directly to stockholders) is in any case a more assured route than buying assets of a going business for stock, which may result in the assumption of undisclosed liabilities by operation of law. Courts have applied a number of theories to hold the buyer who pays with stock liable for obligations not expressly assumed. One is the trust fund theory, which applies primarily in situations where stock of the buyer is distributed to shareholders of the seller. Another theory, that the purchase of assets for stock is in effect a merger, would lead to the same result, and still another theory may be nothing more than that the state should protect creditors of corporations organized under its laws. Indemnification agreements backed with security and withheld purchase price and escrow agreements can be useful in reaching solutions here. Another problem area is "product line" successor liability in tort actions. *Griggs v. Capital Machine Works, Inc.*, 690 S.W.2d 287 (Tex. Ct. of App., 1985). Areas where liability may suddenly be found to exist include pension liabilities, union obligations, and not least, a 10 percent New York State real estate tax imposed on gains (measured by the excess of consideration for real estate over original purchase price) from the transfer of real property (including acquisition of a controlling interest in entities with an interest in New York real property) which applies where the consideration for property is $1,000,000 or more. N.Y. Tax Law Art. 31-B.

The buyer will want representations and warranties that the ownership and use of any real property in the conduct of the business are in compliance with the environmental requirements of applicable federal, state and local statutes, laws, regulations and rules, including the Clean Air Act, the Clean Water Act, the Federal Water Pollution Control Act of 1972, the Resource Conservation and Recovery Act of 1976, the Comprehensive Environmental Response, Compensation and Liability Act of 1980 ("CERCLA") and the Toxic Substances Control Act. Representations will also cover release of hazardous substances, removal thereof, the existence and good standing of all required environmental permits such as National Pollutant Discharge Elimination System ("NPDES") permits, air quality permits, permits for storage and transportation of hazardous wastes and similar representations. Liabilities under some of these laws follow the land and business. The buyer and seller may both hire experts to do tests which may show a possible need for very expensive remedial action now or in the future. Dealing with these problems in a manner satisfactory to buyer and seller can be difficult. As opposed to seller liability to the government and third parties, the liability of a seller to a buyer under the representations and the warranties may be dealt with by limiting it to a fixed time period and a specific escrow amount taken from the purchase price.

C. Antitrust Considerations

This chapter does not cover antitrust considerations under the Clayton Act, Sherman Act, Federal Trade Commission Act, and similar laws; however, where the price is large enough, thought should be given to the Hart-Scott-Rodino Antitrust Improvements Act, 15 U.S.C. § 18a(a). This pre-merger notification statute requires reporting of all mergers and acquisitions where one of the persons involved is engaged in "United States commerce," the transaction is between persons with minimum sizes of $100 million and $10 million, respectively, in gross assets (or, for manufacturing companies, in sales) and as a result of the transaction the acquiring person will hold either more than $15 million of the acquired person's voting securities and assets or 50 percent or more of the voting securities of a person who, together with all entities it controls, has annual sales or gross assets of $25 million or more.

D. Securities and Exchange Commission and Stock Exchange Acts, Rules and Regulations

These problems are outside the scope of this chapter, but even where a public issue of securities is not outstanding as to either buyer or seller or contemplated as part of the transaction, securities laws can become relevant in situations where a seller, a buyer or a subsidiary of the buyer delivers new stock as consideration in a purchase or sale.

E. State Law Requirements

On the corporate level, state law requirements relate to dissenter appraisal rights and director and shareholder approval in a number of situations including sale of substantially all assets, dissolution, merger and other certificate of incorporation amendments.

1. In General

The Business Corporation Law's requirements for business combinations are set forth primarily in Article IX, although other sections of the statute are relevant in this area—particularly, Sections 605 (which governs the procedure for giving notice of a meeting of shareholders), 616 (which specifies some corporate transactions that require a greater quorum or approval percentage vote than is required elsewhere in the statute), and 623 (which governs the procedure for enforcing a shareholder's appraisal rights). Article IX has been considerably "active" in recent years, as the state legislature has sought various ways (some of them unconstitutional) to protect New York corporations against attack by corporate raiders. Although the resulting statutes (including Section 912 and Article XVI of the BCL) are intended to apply exclusively to publicly held New York corporations, counsel should keep a close watch on developments in this area, as even a minor error in drafting a statute could result in unintended "spillover" effects that could require compliance by closely held corporations.

The BCL recognizes four types of business combinations—mergers, consolidations, asset dispositions, and share exchanges—and creates a separate statutory scheme for each type, although the procedural requirements for each type of combination are very similar. Essentially, qualifying a business combination under the BCL involves four steps: the adoption of a "plan" by the board of directors, approval of the "plan" by a vote of shareholders, the filing of a certificate with the New York Department of State, and the filing of certified copies of the certificate in certain locations (counsel should always be sure that he/she orders a sufficient number of certified copies from the Department of State in order to fulfill this last requirement).

In negotiating and drafting documents for a business combination involving one or more New York corporations, counsel should keep in mind at all times that mere compliance with the BCL is not sufficient to ensure a legally successful combination. Counsel should be certain beyond all doubt that the transaction qualifies under the applicable federal and state securities laws and that the federal income tax consequences of the transaction (discussed in Chapter 12) are those desired by his/her client.

2. Mergers and Consolidations

The BCL distinguishes between "mergers" and "consolidations" in Section 901, although for most purposes these two terms are synonymous. A "merger" is defined as a business combination in which two or more corporations (each called a "constituent corporation") meld into each other such that the resulting corporation (called the "surviving corporation") is one of the constituent corporations. A "consolidation," on the other hand, requires the formation of a new corporation and the melding of the constituent corporations into the new corporation such that the new corporation is the "consolidated corporation."

Having made this distinction, however, the statute mandates extremely similar procedures for mergers and consolidations. First, the board of directors of each constituent corporation must approve a plan of merger or consolidation. BCL § 901(a). The contents of the plan, specified by Section 901(a)(1) through (5) of the BCL, should include, for each constituent corporation, the name of the corporation, the original name of the corporation (if different), the name of the surviving or consolidated corporation, the designation and number of outstanding shares of each class and series whether or not entitled to vote on the merger or consolidation (although voting classes and series must be broken out, as well as any class or series entitled to class voting), the terms and conditions of the proposed merger or consolidation (including the consideration to be received by shareholders of the corporation), (for a merger) a statement of any amendments or changes in the certificate of incorporation of the surviving corporation, (for a consolidation) all statements required to be included in a certificate of incorporation under BCL § 402 (*see* discussion in Chapter 4) "except statements as to facts not available at the time the plan of consolidation is adopted by the board," and "such other provisions with respect to the proposed merger or consolidation as the board considers necessary or desirable."

In drafting a plan, counsel should track the statutory requirements closely and should not liberally add other provisions. If, for example, counsel includes a provision that, if contained in an amendment to the certificate of incorporation, would entitle a nonvoting class or series of shares to vote, Section 903(a)(2) of the BCL requires that the plan be approved by a majority vote of such nonvoting shares "notwithstanding any provision in the certificate of incorporation." Counsel should, however, add a provision specifying the circumstances under which the plan can be abandoned prior to the filing of the certificate of merger or consolidation. *See* BCL § 903(b).

Once adopted by the board, the plan must be approved by a two-thirds vote of the shareholders. BCL § 903(a)(2). The notice for the shareholders' meeting should be delivered to all shareholders, whether or not entitled to vote on the merger or consolidation, and should be accompanied by a copy of the plan. BCL § 903(a).

The final step in a merger or consolidation under the BCL is for the constituent corporations to file a certificate of merger or consolidation with the New York Department of State. BCL § 904. The certificate should be captioned "Certificate of Merger (or Consolidation) of ____ and ____ into ____ under Section 904 of the Business Corporation Law," should be signed and verified on behalf of each constituent corporation, and should contain provisions setting forth, with respect to each constituent corporation, the name of the corporation, the original name of the corporation (if different), the designation and number of outstanding shares of each class and series (again, breaking out voting shares and classes and series entitled to class voting), (for a merger) a statement of any amendments or changes in the certificate of incorporation of the surviving corporation to be effected by the merger, (for a consolidation) all statements required to be included in a certificate of incorporation under BCL § 402 (*see* Chapter 4), the effective date of the merger or consolidation (if other than the date the certificate is filed with the Department of State), (for a consolidation) any statement required to be included in a certificate of incorporation under BCL § 402 if omitted from the plan, the date when the certificate of incorporation of each constituent corporation was filed by the Department of State, and the manner in which the merger or consolidation was authorized by each constituent corporation. BCL § 904(a). Once the certificate of merger or consolidation is filed with the Department of State and counsel receives back certified copies, he/she must arrange to have certified copies of the certificate filed (1) in the office of the clerk of each county where each constituent corporation (other than the surviving corporation) has its office, and (2) in the office of the recording officer of each

BUYING AND SELLING THE SMALL BUSINESS

county in New York (and in any other state which requires a similar filing) in which real property of each constituent corporation (other than the surviving corporation) is located. BCL § 904(b).

The merger or consolidation is deemed effective upon the filing of the certificate. BCL § 906(a). Once the merger or consolidation is effective, the surviving corporation (1) has all of the rights, powers, purposes, etc. of each constituent corporation consistent with its certificate of incorporation, (2) has title to all assets of each of the constituent corporations, and (3) assumes and is liable for all of the liabilities, obligations and penalties of each of the constituent corporations (the statute is very clear that a merger or consolidation without more does not relieve a corporation from any liability, obligation or claim "due or to become due"). For both mergers and consolidations, no further amendment of the certificate of incorporation of the surviving corporation is necessary: the original certificates of incorporation, as amended by (in the case of a merger) or as supplemented by (in the case of a consolidation) the certificate of merger or consolidation, constitutes the certificate of incorporation of the surviving corporation. BCL § 906(b). Nevertheless, it is good practice for counsel to restate the entire certificate of incorporation of the surviving corporation in the certificate of merger or consolidation, to avoid confusion later on.

3. Short-Form Mergers

If a New York corporation merges its 90-percent-or-more-owned subsidiary into itself as the surviving corporation, it can avoid obtaining shareholder approval by following the procedure for a "short-form merger" set forth in Section 905 of the BCL. In a "short-form merger," the board of the corporate parent adopts an abbreviated plan containing some but not all of the information required in a plan of merger or consolidation of unrelated companies, BCL § 905(a), delivers "personally or by mail" to all minority shareholders of the subsidiary a copy of such plan "or an outline of the material features thereof," BCL § 905(b), files an abbreviated certificate of merger with the New York Department of State, BCL § 905(c), and files certified copies of the filed certificate of merger in the same locations required by Section 904(b) of the BCL. BCL § 905(d). Clearly, a short-form merger is one of the devices by which the shareholders of a corporate parent (if it holds 90 percent or more of the outstanding shares of a subsidiary) may "freeze out" minority shareholders of the subsidiary.

4. Mergers and Consolidations of Foreign and Domestic Corporations

If the merger or consolidation is between a New York corporation and a foreign corporation, the procedure to be followed is somewhat different. Under Section 907 of the BCL, if the surviving or consolidated corporation is the New York corporation, the procedure is basically the same as in a merger or consolidation of two or more unrelated New York corporations, except that (1) the merger or consolidation must be authorized by the shareholder vote and pursuant to the procedure required by the foreign jurisdiction, BCL § 907(b), and (2) the certificate of merger or consolidation must set forth the jurisdiction and date of incorporation of each constituent foreign corporation, the date its application for authority to do business in New York was filed by the Department of State, and (if any) its fictitious name used in New York under Article XIII of the BCL. BCL § 907(d).

If, on the other hand, the surviving or consolidated corporation is the foreign corporation, the procedure to be followed is the more cumbersome one set forth in Section 907(e) of the BCL. The domestic corporation must adopt a plan pursuant to Section 902 of the BCL, and the foreign corporation must follow the procedure required by its jurisdiction of incorporation. BCL § 907(b). Both corporations must obtain the shareholder approval required by its jurisdiction of incorporation. BCL § 907(b). The foreign corporation must comply with the provisions of Article XIII of the BCL relating to qualification to do business in New York. BCL § 907(e)(1). The consent of the New York State Tax Commission to the filing of a certificate of merger or consolidation must be obtained. BCL § 907(f). A certificate of merger or consolidation meeting the requirements of Section 907(e)(2) of the BCL must be filed, with the consent of the State Tax Commission attached thereto. If the effective date of the merger or consolidation is other than the date the certificate is filed with the Department of State, the effective date must be set forth in the certificate and must not exceed 90 days. BCL § 907(g).

Certified copies of the certificate must be filed in each location specified by Section 904(b) of the BCL. BCL § 907(h). The effect of a merger or consolidation upon the surviving or consolidated corporation will be determined by New York law, except (in cases where the foreign corporation is the surviving or consolidated corporation) insofar as the law of the foreign jurisdiction provides otherwise.

5. Sales of Assets

The procedure for a sale or other disposition of "all or substantially all" of a New York corporation's assets, if "not made in the usual or regular course of business," is set forth in Section 909 of the BCL, which requires authorization of the disposition by the board of directors, delivery to all shareholders (whether or not entitled to vote) of notice of the shareholders' meeting to approve the disposition, and approval of the disposition by a two-thirds vote of shareholders. BCL § 909(a). Whether a disposition is made in "the usual or regular course of business" or disposes of "all or substantially all" of the corporation's assets will depend, of course, upon the facts and circumstances of each case. Section 909(b) of the BCL provides that if the instrument (such as a deed or bill of sale) conveying the assets recites that the property described therein does not constitute all or substantially all of the corporation's assets, or that the conveyance is made in the usual or regular course of the seller's business, such a recital will be deemed "presumptive evidence" of the fact so recited, but the presumption is rebuttable. Finally, the board of directors may abandon the sale or disposition after obtaining shareholder approval without further action by the shareholders. BCL § 909(f).

Sections 909(d) and (e) of the BCL set forth a procedure whereby a corporation which disposes of "all or substantially all" of its assets, together with its corporate name, to a newly formed corporation with the same name, may be deemed automatically dissolved on the 30th day after the filing of the new corporation's certificate of incorporation if the disposing corporation does not change its name within the 30-day period, the consent of the New York State Tax Commission is obtained and attached to the new corporation's certificate of incorporation and the disposing corporation winds up its affairs and liquidates in accordance with Article X of the BCL (*see* Chapter 16). In other words, by following the procedure set forth in Section 909(d) of the BCL, and by making sure the new corporation's certificate of incorporation contains the provisions specified by Section 909(e) of the BCL, the disposing corporation need not file a certificate of dissolution under Section 1003 of the BCL. Since the disposing corporation will have to give its consent to the new corporation's use of the same corporate name (*see* Chapter 4), the reader may well question whether Sections 909(d) and (e) of the BCL offer a less burdensome alternative to voluntary dissolution under Article X.

6. Exchanges of Shares

Section 913 of the BCL, which was added in 1986, specifies the procedure to be followed when two corporations combine by exchanging their shares. If the two corporations are New York corporations, the procedure specified by Section 913 is essentially the same as that for a merger or consolidation under Sections 901 through 904 of the BCL, except that if the exchange is to be deemed effective on a date other than the date the certificate of exchange is filed with the Department of State, such effective date must be not more than 30 days after such filing date. BCL § 913(e). When an exchange of shares pursuant to Section 913 is effected, ownership of the shares acquired pursuant to the plan of exchange vests in the acquiring corporation, "whether or not the certificates for such shares have been surrendered for exchange." *Id.* This means that shareholders in the acquired corporation who fail to tender their shares in accordance with the plan of exchange are no longer shareholders of the acquired corporation and are entitled only to receive the consideration for their shares specified in the plan of exchange.

If the exchange is between a New York corporation and a foreign corporation, the provisions of Section 913(f) of the BCL, which parallel closely those of Section 907, will govern the transaction, while if the exchange is between a New York corporation and its 90-percent-or-more-owned New York subsidiary, the provisions of Section 913(g) of the BCL, which closely parallel those of Section 905, will govern the transaction.

BUYING AND SELLING THE SMALL BUSINESS

7. Appraisal Rights of Dissenting Shareholders

Section 910 of the BCL provides that, by complying with Section 623 (which governs the procedure by which shareholders may enforce appraisal rights), some but not all dissenting shareholders are entitled to receive payment of the fair value of their shares, among other things, upon a merger, consolidation, asset disposition or share exchange.

A shareholder who (a) is entitled to vote on a plan of merger or consolidation and (b) "does not assent" to the plan, qualifies under Section 910 except if such shareholder is a shareholder of the surviving corporation in a short-form merger under Section 905; a shareholder of a domestic parent which merges with its 90-percent-or-more-owned foreign subsidiary under Section 907(c); or any shareholder of the surviving corporation in a merger (as opposed to a consolidation) under Article IX unless the merger effects one or more of the changes in the surviving corporation's certificate of incorporation authorized by Section 806(b)(6) of the BCL (*see* discussion in Chapter 14).

A shareholder who (a) is entitled to vote on a plan of asset disposition and (b) "does not assent" to the plan, qualifies under Section 910 except in the case of certain acquisitions for cash where the shareholders' approval is conditioned upon the liquidation of the acquired corporation and distribution of substantially all of its net assets to the shareholders within one year after the effective date of the acquisition.

A shareholder who (a) is entitled to vote on a plan of share exchange and (b) "does not assent" to the plan, qualifies under Section 910 except if the shareholder's shares are not acquired in the exchange. The exception is intended to give effect to the provisions of Section 913, which effectively convert a dissenting shareholder's shares into rights to receive his/her pro rata share of the consideration to be received in the exchange by shareholders of the acquired corporation. The intent of Section 913 would clearly be defeated if dissenting shareholders who refuse to tender their shares could thereby force a valuation of their respective interests in the acquired corporation.

F. Insider Information, Minority Stockholder Rights (Selling Control)

Mike and John together own 60 percent of a corporation. Sales of the stock have been at $13. George tells Mike and John he will buy substantially all the assets of the corporation at a price equivalent to $21 per share. Mike and John, without telling the 40-percent shareholders about George's offer, begin buying up their stock at $13. There has probably been a violation of at least SEC Rule 10b-5 under the Securities Exchange Act of 1934, subjecting Mike and John to a suit for damages by selling shareholders to recover the illegal profits.

If George simply offers to buy just the stock of Mike and John at $21 per share, it may seem there is no problem, but this may not be the case. The circumstances under which the sale of a stock block at a premium, because it represents "control" of the corporation, will be deemed proper are not altogether clear. Courts may find that other circumstances are present in addition to the sale of "control" which may subject the sellers to liability. Where the sellers resign from management as a condition of sale, for example, some courts may find that some or all of the premium was paid for the corporation's offices and thus constitutes a violation of fiduciary duty to the corporation. If the sellers lie to minority holders by concealing the premium and saying that all of the stockholders are being offered the same price, or the corporation is looted by the buyer after exchange of control, or the buyer uses corporate control to the buyer's own advantage, there may be legal liability. If the corporation has substantial liquid assets or other assets and the buyer has a reputation for acquiring corporations primarily to siphon these assets off, there may be problems. A lawyer representing Mike and John should consider insisting that George make the same offer to all of the shareholders. The law in this area is constantly growing and changing and should be reviewed frequently. Some helpful cases are *Pearlman v. Feldman*, 219 F.2d 173 (2d Cir. 1954); *Essex Universal Corp. v. Yates*, 305 F.2d 572 (2d Cir. 1962); *Beacher v. Gregg*, 89 Misc. 2d 457 (Sup. Ct. N.Y. Co. 1975); and *Zetlin v. Hanson Holdings*, 65 A.D.2d 544 (2d Dep't 1976).

BUYING AND SELLING THE SMALL BUSINESS

G. Fraudulent Conveyances

If a seller goes bankrupt within one year after the sale of assets to buyer, there may be fraudulent conveyance problems under Section 548 of the Federal Bankruptcy Code and Article 10 of the New York Debtor and Creditor Law if the sale is for less than a reasonably equivalent value and the other conditions of the statute respecting fraudulent conveyances are met. The purchase of a business or of some or all of its assets under Chapter 9 or 18 of the Bankruptcy Code is a subject not covered in this chapter.

H. Binding the Deal

Letters of intent, options, restrictive letters, oral understandings and similar things are often spoken of as binding buyer and seller to do the deal. This is not surprising given the fears of buyer and seller that the deal will fall through, but it is sometimes hard to know exactly when the parties are sufficiently bound.

After agreeing on a price, the buyer and/or the seller often desire an immediate binding agreement. Objections to haste may result in a call for a short agreement. This should be resisted as it can lead to litigation and other problems. A short form properly drawn will contain so many conditions that the parties may not be legally bound anyhow.

An option is generally disadvantageous to the seller, and relative bargaining strength is a factor here. An option may not be binding on the seller unless it contains many details or a detailed form of agreement is attached. To do this, as a practical matter, may take as long as doing an actual acquisition agreement.

A restrictive letter binding the seller not to negotiate with third parties for a fixed period while the buyer investigates the business is a possibility.

"Lockup" provisions are sometimes considered here providing for no other negotiations and injunctive relief against the seller's acceptance of a better bid by a third party. There may be an exception based on compliance by the seller's board of directors with its fiduciary duties. In the case of publicly traded corporations or where ownership of a privately held corporation is widely dispersed, limited options to purchase certain blocks of stock or to purchase newly issued stock may be granted. Options to purchase certain key assets, sometimes called "crown jewels," are also sometimes granted.

A letter of intent is another approach to the problem. After the parties reach agreement in principle, the letter is usually sent by buyer and accepted by seller. If it is desirable to be less formal, the negotiated points can be listed on a sheet of paper and the parties can initial the sheet. A letter of intent is particularly useful where a long time is expected to elapse in negotiating and closing the transaction, where certain points of the transaction are complicated and better stated in writing, or where a press release or other formal announcement is to be made prior to signing an agreement.

Advantages of the letter of intent are that it memorializes the basic understanding of the parties, may create moral obligation and can be helpful to the buyer in obtaining financing for the purchase. Disadvantages of the letter of intent are that it may weaken the parties' negotiating posture for items still open, may put the seller in a difficult position requiring announcement to employees, customers and suppliers, and may waste time and energy that could better be spent on the acquisition agreement itself.

In any case, the letter of intent should say more than that the agreement is subject to signing a definitive contract and to the approval of the seller's and buyer's boards of directors. If it is intended to be nonbinding, it should say so, except for portions intended to be binding, such as confidentiality provisions and restrictions on negotiations with third parties. The seller may be more bound than the buyer. The letter should specify the form of purchase and exactly what is being bought, the price and how determined, how and when paid, significant security for a deferred price, special arrangements such as employment and consulting contracts, existence of a broker, possibly the agreed-upon accounting or tax treatment, and any IRS and other government approvals that may be required as a condition to closing. From at least one party's point of view, it is probably best not to put in more than necessary as this may jeopardize the ability to bring up a point later. There may still be a suit based on lack of good faith and other factors even though the letter of intent says it is not binding, but in such a case, damages may be limited to costs incurred by the nondefaulting party prior to breach.

Many acquisition agreements are successfully negotiated and signed on only an oral understanding or exchange of messages. A handwritten list of major points, with no signatures or initials, may do the job. As investigation proceeds and problems become apparent, the acquisition agreement is tailored accordingly and of necessity becomes more detailed. Even though not always planned that way, the detailed acquisition agreement with provision for closing when certain conditions are met may end up being signed and the transaction closed on the same day.

In general, attempts to bind buyer and seller fully as soon as an agreement is reached in principle are impractical.

IV. INVESTIGATION

The greatest need and the greatest help are the facts. A team effort and communication are needed here, and the nature of the business will shape the extent and form of inquiry. Balancing the need for full disclosure, however, is the (presumed legitimate) desire for secrecy. A seller may reasonably believe, for example, that news of the possible transaction will have an adverse effect on employee morale, customers and suppliers, and the buyer will of course want the seller's business to continue smoothly. Where secrecy is important, the parties and the lawyers should all try very hard to accomplish this. This is very difficult but possible. It is often necessary to submit information to others, such as a bank that may be asked to arrange loans to cover part of the purchase price. Use of a "confidentiality letter" signed by the recipient of the information can be very helpful here and is recommended. Experience shows that despite all precautions, rumors of negotiations generally begin to circulate at some point in time. The buyer and seller should be prepared to accept this and to take steps dictated by the circumstances in order to cope with the situation, not permitting strong feelings on the part of either to cause a breakdown in negotiations. In the case of publicly owned companies, press releases are often involved and there is a large body of law surrounding the timing and content of these. In the private business acquisition area, there are no such hard and fast rules. Written or oral statements to officers and employees, lenders, creditors, customers and suppliers should be considered, but each case will be different. Typically the parties are not engaged in this type of transaction on a frequent basis and are accordingly nervous. During negotiations emotions often become taxed but should never be permitted to interfere with the fundamental goal of the parties: to do the deal.

Three basic investigations that should be performed in any sale or purchase of a business are business, legal and accounting.

A. Business Investigation

Depending very much on the facts of each case, this review (performed primarily by the business parties) should cover products, markets and marketing, sales, management, industrial relations, facilities, equipment, production methods and processes, engineering and research, quality controls, financial controls and systems, competition, outlook, customers, distributors, personnel and other basic business functions. Some of these investigations can indeed be delicate, and a checklist is of help here in tailoring the investigation to the particular case.

B. Legal Investigation

Depending on the facts of the particular case, this investigation (performed primarily by or at the direction of lawyers) should include review of the certificate of incorporation; by-laws; minutes; stock record book; qualification to do business in various states; tax returns; SEC filings; all government reports, filings and correspondence; OSHA, ERISA and Fair Labor Standards Act compliance; tax audit history; assets (including leases, deeds, equipment, inventory, work in process); contracts (including purchase orders, sales contracts, agreements with sales personnel or distributors, supplier contracts, advertising commit-

BUYING AND SELLING THE SMALL BUSINESS 263

ments, etc.); labor relations (union contracts); employee rules and policy statements; confidentiality and noncompetition agreements; accounts receivable and aging thereof, mortgages and other encumbrances (e.g., UCC, judgment and tax searches, which can be done by organizations such as Illinois Code Company in Springfield, Illinois, tel. 800-637-8605, and Nationwide Information Service in Albany, tel. 800-833-3482); unsecured liabilities; unfilled orders; correspondence from customers; employment and deferred compensation agreements (including qualified plans); fringe benefit packages; bank accounts; resolutions and banking relationships (e.g., lines of credit, letters of credit, interest rates, borrowing history); patents; trademarks; copyrights; insurance coverage; litigation files; claims (actual, threatened and possible) against the corporation; legal operating restrictions; licenses; etc. *See generally, Kury, Acquisition Checklist*, 36 Business Lawyer 207 (1981). Many of these points will overlap the business investigation, so counsel should work out responsibilities with his client before digging in.

C. Accounting Investigation

Experienced auditors and internal finance personnel can be of tremendous help here in getting the facts so the problems can be put on the table and solutions worked out. No matter how this is done, some of the basic issues are:

(1) Do seller's financial statements fairly present income and financial position?

(2) What differences exist between seller's and buyer's accounting methods? The broad range of generally accepted accounting principles can produce a similarly broad range of profit and balance sheet results.

(3) The search for hidden values, liabilities, costs and reserves.

(4) Valuation of inventory particularly to identify slow-moving and obsolete inventory.

(5) The scope of an audit, which may be from cursory up to a full audit.

(6) The desirability of obtaining a "cold comfort" letter from outside auditors for the seller.

The degree of need for any of the foregoing will be dictated very much by the size and facts of the transaction.

Discussion of the purchase and sale of a business tends to focus on investigation and legal matters from the point of view of the buyer and there is some reason for this. There is something to be said for the view that the seller receiving cash for a business, whether it be for stock or sale of the assets, has not much to do but sit there and be paid. However, notwithstanding the ever-present and vital tax matters affecting the seller, discussed in Chapter 12, there are a number of points of particular interest to a seller, such as employment and consulting agreements where personnel of the seller are to continue on in the business.

The degree and extent of protection to be afforded here can be difficult to determine. Where payment to the seller of a portion of the purchase price is contingent on post-closing earnings, and this amount has not been put into escrow, the seller may have good reason to receive continuing information about the buyer, its ability and willingness to perform, and indeed to have some sort of input and control. The seller in this situation should conduct more than a cursory examination of the buyer, including its history and financial condition. Another broad area of seller concern, which continues past a closing even where the full purchase price is paid in cash at closing, are warranties and indemnification. This can give rise to much negotiation as to the extent of warranties, indemnification or breach thereof resulting in damage to the buyer, dollar and time limits to indemnification, escrow of funds and similar matters. Obviously, the extent of concern by an individual seller who is simply selling a small business so that the seller can retire, as opposed to a younger-still entrepreneurial seller who is interested in joining with a stronger group so as to expand the business and achieve the economies of scale and financial resources of a large corporation or group of corporations, while remaining actively involved in management, will vary. If seller may in the future want to engage in a competing or similar business, the noncompete language may become important and a price factor.

V. SALE OF ASSETS OR SALE OF STOCK

Whether the buyer should buy the assets of the selling company or the stock issued by it can be a difficult question but often is not. The answer may literally leap out as the considerations above are worked on and investigation proceeds. This is not always true, however, and more than one acquisition has started out in one form and been changed to another even rather late in the game. Contract forms will change although differences may be more apparent than real. Whether stock is sold or assets are sold, the buyer will want to know about contingent liabilities of the seller corporation. Both tax and nontax factors will influence the decision, and there may indeed be a conflict between the buyer and the seller. An asset sale may be somewhat more difficult in terms of paperwork but is often best. The position of minority holders may dictate an asset purchase. If the business to be sold is a division of a business to be retained, an asset sale may also be best. Consideration should be given to state corporation laws, dissenting shareholder problems, the number of shareholders, contingent liabilities, pension plans, profit-sharing and stock option plans, bank loan agreements, litigation, nonassignability of contracts, bulk sales laws, parts of a business which may or may not be wanted, and a host of other factors. If the business is operating under Chapter XI of the Bankruptcy Code, an asset sale is generally indicated. The basic need is to recognize the question and discuss the factors with the client.

VI. DRAFTING THE AGREEMENT: SOME PRACTICAL SUGGESTIONS

A. Drafting Responsibility

The first draft should generally be prepared by the buyer's attorney. The buyer is generally the party seeking the most protection. Although the facts of the case may make it more appropriate that the seller's attorney prepare the first draft, there may be cause to be slightly suspicious of a seller's attorney who insists on preparing the initial draft.

B. Desired Length

The purchase for, say, $40,000 in cash of some gigs and tools, a corporate name, goodwill, customer lists and know-how, all to be incorporated into the operations of the buyer together with the transfer of a few key personnel, may well be handled with four or five pages and attached exhibits. On the other hand, even the purchase of a relatively small business involving payments over a period of time, escrows, indemnification, need for full knowledge of receivables, lawsuits, inventory, outstanding contracts, possible environmental and other liabilities, etc. will require more paper. In the author's view, it is preferable to favor the longer route because this will provide better protection and in the end result in a more orderly, happy closing at what may not be greater cost in the end. With some effort and the use of the numerous forms available and today's word-processing machines, this can be done in a span of time and at a cost reasonably related to the size of the transaction.

C. Closing Date

Whether the purchase and sale agreement should provide for a closing to take place simultaneously with the signing of the agreement or for a delayed closing, i.e., on a set date after terms and conditions are met, is a common question. Each case is different. The facts may clearly point to a simultaneous closing. On the other hand, many agreements reflect the delayed closing format. Sometimes negotiation and drafting of the agreement takes so long that the agreement is signed simultaneously with the closing although this was not the original intent of the parties.

D. Terms of Purchase and Sale

The agreement should describe the structure of the transaction. If there is negotiation on the description of the transaction, the basic terms may still be unnegotiated. The consideration to be received and given by buyer and seller (cash, stock, other property), the calculation and amount of the purchase price, the continued involvement of the seller or specified individuals in the management of the acquired business, the assets if any to be retained by the seller, and the tax structure of the transaction should all be spelled out in detail in this section. The drafter should think very carefully about the identity of the parties, which may include on either the buyer's or seller's side parent and subsidiary companies, shareholders, guarantors and others. The agreement should clearly describe the security arrangements if payment is to be deferred, allocation of the purchase price and which liabilities are to be assumed and not assumed.

E. Some Basic Agreement Provisions

A basic view of the purchase and sale agreement is to think of it as a disclosure document, and this is true whether the purchase is of assets or stock. Whether in the end the information is part of the text of the agreement or is presented in exhibits or schedules or in a collateral document may not matter much. Basically the agreement should reveal

1. the organization and standing of the parties;

2. the capitalization of the seller if it is a purchase of stock and possibly even if it is a purchase of assets, and a description of the assets to be transferred and of the liabilities to be assumed and not assumed;

3. the names of any subsidiaries and affiliates that may be involved and information as to them;

4. full information as to the financial statements of the seller and any material changes which have occurred since the date of the statements; there may be provision for financial statements to be prepared post-closing as of the closing date and for price adjustments to be made based on differences between the closing date and pre-closing financial statements;

5. information as to tax reserves, tax payments, tax returns, audits and claims including all income taxes, sales taxes, real estate and other taxes, federal and state;

6. information as to pending or threatened litigation;

7. information as to accounts receivable, reserves for bad accounts and similar information as to accounts payable, including an aging schedule;

8. information as to inventories and any item of inventory which may not be usable or salable or obsolete, and write-downs, reserves and valuation policies for accounting purposes;

9. information as to material agreements including all those not arising in the ordinary course of business; those which cannot be performed within, say, six months; all agreements evidencing ownership of or title to or leases with respect to real estate; all licensing agreements and other agreements relating to patents, trademarks, trade names, trade secrets, inventions, technical assistance, know-how, copyrights, and other like items;

10. information as to agreements relating to employment, consulting, termination or severance, profit sharing, deferred compensation, bonus, incentive compensation, stock options, stock purchase plans, pension plans, hospitalization insurance, retainers and retirement contracts or agreements;

11. information as to agreements with officers, employees, agents, consultants, advisors, salesmen, sales representatives, distributors, or dealers including cancellation terms, all collective bargaining or other agreements with labor unions, any agreements providing for payments based in any manner upon sales or profits, all agreements not in the ordinary course involving future payments in excess of a certain amount, and generally all agreements which are materially adverse to the assets, operations or financial condition of the business to be acquired;

12. information as to any liens on, or title defects in, tangible personal property including machinery and equipment and transportation equipment, and a full description of all real estate and leasehold interests and liens thereon;

13. information as to all intellectual rights including patents, trademarks, trade names, etc., and any pending or threatened claims regarding infringement thereof;

14. information about the results of environmental investigations and reports;

15. full information as to insurance policies maintained by seller, including any pending claims;

16. information as to all key employees, including salary over a certain dollar amount, and information as to any indebtedness between the seller and its employees;

17. identity of all bank accounts, safe deposit boxes, and persons authorized to draw thereon;

18. a complete listing of all lines of credit and loans;

19. identification of any conflicts of interest between the seller and any employee or other party;

20. a complete disclosure as to employee benefit plans, funding and ERISA compliance;

21. provisions as to the conduct of the parties and the business until the closing; and

22. information as to the financing of the transaction.

F. Other Documents

In addition to a basic purchase and sale agreement and schedules attached thereto, the typical acquisition will involve a number of other documents, many of which will require drafting. These might include the following: promissory notes; employment agreements; noncompetition agreements; escrow agreements; mortgages; loan and security agreements; guaranty agreements; transfer instruments, such as bills of sale, deeds, assignments of patents and trademarks, lease assignment and assumption agreements; side letters; releases; consents of banks, lessors, trustees and others; certificates of appropriate officers of seller and buyer regarding corporate action, certificates of incorporation, by-laws, incumbency, compliance and bring-up, amendment of certificates of incorporation and by-laws; name change certificates; stock powers;

powers of attorney; resignations; legal opinions; shareholder agreements and other agreements and forms dictated by the special facts of the transaction.

G. Forms

The "Forms and Materials" section of this volume contains forms which could serve as prototypes for most purchases or sales of a corporation's stock or assets. At the risk of repetition, simply looking through a sampling of forms at the very beginning of a transaction can be the most helpful exercise of all. Sources are numerous and some are listed in Chapter 21.

H. Practice and Drafting Techniques and Hints

Much has been written and said on this subject and experience remains the best teacher. However, it is hoped the following, which includes some ideas expressed by Gary R. Germain of Syracuse, New York, in an article entitled *Techniques of Drafting Acquisition Agreements* published by the New York State Bar Association in 1984 for a lecture series, will be helpful.

1. Preparation—Preparation of even a brief outline will often save considerable time. Use of appropriate language and provisions from several forms may be better than simply taking a single form and marking it up.

2. Fairness—It is better not to overreach in the first draft, but you must nevertheless be firm in getting your client the benefit of the bargain that has been made. Asset values are important and strong representations guarding them are in order. This is similarly true as to the income statement. Earnings are important in the continued conduct of the business and the protection of goodwill. Where payment of part of the purchase price is to be delayed, the seller is entitled to the benefit of the price he expects to receive and in some cases to guarantees or security regarding this.

3. Negotiating—Hard negotiating usually follows drafting of the agreement. To facilitate this, the lawyer should explain to his client in realistic terms what representations and conditions the other party may be willing to give and what he may not be willing to give, and why, and should elicit from his client the same sort of information. Particularly, you should find out what your client thinks he needs for adequate protection. Most often the buyer will have some idea of how honest the seller is, how accurate the financial statements may be, and what sorts of disclosure he will really need to adequately understand the business. The lawyer should know why various terms are in the contract and the reasons behind changes requested by the opposing party's lawyer. It is certain that the parties will not agree on some representations. Understanding the logic behind each position usually makes it possible to reach a compromise. Allocation of the purchase price to various assets may affect depreciation recapture and future depreciation expense, payment of sales taxes and possible payment of New York State Real Estate Gains Tax. Each party may prefer to make its own allocation outside of the agreement, although allocation within the agreement is good evidence of fair allocation because of the adverse interest of the parties.

4. Liabilities—The agreement should be totally clear as to assumed liabilities which may include the assumption of no liabilities or just liabilities on a schedule, liabilities disclosed in a balance sheet, or liabilities incurred in the ordinary course of business only.

5. Representations and Warranties Generally—The purposes behind representations and warranties include seller's disclosure of business conditions, provision of a basis for seller's indemnification undertakings, and provision of an excuse for buyer not to proceed to closing if unforeseen problems arise. These are typically affirmative statements of a given condition with exceptions noted on a disclosure schedule; for example, "There are no liens or security interests of any kind on or in the property or assets of seller except such as are set forth on Schedule I attached hereto and made a part hereof." Where there is a closing deferred until after the signing of the agreement, the seller should be required to give a certificate at the closing which restates the representations generally, except for changes which have occurred in the ordinary course of business. If there is a sale of assets followed by liquidation of the seller, the principal shareholders may be included in the representations on a joint and several basis so that they can be held responsible if the buyer does not get the benefit of its bargain.

6. Financial Statements—This representation by seller is probably the most important. While it is helpful that financial statements are certified by a Certified Public Accountant, this is no guaranty and a detailed representation from the seller should be obtained. Many specific representations in the agreement relate back to the financial statements. A typical representation is that seller's financial statements have been prepared in accordance with generally accepted accounting principles, consistently applied, are true and correct and present fairly, completely and accurately seller's financial position, assets and liabilities as of the balance sheet date and the results of operations for the period covered by the income statement. Particularly where statements are unaudited, the buyer should conduct an extensive investigation of seller's business with respect to the financial statements, or a Certified Public Accountant should be engaged to do this and to report as to important parts of the statements.

7. Assets—A seller may resist representing that properties are in good condition and may want to sell them "as is." However, seller should at least be willing to say the assets are sufficient for conducting the business in its current state. It may be possible to get statements that, to the best knowledge of seller, properties both real and personal are structurally sound, with no known material defects, and are in good and usable operating condition and in a good state of maintenance and repair in accordance with standards generally accepted in the industry and are adequate and sufficient for all current operations.

8. Accounts Receivable—If a seller is guarantying collection of accounts receivable, this should be stated in very specific language.

9. Inventory—If the purchase price is related to seller's net worth, there should be a review as to whether the method of accounting is LIFO or FIFO, as this could make a substantial difference in some cases. Buyer's concern that inventory is of marketable quality and salable in the ordinary course is natural. If special production items are involved, such as a custom-engineered machine taking many months to build, it

BUYING AND SELLING THE SMALL BUSINESS

may be best to say something about accumulated costs as compared to seller's initial cost estimates for production given the status of completion of the item where it is of substantial size. Where finished goods are substantial, the buyer should receive a representation that they will conform to sales warranties generally given. It may be desirable to take a new inventory just before the closing.

10. Liabilities—Representations here will vary depending on whether the buyer is assuming only specific liabilities, assuming liabilities in general, or buying stock. Particular attention should be given to liabilities not reflected in the balance sheet but uncovered by the accounting investigation, and obligations which are incurred by the seller after the most recent balance sheet of the seller is dated but before the date of closing and which are not in the ordinary course of business. A seller should want to disclose liabilities in the drafting process because many minor problems may be overlooked and accepted by buyer. After the closing, problems that are not adequately disclosed may be recoverable by the buyer in an action against the seller.

11. Taxes—Tax provisions in an agreement can become very complex. Besides the buyer wanting to be sure that all necessary returns have been filed by the seller and taxes paid or provided for as set forth in the balance sheet, buyer should be very concerned about whether there are grounds for a taxing authority claiming additional balances due. The question here is who assumes the risk with respect to an audit. If the seller is responsible for tax adjustments, the agreements should describe the procedure for determining who will handle the tax audit. Where an adjustment is simply a timing adjustment and buyer will get the benefit of a deduction in a subsequent year, something should be said about buyer's measure of damages.

12. Commitments and Agreements—A buyer wants to know about agreements it will have to perform or satisfy and will want assurance that beneficial agreements are enforceable and not in default. Although a seller is often concerned about providing details on many small agreements, this can generally be handled by limiting representations to agreements with a specific term and of more than a stated dollar amount. Generally all licenses, labor contracts, employment agreements, etc., should be within the representation. With respect to enforceability of agreements and existence of default, seller may want to qualify his representation to the best of his knowledge, and buyer will in turn want the qualification to read "to the best of his knowledge after due investigation and inquiry." This becomes a question of who bears the risk for these problems and in some cases, as for example with enforceability, it may be simply too difficult to determine accurately.

13. Sales Warranties—In addition to the buyer normally wanting to know what the express sales warranties are, what past experience has been and what reserves, if any, have been set up, the buyer should look into the adequacy of seller's insurance for personal injury claims with respect to each product line and possibly obtain representations as to the extent of coverage for at least the period of the statute of limitations.

14. Other Representations—These may include a whole host of items depending upon the facts and circumstances, including seller's sources of supply, relationship with employees, relationship with principal customers, adequacy of insurance, outstanding powers of attorney, and compliance of seller's business operations with all applicable laws and regulations, including environmental laws. Broad representations may cover statements from the principals of seller that they have no knowledge of material circumstances that will adversely affect business earnings or properties and that no representation contains an untrue statement of material fact or omits to state a material fact necessary to make the statements made not misleading.

15. Waiver—The period between signing of a purchase and sale agreement and closing requires covenants and agreements. Seller may want to prevent the buyer from refusing to close because of seller's breach of a minor representation, and this can often be handled by use of a materiality provision along with a condition that seller restate all representations at the closing. If the buyer waives a condition at closing, buyer may still recover damages because of the breach. The agreement should probably limit buyer's ability to recover damages for a waived condition, so that the buyer in waiving the condition will seek a decrease in the purchase price at closing to compensate buyer for any increased risk.

16. Affirmative and Negative Covenants—The extent of affirmative covenants requiring a seller to do something, such as permit access by buyer to books and premises, or negative covenants which require a seller not to do something, such as pay dividends, will depend on the complexity of the business, the length of time between the signing of the agreement and closing, and other factors.

17. Special Conditions to Closing—In addition to conditions normally thought of, such as that representations be true at the closing and that all covenants in the agreement be duly and faithfully performed, these may include execution of employment agreements by key employees, obtaining necessary consents to contract assignment, obtaining Internal Revenue Service rulings, obtaining board of director and shareholder approval, obtaining necessary licenses or certificates of governmental authority, making satisfactory arrangements for financing by a date certain, delivery of opinion letters, and final review by a CPA and delivery of a comfort letter.

18. Survival of Representations—The agreement should state whether representations survive the closing and for how long. Where the survival period is unstated, the applicable statute of limitations will generally govern. Whether and for how long particular representations are permitted to survive may vary depending on the likelihood of a problem down the road.

19. Limitation of Representations—The seller is naturally concerned with its exposure to substantial liability, having to deal with minor discrepancies and omissions in representations, and not allowing buyer to avoid closing because of misrepresentations. If seller wants to make exceptions as to matters of which seller has no actual knowledge, the issue is who bears the risk of loss. Buyer should accept such a limitation only where seller should not be required to stand behind a representation unless he possesses actual information regarding a problem. If buyer is looking for a seller guaranty on the point, the knowledge limitation is not acceptable. A knowledge limitation may be acceptable with respect to some matters. A representation as to threatened litigation can be limited to seller's knowledge but not as to pending litigation. A representation that there is no event or condition which may adversely affect the business or its assets may also be limited to knowledge.

20. Materiality—The concept of materiality is one which eliminates from the representation facts which are minor and therefore not within materiality standards. Materiality has its place in some representations. It is a concept which may be in the eye of the beholder. In some cases it can be defined as, for example, contracts exceeding $10,000 in amount and/or to be performed over a period in excess of six months. Where seller is worried about damages for breach, the materiality concept may be applied to specific representations only or as to all of them. If seller's worry is about buyer not closing because of a condition precedent that representations be true at closing, then the agreement can provide that at closing all seller representations need only be "materially" true. Counsel should be careful about "double materiality" where the concept is used in various representations and then again as part of the condition precedent that all representations be true at closing.

21. Indemnification—Indemnification will generally be for any damage, loss or claim against buyer arising out of the operation of the business which was not assumed by or disclosed to buyer, and generally includes attorney fees and other costs related to settling or liquidating a claim. Indemnification may come from persons other than those making the representations. There may be a deductible relieving seller from liability to buyer until buyer's damages exceed a certain dollar amount. At that point buyer's recovery can either be limited to the extent damages exceed the deductible amount, or once the deductible amount is exceeded, buyer may be entitled to recover for all damages. Indemnification language may contain a ceiling on the total amount of indemnification and a time period within which possible claims may be made. In some cases there may be liquidated damage provisions or special formulas for calculating damages based on earnings, and damages may be limited to the tax cost resulting from a breach. Each of these points may require a considerable amount of language. There should be specific language as to the handling of indemnification claims by third parties, and generally a party should not be entitled to an indemnification claim if such party's loss was due to its own willful misconduct or gross negligence.

22. Escrow or Setoff—The desirability of an escrow and/or a right to setoff is measured by numerous factors including the potential for buyer's damages, the financial responsibility of the seller and the number of sellers. If the purchase price is being made in installments, setoff against installments will be appropriate, and, in such a case, a note given to evidence such an obligation should not be negotiable. If an escrow is established, the period thereof may be tied in with the indemnification period. The escrow agent may be a bank or, in small cases, one of the lawyers.

23. Covenant not to Compete—A covenant not to compete may be quite important in some cases and easier to enforce than an identical covenant in an employment agreement because it may be considered a protection of goodwill which has been purchased. The covenant must be reasonable in time, nature of the restricted activity and geographic area. *See* discussion in Chapter 8.

24. Installment Sales—Deferred payment may help finance the purchase or sale, provide security for breaches of representations and allow seller to pay taxes over a period of time. An installment obligation is generally evidenced by a note, which should not be negotiable if buyer is intended to have a right of setoff, and should be at an interest rate high enough to avoid imputation of interest by the IRS (in other words, the interest rate charged should be comparable to the prevailing market rates of interest). In the event of default by the buyer or if buyer resells the business or assets acquired, the note should become immediately due and payable. If the installment obligation complies with Section 453 of the Internal Revenue Code, seller will be able to defer recognition of a substantial portion of its gain upon the sale of the business to future tax years.

25. Security—Where payment is deferred, the seller is acting like a lender and should think like a banker. There may be extensive default provisions in the note or acquisition agreement. Security may include mortgages and other liens on the buyer's assets, a pledge of stock, and a guaranty by the buyer's shareholders, among other things. A provision requiring maintenance of a certain net worth can be helpful. A first secured position in buyer's assets is good security and protection against other lenders or creditors taking the property. Where stock is sold and taken back in pledge, this may be helpful, but if seller simply gets a business back in poor condition, this is not always much help and other forms of security should be considered. The pledged shares may be held in escrow.

26. Bulk Transfers—The law allows creditors of the seller to pursue inventory and equipment in the hands of the buyer unless they receive notice prior to the transfer. Usually the buyer and seller want to avoid giving such notice and so the bulk transfer notice provision is waived. As a result buyer bears the risk of a claim by seller's creditors and relies upon the representations and indemnification of the seller for protection.

27. Union Pension Withdrawal Liability—Union pension withdrawal liability where seller is contributing to a multi-employer pension fund on behalf of union employees should be carefully reviewed, because if the seller is deemed to have withdrawn from the fund and is accordingly assessed withdrawal liability under the applicable provisions of ERISA, such liability may be deemed to be assumed by the buyer. This can be handled in a number of ways, including the buyer's agreement to continue at least the same contributions as seller made prior to the transfer and the posting of a bond by the buyer. The problems generally associated with other employee retirement plans deserve particular attention.

28. Opinion Letters Delivered at Closing—Where the purchase price is paid in cash, the opinion of buyer's attorney is normally limited to buyer having the authority to enter into and complete the agreement, the binding effect thereof, and the nonexistence of litigation concerning the transaction. Seller's attorney is normally asked to opine on these and other aspects of the transaction. Depending on the facts, the opinion should cover the incorporation, corporate existence and good standing of seller; qualification to do business in all jurisdictions where necessary; pending litigation; nonconflict with other agreements; laws applicable to seller and the various seller representations. Seller's counsel may be reluctant to do some of this if he believes he should not be required to make investigations into the law and various facts which can just as easily be made by buyer's counsel, or if he believes the requested opinion requires him to guarantee the truth of statements of fact made in the agreement. An opinion based on knowledge of seller's counsel may give comfort that at least seller's counsel has no knowledge of a problem which may exist.

29. Employment Agreement—If seller's stockholder is being employed in some meaningful capacity and his employment will survive closing, the agreement should provide for methods of termination, compensation increases, fringe benefits, etc. Employment agreements are discussed in greater detail in Chapter 8.

CHAPTER TWELVE

TAX ASPECTS OF BUYING AND SELLING THE SMALL BUSINESS

Henry M. Cohn

TAX ASPECTS—BUYING & SELLING SMALL BUSINESS 283

I. INTRODUCTION AND OVERVIEW

The federal income tax consequences of corporate mergers, acquisitions and buyouts (or "reorganizations" as the Internal Revenue Code calls them) are extremely complex, especially when we consider that many tax consequences are dictated by the particular form that a reorganization takes. Often, in the unorganized process of negotiating the purchase or sale of a closely held corporation, the structure of the transaction envisioned by counsel will fall between the "pure" examples set forth in the Code, and an effort must be made to characterize the reorganization as wholly or partially "taxable" or "tax-free," and if tax-free, to identify the particular Code provision under which the claim for tax-free status can be made. Generalizations in this area are extremely difficult to make, and it is strongly recommended that counsel engage competent tax counsel in the earliest stages of planning a reorganization of a closely held corporation.

That being said, it is useful to distinguish three types of reorganization for purposes of the Code: "taxable," "tax-free" or "hybrid" (partially taxable and partially tax-free). Within the category of "tax-free" reorganizations are seven distinct subcategories, which are listed as subsections A through G, inclusive, of Section 368(a)(1) of the Code, and are commonly identified by subsection number (for example, "Type A," "Type B" and so on). In addition, the Code also describes certain "triangular" reorganizations in which a subsidiary is merged with or otherwise acquires the stock or assets of a corporation, and the selling corporation's shareholders receive securities of a corporation controlling the subsidiary. It is fair to say that if a transaction does not precisely fit one of these subcategories of "tax-free" reorganization, it is a "taxable" reorganization or at best a "hybrid." The following paragraphs will discuss the various forms of "tax-free" reorganization and identify some of the more common forms of "taxable" and "hybrid" reorganizations.

Although a reorganization is considered "tax-free" by the Code, this does not mean that it is inherently desirable or that the parties to a particular transaction will necessarily want a transaction that is "tax-free." The overwhelming majority of acquisitions in the United States are either "taxable" or "hybrid." Each transaction is different, and counsel's first task is to identify as early as possible the specific tax objectives of four players in the reorganization game: the corporation to be acquired (the "selling corporation"), the corporation that is doing the acquiring (the "buying corporation"), the shareholders of the selling corporation (the "selling shareholders"), and, in some but not all forms of reorganization, the shareholders of the buying corporation (the "buying shareholders"). Once the tax objectives of each player have been determined (and, as will be seen, some give-and-take may be necessary to resolve conflicting tax objectives), a form of reorganization should be selected that will best realize those objectives. If a "tax-free" reorganization is desired, counsel should adhere as closely as possible to the appropriate Section 368 or 355 provision to avoid an adverse characterization by the IRS or the courts.

Assuming that the form of transaction ultimately decided upon does not precisely fit within one of the Section 368 models, counsel may wish to consider whether the buying corporation should form a subsidiary to act as the nominal buyer in the transaction. The use of a subsidiary can often help resolve a conflict between a Section 368 model and the tax and nontax objectives of the parties.

Finally, it must be pointed out that the term "tax-free" is somewhat misleading. While gain or loss is not recognized at the time a tax-free reorganization is consummated, a buying corporation and the buying shareholders in most cases will have a carryover basis in the stock or assets of the selling corporation acquired in the reorganization, and will be required to pay tax on any inherent gain upon a subsequent sale of the stock or assets. Perhaps the term "tax-deferred" rather than "tax-free" should be used to describe the seven transactions listed in Section 368, but the author will stick to traditional usage.

II. DETERMINING THE TAX OBJECTIVES OF BUYER AND SELLER

The first step in any reorganization is to determine the tax and nontax objectives of the parties. Generally, the selling corporation and its shareholders will want recognition or nonrecognition of gain or loss, depending upon their respective positions. For example, given a selling corporation with two shareholders, one shareholder may have extensive capital losses from other endeavors and may be willing to recognize gains that will be offset by these losses, while the other may be looking for nonrecognition of gain. Older shareholders receiving shares (as opposed to cash, securities or other property) will be concerned that gain not be recognized so that their carryover basis will "step-up" under Section 1014(a) of the Code upon their death. In addition, a selling corporation will normally wish to sell its stock rather than its assets, because in a stock sale the buyer acquires the business subject to known and contingent liabilities of the selling corporation. Finally, the selling corporation will desire a structure that will minimize any gain or loss to it on assets that have appreciated in value since they were acquired.

The buying corporation and (in some reorganizations) its shareholders will normally be concerned that the desirable tax attributes of the selling corporation (e.g., net operating losses) not be jeopardized. On the other hand, the buyer will seek to avoid assuming any unknown tax or other liability of the selling corporation and will want a stepped-up or fair market value basis in the assets of the selling corporation. Thus a buying corporation will often prefer to purchase the assets rather than the stock of the selling corporation.

III. TAX-FREE REORGANIZATIONS

Generally, in order to qualify as a "tax-free" reorganization, a transaction must fit squarely within one of the seven forms described below. For purposes of organization, the seven forms may be divided into three groups: "acquisitive" reorganizations (Types A, B and C and their recognized variations); "divisive" reorganizations (Type D); and "neutral" reorganizations (Types E, F and G).

A. Tax-Free Reorganizations: In General

In addition to complying with the requirements of one of the seven models set forth in Section 368, a tax-free reorganization must comply with a number of other, more general requirements. The reorganization must be entered into for a valid "business purpose" (e.g., reallocation of tax benefits must not be the sole motive behind the reorganization), there must be a "continuity of the business enterprise" in the modified corporate form (the buying corporation must use a "significant portion" of the selling corporation's "historic business assets" after the reorganization in a business), and there must be a "continuity of interest" in that the selling shareholders must continue to have an interest in the business of the selling corporation through ownership of stock of the buying corporation (or a corporation controlling the buying corporation). Although there are no precise quantitative statements of these requirements, the IRS has provided a 50 percent safe harbor for "continuity of interest": the "continuity of interest" requirement will be satisfied if the selling shareholders receive stock of the buying corporation (or its parent) equal or greater in value to 50 percent of the value of the stock of the selling corporation. Case law permits a somewhat lower percentage, but it is prudent to satisfy the safe harbor if at all possible. See Reg. § 1.368-1(c) (business purpose); Reg. § 1.368-1(d) (continuity of business enterprise); Rev. Proc. 77-37, 1977-2 C.B. 568 (continuity of interest). If one of the parties to a tax-free reorganization is other than a United States corporation or entity, Section 367 of the Code should be consulted for additional requirements.

Counsel should also be aware of the "step transaction" doctrine by which two or more related transactions involving the same buyer and seller may be "integrated" by the IRS in determining whether the appropriate requirements of Section 368 have been met. For example, if the buying corporation purchases 10 percent of the selling corporation's stock on January 1 for cash, another 10 percent for cash on April 1, another 10 percent for cash on July 1, and another 50 percent for stock in a purported Type B reorganization on October 1, the IRS may view all four purchases as one transaction such that the "solely for voting stock" requirement in a Type B reorganization (*see* discussion below) will be deemed not met.

A formal, written plan of reorganization, specifying among other things the type of tax-free reorganization sought to be achieved, should

TAX ASPECTS—BUYING & SELLING SMALL BUSINESS 287

be prepared by each party to the reorganization. *See* I.R.C. § 1.368-3. Usually the plan required by Article IX of the BCL to be adopted will be sufficient to satisfy this requirement, although the plan should specify the form of reorganization under which the parties intend the transaction to qualify.

B. Acquisitive Reorganizations

1. Type A: Merger or Consolidation under State Law

Under Section 368(a)(1)(A) and the relevant regulations, whether a transaction is a merger or consolidation is determined by state law (Article IX of the BCL in New York). Generally, a merger is the union or "pooling" of two or more corporations in which one of the corporations retains its corporate existence and effectively "absorbs" the other. In a consolidation, on the other hand, a new corporation is created to take the place of two or more corporations which by operation of law surrender their corporate existence.

The major advantage to a Type A reorganization is that, unlike the "solely for voting stock" requirement in Type B and C reorganizations, only the continuity of interest requirement restricts the type of consideration that the selling corporation or its shareholders may receive. The major disadvantage of a Type A reorganization is that both parties to the merger or consolidation must comply with all requirements of state law, which may require shareholder meetings and appraisal rights for dissenting shareholders. Moreover, in a merger or consolidation the buying corporation must assume all liabilities of the selling corporation.

A common way of avoiding some of the negative consequences of a Type A reorganization is to form a subsidiary of the buying corporation and to have it merge or consolidate with the selling corporation. Generally, the buying corporation will form the subsidiary under appropriate state law, exchange a portion of its voting stock for all of the voting stock of the subsidiary, and then "step back" while the subsidiary exchanges the parent's stock (NONE of the subsidiary's stock) for the stock or assets to be purchased from the selling corporation in a transaction that would be considered a merger or consolidation under state law. By following this procedure, the subsidiary (not the parent) assumes all of the liabilities of the selling corporation, and, because the parent is the sole shareholder of the subsidiary, the consent of the parent's board of directors is required, but the consent of the parent's shareholders will not be required.

In the above situation, if the subsidiary is the surviving corporation in the merger or consolidation (a so-called "forward triangular merger"), that is the end of the story. If the selling corporation is the surviving corporation (a so-called "reverse triangular merger"), however, which is sometimes done if the selling corporation has valuable assets that are difficult to transfer (such as leases or licenses that may require the consent of the lessor or licensor to the transfer), two additional requirements apply: (1) the surviving corporation must hold not only its own properties but also those of the subsidiary; and (2) the selling shareholders must surrender control (defined as 80 percent of the voting power and 80 percent of all nonvoting classes of stock) of the surviving (selling) corporation in exchange for voting stock of the parent. *See* I.R.C. § 368(a)(2)(E).

Generally, the tax consequences of a Type A reorganization are:

a. *to the selling shareholders:* no recognition of gain or loss to the extent that stock of the buying corporation (or its parent) is received in exchange for stock in the selling corporation surrendered; if, in addition, selling stockholders receive cash, warrants, securities, or other property (called "boot"), gain will be recognized to the extent of the fair market value of the "boot" received or, if receipt of "boot" is equivalent to a dividend (*see* discussion in Chapter 10), fair market value of the "boot" will be taxable as a dividend to the extent of the selling stockholder's share of earnings and profits. *See* Section 356 of the Code;

b. *to holders of the selling corporation's debt securities:* no recognition of gain or loss upon a surrender of debt securities for shares or debt securities of the buying corporation (or its parent), except that if the principal amount of debt securities delivered by the buying corporation

TAX ASPECTS—BUYING & SELLING SMALL BUSINESS

exceeds the principal amount of debt securities surrendered by the selling corporation's debtholders, the excess will be treated as "boot" under Sections 354 and 356 of the Code;

c. *to the selling corporation:* generally no recognition of gain or loss, although the selling corporation may recognize gain on the distribution of "boot" other than stock, stock rights or debt obligations of a party to the reorganization; and

d. *to the buying corporation:* the buying corporation will have a basis in acquired assets equal to the basis of such assets in the hands of the selling corporation—in other words, a "carryover" basis; in addition, if the transaction was a "triangular merger," the parent of the buying corporation will have a basis in the stock of the buying corporation (in a "forward triangular merger") or the buying corporation will have a basis in the stock of the selling corporation (in a "reverse triangular merger") that is computed by reference to the selling corporation's basis in its assets.

2. Type B: Stock for Voting Stock Exchange

In a Type B reorganization, the buying corporation acquires stock in the selling corporation "solely in exchange for" its own voting stock, provided that when the dust settles, the buying corporation must have "control" of the selling corporation after consummation of the reorganization. I.R.C. § 368(a)(1)(B). "Control" for purposes of a Type B reorganization means at least 80 percent of the total combined voting power of all classes of stock entitled to vote and at least 80 percent of the total number of shares of all other classes of stock of the buying corporation. Although the buying corporation is not required to actually acquire 80 percent control in the transaction, it must have an 80 percent ownership after all is said and done. I.R.C. § 368(c). Moreover, stock delivered by the buying corporation to the selling corporation or its shareholders must be "voting" stock, and there must be no other consideration flowing from buyer to seller. This requirement is strictly construed. Voting preferred stock may be used as long as the voting rights afford a "significant participation in management." Rev. Rul. 63-234, 1963-2 C.B. 148. Counsel should be careful to determine in advance that the buying corporation or its shareholders have not previously acquired shares in the selling corporation for cash or other nonvoting stock consideration under circumstances where the two transactions may be "integrated" under the step transaction doctrine.

A Type B reorganization may be structured by merging a newly formed subsidiary of the buying corporation into the selling corporation in a transaction in which the selling company survives and the selling corporation's shareholders receive voting stock of the buying company. If properly structured, the existence of the merger subsidiary will be ignored. Rev. Rul. 67-448, 1967-2 C.B. 144. This transaction might also qualify as a "reverse triangular merger."

The biggest advantage of the Type B reorganization is simplicity. Because the buying corporation's shareholders are acting in their individual capacities by transferring their stock to the selling corporation or its shareholders, no formal shareholder action of the buying corporation is required, and the affairs of the buying corporation are otherwise not affected. The greatest disadvantage of the Type B reorganization is the limitation on the consideration that may flow from buyer to seller. Because no "boot" can be used, selling shareholders wishing to be cashed out cannot be accommodated by the buying corporation, although the selling corporation can redeem dissenting shareholders, so long as the cash used for the redemption is not furnished by the buying corporation. Also, because the stock used must be voting stock, shareholders of the buying corporation may be unwilling to part with a significant minority (or, depending on the relative sizes of the buying and selling corporations, a majority) voting position in their own corporation. Moreover, if the buying corporation acquires only between 80 and 100 percent of the selling corporation's stock, it may be compelled to deal with minority interests.

Generally, the tax consequences of a Type B reorganization are as follows:

a. *to the selling shareholders:* nonrecognition of gain or loss. *See* Section 354 of the Code;

b. *to the buying corporation:* nonrecognition of gain or loss and a basis in the selling corporation's shares equal to the basis of the selling shareholders (i.e., a "carryover" basis); and

c. *to the selling corporation:* generally no effect because the selling corporation remains in existence (*but see* the discussion of Section 382 below). If the selling corporation subsequently liquidates under a plan of liquidation adopted prior to the reorganization (or soon enough thereafter that the IRS can prove that liquidation of the selling corporation was contemplated by the parties at the time of the reorganization), the reorganization will be treated as a Type C rather than a Type B reorganization. *See* Rev. Rul. 67-274, 1967-2 C.B. 141.

3. Type C: Acquisition of Assets for Stock

A Type C reorganization is an acquisition by a buying corporation of "substantially all" of the assets of a selling corporation "solely" in exchange for its voting stock. I.R.C. § 368(a)(1)(C). The selling corporation must promptly distribute any and all remaining assets and any and all consideration received by it in the reorganization to its shareholders (i.e., liquidate). I.R.C. § 368(a)(2)(G). IRS ruling guidelines define "substantially all" in this context as 90 percent of the fair market value of the net assets of the selling corporation and 70 percent of the fair market value of its gross assets immediately prior to the transaction. Rev. Proc. 77-37, 1977-2 C.B. 568.

The "solely for voting stock" requirement in Type C reorganizations is construed in much the same way as in Type B reorganizations, except that in a Type C reorganization the buying corporation may assume all or only specified liabilities of the selling corporation. In other words, an assumption of all or some of the liabilities of the selling corporation is disregarded in determining whether the transaction is solely for voting stock, where 100 percent of the consideration flowing from buyer to seller is voting stock of the buying corporation (or its parent). In addition, the "boot relaxation" rule of Section 368(a)(2)(B) of the Code provides that up to 20 percent of the selling corporation's assets may be transferred in exchange for cash, securities or property other than voting stock. In such case, however, any liabilities of the selling corporation assumed by the buying corporation will be counted as part of the "nonstock" consideration. As in a Type A or Type B reorganization, a Type C reorganization may take the form of a "forward triangular merger" or a "reverse triangular merger."

The primary advantage of a Type C reorganization is that the buying corporation may select which of the selling corporation's liabilities it chooses to assume. By contrast, in a Type A reorganization the buying corporation, as a consequence of state law, will usually be required to assume all of the selling corporation's liabilities. Moreover, in some states, only the approval of the selling stockholders and not the buying stockholders will be required, and only the dissenting stockholders of the selling corporation will be afforded appraisal rights. The biggest disadvantage of the Type C reorganization is the "solely for voting stock" requirement. Although Section 368(a)(2)(B) of the Code appears to offer some leeway by permitting up to 20 percent of the consideration flowing from buyer to seller to take a form other than voting stock, in practice liabilities assumed by the buying corporation will usually exceed 20 percent of the fair market value of the assets acquired. Since such liabilities would be included in calculating the 20 percent allowable nonstock consideration, the "leeway" afforded by Section 368(a)(2)(B) is more illusory than real. Moreover, a Type C reorganization requires the selling corporation to liquidate promptly after the transaction is consummated—a move which the selling shareholders may not desire for business reasons.

Generally, the tax consequences of a Type C reorganization are:

a. *to the selling shareholders:* nonrecognition of gain or loss to the extent that stock of the buying corporation was received for stock of the selling corporation; if, in addition, selling stockholders receive cash or other nonstock property, it will be treated as "boot" and gain or loss will be recognized to the extent of the fair market value of "boot" received (or, if applicable, "boot" will be treated as a taxable dividend);

b. *to the buying corporation:* nonrecognition of gain or loss and a "carryover" basis in the transferred assets; and

c. *to the selling corporation:* generally, nonrecognition of gain or loss, but gain might be recognized with respect to "boot" other than stock, stock rights or debt obligations of a party to the reorganization.

C. Divisive Reorganizations

The Type A, Type B and Type C reorganizations are sometimes characterized as "acquisitive" reorganizations, in that the buying corporation has "gotten bigger" by acquiring the stock and/or assets of the selling corporation. In a divisive reorganization, just the opposite occurs: the selling corporation "gets smaller" or, more precisely, divides itself into smaller units. Section 368(a)(1)(D) sets out the requirements for divisive reorganizations, and although transactions carried out under that subsection are commonly referred to as "Type D reorganizations," there are really four (and possibly more) types of divisive reorganization: the "asset transfer downward," the "spin-off," the "split-off," and the "split-up." Distinctions between the various types of divisive reorganization are set forth in Section 355 of the Code.

1. Type D: General Considerations

Sections 354, 355 and 356 of the Code set forth several requirements applicable to divisive reorganizations generally. Section 354 essentially provides that, in a divisive reorganization where substantially all of the property of the selling corporation is transferred to the buying corporation, all property received by the selling corporation in return and any property of the selling corporation not transferred to the buying corporation must be promptly distributed to its shareholders (in other words, a liquidation). Section 355 provides that, in a divisive reorganization where less than substantially all of the property of the selling corporation is transferred to the buying corporation in exchange for control of the buying corporation, all stock and securities received by the selling corporation must be distributed promptly to its shareholders. Section 355 further requires that, in such a reorganization, both the selling corporation and the buying corporation be engaged in the active conduct of a trade or business for at least five years before the distribution. In other words, a divisive reorganization involves the restructuring of a going concern that has been transacting business for at least five years and the parties intend to continue—albeit in restructured form—the business. Generally, what constitutes an "active trade or business" is difficult to determine, but clearly the holding of stock, securities, land or other property, or other "passive investment" pursuits, are not sufficient. *See* Reg. § 1.355-1.

A more difficult question is whether less than all of an "active trade or business" may be the subject of a tax-free divisive reorganization. It is clear that if a corporation has two or more readily identifiable product lines, each may be the subject of a tax-free divisive reorganization under Section 355. Similarly, if a corporation has only one product line but several plants, each plant (or group of plants) may be the subject of a tax-free divisive reorganization. Where the assets sought to be transferred in a divisive reorganization are not as easily identified, however, the issue is not as clear. Counsel should examine carefully the examples set forth in the Section 355 regulations and, if still in doubt, should consider obtaining a private letter ruling from the IRS if time permits and the client is willing to pay the cost.

Finally, in a divisive reorganization, selling shareholders may receive "tax-free" only stock in the buying corporation or securities in the same principal amount as securities in the selling corporation surrendered in exchange. If other property is received, or if securities in a principal amount greater than those transferred by the selling shareholders are received, the selling shareholders receive "boot" that is subject to taxation under Section 356 of the Code. In analyzing a divisive reorganization, counsel should examine the provisions of both Sections 355 and 368, and regulations thereunder, as the two sections interact vigorously.

2. Type D: Asset Transfer Downward

In this type of reorganization, the selling corporation forms a subsidiary and transfers substantially all of its assets to the subsidiary in return for "control" of the subsidiary. Unlike the usual 80 percent definition of "control," in these circumstances Section 368(a)(2)(H) defines "control" as 50 percent of the total voting stock or 50 percent of the total value of all classes of stock of the subsidiary. The selling corporation (or

TAX ASPECTS—BUYING & SELLING SMALL BUSINESS 295

parent, if you will) then liquidates, distributing all of the subsidiary's stock and any retained assets to its shareholders. At first glance, there appears to be little distinction between a Type C reorganization and this type of Type D reorganization, but Section 368(a)(2)(A) of the Code provides that if a transaction may be viewed as both a Type C and a Type D reorganization, the Type D classification will prevail such that the transaction must comply with Sections 354 and 355.

3. Type D: Spin-Offs

In the spin-off, a selling corporation forms a subsidiary and transfers to it less than substantially all of its assets in exchange for "control" (as defined in Section 368(c) of the Code) of the subsidiary. The selling corporation then distributes the subsidiary's stock to its shareholders under Section 355, in much the same manner as a normal dividend distribution. The shareholders of the selling corporation do not part with any of their stock in the selling corporation. Counsel should note that the "control" required in a spin-off is the usual 80 percent of voting and nonvoting stock, since Section 368(a)(2)(H) does not apply.

4. Type D: Split-Offs

The split-off is substantially identical in form to the spin-off, except that the selling corporation's shareholders must surrender a portion of their shares in the selling corporation in return for the subsidiary's stock. "Control" is defined using the 80 percent test.

5. Type D: Split-Ups

In a split-up, the selling corporation forms two or more subsidiaries, transfers all of its assets to the newly formed subsidiaries, and then liquidates by distributing the stock of the subsidiaries to its shareholders in return for all outstanding stock in the selling corporation. This device is commonly used where a corporation has two or more lines of business and the shareholders wish to "go their separate ways"—one group taking control of one line of business, another group taking control of the second line of business. "Control" is defined using the 80 percent test.

6. Tax Consequences of Divisive Reorganizations

The tax consequences of Type D reorganizations for selling shareholders, the selling corporation and the buying corporation are generally the same as in Type A reorganizations.

D. "Neutral" Acquisitions

If an acquisitive reorganization is one in which the buying corporation "gets bigger," and if a divisive reorganization is one in which the selling corporation "gets smaller," a "neutral" acquisition is one in which the selling corporation stays put or, more accurately, one in which the selling corporation and the buying corporation are one and the same.

1. Type E: Recapitalization

Neither the Code nor the regulations provide a specific definition of a "recapitalization" or Type E reorganization. The regulations do, however, give several detailed examples of Type E reorganizations. These involve exchanges of debt for stock (common or preferred), exchanges of preferred stock for common stock, or exchanges of preferred stock or debt for preferred stock or debt having different terms and conditions. Regs. § 1.368-2(e). Generally, a Type E reorganization has no tax consequences for the corporation. Shareholders may, however, recognize gain or loss on the transaction to the extent of "boot" described in Section 356 of the Code.

2. Type F: A "Mere Change"

The Type F reorganization is a "mere change in identity, form or place of organization, however effected." I.R.C. § 368(a)(1)(F). Examples include changes in corporate name or state of incorporation.

3. Type G: Insolvent Corporations

A Type G reorganization is a transfer of all or part of the assets of a corporation in a bankruptcy, receivership, insolvency or other similar proceeding in federal or state court to a buying corporation which subsequently distributes stock or securities in the insolvent corporation to its shareholders under Sections 354, 355 and 356 of the Code (i.e., in a divisive reorganization). A Type G reorganization can take a number of

TAX ASPECTS—BUYING & SELLING SMALL BUSINESS

forms, including a forward or reverse triangular merger. If it takes the form of a reverse triangular merger, under Section 368(a)(3)(E) stockholders of the insolvent corporation may not receive any consideration, and the insolvent corporation's creditors must receive voting stock of the buying corporation equal to at least 80 percent of the total fair market value of the debt of the insolvent corporation.

IV. TAXABLE REORGANIZATIONS

Generally, any transaction that does not fit squarely into one of the "pigeonholes" created by Section 368 of the Code is a taxable reorganization. Some of the more common forms of taxable reorganization are discussed below, but all share the same basic structure: a sale of the stock or assets of a selling corporation to a buying corporation for cash, securities or property other than stock in a manner that results in recognition of gain or loss to the selling corporation or its shareholders.

A. Taxable Asset Purchases

If the buying corporation purchases *assets*, the following tax consequences result:

1. *to the selling shareholders:* no consequences unless their shares in the selling corporation are redeemed, in which case tax consequences will depend on an analysis under Section 302 of the Code (*see* discussion in Chapter 10);

2. *to the buying corporation:* if the consideration paid to the selling corporation exceeds the value of the assets transferred, the excess will be allocated to goodwill or "going concern value," which are nonamortizable capital assets; buying corporation will acquire a "step-up" (or "step-down," as the case may be) in the basis of the assets to the total purchase price paid by buyer to seller (including any liabilities assumed); and

3. *to the selling corporation:* recognition of income, or gain or loss, on the sale of the assets, including depreciation recapture under Section 1245 of the Code, and possible readjustment of bad debt reserves, regardless of whether the corporation is liquidated; otherwise all tax

attributes remain in the selling corporation. Because of the repeal of the *General Utilities* doctrine, gain is recognized even if the selling corporation liquidates. *See* Chapter 18.

B. Taxable Stock Purchase if no Section 338 Election is Made

If the buying corporation purchases shares in the selling corporation in a manner that does not qualify as a Type A or Type B reorganization, the following tax consequences will result:

1. *to the selling shareholders:* recognition of gain or loss; if selling shareholders accept debt instruments payable over several years, the selling shareholders report the sale using the installment method of Section 453 of the Code and thereby spread recognition of the gain over several years, but only if the conditions imposed by Section 453 are met (e.g., at least one payment under the instrument must be made after the close of the taxable year in which the reorganization occurred, debt instruments must not be payable on demand or be in a form that is tradable in an established securities market, and the stock of the selling corporation cannot be traded on an established securities exchange);

2. *to the buying corporation:* buying corporation receives a "step-up" or "step-down" in basis of shares acquired; interest on debt instruments issued to selling shareholders is deductible under Section 163 of the Code. The deduction of interest on indebtedness incurred to purchase stock may be limited if the indebtedness satisfies the four criteria of the definition of "corporate acquisition indebtedness" found in Section 279 (very generally, these criteria are that the debt be used for an acquisition, that it be subordinated to unsecured indebtedness or trade creditor, that it be convertible or sold with a warrant or option, and that certain debt-to-equity or interest-to-earnings ratios be exceeded); and

3. *to the selling corporation:* generally, tax attributes of the selling corporation remain in place, but certain limitations on net operating losses apply (*see* discussion below).

C. Taxable Stock Purchase with Section 338 Election by Buyer

Section 338 of the Code permits a buying corporation which purchases at least 80 percent of the stock of a selling corporation (both in voting power and total value; see § 1504(a)(2)) within a 12-month period to have the consideration paid be its basis in the selling corporation's assets without liquidating the selling corporation. Prior to the adoption of the Tax Reform Act of 1986, this was an extremely popular transaction because the buying corporation achieved a "step-up" in the basis of the acquired, appreciated assets while the selling corporation (as opposed to the selling shareholders) did not recognize gain. Because of changes in the Code wrought by the Tax Reform Act of 1986, particularly the repeal of the *General Utilities* doctrine described in detail in Chapter 18, this transaction will now only be used in certain limited situations.

D. Taxable Stock Purchase with Section 338(h)(10) Election by Buyer and Seller

If the selling corporation is a member of a group of corporations that files a consolidated return for federal income tax purposes, the buyer and the selling consolidated group may agree to file an election under Section 338(h)(10) pursuant to which the purchase of the stock of the selling corporation is treated as if the selling corporation had sold its assets in a single transaction to a successor corporation (the "new" selling corporation). The gain or loss thereby recognized by the selling corporation is included in the consolidated return of the selling corporation, and the selling consolidated group does not recognize gain or loss on its sale of the stock of the selling corporation. The basis of the new selling corporation in its assets is stepped up (or down), based on the purchase price for the stock of the selling corporation.

This 338(h)(10) election combines the tax benefits of an asset sale (cost basis for assets) with the corporate benefits of a stock sale (ease of transfer of assets and liabilities). Unlike the regular 338 election, which is generally not viable after the repeal of the *General Utilities* doctrine, the 338(h)(10) election should always be considered when buying the stock of the member of a consolidated group. Unfortunately, the election is not available when the selling corporation is not a member of a consolidated group (although under regulations yet to be promulgated, the election may be available if the selling corporation is a member of an affiliated group of corporations that does not file a consolidated return). Also, the election is only available when the other requirements of Section 338 are satisfied, i.e., there must be a "qualified stock purchase," with the buying corporation ending up with at least 80 percent of the stock of the selling corporation. Also, as noted above, the selling consolidated group must consent to the election, and such an election may increase the tax costs of the transaction to the selling group.

E. Taxable Asset Purchase Followed by Liquidation of the Selling Corporation

Because of the repeal of the *General Utilities* doctrine in the Tax Reform Act of 1986, this transaction makes sense in two situations only: where the selling corporation has significant losses, and in the case of certain defined "small businesses," where the transaction takes place in the next two years. Generally, the tax consequences of this transaction are as follows:

1. *to the selling shareholders:* the transaction is treated as a fully taxable sale or exchange of stock in the selling corporation such that the tax consequences to the selling shareholders will be the same as in a taxable stock purchase; in the case of certain defined "small businesses," by accepting debt instruments in return for shares the selling shareholders may, under certain conditions, be able to report gain on the sale using the installment method of Section 453 of the Code;

2. *to the selling corporation:* because of the repeal of the *General Utilities* doctrine, the selling corporation normally will recognize gain or loss at the corporate level—while theoretically the installment method is available to the corporation if it accepts debt instruments in return, it will recognize the full amount of gain upon distribution to shareholders in liquidation; if the selling corporation is a defined "qualified corporation" (value is not more than $5 million—the benefit of the

TAX ASPECTS—BUYING & SELLING SMALL BUSINESS

transitional rule is phased out for corporations valued between $5 million and $10 million—and more than 50 percent of the corporation's stock is owned by ten or fewer natural persons who have owned their stock for at least five years), the selling corporation will generally not recognize gain or loss at the corporate level if the transaction is consummated before December 31, 1988 (certain recapture and short-term capital gains and loss will be recognized).

V. "HYBRID" REORGANIZATIONS

As the name implies, a "hybrid" reorganization is designed to combine some features of both a taxable reorganization and a tax-free reorganization in an effort to reconcile conflicting demands of the parties to the transaction. For example, the selling shareholders may want a tax-free reorganization while the buying corporation's shareholders do not wish to surrender their shares in the buying corporation, or some selling shareholders may want cash while others want a tax-free reorganization. Some of the more common forms of "hybrid" reorganizations are summarized below.

A. The "Cash-or-Stock" Merger

Where some of the selling shareholders desire cash and others desire stock, the selling corporation may merge into the buying corporation (or a subsidiary in a "forward triangular merger" under state law), with the selling shareholders receiving either cash or stock in the buying corporation. The total cash payable to the selling shareholders should not exceed 50 percent of the total consideration flowing from buyer to seller in order to ensure satisfaction of the "continuity of interest" test. If too many shareholders elect cash, the transaction documents should provide for a proration of cash to all shareholders electing cash. The tax consequences of this transaction are as follows:

1. *to the selling corporation, the buying corporation, and selling shareholders who receive stock only:* the tax consequences will generally be the same as in a Type A reorganization;

2. *to the selling shareholders who receive cash only:* the transaction is fully taxable; and

3. *to the selling shareholders who receive some stock and some cash:* the cash will be treated as "boot" under Section 356 of the Code, and the selling shareholders will therefore recognize gain to the extent that the sum of the value of the stock they receive and the cash they receive exceeds their adjusted tax basis in their stock of the selling corporation, but the selling shareholders will only recognize gain up to the amount of cash they receive. The gain recognized will be treated as capital gain or as a dividend under Section 356(a)(2) depending on whether it "has the effect of a dividend." *See Commissioner v. Donald E. Clark*, 109 S. Ct. 1455 (1989) (payment of boot in reorganization should be analyzed as if acquiring corporation issued only acquiring corporation stock and then redeemed the stock for boot).

B. The "Preferred Stock Forward Triangular Merger"

When the buying shareholders do not wish to part with shares and the selling shareholders desire a tax-free transaction, the selling corporation may be merged in a "forward" Type A reorganization into a subsidiary of the buying corporation. The selling shareholders will receive nonconvertible preferred stock of the subsidiary in return for their shares (recall that in a forward triangular reorganization, described in Section 368(a)(2)(D), selling shareholders receive stock of the parent of the merged subsidiary), redeemable both at the option of the holder and automatically upon the occurrence of certain events (such as the death of the holder). If the selling shareholders desire some assurance that funds will be available to redeem the preferred shares, the buying corporation could agree to make specified contributions to the capital of the subsidiary sufficient to enable it to redeem the shares (although the contributions would be subject to the claims of creditors of the subsidiary). However, the parties should avoid giving the preferred stock too many debt characteristics, because a successful recharacterization of the preferred stock as debt by the IRS (*see* Chapter 7) destroys the tax-free status of the transaction. If the transaction is structured properly, it will qualify as a Type A reorganization. Counsel should be certain that the preferred stock is the only consideration flowing from buyer to seller in

TAX ASPECTS—BUYING & SELLING SMALL BUSINESS

the transaction; otherwise the preferred stock may be deemed "Section 306 Stock" subject to taxation (*see* discussion in Chapter 10).

C. Recapitalization Followed by Cash Purchase of Shares

Where the shareholders of the buying corporation are reluctant to part with shares, but the selling shareholders want a tax-free reorganization and 50 percent or more of the selling shareholders want cash (thereby possibly running afoul of the "continuity of interest" requirement of a tax-free reorganization), the selling corporation may adopt a plan of recapitalization. In a recapitalization or Type E reorganization, the "continuity of interest" requirement is not applicable. *See* Rev. Rul. 77-479, 1977-2 C.B. 119. In the recapitalization, those selling shareholders desiring tax-free treatment receive preferred stock, possibly with an optional or mandatory redemption feature in exchange for common shares. The buying corporation then purchases the remaining outstanding common stock directly from the selling shareholders, so that the selling shareholders are in the same position as they would be in a "preferred stock forward triangular merger." The tax consequences of this transaction are generally as follows:

1. *to the selling shareholders:* recognition of gain for common stock purchased directly by buying corporation; if a selling shareholder sells all of his/her common stock, although the shareholder will not recognize gain upon receipt of the preferred stock, the preferred stock is not "Section 306 Stock," but if he/she retains any common stock in the selling corporation, the preferred stock is "Section 306 Stock." *See* Rev. Rul. 59-84, 1959-1 C.B. 71; and

2. *to the buying corporation:* this transaction is a taxable purchase of common shares for cash.

D. The Two-Tiered "Freeze Out" Cash Merger

If the shareholders of the buying corporation are reluctant to part with shares (most selling shareholders want a tax-free reorganization but some shareholders do not want to sell), this somewhat complicated transaction can get the job done. The buying corporation begins by forming a subsidiary and contributing cash in exchange for all of the common stock of the subsidiary. The subsidiary then forms a second-tier subsidiary, contributing cash in exchange for all of the common stock of the second-tier subsidiary. The second-tier subsidiary then enters into a merger agreement with the selling corporation, which agreement provides that the second-tier subsidiary will merge into the selling corporation in a transaction in which the selling corporation survives, electing shareholders of the selling corporation receive voting preferred stock of the first-tier subsidiary (perhaps with a mandatory or optional redemption feature), and the nonelecting shareholders of the selling corporation receive cash. The merger is conditioned upon 80 percent of the selling shareholders electing to take preferred stock. The nonelecting shareholders would in most states receive appraisal rights. The tax consequences of this transaction are generally as follows:

1. *to the electing selling shareholders who exchange common stock for preferred stock of the first subsidiary:* nonrecognition of gain or loss;

2. *to the nonelecting selling shareholders who do not participate in the exchange and receive cash in the merger:* recognition of gain or loss;

3. *to a selling shareholder who receives both preferred stock and cash in the merger:* the cash received in the merger will be treated as "boot," gain will be recognized to the extent of the boot, and the preferred stock may be treated as "Section 306 Stock";

4. *to the selling corporation, the buying corporation, and the first-tier subsidiary:* nonrecognition of gain or loss; and

5. *to the second-tier subsidiary:* a "carryover" basis in the selling corporation's shares acquired by it in the merger, computed with reference to the selling corporation's basis in its assets, but increased by the cash contributed to the second-tier subsidiary.

VI. CARRYOVER OF TAX ATTRIBUTES IN CORPORATE REORGANIZATIONS AND ACQUISITIONS

The Tax Reform Act of 1986 substantially revised the rules relating to the carryover of net operating losses and other tax benefits in corporate reorganizations and acquisitions. The rules, which are set forth primarily in Sections 381, 382, 383 and 384 of the Code, are extremely technical and should be examined by counsel only in conjunction with an experienced tax practitioner.

A. Net Operating Loss Carryovers

Generally, in the absence of a corporate reorganization, the taxable years to which a net operating loss can be carried back or forward are set forth in Section 172(b)(1) of the Code. If a reorganization occurs: (1) Section 269 of the Code will disallow the loss altogether if the "principal purpose" of the reorganization was to carry over the loss; (2) Section 381(c)(1) of the Code imposes limitations on the amount of the loss that can be carried over to the first tax year ending after the effective date of reorganization; and (3) Section 382 of the Code imposes additional limitations on the amount of carryover if the reorganization constitutes either a defined "owner shift" or "equity structure shift" which causes a change of 50 percent or more in the ownership of the corporation having the net operating loss. If the Section 382 limitation is applicable, the taxable income of the successor corporation may be reduced each year by the net operating loss carryover only to the extent of the value of the selling corporation's stock on the effective date of reorganization multiplied by the "long-term tax-exempt rate," which is defined as the highest of the adjusted federal long-term interest rates in effect in the three calendar months immediately preceding the effective date of reorganization (published monthly in the IRS Internal Revenue Bulletins).

For example, if the value of the stock of XYZ Corporation (a calendar-year taxpayer) on the effective date of a reorganization (which for the sake of simplicity is assumed to occur on January 1), constituting either an "owner shift" or an "equity structure shift," is $100,000 and the "long-term tax-exempt rate" is 10 percent, the Section 382 limitation for that year will be $10,000 ($100,000 multiplied by 10%). Thus, if the amount of net operating loss carryover acquired in the reorganization is $100,000, and if in that calendar year XYZ Corporation has taxable income of $5,000 (before any carryover), $5,000 of the net operating loss can be used to offset taxable income, because the $5,000 is less than the Section 382 "ceiling" of $10,000. The $5,000 remaining portion ($10,000 minus $5,000) can be carried over and will increase the Section 382 limitation in the following calendar year to $15,000 ($10,000 plus $5,000). If in the following year XYZ Corporation has taxable income of $20,000, only $15,000 of the unused net operating loss carryover of $95,000 ($100,000 minus $5,000) may be used to offset the taxable income, and the Section 382 limitation for the next calendar year will be $10,000 (the original Section 382 limitation), and so on until either the entire net operating loss carryover is used up or the carryforward period expires, whichever is earlier.

What is an "owner shift" or an "equity structure shift"? An "owner shift" is any change in the ownership of stock of a loss corporation that affects the percentage of such stock owned by any "5-percent shareholder" (generally, all less-than-5-percent shareholders are treated as a single "5-percent shareholder" for purposes of this calculation). An "equity structure shift" is a tax-free reorganization other than Type F reorganizations and certain divisive and Type G reorganizations. If an owner shift or equity structure shift causes any 5-percent shareholder or shareholders to increase their percentage ownership of the loss corporation by more than 50 percentage points, when compared to each 5-percent shareholder's lowest percentage ownership during the testing period, an "ownership change" occurs; the loss corporation's use of its net operating loss is limited as discussed above. A "testing period" is the shorter of the prior three years or the period following the most recent ownership change (but in no event before the loss arose). Stock sales, public offerings, redemptions, reorganizations and the issuance of options can all trigger an ownership change. Thus virtually all of the transactions described in this chapter would result in an ownership

TAX ASPECTS—BUYING & SELLING SMALL BUSINESS

change if the selling corporation were a loss corporation. In fact, many of the transactions described herein could result in an ownership change if the buying corporation were a loss corporation. As Section 382 and its incredibly detailed regulations are one of the most complex areas of tax law, an expert should be consulted if either party to a transaction has substantial net operating losses.

B. Earnings and Profits

Under Section 381(c)(2) of the Code, earnings and profits of a selling corporation or deficits in the earnings and profits account carry over to the buying corporation in a reorganization. While a positive earnings and profits balance is deemed received by the buyer as of the effective date of reorganization, a negative balance may be used to offset earnings and profits accruing to the buyer after the effective date of reorganization.

C. Capital Losses

Sections 381(c)(3) and 383 basically impose the same limitations on capital loss carryovers as those which Sections 381 and 382 impose on net operating loss carryovers.

D. Method of Accounting; Depreciation

Section 381(c)(4) of the Code requires the buying corporation to use the same accounting method as the selling corporation if both used the same method immediately prior to the reorganization. If both used different methods immediately prior to the reorganization and the selling corporation is operated as a "separate and distinct business" by the buying corporation after the reorganization, the buying corporation is required to maintain the different methods. Generally, the buying corporation must determine depreciation on acquired assets in the same manner as did the selling corporation. *See* I.R.C. § 381(c)(6).

E. Limitation on Excess Credit

Generally, Section 383 of the Code imposes limitations on the amount of credits that may be carried over if an "owner shift" or an "equity structure shift" causes a more-than-50-percent change in the ownership of the corporation that originally incurred the loss.

F. Built-In Gains and Losses

Section 382 limits certain "built-in losses" (essentially accrued but not yet realized losses) if an ownership change occurs, just as it limits the use of net operating losses. Section 384, added by the Revenue Act of 1987, prohibits the use of "preacquisition losses" to offset "built-in gains." For example, if a buying corporation with net operating losses acquires, by purchase or in a Type B reorganization, the stock of a selling corporation, and the selling corporation owns assets with a fair market value of twice their adjusted basis, gain recognized upon the sale of the assets could not be offset (in a consolidated return) by the net operating losses of the buying corporation that accrued prior to the acquisition.

CHAPTER THIRTEEN

THE EFFECTUATION OF A CORPORATE EVENT— A PRACTITIONER'S OVERVIEW*

Raymond W. Merritt

---

* The author is indebted to Peter H. Jakes, Thomas M. Cerabino and Daniel D. Rubino, his colleagues in the corporate department of Willkie Farr & Gallagher, for their constructive advice and assistance in the preparation of this chapter.

I. INTRODUCTION: THE THREE PHASES OF A CORPORATE TRANSACTION

Most textbooks on corporate practice do not include chapters on the techniques involved in an acquisition or sale of a corporate entity and in raising corporate capital. The reasons for this are not readily apparent. Perhaps the subject needs more exhaustive treatment than a chapter could provide. Perhaps the answer may lie in the reality that experience in this area is clearly the best teacher.

The success of a corporate transaction requires a combination of disciplines and skills in areas outside the law—street smarts, business acumen, accountant's knowledge, etc. With that caution, what follows is a practitioner's overview which ideally will be germane to all major corporate events—sale, purchase, merger or capital infusion through a private placement or public offering.

Every corporate event has *three* phases: planning, negotiation and effectuation. Often a client will indicate that he has, or desires to, come to terms to buy, sell or combine a business or to raise additional capital privately, publicly or institutionally.

The *first* task of the lawyer is to determine why. If your client is a buyer, explore with him the goals he hopes to achieve. Typical goals are diversification, augmentation, the purchase of earnings, the purchase of cash, capture of tax benefits or the irresistible bargain. When your client is a seller, the reasons are normally retirement, realization of profits at a point when the client's business is peaking, concern about competitive disadvantage, personal or family concerns or the general perception of dark clouds on the business horizon. Once you have elicited the reasons for the purchase, sale or financing, then you will be better able to facilitate the transaction.

When dealing with the closely held corporation, special concerns often come to the fore. *First*, one normally finds a lack of accurate records. Informality and oft-claimed inventory cushions or other hidden assets often require paying special attention to the nature and extent of warranties, the necessity of a holdback of purchase price or the establishment of an escrow account. *Second*, one must be sensitive to the loss of the seller's patronage or involvement. Many closely held corporations survive and flourish because of the interpersonal loyalties developed over the years between the owner and the corporation's customers and suppliers. Consequently, many closely held corporations do not reach their maximum potential because of those very relationships. Carefully consider the desirability of retaining the seller's involvement for a period of time in order to mitigate his eventual absence. *Third*, be vigilant in your search for hidden values or liabilities. As previously noted, the books and records as well as the financial statements of closely held corporations often fail to highlight factors such as the aggregate compensation received by all the members of the seller's family as well as the extent to which perquisites or "perks," such as personal insurance, personal travel and entertainment and the personal use of the corporation's lawyer and accountant, diminish the true profit margins of the company. Conversely, the lack of appropriate executive salary and perks or the absence of appropriate levels of legal and accounting services might well inflate the true financial picture of a closely held corporation.

The next phase for the lawyer in a corporate event is to determine what the client is getting into. This is achieved through what is popularly styled "due diligence" or perhaps more aptly referred to as "lawyer's homework." In the excitement of any deal, the client is apt to consciously or unconsciously overlook or discount defects or problems that will loom larger after closing. A good lawyer will persist in unearthing and evaluating them, often to the client's annoyance. In doing so, there are no shortcuts; it is dogged attention to detail that consistently bears fruit.

Until recently, information concerning a private company was only obtainable from company insiders. Information concerning a public company was more readily available through its SEC filings. However, information concerning the company's business, such as industry data and surveys, was often difficult and expensive to obtain. Today, computerized data bases have vastly simplified and expanded the scope of the information-gathering process for both private and public compan-

THE EFFECTUATION OF A CORPORATE EVENT 313

ies. They are therefore an important tool in today's due diligence process, one which can only be ignored at great peril by the practitioner.

Set forth below in outline form is a due diligence guide which can be adapted to most corporate events. This outline was prepared originally by George A. Blackstone, Esq., of Carmel, California, and is reproduced here with minor editorial revisions.

II. GETTING BACKGROUND INFORMATION

A. In General: Where to Look

1. Review of Consultants' Reports

Review any reports prepared for the Company during the last three years by experts (either employees or independent) which describe or evaluate important aspects of its business and future plans.

2. Review of SEC Filings and Offering Circulars

a. If the Company is a public company with equity securities registered under Section 12(b) or (g) of the Securities Exchange Act of 1934, examine the Form 10 registration statement, the Form 10-K, 10-Q and 8-K reports and proxy statements filed with the SEC during the last three years with a view to determining matters of importance that might not otherwise come to your attention.

b. Is the Company current in all required filings with the SEC?

c. If the Company has filed one or more registration statements under the Securities Act of 1933, review all those filed during the last five years (and possibly earlier filings) as a check on matters to be disclosed and to determine the extent to which previously filed exhibits may be incorporated by reference.

d. If the Company has made any offering of securities during the past three years under an exemption from SEC registration, examine the offering circular.

e. If the Company has copies of insiders' Form 4 stock ownership reports (also discussed in Chapter 8) and Schedules 13D and 13G as filed with the SEC, review those reports to corroborate information supplied on questionnaires from insiders.

3. Review of Corporate Minutes

a. Review minutes of meetings of directors (including executive committee meetings, if any) for the last three years to determine the following: appropriate election of officers, the kinds of management problems discussed, what major policy directions have been given by the board and whether the following important transactions were properly approved by a quorum of the board: loans, leases, asset acquisitions and dispositions, stock issuance, dividends, retirement plans, officers' compensation, etc.

b. Are there minutes for all meetings? If not, see that they are prepared.

c. Review minutes of stockholders' meetings for the last three years to determine if proper action was taken to elect directors and to approve other transactions requiring stockholders' approval.

d. Review minutes of the audit committee meetings (if any) for the last three years with reference to the adequacy of internal accounting controls and accounting policies.

4. Review of Filings with Other Regulatory Agencies

Examine reports filed with government agencies which have specific regulatory power over the Company (or a major subsidiary) such as the Interstate Commerce Commission for a trucking company or a railroad, a state insurance commissioner for an insurance company, the Comptroller of the Currency for a national bank, etc.

5. Review Data Bases

Public data bases (e.g., Lexis, Nexis, Dow Jones Information/Retrieval, Dun & Bradstreet Credit Reports and certain files from DIALOG) should be reviewed for (a) news reports referring to or discussing the company or its officers and directors; (b) press releases and other

THE EFFECTUATION OF A CORPORATE EVENT 315

public filings (e.g., SEC filings) by the company; (c) litigations in which the company or its officers and directors are named; and (d) analyst reports concerning the company or major developments (legal or commercial) affecting its industry. Information concerning other companies in the same industry, and industry ratios, are also readily available via these data bases.

B. Formation and Good Standing

1. Articles of Incorporation

a. Obtain and examine a copy (certified by the Secretary of State) of the Articles of Incorporation as originally filed.

b. Are the Articles in the form prescribed by law for filing? (Check law as in effect at date of filing.)

c. Are the Articles properly executed and acknowledged or verified (if required by the law as in effect at time of filing)?

d. Obtain and examine a long-form certificate from the Secretary of State as to the good standing of the Company and identifying all documents on file with the Secretary of State.

e. Obtain and examine a copy (certified by the Secretary of State) of each document referred to on the Secretary of State's good standing certificate to determine (i) if each certificate was prepared in accordance with statutory requirements in effect at the time of filing and (ii) if each amendment was properly executed and acknowledged or verified, if required by law as in effect at the time of filing.

f. For each certificate so examined, do the minutes show appropriate action was taken by the directors and stockholders (if required)? Is any curative action required to correct legal irregularities?

g. Do the Articles unduly restrict the power or business of the Company or limit the life of the Company? If so, action should be taken now to remove the restriction.

2. Franchise Taxes

If nonpayment of state franchise or income taxes would jeopardize the good standing of the Company in its state of incorporation or principal place of business, obtain a certificate of compliance from the appropriate taxing authority.

3. Qualification in Other States

a. Obtain a list from a responsible officer of the Company as to each state where the Company transacts intrastate business. In general, this means purely local business such as maintaining a warehouse or wholesale or retail outlets, operating a manufacturing plant, maintaining a sales office with authority to make binding sales, rendering local maintenance services, etc.

b. If qualification as a foreign corporation was handled by a corporation services company, contact it to find out the status of qualification in each state where intrastate business is being conducted. If the Company or outside counsel handled the qualification, check their files.

c. If qualification has not been effected in any state where the Company is transacting business, advise the Company with reference to the necessity of qualifying there, the costs of doing so and the consequences of not doing so.

(i) Consider whether the state is a "noncure" state so that the Company could never sue on contracts made in that state prior to qualification.

(ii) Will the underwriters require qualification in every state where legally required even if an adverse legal consequence is remote?

d. Prior to rendering any opinion on qualification at the closing, good standing telegrams should be obtained from the various Secretaries of State where the Company is qualified to do business.

C. Capital Stock

1. Authorized Capital Structure

a. What classes of capital stock are authorized by the Articles of Incorporation and how many shares of each class are authorized?

THE EFFECTUATION OF A CORPORATE EVENT 317

b. What are the material provisions of each class of capital stock?

c. May directors authorize the issuance of additional shares without stockholder approval?

d. Do any shares carry preemptive rights by virtue of the Articles or statute? (Check the statute as it existed at the date of incorporation, as well as at present.)

e. Are shares entitled to cumulative voting rights for directors by virtue of the Articles or by statute?

f. Will an amendment of the Articles be required in connection with the offering to increase or decrease the authorized number of shares or to create a new class, to split the stock, to reclassify shares or to make other changes in the capital structure?

2. Stockholder Restrictions

a. Is there any eligibility requirement (such as United States citizenship, active participation in the business, etc.) for stock ownership imposed by the Articles or by-laws? If so, action must be taken to remove any requirement that would impede the corporate event or offering.

b. Is there any restriction on the transfer of stock (including a right of first refusal) imposed by the Articles, by-laws, shareholder agreements, legend conditions imposed by state blue-sky administrators, agreement with underwriters, etc.? Consider the effect on the corporate event or offering and take action to remove restrictions where necessary.

3. Voting Control

a. Who are the controlling persons ("affiliates") of the Company?

b. What is the basis for their control?

c. Is there any voting trust agreement which may affect control of the Company or give voting trustees control of 5 percent or more of the outstanding stock? If so, summarize its contents for disclosure in the prospectus.

d. Similarly, summarize any buy-sell or option agreements among shareholders that may affect control of the Company.

e. Determine if any person holds a proxy to vote a significant number of shares which may give him the status of a 5-percent shareholder.

4. Issuance of Stock

a. How many shares of each class are validly issued, fully paid and outstanding? Check with the stock transfer agent or, if none, examine the Company's own stock record books to determine if there are any irregularities in the issuance or transfer of shares.

b. Has each issuance of stock been authorized by appropriate resolution of the board of directors? If not, corrective action should now be taken.

c. Do the corporate records reflect payment of the consideration for the stock? (Check with the controller and/or outside auditor. Consider whether any shares were issued for impermissible consideration, such as promissory notes or future services. Take whatever corrective action is feasible.)

d. Was each issue of stock qualified with the appropriate blue-sky administrator? (Review applications for qualification, orders and correspondence concerning same.)

e. If required by a blue-sky administrator, have legends been printed on stock certificates that have been issued? If so, seek the consent of the administrator for removal of the legends.

f. What exemption from SEC registration was relied on for each stock issue? Absent special circumstances, this inquiry may be limited to the last three years.

g. Do any securities holders have registration rights (by demand or by "piggyback") which will come into play in connection with the proposed offering?

h. If the Company's stock is listed on any stock exchange, review the listing application and additional listing applications, if any, to determine (1) that all outstanding shares are listed, (2) whether any shares previously listed should be delisted, and (3) that all shares reserved for issuance have been listed subject to notice of issuance.

5. Dividends

a. If preferred stock is outstanding, has the Company been in arrears in the payment of cumulative dividends at any time during the past three years?

b. If dividends are in arrears on a class of preferred stock, does that class have special rights to elect directors or to take any other action? If so, will such action in fact be taken?

c. Are there any restrictions on the payment of dividends? (Check Articles, by-laws, loan agreements, indentures, financing leases and security agreements.)

6. Repurchase of Stock

a. Has the Company repurchased any of its stock during the past three years? If so, was such purchase made out of funds legally available and was appropriate corporate action taken to authorize the repurchase?

b. If repurchased shares are carried as treasury stock, should the board authorize its retirement to the status of authorized but unissued shares?

7. Trading Market

a. Is there an active trading market for the Company's stock? If so, obtain high and low market prices from the stock exchange (if listed), NASDAQ or The National Quotation Bureau (if unlisted) for each quarter during the past two years and for as current a date as possible prior to filing of the registration statement. Depending upon the size of the company, a complete trading history of its securities may be more readily available via one of the public data bases (e.g., Dow Jones Information/Retrieval).

b. If the market has behaved erratically, what is the explanation?

c. Is there any evidence of insider selling or buying in conjunction with price changes?

d. Have Company press releases had any immediate impact on the trading market?

e. Are a significant number of previously restricted shares "overhanging" the market that may be freed up for sale under SEC rule after completion of the offering?

D. Indebtedness and Obligations

1. Borrowings from Banks and Other Outsiders

a. Summarize important features of all loan agreements, trust indentures and debt instruments relating to outstanding loans and lines of credit. Give particular attention to affirmative and negative covenants, events of default and conditions. Do they restrict in any way the proposed offering or limit the Company's payment of dividends or freedom of operations?

b. Is the Company in default in the payment of interest or principal on any of its debt? If so, what curative measures will be taken or will waivers be obtained?

c. Is the Company in default of any covenants or conditions in loan agreements? If so, what curative measures will be taken or will waivers be obtained?

d. Review all security agreements (trust indentures, mortgages, deeds of trust, guaranties, installment purchase agreements, financing leases, etc.) to determine the extent of liens on Company property, restrictions on business, etc.

e. Does the corporate event you are handling require the consent of any lender? If so, follow up on obtaining such consent and be sure the consent is in proper form (i.e., complies with the underlying agreement).

f. Have loan agreements and borrowings been properly authorized by the board of directors? (Check the minutes.)

2. Borrowings from Insiders

a. Has the Company borrowed any funds from insiders (officers, directors, employees or stockholders)?

THE EFFECTUATION OF A CORPORATE EVENT 321

b. If so, are any such loans made on terms more favorable to either the lender or the Company than terms obtainable in an arm's-length transaction?

c. Was excessive security given for any such loans?

d. Has any insider guaranteed any loans or indebtedness owed by the Company? (Check loan documentation, discuss with controller, review questionnaires.) If so, on what terms and are such terms prudent?

3. Loans to Insiders

a. Has the Company made any loans over the past three years to officers, directors or stockholders?

(i) If so, on what terms; what was the highest unpaid balance outstanding at any time for each loan; and what is the present outstanding balance of each loan?

(ii) If so, were such loans properly authorized and legal in all respects?

b. Does the Company make loans to rank-and-file employees?

(i) If so, on what terms and what was the highest aggregate amount outstanding during the past three years and at present?

(ii) Were such loans properly authorized and legal in all respects?

E. Property

1. Leases

a. Review leases of the significant properties leased to the Company and summarize their important terms: expiration date, size and location of property, description of improvements, rent, options to renew or buy, restrictions on use and unusual provisions. Be sure to watch for any provisions which would restrict the proposed corporate event or offering.

b. Is the Company in default in payment of rent or in performance of any covenants or conditions? If so, what curative action will be taken or will waivers be obtained?

c. If any proceeds of the offering are to be used for leasehold improvements, is the lessor's consent necessary and has it been obtained? Follow up on obtaining such consent and be sure the consent is in proper form.

d. If the Company is the subtenant of any significant properties, determine that the underlying lease is not in default and that the sublease to the Company is not inconsistent with the main lease.

e. If material to the Company's operations, review equipment leases to determine unusual conditions, renewal or purchase options, defaults, etc.

2. Fee Title

a. Does Company have title insurance policies or abstracts of titles on all material real property held in fee? (Examine the policies and abstracts.)

b. Is there any defect in title (exceptions in title policy or abstract) which would affect the usability or marketability of any significant property?

3. Easements and Licenses

a. Does the Company own any easements or licenses necessary for the access or use of its significant properties? If so, examine the documentation to determine the extent, duration and enforceability of the easement or license.

b. Are any of the Company's significant properties subject to an easement, license or adverse use in favor of a third party? Is it probable that such easement, license or adverse use will preclude further development or use of the property by the Company?

4. Patents, Trademarks, Copyrights and Other Intangibles

a. If a material part of the Company's business is dependent on ownership or use of a patent, trademark, copyright, invention or other intangible, examine the evidence of ownership or license to determine its scope and restrictions.

THE EFFECTUATION OF A CORPORATE EVENT   323

b. Has the Company vigorously defended its ownership and taken action to stop infringement?

c. Is anyone challenging the validity of any such patent, trademark or copyright?

d. Has the Company received opinions from patent/trademark/copyright counsel as to the enforceability of its patents, trademarks and copyrights?

e. Does the Company have valid licenses to use patents and trademarks owned by others?

f. Has anyone claimed that the Company is infringing on patents, trademarks or copyrights owned by others?

g. Has the Company granted licenses to others to use its patents, trademarks, copyrights, inventions, etc.? If so, on what terms?

h. Has the Company improperly appropriated a trade secret or invention owned by another?

i. Has the Company taken appropriate steps to protect its trade secrets and inventions from appropriation by others?

j. Examine employment contracts to determine the extent to which the Company is entitled to own the inventions of its employees and the restrictions on their disclosure of the Company's trade secrets and inventions. (If the Company places substantial reliance on such contracts, consider the enforceability of such contracts under state law.)

5. Use of Properties

a. Is the Company's use of its property consistent with the rights conferred by leases and deeds? If not, what is the likely consequence and what can be done about it?

b. Is the Company interfering with an easement or mineral right of a third person?

c. Does the Company claim ownership of significant land or an easement by adverse possession or adverse use?

d. Is the Company's use of its properties in compliance with applicable zoning ordinances?

(i) If not, what is the likely consequence of violation?

(ii) Should a variance be applied for?

e. Is the Company in compliance with all state and federal environmental protection laws and regulations?

(i) If not, what curative action is planned?

(ii) What is the likely penalty for the violation?

6. Condition and Adequacy of Buildings and Equipment

a. Are buildings and equipment in good condition?

b. Are buildings used to capacity?

c. Are buildings adequate for anticipated growth?

7. Insurance

a. Are the significant properties covered by adequate extended coverage fire insurance?

b. On leased properties, if the lessor has the obligation to carry fire insurance, is the lessor, in fact, carrying such insurance?

F. Business Operations

1. Financial Statements

a. Review the financial statements for the last five years with particular reference to

(i) trends in sales and earnings;

(ii) liquidity;

(iii) choice in accounting policies;

(iv) capital stock account; and

(v) notes re contingencies.

THE EFFECTUATION OF A CORPORATE EVENT 325

b. Review the "management letters" of the outside auditor commenting on adequacy of accounting controls, etc. If any serious deficiencies are noted, have they been corrected?

c. Discuss the financial statements with the Company controller and outside auditor to determine any weaknesses in the accounting system or controls.

d. If the Company has changed auditors within the past two years, determine the reason and corroborate with the former auditor.

2. Budgets and Sales Data

a. Compare the Company's budget for the ensuing year with the budget for the prior year and the actual results of the prior year. Does the budget indicate results for the ensuing year that are inconsistent with the earnings trends of prior years?

b. Compare the Company's current backlog with the last two year-end backlogs.

(i) Were backlogs computed on a consistent basis during the periods under review?

(ii) Do backlogs represent noncancellable orders from customers?

(iii) What is the Company's experience in cancellation of backlogs?

(iv) Has there been any noticeable change in the time lag between receipt of orders and shipment? If so, why?

(v) Has the Company experienced any recent increase in cancellation of orders?

c. Did the Company use projections when negotiating with the clients? If so, review the reasonableness of the underlying assumptions.

d. Examine the Company's forms of sales contracts. Are the sales terms standard for the industry? Are there provisions for cancellation or returns by customers?

e. When are sales recorded as sales on the books? Is there any question that recorded sales may not be firm?

f. Are the Company's warranties overly broad? What is the Company's experience on claims for breach of warranty?

g. Who are the Company's largest customers and what is the trend in sales to them?

h. Do sales to any one customer (including the government) account for 10 percent or more of total sales? What is the partnership based on? To what extent are government contracts subject to renegotiation? What is the Company's experience in renegotiation?

3. Purchases and Inventory

a. Examine the Company's form of purchase order. Are the terms standard in the industry? Are there reasonable provisions for cancellation or return by the Company?

b. Are the relations with suppliers satisfactory?

c. Is the Company dependent on only a few suppliers for a significant amount of raw materials or inventory?

d. Are there any recent developments which may make inventory obsolete or may require a write-off?

e. Is inventory being built up at a faster rate than normal?

4. Accounts and Notes Receivable

a. Does the Company have perfected security interests in collateral securing accounts and notes receivable?

b. Has the Company encountered any recent slowdown in payment of accounts or notes receivable?

c. Is the Company's bad debt reserve adequate?

5. Liability Insurance

a. Does the Company have adequate product liability insurance? (Examine policies to determine amount, deductibles, scope of coverage and exclusions.)

b. Does the Company have adequate business interruption insurance? If not, is disclosure required on grounds of imprudent practice?

c. Does the Company have adequate public liability insurance?

d. Determine what other types of insurance coverage the Company has and their adequacy.

e. If the Company carries officers and directors' liability insurance, what is the amount of coverage? Does the policy protect officers and directors against liability under the Securities Act of 1933?

6. Business Licenses and Permits

a. Does the Company have all the business licenses and permits required of it

(i) under federal law?

(ii) under state law?

(iii) under local ordinances?

b. If not, what are the consequences of the violation and what curative action is being taken?

7. Joint Ventures and Partnerships

a. Review and summarize all joint venture and partnership agreements to which the Company is a party.

b. Who controls the business of the joint venture or partnership?

c. Does the Company have unusual exposure to liability under any such agreements?

8. Competition and Marketing Policies

a. Inquire of the Company officers as to the competitive situation.

(i) What is the extent of competition?

(ii) Who are the leaders in the industry?

(iii) What is the Company's relative position?

(iv) How does the Company compete as to both price and quality?

(v) What share of the market does the Company have or hope to capture?

b. Pricing policies.

(i) How does the Company determine its prices?

(ii) Does the Company discriminate in prices to customers? Does the Company grant quantity discounts? If so, are they legal under the Robinson-Patman Act?

(iii) Have there been customer complaints as to discriminatory pricing?

(iv) Is there any collusion with competitors in setting prices?

c. How does the Company market its products?

(i) Through its own sales force?

(ii) Through independent sales representatives?

(iii) Through dealers?

d. Arrangements with dealers.

(i) Does the Company grant exclusive market areas to its dealers?

(ii) How does the Company enforce exclusive dealer arrangements?

(iii) Are dealers precluded from handling competing products?

(iv) Does the Company suggest resale prices?

(v) Does the Company enforce suggested resale prices?

e. Trade associations.

(i) Does the Company belong to any trade associations?

(ii) Do the associations have legal counsel at meetings and take reasonable precautions to avoid price setting and other illegal anticompetitive practices?

f. Are there any areas in which the Company's marketing policies and practices may violate antitrust laws?

9. Pending Negotiations

Are any negotiations pending for asset acquisitions or dispositions, mergers, joint ventures or other material transactions?

THE EFFECTUATION OF A CORPORATE EVENT 329

G. Management and Employees

1. Management

a. Have the ostensible directors been properly elected and do they meet the qualifications, if any, for directors imposed in the Articles or by-laws?

b. Who are the properly elected officers? What persons other than officers perform equivalent top management functions?

c. In connection with an offering, prepare and circulate a questionnaire to officers (and persons performing top management functions), directors and 5-percent stockholders designed to elicit the information called for by items 3, 4 and 6 of SEC Regulation S-K.

d. Review completed questionnaires carefully and compare with information known to the Company (stock holdings, remuneration, stock options, perquisites, contracts, material transactions, etc.).

e. If the board of directors has an executive committee, who are its members?

f. Obtain and review copies of contracts and descriptions of transactions between the Company and officers, directors, 5-percent stockholders and their associates (i.e., spouse, relatives and in-laws having the same home as such person or who is a director or officer of any parent or subsidiary of the Company; any partnership in which the person is a general partner; any corporation in which the person is an officer; any limited partnership or corporation in which such person and related persons own 10 percent or more of the equity).

g. Did an independent majority of the board approve conflict-of-interest transactions involving insiders and their associates? Are such transactions fair to the Company and on terms similar to transactions entered into at arm's length?

h. Has any insider seized a corporate opportunity without approval by vote of disinterested directors made after full disclosure to them?

i. Are officers and directors entitled to be indemnified against liabilities incurred in the performance of their duties (including liabilities under Section 11 of the Securities Act of 1933)?

(i) Summarize indemnity provisions in Articles, by-laws, resolutions or contracts.

(ii) Summarize applicable statutory provisions.

j. Review and summarize material features of stock option plans and other management incentive plans.

2. Employee Relations

a. How many total employees are there? How many are unionized? How many are professionals (if business is dependent on them)?

b. What union contracts are about to expire?

c. If the Company anticipates any strikes in the near future, what disclosure problems are involved? What will be the Company's strategy and how long is the strike likely to last?

d. Does the Company's wage and fringe benefit structure for employees present a problem?

e. Is there any unionizing activity going on in a major plant which may result in a work stoppage?

f. Is the Company presently subject to any unfair labor practice charge before the NLRB?

g. Is the Company the subject of any arbitration proceeding under a union contract which might result in a materially unfavorable result as to wage costs, hiring, promotions, welfare benefits or retirement?

h. Do the Company's retirement plans comply with ERISA? If not, what are the likely consequences?

i. Is the Company under investigation or charged with unlawful discrimination in its employment practices? If so, what is the Company's position and the probable outcome?

j. Is the Company in compliance with minimum wage and hour laws, OSHA and other laws designed to protect employees?

H. Litigation

1. Review of Pending and Threatened Litigation and Administrative Proceedings

a. Determine current status of each suit, proceeding and asserted claims.

b. What is the Company's position as to each case and the likelihood of a material adverse result?

c. Give special consideration to administrative or judicial proceedings involving violation of environmental protection laws.

d. To what extent does the Company have any claim against an insider or the insider against the Company?

2. Review of Unasserted Claims

a. Discuss with management the probability of assertion of any claims against the Company for negligence, breach of contract, violations of law, infringement of property or other rights and violations of fiduciary duties owed to others.

b. Has the Company discovered any evidence of commercial bribery to obtain business or other improper payments?

c. Has the Company violated the Foreign Corrupt Practices Act?

3. Review Data Bases

Public data bases (e.g., Lexis) should be reviewed to determine if the company or its officers and directors have been named in any material litigation.

III. DRAFTING AN ACQUISITION AGREEMENT

Once you have determined why your client is buying, selling or raising capital and what he (or she) is getting, you must then assist in determining how best to effectuate the transaction in writing. It is at this juncture that most practitioners need help and should recognize their limitations. The Code of Professional Responsibility in the state of New York dictates that a lawyer should represent his client competently, that he should strive to become and remain proficient in his practice and that he should accept employment only in matters which he is or intends to become competent to handle. Completing a given corporate event requires knowledge of many legal disciplines. The tax ramifications require careful analysis. At this stage of the transaction, be sure that you have the active and knowledgeable support and counsel of a competent accountant and tax lawyer. Consider suggesting to your client the special engagement of experienced tax and accounting experts. The cost is not unduly burdensome and will invariably be outweighed by the benefits.

Given the above warning, set forth below is a prototype acquisition agreement which has been annotated, with comments in the form of practice guides, to illustrate the issues raised by each section. As you prepare the first draft of the document, each paragraph in the prototype acquisition agreement should help you tailor your agreement to fit your client's needs and objectives.

The form of an acquisition agreement depends, among other factors, on whether the transaction has been structured as a merger, a sale of stock or a sale of assets. Each acquisition agreement will, however, contain representations and warranties of the seller (to provide assurance to the buyer that it will be getting what it thinks it is paying for), representations and warranties of the buyer (which may be minimal if the consideration is cash or extensive if the consideration is securities of the buyer), covenants of the seller and buyer and conditions to the seller's and buyer's obligations to consummate the transaction. The nature and scope of the specific provisions to be included in an acquisition agreement depend, of course, on the particular businesses in which the buyer and seller are engaged and the resulting assurances that each party will seek to include in the agreement during the course of negotiations. Exhibits to the acquisition agreement, which contain exceptions to the representations and warranties, will also vary depending on the transaction.

In light of the foregoing, the following acquisition agreement should only be viewed as a basic model requiring significant revisions necessitated by the particular transaction. For this reason, the following commentary will include not only a discussion of the basic model but other provisions that the draftsperson should consider.

IV. AGREEMENT FOR PURCHASE OF ASSETS (ANNOTATED)

[The exhibits referred to in this agreement are for illustrative purposes only and are not actually included herein.]

AGREEMENT, dated as of ____, 19____, among ____, a New York corporation ("Buyer"), ____, a ____ corporation ("Seller") and [Name of Parent or Other Entity Controlling the Seller] ("Parent").

WITNESSETH:

WHEREAS, Seller desires to sell, and Buyer desires to purchase, all of the assets of Seller, including the assets more particularly described herein, all upon the terms and subject to the conditions herein set forth;

NOW, THEREFORE, in consideration of the premises and the mutual agreements herein set forth, the Seller, Buyer and the Parent hereby agree as follows:

A. Definitions

As used herein the following terms shall, unless the context clearly indicates otherwise, have the following meanings:

(1) **"Assorted Tools"** shall mean all hand tools and machine tools in which the Seller has on the Purchase Date any right, title and interest, including, without limitation, the hand tools and machine tools listed on Exhibit A annexed hereto.

(2) **"Assumed Contracts"** shall mean the Business Space Lease, Sales Contracts, Purchase Orders and such other contracts and agreements listed on Exhibit B hereto.

(3) **"Business Space"** shall mean the office, warehousing and manufacturing space presently occupied by Seller and located at ____, a lease with respect to which is annexed hereto as Exhibit C.

(4) **"Business Space Lease"** shall mean the lease between the Seller and [Name of Lessor] with respect to the Business Space, annexed hereto as Exhibit C.

(5) **"Closing Date"** or **"Closing"** shall mean 10:00 A.M. Eastern Standard Time on such date as shall be mutually agreed to by the parties hereto, provided that such date shall not be later than ____, 19____.

(6) **"Inventory"** shall mean all of the raw materials, work-in-process and finished goods and other inventory and all other supplies used in the operation of its business in which the Seller shall have any right, title and interest on the Purchase Date (a list of which has previously been provided by Seller to Buyer), together with any rights of the Seller to the warranties received from its suppliers with respect to such inventory and any related claims, credits, rights of recovery and setoff with respect thereto.

(7) **"Machinery and Equipment"** shall mean all of the machinery, equipment, furniture, fixtures and improvements, spare parts, supplies and motor vehicles used by the Seller in connection with the operation of its business and located on the Business Space or elsewhere on the Purchase Date and all of the replacement parts for any of the foregoing, in which the Seller has on the Purchase Date any right, title or interest, and the tools and dies, the punch presses and the assorted tools, together with any rights of the Seller to the warranties and licenses, if any, received from manufacturers and sellers of the aforesaid items and any related claims, credits and rights of recovery with respect to such Machinery and Equipment.

(8) **"Patents and Trademarks"** shall mean all of the inventions, patent applications, patents, trademarks, trademark registrations and applications, copyrights, know-how, formulae, trade secrets and trade names in which Seller has on the Purchase Date any right, title or interest, including, without limitation, the patents, trademarks and copyrights listed on Exhibit D annexed hereto.

THE EFFECTUATION OF A CORPORATE EVENT 335

(9) **"Punch Presses"** shall mean all of the punch presses in which the Seller has on the Purchase Date any right, title and interest, including, without limitation, the punch presses listed on Exhibit E annexed hereto.

(10) **"Purchase Date"** shall mean ____, 19____.

(11) **"Purchase Orders"** shall mean those purchase orders and purchase commitments of Seller outstanding on the Purchase Date which are listed in Exhibit F annexed hereto, and such purchase orders and purchase commitments of Seller outstanding on the Purchase Date not so listed which do not in the aggregate exceed $1,000.

(12) **"Purchased Property"** shall mean collectively the Machinery and Equipment, Punch Presses, Tools and Dies, Assorted Tools, Inventory, Patents and Trademarks, the Business Space Lease and all of the tangible and intangible property of every kind and description, including without limitation all of the assets, receivables, cash, contract rights, name and goodwill, properties, real and personal, engineering data, drawings, cuts, plates, stationery, office supplies and forms, catalogues, manuals, customer lists and data, and all of the tangible and intangible assets (including patent and trademark rights) assigned, transferred or sold to Seller or the Parent by [Name of Seller] or the Trustee in Bankruptcy thereof, and other rights and interests, in which the Seller has on the Purchase Date any right, title or interest or which are used in connection with the business of the Seller on the Purchase Date, it being understood that the business of the Seller includes, without limitation, the following: (a) the ____ division of Seller which manufactures and distributes hardware for the electronics and defense industries, including, without limitation, component clips, printed circuit board holders and bus bars; (b) the ____ division of Seller which is involved in the business of re-inking its machine rolls, supplying spare parts for and providing other services to users of its machines; and (c) the ____ division of Seller which manufactures and distributes a proprietary annular power saw and accessory equipment.

(13) **"Tools and Dies"** shall mean all of the tools and dies in which the Seller has on the Purchase Date any right, title and interest, includ-

ing, without limitation, all tools and dies used in connection with the manufacture of clips and bus bars and including, without limitation, the tools and dies listed on Exhibit G annexed hereto.

(14) "**Sales Contracts**" shall mean those unfilled sales contracts, customer orders and commitments between Seller and its customers listed in Exhibit H annexed hereto, and such sales contracts, customer orders and commitments unfilled as of the Purchase Date and not so listed which do not in the aggregate exceed $_____.

The function of this section is to identify the principal categories of assets to be purchased and to provide certain definitions of related terms used in the agreement. Asset categories should be defined in broad terms (if all assets of that type are being sold) and should include all such assets existing at the closing date, whether or not scheduled elsewhere or reflected on a balance sheet. In addition, if an entire operating business is being sold, the definition of "Purchased Property" should include all tangible or intangible property used in the business that is not covered elsewhere or specifically excluded. While the definitions outline all major asset categories, it is customary within each category to require a schedule listing specific material assets in such category, for example, parcels of real estate or material purchase orders, supply contracts or equipment leases. By requiring the seller to list material assets in a schedule, the buyer and its counsel will be aided in conducting a business and legal review of the acquired business and will have readily available information which will be required to be provided to a lender providing financing for the acquisition. Any assets not being sold should be specifically identified as "excluded assets." In this regard, a buyer may elect not to assume certain types of contracts (for example, collective bargaining agreements).

In defining the assets to be purchased, problems may arise in situations when the business being sold is not easily divisible from other assets of the seller. This may occur if the seller conducts more than one business from the same facility or if other common assets are used to service the business being sold and the seller's other businesses. In these

THE EFFECTUATION OF A CORPORATE EVENT 337

cases, care must be taken in framing the definitions to ensure that the assets being transferred are sufficient to operate the business after the closing.

B. Balance Sheet

All references in this Agreement to the balance sheet of Seller or to the balance sheet of Seller as included in Exhibit K hereto shall mean the balance sheet of Seller as at ____, 19____, included in such Exhibit K.

This section establishes a reference point for various representations and warranties contained in the agreement. In addition to obtaining appropriate representations and warranties on this balance sheet, the buyer will seek to obtain representations and warranties covering material changes in the business after this date. Typically, the balance sheet date will serve as the starting point for such representations, which may cover undisclosed liabilities, the absence of a material adverse change in the business and other specified matters.

C. Purchase and Sale of the Purchased Property

(1) **Purchase.** Subject to the terms and conditions herein set forth, on the Closing Date Seller shall sell (and the Parent shall cause Seller to sell) and Buyer shall purchase all of the Purchased Property as of the Purchase Date, free and clear of all mortgages, liens, charges, encumbrances or defects of any nature whatsoever except as described on Exhibit I.

(2) **Sale at Closing Date.** The sale, transfer, assignment and delivery by Seller of the Purchased Property to Buyer, as herein provided, shall be effected on the Closing Date by full warranty deeds, bills of sale, endorsements, assignments and such other instruments of transfer and conveyance satisfactory in form and substance to counsel for Buyer. To the extent that any sales or other similar taxes may be imposed by reason of such sale, transfer, assignment and delivery of the Purchased Property, Seller shall pay any excess of such taxes over $____.

(3) **Subsequent Documentation.** Seller shall, at any time and from time to time after the Closing Date, upon the request of Buyer and at the expense of Seller, do, execute, acknowledge and deliver or will cause to

be done, executed, acknowledged and delivered all such further acts, deeds, assignments, transfers, conveyances and assurances as may be reasonably required for the better assigning, transferring, granting, conveying, assuring and confirming to Buyer, or to its successors and assigns, or for aiding and assisting in collecting and reducing to possession any or all of the Purchased Property to be purchased by Buyer as provided herein.

(4) **Assignment of Contracts.** On the Closing Date, the Seller shall assign to Buyer, and Buyer shall assume, as of the Purchase Date, all of the Assumed Contracts by means of an Assignment and Assumption Agreement in the form of Exhibit J annexed hereto and made a part hereof. To the extent that the assignment of any Assumed Contract shall require the consent of the party thereto, this Agreement shall not constitute an agreement to assign the same if an attempted assignment would constitute a breach thereof. The Seller will use its best efforts to obtain the consent of the other parties to such contracts for the assignment thereof to the Buyer. If such consent is not obtained in respect of any such Assumed Contract, the Seller will cooperate with the Buyer in any reasonable arrangement requested by the Buyer to provide for the Buyer the benefits under any such Assumed Contract, including enforcement, at the cost of and for the benefit of the Buyer, of any and all rights of the Seller against the other party thereto with respect to such Assumed Contract.

(5) **Assumption of Liabilities.** At the Closing the Buyer shall assume, and agree to pay, perform or discharge, subject to the provisions of Paragraph C(4) above, the obligations of Seller under the Assumed Contracts accruing from and after the Purchase Date, all sales contracts, customer orders, customer commitments, purchase orders, purchase commitments and liabilities of Seller arising in the ordinary course of business between the Purchase Date and Closing Date, and all liabilities of Seller disclosed on the balance sheet of Seller included as part of Exhibit K annexed hereto except for the amount of $____ of "income taxes to parent company" reflected on such balance sheet. Except as specifically provided in the foregoing sentence, the Buyer shall not assume or agree to pay, perform or discharge, nor shall the Buyer be

responsible, directly or indirectly, for any debts, obligations, contracts or liabilities of the Seller wherever or however incurred, including, without limitation, all federal, state and local tax liabilities for all periods ended on or prior to ____, 19____.

(6) **Collection of Receivables.** Seller agrees that Buyer shall have the right and authority to collect, for the account of Buyer, all receivables and other items which shall be transferred to Buyer as provided herein, and to endorse with the name of Seller any checks received on account of any such receivables or other items. Seller agrees that it will transfer and deliver to Buyer or its designee any cash or other property that Seller may receive in respect of such receivables or other items. A list of all receivables of Seller as of the Purchase Date, broken down by name of customer, date incurred and amount, is contained in Exhibit L attached hereto.

(7) **Conduct of Business.** All operations of the Seller between the Purchase Date and the date hereof have been, and all operations of the Seller between the date hereof and the Closing Date shall be, conducted in the ordinary course of business consistent with its prior business practice by the Seller for the account and benefit, and at the expense, of the Buyer as if this Agreement had been consummated on the Purchase Date, provided that if for any reason the Closing shall not occur hereunder, the Buyer shall have no rights or liabilities with respect to such operations, and in such event the business of Seller from and after the Purchase Date shall be conducted at the expense and for the account and benefit of the Seller. For purposes of the foregoing sentence, all income received or receivable from and after the Purchase Date, and all expenses incurred, accrued or paid in the ordinary course of business from and after the Purchase Date shall, as to such income, be the property of, and as to such expenses, be the obligations of, the Buyer if the Closing hereunder shall occur or of the Seller if the Closing hereunder shall not occur. The Seller has not taken from and after the Purchase Date, and shall not take from and after the date hereof through the Closing Date, any action in connection with the conduct of the business of Seller other than in the ordinary course of business without the written consent of Buyer, and, except as approved by the Buyer, has not from and after the

Purchase Date sold, leased, disposed of or encumbered or entered into any commitment to sell, lease, dispose of or encumber and shall not from and after the date hereof through the Closing Date, sell, lease, dispose of or encumber or enter into any commitment to sell, lease, dispose of or encumber, any item of Purchased Property, except items of finished goods Inventory sold only in the ordinary course of business. Without limiting the generality of the foregoing, the Seller has not from and after the Purchase Date and shall not from and after the date hereof through the Closing Date, without the consent of the Buyer:

(a) changed or change the type of business conducted by it;

(b) hired or hire any additional employees except for ____;

(c) terminated or terminate any employee;

(d) changed or change any salary of any employee, except for: ____ (increased from $____ to $____ per annum as of ____, 19____), ____ (increased from $____ per week to $____ per week as of ____, 19____) and ____ (increased from $____ to $____ per annum as of ____, 19____);

(e) made or make any general or uniform increase in the rate of pay of its employees or entered or enter into any collective bargaining agreements pertaining to its employees;

(f) entered or enter into any commitment, contract or lease with respect to the purchase, lease or sale of capital assets;

(g) failed or fail to repair, maintain or replace all its equipment in accordance with practices and procedures theretofore followed and failed or fail to maintain its equipment and the Business Space in its present operating condition; and

(h) paid or pay or included or include in any expenses for which Buyer shall be liable for the period between the Purchase Date and the Closing Date any expenses incurred by Seller for the purpose of consummating this Agreement and the transactions contemplated hereby, including but not limited to any expenses for attorneys' or accountants' fees, except for expenses accrued on the balance sheet of Seller included as part of Exhibit K.

THE EFFECTUATION OF A CORPORATE EVENT 341

This section provides the mechanics for transferring the acquired business from the seller to the buyer. Subsection (1) sets forth the buyer's agreement to buy and the seller's agreement to sell, and requires any liens, mortgages or similar encumbrances on the assets to be listed. In addition to requiring the seller to list these items, it generally would be prudent for the buyer to engage a search bureau to conduct a search of public records for liens filed against the seller in the jurisdictions where the assets are located. With respect to real estate assets, the buyer may elect to have a title search done and to obtain title insurance.

Subsection (2) establishes the date of closing and requires the seller to deliver documentation satisfactory to buyer with respect to transferring legal title to the assets sold. Personal property generally may be transferred by delivering a single bill of sale. Certain types of assets, such as patents, trademarks and other types of intellectual property, should be transferred pursuant to separate forms of assignment which comply with requirements for recording the same with the United States Patent and Trademark Office or other similar agencies. Real estate should be transferred by separate deeds or lease assignments in proper form for recording in the jurisdictions where the properties are located. The agreement should specifically allocate between the buyer and seller the responsibility for sales and transfer taxes relating to the sale. Generally, exemptions from state sales taxes should be available for certain categories of assets transferred in bulk or to be held by the buyer for resale. Where the transfer of real estate (including leased real estate) located in New York is involved, particular attention should be given to the applicability of the New York State Real Property Gains Tax. In light of special requirements which may be applicable to transferring legal title to particular categories of assets as noted above, subsection (3) generally requires the seller to deliver any further documents which may be necessary to vest title to the purchased assets in the buyer.

Subsection (4) provides for the assignment and assumption of contracts relating to the business being sold. Typically, purchase orders, long-term supply contracts, equipment leases, real property leases and other types of third-party contracts will not be assignable without the consent of the other parties to such contracts. Buyer and seller should specifically identify which consents are required as a condition to closing. However, since it is almost always impractical to obtain consents for all nonassignable contracts, the agreement will provide that if a required consent is not obtained by closing for any nonessential contract, the contract will not be assigned. Instead, the seller will nominally remain on the contract and provide the benefits of the contract to the buyer. One area where this procedure is frequently used is in the case of government contracts, when novations of such contracts with the buyer generally cannot be accomplished within the contemplated closing period.

Subsection (5) specifies what liabilities are being assumed by the buyer. This provision generally is subject to substantial negotiations between the parties. Typically, the buyer wants to assume specified liabilities and be indemnified by the seller for undisclosed liabilities. On the other hand, the seller generally seeks to have the buyer assume all liabilities relating to the business being sold and may only be willing to represent that, to the best of its knowledge, no undisclosed liabilities exist. The outcome of this negotiation and the level of risk a buyer is willing to assume generally are functions of the price being paid. (For example, if the price is a bargain price, the buyer may be more willing to take the business "as is.") Negotiation of this provision must be undertaken in conjunction with the discussion of the representations and warranties generally.

Subsection (6) provides a mechanism for ensuring that collections of receivables are made for the account of the buyer. By requiring seller to list significant receivables, the buyer is able to identify important customers. It is often prudent for the buyer (together with the seller) to contact such customers prior to closing to ensure an orderly transition of the business.

Subsection (7) provides limitations on actions which may be taken by seller between the date the agreement is assigned and the closing date and, accordingly, is not necessary where signing and closing are done simultaneously. The thrust of this provision is to require the seller to conduct the business substantially as it had been conducted in the past *and to give the buyer the right to approve certain material events, such as capital commitments over a specified amount and increases in compensation to employees. From the seller's perspective, this provision must be broad enough to permit it to run its business in the ordinary course since, if the transaction does not close, the seller will bear the results of any degradation in the business arising from the buyer's failure to give a required consent. The buyer, on the other hand, needs to ensure that it has a say in decisions that affect the future value of the business and that the seller does not engage in certain questionable practices such as accelerating the collection of receivables or delaying payment of payables. As a practical matter, when the business will be managed on a day-to-day basis after the closing by existing employees, the buyer often will rely on such employees' self-interest (through equity or other incentive arrangements) to ensure that the business has not been materially harmed during this period.*

D. Payment of Purchase Price

The purchase price for the Purchased Property shall be $____. Subject to the terms and conditions herein set forth, the Buyer will pay the purchase price as follows:

(1) On the Closing Date Buyer shall deliver to Seller a certified or bank check payable to the order of Seller, in the amount of $____.

(2) On the Closing Date Buyer shall deliver to Seller the Note (the "Note") of the Buyer in the principal amount of $____ in the form annexed hereto as Exhibit M.

This section encompasses the basic economic arrangement between the buyer and seller in respect of the business and assets being sold. All components of the purchase price, including any deferred portion and any post-closing adjustments, should be set forth. It is common for asset sales to be priced in relation to the most recent balance sheet for the business. Since the composition of that balance sheet undoubtedly will change during the period prior to closing, many asset transactions require a "closing balance sheet" which serves to verify, within specified limits, that the business actually conveyed at closing is not materi-

ally different, either in terms of total assets and liabilities or in the allocation of assets and liabilities among the various categories, from the business reflected in such earlier balance sheet. If material differences are found, a post-closing adjustment typically will require either a refund of part of the purchase price paid at closing or the payment to the seller of additional amounts.

Where the seller agrees to take back a promissory note of the buyer for all or part of the purchase price, the form of the note should be attached as an exhibit to the agreement. If the buyer is obtaining senior financing for the acquisition, the terms of the seller note should be reviewed and approved by the senior lender prior to signing the agreement, if feasible. To the extent this is not done, the buyer risks that the transaction may not close because of disputes arising between the senior lender and the seller over the schedule of payments under the seller note, the terms of subordination or other terms of the note. This risk is heightened where the buyer's obligation to close is not subject to receipt of financing and, accordingly, a breach by the buyer (or, more likely, a renegotiation of price) would result if any such dispute could not be resolved.

E. Closing

The Closing under this Agreement shall take place at the offices of [Name and Address of Buyer's Attorney] on the Closing Date.

This section specifies the date, time and place of closing. The date specified for closing generally is set with regard to the nature of the conditions to closing (e.g., arrangement of financing or obtaining third-party approvals and consents) and should specify an outside (or "walk-away") date. The closing date may be written as a specific date or a certain number of days following satisfaction or waiver of the conditions to closing. Where a specific date is set, the agreement should clearly delineate what rights the parties have if the closing does not occur by such date (for example, liquidated damage payments).

THE EFFECTUATION OF A CORPORATE EVENT

F. Representations and Warranties of Seller and the Parent

The Seller and the Parent, as a material inducement to Buyer to execute and deliver this Agreement, jointly and severally represent and warrant to Buyer as follows:

(1) **Organization and Standing.** Seller is a corporation duly organized, validly existing and in good standing under the laws of the State of ____, is qualified to do business as a foreign corporation and is in good standing in all states wherein the character of the property owned or the nature of the business transacted by Seller makes qualification by Seller as a foreign corporation necessary. The Parent is a corporation duly organized, validly existing and in good standing under the laws of the State of ____.

This standard provision concerning the corporate organization and qualification of the seller customarily allows the seller to qualify its representation by stating that it is qualified to do business as a foreign corporation in all states in which its failure to be so qualified would have a material adverse effect on its business.

Acquisition agreements also include representations as to business entities owned by the seller and the organization of such entities and their qualifications to do business as foreign corporations.

Representations as to the capitalization of the seller and its subsidiaries are common contractual provisions.

(2) **Authority.** Seller and the Parent have full corporate authority to operate their respective businesses as conducted on the date hereof and to execute and perform in accordance with this Agreement, and this Agreement constitutes a valid and binding obligation of Seller and the Parent enforceable in accordance with its terms, and each document of transfer contemplated by this Agreement, when executed and delivered by Seller in accordance with the provisions hereof, shall be valid and legally binding upon Seller in accordance with its terms; this Agreement and all transactions contemplated hereby have been duly authorized by all requisite corporate action by Seller and the Parent.

Acquisition agreements commonly require delivery of the board of directors' minutes approving the transaction.

(3) **Conflicting Agreements; No Liens.** Neither the execution nor delivery of this Agreement nor fulfillment nor compliance with the terms and conditions hereof will constitute a breach by Seller or the Parent of their respective certificates of incorporation or by-laws or result in a breach of the terms, conditions or provisions of, or constitute a default under or result in a violation of any agreement, contract, instrument, order, judgment or decree to which Seller or the Parent is a party or by which any of them is bound except for items specified on Exhibit N, or result in a violation by Seller or the Parent of any existing law or statute or any material rule or regulation of any jurisdiction or of any order, decree, writ or injunction of any court or governmental department, bureau, board, agency or instrumentality or result in the creation or imposition of any lien, charge, restriction, security interest or encumbrance of any nature whatsoever on the Purchased Property, except as listed on Exhibit I.

This representation could be expanded to include references to subsidiaries of the seller.

(4) **Consents.** Except for items specified on Exhibit N, no consent from or other approval of any governmental entity or other person is necessary in connection with the execution of this Agreement or the consummation by Seller or the Parent of the transactions contemplated hereby or the continuation of the business of Seller by Buyer in the manner previously conducted by Seller.

Obtaining such consents would in all likelihood constitute a condition to closing.

(5) **Real Property; Leaseholds.** No real property is owned or held under lease by Seller or is used in connection with or, to the knowledge of Seller or the Parent, necessary for the business of Seller as such business is now conducted except for the Business Space. Seller is the owner and holder of all leasehold estates purported to be granted by the Business Space Lease, and Seller has not been notified of any default under or termination of such lease.

(6) **Title to Purchased Property.** Seller owns all of the right, title and interest in and to all of the Purchased Property and shall own such property on the Closing Date free and clear of all mortgages, liens, charges, encumbrances or title defects of any nature whatsoever except as specified on Exhibit I.

These representations (5) and (6), collectively, would include statements concerning (a) the ownership and location of all real property owned by the seller and its subsidiaries, (b) the lessor and location of all real property leased by the seller and its subsidiaries and (c) the validity and enforceability of such leases.

(7) **Inventory.** The Inventory is merchantable and fit for intended use and is free of any material defects in workmanship. The finished goods Inventory is of a type, quantity and quality usable and salable in the ordinary course of business of Seller. This subparagraph (7) shall not be applicable with respect to Inventory which is not valued or which is written down or reserved against (to the extent of such write-down or reserve) on the balance sheet included as part of Exhibit K. This subparagraph (7) shall not be applicable with respect to the ____ division of Seller, and the second sentence of this subparagraph (7) shall not be applicable with respect to the ____ division of Seller.

This representation may be omitted where the seller is engaged in a service business. In such cases, it is common to include a representation that the seller's accounts receivable are bona fide accounts receivable created in the ordinary course of business and have been collected or are fully collectible. Such a representation would normally define an uncollectible account receivable as one not being collected within a specified period of time. The acquisition would provide for the buyer to be indemnified for such uncollectible accounts.

(8) **Compensation Due Employees.** Except as shown in Paragraph C(7) hereof, Exhibit O annexed hereto and made a part hereof is a true and complete list showing the names and job descriptions of all persons employed by Seller or employed in connection with the business of Seller together with a statement as to the full amount of compensation paid or payable to, or on behalf of, each person for services rendered

during the period from ____, 19____, through ____, 19____, and the current aggregate base compensation rate for each such person.

Neither Seller nor the Parent has any outstanding liability other than amounts included in the $____ of accrued expenses on the balance sheet included as part of Exhibit K annexed hereto with respect to such employees for payment of wages, vacation pay (whether accrued or otherwise), salaries, bonuses, reimbursable employee business expenses, pensions, contributions under any employee benefit plans or any other compensation, current or deferred, under any labor or employment contracts, whether oral or written, based upon or accruing with respect to those services of such employees performed prior to the date hereof except for (a) any payment due at the rate specified for an employee listed on Exhibit O with respect to any period after the Purchase Date, (b) amounts accrued with respect to vacation pay for periods after the Purchase Date, and (c) amounts accrued with respect to periods after the Purchase Date for any pension plan or insurance policy listed on Exhibit U. Seller or the Parent has not, because of past practices or previous commitments with respect to such employees, established any rights on the part of such employees to receive additional compensation with respect to any period after the Purchase Date, except for commissions as described on Exhibit O. Any outstanding liabilities or amounts payable with respect to such employees or rights to receive additional compensation of the types described in the preceding two sentences (other than amounts included in such $____ or described in clauses (a), (b) and (c) above) shall be paid by the Parent.

As with all representations, this representation must be revised to elicit the specific information that the buyer requires.

(9) **Union Agreements and Employment Agreements.** Seller or the Parent is not a party to any union, collective bargaining or similar agreements covering any employees employed in the conduct of the business of Seller nor does Seller have any employment agreements with any employees that are not terminable at will on 30 days' notice at the election of Seller, without extra payment of penalty. The Seller does not have any policy arrangement of any kind with any of its employees

THE EFFECTUATION OF A CORPORATE EVENT 349

regarding the payment of termination pay irrespective of the reason or cause of termination other than the payment of two weeks' pay in the case of layoff. There are no pending or threatened labor disputes between the Seller or the Parent and any of the employees employed in the conduct of the business of Seller, and Seller has not received any claim affecting labor relations or threat of strike or other interruptions of work. No union has attempted, is attempting or has threatened to unionize the employees employed in the conduct of the business of Seller.

Sellers usually try to limit this representation to written employment agreements, while buyers usually attempt to expand the representation to relate to all employment contracts other than those terminable at will (which is a matter of state law).

(10) **Contracts and Agreements.** Seller has performed all of its obligations under the Assumed Contracts required to have been performed by it on or prior to the date hereof, and Seller has not received any notice of default, nor is Seller in default, nor does any condition exist which with notice or lapse of time, or both, would render Seller in default under any Assumed Contract. The assignment of the Assumed Contracts does not require the consent of the other party thereto except as specified on Exhibit N.

References in this representation to assumed contracts relate to an assets acquisition in which only specific liabilities are assumed. In the context of an acquisition of stock, this representation would require the listing of all contracts in specified categories and include statements concerning the validity and enforceability thereof.

(11) **Insurance.** Exhibit P annexed hereto lists and describes all insurance policies now in force with respect to the Purchased Property and the business of Seller. Copies of all of such policies have previously been delivered to Buyer. The Seller will continue in full force and effect through the Closing Date all of such policies of insurance. Seller has not been refused any insurance with respect to the Purchased Property during the last three years.

This representation could be expanded to include information concerning the claims history of the seller under the listed policies and the coverage of such claims by the insurance carrier.

(12) **Licenses, Permits and Consents.** There are no licenses or permits currently required by Seller for the operation of the business of Seller. Seller is not aware of any circumstances relating to Buyer's proposed use of the Purchased Property which would require Buyer to obtain any licenses or permits except for permits relating to its _____ division.

This representation could be expanded to include information concerning licenses and permits required by the seller's employees. Information could also be included concerning the validity of licenses, the absence of any notice from the licensing authority regarding the termination or cancellation of such licenses and the licensing history of the seller's employees (whether any such person has been barred from or ordered to cease and desist from any activities or has had any license denied, revoked, restricted or suspended).

(13) **Litigation.** Except as described on Exhibit Q annexed hereto, there are no actions, suits, proceedings or investigations pending or, to the knowledge of Seller or the Parent, threatened against or involving Seller or brought by Seller or affecting any of the Purchased Property at law or in equity or admiralty or before or by any federal, state, municipal or other governmental department, commission, board, agency or instrumentality, domestic or foreign, nor has any such action, suit, proceeding or investigation been pending during the 24-month period preceding the date hereof; and Seller is not operating its business under or subject to, or in default with respect to, any order, writ, injunction, or decree of any court or federal, state, municipal or governmental department, commission, board, agency or instrumentality, domestic or foreign.

The buyer may wish to expand this representation to include a statement by the seller that there are no disputes or circumstances which might ultimately result in a claim being asserted against the seller or any of its subsidiaries.

THE EFFECTUATION OF A CORPORATE EVENT 351

(14) **Compliance with Laws.** To the best of its knowledge, Seller has complied with and is operating its business in compliance with all laws, regulations and orders applicable to the business conducted by it, and the present uses by the Seller of the Purchased Property do not violate any such laws, regulations and orders. Seller has no knowledge of any material present or future expenditures that will be required with respect to any of Seller's facilities to achieve compliance with any present statute, law or regulation, including those relating to the environment or occupational health and safety.

The buyer would certainly attempt to have this representation made by the seller without the "to the best of its knowledge" qualification.

(15) **Pension Plans.** Except for plans specified on Exhibit U, there are no profit-sharing, pension plans or other plans of indirect or deferred compensation or employee benefit plans for any of Seller's employees or employees engaged in the conduct of Seller's business except for an option granted to ____ under the Parent's Non-Qualified Stock Option Plan. The Parent agrees that so long as he continues to be employed by Buyer, such employment shall be treated as employment by Seller for purposes of options held by him, which are vested or which will become vested in the future under the Parent's Non-Qualified Stock Option Plan.

This representation could be expanded by the buyer to include information with respect to the operation of the referenced plans. This representation must be drafted and the seller's benefit plans reviewed by counsel experienced in employee benefit matters.

(16) **Disclosure.** No representation or warranty by the Seller contained in this Agreement, and no statement contained in any certificate or other instrument furnished or to be furnished to Buyer pursuant hereto, or in connection with the transactions contemplated hereby, contains or will contain any untrue statement of a material fact, or omits or will omit to state any material fact which is necessary in order to make the statements contained therein not misleading.

This representation is frequently the source of considerable controversy. Sellers often object to this representation on the ground that it imposes a "10b-5" form of contract liability in addition to the obligations imposed by the individual representations and warranties.

(17) **Subsidiaries.** There are no wholly or partly owned subsidiaries of Seller or other entities in which Seller has a proprietary interest. Each division or type or major subdivision of Seller's operations and business is disclosed in items (a) through (c) of Paragraph A(12).

See comments to F(3) above.

(18) **Bank Accounts.** Exhibit R annexed hereto specifies accurately and completely each and every bank account, banking arrangement and safe deposit box used in connection with the business or operations of Seller at the Purchase Date, specifying the bank or type of account or other arrangement and the balance or amount of funds in such account or deposit box or subject to such arrangement.

(19) **Purchase Order and Commitments of Seller.** Exhibit F annexed hereto lists all unfilled purchase orders and purchase commitments of Seller outstanding as of the Purchase Date, all of which were made in the usual and ordinary course of business; to the best of Seller's knowledge, the suppliers under said orders and commitments are not in default, pursuant to the terms of said orders and commitments, as to product quality and time of delivery as of said date except as set forth in Exhibit F.

See comments to F(7) above.

(20) **Customer Orders and Commitments.** Exhibit H annexed hereto lists all unfilled customer orders and commitments pertaining to Seller's business received by Seller and on hand as of the Purchase Date; none of the orders of the ten largest customers listed on Exhibit H has been cancelled or has cancellation thereof been threatened except as shown on Exhibit T. Buyer shall be entitled to receive on the Closing Date all advances or prepayments received by Seller from such customers under the provisions of such orders or otherwise for products to be delivered by Buyer (or by Seller for the account of Buyer) after the Purchase Date.

See comments to F(7) above.

THE EFFECTUATION OF A CORPORATE EVENT   353

(21) **Medical, Hospitalization, Life Insurance, etc.** The Seller has set forth in Exhibit U annexed hereto a list of all medical, health, hospitalization and life insurance plans, programs and policies in effect pertaining to any of the employees of Seller.

This representation is important for informational reasons so the buyer can assess the cost of the seller's insurance program and determine whether such program should be terminated or maintained.

(22) **Necessary Property.** Seller is selling Buyer all machinery and equipment and other assets required by Buyer to manufacture the product lines and continue the business of Seller in the same manner as heretofore conducted by Seller. Seller has the full right to produce, manufacture, sell and distribute such products produced, manufactured, sold and distributed by it without incurring any liability for license fees, royalties or other compensation, or for any claims of infringement of patent or trademark rights. All of the business described in items (a) through (c) of Paragraph A(12) hereof is conducted by Seller and not by the Parent itself or any other subsidiary, division or entity of the Parent.

This representation would be omitted for a seller engaged in a service as opposed to a manufacturing business.

(23) **Patents and Trademarks.** Seller owns no patents, trademarks, inventions, patent rights, trade secrets, formulae, trade names or copyrights nor has Seller applied for any patents or trademark registrations except those listed on Exhibit D hereto which are to be assigned to Buyer at the Closing without additional consideration and which are not subject to any royalty or license arrangements whatsoever, except as related to the Agreement between Seller and _____. If Seller hereafter learns of the existence of any additional patents, patent rights, trademarks, trade secrets, inventions, trade names or copyrights intended to be sold hereunder, Seller shall promptly assign the same to Buyer. Except as shown on Exhibit D, Seller or the Parent has not received any notice or claim of infringement of any patents, inventions, rights, trademarks, trade names or copyrights of others with reference to the processes, methods, formulae or procedures used by Seller in the operation

of its business, and Seller or the Parent has no actual knowledge not generally available in the trade of any new products, inventions, procedures or methods of manufacturing developed by any of Seller's competitors or any other information concerning same which could reasonably be expected to supersede or make obsolete the products of Seller or the procedures or methods of manufacturing used by Seller or the significant suppliers of Seller.

In situations where intellectual property is material to a seller's business, the buyer should require as a condition to closing an opinion concerning the ownership of such property.

(24) **Contracts, Agreements and Commitments.** There are no material contracts, agreements or other commitments, written or oral, not listed herein or in the Exhibits hereto, to which Seller is a party, or by which it is bound or which pertain in any way to Seller's business.

This representation could be combined with F(10).

(25) **Liabilities.** Seller has as of the Purchase Date and shall have on the Closing Date no liabilities of any kind whatsoever, contingent or otherwise, except liabilities under the Assumed Contracts, such liabilities which are disclosed on the balance sheet of the Seller annexed hereto as Exhibit K, liabilities relating to the litigation described on Exhibit Q hereto and liabilities incurred in the ordinary course of business between the Purchase Date and Closing Date.

This representation could be expanded by the buyer to refer to "liabilities or obligations of any nature, whether absolute, accrued, known or unknown, contingent or otherwise and whether due or to become due, including, without limitation, liabilities for taxes (with interest and penalties thereon)."

Acquisition agreements customarily include representations concerning the preparation and presentation of interim and year-end financial statements, which representations form the basis of the representation discussed in the preceding paragraph.

THE EFFECTUATION OF A CORPORATE EVENT 355

(26) **Capital Stock.** All of the issued and outstanding capital stock of Seller is owned, beneficially and of record, by the Parent. No options, warrants or other rights to subscribe to or purchase any shares of capital stock of Seller exist.

This representation could be expanded to include statements concerning agreements, commitments or understandings relating to the seller's issued and outstanding capital stock.

(27) **Conduct of Business since Purchase Date.** During the period between the Purchase Date and the date hereof, Seller has not taken any action with respect to the conduct of Seller's business other than in the ordinary course of business, and there has been no material adverse change in the assets or liabilities or in the condition, financial or otherwise, or in the business, properties, earnings or net worth of Seller.

In the context of an acquisition of stock, an acquisition agreement would customarily provide that between a specific balance sheet date and the closing date the seller has not taken and will not take, without the buyer's prior written consent, certain actions (including issuing stock, incurring indebtedness and declaring dividends).

In addition to the representations and warranties discussed above, common representations and warranties include those relating to (a) taxes; (b) liabilities as guarantor; (c) the interest of officers and directors in clients, suppliers and customers; (d) actual and threatened terminations by employees and clients; and (e) customer lists.

G. Representations and Warranties of Buyer

The Buyer represents and warrants to the Seller as follows:

(1) **Organization and Standing.** Buyer is a corporation duly organized, validly existing and in good standing under the laws of the State of New York.

(2) **Corporate Authority.** Buyer has full corporate authority to execute, deliver and perform this Agreement, the Note and all of the documents required to be executed by Buyer hereunder, and this Agreement and the Note will constitute valid and binding obligations of Buyer; this

Agreement and the Note and all transactions contemplated hereby have been duly authorized by all requisite corporate action.

(3) **Conflicting Agreements.** Neither the execution nor delivery of this Agreement or the Note nor fulfillment nor compliance with the terms and conditions hereof or thereof will constitute a breach by Buyer of its certificate of incorporation or by-laws or result in a breach of the terms, conditions or provisions of or constitute a default under or result in a violation of any agreement, contract or instrument to which Buyer is a party or by which it is bound, or result in a violation by Buyer of any existing law or statute or any rule or regulation of any jurisdiction or of any order, decree, writ or injunction of any court or governmental department, bureau, board, agency or instrumentality.

(4) **Consents.** No consent from or other approval of any governmental entity or other person is necessary in connection with the execution of this Agreement or the consummation by Buyer of the transactions contemplated hereby or the continuation of the business of Seller by Buyer in the manner previously conducted by Seller.

(5) **Insurance.** Buyer shall maintain reasonable insurance with respect to its assets, including product liability insurance.

(6) **Disclosure.** No representation or warranty of Buyer contained in this Agreement, and no statement contained in any certificate or other instrument furnished or to be furnished to Buyer pursuant hereto, or in connection with the transactions contemplated hereby, contains or will contain any untrue statement of a material fact, or omits or will omit to state any material fact which is necessary in order to make the statements contained therein not misleading.

(7) **Capital Stock.** All of the issued and outstanding capital stock of Buyer is owned beneficially and of record by _____. No options, warrants or other rights to subscribe to or purchase any shares of capital stock of Buyer exist.

As noted above, the nature and scope of a buyer's representations and warranties are primarily functions of the consideration in the transaction. If the consideration is cash, the buyer's representations can be as limited as those relating to the organization of the buyer and its approval of the acquisition. If the consideration consists of the buyer's securities, the buyer's representations and warranties can be as extensive as those of the seller discussed above.

H. Covenants of Seller and the Parent

(1) **Interference.** Seller shall not interfere with, disrupt or attempt to disrupt the relationship, contractual or otherwise, between the Buyer and any supplier or customer of the Seller which was such on or prior to the Closing Date or any supplier or customer of Buyer.

(2) **Investigation.** From and after the date hereof through the Closing Date, the Seller will afford to the officers and representatives of the Buyer free access to the Business Space and Seller's books and records relating to its business during normal business hours in order that the Buyer may have full opportunity to make such investigation as it shall desire with respect to the condition of the Purchased Property and the business of Seller.

(3) **Working Papers.** Seller shall cause Messrs. _____ to preserve for at least two years after the Closing Date their working papers relating to their audit of Seller's financial statements for the period ended _____, 19___, and their working papers relating to Seller in connection with their audit of the Parent's financial statements for the period ended ____, 19___. Seller shall cause Messrs. ____, during such period, to grant the auditors of Buyer reasonable access to and the opportunity to make copies of such papers at Buyer's expense during normal business hours. If after such two-year period ____ wishes to dispose of such papers, it shall turn them over to Buyer.

(4) **Customers; Employees.** Seller shall use its best efforts through the Closing Date to preserve the customers and suppliers of its business. In addition, Seller will use its best efforts through the Closing Date to keep available Seller's present employees now employed for employment by the Buyer, without making any increase after the date hereof in the compensation, current or deferred, payable to such employees without the prior consent of Buyer, and Seller will cooperate fully with Buyer so that Buyer may, in its discretion, retain some or all of such

employees. Seller shall not hire any employees during the period between the date hereof and the Closing Date without the consent of Buyer.

(5) **Names.** Seller and the Parent shall, from and after the Closing Date, cease to use the words ____ or any variations thereof or any other trademarks, trade names or copyrights listed on Exhibit D.

(6) **Books and Records.** Seller shall preserve its books, records, files and correspondence relating to its business conducted prior to the Closing Date and Buyer shall have reasonable access to them and to make copies thereof. Seller shall turn over to Buyer such books, records, files and correspondence when Seller wishes to dispose of them.

(7) **Dividends and Distributions; Liabilities to Parent.** During the period from the Purchase Date through the date hereof Seller has not made, and during the period from the date hereof through the Closing Date Seller shall not make, any dividend payments to its stockholders, any distributions of assets of any kind on its stock or any redemption or retirement of any of its stock. Except as specified in Exhibit V, during the period from the Purchase Date through the date hereof Seller has not, and during the period from the date hereof to and including the Closing Date Seller shall not, incur any liability to the Parent except for the $____ of "income taxes to parent company" reflected on the balance sheet included as part of Exhibit K annexed hereto, which $____ liability the Parent hereby agrees to pay.

(8) **Computer Accounts.** The Parent at its expense shall maintain on its computer system for ninety (90) days after the Closing the general ledger computer-based accounts of the business of Seller purchased by Buyer hereunder.

A basic covenant or group of covenants in an acquisition agreement pertains to the interval between the execution of the agreement and the closing date. These covenants typically provide that the seller will conduct its business in the ordinary course and will not engage in unusual transactions, impair its assets or diminish its goodwill. Covenants (1), (4), (6) and (7) are of this nature. Covenants (5) and (8) are designed to preserve the goodwill purchased by the buyer after the closing date.

Covenants (2) and (3) are typical covenants and are frequently accompanied by a covenant on the part of the buyer to treat such books and records as confidential in the event that the transaction is not consummated.

(9) **Covenant Not to Compete.** From and after the Closing Date for a period of five (5) years, Seller, the Parent and any of their subsidiaries and any business in which either of them owns directly or indirectly more than 20 percent of the equity interest thereof shall not compete with Buyer or its subsidiaries in any business of the type carried on by Seller prior to the Closing Date in any area in which Buyer or its subsidiaries are engaged in business. The term "compete," as used herein, means to engage in competition, directly or indirectly (including, without limitation, soliciting or selling to any customer with which Buyer has or Seller had any direct or indirect business contacts), either as a proprietor, partner, employee, agent, consultant, stockholder or in any capacity or manner whatsoever. The parties hereby acknowledge that remedies at law for violations of this paragraph are inadequate and that only injunctive relief is an adequate remedy for such violations. The provisions of this paragraph are severable; if any provision of this paragraph or application thereof to any circumstance is held invalid, such invalidity shall not affect other provisions or applications of this paragraph which can be given effect without the invalid provision or application.

Covenants not to compete on the part of selling stockholders are frequently included in acquisition agreements because, as a general matter, such covenants are more easily enforceable if executed in connection with the sale of a business. The duration and scope of the covenant must be carefully examined under applicable state law to ensure, to the greatest extent possible, that such covenant is enforceable.

The opinion of seller's counsel required as a condition to closing should address, even if in a reasoned manner, the covenant's enforceability.

(10) **Accounts Receivable.** The Parent shall buy for cash at face value from Buyer on the first anniversary of the Closing Date the

amount of receivables, net of bad debt reserve, reflected on the balance sheet included as part of Exhibit K which is not collected in full by Buyer within one year after the Closing Date.

I. Covenants of Buyer

From the Closing Date until payment in full of the Note, Buyer agrees that unless Seller shall otherwise consent in writing:

(1) within thirty (30) days of the Closing, the Buyer shall cause the Parent to be released from all liabilities under its guarantees of the Seller's indebtedness to banks referred to in this Agreement;

(2) Buyer shall not pay any dividends (other than dividends payable solely in shares of any class of its stock) on any shares of its stock if the Note is in default. If the Note is not in default, Buyer shall not pay any such dividends unless at the time of such payment after giving effect to such payment the debt/equity ratio of Buyer is equal to or less than one-to-one;

(3) unless at the time of any payment referred to in this sentence after giving effect to such payment the debt/equity ratio of Buyer is equal to or less than one-to-one, (a) Buyer shall not use the cash flow derived from the assets purchased hereunder to make any payment of a material amount for matters or expenses unrelated to the business or expansion plans of Buyer of corporations in which it owns directly or indirectly a majority interest; (b) the aggregate of any payments derived from such cash flow made by Buyer to its affiliates in connection with such business or expansion plans shall be reasonable; (c) the financial statements referred to in the Note attached hereto as Exhibit M shall be accompanied by a statement of the aggregate amount of any such payments to affiliates; and (d) Seller shall have the right to make reasonable requests to examine at reasonable times records or information pertaining to such payments;

(4) for purposes of calculating the debt/equity ratio with respect to paragraphs I(2) and (3) above, (a) the debt/equity ratio shall refer to the debt/equity ratio on an equity accounting basis of Buyer and (b) "debt"

shall mean the difference between (i) the sum of long-term debt and other indebtedness or borrowed money and (ii) the excess of current assets over current liabilities;

(5) on the Closing Date, Buyer shall have $____ of equity.

As discussed above, these covenants assume the issuance of the buyer's securities as consideration in the acquisition.

In addition to the covenants discussed above, common covenants include those relating to (a) calling a meeting of stockholders and using one's best efforts to secure the necessary stockholder vote to approve the transaction if such action is required under applicable state law; (b) making all required regulatory filings; (c) maintaining existing insurance policies; (d) taking certain action with respect to benefit plans; and (e) using one's best efforts to cause the conditions precedent for which a party is responsible to be fulfilled.

J. Conditions Precedent of Buyer

The obligations of the Buyer hereunder are subject to the conditions that on or prior to the Closing Date:

(1) **Representations and Warranties True at Closing.** The representations and warranties of the Seller contained in this Agreement or in any certificate or document delivered pursuant to the provisions hereof or in connection with the transactions contemplated hereby shall be true on and as of the Closing Date as though such representations and warranties were made at and as of such date, except if such representations and warranties were made as of a specified date and such representations and warranties shall be true as of such date.

(2) **Seller's Compliance with Agreement.** The Seller shall have performed and complied with all agreements and conditions required by this Agreement to be performed or complied with by it prior to or at the closing of this Agreement.

(3) **Resolutions and Seller's Certificate.** The Seller shall have delivered to the Buyer copies of the resolutions of the Board of Directors of the Seller authorizing the transactions contemplated herein, with such

resolutions to be certified to be true and correct by its Secretary or Assistant Secretary, together with a certificate of an officer of the Seller, dated the Closing Date, certifying in such detail as the Buyer may request to the fulfillment of the conditions specified in subparagraphs (1) and (2) above.

(4) **Opinion of Seller's Counsel.** Seller shall have delivered to Buyer an opinion of Messrs. ____, dated the Closing Date, to the effect that

(a) Seller is a corporation duly organized, validly existing and in good standing under the laws of the State of ____; has the legal and corporate power to own or lease and operate the Purchased Property and carry on the business of Seller as and where such assets are now owned or leased and operated and such business is now conducted, and has the legal and corporate power and authority to make, execute, deliver and perform this Agreement; the Parent is a corporation duly organized, validly existing and in good standing under the laws of the State of ____ and has the legal and corporate power and authority to make, execute, deliver and perform this Agreement;

(b) all corporate and other proceedings required to be taken by the Seller and the Parent to authorize them to execute and carry out this Agreement and the transactions contemplated herein have been duly and properly taken, and this Agreement has been duly and validly executed and delivered and constitutes the valid and binding obligation of the Seller and the Parent enforceable in accordance with its terms;

(c) the instruments of conveyance delivered by Seller to Buyer at the Closing have been duly authorized and validly executed and delivered and constitute valid and binding obligations of the Seller enforceable in accordance with their respective terms; and

(d) the execution and delivery of this Agreement, and the performance by the Seller and the Parent of their respective obligations hereunder, will not conflict with or violate any provision of the Certificate of Incorporation or By-laws of Seller or the Parent or conflict with or violate any provisions of, or result in a default or acceleration of any obligation under, any mortgage, lease, contract, agreement, indenture, or other instrument or undertaking, of which such counsel has knowledge, or any order, decree or judgment, of which such counsel has knowledge, to which the Seller or the Parent is a party or by which the Seller or the Parent or the property of either of them is bound or, to the best of such counsel's knowledge, result in the creation or imposition of any lien, charge, restriction or security interest on the Purchased Property except to the extent contemplated by this Agreement.

In many respects, the legal opinion is the most sensitive of all the documents a lawyer is called on to draft. Lawyers render opinions every day, often in situations which require giving advice from the "seat of one's pants," without research or the benefit of prior consultation with colleagues. It cannot be avoided. Such advice is better characterized as "reactions" or "views." However, when set to paper in the context of a significant corporate event, a lawyer's opinion takes on significantly different import. It comes closer to assurance than opinion. Persons other than your client will rely on it, and if the opinion contains factual or legal inaccuracies, liability may result which far exceeds the remuneration received for one's effort. Consequently, a written legal opinion should be drafted with great care and thorough preparation.

In negotiating and drafting legal opinions, a few basic guidelines should be observed:

a. Clearly state all assumptions (including any limitations or conflicts) upon which the opinion is based.

b. Do not accept factual assumptions about the client or take the transaction at face value. Probe the client and confirm the answers the client gives. To the extent that facts which are the subject of the opinion (e.g., that the transaction was duly authorized by the board of directors) can be verified, be sure to perform appropriate due diligence. In the event that the opinion refers to facts that the lawyer cannot practically verify (e.g., a company's sales figures), the opinion should clearly state that independent verification was not undertaken with regard to such information. Obtain and keep on file all documentation related to this information due diligence.

c. If no opinion is being given with regard to certain factual or legal matters, or if another lawyer's opinion is being relied on in the opinion, then this should be explicitly stated.

d. When the law is not clear, do not hesitate to say so. More and more, lawyers are restricting their opinions by including language to the effect that "the status of the law is unsettled, and consequently we are unable to give a legal opinion on this matter." When appropriate, they may then proffer a "view" as to how they feel the issue will be resolved.

e. If possible, establish a "cold review" procedure within your firm. Having another partner who is not involved with the transaction review the opinion will bring a more dispassionate (and therefore more objective) perspective to the issue.

f. Maintain all opinions in one central file to maintain better consistency.

g. React with great caution when the client suggests language changes in the opinion.

h. Periodically consult with your insurance advisor to determine whether new policy provisions negatively affect the coverage on legal opinions.

(5) **Injunction.** On the Closing Date, there shall be no effective injunction, writ, preliminary restraining order or any order of any nature issued by a court of competent jurisdiction directing that the transactions provided for herein or any of them not be consummated as herein provided.

(6) **Approval of Proceedings.** All actions, proceedings, instruments and documents required to carry out this Agreement, or incidental thereto, and all other related legal matters shall have been approved by Messrs. ____, counsel for the Buyer.

(7) **Casualty.** The Purchased Property or any substantial portion thereof shall not have been adversely affected in any material way as a result of any fire, accident, flood or other casualty or act of God or the public enemy, nor shall any substantial portion of the Purchased Prop-

erty have been stolen, taken by eminent domain or been subject to condemnation. If the Closing occurs hereunder despite such casualty as a result of the waiver of this condition by Buyer, the Seller shall assign or pay over to the Buyer the proceeds of any insurance or any condemnation proceeds with respect to any casualty involving the Purchased Property which occurs after the date hereof.

(8) **Adverse Change.** There shall have been between the Purchase Date and the Closing Date no material adverse change in the assets or liabilities, or in the condition, financial or otherwise, or in the business, properties, earnings or net worth of Seller.

(9) **Consent.** Buyer shall have received a copy of the consent of ____ Bank to this Agreement and the transactions contemplated hereby.

(10) **Employment Agreement.** Buyer shall have entered into an employment agreement with ____.

(11) **Dismissal of Action.** The action entitled ____ and counterclaims in such action and the other actions and counterclaims referred to in Exhibit W attached hereto shall have been dismissed with prejudice and settled pursuant to Exhibit W attached hereto.

(12) **Audited Financial Statements.** Seller shall have delivered to Buyer a signed opinion of Seller's auditors reporting on an examination of the financial statements of Seller for the years ended ____, 19____, and ____, 19____, identical to the opinion included as part of Exhibit K annexed hereto. Such opinion shall have reported on the balance sheets of Seller as at such dates and the related statements of income, stockholders' equity and changes in financial position of Seller for the years then ended, including the notes thereto, which shall be identical to the financial statements included as part of Exhibit K annexed hereto.

(13) **Assignment of Business Space Lease.** Seller shall have assigned the Business Space Lease to Buyer and shall have obtained the necessary approval of any party thereto.

K. Conditions Precedent of Seller

The obligations of the Seller hereunder are subject to the conditions that on or prior to the Closing Date:

(1) **Representations and Warranties True at Closing.** The representations and warranties of the Buyer contained in this Agreement or in any certificate or document delivered pursuant to the provisions hereof or in connection with the transactions contemplated hereby shall be true on and as of the Closing Date as though such representations and warranties were made at and as of such date, except as otherwise contemplated herein.

(2) **Buyer's Compliance with Agreement.** The Buyer shall have performed and complied with all agreements and conditions required by this Agreement to be performed or complied with by it prior to or at the Closing.

(3) **Resolutions and Buyer's Certificate.** The Buyer shall have delivered to the Seller copies of the resolutions of the Board of Directors of the Buyer authorizing the transactions contemplated herein, with such resolutions to be certified to be true and correct by its Secretary or Assistant Secretary, together with a certificate of an officer of the Buyer, dated the Closing Date, certifying in such detail as the Seller may request to the fulfillment of the conditions specified in subparagraphs (1) and (2) above.

(4) **Opinion of Buyer's Counsel.** Buyer shall have delivered to Seller at the Closing an opinion of Messrs. _____, dated the Closing Date, to the effect that

(a) Buyer is a corporation duly organized, validly existing and in good standing under the laws of the State of New York;

(b) Buyer has full power and authority to enter into this Agreement and to purchase the Purchased Property from Seller;

(c) all corporate action required to be taken by the Buyer to authorize it to carry out this Agreement and the transactions contemplated herein has been duly and properly taken; and

(d) the execution and delivery of this Agreement and the performance by the Buyer of its obligations hereunder will not conflict with or violate any provision of the Buyer's Certificate of Incorporation or its By-laws or conflict with or violate any provisions of, or result in a default or acceleration of any obligation under, any mortgage, lease, contract, agreement, indenture or other instrument or undertaking, of which such counsel has knowledge, or any order, decree or judgment, of which such counsel has knowledge, to which the Buyer is a party or by which it or its property is bound.

See comments to J(4) above.

(5) **Injunction.** On the Closing Date, there shall be no effective injunction, writ, preliminary restraining order or any order of any nature issued by a court of competent jurisdiction directing that the transactions provided for herein or any of them not be consummated as herein provided.

(6) **Approval of Proceedings.** All actions, proceedings, instruments and documents required to carry out this Agreement, or incidental thereto, and all other related legal matters shall have been approved by Messrs. ____, counsel for Seller.

An acquisition agreement will contain a series of conditions precedent to the buyer's and the seller's obligations to close. Common conditions precedent normally include (a) the obtaining of necessary regulatory approvals; (b) the delivery of legal opinions; (c) the delivery of accountants' letters; (d) the obtaining of stockholder approval; (e) the obtaining of consents from third parties; (f) the delivery of certificates as to the truth of the buyer's and the seller's representations and warranties as of the closing date; (g) the absence of certain litigation or injunctions; and (h) the execution and delivery of employment or noncompetition agreements.

These provisions are styled as conditions to closing rather than as covenants because it may be beyond the ability of either party to satisfy a condition. In such an event, the buyer or the seller may wish to cancel the transaction without being liable for the breach of a covenant.

L. Indemnification

(1) The Seller and the Parent jointly and severally shall indemnify and hold Buyer harmless from and against and in respect of any and all

liabilities, losses, damages, claims, costs and expenses, including, but not limited to, attorneys' fees, arising out of or due to

(a) a breach of any representation, warranty, covenant or agreement of the Seller or the Parent contained in this Agreement or in any statement or certificate furnished to Buyer pursuant hereto or in connection with the transactions contemplated hereby;

It is important to specifically identify in the agreement the information upon which indemnification liability can be based. References to "statements or certificates furnished to the buyer in connection with the transactions contemplated hereby" can be deemed to include every document ever transmitted between the buyer and the seller. In many cases, not all information so transmitted (e.g., certain projections, estimates and pro forma financial statements) is intended by the parties to form the basis of liability. It is suggested, therefore, that the agreement specify the information by referring to "exhibits, schedules or certificates furnished to the Buyer pursuant to the terms of this Agreement." In this manner, all information which can form the basis of liability will be identified and either attached to the agreement or presented at the closing.

(b) any claim by customers of Buyer or the ultimate users with respect to the finished goods Inventory assigned to Buyer on the Closing Date based upon defects or alleged defects therein; except that as to Inventory which is not valued or which is a write-down or reserved against (to the extent of such write-down or reserve) on the balance sheet of Seller included as part of Exhibit K, indemnification may not be had hereunder for any claims by any such user or customer for a refund or credit of the price paid for such goods;

Depending upon the size of the business sold, inventory may not be valued on a per-item basis, and write-downs or reserves on the seller's balance sheet may only refer to inventory as a whole. Consequently, the second clause of L(1)(b) would be impossible to monitor. Moreover, if inventory has been either written down or reserved against, one would assume that would have been taken into consideration when negotiating the purchase price. The buyer and the seller would rely upon the repre-

THE EFFECTUATION OF A CORPORATE EVENT 369

sentation that the "finished goods inventory (except to the extent written down or reserved against) is saleable in the ordinary course of business of the Seller."

(c) any liabilities of Seller which are not expressly assumed by Buyer under the terms of this Agreement; or

To eliminate any uncertainty or confusion, liabilities which are to be assumed by the buyer should be defined terms and be specifically listed in a schedule or exhibit attached to the agreement (which will be further updated on the closing date). Liabilities which are not expressly assumed by buyer would therefore refer to all other liabilities.

(d) the action captioned ____, and any counterclaims in such action, and any other actions or counterclaims referred to in Exhibit W or other actions or counterclaims brought by ____, ____ or any affiliate of either of them relating to or arising out of the same or similar facts as that of such actions or counterclaims and any and all actions, suits, proceedings, demands, assessments or judgments, costs and expenses incidental to any of the foregoing, provided, that with respect to item (a) above, indemnification may be had pursuant to this paragraph L(1) only if a claim is made by Buyer in respect thereof prior to the second anniversary of the Closing Date.

(2) Buyer shall indemnify and hold harmless the Seller from and against and in respect of any and all liabilities, losses, damages, claims, costs and expenses, including but not limited to attorneys' fees, arising out of or due to a breach of any representation, warranty or covenant of Buyer contained in this Agreement and any and all actions, suits, proceedings, demands, assessments or judgments, costs and expenses incidental to any of the foregoing, provided, that such indemnification may be had hereunder only if a claim is made by Seller in respect thereof prior to the second anniversary of the Closing Date.

It is necessary to ensure that the buyer's representations, warrants and covenants specifically cover and apply to ongoing liabilities of the business purchased (which may not be recorded on the balance sheet), as well as "Assumed Liabilities" (as defined in the agreement). Otherwise, paragraph L(2), relating to the buyer's obligation to indemnify, will be of little value. In this regard, releases of the seller from certain ongoing liabilities assumed by the buyer will afford additional protection for the seller.

(3) (a) Promptly after the receipt by any party hereto of notice under this paragraph L of (x) any claim or (y) the commencement of any action or proceeding, such party (the "Aggrieved Party") will, if a claim with respect thereto is to be made against any party obligated to provide indemnification pursuant to this paragraph L (the "Indemnifying Party"), give such Indemnifying Party written notice of such claim or the commencement of such action or proceeding and shall permit the Indemnifying Party to assume the defense of any such claim or any litigation resulting from such claim. Failure by the Indemnifying Party to notify the Aggrieved Party of its election to defend any such action within a reasonable time, but in no event more than fifteen (15) days after notice thereof shall have been given to the Indemnifying Party, shall be deemed a waiver by the Indemnifying Party of its right to defend such action.

(b) If the Indemnifying Party assumes the defense of any such claim or litigation resulting therefrom, the obligations of the Indemnifying Party as to such claim or litigation shall be limited to taking all steps necessary in the defense or settlement of such claim or litigation and to holding the Aggrieved Party harmless from and against any and all losses, damages and liabilities caused by or arising out of any settlement approved by the Indemnifying Party or any judgment in connection with such claim or litigation. The Aggrieved Party may participate, at its expense, in the defense of such claim or litigation provided that the Indemnifying Party shall direct and control the defense of such claim or litigation. The Indemnifying Party shall not, in the defense of such claim or litigation, consent to entry of any judgment, except with the written consent of the Aggrieved Party, or enter into any settlement, except with the written consent of the Aggrieved Party, which does not include as an unconditional term thereof the giving by the claimant or the plaintiff to the Aggrieved Party of a release from all liability in respect of such claim or litigation.

(c) If the Indemnifying Party shall not assume the defense of any such claim or litigation, the Aggrieved Party may defend against such claim or litigation in such manner as it may deem appropriate and, unless the Indemnifying Party shall deposit with the Aggrieved Party a sum equivalent to the total amount demanded in such claim or litigation, or shall deliver to the Aggrieved Party a surety bond or an irrevocable letter of credit in form and substance reasonably satisfactory to the Aggrieved Party, the Aggrieved Party may settle such claim or litigation on such terms as it may deem appropriate, and the Indemnifying Party shall promptly reimburse the Aggrieved Party for the amount of all expenses, legal or otherwise, incurred by the Aggrieved Party in connection with the defense against or settlement of such claim or litigation. If no settlement of such claim or litigation is made, the Indemnifying Party shall promptly reimburse the Aggrieved Party for the amount of any judgment rendered with respect to such claim or in such litigation and of all expenses, legal or otherwise, incurred by the Aggrieved Party in the defense against such claim or litigation.

The aggrieved party may not want to permit the indemnifying party to assume the defense of any claim because, among other reasons, the aggrieved party may have a special interest it may want to protect (e.g., reputation) which the indemnified party may not want to vigorously defend—a classic example of divergence of interests. As a compromise, it may be appropriate to allow the indemnifying party the opportunity to "participate in" rather than "assume" the defense.

Additionally, the following points regarding indemnification generally should also be considered:

● *Dollar Limitation. It is not unusual to limit the indemnification liability of the seller to a specific dollar amount—a percentage of the purchase price. Although the amount will vary from transaction to transaction, the greater the percentage of tangible assets to be sold (e.g., cash, accounts receivable, plant, property and equipment), the better the argument that indemnification should be limited. This is especially true where the tangible assets sold bear a direct relationship to the purchase price. In addition, to curtail the potential number of indemnification claims, it is suggested that a "basket" or "minimum indemnity"* *clause be negotiated. This clause provides that no single claim for indemnity would be required to be honored unless it exceeds $X and/or that claims for indemnity must aggregate at least $Y for the indemnification obligation to become operative.*

- *Time Limitation.* *Obviously, it is in the seller's best interest to shorten the period in which the buyer can make an indemnification claim. Two years following the closing date may be too long, because in most instances the "indemnifiable liability" will be identified within one year of the closing. On the other hand, certain liabilities (e.g., taxes and other governmental claims) can survive well beyond the two-year period following the closing. Thus, different periods for different types of claims may be appropriate. In any event, the time limitation agreed upon should be parallel to and consistent with the period in which the representations are to survive as set forth in Section Q of the agreement. To secure the indemnification obligations, an escrow of a portion of the purchase price or a bond or letter of credit should be obtained.*

M. Guaranty

The Parent hereby unconditionally guarantees to the Buyer the prompt, full and faithful performance of the obligations of Seller to be performed under this Agreement and all agreements ancillary thereto, as if the Parent were the primary obligor hereunder and thereunder. The Buyer may proceed against the Parent under this Guaranty independently of and without recourse to any action against Seller, provided, that the Parent shall have any and all rights of defense, set-off and counterclaim which are available to Seller.

The Parent's maximum liability under this Agreement shall be $____, except that if its total liability under this Agreement (without giving effect to such maximum) exceeds $____ and the Parent is liable under this Agreement (without giving effect to such maximum) for a breach of warranty under paragraph F(7) hereof, or for the indemnification under paragraph L hereof with respect to a breach of a warranty under paragraph F(7) hereof, the Parent's maximum liability shall be

(1) the sum of $\_\_\_$, and (2) the amount of all liabilities for all such breaches or all such indemnifications not included in the $___ referred to in clause (1) above.

If negotiating leverage exists, guaranty liability of the parent should be limited to the monetary obligations of the seller (in contrast to the performance obligations in covenants), which, in turn, should be limited to a specific dollar amount. Thought should also be given to whether the guaranty of the parent is required to be a liability recorded on the parent's balance sheet.

From the parent's perspective, it is preferable to require the buyer to first proceed against the seller and then against the parent. In general, paragraph M circumvents the protections afforded to a parent in a parent/subsidiary relationship.

N. Brokerage

Seller, Buyer and the Parent represent and warrant to each other that all negotiations relative to this Agreement and the transactions contemplated hereby have been carried on by Seller and the Parent directly with the Buyer and without the intervention of any broker, finder or other third party.

Many brokers/finders serve specific industries (e.g., health care, travel, etc.) and may have represented, at one time or another, most of the companies in a given geographic location. If a broker/finder has been employed in the transaction and has represented the parties in the past, a splitting of fees may be appropriate. In any event, if a broker/finder is present in the transaction, explicit mention should be made in this section as to which party will be obligated for its fees and expenses.

O. Notices

All notices, requests, demands and other communications hereunder shall be in writing and shall be deemed to have been duly given upon delivery, if delivered in person, or on the third business day after mailing, if mailed, by registered mail, postage prepaid, return receipt requested:

(1) To Seller:
    [ADDRESS]
    With a copy to:
    [ADDRESS OF SELLER'S ATTORNEY]
(2) To Buyer:
    [ADDRESS]
    With a copy to:
    [ADDRESS OF BUYER'S ATTORNEY]

or to such other address or to such other person as Seller or Buyer shall have last designated by notice to the other party.

Controversy and debate typically steer clear of the notices provision. This one appears to have all the essential ingredients, although telex and telecopy information could be included.

P. Entire Agreement; Modification

This Agreement contains the entire agreement between the parties hereto with respect to the transactions contemplated herein, and no representation, promise, inducement or statement of intention relating to the transactions contemplated by this Agreement has been made by any party which is not set forth in this Agreement. This Agreement shall not be modified or amended except by an instrument in writing signed by or on behalf of the parties hereto.

The importance of this section cannot be overstated because it defines the parameters of the parties' intentions and agreement. Indirectly, it limits the scope of liability to the agreement. If schedules and exhibits are attached to the agreement, specific reference to them should be made here. Also, the scope of this section (i.e., limiting representations, etc., to those set forth in the agreement) should be consistent with the Indemnification section (see Section L(1)(a)) and the Survival of Representations section (see Section Q).

Q. Nature and Survival of Representations

All statements contained in any certificate or other instrument delivered by or on behalf of the Buyer or Seller pursuant to this Agreement or in connection with the transactions contemplated hereby shall be deemed representations and warranties respectively by the Buyer and Seller hereunder. All representations and warranties and agreements made by the parties hereto in this Agreement or pursuant hereto shall survive the Closing hereunder and any investigation at any time made by or on behalf of any party hereto.

The survival of representations and warranties is often limited to specific time periods. The time limitation comments to the Indemnification section apply here. Also, the first sentence of this section is inconsistent with Section P and should be revised to limit the representations made to those set forth in the agreement or in schedules or exhibits attached thereto.

R. Bulk Sales Law

Buyer waives compliance by Seller with the bulk sales law of the State of ____ and any state or jurisdiction in which Seller (1) was doing business, (2) had property located or (3) had existing creditors on the Closing Date.

It is imperative that an analysis be made of all applicable bulk sales laws. They vary from state to state and, in most instances, impose the burden of compliance on both the buyer and seller. Thus, unless the buyer is willing to assume the risk of noncompliance, it may be inappropriate to waive compliance.

S. Specific Performance

Without limiting or waiving in any respect any rights or remedies of any party given under this Agreement, or now or hereafter existing at law or in equity or by statute, any party, upon its fulfillment of the conditions precedent to the other party's obligations as provided in this Agreement, shall be entitled to specific performance of the obligations to be performed by the other party in accordance with the provisions of this Agreement.

Specific performance may be an improbable remedy depending upon the type of business which is being sold. As an alternative, a monetary "break-up" or "liquidated damages" provision should be agreed to by the parties. In most cases, such a provision will eliminate the uncertainties associated with specific performance proceedings and maximize the aggrieved party's potential for being made whole if the deal is not consummated.

T. Compliance with Closing Conditions

The parties hereto shall use their best efforts to comply with the respective closing conditions to be performed on their part.

A covenant to use best efforts is probably the only effective (and realistic) means by which one party can force another to comply with closing conditions.

U. Termination

Buyer and Seller may, at any time prior to the Closing Date, mutually consent to the termination of this Agreement. If the Closing hereunder is not held, or an action or proceeding for specific performance as provided above is not commenced on or before ____, 19___, this Agreement shall be terminated as of that date and neither Buyer nor Seller shall have any further obligation thereunder.

Having an automatic termination provision may not be conducive to completing a transaction. If the transaction is automatically terminated, a new agreement entered into by both parties would be needed to revive the basic document. Often a provision which allows the agreement to survive beyond a certain date, but which also allows for the unilateral termination of the agreement by one party upon written notice, is preferable. It permits the parties to continue with the status quo (hopefully, allowing time for a deal to be consummated), while giving each side the right to terminate at any time.

V. Parties

Nothing contained in this Agreement is intended or shall be construed to give any person or corporation, other than the parties hereto and their respective successors, any legal or equitable right, remedy or claim under or in respect of this Agreement or any provision herein contained;

this Agreement being intended to be and being for the sole and exclusive benefit of the parties hereto and their respective successors and for the benefit of no other person or corporation.

This section and Section X are interrelated and therefore need to be consistent. If the acquisition is to be accomplished by an acquiring subsidiary or other entity, the buyer must be given the ability to assign the agreement to such entity, thereby affording it the rights and remedies of the agreement.

In addition, it may be appropriate to state that the agreement may not be assigned without the consent of the other party, which consent shall not be unreasonably withheld. Depending upon the parties to the transaction, it may also be unimportant to whether the buyer or seller has the ability to assign the agreement, as long as the other party's rights and expectations are not negatively impacted.

W. New York Law to Govern

This Agreement shall be governed by and construed and enforced in accordance with the laws of the State of New York.

Choice of law is becoming increasingly important. Practitioners should be cognizant of the legal implications of the selection and the probability of the court enforcing this provision. Of course, there must be some relationship between the state whose law is chosen and the transaction. To further ensure that the law of a particular state will be applied, it is suggested that the choice-of-law provision specifically exclude the state's choice-of-law principles.

X. Assignment

This Agreement shall not be assignable by either party hereto.

Y. Counterparts

This Agreement may be executed simultaneously in any number of counterparts, each of which shall be deemed an original but all of which together shall constitute one and the same instrument.

Z. Paragraph Headings

The paragraph headings in this Agreement are for convenience of reference only and shall not be deemed to alter or affect any provision thereof. Reference to numbered "paragraphs," "subparagraphs," and "Exhibits" refers to paragraphs and subparagraphs of this Agreement and Exhibits annexed hereto.

See comments to Section V above. While signing in counterparts provides convenience, it is always preferable, if feasible, to have at least one agreement executed by each party to the transaction. "Paragraph headings," like the "Notices" provision, is seldom controversial.

AA. Taxes

(1) Buyer shall deliver to Seller at the Closing a check in the amount of $____. It is agreed that upon payment of such amount, Seller hereby assumes, and releases Buyer from, all liability with respect to any and all federal, state and local tax liability of Seller (a) relating to the period between the Purchase Date through and including the Closing Date, including, without limitation, all liability for income taxes, and (b) for sales taxes in excess of $____ relating to the sale of assets hereunder.

Said payment shall not be subject to any later adjustment by either party.

(2) Buyer shall be liable for all federal, state and local taxes of any kind for any period commencing from and after the Closing Date. Seller shall be liable for, and hold Buyer harmless with respect to, all federal, state and local taxes of any kind for all periods ended on or prior to the Purchase Date.

The issue of who assumes the liability for taxes of the seller, as well as the amount of such liability, for the period commencing on the purchase date through the closing date is subject to negotiation. It is difficult, however, to determine accurately the amount, and any attempt to agree to a settlement payment by the buyer to the seller may ultimately be found to prejudice one of the two parties. A post-closing determination may better serve the interests of the buyer and the seller in this regard. It is important to recognize that unless the effective date of the acquisition is the purchase date, the buyer would not be liable for taxes of the seller prior to the closing date.

IN WITNESS WHEREOF, Seller and Buyer have caused this Agreement to be executed as of the day and year first written above.

[NAME OF SELLER]

By:_____

[NAME OF BUYER]

By:_____

[NAME OF PARENT]

By:_____

V. CONCLUSION

In conclusion, a few observations are worth noting:

(1) **Achieve the expected.** Know what your client's objectives are and make sure the agreement achieves them.

(2) **Protect against the unexpected.** Consider carefully the nature and extent of indemnification and ask how the seller will back up his representations, covenants and warranties. Some of the more commonly used mechanisms involve putting a portion of the purchase price in escrow, deferring a portion of the purchase price with non-negotiable notes and having the seller's available net worth identified and verified by an expert who is independent of the parties to the transaction.

(3) **Volunteer to write the first draft.** It is always easier to negotiate from your own draft than to agonize over your opponent's draft. Often lawyers pressed for time will too readily acquiesce to a voluntary undertaking by their opponent to work up the first draft. Invariably one finds that the moments saved do not outweigh the moments spent on revision.

(4) **Keep your objectivity.** Avoid acting in dual capacities. If the lawyer serves as a "finder" in the transaction, then he should not act as the attorney. The inherent conflicts are often insurmountable.

(5) **Involve the client.** Unlike many other documents, acquisition agreements should be understandable to the business layman. Be sure the client has signed off and understands the documents.

(6) **Observe the corporate niceties.** If shareholder or board approval is required, obtain it. If opinions of counsel are required, back them up with appropriate written information and certificates.

(7) **Do not be intimidated by the client's insensitivity to the amount or complexity of the work involved.** Clients invariably set time limits; most are arbitrary. Buying, selling and raising capital for a company requires the interplay of so many disciplines that the transaction dictates the expenditure of significant time and energy to acquit yourself responsibly.

(8) **Involve others in your office.** Do not rely solely on your own knowledge, wit or instinct. Discuss points and issues with your partners. Often someone who is not directly involved will see priorities differently and may provide you with useful information on the transaction.

CHAPTER FOURTEEN

CORPORATE OPERATIONS I: SOME CORPORATE LAW ASPECTS OF DAY-TO-DAY MANAGEMENT

Clifford R. Ennico

ASPECTS OF DAY-TO-DAY MANAGEMENT 383

I. INTRODUCTION AND OVERVIEW

As has been discussed elsewhere in this volume (*see* Chapters 8 and 9), decision making can take place at one (or more) of three levels in the small business corporation—at the officer level, at the director level, and at the shareholder level. Some business decisions are of such magnitude as to require changes in the corporation's organizational documents—the certificate of incorporation or by-laws.

Traditionally books on corporate law and practice emphasize counsel's role in the management process at three stages in the corporation's life cycle: birth (formation, incorporation, organization); marriage (acquisition, reorganization, business combinations); and death (dissolution, liquidation, termination). Too often counsel comes away from such books with the impression that he/she can "go to sleep" in between these three stages, at least with respect to corporate law matters. This is partly because the vast majority of day-to-day business decisions made by the shareholders, directors and officers of a closely held corporation will normally fall outside the traditional field of "corporate law" and take the practitioner into such diverse areas as antitrust law and trade regulation (dealings with competitors, agreements with sales distributors and franchisees); environmental law (the disposal of industrial wastes); real estate (acquiring or leasing plant and office space); securities law (selling shares in the corporation); Uniform Commercial Code (borrowing money for the corporation and encumbering corporate assets); and labor law (hiring and, especially, firing employees; compensation and benefits packages; compliance with federal labor and antidiscrimination statutes). Today's corporate counsel must be knowledgeable in these and indeed many other areas of the law, not just in "corporate law" as traditionally defined.

What is sometimes overlooked, however, is that even between the "peaks" of birth, marriage and death of a closely held corporation, there are matters where the provisions of the New York Business Corporation Law and the federal Internal Revenue Code impact heavily. This chapter addresses some of the corporate law aspects of day-to-day management decision making, and ideally will furnish the practitioner with a framework for analyzing some of the myriad business decisions he/she will be called upon to review. Chapter 15 discusses some of the federal income tax pitfalls which counsel must take into account in analyzing the consequences of individual decisions.

To accomplish its objective, this chapter will be divided into two parts: the first part addresses the role of counsel as corporate "manager" and focuses upon the corporate secretary's function, where counsel can assert some influence on the decision-making process; while the second part discusses the appropriate level of management (officer, director, shareholder) which should make and implement specific management decisions and focuses on the Business Corporation Law provisions governing amendments to the certificate of incorporation.

II. COUNSEL AS CORPORATE MANAGER: THE SECRETARY'S FUNCTION

When first called upon to incorporate a small business, counsel will have to determine the extent of his/her ongoing involvement with the client.

A. Counsel as Shareholder

If the individuals forming the business do not have much money, counsel may be asked to accept stock in the newly formed corporation as payment, thereby becoming a minority shareholder. While there is no legal restriction on counsel's ability to do so, the ethical guidelines in this area are only beginning to take shape and counsel should seek guidance from the professional ethics committee of a state or local bar association before agreeing to accept payment in this form (the procedure for doing so is outlined in Chapter 20). More importantly, it is generally not good business for counsel to become a minority shareholder in a small corporation; due to the high failure rate of new businesses in general (one leading magazine for entrepreneurs estimates that only one in five small businesses survives the first five years of operations) and the lack of a market for shares in closely held corporations, counsel's "compensation" may be virtually worthless from the day it is

ASPECTS OF DAY-TO-DAY MANAGEMENT

accepted. Moreover, as a minority shareholder, counsel may well find himself/herself "frozen out" if the corporation's business "takes off" and the majority shareholders decide to arrogate the spoils to themselves. Counsel may even have the ill luck to hold the "tie-breaking" shares that will be called upon to resolve any dispute or deadlock among the other shareholders; in such a situation counsel will make enemies and lose potential clients no matter which way he/she votes on a matter. Finally, counsel's acceptance of stock in exchange for services rendered may prevent the other shareholders from qualifying the incorporation for tax-free treatment under Section 351 of the Internal Revenue Code (*see* discussion in Chapter 5).

B. Counsel as Director

Similarly, it is not a good idea for counsel to serve as a director of the corporation if asked by the client to do so. A corporate director is exposed to numerous liabilities under the Business Corporation Law (*see* discussion in Chapter 8) and under the federal securities laws (*see* discussion in Chapter 8) to which he/she would not be subject in his/her capacity as counsel. Moreover, while counsel may (and indeed should) develop some familiarity with the client's business, he/she will usually have little time (short of leaving the practice of law altogether) to devote to corporate matters, especially if he/she serves on more than one board. Counsel may have the ill fortune to become the board's "tie-breaker" in case of dispute or deadlock among the other directors—a position in which counsel can only lose. Finally, even counsel with significant business experience or training (such as a master's degree in business administration) may discover that the other directors will continue to look upon him/her as the corporation's counsel first and foremost, such that his/her attempts to raise points or objections on matters other than "legal issues" (the businessperson's and lawyer's definitions of the quoted term may be significantly different) will be disregarded or at best suffered by the non-lawyers at the table.

C. Counsel as Officer

Counsel may finally wish to consider serving as an officer of the corporation, and indeed there is one position—that of corporate secretary—where counsel cannot only perform valuable service to the corporation but also be in an advantageous position to influence management decisions.

D. The Corporate Secretary's Function

Generally, the corporate secretary is the officer responsible for determining that the proper procedures are being followed in making management decisions and for keeping appropriate records of those decisions. As such, the corporate secretary has three important jobs: keeping the corporation's books and records, particularly the minute book and share transfer ledger; preparing and reviewing communications by the corporation to its shareholders, particularly the annual report; and overseeing meetings of directors and shareholders (including the drafting of minutes of each such meeting). The following paragraphs summarize some of the more important aspects of each job.

1. The Recordkeeping Function

The job of collecting all corporate records and keeping them in one place such that they may be accessed on short notice when necessary is deceptively simple. In practice, it is probably the secretary's most difficult task. The Business Corporation Law requires every domestic corporation to keep and maintain the following internal records: correct and complete books and records of account; minutes of the proceedings of its shareholders, board of directors and executive committee, if any; a record containing the names and addresses of all shareholders, the number and class of shares of stock held by each of them, and the time when each shareholder became the owner of his/her shares; a financial statement, consisting of an annual balance sheet and profit and loss statement; and a list of directors and officers. BCL § 624(a). With the exception of the first, which will in all likelihood be maintained by the corporation's accountants, these documents should be kept in the secretary's office and updated promptly whenever necessary. In addition to the documents required by the BCL, the secretary should also have on hand the executed originals of every agreement to which the corporation is a party; copies of all federal, state and municipal tax returns; copies of

ASPECTS OF DAY-TO-DAY MANAGEMENT 387

all filings made with federal, state and municipal government agencies; and an adequate number of copies of the standard secretary's "incumbency and authorization certificate" showing, on the given date, the names and specimen signatures of all officers who are authorized to commit the corporation to a given course of action. A sample of such a certificate is included in the "Forms and Materials" section of this book.

The basic corporate records are contained in the minute book, which is usually procured upon incorporation, and the share transfer ledger, which is usually a part of the minute book. Anyone attempting to determine what a corporation did, when it was done, and whether it was properly authorized will look to these records first. The minute book, which should be kept by the secretary in duplicate and in separate places (in case one should be lost or destroyed), should contain all organizational documents of the corporation and all amendments thereto in one section, and the minutes of all director and shareholder meetings (in chronological order) in another, with copies of all documents, instruments and certificates referred to in the minutes attached as "exhibits" thereto for quick and easy reference.

Should counsel be named secretary of a corporation which has been in existence for some time and notices that the records in the minute book are deficient (or nonexistent), he/she should do three things right away: write to the New York Department of State requesting certified copies of the certificate of incorporation of the corporation and all amendments thereto; write to the New York State Tax Commission to determine whether the corporation is current in the payment of franchise taxes (if it is more than two years delinquent it may have been dissolved by the New York Department of Law under Section 203-a of the New York Tax Law—*see* discussion in Chapter 16); and call a special meeting of shareholders requiring 100 percent attendance in person or by proxy. At the special meeting, which should be transcribed by a stenographer at the corporation's expense, the corporation's president should describe in reasonable detail all transactions outside the ordinary course of business during the period for which records are nonexistent, particularly issues and repurchases of corporate stock and transactions with related parties under Section 713 of the BCL. The secretary should draft minutes of this special meeting by which the shareholders approve, authorize, ratify and confirm all of the acts, decisions and transactions of the directors and officers during the "gap period," not just those summarized by the president at the meeting, and such minutes should be adopted at the meeting by not less than all of the shareholders. While a less burdensome procedure may be adopted for short "gap periods," or "gap periods" during which nothing of significance happened in the corporation's life, under no circumstances should counsel ever draft fictitious minutes of meetings that never in fact took place, as this is a criminal offense in New York. *See* N.Y. Penal Law § 175.

The businesses that specialize in preparing corporate "packets" consisting of a minute book, corporate seal, share certificates and share transfer ledger (*see* discussion in Chapter 4 of this volume for names and addresses of several such businesses) generally do a creditable job of determining that share certificates comply with the requirements of Section 508 of the BCL, but counsel should never take this for granted. Particularly, if the corporation has taken action which must be noted on the face and/or the back of each share certificate under Section 505(e), 609(h), 616(c), 620(g), 709(c) or 1002(c) of the BCL, this should be mentioned when ordering the minute book, and counsel should furnish the minute book manufacturer with the required language. Counsel should read the instructions provided by the minute book publishers carefully to determine the proper method of filling out both the stubs attached to each share certificate and the share transfer ledger (an alphabetical list of shareholders which usually appears in the same section of the minute book as the share certificates themselves).

In addition to the minute book and the share transfer ledger, the corporate secretary should (but seldom does) keep handy a "cross-reference" file for each important document or agreement executed by the corporation, cross-referenced by category (e.g., real estate, employment, tax returns) and by the name of each party thereto other than the corporation.

ASPECTS OF DAY-TO-DAY MANAGEMENT

As a final suggestion, it is seriously suggested that counsel develop the practice of inserting a sheet of colored paper in the minute book after each year's minutes, to distinguish the transactions entered into by the corporation each year, or use index tabs to separate the years. Minute books have a habit of expanding in geometric proportion to the number of matters approved by the directors and shareholders, and any method of organization which can assist the secretary (or his/her successors) to find a document quickly and easily is worth the time and trouble.

2. Communicating with Shareholders

The BCL requires a corporation to give notice to its shareholders of, and certain information in connection with, certain corporate actions relating to dividends, share distributions, reacquired shares, reduction of capital, surplus and reserves, and convertible shares and bonds. BCL § 520. A New York corporation is also required to furnish financial statements to a shareholder who either has held his/her stock for six months or more, or holds five percent or more of the corporation's stock, but only if such shareholder asks for the statements in writing. If such a shareholder asks for financial statements in writing, however, he/she must get them. BCL § 624(e). Similarly, if a shareholder or creditor of a New York corporation asks in writing to inspect a list of corporate officers and directors, the corporation must within two days after receiving the demand make the list available for inspection at its office during usual business hours. BCL § 718.

Generally, shareholders who either have held their stock for more than six months or who hold more than 5 percent of the corporation's stock have the right, on five days' notice, to examine the corporation's minutes and the record of shareholders and to make copies. A corporation's directors and president have the absolute right to inspect the books and records of the corporation. Whether the corporation's books and records should be opened to lower-level employees of the corporation is largely a matter of discretion. If the corporation has failed to pay wages to laborers, servants or employees, or if documents are required to be produced by court order or in a labor dispute, they must be produced. BCL § 624(b). A number of corporations have added provisions to their labor contracts to permit workers and union officials the right to inspect corporate books and records to verify management's claims in labor contract negotiations. While creditors in general do not have the right to inspect corporate books and records, a corporation may by amending the certificate of incorporation or by-laws give bondholders the right to inspect books and records. BCL § 518(c).

Although the Business Corporation Law does not require the delivery to shareholders of an annual report, corporations with more than a handful of shareholders should consider preparing and distributing such a document, together with financial statements reviewed or audited by the corporation's accountants, as it is probably the most important method of improving shareholder relations, especially in good times. Useful guidelines for preparing an annual report may be found in the federal securities laws and regulations of the Securities and Exchange Commission, particularly Regulation S-K, which specifies the contents of annual reports filed with the SEC by publicly held corporations.

Beyond that it is well worth the time and trouble for a corporation to take advantage of any opportunity to send "goodwill" letters to its shareholders. Regrettably, there is usually little time for such "extracurricular" ventures. The corporate secretary will usually spend a considerable amount of his/her time responding to shareholder inquiries and complaints. Generally, responses to shareholder inquiries and complaints are drafted by the corporate secretary, reviewed and approved by management (it is wise for the secretary to preserve all internal memoranda for future reference), and sent to the shareholder over the secretary's signature. Among the subjects of shareholder inquiries and complaints are the salaries, pensions, terms of office and perquisites of corporate officers; dividend payment policy; the composition and stock ownership of the corporate directors; stock splits; stock dividends; stock option and purchase plans; proxies; reports of meetings and reports required by the BCL; advertising expenses; requests for charitable contributions to tax-exempt organizations favored by the shareholder; and retirement policy. If the corporate secretary is one of those whose salaries, benefits, etc. are questioned by the shareholder, it may be wise to have the response letter sent out over the signature of someone unaffected by the subject matter of the inquiry/complaint, such as a non-officer director. A number of manuals, guides and "encyclopedias" for the corporate secretary exist (some are referred to in Chapter 21), which contain forms for letters responding to most of the common areas of shareholder inquiry and complaint. Generally, however, such a letter must be written in tactful if not deferential prose. The corporate secretary is, after all, writing to the "boss."

3. Meetings and Minutes

The procedure for conducting meetings of directors and shareholders required by the Business Corporation Law is discussed at length in Chapter 8 (directors) and Chapter 9 (shareholders). As a general rule, the corporate secretary should draft a "script" to assist management in conducting those portions of a meeting which can be reasonably anticipated in advance (e.g., discussion of and voting on motions known in advance to be raised at the meeting), with the understanding that there will always be a certain amount of discussion (e.g., shareholder inquiries) which cannot be "scripted" in advance.

The drafting of minutes has become a lost art. In the past, law firms would delegate this task to the juniormost associate, who would prepare numerous drafts, every comma and semicolon of which would be intensely scrutinized by senior personnel before delivery to the client. Given the velocity with which business decisions must be made in these fast-paced times, and given the cost constraints which prevent most firms from spending a great deal of time on matters which the client perceives as "routine," minutes of director and shareholder meetings have become ever shorter and simpler. Numerous publications exist, some of which are referred to in Chapter 21, which contain forms of resolution for many types of corporate transactions, and counsel should avail himself/herself of these resources to save time and cost to the client. The following paragraphs suggest a uniform approach to drafting minutes of corporate meetings which should apply to the vast majority of transactions not covered by these "formbooks."

As a general rule, meetings of directors or shareholders to approve a particular transaction are not held until fairly well along in the game, usually after substantial negotiation and review of draft documents.

When drafting minutes, the corporate secretary is advised to wait until all of the principal transaction documents are in substantially final form, with perhaps a few blank spaces remaining to be filled in. These "substantially final" drafts may then be appended as "exhibits" to the minutes, which will contain four resolutions for each transaction to be approved by the directors or shareholders at the meeting:

a. a paragraph resolving that the appropriate officers of the corporation are authorized to execute and deliver each of the principal transaction documents, which will be listed in the resolution as follows: "____ Agreement, dated as of ____, 19____, between the Corporation and XYZ Gaming Co., a Nevada corporation, relating to the lease by the Corporation of 1,000 red, white and blue poker chips more particularly described therein, in substantially the form presented to this meeting which form is attached hereto as Exhibit ____, together with such additions, deletions and revisions as such officers may deem necessary and appropriate";

b. a paragraph resolving that the appropriate officers of the corporation are authorized to perform and carry out any and all duties, obligations and responsibilities required to be performed and carried out by the Corporation pursuant to the principal transaction documents or (if the directors/shareholders intend an especially broad delegation of authority) "reasonably incidental thereto";

c. a paragraph resolving that the appropriate officers of the corporation are authorized to do any and all things "necessary or appropriate to effectuate the transactions described in and contemplated by the foregoing resolutions"; and

d. a paragraph ratifying and confirming "in all respects" any actions taken by the appropriate officers of the Corporation "on or before the date hereof, in furtherance of the transactions described in and contemplated by the foregoing resolutions."

The above approach is useful where the directors or shareholders intend to delegate broad authority to the appropriate officers of the corporation, and want to be sure there will be no question down the road as to whether a particular action by an officer was authorized. Obviously, where the intent is instead to delegate narrow authority, the above approach will not be useful, and the corporate secretary should draft the minutes so as to describe the transaction in as "minute" detail as possible, omitting the last two resolution paragraphs.

III. DETERMINING THE LEVEL OF MANAGEMENT AT WHICH A DECISION SHOULD BE MADE: AMENDING THE CERTIFICATE OF INCORPORATION

A. In General

Where counsel serves as secretary to a corporation, he/she will be called upon not only to handle the "paperwork" aspects of the job, but will also be asked to determine whether meetings of the corporation's directors or shareholders are necessary to authorize a particular transaction or strategic decision. Another question which the secretary-counsel must resolve in his/her own mind is whether the transaction or decision is such as to require amendments to the corporation's organizational documents, particularly the certificate of incorporation. This section offers guidance to the secretary-counsel in resolving these difficult and judgmental questions, for which there are few mechanical or statutory solutions.

B. Decisions Requiring a Meeting of Directors

The Business Corporation Law permits or requires the board of directors to make a vast number of decisions (too many to be discussed in detail in this volume, much less this chapter), either (1) without restriction, (2) only when authorized by the certificate of incorporation, the by-laws or the shareholders, or (3) unless the certificate of incorporation or the by-laws provide otherwise. In analyzing the appropriate level at which a business decision must be made, counsel should begin by researching the relevant BCL provisions to determine if the decision is one regulated by statute, and, if the decision is one falling into category (2) or (3) above, researching the certificate of incorporation and by-laws (including all amendments) of the client.

Unfortunately, the Business Corporation Law does not specify all the types of corporate action or decision which may require approval of the board of directors. In some cases extraordinary action is permitted to be taken by board action only. For example, upon a finding that a corporation is insolvent, the board may petition the supreme court of the State of New York to dissolve the corporation, *see* BCL § 1102, and the board may reduce the stated capital of a corporation under the circumstances set forth in BCL § 516(a). *See* BCL § 802(b).

Generally, board approval should be obtained, at the very least, for decisions which (1) determine or alter the corporation's product development, marketing or competitive strategy, (2) impact materially on the corporation's financial structure or condition, (3) involve a business combination with another corporation or entity or otherwise change the corporate structure, or (4) involve the purchase or lease, or the sale or disposition, of a material amount of the corporation's assets (for example, over $100,000 or causing an increase/decrease of 5 percent or more in value of the assets set forth in the corporation's most recent balance sheet). Counsel is best advised to learn as much as possible about his/her client's business so as to make an informed decision in each case whether a particular decision or transaction falls within or outside the ordinary course of the client's business.

C. Decisions Requiring a Meeting of Shareholders

The Business Corporation Law is more specific about the types of corporate action or decision which require approval by the shareholders. As in the case of directors' decisions, the shareholders are required or permitted to act either (1) without restriction, (2) only when authorized by the certificate of incorporation or the by-laws, or (3) unless the certificate of incorporation or the by-laws provide otherwise. In analyzing the appropriate level at which a business decision must be made, counsel should begin by researching the relevant BCL provisions to determine if the decision is one regulated by statute, and, if the decision is one falling into category (2) or (3) above, researching the certificate of incorporation and by-laws (including all amendments) of the client. Where the BCL is silent on a particular decision, counsel has somewhat

ASPECTS OF DAY-TO-DAY MANAGEMENT

greater comfort than in the area of directors' decisions that the decision in question may properly be made by the next-lower level (i.e., the directors). However, any decision not expressly regulated by the BCL which either affects the rights of the shareholders as shareholders (other than the declaration of a dividend on common stock, which is the prerogative solely of the board of directors), or effects a change in the structure of the corporation, should be submitted to shareholder vote. In each case counsel should examine the BCL and the corporation's by-laws carefully to determine the percentage of shareholders necessary to constitute a quorum and to approve a particular decision, as these will vary widely depending on the gravity of the particular decision. If the necessary percentage vote for quorum or approval is not specified in the BCL or the by-laws, an amendment to the by-laws, which itself will require a shareholder vote, may be necessary.

Often the client will question the necessity of holding shareholder meetings at all, even the annual meeting required by the BCL, since in many small corporations the officers, directors and shareholders are the same persons (or person). While it is true that the failure to hold an annual meeting of shareholders does not in any way affect the validity of the acts of the officers or directors, because of the "holdover" provisions of the BCL discussed in Chapter 9, it is nonetheless a good idea to hold such a meeting at least once a year (1) to ratify any transactions between the corporation and related parties which may be subject to Section 713 of the BCL and (2) to make absolutely certain that all shareholders are being adequately informed of management activities. There is also a common practice (although it is not recommended) of having shareholders at the annual meeting give a "blanket" ratification of all actions taken by the directors and officers of the corporation during the preceding year.

D. Decisions Requiring Amendment to the Certificate of Incorporation

Under Section 801 of the BCL, a New York corporation may amend its certificate of incorporation at any time and for any purpose as long as the amended certificate of incorporation could have been filed as an original certificate of incorporation under Section 402 of the BCL. In addition, under Section 803(b) of the BCL, a corporation may without shareholder approval "change" its certificate of incorporation to specify or change the location of its corporate office; specify or change the post office address to which the Secretary of State shall mail a copy of any process against the corporation served upon him/her; make, revoke or change the designation of a registered agent; or specify or change the address of its registered agent. Finally, under Section 807 of the BCL, a corporation may "restate" its certificate of incorporation in whole so that all amendments made to the original certificate of incorporation may appear in a single document.

Section 801(b) specifies a number of situations in which a corporation may desire to amend its certificate of incorporation: to change its corporate name; to enlarge, limit or otherwise change its corporate purposes; to specify or change the location of the corporate office; to specify or change the post office address to which the Secretary of State shall mail a copy of any process against the corporation served upon him/her; to make, revoke or change the designation of a registered agent or to specify or change its registered agent's address; if the corporation's existence was limited in the original certificate to a term of years, to extend its duration or to revive its existence if such duration has expired; to increase or decrease its authorized shares; to remove a class or classes of shares; to increase or reduce the par value of any authorized shares; to change the number or class of any authorized class of shares (i.e., to permit stock dividends and splits); to fix, change or abolish either the designation of any authorized class or series of shares or any of the relative rights, preferences and limitations of any shares of any authorized class or series of shares (i.e., to alter the cumulative dividend provisions of preferred shares); to permit the board of directors to establish and designate series (not classes) of preferred shares and to determine their rights and number of shares; and to strike out, change or add any provision, not inconsistent with the BCL or other applicable law, relating to the business of the corporation, its affairs, its rights or powers, or the rights or powers of its shareholders, directors or officers.

If the corporation seeks to increase, decrease or alter its stated capital by an amendment to the certificate of incorporation, it must comply with several statutory limitations which are discussed in Chapter 4. If the corporation seeks to change the rights, preferences and limitations of authorized shares, counsel should be careful to examine the federal and state securities laws as well as the BCL to determine that its action will not be deemed a new issue of stock subject to those statutes. *See* BCL § 806(b)(4). Finally, the certificate of incorporation may not be amended so as to affect the rights of any person having a claim against the corporation (other than a shareholder). BCL § 806(b)(5).

E. Procedure to Amend or Change the Certificate of Incorporation

An amendment to the certificate of incorporation requires the approval of both the board of directors and a majority of the shareholders. BCL § 803(a). A "change" to the certificate of incorporation, on the other hand, need be approved only by the board of directors. BCL § 803(b). If the change to be wrought by an amendment has the effect of (1) excluding or limiting the right to vote, (2) changing the conversion features of the shares, or (3) subordinating the rights to a newly authorized issue of shares of the holders of a class or series of shares which would not ordinarily be entitled to vote on an amendment, Section 804 of the BCL requires an affirmative vote of a majority of each class and series of shares affected by the proposed amendment, in addition to the requisite majority of all shareholders, before the amendment shall be deemed properly authorized. A restated certificate of incorporation which does not amend the certificate of incorporation (or which makes only those "changes" set forth in Section 803(b)) may be authorized by the board alone, but if a restatement also purports to amend the certificate of incorporation, it must be authorized as if it were an amendment. BCL § 807(a).

Upon receiving such approval, the corporation must file with the New York Department of State, in the case of an amendment, a certificate of amendment meeting the criteria of Section 805 of the BCL; in the case of a change, a certificate of change meeting the criteria of Section 805-A of the BCL; and, in the case of a restatement that does not contain amendments, a restated certificate of incorporation meeting the criteria of Section 807(b) of the BCL. A certificate of change which either changes the address to which service of process upon the Secretary of State may be forwarded or the address of the corporation's registered agent may be filed by the registered agent under the circumstances set forth in Section 805-A(b) of the BCL. Forms of a certificate of amendment and a certificate of change are included in the "Forms and Materials" section of this book.

Section 806(b)(6) of the BCL provides that shareholders who dissent from a vote approving an amendment to the certificate of incorporation which adversely affects the shares held by them are afforded appraisal rights if they comply with the provisions of Section 623 of the BCL (*see* discussion in Chapter 9).

Finally, special provisions apply in the case of New York corporations which file certificates of amendment as part of a plan of reorganization or liquidation under the federal Bankruptcy Code. *See* BCL § 808.

CHAPTER FIFTEEN

CORPORATE OPERATIONS II: FEDERAL INCOME TAX PITFALLS

Orrin E. Tilevitz

I. SCOPE OF THE CHAPTER

Doing business in a corporate form presents numerous apparent tax-saving opportunities for clever taxpayers. When corporate tax rates are lower than personal tax rates (true historically but generally not now), current taxes may be reduced by incorporating a business or individual investment assets. Taxes on distributions to shareholders may be deferred by deferring the distributions to a subsequent tax year. The shareholders' heirs will ultimately take a stepped-up basis in the corporation's stock, and the stock may then be sold without the shareholders' recognizing income. The corporation may avoid tax on operating income by engaging in various tax-sheltering techniques, including owning (and depreciating) property used by shareholders for personal purposes and purchasing assets for high (although not demonstrably excessive) prices using nonrecourse debt. Ordinary income which cannot be sheltered can be converted to capital gain (historically taxed at a much lower rate, although today the differential is small) by liquidating the corporation or selling its stock.

This chapter discusses various statutory attempts to curb these techniques, which provisions, alas, frequently apply to perfectly innocent, nontax-motivated transactions as well. Some of these provisions are highly technical and impossible to describe in simple terms, and the reader should not rely on any simplified treatment of any of these topics. A useful additional reference is the applicable chapter of B. Bittker and J. Eustice, *Federal Income Taxation of Corporations and Shareholders* (5th edition, 1987, with current supplements). However, given the baroque complexity of many of these provisions, a nonspecialist trying to circumvent them should probably seek professional guidance from a specialist in this area.

II. PERSONAL HOLDING COMPANY TAX

As one attempt to curb the "abuse" of corporate tax rates which are (or were) lower than individual rates and the deferral of individual taxes which results when a corporation pays no dividends, in addition to the regular corporate tax a tax is imposed at a rate of 28 percent (which will undoubtedly be raised to 31 percent to match the current maximum marginal individual rate) on, essentially, the undistributed after-tax income of a "personal holding company" ("PHC"). A PHC is a closely held corporation with income which is (1) primarily passive (an "incorporated pocketbook" if you will), (2) primarily from personal services ("incorporated talent" if you will), and/or (3) primarily from property used by shareholders for personal purposes (the "incorporated yacht" if you will). Specifically, to be a PHC, a corporation must meet both an earnings test and an ownership test.

A. Earnings Test

The earnings test under Section 542(a)(1) of the Internal Revenue Code of 1986, as amended (the "Code"), is met if at least 60 percent of the corporation's "adjusted ordinary gross income" ("AOGI") for the taxable year is "personal holding company income" ("PHCI"). AOGI is essentially ordinary gross income (i.e., income other than capital gain), with limited exclusions and reduced by certain deductions relating to the receipt of rents and royalties, such as depreciation, depletion, property taxes, interest and rent. I.R.C. § 543(b)(2). PHCI generally includes dividends, interest, rents and royalties (less certain deductions relating to the rents and royalties), except that rents and royalties are not included in PHCI if they constitute at least 50 percent of the corporation's ordinary gross income and certain other tests are met. Also, certain royalties received by a computer software company are excluded from PHCI. I.R.C. § 543(a)(3)(E). PHCI also includes income from personal service contracts where a 25-percent-or-more shareholder is designated in the contract (or may be designated by a person other than the corporation) as the person who is to perform the contract, and, in certain cases, includes income from corporate property used by 25-percent-or-more shareholders.

In general, corporate landlords with only nominal investment income or which distribute any investment income as dividends will not meet the earnings test. Other corporations with significant rental and investment income (which may simply result from the installment disposition of a corporate asset or its temporary lease pending sale) may very well meet the earnings test in a particular year. Incorporated consultants, lawyers, actors, athletes and employees will almost certainly meet the earnings test unless extreme care is taken in drafting any retainer agreement or employment contract. Incorporated employees and service partners may also be subject to Section 269A of the Code, discussed below, and certain incorporated employees and professionals may also be subject to the denial of graduated rates under Section 11(b)(2), as discussed below.

B. Ownership Test

The ownership test under Section 542(a)(2) of the Code is met if "at any time during the last half of the taxable year more than 50 percent in value of [the corporation's] outstanding stock is owned, directly or [by attribution], by or for not more than 5 individuals," including pension plans and private foundations (note that under 26 C.F.R. § 1.542-3(b) treasury stock is not "outstanding" for this purpose). The attribution rules set forth in Section 544 of the Code are limited but quirky. An individual is considered to own the stock owned by his/her family, defined as siblings, spouse, ancestors, and lineal descendants, and by his/her partner(s). Stock owned by a corporation, partnership, estate or trust is considered to be owned proportionately by its shareholders, partners, or beneficiaries. Options to acquire stock and convertible securities are generally considered actual stock. Finally, "double attribution" rules generally apply. For example, if one brother owns stock and another an option, each brother will be considered to own the stock owned (or deemed owned) by the other.

The language of the ownership test bears careful attention, particularly since inadvertence will not be excused. For example, since the "last half of the taxable year" is the key, a calendar-year corporation which meets the earnings test, and meets the ownership test until June 30 but not thereafter, will not be a PHC for the year *provided* it is still in existence on December 31. If it liquidates on December 29, it will be a PHC for the whole year because it met the ownership test on one day during the last half of *its* taxable year. *Lane-Wells Co.*, 43 B.T.A. 463 (1941). Similarly, a calendar-year corporation with ten equal shareholders, two of whom marry on December 31, will suddenly meet the ownership test for the whole year. To avoid unpleasantness, a corporation less than 60 percent or so of whose stock is publicly held should be presumed to meet the ownership test until it is established otherwise.

C. Exemptions

Banks, life insurance companies and corporations in bankruptcy proceedings are generally not PHCs even if they meet the earnings and ownership tests. Also, a corporation deriving 60 percent or more of its ordinary gross income from the active and regular conduct of a lending or finance business will not be a PHC if certain requirements are met. I.R.C. § 542(c) and 542(d).

D. Computation of Tax

The tax is imposed on a PHC's "undistributed personal holding company income" ("UPHCI"), which should not be confused with PHCI. I.R.C. § 545. UPHCI is taxable income, less federal income taxes paid and dividends paid or deemed paid, and plus certain adjustments. To receive the deduction, the corporation may pay the dividend anytime during the taxable year or 2-1/2 months thereafter (March 15 for calendar-year corporations). Alternatively, the corporation may avoid paying an actual dividend by declaring a "consent dividend," under Section 565 of the Code, which is treated for tax purposes as a dividend followed by a capital contribution. There is also a limited carryover of excess dividends paid. I.R.C. § 564.

E. Avoiding the Tax

The PHC tax is avoided by deliberately failing either test or both of them. Typically, the corporation can fail the earnings test by acquiring a going business, thereby reducing the percentage of its income which is passive. A landlord can fail the test by investing surplus cash in tax-exempt obligations, thereby eliminating any investment "income." Occasionally, the ownership test can be avoided by the shareholders' conveying stock to (friendly) outsiders.

FEDERAL INCOME TAX PITFALLS 405

Finally, since the PHC tax is based on the corporation's UPHCI, the corporation can, if all else fails, avoid the PHC tax by paying out its UPHCI. In fact, the PHC tax itself will rarely be imposed because, if the Internal Revenue Service ("IRS") successfully assesses a PHC tax, the corporation can still avoid the tax by then distributing the UPHCI as a "deficiency dividend," in which case it will owe only interest and penalties on the PHC tax. I.R.C. § 547.

The effect of the PHC tax is thus simply to force corporations which cannot otherwise avoid the tax to distribute their income, concomitantly forcing shareholders to pay a second tax (and possibly enriching hostile outside shareholders who otherwise would have been paid no dividends). Merely being a PHC, or even merely meeting the PHC ownership test, however, may have collateral tax consequences such as subjecting the corporation to the at-risk rules (discussed below) or the passive activity loss rules (discussed below). A corporation with a PHC problem which can be solved only by distributing substantial dividend income perhaps should not be operating as a regular corporation at all.

III. ACCUMULATED EARNINGS TAX

A corporation which is not a personal holding company faces a further hurdle in attempting to retain earnings: the accumulated earnings tax ("AET"), imposed by Sections 531-537 of the Code. The AET is imposed on a corporation (other than a PHC) "formed or availed of for the purpose of avoiding the income tax with respect to its shareholders . . . by permitting earnings and profits to accumulate instead of being . . . distributed." I.R.C. § 532(a). In general, a corporation which permits earnings and profits "to accumulate beyond the reasonable needs of the business" is deemed to have the forbidden tax-avoidance purpose, although in theory the corporation could prove it had some other purpose. I.R.C. § 533(a). Since tax avoidance will be deemed the forbidden purpose if it is any purpose of the accumulation, *United States v. Donruss Co.*, 393 U.S. 297 (1969), in fact the issue will almost always be whether the accumulation was reasonable. Also, the fact that a corporation is a "mere holding or investment company" is *prima facie* evidence of the forbidden purpose.

The regulations, which are set forth in 26 C.F.R. § 1.533-1(a)(2), provide that the following factors, among others, may indicate the existence of the forbidden purpose to accumulate earnings: withdrawals by shareholders in the form of loans; investment by the corporation of undistributed earnings in unrelated assets; and a tendency not to distribute earnings. The regulations also list examples of grounds for determining that accumulations were reasonable or unreasonable. Reasonable accumulations, which are enumerated in 26 C.F.R. § 1.537-2(b), include provision for expansion or replacement of plant, acquiring a new business, retirement of business debt, working capital, loans to suppliers, and product liability losses. Certain other accumulations are also deemed to be reasonable, *see* I.R.C. § 537, and case law has provided still others.

Unreasonable accumulations, which are enumerated in 26 C.F.R. § 1.537-2(c), include provision for loans to shareholders, nonbusiness loans to relatives or friends of shareholders, or loans to other corporations controlled by the taxpayer's shareholders; investment in unrelated properties or securities; and retention of earnings to provide against unrealistic hazards. Case law generally permits a corporation to accumulate earnings to cover working capital needs for a single operating cycle. *See Bardahl Manufacturing Corp.*, 24 T.C.M. (CCH) 1030 (1965) and *Bardahl International Corp.*, 25 T.C.M. (CCH) 935 (1966).

The tax is computed at a rate of 28 percent (undoubtedly to be raised to 31 percent to match the current maximum marginal individual rate) on a corporation's "accumulated taxable income" ("ATI"). ATI is defined in Section 535 of the Code as taxable income, less the dividends-paid deduction (*see* personal holding company discussion above; however, there is *no* deduction for deficiency dividends), the "accumulated earnings credit" ("AEC"), and federal income taxes paid, and increased by certain adjustments set forth in Section 535(b) of the Code. For operating companies, the AEC is (a) $250,000 ($150,000 for certain personal service corporations), reduced by the corporation's accumulated earnings and profits (*see* Chapter 10) at the end of the previous year, or (b) the amount of current earnings and profits retained for reasonable business needs. Holding and investment companies, which

FEDERAL INCOME TAX PITFALLS

by definition have investment requirements but not "business needs," receive an AEC of $250,000, less the accumulated earnings and profits at the end of the previous year. The credit is not allowed in certain circumstances where multiple corporations are formed to avoid tax, *see* I.R.C. § 1551, and is limited in the case of controlled corporations. I.R.C. §§ 1561 and 1564. If tax is determined to be due, interest will be imposed from the due date of the income tax return for the year the tax is imposed. I.R.C. § 6601.

As a result of the AEC, a corporation may retain earnings of up to $250,000 for any reason ($150,000 for certain personal service corporations) without being subject to the AET. In addition, counsel representing an operating company ordinarily need not be overly concerned about the AET unless the company begins to turn into an investment company. So long as corporate tax rates exceed individual tax rates, it will generally be relatively difficult for the IRS to argue that tax avoidance has motivated an accumulation of earnings. In any event, "it is often a good gamble to refrain from paying dividends. The corporation may win its [AET] case, or be able to settle it on terms that leave the shareholders in a better position than if the corporate earnings had been distributed." B. Bittker and J. Eustice, *supra*, at 8.01.

IV. SECTION 269A

During the early 1980s, the IRS lost several cases challenging the ability of doctors and other individuals to incorporate primarily in order to take advantage of favorable corporate employee benefit rules. Instead of Doctor receiving a $100,000 salary and making a $10,000 non-deductible medical expense payment, Doctor Inc. would receive $100,000 for services, pay $90,000 to Doctor as salary and pay $10,000 of Doctor's medical expenses, which payment was tax-deductible by Doctor Inc. and tax-free to Doctor. The IRS unsuccessfully claimed that it had the authority to treat Doctor as having received $100,000 in salary and having paid the medical bill on his/her own.

In 1982, Congress gave the IRS the authority it had unsuccessfully claimed in the courts (and more) by enacting Section 269A of the Code, which is aimed at "personal service corporations," defined as corporations principally performing personal services where the services are "substantially performed by employee-owners." Under Section 269A, if substantially all of the services of a personal service corporation are performed for or on behalf of one other entity (or more than one related entity), and if the principal purpose of using the corporate form is to reduce federal income taxes by securing a tax benefit which would not otherwise be available, then the IRS may allocate some or all of the corporation's income or tax benefits to its employee-owners. The provision is thus directed primarily at incorporated management and incorporated service partners, and could apply to incorporated employees as well. For example, if a doctor who is in partnership with other doctors incorporates principally to receive a tax-deductible medical plan (self-employed persons must otherwise pay for medical insurance and expenses after taxes), then the IRS may treat the doctor as having received extra income equal to the cost of the medical plan. But the IRS could not do so if the doctor showed a principal business purpose for incorporating.

For purposes of Section 269A, an employee-owner is defined as any employee who owns, directly or by attribution, more than 10 percent of the outstanding stock of the corporation. There is some question as to whether "substantially all" (90 percent?) of the services must be performed by the employee-owners (as the legislative history of Section 269A states) or whether it is sufficient that the services be "substantially" (10 percent?) performed by owner-employees, as the statute reads literally. The IRS's position is that the latter interpretation is correct. 26 C.F.R. § 1.441-3T(b)(3).

Since the ultimate application of this provision depends entirely on the taxpayer's subjective intent to avoid taxes, and since a taxpayer subject to Section 269A will be, at worst, in the same position as if he/she had never incorporated, Section 269A should not prevent a professional or employee from incorporating if there are sound business reasons to do so. However, in addition to Section 269A, the personal holding company rules (discussed above) and the passive activity loss rules (discussed below) may substantially diminish any tax flexibility for an incorporated professional or employee.

V. AT-RISK RULES

Assume the following facts: a small, profitable manufacturing corporation pays too much in taxes. It purchases a master recording of an unknown artist for $200,000, with $20,000 down and the rest in the form of a nonrecourse note which is payable only when, and if, any records are sold. The price is way too high, but the corporation does not care because it will never pay the note and the taxes it saves after depreciating this $200,000 asset far exceed its cash investment. The corporation prints a few records, sells them to its staff and their families, and dutifully pays the proceeds to the seller.

Unless the passive activity loss rules (discussed below) make this scheme uneconomic—and they may not apply here—the major statutory impediment to this transaction is (if they apply) the "at-risk" rules. To prevent taxpayers from deducting paper losses which they may never bear economically and, more specifically, to discourage taxpayers from purchasing property at an inflated price using nonrecourse financing, Section 465 of the Code generally prevents taxpayers from deducting losses which exceed the amount in which they are "at risk" in an activity.

Section 465 applies primarily to individuals, but also applies to closely held C (as opposed to S) corporations which meet the stock ownership test for a personal holding company (discussed above) and which do not fall into one of the exemptions discussed below. (S corporations, discussed in Chapter 3, are subject to the at-risk rules at the shareholder level.) That is, a corporation which is not otherwise exempt will be subject to the at-risk rules if more than half of its stock is owned, directly or indirectly, by five or fewer individuals, including pension plans and private foundations. Again, the personal holding company ownership attribution rules apply, except that stock owned by one partner is not attributed to another partner.

Two classes of corporations which meet the ownership requirement may nonetheless be exempt from the at-risk rules. The first exemption is of limited applicability but the second is broad enough to cover many sizable corporations.

First, the at-risk rules do not apply to losses from equipment leasing (which includes purchasing, servicing and selling the equipment) by a corporation principally engaged in equipment leasing. I.R.C. § 465(c)(4). To be covered by the exemption, at least 50 percent of the total gross receipts of the corporation and (with a limited exception) all other corporations under common control must be from equipment leasing. However, the corporation's other activities could still be subject to the at-risk rules.

Second, certain active businesses conducted by a corporation are exempt from the at-risk rules. I.R.C. § 465(c)(7). This exemption does not apply to personal holding companies (discussed above), or to personal service corporations as defined in Section 269A of the Code (discussed above) but including 5-percent shareholders as employee-owners. Also, the exemption does not apply to (1) equipment leasing businesses (which may be exempt anyway under the first exemption) or (2) generally, any business involving the exploitation, sale, or lease of master sound recordings, films, videotapes or other similar tangible and intangible assets. However, the provision of radio, television, cable television or similar services under a Federal Communications Commission license or local franchise is not excluded from the exemption. The exemption applies to losses from a particular active business only if during the entire 12-month taxable year the corporation has at least one full-time employee who devotes substantially all of his/her time to actively managing the business *and* at least three full-time non-owner (i.e., 5-percent-or-less stockholders, taking into account ownership attribution) employees devoting substantially all of their time directly to the business. Also, pension plan contributions and deductions for business expenses attributable to the business (but excluding compensation paid to owner-employees and their families) must exceed 15 percent of the gross income from the business. (This provision is designed to make sure the corporation's business is "active.") Thus, a corporation with a single shareholder who spends all of his/her time running the business and with several other employees who aren't related to him/her and who also work full-time on the business probably will not be subject to the at-

FEDERAL INCOME TAX PITFALLS

risk rules on the corporation's principal business, although it still could be subject to the at-risk rules if it invested in a limited partnership tax shelter.

If a corporation is nevertheless subject to the at-risk rules, it may deduct losses from an activity up to its amount at risk, which is the sum of (1) the amount of money and the adjusted basis of other property contributed to an activity and (2) certain borrowed amounts, less (3) losses deducted previously. With certain exceptions, *see* I.R.C. § 465(c)(3)(D) and *Alexander v. Commissioner*, 95 T.C. 467 (1990), borrowed amounts are included only if the lender has no interest, and is unrelated to any person having an interest, in the activity (other than as a creditor), and the borrower either is personally liable or has pledged property not used in the activity as security for the loan. However, if the borrower's business is owning rental real estate, the borrower may generally include in the amount at risk nonrecourse loans from unrelated commercial lenders and commercially reasonable nonrecourse loans from related commercial lenders provided the loans are secured by the real estate.

Losses disallowed in one year because of the at-risk rule are carried forward and may be used if a corporation is at risk in later years. The at-risk rules are applied separately to certain activities such as farming and equipment leasing; other activities are aggregated provided the corporation actively manages them. I.R.C. § 465(c). For example, if a corporation has $100 of tax losses from a manufacturing business and is not at risk for those losses, and has $100 of income from a consulting business, it may deduct the losses against the income, but if the losses are from a farming business, it may not. A specific provision in Section 465(b)(4) of the Code prevents taxpayers from creatively avoiding the at-risk rules by pretending to be at risk when they really are not.

VI. PASSIVE ACTIVITY LOSSES

The passive activity loss ("PAL") rules in Section 469 of the Code were enacted in 1986 to prevent taxpayers from sheltering active business income and portfolio income with losses from passive activities such as limited partnership investments, although Section 469 casts a somewhat wider net. Like the at-risk rules in Section 465 (discussed above), the PAL rules are aimed primarily at individuals but also apply to certain corporations. The statute and its absurdly voluminous and intricate (though so far temporary and incomplete) regulations have spawned almost 200 articles in professional tax publications and the accusation that draftsmen of Treasury Regulations deliberately complicate them in order to capitalize on the draftsmen's unique expertise when they leave the IRS for private practice. Nonspecialized counsel here would best identify any issues and call for help.

A. Coverage

In addition to individuals, the PAL rules apply to any "personal service corporation" and, in a more liberal fashion (discussed below), to any "closely held C corporation." A "personal service corporation" is essentially as defined in Section 269A of the Code (discussed above), i.e., a corporation principally involved in performing personal services, which services are "substantially performed by employee-owners," except that for purposes of the PAL rules an "employee-owner" is an employee who owns *any* stock of the corporation, and at least 10 percent of the corporation's stock must be held (directly or through ownership attribution) by employee-owners. A "closely held C corporation" is one which meets the ownership test for being subject to the at-risk rules (discussed above), i.e., more than half of the stock is owned (directly or through ownership attribution) by five or fewer individuals, including pension plans and private foundations. Also like the at-risk rules, in the case of an S corporation (*see* Chapter 3), the PAL rules generally apply at the shareholder level.

B. Loss Limitation

1. Personal Service Corporations

Personal service corporations (and individuals) may deduct a loss from a passive activity (i.e., a PAL) only against income from that activity or another passive activity. The PAL is not deductible against either "active" income or portfolio income, such as dividends and inter-

FEDERAL INCOME TAX PITFALLS 413

est not derived in the ordinary course of business and gains from the sale of portfolio investments. (However, portfolio income may be offset with related expenses, losses, and, in the case of a corporation, the dividends-received deduction). Also, to prevent taxpayers from avoiding the PAL rules, the IRS has the regulatory authority to classify other passive income as portfolio income. *See* 26 C.F.R. § 1.469IT(f). Unused PALs are not lost: they may be carried forward, indefinitely, and deducted against passive income in succeeding years or in full when the taxpayer disposes of his entire interest in the activity. (Net income and loss from publicly traded partnerships are accounted for separately.)

A "passive activity" is any business activity in which the taxpayer does not materially participate and any rental activity, regardless of the taxpayer's material participation. (There is a limited exception, not discussed here, for rental real estate owned by an individual.) Also, regardless of the taxpayer's material participation, an investment as a limited partner is almost always a passive activity, while, provided the taxpayer's liability is unlimited, a working interest in oil or gas property never is.

"Material participation" in an activity requires involvement which is "regular," "continuous," and "substantial." I.R.C. § 469(h)(1); 26 C.F.R. § 1.469-5T. Normally, a taxpayer will have materially participated in an activity where involvement in the activity is the taxpayer's main business. Also, since working as an employee and providing services as part of a personal service business intrinsically require the taxpayer to be personally involved, the major part of a personal service corporation's business should not be a passive activity. However, for a personal service corporation to be materially participating in an activity, one or more shareholders holding stock which together represents more than 50 percent (by value) of the corporation's outstanding stock all must materially participate in the activity personally. Although the legislative history indicates that personal service corporations were subjected to the PAL rules to prevent individuals from sheltering personal service income simply by incorporating and purchasing tax shelters at the corporate level, the requirement that a majority of shareholders materially participate could present a very different problem for a personal service corporation with a second business run exclusively by a minority shareholder. For example, if a consulting corporation's stock is owned 40 percent by a shareholder who runs the corporation's ancillary restaurant business and 60 percent by the consultants, any loss from the restaurant business would be a PAL, which the corporation could not offset against portfolio income or against income from the consulting business.

Since losses from a passive activity may offset income from the same activity (or a different passive activity) but may not offset income from different "active" activities, one must determine the scope of an "activity" when there are arguably multiple "activities." Recent (May 15, 1992) proposed regulations drastically simplify the definition of "activity" contained in 26 C.F.R. § 1.469-4T.

Under the proposed regulations, the taxpayer may group activities into a single "activity" using any reasonable method considering all relevant facts and circumstances, including, among others, a) similarities and differences in types of businesses, b) the extent of common control, c) the extent of common ownership, d) geographic location, and e) interdependence among the activities. However, the IRS may regroup the activities if the taxpayer's grouping fails to reflect an appropriate economic unit and the purpose of the taxpayer's grouping is to circumvent the PAL rules.

2. Closely Held C Corporations

For a closely held C corporation (defined above) which is not a personal service corporation, any PAL may be deducted against active business income but not against portfolio income, although, as in the case of an individual or personal service corporation, portfolio income may be offset by related expenses, losses, and the dividends-received deduction. See 26 C.F.R. § 1469-IT(g)(4) and (5); D.J. Mason and K. Horne, "The Passive Activity Loss Rules and Closely Held C Corporations," 21 *The Tax Adviser* 280 (May, 1990).

To be materially participating in an activity, a closely held C corporation must meet one of two tests. The first test is met if, as in the case of a personal service corporation, one or more shareholders holding stock which together represents more than half of the corporation's outstanding stock materially participate in the activity personally. Alternatively, the second test is generally met if each of the following conditions is satisfied: (a) during the entire 12-month taxable year, the corporation has at least one full-time employee who devotes substantially all of his/her time to actively managing the activity *and* at least three full-time nonowner (i.e., 5-percent-or-less stockholders, taking into account ownership attribution) employees devoting substantially all of their time directly to the business, and (b) pension plan contributions and deductions for business expenses attributable to the activity (excluding compensation paid to owner-employees and their families) exceed 15 percent of the gross income from the activity.

If a closely held C corporation (as defined) meets neither of these tests, tax losses from a business activity which ordinarily would clearly be "active" will now be "passive" and will not be available to shelter portfolio income. The result of these rules is that corporate landlords and equipment lessors (whose losses are, by definition, passive) and very closely held corporations with either absentee ownership or only family employees should not plan on sheltering portfolio income with corporate business losses. Also, regardless of whether one of the tests is met, no closely held C corporation should plan on sheltering portfolio income with tax shelter losses.

VII. COLLAPSIBLE CORPORATIONS

A. Introduction and Overview

Let's say you are going into vegetable farming. You incorporate and have the corporation lease land and equipment, and plant your crops. But at harvest time, instead of simply selling the vegetables and recognizing ordinary income, you sell the corporation's stock (at capital gains rates) and have the buyer liquidate the corporation tax-free. Or, instead, you have the corporation adopt a plan of liquidation and sell the crops tax-free, and then pay a tax—at capital gains rates—when the corporation liquidates. What you have done is magically convert ordinary income into capital gain.

This scheme does not work.

Under Section 341 of the Code, a corporation is "collapsible" if its purpose is to convert ordinary income into capital gain through the sale of stock by shareholders, distributions to shareholders, or the liquidation of the corporation, before the corporation has realized substantial taxable income. Under Section 341, if a shareholder disposes of stock in (or receives a distribution from) a collapsible corporation in a transaction which would otherwise produce capital gain, the gain will be taxed as ordinary income. Worse, a collapsible corporation cannot engage in a tax-free liquidation, making sales of property in a corporate liquidation fully taxable at the corporate level. So here the sale of the "croporation's" [sic] stock will produce ordinary income, not capital gain, and the corporation will be taxed on the sale of its crops.

Of course, there are other reasons why today (1992) this scheme makes little sense. Capital gain is now taxed at a rate only slightly lower than ordinary income and all corporate liquidations are now taxable to both the corporation and its shareholders (*see* Chapter 17). Therefore, the main effect of the collapsibility rules today is to prevent a shareholder from offsetting capital gain from a sale of stock or a corporate distribution against other capital losses, and even this penalty may be avoidable by proper planning.

In fact, one is fortunate not to need to be concerned with Section 341. The collapsibility rules are blunt and harsh, for they penalize shareholders who do not benefit from corporate-level shenanigans. They also go so far beyond the "classic" collapsible corporation illustrated earlier that Congress has continually had to graft new exceptions to the rules to prevent (not always successfully) injury to innocent taxpayers. Moreover, Section 341 is almost impenetrably dense, containing what at least at one time was reputedly the longest sentence in the Internal Revenue Code. Still, because someday capital gain will certainly again be taxed at a much lower rate than ordinary income, the following paragraphs contain a (mercifully) abbreviated discussion of collapsible corporations.

FEDERAL INCOME TAX PITFALLS 417

B. Definition of "Collapsible Corporation"

A "collapsible corporation" is defined as a corporation formed or availed of (corporate longevity is no defense) principally for the manufacture, construction, or production of property, for the purchase of certain "tainted" assets (primarily inventory, accounts receivable, and real estate used by the corporation), or for the holding of stock in a corporation so formed or availed of, "with a view to" (1) the disposition of stock by the shareholders (in liquidation or otherwise), or a distribution to shareholders, before the corporation realizes at least two-thirds of the taxable income to be derived from the property, and (2) the realization by the shareholders of gain attributable to the property. Given the breadth of this definition, nearly every corporation could be a collapsible corporation, and stockholders of publicly held corporations would have much to fear. Therefore, Congress and the IRS have thoughtfully provided various exceptions.

C. Exceptions

1. Inventory

Although inventory is a "tainted asset," 26 C.F.R. § 1.341-5(c)(1) confers immunity on a corporation holding inventory which is normal for the purposes of the business activities of the corporation, if the corporation has a substantial prior business history involving such property and continues in business.

2. Minority Shareholders

The penalties for collapsibility do not apply to a shareholder who has never owned more than 5 percent (directly or by attribution) of the corporation's outstanding stock. The personal holding company (discussed above) ownership attribution rules generally apply except that stock ownership is also attributed to and from spouses of siblings and spouses of one's lineal descendants. I.R.C. § 341(d)(1).

3. 70-30 Rule

Capital gain recognized during the year is not treated as ordinary income unless more than 70 percent of the gain is attributable to the "tainted" assets. I.R.C. § 341(d)(2). Under 26 C.F.R. § 1.341-4(c)(2), the gain attributable to tainted assets is the difference between the gain actually recognized and that which would have been recognized had the tainted assets not existed.

4. Three-Year Rule

Gain realized more than three years after the completion of production or purchase of tainted assets is not treated as ordinary income. I.R.C. § 341(d)(3).

5. Section 341(e)

A shareholder or the corporation may avoid the collapsibility penalties if the net appreciation in certain corporate assets (called, appropriately enough, "subsection (e) assets") which would produce ordinary income if sold is *de minimis*. I.R.C. § 341(e).

6. The Section 341(f) Consent

A shareholder may sell stock without fear of being taxed at ordinary income rates if the corporation consents to be taxed on "subsection (f) assets" (mainly real estate and noncapital assets) when it disposes of them in a transaction on which gain would otherwise not be recognized.

In addition, the corporation can avoid collapsibility by recognizing the potential income at the corporate level, and a shareholder can avoid problems of any sort by holding his/her shares until death; his/her heirs will receive a stepped-up basis and the stock appreciation will never be taxed to anyone.

VIII. DENIAL OF GRADUATED RATES

One benefit of operating a small business as a C corporation is that income may be accumulated while being taxed at graduated rates beginning at 15 percent. Section 11(b)(2) of the Code reduces the availability of this strategy by taxing all income of a "qualified personal service corporation" at the maximum corporate tax rate of 34 percent, thus denying the corporation the benefit of graduated corporate tax rates. Such a corporation is one substantially all of whose activities involve performing services in the fields of health, law, engineering, architecture, accounting, actuarial science, performing arts, or consulting, and substantially all of the stock of which is owned by employees performing services in these fields, retired employees, or their estates and certain heirs.

IX. ALTERNATIVE MINIMUM TAX

Your corporation is not a personal holding company, a personal service company, or a collapsible corporation. It is taxed, if at all, at graduated rates like everyone else's. You have avoided the accumulated earnings tax, the at-risk rules, the passive activity loss rules, and everything else the Internal Revenue Code has to throw at you. Your corporation has a negative taxable income, but has a financial statement which makes lenders salivate. You forgot one thing: the alternative minimum tax ("AMT").

The AMT, which is set forth in Section 55 of the Code, exists to tax a corporation on its economic income if its taxable income is too small. It does this by imposing a 20 percent tax on a corporation's "alternative minimum taxable income" ("AMTI"); the corporation pays this tax if it is greater than its regular tax liability. AMTI is equal to taxable income, subject to certain adjustments and increased by certain "tax preferences." Among the adjustments are slower depreciation, I.R.C. § 56(a)(1), the inclusion of some gain deferred under the installment sale rules, I.R.C. § 56(a)(6), and the addition of the "adjusted current earnings" ("ACE") adjustment, discussed below. I.R.C. § 56(g). Also, certain losses are disallowed in determining AMTI. I.R.C. § 58. Tax preference items include certain tax-exempt interest, I.R.C. § 57(a)(5), charitable deductions for gifts of appreciated property, I.R.C. § 57(a)(6), and certain accelerated depreciation. I.R.C. § 57(a)(7).

The ACE adjustment is 75 percent of the difference, if positive, between the corporation's "adjusted current earnings" and its AMTI, computed without regard to the ACE adjustment. "Adjusted current earnings" are a modified form of "earnings and profits," which are in turn a measure of economic income used to determine whether a distribution is a dividend or a return of capital (*see* Chapter 6). For example, adjusted current earnings include all tax-exempt interest and the inside buildup in life insurance contracts. A corporation's adjusted current earnings are not necessarily equal to either its earnings and profits or its book income.

The effect of the ACE adjustment is primarily to impose an absolute minimum tax equal to 15 percent of a corporation's economic income, but that is a gross oversimplification. Because of the manifold implications of the ACE adjustment and the complex issues involved in its computation (simplified somewhat by the Revenue Reconciliation Act of 1989 and likely to be amended by future legislation), an extended discussion of the ACE adjustment is far beyond the scope of this chapter. For a fuller discussion, counsel is referred to Treasury Regulations at 26 C.F.R. § 1.56(g)-1 and any of several recent articles dealing with the ACE adjustment, including C.K. Craig, "The ACE Adjustment to AMTI: An Update," 68 *Taxes* 206 (March, 1990).

CHAPTER SIXTEEN

DISSOLUTION, "WINDING UP" AND LIQUIDATION OF THE CLOSELY HELD CORPORATION

Clifford R. Ennico

I. INTRODUCTION AND OVERVIEW

The differences between corporations and human beings are, of course, too numerous to mention. In one fundamental respect, however, corporations and human beings are exactly alike: while there is only one way each can enter the world (Shakespeare's *MacBeth* notwithstanding), there are many ways each can leave it. Moreover, like their human counterparts, corporations can leave this world voluntarily or involuntarily. This chapter describes the varied ways in which New York corporations cease to exist.

The decision to terminate a client is never an easy one for an attorney. Generally, there will be four common situations in which your client will consider corporate destruction. First, if the corporation was formed as a "shell" to reserve a corporate name for a planned business enterprise that never came to fruition, the cost of keeping the corporation alive (e.g., the annual franchise taxes and quarterly estimated franchise taxes discussed in Chapter 18) may be greater than the cost of dissolving it. Second, if the corporation has been steadily losing money for a number of years, its officers, directors and shareholders may concur that "getting out while the getting is good" will avoid possible insolvency and bankruptcy proceedings down the line. Third, the key employee who cannot be replaced (and for whose benefit the corporation may have been formed) may die or retire. Finally, relationships among the shareholders, directors and officers of the corporation may have deteriorated to the point that they can no longer collectively function as a viable entity (a situation which the BCL calls "deadlock").

As you can see, the circumstances surrounding a decision to terminate the corporation's existence are likely to be emotionally charged, and the attorney will do well to sit down with officers and directors of his/her client to discuss possible alternatives to dissolution before taking action. In the BCL, as in life, a corporation, once dead, is extremely difficult to resurrect.

Of course, the decision to terminate the corporation's existence may not be made by you or your client. Under certain circumstances, the shareholders of the corporation can force a termination. The corporation may no longer be able to pay its debts when due, in which case corporate existence may be terminated by the corporation's creditors under the federal bankruptcy and state insolvency laws. Or the officers and directors of the corporation may have committed such foul and dastardly acts that the New York Attorney General or some other governmental official will step in to terminate the corporation.

Articles 10 and 11 of the BCL deal respectively with voluntary and involuntary dissolution of the corporation. This chapter will not discuss the applicability of the federal bankruptcy and state insolvency laws, which are beyond the scope of this book.

Although the words "termination," "dissolution" and "liquidation" are often used in the BCL as if they are interchangeable, it is helpful to think of corporate termination as occurring in three distinct stages: cessation of the corporation's business (which this chapter will refer to as "dissolution"); conclusion of the corporation's predissolution business arrangements and reduction of all corporate assets to liquid form (which this chapter will refer to as "winding up"); and distribution of these liquid assets to the corporation's creditors and shareholders and other claimants (which this chapter will refer to as "liquidation").

II. EXPIRATION OF TERM

In general, corporations do not die of old age. The certificate of incorporation of a New York corporation will normally provide for perpetual existence of the corporation. If you represent a New York corporation whose certificate of incorporation was adopted long ago, however, you may find that the corporation was created for a period of years subject to periodic renewal. If this provision has not been amended to permit perpetual existence under Section 202 or 801 of the BCL, and if the corporation's expiration date has passed, you may find that your client has died without its knowledge. You will then be in the unfortunate position of re-creating it, and the tax and other consequences of business your client conducted after the expiration date may be called into question.

DISSOLUTION, "WINDING UP" AND LIQUIDATION

A recent amendment to the BCL provides that in just this situation corporate existence may be "revived" by filing an amendment to the certificate of incorporation, provided that the consent of the New York State Tax Commission is obtained beforehand (counsel may anticipate that such consent will not be given if the deceased corporation is delinquent in paying its franchise taxes, and all arrearages will have to be brought current) and provided that the corporate name remains available. BCL § 801(b)(6).

III. VOLUNTARY DISSOLUTION UNDER ARTICLE 10 OF THE BCL

Under the BCL, a corporation may be dissolved for any reason by a two-thirds vote of its shareholders. BCL § 1001. Although it is customary to have the board of directors pass a resolution affirming the results of the shareholders' vote and authorizing the commencement of "winding up," this is not required by the BCL. The corporation's original certificate of incorporation may provide for dissolution at the instance of any shareholder, or any specified number or proportion of total shares, or of any class or series, either at any time or upon the happening of a specified event (e.g., the death of a shareholder or a defined "deadlock" of the board of directors). BCL § 1002(a). If the certificate of incorporation contains such a provision, however, the existence of the provision must be noted conspicuously on the face or back of every stock certificate issued by the corporation. BCL § 1002(c). Because stock certificates are usually preprinted, this will most likely have to be done by hand.

If such a provision is added by amendment (or if such a provision in the original certificate is later deleted by amendment), the holders of all outstanding shares (including nonvoting shares) must approve the amendment by unanimous vote, unless the original certificate of incorporation specifically provides that such a provision may be added or deleted by vote of a lesser number of shareholders (but in no event less than a majority). BCL § 1002(b). Section 1002 of the BCL thus emphasizes the unique importance of a corporation's decision to terminate its existence. When drafting an original certificate of incorporation, you should seek guidance from your client as to how the "dissolution clause" should be drafted. This is difficult in practice, however, since dissolution is usually the last thing on the mind of a promoter who is actively involved in starting a business, and you will have to alert him/her to the problems which arise in dissolution.

Once the requisite number of shareholders has approved the dissolution, you will be asked to draft a certificate of dissolution meeting the requirements of Section 1003 of the BCL. The contents of such a certificate are as follows:

(1) a caption identifying the document as "Certificate of Dissolution of [NAME OF CORPORATION] under Section 1003 of the Business Corporation Law";

(2) the date the corporation's original certificate of incorporation was filed with the New York Department of State;

(3) the name and address of each of its officers and directors;

(4) that the corporation elects to dissolve;

(5) a brief discussion of the manner in which the dissolution was authorized (it is generally good practice to attach a copy of the minutes of the shareholders' meeting or unanimous written consent of shareholders authorizing the dissolution; if properly drafted, the "whereas" clauses of this document should contain enough information that the New York Department of State will be able to tell at a glance whether the voting requirements of Section 1001 of the BCL have been satisfied); and

(6) signatures of appropriate officers of the corporation, with a verification of such signatures (although the BCL does not deal with the manner of verification, normally a standard New York notary form is sufficient).

Once completed, the certificate of dissolution must be delivered to the New York Department of State for filing. Note, however, that you are required to obtain the consent of the New York State Tax Commission before filing the certificate of dissolution. If the Tax Commission concludes that your client owes franchise or other state taxes, it will

DISSOLUTION, "WINDING UP" AND LIQUIDATION

withhold its consent to the filing until your client has paid all such taxes in full. Once the Tax Commission has given its consent, and you have attached the consent to the certificate, the Department of State will usually file the certificate of dissolution as a matter of course. The corporation is dissolved when the certificate of dissolution is filed. BCL § 1004.

The Department of Taxation and Finance, in its Publication 110 entitled "Information and Instructions for Termination of Business Corporations," spells out the procedure for obtaining the consent of the Tax Commission. Publication 110 is reprinted in the "Forms and Materials" section of this book.

If the dissolution of a New York corporation occurs as part of a sale of all or substantially all of the corporation's assets, counsel should be aware of Sections 909(d) and (e) of the BCL, which permit a "short form dissolution" for which the filing of a Section 1003 dissolution certificate will not be necessary. These provisions are discussed in greater detail in Chapter 11. Note, however, that even in a "short form" dissolution the consent of the Tax Commission is required.

IV. INVOLUNTARY DISSOLUTION UNDER ARTICLE 11 OF THE BCL

A. In General

The BCL provides that the New York State Supreme Court in the judicial district in which the office of a corporation is located may, either in an action or in a special proceeding under Article 78 of the Civil Practice Law and Rules ("CPLR"), order the dissolution of the corporation upon receiving a petition to do so and upon giving all parties notice and an opportunity to be heard as provided in Article 11 of the BCL. The petition may be filed with the court by the New York Attorney General, by a specified percentage of the shareholders, or by resolution of the board of directors.

B. By the Attorney General

Section 1101 of the BCL provides that the Attorney General may petition the supreme court to dissolve a corporation upon one or more of the following grounds: (1) that the corporation was formed through fraud; (2) that the corporation has committed *ultra vires* acts; (3) that the corporation has "carried on, conducted or transacted its business in a persistently fraudulent or illegal manner"; or (4) the corporation has "violated any provision of law whereby it has forfeited its charter." BCL § 1101(a).

Generally, if the corporation has failed to file annual franchise tax reports and pay such taxes for two consecutive years, the Attorney General may petition to dissolve the corporation under (4) above. *See* N.Y. Tax Law § 203-a. This is commonly known as "dissolution by proclamation," and it is estimated that some 5,000 corporations are dissolved for nonpayment of franchise taxes each year in New York. Section 203-a(7) of the New York Tax Law sets forth a procedure whereby a corporation that is dissolved by proclamation may be reinstated upon paying the accrued franchise taxes, with interest and penalties. For this purpose, the Department of State is required to reserve the name of any corporation dissolved by proclamation for a period of three months after the effective date of dissolution. N.Y. Tax Law § 203-a(6).

Because a corporation may not know that it has been dissolved by proclamation for some time after the fact, and may continue its business for months or even years without knowing it has been dissolved, counsel may well wonder whether its post-dissolution business is legally valid and what the consequences are of simply "letting the corporation die" for nonpayment of franchise taxes. A number of recent New York cases have addressed this problem, the difficulty of which was summarized by one court as follows:

> Pursuant to Tax Law sec. 203-a(6), the [defendant corporation's] name was reserved for a period of three months and unavailable for use as a corporate name by any other entity. After three months, however, there is no prohibition on the reuse of the name. This seemingly enables the holder of business assets at the conclu-

DISSOLUTION, "WINDING UP" AND LIQUIDATION 429

sion of the corporate dissolution to avoid payment of the overdue franchise taxes by simply refiling in the same name after three months.

. . .

It should be noted . . . that for the enforcement of the Tax Law and collection thereunder from corporations dissolved by proclamation the [New York Department of Taxation and Finance] must be made aware of such dissolutions by the [New York Department of State] . . . . Such communication between the two governmental entities is not statutorily required . . . , and it appears that no expedient informal procedure exists to accomplish such notice as evidenced by the fact that it has taken the Department several years to proceed on the delinquent franchise taxes of [defendant]. . . . The need for a notice system change, either statutory or by cooperation within the government, is obvious.

Costello v. New York State Dep't of Taxation and Finance, 129 Misc. 2d 285, 493 N.Y.S. 2d 88, 88-90 (Sup. Ct. 1985).

Given the lack of communication between the Department of State and the Department of Taxation and Finance, it is unlikely as a practical matter that a corporation dissolved by proclamation will be "called on the carpet" if it promptly terminates its business and if its principals do not subsequently try to resume the same business under a different name. If, however, the dissolved corporation continues to conduct business in the corporate name, it does so as a *de facto* corporation—an association of persons holding itself out to the outside world as a legally incorporated company, and exercising the powers and functions of a corporation, but without actual lawful authority to do so—and may not avoid its post-dissolution obligations to third parties. *D & W Central Station Alarm Co., Inc. v. Copymasters, Inc.*, 122 Misc. 2d 453, 471 N.Y.S.2d 464 (N.Y.C. Civ. Ct. 1983). Although the dissolved corporation's principals will continue to enjoy limited liability at least as against claims by persons other than the State of New York, it will not be allowed access to New York State courts to enforce post-dissolution claims against third parties. *Lorisa Capital Corp. v. Gallo*, 119 A.D.2d 99, 506 N.Y.S.2d 62 (2d Dep't 1986).

Such *de facto* status will be recognized, however, only as long as the dissolved corporation acts in good faith. If, for example, the corporation's principals do not know (in good faith) that the corporation has been dissolved by proclamation, and promptly upon learning of such dissolution take steps to reinstate the corporation under Section 203-a(7) of the New York Tax Law, a New York court is likely to treat the dissolved corporation as if it had never dissolved. *See, e.g., Prentice Corp. v. Martin*, 624 F.Supp. 1114 (E.D.N.Y. 1986). If, however, the corporation's principals upon learning of the dissolution by proclamation take no steps to reinstate the corporation and either (1) continue to conduct business in the corporate name as if nothing had happened or (2) reincorporate the same business under another name without paying the delinquent franchise taxes, the consequences (if they are caught) are most severe. Not only will the dissolved corporation and any successor corporation be liable for the delinquent franchise taxes, *see Costello v. New York State Dep't of Taxation and Finance, supra*, but the corporation's principals will become personally liable for all obligations of the dissolved corporation to third parties which are incurred after they learned of the dissolution by proclamation. *Prentice Corp. v. Martin, supra*.

As long as the Department of State and Department of Taxation and Finance fail to coordinate their efforts to enforce the franchise tax statutes, it will be difficult to "catch" individuals who allow their corporations to be dissolved by proclamation, continue in business after dissolution, and reincorporate the same business under a different name (having no similarity to the earlier name) after three months have passed. Such individuals do so, however, at their peril, and counsel who condones or tacitly permits such a scheme to avoid franchise taxes may be exposing himself/herself to an ethical challenge. As the computer systems used by the Department of Taxation and Finance and the Department of State become more sophisticated, and as the state (ever desiring to avoid having to raise taxes) steps up its enforcement efforts so as to squeeze every drop of revenue it can out of the existing system, it will become increasingly difficult for corporate principals to use this device to evade franchise taxes. Counsel should request a good standing certificate for each corporate client from the Department of State at least once a year, and notify the corporation's principals immediately upon learning that such a certificate cannot be given.

C. By the Shareholders: the "10% Majority Rule" of Section 1103

Section 1103 of the BCL provides that the holders of a majority of the outstanding voting shares of a corporation may adopt a resolution to petition the supreme court to dissolve the corporation, on the ground either that (1) the corporation's assets are not sufficient to discharge its liabilities, or (2) they believe a dissolution to be "beneficial to the shareholders." BCL § 1103(a). A meeting of shareholders to consider such a resolution may be called, notwithstanding any provision in the certificate of incorporation, by the holders of 10 percent of all outstanding voting shares, or, if the certificate of incorporation authorizes a lesser proportion of shares to call the meeting, by such lesser proportion. A meeting for this purpose may not be called more often than once in any year. BCL § 1103(b). The effect of this rule is to require a three-step procedure: (1) 10 percent of the shareholders call a meeting to consider whether a resolution to dissolve the corporation should be drafted; (2) after discussion, 50 percent of the shareholders (at the same meeting or a subsequent meeting) vote to pass the resolution; and (3) the petition is drafted and filed with the supreme court according to the resolution.

In construing whether dissolution is "beneficial to the shareholders" under Section 1103(a) of the BCL, the test to be applied is whether it is more in the interest of the shareholders to end the corporate existence than it is to continue it. Accordingly, there are limitations on the shareholders' ability to petition the court for dissolution because they disagree with the way in which the corporation is managed. Similarly, the shareholders' belief that the directors are wasting corporate assets will generally not be enough to support a petition. If, however, a minority of shareholders believes that majority shareholders are wrongfully diverting or looting corporate assets and are maintaining the corporation's existence solely for that purpose, a resolution to dissolve the corporation on the ground that dissolution will be "beneficial to the shareholders" will probably be sustained (provided, of course, the shareholders can muster a majority vote to pass the resolution).

Because of the requirement of a majority vote, it is not likely that disgruntled minority shareholders will be able to take advantage of the "10% Majority Rule" in Section 1103(a) of the BCL. The preferred approach would be either to commence a shareholder derivative suit (discussed in Chapter 9) or to petition for dissolution under the "20% Rule" of Section 1104-a of the BCL, discussed below. The requirement that a meeting to discuss a resolution to petition for an involuntary dissolution may be called by only 10 percent of shareholders may be a useful device to air the grievances of minority shareholders, provided it is not utilized more than once a year. In general, however, a petition to dissolve a corporation involuntarily is a serious matter and should not be used as a vehicle to protest management (or majority shareholder) practices.

D. By the Shareholders: Deadlocks

Section 1104 of the BCL contains special rules in the event of management or shareholder "deadlocks" that prevent the efficient operation of the corporation. Unless the certificate of incorporation contains provisions calling for a greater percentage vote for election of directors than is required by the BCL, the holders of one-half of the outstanding voting shares of the corporation may petition the supreme court for an involuntary dissolution if (1) the directors are so divided respecting the management of the corporation's affairs that the votes required for action by the board cannot be obtained, (2) the shareholders are so divided that the votes required for the election of directors cannot be obtained, or (3) two or more factions of shareholders are so divided that dissolution is "beneficial to the shareholders" (i.e., as in the "10% Majority Rule," that the corporation is worth more to the shareholders dead than alive). BCL § 1104(a). If the certificate of incorporation calls for a two-thirds vote of shareholders to elect directors, the holders of

DISSOLUTION, "WINDING UP" AND LIQUIDATION 433

over one-third of the outstanding voting shares of the corporation can petition the supreme court in the event of any of the above "deadlocks." BCL § 1104(b). Finally, if a "deadlock" of the shareholders has prevented the election of directors at two consecutive annual meetings, the petition can be filed by any voting shareholders of the corporation. BCL § 1104(c).

Of course, not every conflict among members of the board of directors or shareholders will trigger the right to petition the supreme court for an involuntary dissolution. The court in its discretion must determine that the deadlock pertains to matters which are material and essential to the existence of the corporation, and render the corporation unable to function. The fact that the corporation has or has not been turning a profit up to the time of the petition is irrelevant, BCL § 1111(b)(3), but as a practical matter a petitioner will have a difficult time proving that dissolution will be "beneficial to the shareholders" if the business of the corporation is actively functioning with large profits.

E. By Minority Shareholders: the "20% Rule" of Section 1104-a

Minority shareholders seeking an involuntary dissolution of the corporation because of alleged mismanagement by the board of directors or alleged oppression by majority shareholders can take advantage of the "20% Rule" found in Section 1104-a of the BCL. Under Section 1104-a, holders of 20 percent or more of the outstanding voting shares of a corporation may petition the supreme court for dissolution if (1) the directors or those in control of the corporation have committed illegal, fraudulent or oppressive actions toward the complaining shareholders, or (2) the assets of the corporation are being looted, wasted or diverted by directors, officers or those in control. In deciding whether to proceed with involuntary dissolution, the court must consider (1) whether dissolution is the only feasible way to achieve a fair return to the complaining shareholders, and (2) whether dissolution is reasonably necessary to protect the petitioners or any substantial number of shareholders. Within 90 days of the filing of the petition, any other shareholders of the corporation may elect to "buy out" the petitioners by paying fair market value for the petitioners' shares of stock upon terms approved by the court. BCL § 1118(a). If an agreement cannot be reached on the fair market value of the petitioners' shares, the court, upon motion by the shareholders who want to "buy out" the petitioners, may stay the proceeding and fix the fair market value itself, presumably using the same criteria to value the shares as would be applied in other contexts (*see* Chapter 12 for a discussion of valuation methods generally). Note, however, that the valuation procedure of Section 623 of the BCL is not available. BCL § 1118(b). For two excellent illustrations of how a court will value a minority shareholder's interest in a closely held corporation, *see Matter of Taines v. Gene Barry One Hour Photo Process, Inc.*, 124 Misc. 2d 529, 474 N.Y.S.2d 362 (Sup. Ct. 1983), *aff'd*, 108 A.D.2d 630, 486 N.Y.S.2d 699 (1st Dep't 1985); and *Raskin v. Walter Karl, Inc.*, 415 N.Y.S.2d 120 (2d Dep't 1987).

The statute requires that the directors, within 30 days after the commencement of a Section 1104-a proceeding, make available for inspection and copying to the petitioning minority shareholders "under reasonable working conditions" the corporate books and records for the three preceding years. BCL § 1104-a(c). In the event the court finds that the directors or majority shareholders willfully or recklessly dissipated or transferred assets or corporate property "without just or adequate compensation therefor," the court may order stock valuations to be adjusted (which will mean an increase most of the time, where directors or majority shareholders have driven down the value) and may provide for a surcharge upon the directors or those in control of the corporation. BCL § 1104-a(d).

Determining whether a minority shareholder has been sufficiently "oppressed" is, as the reader may suspect, not an easy task. A minority shareholder is oppressed within the meaning of Section 1104-a when "the majority conduct substantially defeats expectations that, objectively viewed, were both reasonable under the circumstances and were central to [the shareholder's] decision to join the venture." *Matter of Kemp & Beatley*, 64 N.Y.2d 63, 484 N.Y.S.2d 799 (1984). The minority shareholder's "expectations" are generally that he/she will continue to be employed by the corporation and have input into its management. *Gunzberg v. Art-Lloyd Metal Products Corp.*, 492 N.Y.S.2d 83 (2d

DISSOLUTION, "WINDING UP" AND LIQUIDATION 435

Dep't 1985). If the majority shareholders, for example, terminate a minority shareholder-employee's salary entirely (and not merely reduce it because of inadequate performance by the shareholder-employee), that alone is sufficient to constitute "oppression." *Matter of Imperatore*, 512 N.Y.S.2d 904 (2d Dep't 1987). Where, however, the minority shareholder is a shareholder only and does not participate in management or perform labor for the corporation, it will be difficult for a court to sustain a finding of "oppression." *See, e.g., Matter of Farega Realty Corp.*, 517 N.Y.S.2d 610 (3d Dep't 1987).

Beyond these clear-cut examples, however, only one general rule can be derived from the cases construing Section 1104-a to date: the more violent his/her treatment at the hands of the majority, the more likely a minority shareholder will prevail. *See Matter of Wiedy's Furniture Clearance Center Co., Inc.*, 487 N.Y.S.2d 901 (3d Dep't 1985) (minority shareholder was discharged as an officer and employee of the family corporation, locked out of the corporation's offices, threatened with criminal prosecution if he ever set foot on the corporation's premises, and majority shareholders published a notice in local newspapers disassociating him from the business; court found minority shareholder was "oppressed"); *Petraglia v. Whirlwind Music Distributors, Inc.*, 511 N.Y.S.2d 718 (4th Dep't 1987) (majority shareholders diverted business opportunities from corporation in which plaintiff was a minority shareholder to affiliated corporations in which he had no interest, failed to pay dividends, and refused to grant minority shareholder access to the corporation's books and records; court found minority shareholder was "oppressed").

The impact of Section 1104-a is to give dissenting shareholders a powerful tool—the threat of dissolution—to force other shareholders to grant them the appraisal rights afforded to them by other sections of the BCL. However, counsel should not petition the court for an involuntary dissolution lightly. If less drastic alternatives to resolve the shareholders' grievances can be utilized, such as a shareholder derivative suit, they should be utilized.

As a final point, there is authority in New York that a minority shareholder who owns less than 20 percent of a corporation's shares (and who therefore cannot petition for a judicial dissolution under Section 1104-a of the BCL) may nonetheless have a common law right to petition the supreme court for judicial dissolution of the corporation based upon allegations of fraud, misappropriation or misuse of corporate assets by the directors and/or the majority shareholders. *See, e.g., Lewis v. Jones*, 107 A.D.2d 931, 483 N.Y.S.2d 868 (3d Dep't 1985).

F. By the Directors

If it appears that the corporation has insufficient assets to discharge its liabilities, or that "dissolution will be beneficial to the shareholders," a majority of the board of directors may pass a resolution to file a petition with the supreme court for an involuntary dissolution of the corporation. BCL § 1102. Note that this is really a voluntary dissolution and is involuntary only in the sense that management can force a dissolution on the shareholders, who may not agree with the board's determination that a dissolution is more beneficial to them than continued operation of the corporation. In the closely held corporation, of course, this is not usually a problem because of the substantial identity of shareholders and directors.

G. Procedure

The attorney representing the petitioner in an involuntary dissolution proceeding must first make sure that the petition is in proper form: that it specifies the particular section of Article 11 of the BCL under which relief is sought and sets forth the reasons why the corporation should be dissolved. The signature of the petitioners or one of them (if many) must be verified (presumably as provided in Sections 3020 to 3023 of the CPLR; a standard New York notary form should be sufficient). BCL § 1105. Counsel should pay particular attention to the possibility of a conflict of interest in any involuntary dissolution proceeding, especially one which arises out of a dispute among factions of shareholders.

When the petition is filed, the Supreme Court must make an order requiring the corporation and all persons interested in the corporation to show cause before it why the corporation should not be dissolved. The

DISSOLUTION, "WINDING UP" AND LIQUIDATION

court may order the corporation, its officers and directors, to provide any information the court requests, including a statement of the corporation's assets and liabilities, and the name and address of each claimant, shareholder and creditor, including any whose claims against the corporation are contingent. BCL § 1106(a). A copy of the order to show cause must be served upon the State Tax Commission (so that it may determine franchise tax liability as in the case of voluntary dissolutions), the corporation, and each shareholder, creditor or claimant, unless his/her address is stated to be unknown and cannot with due diligence be ascertained by the corporation. BCL § 1106(c).

The court acquires jurisdiction of the property of the corporation upon presentation of the petition, which may be amended at any time up to the entering of the judgment or final order of involuntary dissolution. BCL § 1107. On the other hand, if at any time during the proceeding the corporation can demonstrate to the court's satisfaction that the cause for dissolution alleged in the petition did not exist or no longer exists, the court must dismiss the action. BCL § 1116. The court can issue injunctions while the action is pending to restrain the corporation from conducting its business, collecting corporate debts, or transferring any corporate property, without the court's permission. Similarly, the court can enjoin the corporation's creditors from bringing actions against the corporation without the court's permission. BCL § 1115.

After the court has heard the arguments of the parties and determined the facts, it must file its decision with the clerk of the court. BCL § 1109. If, in the court's discretion, the corporation should be dissolved, it shall make a judgment or final order accordingly. BCL § 1111(a). The court, in making this decision, must take into consideration the following: (1) if the petition was filed by shareholders or by directors, the benefit to the shareholders of a dissolution must be of paramount importance; (2) if the petition was filed as a result of a "deadlock," dissolution is "not to be denied merely because it is found that the corporate business has been or could be conducted at a profit"; and (3) if the Attorney General commenced the action, the interest of the public must be of paramount importance. BCL § 1111(b). If the judgment or final order provides for a dissolution of the corporation, the court may in its judgment or final order provide for the distribution of the property of the corporation to those entitled thereto. BCL § 1111(c).

The court is required to submit certified copies of the judgment or final order of dissolution to the New York Department of State and to the clerk of the county in which the office of the corporation is located, for appropriate filing. When the Department of State files its certified copy of the judgment or final order, the corporation is dissolved. BCL § 1111(d).

H. The Problem of Assessable "Nonassessable" Stock

In dissolving a closely held corporation, whether voluntarily or involuntarily, a pitfall for the unwary lies in Section 630 of the BCL, which will hold the ten largest shareholders of the corporation personally liable for all debts, wages or salaries due and owing to any laborers, servants or employees, other than independent contractors, for certain services performed by them for the corporation. BCL § 630(a). This section would apply in spite of the assurance given by Section 628(a) of the BCL that "a holder of . . . shares of a corporation shall be under no obligation to the corporation for payment for such shares other than the obligation to pay the unpaid portion of his subscription which in no event shall be less than the amount of the consideration for which such shares could be issued lawfully." Thus, a victorious minority shareholder in an involuntary dissolution proceeding, if he/she were one of the ten largest shareholders of the closely held corporation, ironically could be compelled to pay out of his/her own pocket his/her pro rata share of the accrued wages and benefits of the very people he/she helped put out of work, to the extent they cannot be paid from proceeds of the dissolution. Such a shareholder should be warned of this possibility before the action begins.

Before commencing any type of dissolution, counsel should also examine the corporation's pension plan, if there is one, to make sure there are no "unfunded pension liabilities" within the meaning of the Employee Retirement Income Security Act of 1974.

V. THE "WINDING UP" PROCESS

When the corporation has been dissolved, either voluntarily or involuntarily, it cannot carry on any business except for the purpose of "winding up" its affairs. BCL § 1005(a)(1). The corporation is required to fulfill or discharge its pre-dissolution contracts, collect its assets, sell its assets for cash at a public or private sale, discharge or pay its liabilities, and do all other things appropriate to reduce its assets (existing and contingent) to liquid form. BCL § 1005(a)(2). A dissolved corporation, its officers and directors, may continue to function as before for the purpose of "winding up," and the corporation may sue and be sued in its corporate name. BCL § 1006. In an involuntary dissolution, of course, the corporation in "winding up" will be acting under the close supervision of the supreme court.

Perhaps the most important task in "winding up" a dissolved corporation is the identification of creditors and claimants of the corporation so that they may partake of their fair share of the corporation's assets. The procedure to be used in both voluntary and involuntary dissolutions is spelled out in Section 1007 of the BCL. First, the corporation publishes a "legal notice" in a local newspaper of general circulation requiring all creditors and claimants, "including any with unliquidated or contingent claims and any with whom the corporation has unfulfilled contracts," to present in writing their claims by a date at least six months after the notice first appears in print. The corporation must also mail copies of this notice to each person it knows to be a creditor or claimant. BCL § 1007(a). Any claim filed within the six-month period which the corporation disputes, in whole or in part, may be submitted to the supreme court for expedited review under Section 1008 of the BCL. Unless the claim is being litigated on the "first publication date," any claim which is not filed within the six-month period and any claim which is so filed but is disallowed by the supreme court under Section 1008 of the BCL, is forever barred against the corporation. The supreme court may, however, allow a tardy claim against remaining corporate assets if the creditor can satisfactorily explain its tardiness. BCL § 1007(b).

VI. LIQUIDATION

Once a corporation has been dissolved and the "winding up" process is complete—i.e., all corporate assets have been reduced to liquid form and all creditors and claimants have been identified—all that remains to be done is the "liquidation" of the corporation, or the distribution of corporate assets to creditors and shareholders of the corporation.

The Internal Revenue Service and the New York State Tax Commission, of course, have the first call on corporate assets to pay tax claims. BCL § 1007(c). Wage claims and unfunded pension liabilities are next in line. BCL § 1007(d). Remember that if corporate assets are not sufficient to pay wage claims, the ten largest shareholders of a closely held corporation will be required to make up the difference. BCL § 630(a).

Next in line are secured and unsecured creditors of the corporation. Secured creditors, of course, are ranked according to the priorities of their respective liens under applicable law. In general, unsecured creditors are then entitled to share "ratably" in the distribution of the assets of the corporation. "Ratably" generally means "proportionately." For example, if a dissolved corporation has three creditors who loaned the corporation $25,000, $25,000 and $50,000, respectively, but there is only $50,000 in remaining corporate assets, each creditor will take as follows: creditor A will take $12,500 (one-fourth of the total), creditor B will take $12,500 (one-fourth of the total), and creditor C will take $25,000 (one-half of the total).

Finally, any remaining assets are distributed among the shareholders according to their respective rights as set forth in the dissolved corporation's certificate of incorporation. BCL § 1005(a)(3).

Special problems arise if the corporation has issued one or more classes of preferred stock. Generally, preferred shareholders are entitled on liquidation to the full par value of their shares before the common shareholders receive anything. But where the language of the corporation's certificate of incorporation is to the effect that upon the dissolution of the corporation and the distribution of its assets, the preferred shares shall be paid in full at par before any amount shall be paid on account of the common stock, preferred shareholders upon such distribution of assets, when paid in full according to the par value of the shares, are not entitled to any further payment, and the common shareholders are entitled to receive the remaining assets, even though they have also received the full par value for their shares. Whether the holders of preferred shares have the right to be paid on liquidation of the corporation dividends which have not been paid to them while the corporation was actively functioning, will depend upon the appropriate language in the contract or indenture under which the preferred shares were issued. However, preferred shareholders will not be entitled to dividends on distribution where the preferred shares have been paid their par value and the remaining assets are less than the capital of the common stock, or, in other words, where there is no surplus or profits.

To sum up, unless preferred shareholders have an express right, either in the dissolved corporation's certificate of incorporation or in the contract or indenture under which the preferred shares were issued, to surplus and profits of the corporation upon liquidation, they have no such rights, and if there are any corporate assets remaining after preferred shareholders have received the par value of their shares, they will go entirely to the common shareholders. In addition, if interest on the preferred shares is owing at the time of dissolution, holders of the "preferred shares" will be "out in the cold" if there is nothing left after holders of common stock have received the par value of their shares. Therefore, in drafting documents for the issuance of preferred shares, counsel should be extremely careful to spell out in detail the rights, if any, of preferred shareholders to accrued and cumulated dividends, surplus and profits upon liquidation.

Bear in mind that if assets other than cash are being distributed in liquidation, minority shareholders have a right to demand an appraisal and payment of their shares in lieu of accepting their pro rata share of such assets. BCL § 1005(a)(3)(A). Otherwise, unless the dissolution proceedings were so improperly conducted that a minority shareholder can prove individual injury (as distinct from injury to the corporation), he/she is entitled to no more than his/her fair share of the remaining assets.

If any shareholder, creditor or claimant is unknown or cannot be located, his/her fair share of remaining corporate assets escheats to the State of New York and must be paid to the New York State Comptroller within six months after the date of the final distribution of corporate assets. BCL § 1005(c).

The problem of escheat can be particularly troublesome where the liquidating corporation is either (a) a corporation or fiduciary holding securities where the true owner has not come forward or cannot be found, or (b) a brokerage house that has purchased shares in various corporations for clients and customers that are either unknown or cannot be located. In such a situation the Bureau of Audit and Control, which is part of the New York State Comptroller's Office, should be contacted.

New York State's Abandoned Property Law, particularly Article V (Sections 500-504) thereof, requires any fiduciary, domestic corporation or foreign corporation to pay to the State Comptroller by March 10 of each year all property "deemed abandoned" on December 31 of the prior year. N.Y. Ab. Prop. Law § 502. Section 501 determines what constitutes "abandoned property." The most important requisite is that the property be unclaimed for a period of three years. If a liquidating corporation holds property that has been unclaimed for a period of less than three years, the liquidation process may be held up. This can be a problem for a company that has debtholders or shareholders it cannot locate.

PRACTICE GUIDES

- *Make sure there is no viable alternative to dissolution before you advise your client to proceed with a voluntary or involuntary dissolution.*

- *Many problems which arise when dissolving a corporation can be avoided by careful drafting of the corporation's certificate of incorporation and certain contracts between the corporation and its shareholders. Your client probably will not be thinking about*

DISSOLUTION, "WINDING UP" AND LIQUIDATION

these problems when these documents are being drafted, and you will have to educate him/her so that the documents can be drafted properly.

- *If your client's certificate of incorporation provides that the corporation shall exist only for a period of years subject to periodic renewal, have the certificate amended to provide for perpetual existence.*

- *Make sure your client files its annual New York State franchise tax report and pays all state taxes on time, and make sure the State Tax Commission is recording the payments properly (clerical errors are not uncommon in Albany) by requesting a good standing certificate for each corporate client from the New York Department of State once a year. These documents will usually indicate whether any franchise or other state taxes are owing.*

- *Although dissolution is one of the last things on your client's mind, when drafting the original certificate of incorporation see if you can persuade your client to spell out the voting procedure for a voluntary dissolution. This will save you and your client many headaches should it ever be deemed desirable to dissolve the corporation.*

- *In a voluntary dissolution, carefully draft the minutes of the shareholders' meeting authorizing the dissolution and make sure the procedure that was followed is documented in detail.*

- *If you are representing a petitioner in an involuntary dissolution proceeding who is one of the ten largest shareholders of the corporation, be sure to warn him/her that he/she may have to pay accrued wages of employees and laborers out of his/her own pocket if the proceeding is successful and corporate assets are not sufficient to pay such wages.*

- *Recognize that an involuntary dissolution proceeding requires as much litigation as corporate skills. Counsel should consider associating himself/herself with litigation experts who can advise him/her as to the intricacies of tactics and procedure in the particular court in which the proceeding takes place.*

- *In any dissolution proceeding, watch out for ERISA problems resulting from "unfunded pension liabilities."*

- *In "winding up" a corporation, conduct or supervise a "due diligence" inquiry to make sure all creditors of and potential claimants against the corporation are accounted for. Nobody reads "legal notices" in newspapers.*

- *If you learn that the corporation has contingent liabilities that have not given rise to actual claims (e.g., due to your client's possible negligence, a ship sinks with all hands aboard the week before dissolution and the next-of-kin have not yet commenced suit), be sure the potential claimants are included in your list of the corporation's creditors, even if the exact amount of the liabilities will not be known until the litigation is concluded.*

- *If the principals of your client intend that preferred shareholders are to receive assets in liquidation in excess of the par value of their shares, be sure this is expressly stated either in the certificate of incorporation or in the documents under which the preferred shareholders acquired their shares.*

- *If the corporation is posting record profits and enjoying phenomenal growth, do not try to dissolve it because your client disagrees with current management practices. Any grievances your client has against the corporation's management or controlling shareholders are probably better resolved by a direct or derivative suit.*

- *In any dissolution proceeding, watch out for possible conflicts of interest, especially where the proceeding pits rival shareholder factions against each other.*

CHAPTER SEVENTEEN

FEDERAL INCOME TAX ASPECTS OF CORPORATE LIQUIDATION

Elizabeth A. Hartnett

I. INTRODUCTION

The Tax Reform Act of 1986 radically changed the tax consequences of corporate liquidations by repealing the sections of the 1984 Internal Revenue Code which, under the so-called *General Utilities* doctrine, had historically provided nonrecognition of gain on liquidation. Now the following Code sections determine the tax consequences of complete liquidation on the corporation and its shareholders.

A. Internal Revenue Code Section 336

Under new Section 336 of the Code, gain or loss is now generally recognized at the corporate level on sales or distributions of property in complete liquidations. This means that liquidation distributions are now taxed twice—once at the corporate level and again at the shareholder level.

Recognition of loss by the corporation is denied for non-pro rata distributions to certain related persons or where the loss property was contributed with a tax avoidance purpose.

B. Internal Revenue Code Section 331

Section 331 of the Code characterizes a corporate liquidation as an exchange. Recognized gain or loss is measured by the difference between the cash and fair market value of the property distributed to the shareholder and the adjusted tax basis of the stock of the liquidating corporation.

A special rule set forth in Section 453(h) of the Code provides limited relief from immediate gain recognition on distribution of certain installment obligations.

C. Internal Revenue Code Sections 332, 334 and 338

Sections 332, 334 and 338 of the Code govern the tax effects to a parent corporation on the liquidation of a subsidiary corporation. Generally, if a parent owns at least 80 percent of the voting stock of a subsidiary, no gain or loss is recognized on distributions to the parent.

II. TAX REASONS FOR LIQUIDATION

The corporation has traditionally been the favored choice of entity for conducting business. The negative tax implications of the corporate form of business can be a sufficient reason to terminate the corporate form of doing business and to continue in an alternate form such as a partnership or sole proprietorship.

The tax reasons for liquidation have included the following:

A. Lowering Tax Rates

The relative tax rates of the shareholder and corporation may make noncorporate forms of business advantageous. The highest marginal individual income tax rate after 1987 is lower than the highest marginal rate for corporations. This change is a reversal of the prior tax rate relationship which favored a buildup of earnings in a corporation at income tax rates lower than those imposed on the individual shareholder.

The corporate alternative minimum tax includes a significant tax preference item not applicable to S corporations or noncorporate taxpayers. After 1989, the calculation of corporate alternative minimum taxable income includes 75 percent of the amount by which adjusted current earnings ("ACE") exceed other alternative minimum taxable income. The ACE adjustment is based on the difference between earnings and profits and reported taxable income. It was added as a tax preference to ensure that corporations with substantial economic earnings could not avoid paying some tax on income.

B. Reducing Double Taxation

Any buildup in asset value and earnings in the corporation will now always be taxed to both the corporation and, when distributed, to the shareholder, regardless of whether it is a dividend or a liquidating distribution.

The dividend versus liquidation distribution decision should be based on the difference in taxation of the dividend at ordinary income tax rates and the liquidation distribution at capital gains tax rates. But, even if the

ASPECTS OF CORPORATE LIQUIDATION

same tax rate applies to dividend and capital gain income, the amount of capital gain will be less than the dividend to the extent of the recovery of the shareholder's tax basis in his stock.

C. Avoiding Constructive Dividends

Traditionally, in a closely held corporation several techniques have been used to shift the incidence of taxation to the shareholder without tax at the corporate level. Salaries to shareholder-employees, rents and royalties on leases with shareholders, and interest payments on corporate loans, if they constitute reasonable and necessary business expenses, are deductible to the corporation and taxable only to the shareholder. Because individual tax rates are now lower than corporate rates, the Internal Revenue Service is more likely to examine the reasonableness of these deductions with an eye to recharacterizing the payments as dividends which are not deductible by the corporation (*see* discussion in Chapter 10).

D. Avoiding Accumulated Earnings Tax

One tax-savings technique used by high-bracket taxpayers has been to accumulate earnings in a corporation over a number of years, paying only the corporate income taxes, and paying out such accumulated earnings as dividends only when the shareholder's tax bracket became lower (for example, upon retirement) or upon liquidation of the corporation under the favorable liquidation rules. The accumulation was not warranted for business purposes and the corporation became an incorporated pocketbook.

A special penalty tax, the "accumulated earnings tax," is imposed on any such unreasonable accumulations of earnings under Section 531 of the Code (*see* Chapter 11 for a more detailed discussion). The accumulated earnings tax is levied in addition to the regular corporate tax at rates equal to 27-1/2 percent on the first $100,000 of accumulated taxable income and 38-1/2 percent on all accumulated taxable income in excess of $100,000, but only if the corporation is deemed by the Internal Revenue Service to be "formed or availed of for the purpose of avoiding the income tax with respect to its shareholders . . . by permitting earnings and profits to accumulate instead of being divided or distributed." I.R.C. § 532(a). "Accumulated taxable income" means taxable income in excess of what is "retained for the reasonable needs of the business," I.R.C. § 535(c), but in no event less than $250,000 for most corporations and $150,000 for personal service corporations (e.g., law, engineering, architecture, accounting, etc.). "Reasonable business needs" is a subjective concept and the determination of unreasonable accumulation occurs only upon a tax audit.

Thus, a corporation which runs afoul of the accumulated earnings tax may accumulate earnings up to the target amount without fear and perhaps more if it can demonstrate to the IRS's satisfaction that at least some of the excess was retained for the reasonable needs of the business. A list of examples of permitted reasons for accumulating earnings appears at Reg. § 1.537-2(b).

To summarize, all corporations having earnings and profits approaching or exceeding the target amounts should analyze and justify the reasonable needs for such accumulation and, if the accumulation is unreasonable, should consider either a taxable dividend or liquidation.

E. Avoiding Personal Holding Company Tax

A closely held corporation that earns passive income may be subject to a penalty tax on "personal holding company" income under Section 541 of the Code (*see* Chapter 18 for a more detailed discussion). The personal holding company tax is assessed at the rate of 28 percent for tax years beginning January 1, 1988, in addition to the regular corporate tax. The tax is imposed on "undistributed personal holding company income," which is defined in Section 545 of the Code to include dividends, interest, royalties, certain rents, trust income and amounts received from contracts for personal services.

The tax, like the accumulated earnings tax, is intended to curtail the use of "incorporated pocketbooks" or "incorporated talent" whereby investment income was left in a corporation to be taxed at a corporate rate lower than the individual rate. Additionally, a corporation going out of business may inadvertently be subject to the personal holding company tax. As the corporation's income from operations decreases during the winding down process, its passive income may increase sufficiently to cause imposition of the personal holding company tax. Distribution of all passive income prior to winding down the business may help to avoid this tax.

III. ALTERNATIVES TO LIQUIDATION

Alternatives to liquidation should always be analyzed and the tax consequences factored into the liquidation costs. The tax objectives to be accomplished by liquidation may often be attained by other means detailed below.

A. Stock Sale

A sale of stock may be more favorable than a sale of assets and liquidation of the corporation. Only the shareholders recognize gain on the sale of stock, which may be structured to comply with the installment reporting basis under Section 453 of the Code. No gain or loss will be incurred at the corporate level.

B. Tax-Free Exchange of Stock

A tax-free exchange of stock for stock under Section 368(a)(1)(B) of the Code (a detailed discussion appears in Chapter 12) may enable the seller of a business to avoid tax and receive stock of a corporation which may thereafter be liquidated or merged. This most likely would occur upon acquisition by a publicly traded company.

C. Tax-Free Divisive Reorganizations

Tax-free spin-offs or split-ups and stock redemptions can be used when the need for a liquidation is occasioned by disputes between co-owners (spin-offs and split-ups are discussed in Chapter 12; stock redemptions are discussed in Chapter 10).

D. Election of S Corporation Status

Election of S corporation status, if possible, will enable the shareholders to avoid taxation of income at the corporate level. To be taxed as an S corporation, a corporation (1) must have no more than 35 shareholders who are either individuals (but not nonresident aliens) or certain qualified trusts or estates (which are qualified only for a limited time), (2) may not have more than one class of stock (but can have varying voting rights within that class), (3) may not be a member of an affiliated group of corporations, and (4) may not be one of certain specialized corporations, such as a financial institution or insurance company.

E. Tax Planning to Avoid Penalty Taxes

Personal holding company status may be maintained and tax planning of income and dividend payments used to avoid the penalty tax on personal holding company income. Accumulated earnings tax may be avoided by timely dividend payments or consent dividends.

F. Qualified Stock Purchase Election

Liquidation of a subsidiary can be avoided and a stepped-up basis for the acquisition cost of the subsidiary can be obtained by making a Section 338 election.

Counseling a corporation on the advisability of liquidating or pursuing an alternative to liquidation requires that both the tax costs and the nontax advantages be determined under each particular set of circumstances.

IV. TAX CONSEQUENCES TO THE CORPORATION

A. The General Rule

Section 336(a) of the Code requires a corporation to recognize gain or loss on liquidating distributions to its shareholders. The fair market value of any property distributed to shareholders is used to determine gain.

Recognition is required regardless of the type of property distributed. Intangible assets such as goodwill, exclusive franchise or other valuable contract rights whose value exceeds the liquidating corporation's bases in those assets will generate gain, as will the distribution of tangible real or personal property. The fair market value of the property is the hypothetical price at which the property would sell between a willing buyer and a willing seller in the market in which it is most commonly sold to the public, neither being under any compulsion to buy or sell and both having reasonable knowledge of all relevant facts. The character of the gain or loss (i.e., ordinary or capital) is dependent on the character of the property distributed. The distinction between capital or ordinary gain or loss is important since capital losses can only offset capital gains and not ordinary income, even though there currently is no tax rate distinction between capital and ordinary income.

Gain or loss is also recognized if property is sold to a third party and the proceeds of sale are distributed in liquidation. Special rules that limit recognition of losses are discussed below.

Section 336 applies to all corporate liquidations except for subsidiary liquidations covered by Section 337.

B. Corporate Liabilities

Section 336(b) of the Code provides special rules for measuring gain where the distributed property is subject to a liability or the shareholder assumes corporate liabilities. This section requires that the fair market value of any such distributed property for purposes of determining gain shall be deemed to be not less than the amount of such liability.

C. Related Parties—Loss Limitation under Section 336

Section 336 permits recognition of loss by a corporation distributing assets whose tax basis exceeds their fair market value at the time of distribution (the repealed *General Utilities* doctrine recognized no losses). The Tax Reform Act of 1986 added several broad anti-tax avoidance provisions, including one which gives regulatory authority to the Internal Revenue Service to proscribe such activities and another which prevents the creation of artificial losses by transactions with related parties. For example, if there is a tax-free transfer by a shareholder to a corporation of property with a tax basis greater than its fair market value (i.e., a "built-in loss") whereby the corporation succeeds to the basis of the shareholder's assets, then, upon subsequent distribution in liquidation, the corporation may not recognize the loss on that asset.

Under the new rules of Section 336(d)(1)(A) of the Code, losses will be disallowed in related party transactions in either of two situations.

First, loss may not be recognized in a liquidation distribution if the distribution is non-pro rata to a "related" party. Loss property must be distributed pro rata to shareholders in order to obtain recognition of the loss. Related parties include individuals who own more than 50 percent of the value of the liquidating corporation stock and corporations who own more than 50 percent of the voting power and more than 50 percent of the value of all classes of stock of the corporation. The constructive ownership rules of Sections 267 and 1563 of the Code apply to determine ownership percentages.

Second, loss may not be recognized when the property distributed is "disqualified property." "Disqualified property" is property acquired by the corporation in a tax-free transfer (a tax-free incorporation or contribution to capital under Section 351 of the Code) during a five-year period ending on the date of the liquidating distribution. "Disqualified property" is also any property whose basis is determined by reference to the basis of other disqualified property (e.g., basis determined in a like kind exchange).

Losses disallowed under these rules cannot be recovered. If a sale to a related party prior to the adoption of the plan of liquidation resulted in a disallowed loss under Section 267 of the Code, the loss could offset subsequent gain recognition. The timing of related party transactions and the adoption of a plan of liquidation (formally or informally) can therefore have important tax effects.

Section 336(d)(2) of the Code disallows losses on the sale, exchange or distribution in liquidation of property acquired with a tax avoidance purpose. Only the loss "built in" at the time of acquisition of the loss property is disallowed. The disallowance is accomplished by a reduction of the tax basis by the excess of the basis of the property upon its acquisition over the fair market value of the property at that time.

ASPECTS OF CORPORATE LIQUIDATION

Additional losses after acquisition which are caused by further decline in fair market value may be recognized by the liquidating corporation.

The adjustment of basis and loss disallowance rule under Section 336(d)(2) of the Code applies to property acquired in a tax-free transfer (a tax-free incorporation or a contribution to capital under Section 351 of the Code) when the principal purpose of the contribution was to provide loss recognition upon liquidation. This tax avoidance purpose is presumed in any contribution of loss property after the date which is two years prior to the adoption of the plan of liquidation and continuing for contributions after the adoption of the plan of liquidation. Loss disallowance under this rule may necessitate an amended return for applicable years prior to the year the plan of liquidation was adopted or, alternatively, the recapture of the disallowed loss in the year of liquidation.

The Joint Committee on Taxation reports indicate that the following exceptions to the disallowed loss rules will apply:

1. Transfers when there is a clear and substantial relationship between the contribution and the corporate business enterprise.

2. A transfer of all assets of an entire trade or business or line of business when there is justification for operating in the corporate form.

3. A transfer to a corporation at any time during the first two years of its existence.

D. S Corporation Liquidation and New "Built-In Gain" Rules of Section 1374

Another anti-tax avoidance rule added by the Tax Reform Act of 1986 limits the general rule that income of S corporations is not taxed twice. Previous law provided that S corporations did not recognize gain or loss on distributions of appreciated property. Without any change in the law, a C corporation could circumvent the new Section 336 by the adoption of S corporation status for the year in which the plan of liquidation was to be carried out. The Tax Reform Act of 1986 modifies the treatment of an S corporation that was formerly a C corporation if there is a "built-in gain" at the time of conversion. Under Section 1374 of the Code, such "net recognized built-in gain" is recognized in a sale, liquidation or other disposition after 1986 during the ten-year period following conversion from a C corporation to an S corporation if the election was made after 1986. 1988 amendments extended this built-in gains rule to any asset acquired by an S corporation where the basis of such asset is determined by reference to the basis the asset had in the hands of a C corporation.

The gain recognition applies whether or not a plan of liquidation has been adopted. The S corporation pays a tax on this gain and the gain (net of tax) is passed through to the S shareholders for taxation on their income tax returns. The corporate tax is the highest rate of tax applied to the lesser of the S corporation's income or the net recognized built-in gain.

The "net realized built-in gain" subject to tax on the S corporation's return is the gain or loss determined by subtracting the adjusted basis of property owned by an S corporation as of the beginning of the first taxable year for which the S election applies from the fair market value of such assets. Such gain is taxable to the corporation upon disposition of the asset during the ten-year period beginning on the effective date of the S election. All gains during that ten-year period are presumed to be taxable built-in gains, so it is important to obtain an appraisal of all property owned by a C corporation upon election of Subchapter S status.

The key factors are the identification of the assets held at conversion and their fair market value. The Internal Revenue Service has issued legislative regulations in Announcement 86-128, 1986-51 I.R.B. 22 and 88-60, 1988-15 I.R.B. 47 to prevent circumvention of these provisions.

Corporations that elected S status before 1987 are subject to the prior Section 1374. A special capital gains tax at the corporate level may be imposed in certain instances if there is a significant capital gain and the S status election has not been in effect for more than three years.

E. Liquidation-Reincorporation

Corporate owners often seek the benefits of liquidating a corporation, such as the elimination of earnings and profits and the avoidance of accumulated earnings tax or personal holding company status, but wish to continue the business operations in the corporate form for other non-tax reasons. The Internal Revenue Service often challenges the tax-free aspects of a liquidation-reincorporation transaction involving the same assets, similar shareholders and a similar business purpose. The Internal Revenue Service contends that the corporation continues to exist and the distributions of the purported liquidation are fully taxable dividends.

Extraordinary caution and careful review of the Internal Revenue Service position should precede any action which could be viewed as a liquidation-reincorporation.

V. TAX CONSEQUENCES TO THE SHAREHOLDER

A. General Rule

The general rule of Section 331 is that property distributed in a liquidation is received in a taxable exchange for the stock of the corporation being liquidated. The shareholder is treated as having sold the stock to the corporation for the cash and the fair market value of the property received. If the shareholder's debt to the corporation is cancelled, the amount of such debt is also considered as a distribution on liquidation. The difference between the fair market value of the property plus the cash received by the shareholder and the adjusted tax basis of the stock is the amount of realized and recognized gain.

In a series of liquidating distributions, the shareholder recovers the basis of his stock allocated on a per-share basis where stock was acquired at different prices. Once the per-share basis is recovered, the excess is gain.

The character of the gain or loss as capital gain or ordinary income is determined by the character of the stock in the hands of the shareholder (normally a capital asset).

The general rule of Section 331 has exceptions for the liquidation of a corporate subsidiary. Those rules are described below.

B. Installment Obligations

If certain requirements are met, the gain on liquidation arising from the distribution of installment obligations can be deferred until payments are made on those obligations. I.R.C. § 453(h). The requirements that must be met are that

1. the installment obligation must be received in a liquidating distribution;

2. the liquidating corporation must have received the installment obligation in connection with a sale or exchange of property during the 12-month period beginning on the date the plan of liquidation was adopted. The tax advantages of this rule do not, however, apply to the sale of inventory and property held by the corporation primarily for sale to customers in the ordinary course of its trade or business unless such property is sold in bulk to one person;

3. the liquidation must be completed within 12 months after the date the liquidation plan was adopted; and

4. the installment sale was not to the spouse of the shareholder or a related party within the meaning of Section 1239(b) of the Code.

C. Collapsible Corporations

The "collapsible corporation" rules were enacted to defeat the conversion of ordinary-income recognition to capital-gain treatment by shareholders on liquidation of a corporation before substantial income had been realized at the corporate level. The application of the rule is automatic and requires no intention to avoid ordinary-income recognition by the shareholders or by the corporation. Section 341 of the Code requires that any gain realized by a shareholder on a liquidating distribution from a collapsible corporation is ordinary income. When the effective tax rate on capital gain and ordinary income is the same, however, the practical effect of the rule is diminished.

D. Tax Basis Rules

Section 334(a) of the Code provides a step-up to fair market value for the basis of property distributed in liquidation to a shareholder. If the property distributed is subject to a rule where recognition by the distributing corporation of gain is avoided or loss is denied, then that property has a cost basis equal to the basis of the stock in the hands of the shareholder.

If the assets acquired after May 6, 1986, constitute a trade or business, then the aggregate basis is allocated under the residual method for Section 338 elections described in VI,D below regarding subsidiary liquidations. If the assets are not a trade or business, then the aggregate basis is allocated based on the relative fair market value of the assets distributed, including goodwill.

VI. LIQUIDATION OF A SUBSIDIARY

A. General Rule

Section 332 of the Code provides that a parent corporation will recognize no gain or loss upon the liquidation of a subsidiary corporation in which it owns at least 80 percent of the voting stock. This nonrecognition provision is mandatory if the following conditions are met:

1. The parent corporation must have at least 80 percent of the voting stock of the subsidiary and must own at least 80 percent of the total value of the subsidiary. These percentage requirements must be met on the date of adoption of the plan of liquidation and at all times until all the property of the subsidiary is distributed.

2. The subsidiary must distribute all its property in complete redemption of all stock within a taxable year or within three years from the close of the taxable year in which the plan was adopted and the first distribution occurred. If the liquidation cannot be completed within one taxable year, the parent corporation must file a waiver of the statute of limitations on tax assessments and may have to post a bond to ensure payment of taxes in the event the technical requirements of Section 332 are not met and the distributions in liquidation are taxable.

3. The subsidiary corporation must be solvent and the parent must receive at least partial payment for the stock. If this requirement cannot be met, the parent may have an allowable loss on a worthless security

under Section 165 of the Code. The loss would be ordinary if more than 90 percent of the gross receipts of the subsidiary for all tax years came from sources other than passive income. Otherwise, the loss is capital.

B. Indebtedness of Subsidiary to Parent

Special rules apply when indebtedness of a liquidating subsidiary to a parent is cancelled. If Section 332 applies, the subsidiary recognizes no gain or loss even though appreciated properties are transferred in satisfaction of the debt (normally gain to the extent of the appreciation would be taxable).

The parent corporation may have to recognize gain or loss if the amount received in payment is different from the parent's tax basis in the debt.

This exception to Section 332 also does not apply if the parent owes money to the subsidiary and that debt is satisfied by appreciated property.

C. Minority Interests

Gain, but not loss, is recognized by a subsidiary corporation that distributes property to its minority shareholders. Gain recognition applies only to the property distributed to the minority shareholder. Distributions of appreciated property to the parent corporation remain protected by Section 332. The minority shareholder recognizes gain or loss equal to the difference between the cash and the fair market value of the property distributed and the minority shareholder's adjusted tax basis in the stock of the subsidiary.

D. Tax Basis Rules

A parent corporation's basis in property received from a liquidated subsidiary is governed by Sections 334 and 338 of the Code. Unless the parent elects under Section 338, the property distributed to the parent has the same basis as it had in the subsidiary corporation. The fair market value of the property and the parent corporation's investment in the subsidiary stock is ignored. If a Section 338 election is made, the

ASPECTS OF CORPORATE LIQUIDATION

basis of the property received is the tax basis that the parent corporation had for the subsidiary's stock (allocated among the tangible assets based on their fair market value, with any excess being goodwill). This election can only be made for specific "qualified stock purchases." The election may be beneficial to the parent corporation if it receives a stepped-up basis for the assets. But, if a Section 338 election is made, the subsidiary recognizes gain or loss as though it had sold its assets.

A minority shareholder's basis in property received in a subsidiary liquidation is subject to the rules set forth in V,D above.

VII. PROCEDURE

A. Federal Income Tax Return

In connection with the filing of the federal income tax return of a liquidated corporation, the following requirements must be met:

1. Form 966 (Corporate Dissolution or Liquidation) must be filed within 30 days after the resolution is adopted to dissolve the corporation or liquidate any of its stock, together with a certified copy of the plan of liquidation. If the resolution or plan is amended, an additional Form 966 must be filed with copies of the amendment.

2. The final income tax return must include a certified copy of the shareholders' meeting in which the plan of liquidation was adopted and a statement listing the assets sold, with dates of sale given and computations of gain or loss, both realized and recognized.

3. Additional materials required to be filed by the parent corporation upon liquidation of its subsidiary include (a) a copy of the plan of liquidation, (b) a list of all properties received showing cost and fair market value, (c) a statement of indebtedness of the subsidiary to the parent, (d) a statement of ownership of all classes of stock of the subsidiary, and (e) if distributions will be received in more than one year, a waiver of the statute of limitations on assessment.

4. Form 1099-DIV must be transmitted to each shareholder (other than a parent corporation in a subsidiary liquidation) on or before January 31 of the year following the liquidation, and Form 1096 must be sent

to the Internal Revenue Service by February 28 of the year following liquidation. These forms inform the shareholders of the values they have received for computation of gain or loss.

B. New York State Requirements

The certificate of dissolution cannot be filed without the approval of the New York State Bureau of Taxation. That approval requires the filing of all tax returns for periods ending on the date of cessation of business and all prior fiscal years as well as the payment of all franchise taxes relating to such periods. The final franchise report may be on an estimated basis if necessary.

The following should be mailed to the Dissolution Unit, Corporation Tax, State Campus, Albany, New York 12227:

1. certificate of dissolution;

2. certified check payable to the "Department of State" in the amount of $60 for the filing fee; and

3. the final franchise tax return and payment of all taxes due.

The filing of a final franchise tax return and certificate of dissolution may not necessarily be the last return filed by a dissolved corporation in New York State. New York Tax Law includes in the definition of taxpayer a corporation which continues to do business after it has been dissolved by the filing of a certificate of dissolution, by proclamation or otherwise. A dissolved corporation is not taxable as a corporate taxpayer if its activities are limited to the liquidation of its business and affairs, the disposition of its assets (other than in the regular course of business) and the distribution of the proceeds.

Although a liquidating corporation is subject to unincorporated business tax, if the liquidation is in connection with a bankruptcy proceeding, neither the trustee in bankruptcy nor the corporation will be subject to tax on the liquidation and distribution of the corporate assets.

CHAPTER EIGHTEEN

A CORPORATE TAX CHECKLIST FOR THE LAWYER REPRESENTING THE SMALL BUSINESS

Orrin E. Tilevitz

CORPORATE TAX CHECKLIST   465

I. SCOPE OF THE CHAPTER

This chapter outlines the principal taxes, other than the federal income tax (and related taxes such as the personal holding company tax, accumulated earnings tax, and alternative minimum tax), to which a corporation doing business in New York State and particularly New York City may be subject. The object is to alert the practitioner to the existence of each tax and to some unexpected instances where the tax could apply. For a more extensive description of these taxes, the reader should consult a general manual such as *Guidebook to New York Taxes*, published annually by Commerce Clearing House, Inc. ("CCH") or the *New York Tax Handbook*, published by Prentice-Hall, Inc. In many cases, the reader should also consult the *New York State and Local Tax Service*, published by Prentice-Hall, or the *New York State Tax Reporter*, published by CCH. These services contain the statutes, any administrative regulations, and annotations to cases and rulings. In referring to these works, be aware that New York tax law is amended continually, so the reader should make sure that the source consulted has been properly updated. Also, since editors of tax services occasionally miss important developments (including legislation), prudent counsel will consult more than one service.

For certain taxes (as noted), the New York Commissioner of Finance has promulgated interpretive regulations. They are published in the Prentice-Hall and CCH tax services or may be ordered as separate pamphlets from the Office of Legal Affairs, New York City Department of Finance, 345 Adams Street, Brooklyn, New York 11201.

II. WHAT THIS CHAPTER DOES NOT COVER

New York State and its local taxing authorities, particularly New York City, impose a formidable variety of taxes on particular industries, sometimes in lieu of, and often in addition to, the generally applicable taxes. Life insurance companies, banks, and public utilities (including transportation and transmission companies) are subject not to the general corporation tax but to separate franchise tax schemes. New York State also imposes a motor vehicle registration tax, a highway use tax on large motor vehicles, a 5 percent tax on car rentals, alcoholic beverage license and excise taxes, a gasoline tax, a cigarette tax, a tax on cooperative agricultural corporations, and gross receipts taxes on importers of petroleum products and natural gas into New York. New York City and many localities impose an *ad valorem* real property tax, a hotel occupancy tax, and an additional utility tax. Some localities impose a restaurant meals tax and a tax on admissions, club dues and cabaret charges. In addition, New York City imposes a cigarette tax, an "annual vault charge" on the maintenance or use of subsurface openings or structures, a tax on the ownership of coin-operated amusement devices, taxes on commercial and passenger motor vehicles, a Waterfront Commission payroll tax, a tax on motor fuels containing lead, alcoholic beverage license and excise taxes, a tax on the transfer of taxicab licenses, and an additional 8 percent parking tax in Manhattan. Some of these taxes can indirectly affect ordinary taxpayers; for example, the price of diesel fuel delivered to a manufacturer may be keyed to taxes paid by the supplier. These taxes, and other taxes which are imposed on individuals and unincorporated entities, are beyond the scope of this chapter.

III. AN INTRODUCTION TO FEDERAL EXCISE TAXES

The many federal "excise taxes" fall roughly into two categories: penalty taxes and particular business taxes. The following discussion is limited to those taxes which could apply to business corporations.

A. Penalty Taxes

Penalty taxes generally exist to deter conduct prohibited by, or encourage conduct required by, other provisions of the Internal Revenue Code of 1986, as amended (the "Code"). For example, Section 4701 of the Code imposes a tax on the issuer of corporate bearer bonds with a term of more than one year, while Section 163(f) denies a deduction for interest paid on these bonds. Following is a list of some commonly encountered penalty taxes.

CORPORATE TAX CHECKLIST 467

1. Employee Benefit Plans

Special penalty taxes are imposed on the improper use or maintenance of employee benefit plans, such as underfunding of plans (§ 4971); overfunding of plans (§§ 4972, 4973 and 4979), inadequate distributions from plans (§ 4974), reversions of plan assets to an employer (§ 4980), and discriminatory funded welfare benefit plans (§ 4976). In addition, Section 4975 imposes an excise tax, which in some cases may be confiscatory, on certain "prohibited transactions" between pension plans and "disqualified persons," including employers, fiduciaries and their officers, directors, shareholders, and relatives. Some transactions will trigger the excise tax even though they are prudent investments for the pension plan. *See, e.g., Alden M. Leib*, 88 T.C. 1474 (1987). Because the tax rules governing pension and other employee benefit plans are arcane and the penalties for failure to comply onerous, a specialist should be consulted before attempting to set up or administer such a plan.

2. Golden Parachutes

Section 4999 imposes a 20 percent nondeductible excise tax on the recipient of "excess parachute payments"; the payments are also nondeductible by the paying corporation under Section 280G of the Code. With certain exceptions, an "excess parachute payment" occurs when an officer, shareholder, or highly compensated employee or independent contractor receives a payment of at least 300 percent of the recipient's average compensation during the previous five-year period, the payment is not demonstrably reasonable compensation for services rendered, and the payment is "contingent" on a change in the ownership or effective control of the corporation or its assets. The tax does not apply to corporations which have or could have elected S corporation status (*see* Chapter 3), or (with limitations) to corporations whose stock is not readily tradable.

The "golden parachute" rules were designed to limit the perceived abuses of management's lining its pockets at the shareholders' expense, attempting to remain in control in a hostile takeover that could potentially benefit shareholders, or recommending proposed takeovers not in the shareholders' interests in the expectation of substantial personal gain. However, the statute and its legislative history can be interpreted to apply in situations ranging far beyond these limited purposes. Unless the corporation is clearly exempt, any agreement to increase salary, pay severance, or accelerate amounts previously deferred, which is entered into within one year before a change in control of the corporation, which takes effect within one year after a change in control, or which arguably might not have been entered into had a change in control not been imminent, must be scrutinized to see if the golden parachute rules apply.

B. Excise Taxes on Specific Business Activities

Federal excise taxes are imposed on the manufacture or sale of certain articles, on certain transactions, on certain occupations, and on the use of certain items. For example, taxes are imposed on the manufacturer or importer of firearms, sport fishing equipment, and tires, and on the sale of certain fuel, heavy trucks, trailers, and tractors. For further information, see IRS Publication 334, *Tax Guide for Small Business* and IRS Publication 510, *Excise Taxes*.

IV. PAYROLL TAXES

An employer must withhold or pay directly the payroll taxes discussed below. For details, see IRS Publication 15, *Employer's Tax Guide* and New York State Form IT2100, "Employer's Withholding Tax Instructions." Draconian penalties are imposed for nonwithholding, nonpayment, or late payment of these taxes. In particular, anyone responsible for paying over withheld taxes to the government, including but not limited to corporate officers, who pays or approves their payment to other corporate creditors instead, is personally liable for the unpaid taxes. Also, an employer that incorrectly treats an employee as an independent contractor and fails to withhold tax may be liable for the tax which should have been withheld, plus penalties and interest.

CORPORATE TAX CHECKLIST

A. Income Tax Withholding

An employer must withhold federal, New York State, and New York City (or city of Yonkers) personal income taxes (or New York City nonresident income taxes) from employees' salaries and must pay those withheld amounts to the government.

B. FICA

An employer must pay social security (FICA) taxes on employees' wages and withhold (and pay over to the federal government) an equal amount of taxes from the employees' wages.

C. Unemployment Taxes

An employer must pay federal unemployment (FUTA) taxes and New York State unemployment insurance tax.

V. NEW YORK STATE BUSINESS TAXES

Following is a synopsis of the principal New York State taxes which a corporation may encounter.

A. Corporate Franchise Tax: N.Y. Tax Law art. 9-A, § 208 *et seq.*

1. Scope

The tax is imposed on all New York State corporations and all foreign corporations doing business, employing capital, or owning or leasing property in New York, unless otherwise exempted. S corporations (*see* Chapter 3) are taxed at a lower rate. To be treated as an S corporation for New York tax purposes, an S corporation must file New York State Form CT-6; federal Form 2553 is insufficient. (New York City does *not* recognize the S election for purposes of the New York City corporation tax, as will be discussed below.)

2. Rate

a. C Corporations

The tax rate for regular C corporations is the highest of (a) 9% of "entire net income" allocated to New York; (b) 0.178% of "total business and investment capital" allocated to New York (0.04% for cooperative housing corporations), but not more than $350,000; (c) 5% (3.5% after 1992) of "minimum taxable income" allocated to New York; or (d) a minimum tax, depending on the corporation's gross payroll, ranging from $325 at a gross payroll of $1 million or less to $1,500. However, if the corporation has a gross payroll, total receipts and gross assets of $1,000 or less each, the minimum tax is $800. An additional tax is imposed equal to 0.09% of "subsidiary capital" (essentially, stock and debt of over-50-percent-owned subsidiaries) allocated to New York. Tax rates are different for some small corporations discussed below.

b. S Corporations

The tax rate for S corporations is the greater of (a) the minimum tax (other than the $800 tax on shell corporations) or (b) entire net income allocated to New York multiplied by the difference between the 9 percent corporate tax rate (plus the additional surcharge; *see* below) and the highest individual tax rate for the year. As a result, the total tax liability for an S corporation and its shareholders will equal the tax computed at the C corporation rate on the S corporation's entire net income.

3. Bases of State Franchise Tax

(a) "Entire net income" is based on federal taxable income, with subtractions, additions and modifications. *Subtractions* include income, gains and losses from subsidiary capital. *Additions* include municipal bond interest and corporate franchise taxes paid to New York or other taxing jurisdictions. *Modifications* include a 50 percent dividends-received deduction, with certain exceptions (instead of the 80 percent or 70 percent federal dividends-received deduction; *see* Chapters 2 and 10). Business income is allocated to New York based on a weighted average of the following percentages: (i) the percentage of the total value of corporate property located in New York State; (ii) *twice* the percentage of the business's gross receipts which are from New York sources; and (iii) the percentage of the business's payroll paid to New York-based employees. Investment income is allocated to New York based on New York activity of the issuer of each investment instrument; allocation percentages for particular issuers are available from the Taxpayer Assistance Bureau, Building 8, State Campus, Albany, New York 12227. The resulting percentage is the taxpayer's own investment allocation percentage. Commercial publishers such as CCH list allocation percentages of major issuers. In some cases, the taxpayer may or must use the business allocation percentage for all income. Regardless of how the allocation percentage is determined, New York State may ignore or adjust allocation factors to reflect true New York activity.

(b) "Business and investment capital" is essentially the fair market value of corporate assets other than subsidiary capital, except for taxable personal property which is valued at accounting book value. It is allocated to New York based on the taxpayer's business allocation percentage and investment allocation percentage, respectively.

(c) "Minimum taxable income" is essentially entire net income plus tax preferences.

Various credits are allowed against the tax liability, including some for investment in an "economic development zone."

4. Small Business Corporations

For a small business corporation (as defined in Section 1244 of the Code; *see* Chapter 7) which is not part of an affiliated group and which has a net income of $290,000 or less, the income tax is 8 percent of the first $200,000 of net income, 9 percent of the excess over $200,000 and 5 percent of the excess over $250,000. The tax on business and investment capital does not apply to small business corporations if it would result in a tax of between 8 percent and 9 percent of entire net income. Finally, certain small business corporations are not subject to the tax on capital during their first two taxable years.

5. MTA Surcharge

A 17 percent surcharge is imposed on the portion of the corporate franchise tax of a C corporation (S corporations are exempt) attributable to business activity carried on within the Metropolitan Commuter Transportation District, which consists of New York City and the counties of Westchester, Putnam, Dutchess, Rockland, Orange, Nassau and Suffolk. The surcharge, which has a nominal expiration date, has been extended repeatedly since its enactment in 1982 and is unlikely to expire anytime soon.

6. Additional Surcharge

The corporate franchise tax is subject to a surcharge of 15 percent for taxable years ending before July 1, 1992, and 10 percent for taxable years ending between July 1, 1992 and June 30, 1993. However, the 15 percent rate will likely be extended indefinitely.

7. Further Information

New York State income tax regulations appear in 20 N.Y.C.R.R. Parts 1-11.

B. Sales and Use Taxes: N.Y. Tax Law art. 28, § 1101 *et seq.*

1. Scope

A sales tax is imposed on the retail sale and rental of tangible personal property, including prewritten computer software; sales of natural gas, electricity, refrigeration and steam; sales of food and beverages by restaurants and caterers; occupancy of hotel and motel rooms; admission charges; storage and safe deposit rentals; social or athletic club dues; and certain services, including various information services (but not advertising), processing and printing services, telephone answering services, and installation and maintenance services (but no tax is imposed on the *inspection* of real property if maintenance or repair is not performed). A compensating use tax is imposed on the use in New York of items which escaped sales tax, generally because they were purchased elsewhere or manufactured by the user.

CORPORATE TAX CHECKLIST

2. Rate

The tax rate is 4 percent, 4-1/4 percent in the Metropolitan Commuter Transportation District (discussed above). Cities and counties may impose an additional tax of up to 4 percent, more in some cases.

3. Basis

The sales tax is applied to the retail sale price (or rental paid), including shipping and delivery charges. For automobile (and certain boat and noncommercial aircraft) leases with a term of one year or more, including renewals, the tax is imposed at the time of the first payment on all payments due under the lease, without deduction for any imputed interest factor. The use tax is applied to the value of the item when brought into the state or, for a manufacturer using its own product, the price at which it is ordinarily offered for sale.

4. Exempt Purchasers

The State of New York, the federal government and their agencies and instrumentalities, and certain nonprofit organizations pay no tax on their purchases.

5. Exempt Transactions

The following transactions are exempt from sales (and use) taxes: sales for resale (including leases for re-lease); generally, food and beverages (*see* New York State Department of Taxation and Finance Publication 880); sales of drugs and medicine; sales for delivery outside New York; sales of machinery and equipment for producing for sale tangible personal property, natural gas, electricity, refrigeration or steam; sales of fuel, electricity, etc., consumed in producing property for sale (the exemption does *not* apply to the New York City sales tax); sales of certain personal property used in farming; sales of property used or consumed directly and predominantly in research and development; and certain other transactions. *Real* property and capital improvements thereto are not subject to the sales tax; however, the sale of personal property which is to be incorporated into real property is subject to tax. Credits against the sales tax are available for property purchased for use in an "economic development zone."

6. Collection

The sales tax is collected by the vendor, but the purchaser is liable if the vendor does not collect the tax. Vendors must register with the state and obtain a certificate of authority. Sales tax information is normally furnished by the State Tax Commission to a New York corporation soon after it is incorporated. A vendor must separately certify to the customer the amount of the tax (i.e., it must be broken out separately on the customer's receipt or invoice) and may not absorb (or state that it is absorbing) the tax. Corporate officers and other responsible persons are personally liable if collected sales tax is not remitted to the state.

7. Further Information

New York State Form ST-150, "General Instructions for State and Local Sales and Use Taxes in New York State," provides a helpful summary of the tax. New York State sales and use tax regulations appear in 20 N.Y.C.R.R. Parts 525-541.

C. Real Property Transfer Gains Tax: N.Y. Tax Law art. 31-B, § 1441 *et seq.*

1. Scope

This tax is imposed on the transfer of real property or an interest therein if the consideration received (including the fair market value of property received and mortgages assumed or to which the property is subject) is $1 million or more. The tax is paid by the transferor. Special rules apply to cooperative conversions and transfers of co-op units.

2. Basis and Rate

The tax is 10 percent of the "gain" realized on the transaction. "Gain" is the difference between the consideration received and the undepreciated basis of the property transferred, including the cost of any capital improvements.

3. Examples of Taxable Transactions

The tax is imposed on a variety of transactions not subject to income tax and can apply to a transaction which seemingly does not meet the $1 million threshold. For example, the following are taxable transactions:

CORPORATE TAX CHECKLIST

the creation of a leasehold exceeding 49 years; the creation of a leasehold coupled with an option to purchase the property; an assignment of a leasehold; an acquisition of a 50 percent interest (by vote or value) in a corporation or partnership owning real property worth $1 million or more; a sale of adjacent parcels for a total consideration of $1 million; a tax-free exchange of property under Section 1031 of the Code; a mortgage foreclosure; a distribution of property by a corporation to the extent that there is a change in beneficial ownership; and an assignment of a lease where the consideration received plus the discounted present value of the remaining rental payments is $1 million or more.

4. Exempt Transactions

Following are examples of exempt transactions: a transfer of the portion of real property occupied as the transferor's residence; transfers of real property to a corporation upon its organization if after the transfer the transferors "control" the corporation; mere changes of form or identity; gifts; and transfers by governmental agencies and certain tax-exempt organizations.

5. Filing Requirements

A deed may not be recorded unless tax is paid or the state issues a "statement of no tax due." The tax is generally due on the date of the transfer, although in limited cases the tax may be paid in installments. The transferee is liable if the transferor does not pay. Also, the state's position is that corporate officers and other "responsible persons" are personally liable for the tax. Transfers for consideration of $500,000 or more, including transfers by tax-exempt organizations, require the submission of transferor and transferee questionnaires at least 20 days in advance of the transfer; a state auditor then determines the tax due.

Transfers for consideration of less than $500,000 and certain exempt transactions require submission of an affidavit.

6. Further Information

Regulations appearing in 20 N.Y.C.R.R. Part 590 must be consulted along with the statute.

D. Stock Transfer Tax: N.Y. Tax Law art. 12, § 270 *et seq.*

1. Scope

This tax is imposed on the sale or transfer of shares of stock and similar instruments if the sale is made, shares are delivered, or record transfer on the corporation's books occurs, within New York State.

2. Basis and Rate

The tax is computed at a rate of from 1-1/4 cents per share to 5 cents per share of stock transferred, depending on the sale price of the stock. There is a $350 maximum tax for a single transaction.

3. Examples of Taxable Transactions

Gifts, transfers between a partnership and its partners or a corporation and its shareholders, and transfers between joint tenants are subject to the tax.

4. Rebate

The statute now provides for a 100 percent rebate of the tax. Therefore, if the tax would otherwise apply, the cost of avoiding it may exceed the interest foregone by paying the tax and waiting for a rebate. The rebate procedure is set out in TSB-M82(6)M.

5. Exempt Transfers

Examples of exempt transfers are the original issuance of stock and loans of stock.

6. Further Information

Regulations appear in 20 N.Y.C.R.R. Parts 440-447.

E. Mortgage Recording Tax: N.Y. Tax Law art. 11, § 250 *et seq.*

1. Scope

The tax is imposed on mortgages on real property located in New York.

CORPORATE TAX CHECKLIST

2. Basis and Rate

The tax is really three separate taxes totaling up to 1 percent of the face amount of the mortgage. Counties may impose an additional tax. Special rules apply to so-called credit line mortgages securing credit line or revolving credit loans secured by a one- to six-family owner-occupied residence.

3. Payment

The tax is paid when the mortgage is recorded.

4. Further Information

Regulations appear in 20 N.Y.C.R.R. Parts 400-404.

F. Real Estate Transfer Tax: N.Y. Tax Law art. 31, § 1400 *et seq.*

1. Scope

This tax is imposed on the transfer of real property or an interest therein if the consideration received (including the fair market value of property received and, with some exceptions, mortgages assumed or to which the property is subject) exceeds $500. An additional tax (the "mansion tax") is imposed on each conveyance of residential real property (or an interest therein) where the consideration for the entire conveyance (including nonresidential real property) is $1 million or more. "Residential" means used as a one-, two-, or three-family house, and an individual condominium or cooperative unit. Special rules apply to cooperative conversions and transfers of co-op units.

2. Basis and Rate

The basic tax is computed at a rate of 0.4 percent of the consideration received. The mansion tax is computed at a rate of 1 percent of the consideration received attributable to the real property.

3. Examples of Taxable Transfers

The transfer tax is imposed on a variety of transactions, some of which are not subject to income tax. For example, the following are taxable transactions: in certain cases, the creation of a leasehold exceeding 49 years; the creation of a leasehold coupled with an option to purchase the property; an assignment of a leasehold; an acquisition of a 50-percent-or-more interest (by vote or value) in a corporation or partnership owning real property worth $500 or more; a tax-free exchange of property under Section 1031 of the Code; a mortgage foreclosure; and a conveyance to a corporation in exchange for its stock or a distribution by a corporation to its shareholders, to the extent there is a change in beneficial ownership.

4. Exempt Transfers

Examples of exempt transfers are transfers without consideration, including gifts; transfers without a change of beneficial ownership; and transfers *to* governmental entities. In a transfer *by* a governmental entity, the transferee must pay the tax. Transfers by (or to) other tax-exempt entities are fully taxable.

5. Payment

The tax is paid by the transferor when the deed is recorded or, if no deed is recorded, within 15 days after the transfer. The transferee is liable if the tax is not paid.

6. Further Information

Regulations appearing in 20 N.Y.C.R.R. Part 575 must be consulted along with the statute.

G. Utility Vendor's Tax: N.Y. Tax Law art. 9, § 186-a

1. Scope

This tax, a statutory afterthought of the corporate franchise tax on public utilities, is imposed on vendors of natural gas, electricity, steam, water, refrigeration, and telephone or telegraph service which are not regulated by the Public Service Commission. The tax is normally a concern primarily for landlords and submeterers of electricity.

2. Basis and Rate

The tax is computed at the rate of 3-1/2 percent, plus the additional surcharge (*see* Part V,A,6, *supra*) on gross receipts from sales (other than for resale) of natural gas, electricity, steam, water, refrigeration,

CORPORATE TAX CHECKLIST

telephone, or telegraph service for ultimate consumption or use by the purchaser in the state. Localities may impose an additional tax. The 17 percent MTA surcharge applies to the portion of the tax attributable to sales within the Metropolitan Commuter Transportation District (*see* discussion above). Receipts subject to this tax are ordinarily subject to the corporate franchise tax too.

3. Further Information

Regulations appear in 20 N.Y.C.R.R. Part 502.

VI. NEW YORK CITY BUSINESS TAXES

Following is a synopsis of the principal New York City taxes which a corporation may encounter.

A. General Corporation Tax: N.Y.C. Admin. Code § 11-601 *et seq.*

1. Scope

This tax, which is substantially the same as the New York State corporate franchise tax except that S corporations and C corporations are taxed at the same rate, is imposed on corporations doing business in New York City.

2. Basis and Rate

The tax is the highest of (a) 8.85% of "entire net income" allocated to New York City; (b) 0.15% of "total business and investment capital" allocated to the city (0.04% for cooperative housing corporations); (c) 2.655% of the taxpayer's net income *plus* salaries and compensation paid to officers and to holders of more than 5% of the issued stock *minus* $15,000 (prorated for short taxable years); or (d) $300. An additional tax is imposed equal to 0.075% of "subsidiary capital" allocated to the city. Income is allocated using the same principles as under the state's franchise tax, but the numbers may differ since the allocation in this case is to New York City. Issuer allocation percentages for corporations may be obtained from the New York City Department of Finance, Business Tax Refund Unit, 25 Elm Place, 3rd Floor, Brooklyn, New York 11201. Commercial publishers such as CCH list allocation percentages of major issuers.

Because of the minimum tax on income plus salaries paid, and because S corporations are not recognized by New York City, a closely held corporation in New York City cannot by paying salaries to its shareholders eliminate totally its taxable income.

3. Further Information

Regulations have been issued by the New York City Commissioner of Finance.

B. Sales and Use Taxes: N.Y.C. Admin. Code § 11-2001 *et seq.*

These taxes, imposed at a rate of 4 percent, are essentially the same as their New York State counterparts and are administered and collected by the state. Additional services subject to the city tax include credit rating and reporting services; protective and detective services; and beauty, barbering, health salons and related services. There is no exemption for natural gas and electricity, etc. used in manufacturing or for residential sales of natural gas, electricity, etc.; however, the city tax on these state-exempted items is credited against any New York City general corporation tax liability.

C. Commercial Rent or Occupancy Tax: N.Y.C. Admin. Code § 11-701 *et seq.*

1. Scope

This tax is imposed on the payer of "rent" (i.e., the tenant) for any "premises" (essentially, any real property) used for business purposes.

2. Basis and Rate

The tax is 6 percent of "base rent," which is essentially rent less any sublease payments received, and includes expenses normally payable by a landlord when paid instead by a "tenant" pursuant to a "lease." In-kind rent is also subject to the tax. The quoted terms are broadly defined and include transactions not normally thought of as leases or as involving a landlord-tenant relationship. Since the city will attempt to tax nearly anything called a "lease" or calling for payments of "rent," counsel is advised to choose terms carefully in drafting agreements to be performed in New York City.

CORPORATE TAX CHECKLIST 481

3. Examples of Taxable Transactions

Leases of advertising signs, office space, automobile parking lots, and safe deposit vaults are subject to the tax.

4. Exempt Transactions

Rent paid by governmental entities and certain tax-exempt organizations is exempt from the tax. Also exempt are rent payments of less than $11,000 per year and certain specified transactions. The tax is reduced for rent on premises located other than in Manhattan below 96th Street.

5. Further Information

Regulations have been issued by the New York City Commissioner of Finance.

D. Real Property Transfer Tax: N.Y.C. Admin. Code § 11-2101 et seq.

1. Scope

This tax is imposed on transfers of real property by deed and "economic interests in real property" located in New York City where the consideration exceeds $25,000. "Consideration" includes the fair market value of property received and, in most cases, any debt encumbering the property. Special rules apply to cooperative conversions and transfers of co-op units.

2. Basis and Rate

The tax is computed at a rate of 1 percent of the consideration received where the property transferred is a one-, two- or three-family house, residential condominium or cooperative unit or where the consideration is $500,000 or less (1.425 percent where the consideration is more than $500,000), at a rate of 1.425 percent for other property transferred where the consideration is $500,000 or less, and at a rate of 2.625 percent for all other transfers.

3. Examples of Taxable Transfers

This tax is similar to the state tax except that there is no specific exemption for purely formal transactions.

4. Exempt Transfers

Transfers to or by governmental entities and certain tax-exempt organizations, transfers of property as collateral for a loan, and transfers by and to nominees are exempt from the tax.

5. Administration

The tax is paid when the deed is recorded or, if there is no deed, within 30 days after the transfer. The transferor is liable for the tax, but the transferee is liable if the tax is not paid.

6. Further Information

Regulations issued by the Commissioner of Finance must be consulted together with the statute.

E. Utility Vendor's Tax: N.Y.C. Admin. Code § 11-1101 *et seq.*

This tax, imposed at a rate of 2.35 percent of gross receipts from sales in New York City, is substantially the same as the state tax.

F. Mortgage Recording Tax: N.Y.C. Admin. Code § 11-2601 *et seq.*

The tax, which is similar (but not identical) to the state tax, is imposed at a rate of 1 percent for mortgages of less than $500,000; 1.125 percent for mortgages of $500,000 or more secured by one-, two- or three-family houses, cooperative and condominium units; and 1.75 percent for all other mortgages. Because of the graduated rates, the statute contains an anti-abuse rule and requires aggregation of related mortgages.

VII. FORMS

For federal tax forms and publications, visit your local Internal Revenue Service office or call 1-800-829-3676. For New York State tax forms and publications, call 1-800-462-8100 (inside New York) or (518) 438-1073 (outside New York). For New York City tax forms, call (718) 935-6739 or go to the third floor of 25 Elm Place, Brooklyn, New York 11201.

VIII. CALLING FOR ASSISTANCE

If you want a federal tax question answered, you might try the telephone number listed under "Federal Tax Information" in your local directory. Statistically, you have between a 50 and an 80 percent chance of getting the correct answer, assuming you can get through to a warm body. If you do not mind these odds, by all means call. Generally, New York State and New York City are more helpful in giving useful tax advice over the telephone. For New York State tax information, call 1-800-225-5829 (inside New York) or (518) 438-8581 (outside New York). For New York City tax information, call (718) 935-6000.

CHAPTER NINETEEN

VALUATION OF CLOSELY HELD CORPORATIONS

Idelle A. Howitt

VALUATION OF CLOSELY HELD CORPORATIONS

I. INTRODUCTION

It might seem that there would be only one situation in which a valuation of a closely held corporation would be needed: the sale of a company. In fact, however, valuation plays a major role in a surprisingly extensive list of other legal and business transactions.

Values established for closely held stock usually form the basis on which estate, gift and income taxes are calculated. For example, federal law mandates independent valuations of stock for charitable donations and for Employee Stock Ownership Plans ("ESOPs"). Valuations are used in management incentive stock option plans, recapitalizations and succession planning. Of course, a valuation is needed in cases where the price of the stock is contested by litigation, such as marital dissolution, corporate dissolution and dissenting shareholder cases.

A valuation for a closely held business, which may encompass the entire business, a block of its stock, or a single share, is based on information collected from the marketplace and the business as of a specific date. The guideline for determining the fair market value of closely held corporations is IRS Revenue Ruling 59-60, which originally was developed for estate and gift calculations and subsequently has served as the standard for other purposes. Each valuation is based on all of the relevant facts and circumstances of the particular situation; business appraisers must use common sense, informed judgment and reasonableness in weighing the facts and determining their significance.

II. DISTINCTIVE FEATURES OF A CLOSELY HELD CORPORATION

Determining the fair market value of publicly traded stock on any given business day can be accomplished by calling a stockbroker or by checking the stock tables in the next day's newspaper.

Since the shares of a closely held company are not traded on an exchange and its financial statements are not disclosed to the public, determining the fair market value of the stock of a closely held company is, unfortunately, not as simple. Although the number of shares outstanding can be obtained from reading the financial statements, by definition there is no marketplace to provide a per-share price. Book value is generally inappropriate because it is an accounting convention that measures the historic costs of assets and liabilities; it is not a measure of fair market value. Therefore, other approaches such as commissioning an independent, qualified financial valuation to obtain the fair market value of the company or a block of its stock must be used.

III. APPRAISALS REQUIRED BY RECENT FEDERAL LAWS

Since the mid-1980s, two federal tax statutes have required independent appraisals of closely held corporations or blocks of their securities to qualify for certain tax benefits. The Tax Reform Act of 1984 requires that the claimed value of all donations of stock of closely held companies be verified by an independent, qualified appraisal, as determined under Section 170 of the Internal Revenue Code (the "Code"). The Tax Reform Act of 1986 requires that the fair market value of stock of closely held companies held by an Employee Stock Ownership Plan or ESOP be determined by an independent, qualified appraisal, also as determined under Section 170 of the Code.

IV. RECOMMENDED APPRAISALS

In addition, there are times when knowing the fair market value of a closely held corporation or a block of its securities is central to effective tax, business and estate planning for a corporation and its owners. The most common situations include determining the fair market value of a decedent's interest in a closely held corporation for estate tax filing or auditing purposes, gift and estate tax planning, sale of the entire corporation (*see* Chapter 11), recapitalizations, buy-sell agreements, going public, adequacy of life insurance, stock options, and compensatory damages. In addition, determining the fair value (as distinguished from the fair market value) of a minority ownership interest can be crucial in matters involving the appraisal rights of minority shareholders under several BCL provisions (*see* Chapter 10).

V. COMMON CORPORATE VALUATION SITUATIONS

Some of the most common situations when a determination of fair market value is required or recommended are discussed in the following sections: buy-sell agreements, estate taxes, the interrelationship between buy-sell agreements and estate and gift values, ESOPs, and charitable donations.

A. Buy-Sell Agreements

The purpose of a buy-sell agreement is to avoid the problems that can occur in the disposition of closely held stock following the death, disability, departure, or incapacity of a shareholder. If any of these circumstances occurs, the agreement conveys to the remaining shareholders or the corporation itself certain priority rights regarding the purchase of the stock.

Many buy-sell agreements contain extensive lists of events that trigger the agreement. However, they often provide only a brief section detailing the method for determining the price at which the securities will change hands.

Traditional methods found in many buy-sell agreements set the transaction price at book value or recommend a formula. The primary advantage of these methods is their simplicity and efficiency; there are, however, disadvantages including the discrepancy between book value and fair market value and the selection of the capitalization multiples used in formulas. Although more costly and more time-consuming than using simple mathematical models, having an independent third party determine the transaction price can minimize the potential for litigation.

B. Estate Taxes

Because estate taxes are calculated on the basis of the fair market value of the gross estate, when a material portion of the value of the estate is a closely held business or a block of closely held securities, it is prudent to obtain a valuation of the business or securities in connection with the preparation and filing of an estate tax return. To be protected properly, the estate should provide thorough documentation of the basis used for the valuation. For estate tax purposes, the valuation guidelines are embodied in Revenue Ruling 59-60, 1959-1 C.B. 237, which was supplemented by Revenue Rulings 77-287, 1977-2 C.B. 319, and 83-120, 1983-2 C.B. 170. An extensive discussion of Revenue Ruling 59-60 appears later in the chapter.

In general, the value determined pursuant to a buy-sell agreement will be binding for estate tax purposes if certain conditions occur. Case law suggests that the most significant factor in this determination is the extent to which the price was established at arm's length. However, the buy-sell agreement price may not be binding for gift tax purposes. The rationale is that the price set can be modified by a living donor for gift purposes, whereas it is binding on the estate.

C. Employee Stock Ownership Plans ("ESOPs")

An Employee Stock Ownership Plan ("ESOP") is a qualified employee benefit plan designed to encourage employees to have an ownership interest in their company. These plans have become more popular in recent years because of increasingly favorable income tax treatment resulting from ESOP formation and financing. Several significant features that have enhanced the appeal of ESOPs include:

1. corporate income tax deductions permitted for the principal portion of repayment of ESOP stock;

2. corporate income tax deductions permitted for dividends paid on ESOP stock;

3. exclusion for banks and other lenders of 50 percent of interest income earned on ESOP loans; and

4. deferral of capital gains tax for the original selling shareholders.

Federal agencies that review ESOPs include the United States Department of Labor ("DOL") and the Internal Revenue Service ("IRS"). As part of the Employee Retirement Income Security Act of 1974 ("ERISA"), Congress directed the DOL to promulgate regulations,

VALUATION OF CLOSELY HELD CORPORATIONS 491

which would provide guidelines for the valuation of ESOP securities. The proposed regulations did not appear until 1988, and as of this writing (1992) have yet to be issued.

In the intervening years, when business appraisers were retained to value ESOP securities, many utilized Revenue Ruling 59-60 which satisfied the IRS. However, the potential for inaccurate valuations continued because many valuations were performed by individuals who were not independent or did not have the necessary qualifications. Moreover, many valuations were calculated with simple mathematical formulas that did not reflect key factors such as changing market conditions.

Congress responded to concern about share price accuracy in the Tax Reform Act of 1986. Section 401(a)(28)(C) of the Code provides that valuations of employer securities which are not readily traded on an established exchange must be performed on an annual basis by an independent, qualified appraiser, as defined in Section 170(a)(1). For a more detailed discussion of Section 170, see Part X,D of this chapter.

The proposed DOL regulation, which generally parallels Revenue Ruling 59-60, lists the criteria to be followed for a valid determination: the value of the securities must reflect fair market value; the value of the securities must be determined in good faith; the value of the securities must be as of the date of the transaction; and written documentation is required.

D. Charitable Contributions

Historically, donors have been permitted to claim income tax deductions equal to the fair market value of their noncash donations to charitable institutions; such donations tended to generate a disproportionate amount of controversy with the IRS. To stem the avalanche of questionable valuations of noncash donations, Congress placed restrictions around the deductibility of donations in the Tax Reform Act of 1984. The law now specifies that charitable deductions in excess of $5,000 are automatically disallowed unless a qualified, independent appraisal of the donations has been performed in a timely fashion. Additionally, the law requires individual or corporate taxpayers to file IRS Form 8283 (a one-page form signed by the appraiser) with their tax returns to verify the fair market value of the donations.

A curious exception exists for donations of closely held securities. If the claimed value of the donation is between $5,000 and $10,000, donors need not obtain a qualified appraisal, but they must attach a partially completed appraisal summary to the tax return. However, when the claimed value of the securities exceeds $10,000, the donor is subject to all the requirements enumerated above. The practical significance of these provisions, however, is that a donation of a block of closely held stock with a claimed value in excess of $5,000 still must be valued by a qualified appraiser, since a summary is still required.

VI. VALUATION METHODS

There are three basic methods for valuing property, including closely held businesses: the cost/net asset approach, the income approach, and the market approach. When valuing closely held businesses, the cost approach takes the form of net asset value analysis. All three are included within the eight-point guidelines of Revenue Ruling 59-60. A discussion of the three basic approaches and a review of the eight points of Revenue Ruling 59-60 follow.

A. The Cost Approach/Net Asset Value Analysis

The cost approach establishes the value of property based on the cost of reproduction or replacement, less depreciation from functional and economic obsolescence as well as physical deterioration, if present and measurable. This approach provides a reliable indication of value when applied to specific assets, such as land improvements, special purpose buildings and structures, special machinery and equipment, and certain intangible assets.

When applying this method to business valuations, a form of the cost approach called net asset value analysis is appropriate, particularly for investment holding companies and asset-rich operating companies. Examples include real estate or oil and gas companies, where assets are most probative of the company's value.

VALUATION OF CLOSELY HELD CORPORATIONS

Using a balance sheet current to the valuation date, the appraiser prepares a list of all assets and liabilities. Then the current values of the operating assets, either individually or by category, are determined, as well as the current values for the liabilities. (Each of these current fair market values may be determined by the cost, market, or income approach.) When the sum of the adjusted liabilities is subtracted from the sum of the adjusted assets, the remainder is the net asset value of the enterprise. This value may then be adjusted through to application of appropriate discounts or premiums to produce the fair market value of the ownership interest being valued.

B. The Income Approach

The income approach is based on the premise that the value of the enterprise is equal to the net present value of future income streams produced by the business. A type of income stream is selected, such as net income or free cash flow, based in part on the type of business being valued. These streams are projected into the future for a reasonable amount of time, often five years. At the end of this time period, a terminal value for the business is determined. Terminal value may be based upon direct capitalization of the income stream which is assumed to continue into perpetuity, liquidation of the business, or the projected sale of the business.

The next step, perhaps the most critical, is selection of the appropriate discount rate to apply to the income projections and the terminal value. This discount rate reflects both the type of income stream selected and the appraiser's judgment of an appropriate return of the perceived risks. The discount rate is then applied to the discrete income streams and the terminal value to yield effectively two subtotals. These subtotals are added together to yield an aggregate freely traded value.

C. The Market Approach

The market approach determines the value of the business by comparing the company or its securities to similar companies or their securities which are publicly traded in the marketplace. To determine comparability, typical items reviewed include

1. type of business;

2. level of revenues and assets;

3. geographic markets; and

4. consistency of profitable operations.

One technique, especially when valuing an entire business, is to select purchases of comparable firms within a reasonable time frame and adjust the purchase prices to reflect significant differences between the comparative companies and the subject company through the use of acquisition price/earnings and price/book value multiples. However, there are situations where sufficient information about comparable purchases is not available, or only minority blocks of common stock, not the entire business, is being valued.

In those instances, it may be more appropriate to calculate a per-share value for the stock as if it were publicly traded, using the technique of comparative analysis. The company's financial performance and operating characteristics are compared with those of comparable companies. These comparisons, together with the investor appraisal ratios (price/earnings, price/book value and dividend yield) of the comparable companies' common shares, provide the basis for determining the freely traded value of the company's stock. To this value, appropriate discounts or premiums may be applied to reflect the liquidity and the degree of control of the ownership interest. This approach is also the essence of Revenue Ruling 59-60, discussed later in this chapter.

D. Comparison of the Three Approaches

The market approach is overwhelmingly favored by the courts, although there are occasions where insufficient comparable transaction data or comparative companies exist to provide meaningful data. The income approach is preferred by many members of the financial community for valuing business enterprises and often is used in transaction analysis. But for tax-related valuations, especially where litigation is contemplated, this approach is viewed as speculative and its conclusions are treated with skepticism by many IRS agents and the courts. The

VALUATION OF CLOSELY HELD CORPORATIONS 495

cost/net asset approach is suited to certain types of corporations. However, because it is asset-oriented, it may not consider adequately the earning power of the business.

A quality valuation should consider all three approaches to value and apply the approaches that are appropriate or possible. In situations where more than one approach is used, each approach usually yields a somewhat different mathematical conclusion. Typically, the appraiser will weigh the various values to determine the conclusion of value.

VII. REVENUE RULING 59-60: THE INDUSTRY GUIDELINE

Revenue Ruling 59-60 describes eight key factors to be considered in a valuation. However, there is no recognized formula or weighting system for the various factors. Earnings, for example, may be a major factor in valuing operating companies, whereas adjusted asset values may be more important for investment companies. It is the circumstances that determine the importance or relative weight of these factors.

A. The Nature of the Business and the History of the Enterprise from its Inception

By reviewing the history of a business, and considering its stability, growth rate, and diversity of operations, an appraiser can form an opinion as to the degree of risk involved in the business.

B. The Economic Outlook in General and the Condition and Outlook of the Specific Industry

An appraisal must consider the current and the future economic conditions of both the general economy and the subject company's industry. The ability of the subject company to be competitive within its industry, and the ability of that industry to be competitive within the general economy, are considered.

C. The Book Value of the Stock and the Financial Condition of the Business

Annual balance sheets for the company for at least two and preferably five years preceding the valuation date should be obtained. Analysis of these financial statements should provide an understanding of basic data, including liquidity ratios, gross and net book value of fixed assets, working capital, long-term debt, capital structure, and net worth. If a company has more than one class of stock, consideration should be given to voting rights, dividend preferences, and liquidation preferences. Trends and influences related to historical net worth also should be analyzed.

D. The Earning Capacity of the Company

Income statements for the company for five years prior to the valuation date as well as future income projections should be obtained. Analysis of these statements should provide an insight into basic data, including gross revenues, operating expenses, net income, and rate and amount of dividends paid. Of particular significance are projected earnings or cash flow since they can be a major factor in valuing closely held stock, especially in service industries.

E. Dividend-Paying Capacity

Dividends paid out by a closely held company may reflect a desire on the part of the owners to avoid taxes on dividend receipts or other personal needs of shareholders, rather than the ability of the company to pay these dividends. Because the control group of the company can, to some extent, substitute salaries and bonuses for dividends, dividends are usually given relatively little weight as indicators of value when valuing a control block or the entire business. However, for valuations of minority interests where the holder does not have control over dividend policy, the declared dividends may take on greater significance.

F. Whether the Enterprise has Goodwill or Other Intangible Value

The value of a business may be greater than the sum of the values of its tangible net assets. For example, goodwill, which is a function of the earnings capacity of the business, can be a significant factor. Other intangible factors that can contribute to value include the prestige and renown of the business, ownership of trade or brand names, patents, copyrights, contract rights, and a history of successful operation over a period of time in a particular location.

G. Sales of the Stock and the Size of the Block to be Valued

Comparisons of sales of stock of closely held corporations should be reviewed carefully to determine whether they represent arm's-length transactions. Forced sales or isolated sales in small amounts usually are not considered probative of value. Arm's-length transactions within two years of the valuation date can be of material assistance.

H. The Market Price of Stocks of Corporations Engaged in the Same or a Similar Line of Business Having Their Stocks Actively Traded in a Free and Open Market, Either on an Exchange or Over-the-Counter

The essential factors are that the companies selected as comparatives be in the same or similar lines of business, with comparable capital structures, operating results, and market position. Their stock must be actively and freely traded in a public market as of the valuation date.

VIII. PREMIUMS AND DISCOUNTS

A. Premium for Control

The concept of "enterprise value" reflects the value of an interest representing total control. This is the usual indicator of a company's value for merger or sale purposes. A "control interest" is defined as more than 50 percent but less than 100 percent ownership of the business.

Typically, a premium for control above freely traded value is paid to gain a controlling interest in the business. The factors affecting the size of the premium include the amount of excess working capital, nonoperating assets, compensation and employee perquisite practices, discretionary expenditures and synergy.

The value of a controlling interest may differ from that of a pro rata share of the company's enterprise value depending on state law, the company's by-laws and the circumstances of the valuation. In most states, such as New York, a 66-2/3 percent controlling interest carries with it the rights to elect directors, set management and operating policy, establish compensation programs, buy and sell assets including the business itself, and liquidate the business.

Under the income approach, the discount rates selected usually result in a value representing enterprise value. Under the market approach, if use of acquisition prices for acquired comparative companies enables the appraiser to determine enterprise value directly, a premium for control is included. Conversely, if the comparative company price/earnings multiples are based on prices of actively traded minority interests in public companies, a premium for control is usually added.

B. Discounts for Minority Interests

The minority shareholder has none of the advantages, or opportunities, enjoyed by a controlling shareholder. Unless large minority interest blocks vote in concert, a minority shareholder is essentially a passive investor. An example of a minority interest basis is the price paid for common stock on a public exchange as reported in the financial section of the newspaper. A freely traded position, by definition, assumes a minority interest position. Therefore, a minority interest discount is not applied to a freely traded position, be it real or hypothetical. A minority interest discount is applied to a control or to an enterprise position to effectively "neutralize" the premium for control that those positions assume.

C. Discounts for Lack of Marketability

Minority shareholders in a privately held company face a liquidity problem if they wish to sell their securities. Without a purchase agreement, such as a buy-sell agreement, there is a risk as to whether a purchaser will be found and if so, how long it will take. This is unlike the situation of a minority shareholder in a publicly traded company, where a purchase within a brief amount of time is virtually assured. To reflect this liquidity risk, valuations of blocks of stock of closely held companies reflect a discount for lack of marketability.

IX. VALUATION PENALTIES

A. Penalties for Valuation Overstatement

Valuation overstatement for tax purposes historically occurred in two major areas: tax shelter schemes and charitable donations. In both of these situations, an overvaluation resulted in higher deductions and lower taxes. In addition, with the advent of the unlimited marital deduction for estate taxes, there was concern that some taxpayers would overstate values on estate tax returns to achieve a higher basis for depreciation or for calculating the gain on a future sale.

In part to counter the perception that valuation controversies could be settled by "splitting the differences," a penalty for valuation overstatement was created by Congress with the passage of the Economic Recovery Tax Act ("ERTA"). I.R.C. § 6659.

B. Penalties for Valuation Understatement

In 1984 Congress increased its monitoring of questionable valuations by taxpayers by adopting then Section 6660 of the Code. This more recent section focused on understatement of value, rather than overstatement, for gift and estate tax purposes.

C. Section 6662

The Tax Reform Act of 1989 added Section 6662 to the Code in an effort to consolidate the penalties for inaccuracies in tax returns. The penalties set forth in Section 6662 will apply to all federal tax returns the due date for which (determined without regard to extensions) is after December 31, 1989.

I.R.C. § 6662 imposes a 20 percent penalty on the portion of any underpayment that is attributable to (1) negligence, (2) any substantial understatement of income tax, (3) any substantial valuation overstatement under Chapter 1 of the Code (I.R.C. §§ 1-1399), (4) any substantial overstatement of pension liabilities, or (5) any substantial estate or gift tax valuation understatement. These penalties apply only in cases where a return is filed. I.R.C. § 6662(b). The penalties do not apply if there is reasonable cause for the underpayment, it was made in good faith, and it was disclosed to the IRS.

The negligence penalty applies only to the portion of the underpayment that is attributable to negligence. Negligence includes any failure to make a reasonable attempt to comply with the Code provisions, and the term "disregard" includes any careless, reckless or intentional disregard of rules or regulations.

A substantial valuation overstatement exists if the value or adjusted basis of any property claimed on the return of a tax imposed by Chapter 1 of the Code is 200 percent or more of the corrected value or adjusted basis. However, no penalty is imposed unless the underpayment for the year attributable to the overstatement is at least $5,000 ($10,000 for a corporation other than an S corporation or a personal holding company). I.R.C. § 6662(e). The rate of the penalty is doubled from 20 percent to 40 percent of the underpayment if the value or adjusted basis claimed is 400 percent or more of the corrected value or adjusted basis. I.R.C. § 6662(h). It should be noted that while reasonable cause generally prevents the penalty (I.R.C. § 6664(c)(1)), in case of an underpayment attributable to a substantial or gross valuation overstatement for charitable deduction property, the reasonable cause exception does not apply unless the claimed value was based on a qualified appraisal made by a qualified appraiser, and, in addition to such appraisal, the taxpayer made a good-faith investigation of the value of the contributed property. *See* I.R.C. § 6664(c)(2).

A substantial estate or gift tax valuation understatement exists if the value of any property claimed on any return is 50 percent or less of the amount determined to be the correct amount of such valuation, provided that the amount of the underpayment attributable to the substantial estate or gift tax valuation understatement is greater than $5,000. I.R.C. § 6662(g).

VALUATION OF CLOSELY HELD CORPORATIONS 501

In the event that an understatement of income is due to one or more gross valuation misstatements, the penalty with respect to the portion of such understatement attributable to the misstatement is 40 percent, not 20 percent. A substantial valuation of overstatement of 400 percent (as opposed to 200 percent), and a substantial estate or gift tax valuation understatement of 25 percent (as opposed to 50 percent) is considered a "gross valuation misstatement." I.R.C. § 6662(h).

If any part of any underpayment of tax required to be shown on a return is due to fraud, an amount equal to 75 percent of the portion of the underpayment which is attributable to fraud will be added to the tax.

D. Exceptions

For both sections, the penalty does not apply if the underpayment is less than $1,000.

In addition, the Secretary of the Treasury is authorized to waive any part or all of the penalty for noncharitable deduction property if the taxpayer can demonstrate a reasonable basis for the valuation and can show that the claim was made in good faith. For charitable donation property, however, a waiver is permitted only if the claimed value was based on a qualified appraisal by a qualified appraiser as defined by Section 170 of the Code, and the taxpayer can show that a good-faith investigation of the value of the contributed property was conducted.

E. Section 170 of the Internal Revenue Code

Section 170 of the Code defines a qualified appraisal as a document indicating that the appraisal was prepared for income tax purposes, was prepared by a qualified appraiser, and did not involve an appraisal fee based on a percentage of the appraised value of the securities.

The regulations under Section 170 define a qualified appraiser as someone who presents himself/herself to the public as an appraiser and is qualified to make appraisals of the type of property being valued. In other words, unless an individual is qualified as an appraiser, it is inadvisable to value securities or other property on behalf of a client.

F. Appraiser Penalties

If an appraiser is found to have aided or abetted in the understatement of the tax liability of a taxpayer, the appraiser may be subject to a $1,000 civil penalty. Additionally, the appraiser may be barred from presenting evidence or testimony in any administrative proceeding before the Department of the Treasury or the Internal Revenue Service. Furthermore, an appraisal submitted by that appraiser would have no probative effect in any Treasury or Internal Revenue Service administrative proceeding.

X. THE VALUATION ENGAGEMENT

The valuation of a business or a block of its stock can produce significantly varied conclusions, depending on the parameters of the assignment. If you or your client hire a third party to value a business, you should review the following items with the appraiser and commit them to writing.

A. Define What Is To Be Valued

One of the least understood facts about the valuation of closely held companies is that a minority interest is rarely worth its pro rata percentage of the value of the total business. This can be true even for majority interests as well. As was explained in Part IX, the value of a minority interest should reflect two separate and distinct discounts from the value of a 100 percent interest—a minority interest discount and a discount for lack of marketability. A majority interest with less than complete control also could have its value affected by discounts resulting from a lack of certain control rights or certain marketability discounts. Therefore, it is important to be clear from the beginning about the interest being valued. Commissioning a valuation of the enterprise and arbitrarily dividing the results into pro rata segments could result in distortions or outright mistakes in interpretation, all with far-reaching consequences.

B. Define the Purpose of the Valuation

A second significant dimension of business valuation is that the value of a block of closely held stock or an entire business can be different, depending on the purpose of the valuation. This is because the purpose

VALUATION OF CLOSELY HELD CORPORATIONS

will dictate the premise of value and the valuation method selected; different methods are appropriate for different purposes.

For example, the purpose determines to a great extent whether the appraiser will rely more heavily on an analysis of historical financial data or on projections of future operating results. The purpose of the valuation also determines the types and amounts of discounts or premiums applied. Valuations of ESOP stock are a case in point. Because of the unique "put" provision required by federal law to be a feature of ESOP stock, a minority interest block of ESOP stock tends to be worth more than an identically sized block of closely held stock valued for other tax purposes because the marketability discount applied to ESOP stock tends to be smaller than the marketability discount applied for non-ESOP purposes.

C. Select the Date of the Valuation Carefully

There are certain valuation engagements whose valuation date is set by law—for example, an estate tax valuation. However, federal law permits valuing the assets of the estate on one of two dates, either as of the date of death or six months later. If a closely held business or block of securities forms a material portion of the estate, and there has been volatility in the stock market or some other material event that could affect the value of the business has occurred within the six-month period, valuation of the business or stock on both dates is recommended.

There are a myriad of other matters, such as gift tax filings, stock option plans, divorce proceedings or damage cases, where the strategic selection of the valuation date is important. For example, if a donor wishes to minimize the amount of gift taxes due when gifting stock in a family-owned business to the next generation, the donor should gift the stock during an adverse economic climate when the value of the stock would be depressed and, hence, the amount of gift tax due would be lessened.

D. Decide on the Standard of Value

Generally speaking, for tax-related matters, the standard of value for closely held corporations is fair market value. For other purposes, such as dissenting shareholder litigation or fairness opinions performed in connection with corporate mergers and acquisitions, the standard of value is fair value.

Fair market value is defined as the price at which a willing buyer and a willing seller agree, neither being under compulsion to buy or sell, and both having reasonable knowledge of relevant facts.

In other words, fair market value ordinarily represents a hypothetical arm's-length purchase price for cash between two parties who are not forced to participate in the transaction (so as not to cause a distortion in the price, e.g., liquidation value), and both parties possess information relevant to negotiating a reasonable price on or before the date of the transaction.

E. Define the Terms and Conditions of the Engagement

A financial valuation of a corporation should fulfill the business objectives as well as the legal needs of the corporation. Key items that should be discussed and committed to writing include:

1. The Valuation Report

A report may be oral or written, or a combination; the format should be determined at the beginning of the engagement. An oral report can be a brief telephone conversation or a formal presentation before a board of directors. A written report can be a one-page document or an extensive narrative buttressed by charts, graphs, and exhibits.

The purpose of the valuation determines the type of report needed. For tax-related engagements, such as ESOPs, estate and gift filings, charitable contributions or recapitalizations, the report should satisfy the requirements of Revenue Ruling 59-60 thoroughly.

2. The Schedule

Often, an appraisal is required to meet a looming tax filing deadline, or the services of an appraiser as an expert witness are needed on a specific and very close trial date. As a general rule, you should allow the appraiser six to eight weeks after he/she has received the necessary

VALUATION OF CLOSELY HELD CORPORATIONS

financial information to complete the valuation and prepare a narrative report. If the parameters of the engagement change during the course of the assignment, additional time may be needed.

3. The Fee

Common sense suggests that any appraisal fee based partially or solely on a percentage of the value of the property being appraised raises, at best, the appearance of a possible conflict of interest. In fact, Section 170 of the Code expressly prohibits such arrangements for tax-related valuations, as do the ethical standards of the business valuation industry. The standard fee arrangement in the industry is either a per-diem rate or a fixed fee per assignment, agreed on at the beginning of the engagement. Naturally, fixed fees may fluctuate subsequently if the nature of the engagement changes during the course of the assignment.

XI. SUMMARY

An estimate of the fair market value of a closely held company or its stock made by a qualified appraiser can be required or recommended in a number of business and legal situations: setting the terms of buy-sell agreements, calculating estate taxes, determining gift values, valuing ESOP stocks, and calculating income tax deductions for charitable contributions.

Because results of a valuation can differ depending on the purpose of the valuation and the method used, the terms of the appraiser's engagement should be specified clearly and in writing. They should state what is to be valued, the purpose of the valuation, the valuation date to be used, the standard of value to be used, and the terms and conditions for the appraiser's work (type and format of the final report, schedule and fee).

The business valuation industry uses at least one of three basic techniques to value any business: the cost or net asset value approach, the income approach, and the market approach. The approach used and the weight given various factors depend upon the circumstances of each situation. In addition, again depending upon the circumstances, factors such as premiums for control, discounts for minority interests, and/or discounts for lack of marketability must be considered. Valuations for tax purposes should follow the guidelines of Revenue Ruling 59-60. In the case of valuations made for tax-deduction purposes, federal law now mandates penalties for overstatement or understatement beyond a specified proportion, with only limited exceptions.

Because valuation is an art, not a science, it cannot be reduced to simple formulas or mathematical calculations. It is an informed judgment based on factual knowledge, common sense, and a reasonable interpretation of the particular circumstances. Unless attorneys are also qualified as appraisers, they should not make valuations on behalf of their clients.

CHAPTER TWENTY

SOME ETHICAL CONSIDERATIONS FOR THE CORPORATE LAWYER*

Clifford R. Ennico

* Reprinted with permission from *A Primer for New Corporate Lawyers: What Business Lawyers Do*, by Clifford R. Ennico (Clark Boardman Company, Ltd., 1990).

I. INTRODUCTION: THE LEGAL LIMITS ON WHAT BUSINESS LAWYERS CAN DO

This book is not a treatise on the ethical obligations of business lawyers. It is important, however, to recognize that there are limitations on a lawyer's conduct when representing the small business corporation. The most important of these rules are imposed not by law but rather by the legal profession itself which, through the American Bar Association, has drafted codes of lawyerly conduct which the states have adopted. This chapter summarizes some of the more important ethical rules that govern the business lawyer's professional life; for a more comprehensive discussion of this important topic, the reader is referred to the books reviewed in Chapter 21.

II. THE SOURCES OF ETHICAL RULES GOVERNING THE BUSINESS LAWYER'S CONDUCT

When a business lawyer is admitted to practice in a particular state, she is expected to become familiar with that state's ethical rules and regulations. Ordinarily these are set out in the state's statute books; the rules governing lawyers admitted to practice in New York, for example, appear in scattered sections of the Judiciary Law and particularly in the Appendix thereto. N.Y. Judiciary Law App. (McKinney 1990-1991). A majority of states require the aspiring business lawyer to take a special examination on these ethical rules as part of the bar admission process.

There are two sets of rules which govern the conduct of American lawyers: the American Bar Association Code of Professional Responsibility (the "CPR") and the Model Rules of Professional Conduct (the "Model Rules"). The CPR was adopted by the ABA in 1968 and has been adopted, with or without some modification, by virtually all of the states. The Model Rules were put forth in 1983 and have met with some resistance from the bar for reasons which need not be discussed here; as a result, the Model Rules have to date been adopted in only about half of the states. Even in the states that have not yet adopted the Model Rules, however, judges and bar association ethics committees may use the Model Rules as guides to lawyerly conduct.

Finally, most state bar associations have ethics committees that issue formal written opinions and telephone advice on ethical issues raised by practitioners in that state, in much the same way as an administrative agency will issue formal and informal advice on compliance with its regulations. Most business lawyers will subscribe to the formal opinions of their state bar association, which are usually published on an irregular basis. This chapter will summarize only the most important rules contained in the CPR and the Model Rules.

III. THE LAWYER'S BASIC DUTIES TO THE CLIENT

The ethical rules to which business lawyers are subject are often not easy to find; the drafters of the CPR and the Model Rules had litigators primarily in mind, and most of their rules apply only in the context of adversarial proceedings. A few of the rules, however, can be applied by analogy to the tasks of client monitoring, client counseling and transaction management.

Both the CPR and the Model Rules impose a number of duties on the business lawyer in his dealings with clients, regardless of the type of work involved. The most important of these are the duty of competence, the duty of diligence, the duty to keep the client informed of developments, and the duty of confidentiality.

First, a business lawyer is required to represent his clients competently. *Model Rules of Professional Conduct,* Rule 1.1; *ABA Code of Professional Responsibility,* DR 6-101. This means that the lawyer cannot neglect his client's matters, must be thoroughly prepared to handle the matters he takes on, and cannot take on work he is unable to do either because he lacks knowledge or because he has insufficient time to handle the matter. Business lawyers have the obligation to stay abreast of current developments in their areas of practice, and in some

ETHICAL CONSIDERATIONS 511

states must attend a certain number of "continuing legal education" courses and seminars each year. *ABA Code of Professional Responsibility*, EC 6-2.

Second, a business lawyer must act on behalf of her client with reasonable diligence and promptness. *Model Rules of Professional Conduct*, Rule 1.3; *ABA Code of Professional Responsibility*, DR 6-101(A)(3). One of the most common complaints clients have about their lawyers is procrastination—the lawyer does not respond in a timely fashion to their letters and telephone calls, or takes weeks to perform a task that the client needs done in days. Often a client will have unreasonable expectations about the time necessary to research a particular question or draft a particular legal document. In such cases it is the business lawyer's ethical responsibility to discuss the necessary time frame with the client up front and, if possible, to reach an agreement with the client as to the lawyer's deadline for rendering the advice or drafting the document.

Closely related to the duty of diligence is the duty to keep the client informed of developments in his matter. *Model Rules of Professional Conduct*, Rule 1.4; *ABA Code of Professional Responsibility*, DR 6-101(A)(3); EC 7-8 and 9-2. Because it is the client, not the lawyer, who must make the ultimate business decisions in a particular matter, the lawyer has a duty to furnish the client all of the information necessary for the latter to make informed decisions, even if this information is adverse to the lawyer's interest or results in inconvenience to the lawyer. *Model Rules of Professional Conduct*, Official Comment to Rule 1.4. Part of the reason for the businessperson's traditionally negative view of the business lawyer probably arises from the simple fact that business lawyers are frequently called upon to be the bearers of bad tidings: "Shooting the messenger" is a natural human response to bad news of any kind.

Finally, the business lawyer owes to his client a duty of confidentiality. *Model Rules of Professional Conduct*, Rule 1.6; *ABA Code of Professional Responsibility*, DR 4-101(B). Simply put, he is not allowed to gossip about his client's affairs at any time whatsoever, in any place whatsoever, under any circumstances whatsoever, unless the client has expressly authorized him to disclose certain aspects of the matter to specific people. This is true even though the lawyer came upon information about his client outside of the attorney-client relationship, or the information does not relate to any matter upon which the lawyer is then working. *Model Rules of Professional Conduct*, Rule 1.6. Some law firms even impose upon their lawyers a rule never to reveal that someone is a client of the firm!

The business lawyer also cannot use confidential information for his own benefit, even if the client is not harmed in any way. This duty may explain why business lawyers are not the most favored guests at cocktail parties or backyard barbecues; a number of lawyers I know make it a rule never to "talk shop" with anyone outside their law offices at any time.

These basic ethical duties apply regardless of the type of activity in which the business lawyer is engaged. Another set of ethical rules which have general application in the business lawyer's world are those which prevent her from engaging in any activity that causes a conflict of interest. These rules will be the subject of the next two sections.

IV. CONFLICTS OF INTEREST WITHIN THE CLIENT ORGANIZATION

A. Who is the Business Lawyer's Client?

The lawyer who represents a corporation or other type of business organization is always on the alert for possible conflicts of interest, because of the peculiar nature of organization clients. For, although the organization is a recognized legal entity that has powers and rights of its own, it can only act through the activities of individual human beings—shareholders, directors, partners, employees, owners, officers, and so forth. As a practical matter, the business lawyer deals only with the individual human beings, and yet in theory he is counsel to the organization itself. Who exactly is the business lawyer's client, and what happens when the interests of the organization and one or more of the individuals who make up the organization are in conflict?

When the business lawyer's client is an organization, both the CPR and the Model Rules require that he be loyal to the organization itself, not the human beings who make it up. If the lawyer learns that an individual within the organization has acted, or is going to act, in a way that violates the law or that violates a duty the individual owes to the organization, the lawyer has an ethical obligation to protect the interests of the organization, not the individual. *Model Rules of Professional Conduct*, § 1.13.

B. The Organization vs. the Human Beings who Make Up the Organization

Ordinarily, the interests of the organization and the human beings who make it up are not in conflict. On the occasions when they are, the business lawyer's challenge is to perform his ethical obligations to the organization without alienating the individual, who may after all be one of the lawyer's regular contacts at the organization. At times, it will be impossible to walk this ethical tightrope; in such cases the lawyer will be required to come down unequivocally on the side of the organization (as he is required to "resolve all doubts against the propriety of the representation"), *Id.* § 1.13(c), disqualify himself from representing either the individual or the organization (a difficult thing to do in practice, since he forgoes a fee and risks losing both the individual and the organization as clients), or proceed after disclosing to both parties the nature of the conflict and obtaining the consent of each (preferably in writing) to the joint representation. *Id.* § 1.13(e).

Perhaps the most common instance of such a conflict occurs when a senior officer's employment contract with a corporate employer comes up for renewal. The corporation's general counsel will be required to represent the employer, and yet the person asking him to do so may well be the senior officer whose contract is up for renewal! In such a case the general counsel probably would advise the senior officer to obtain other counsel, for whose services the corporation most likely would pay.

Another common instance of a conflict of interest between the organization and its individual constituents occurs when a new corporation is being formed. At such a time the individuals who will run the corporation will enter into a shareholders' agreement, which will determine such matters as the amount of control each shareholder will have over the corporation's activities, how much stock each shareholder will receive, what each shareholder will contribute to the corporation in return for her shares, and so forth. It is common also for such agreements to require the corporation to buy the shares of any shareholder upon her death, retirement or termination of employment by the corporation. The potentials for conflict in such an agreement are obvious, yet it is often not economically possible for each of the individuals *and* the corporation to retain separate counsel. In such a case the business lawyer will point out the possible conflicts, obtain the written consent of each shareholder (and the corporation, by a letter signed by an authorized officer) to the joint representation, and agree to withdraw if the going gets too rough during the negotiations.

C. When the Human Beings Fail to Follow the Business Lawyer's Instructions

A special case involving a conflict of interest between an organization and one of its individual constituents is that of the corporate officer or employee who has engaged, or proposes to engage, in conduct that is contrary to the corporation's interests. Generally, under both the CPR and the Model Rules, a lawyer may withdraw in certain instances where the client refuses to follow the lawyer's recommendations or instructions, but is not required to withdraw unless continuing the representation would result in a course of action that is either fraudulent or criminal in nature. *Id.* § 1.13(b).

What if the lawyer is not required to resign, but is uncomfortable with the conduct proposed by the individual officer or employee? Here the CPR and the Model Rules part company, and the approach taken by the Model Rules is one of the reasons that many states have refused to adopt the Model Rules. The CPR in such a case leaves it up to the lawyer's discretion whether to withdraw (if he is an in-house counsel, this would mean resigning from the company), taking into account his ability to render independent advice to the organization in the future and the extent to which the individual's behavior has undermined the lawyer's trust and confidence in him. *Id.* In addition, the Model Rules require the business lawyer to decide whether he must go over the individual's head to a superior officer, the board of directors, or even the shareholders of the corporation. *Id.* Model Rule 1.13 requires a lawyer for an organization to take such action as is "reasonably necessary in the best interests of the organization" when the individual "is engaged in an action, intends to act or refuses to act in a matter related to the representation that is a violation of a legal obligation to the organization, or a violation of law which reasonably might be imputed to the organization, and is likely to result in substantial injury to the organization." *Id.* In such a case the lawyer, after using all the arts of persuasion at his disposal to try to talk the individual out of the harmful conduct, is required to go over the individual's head, and if the senior policy-making body in the organization backs the individual up, the lawyer in such a case may resign (indeed if the individual is a senior officer he almost will be required to do so). *Id.* Needless to say, many lawyers are reluctant to play the role of whistle-blower in an organization, and as a result many state bar associations are reluctant to recommend to their state legislatures that Model Rule 1.13 be adopted without some modification that would not put the business lawyer in such a difficult position.

V. CONFLICTS OF INTEREST BETWEEN THE BUSINESS LAWYER AND THE ORGANIZATION CLIENT

In addition to the conflicts that often occur between an organization client and the client's personnel, it is possible for conflicts to occur between the business lawyer's interest and those of its organization client. This situation usually occurs when the lawyer has other ties to the organization, as a shareholder, director or employee.

A. The Lawyer-Director and the Lawyer-Executive

The general counsel of a privately held corporation is often asked to serve on the board of directors. It is often believed that by doing so counsel will be in a better position to practice preventive corporate law, since he will be a part of the decision-making process rather than an outsider who merely reacts to management's proposals. It is also believed that having a lawyer on the board reduces the overall cost and delay of making management decisions, since executives will not have to consult with counsel separately and then report counsel's advice back to the full board. Generally, neither the CPR nor the Model Rules prevents a lawyer from doing so. H. Haynsworth, *The Professional Skills of the Small Business Lawyer* § 2.03 (1984).

The practical wisdom of doing so is another matter. The business lawyer who serves as a corporate director is subject to individual liability for his actions as a director; since he is a lawyer, there is the risk he will be held to a higher degree of diligence and due care than a non-lawyer would. Moreover, in the event of a dispute among factions of directors on the board, the business lawyer will be placed in an awkward position, as he will invariably have to take sides in the matter and risk alienating one faction. He may even find himself in the awkward position of casting the tie-breaking vote on a particular matter.

The best approach for the business lawyer who is asked to serve on a board of directors is not to "just say no," as this might antagonize an otherwise friendly and profitable client. Instead, if the business lawyer is squeamish about assuming a director's responsibilities, he will suggest that he be present at board meetings in a nonvoting capacity. This will accomplish the businesspeople's objective of having the lawyer ready at hand to render on-the-spot legal advice and discover legal issues before management commits itself to a course of action, and will also accomplish the lawyer's objective of avoiding responsibility for business decisions. If the lawyer does indeed wish to serve as a director, believing himself competent to do so, he is well advised to take out (or have the corporation take out) a policy of directors' and officers' liability insurance.

Traditionally, the business lawyer who also serves as a corporate executive runs little risk of a conflict of interest with her client, since she will be either the corporation's general counsel, in which case she is not, strictly speaking, performing a management function but rather is acting solely in a legal capacity; the corporation's secretary, whose role as was seen in Chapter 6 is well defined; or a nonlegal executive, in which case she is not engaged in the practice of law. The business lawyer who serves as both general counsel and corporate secretary (a common combination), however, will be concerned that in preparing minutes of meetings of the corporation's board of directors or shareholders she will not be called upon to falsify or invent from her own imagination official records, documents or evidence.

B. Investing in Stock or Securities of a Client Organization

Generally, a business lawyer is careful when he is called upon either (1) to accept stock or other securities of an organization client in lieu of a fee, (2) to invest in a client organization's stock or securities, or (3) to perform legal work for an organization in which the lawyer is already a significant stockholder or owner. Most law firms have detailed policies that require their lawyers to disclose their holdings of stock or securities in corporations, whether or not they are clients of the firm, and prevent the fees from any one client from being greater than a certain percentage of the firm's total fees. *Id.* § 2.04.

In the case of smaller corporations, which are normally strapped for cash, there may be no practical alternative to accepting stock or other securities in lieu of cash as payment for legal services. Since there is no ready market for the stock or securities, however, and given the fact that most new business startups in the United States fail in the first five years of operations, A. Lipper III, *Venture's Guide to Investing in Private Companies* (1984), the lawyer who accepts client securities as payment may find to her dismay that the securities are worthless in later years. It should also be pointed out that accepting corporate stock for services rendered to the newly formed corporation could cause the incorporation to lose its tax-exempt status under Section 351 of the Internal Revenue Code. I.R.C. § 351 (1991).

VI. ETHICAL ASPECTS OF THE CLIENT MONITORING FUNCTION

A. The Ethical Duties of Diligence and to Keep the Client Informed Do Not Apply

To avoid confusing the reader, it is necessary to point out that the general ethical duties of diligence and "keeping the client informed," discussed earlier in this chapter, do not apply in the context of the business lawyer's client monitoring function. These general rules apply only *after* a client has brought a legal matter to the attention of an attorney and has retained that attorney's services. The client monitoring function occurs before the client has become aware of a legal problem or risk and has approached an attorney for assistance.

Generally, while a business lawyer has no ethical obligation to render legal advice until asked to do so, she may volunteer legal advice without being asked. *Model Rules of Professional Conduct*, Rule 2.1; *ABA Code of Professional Responsibility*, DR 2-104(A)(1).

B. The Prohibition on Soliciting Legal Business

Traditionally, there have been strict rules prohibiting lawyers from soliciting legal business from a potential client who has not sought the lawyer's services. The term "solicitation" has not, however, been construed to mean the volunteering of legal advice to a relative, close friend, or present client, or the volunteering of legal advice to a former client if the advice concerns the subject of a former representation of that client. *Model Rules of Professional Conduct*, Rule 7.3; *ABA Code of Professional Responsibility*, DR 2-104(A)(1).

The rules prohibiting solicitation have been relaxed somewhat in recent years, as courts and bar associations have grown generally more comfortable with the idea that lawyering is a service business and should not be treated differently than other service businesses. The United States Supreme Court, for example, issued a ruling in 1988 that lawyers may send truthful, nondeceptive letters to potential clients known to face particular legal problems. *Shapero v. Kentucky Bar*

Ass'n, 108 S.Ct. 1916 (1988). The Model Rules, however, prohibit lawyers from engaging in any person-to-person contact where a significant motive for the lawyer's conduct is pecuniary gain; this rule will, of course, have to be modified at least somewhat in light of the Supreme Court's 1988 decision on direct mail solicitation. *Model Rules of Professional Conduct*, Rule 7.3. Even under the Model Rules, however, a lawyer can send out letters, brochures or other printed materials to a group of people who "are not known to need legal services of the kind provided by the lawyer in a particular matter, but who are so situated that they might in general find such services useful." *Id*. Until these rules have been clarified, most business lawyers will take a conservative position and have their direct mail brochures approved by the ethics committee of their state bar association before sending them to potential clients.

VII. Ethical Aspects of the Client Counseling Function

A. The Business Lawyer as Advisor

When acting as advisor to a client, a lawyer must exercise independent judgment and render candid advice, no matter how unpleasant that task may be. A lawyer may give a client not only legal advice, but also moral, economic, social, or political advice where that is relevant to the client's situation. *Model Rules of Professional Conduct*, Rule 2.1; *ABA Code of Professional Responsibility*, EC 7-3, 7-8 and 7-9.

B. The Business Lawyer's Evaluation of a Client for Use by Third Parties

Often a business lawyer is called upon to analyze or evaluate the client's affairs from a legal standpoint and then present a report or opinion letter summarizing her findings to a third party. Under Model Rule 2.3 (there is no corresponding provision in the CPR), a lawyer may evaluate a client's affairs for the use of a third person if both (1) the lawyer reasonably believes that making the evaluation is compatible with the lawyer's other responsibilities to the client, and (2) the client consents after consultation with the lawyer. *Model Rules of Professional Conduct*, Rule 2.3.

C. The Business Lawyer's Association with Specialists

Often a business lawyer is presented with a matter or client question that is beyond her ability to handle effectively, or that requires knowledge of the law of a jurisdiction in which she is not admitted to practice. In either of these situations, a business lawyer has an ethical obligation to associate with a specialist, or with a lawyer or law firm that is qualified to render an opinion on the law of the other jurisdiction. *ABA Code of Professional Responsibility*, DR 6-101(A)(1) and EC 6-3. Obviously, business lawyers will be concerned about the possibility that their clients will be stolen by the attorney or law firm to whom the matter is referred, but most law firms in practice limit this risk by establishing long-term working relationships with firms in other cities and in certain specialized areas (such as patent or admiralty law), and will publish periodic "lists of recommended counsel" for distribution to all lawyers in the firm to make sure that only those "friendly" firms are used.

A lawyer who is forced to relinquish control of a matter to another lawyer or law firm usually will not be able to charge a referral fee for this service, and the lawyer or law firm to whom the matter is referred will be entitled to retain the entire fee. *Model Rules of Professional Conduct*, Rule 1.5(e); *ABA Code of Professional Responsibility*, DR 2-107.

VIII. ETHICAL ASPECTS OF THE TRANSACTION MANAGEMENT PROCESS

A. The Duty of Fairness to the Opposing Party and its Counsel

While the CPR and Model Rules provisions regarding the lawyer's duty of fairness to opposing parties and their counsel apply primarily in litigation, the business lawyer will find these provisions applicable as well when negotiating or drafting legal documents for a client's business transaction. Generally, when dealing on behalf of a client with a third person, a lawyer must not knowingly make a false statement of law or material fact. While a lawyer has no duty to inform a third person of

ETHICAL CONSIDERATIONS 521

relevant facts, he must not misrepresent the facts. *Id.* In some cases, the lawyer's failure to speak or act—usually the failure to correct the opposing party's mistaken statement or assumption of fact—may constitute a misrepresentation that will run afoul of this rule. *Id.*

Certain types of exaggerated statement which are ordinarily made during negotiations, such as an initial bargaining position that everyone at the table knows is unrealistic, do not come under the heading "misrepresentation" but are instead called "puffery" and are permissible. *Model Rules of Professional Conduct*, Official Comment to Rule 4.1. The line separating permitted puffery from prohibited misrepresentation, however, can sometimes be quite thin.

Finally, while these rules can easily be applied to a negotiation setting, the business lawyer must be aware that in drafting transaction documents, these rules may come into play as well. The lawyer who sees a provision in a term sheet that he does not like and who willfully omits the offensive provision from the first draft in the hopes the other party's counsel will not notice its absence, is as much at fault as the negotiating business lawyer who tells an outright lie to the other side. Similarly, when the businesspeople agree to a point during negotiations, it is the drafting lawyer's responsibility to be sure the language accurately reflects the agreement of the parties and is not twisted to favor his client's side in a way the parties did not anticipate. Of course, if in reaching the agreement the parties failed to discuss a particular detail of their agreed-upon point, there is nothing wrong with drafting language resolving the detail in favor of one's client.

B. Communication with Persons Represented by Counsel; Dealing with Unrepresented Persons

Simply stated, a business lawyer never, ever, ever talks to a businessperson on the opposite side of the table unless the opposing party's lawyer is present (in person or on the telephone) or has consented to the communication. *Model Rules of Professional Conduct*, Rule 4.2; *ABA Code of Professional Responsibility*, DR 7-104(A). Where an organization is the opposing party, the business lawyer cannot contact most of the organization's executives or employees without first contacting the organization's counsel and seeking permission to communicate directly. *Model Rules of Professional Conduct*, Official Comment to Rule 4.2. The reader should note that this rule only applies to business lawyers; it does not prevent businesspeople on opposite sides of the table from meeting or talking separately without their lawyers' presence or permission. *Id.*

C. Dealing with Other Professionals; Preventing the Unauthorized Practice of Law

In negotiating a complicated business transaction, an organization client will be served not only by business lawyers but by accountants, investment bankers, underwriters, insurance agents and management consultants as well, and it behooves the lawyer to work together, and not at cross-purposes, with these other professionals who may after all be useful contacts for future business. Often a lawyer and another professional will give a client conflicting advice, and it is the lawyer's task to persuade the client to accept his (the lawyer's) point of view in a way that does not cast the other professional in a negative light. If the client's decision is one that ultimately does not have a legal component (such as the amount of life insurance each shareholder of a closely held corporation should buy to fund the mutual buyout provisions in their shareholders' agreement, a point as to which lawyers and insurance agents are likely to disagree), most business lawyers will accept their limitations and decline comment on the matter even if they disagree with the other professional's advice.

In most states it is a criminal misdemeanor, if not a felony, to practice law without being admitted to the bar of that state. Accordingly, the business lawyer has an ethical obligation to make sure that other professionals, in performing their customary tasks in a business transaction, do not engage in the unauthorized practice of law. *Model Rules of Professional Conduct*, Rule 5.5(a); *ABA Code of Professional Responsibility*, DR 3-101(B). Thus if an accountant, for example, attempts to persuade an entrepreneur to form his new enterprise as a partnership rather than a corporation, and begins discussing the legal consequences of this course of action, the business lawyer, if present, should blow the whistle and make sure his view of the matter is heard.

IX. CROSS-BORDER PROBLEMS

The reader will recall that a business lawyer admitted to practice in State X who is called upon to render advice on the law of State Y normally will associate herself with a lawyer or law firm in State Y who will render the advice and, if requested, an opinion letter on the application of State Y law to the matter. What if the business lawyer does not do this? What if the business lawyer plows ahead, researches thoroughly the law of State Y, and renders the advice on State Y law herself to the client?

Technically, she has done nothing wrong; a lawyer in one state can give advice on the law of another state (or country) if she is diligent and thorough in her work. H. Haynsworth, *The Professional Skills of the Small Business Lawyer* § 2.09 (1984). Customarily in business transactions, most New York law firms will render opinions on Delaware's corporate law, even though neither they nor anyone else in their firm is admitted in Delaware. It is also customary for any lawyer in a law firm to sign an opinion letter on the law of another state if at least one other lawyer in the firm is admitted to the bar in that other state.

The lawyer who renders such an opinion, however, will often be held to the same standard of competence and due care as a lawyer admitted to practice in the other state. *Id.* If the opinion is rendered (i.e., the transaction closes) in the other state, moreover, she may be subject to liability for the unauthorized practice of law in that state.

X. SOME ETHICAL ASPECTS OF IN-HOUSE LAWYERING

The proliferation of corporate legal departments and in-house counsel has spawned new and difficult ethical issues for business lawyers which are only now beginning to be sorted out in the courts. Most of these issues stem from the in-house counsel's dual role as independent professional and corporate employee.

For example, what if an in-house counsel discovers impropriety in his employer's conduct? Under the Model Rules of Professional Conduct, he is obligated to alert senior management to the problem, and if they fail to take action, he may under some circumstances go to the board of directors. Obviously, by doing so he puts his career at risk, but what if the company still fails to take action? Most states have adopted "whistle-blowing" statutes which allow employees to sue their employers if they are fired for making public disclosure of alleged violations of law. Clearly the in-house counsel's status as a corporate employee with perhaps the best access to the sort of internal information that will uncover improprieties and illegal conduct within the organization supports that argument that he should be entitled to release information to the public. The in-house counsel, however, is also under a professional duty to keep his client's matters strictly confidential. If that duty of confidentiality is overridden by the employee's duty to "blow the whistle" on illegal conduct, there is a real risk that businesspeople will fear to entrust their in-house counsel with sensitive information, and thereby render them second-rate attorneys. How to reconcile these conflicting duties?

The few cases involving whistle-blowing by in-house attorneys are in conflict. Compare *Parker v. M&T Chemical Inc.*, 566 A.2d 215 (New Jersey 1989) (an in-house attorney who refused to photocopy a business competitor's confidential documents could sue the employer for retaliatory discharge) with *Willy v. Coastal Corp.*, 647 F. Supp. 116 (S.D. Texas 1986) (an in-house counsel who was fired for telling his employer to comply with environmental laws had no action to sue for wrongful discharge). Two recent cases found for the employer. In *Balla v. Gambro Inc.*, 145 Ill. 2d 492, 584 N.E.2d 104 (1991), an in-house attorney learned that his employer, a distributor of dialysis machines, would shortly be receiving a shipment of defective machines from an overseas manufacturer. The attorney notified the company president that the sale would have to be reported to the Food and Drug Administration ("FDA"), but the machines were sold to customers anyway and the attorney was fired. Shortly after his firing, the attorney reported the sale to the FDA, which confiscated the defective machines. The appellate

ETHICAL CONSIDERATIONS

court, holding for the fired attorney, found it necessary to determine whether the firing resulted from information learned in a nonlegal capacity or as a lawyer, whether the information was privileged, and whether the privilege was waived. Even if the privilege exists and is not waived, the appellate court added, the court is obliged to balance the public policy of the privilege against the competing policy of protecting individuals (users of the defective dialysis machines) from serious bodily harm or death. *Id.* at 2187. The fact that the sale of the defective machines posed serious risk to bodily harm or death seems to have weighed heavily in the appellate court's decision.

The Illinois Supreme Court reversed the appellate court, citing ABA Formal Opinion No. 328, which addresses the dual role situation: "If the second occupation is so law-related that the work of the lawyer in such occupation will involve, inseparably, the practice of law, the lawyer is considered to be engaged in the practice of law while conducting that occupation." ABA Formal Opinion No. 328, at 65 (June 1972). The Court held that "if extending the tort of retaliatory discharge might have a chilling effect on the communications between the employer/client and the in-house counsel, we believe that it is more wise to refrain from doing so."

The court in *IBM v. Murray*, Stamford (Conn.) Superior Court No. DN CV 90-0107445 S, *summarized in* NATIONAL L.J., Nov. 5, 1990 at S1 and S12, found for the employer. In this case the in-house attorney warned company officers that an IBM regional office was treating black workers engaged in threatening behavior significantly harsher than white employees accused of similar actions. Although the in-house attorney availed himself of an internal company policy favoring such disclosures, he was promptly transferred to a location thousands of miles away that he described as "disciplinary barracks for attorneys." *Id.* IBM put the attorney on a paid leave of absence, offering him the opportunity to return if he promised in writing not to disclose confidential IBM documents to the public. The attorney refused and was promptly dismissed. The attorney sued IBM for wrongful termination, and IBM moved to seal all IBM documents in the attorney's possession, winning a temporary restraining order from the court preventing the attorney from disclosing IBM documents to anyone except his attorney. Both before and after the temporary restraining order issued, the attorney released copies of the lawsuit to two local newspapers. IBM has since filed motions for the adjudication of civil contempt, and a criminal contempt motion is pending. *Id.* at S12.

Another ethical problem for in-house attorneys involves the unauthorized practice of law. Like all corporate employees, in-house attorneys are subject to transfer from one corporate location to another on little or no notice. If the attorney is not admitted in the state of his new corporate location, what can he do, and what must he not do, without engaging in the unauthorized practice of law in that state? Clearly he cannot represent his employer in a court of that state, or issue a written opinion on the law of that state. Arguably he should not give verbal advice on the law of that state. The in-house attorney's work involves a lot of "gray areas" that only partially entail the practice of law as traditionally viewed. Situations may well arise where an in-house attorney, in the heat of getting a deal done or getting a rush question answered, may engage in conduct that a court or state bar association may look upon as the practice of law.

PRACTICE GUIDES

- *When a business lawyer is admitted to practice in a particular state, he is expected to become familiar with that state's ethical rules and regulations.*
- *There are three sets of rules which govern the conduct of American lawyers: the American Bar Association's Code of Professional Responsibility (or the "CPR"), the Model Rules of Professional Conduct (or the "Model Rules"), and those state statutes that amend, overrule or add to the CPR or the Model Rules (such as the Appendix to New York's Judiciary Law).*
- *The ethical rules of a particular state are usually interpreted by that state's bar association, in the form of written opinions which are published irregularly.*
- *The drafters of the CPR and the Model Rules had litigators, not business lawyers, in mind.*

ETHICAL CONSIDERATIONS 527

- *A business lawyer is required (1) to represent his clients competently, (2) to act on behalf of his client with reasonable diligence and promptness, (3) to keep the client informed of developments, and (4) to keep the client's affairs and information relating to the representation confidential (this may include even the fact that someone is a client of the firm).*

- *When the business lawyer's client is an organization, both the CPR and the Model Rules require that he be loyal to the organization itself, not the human beings who make it up.*

- *When the interests of an organization and one or more of its principals is in conflict, the business lawyer's challenge is to perform his ethical duties to the organization without alienating the principal.*

- *Under both the CPR and the Model Rules, a lawyer may withdraw in certain instances where the client refuses to follow the lawyer's recommendations or instructions, but is not required to withdraw unless continuing the representation would result in a course of action either fraudulent or criminal in nature.*

- *Under the Model Rules (not the CPR), a business lawyer may be required to "blow the whistle" within his organization if he discovers illegal or harmful conduct.*

- *The best approach for the business lawyer who is asked to serve on a board of directors is not to "just say no" and risk antagonizing an otherwise friendly and profitable client.*

- *Most law firms have detailed policies requiring their lawyers to disclose any personal holdings of stock or securities in corporations, whether or not they are clients of the firm, and prevent the fees from any one client from being greater than a certain percentage of the firm's total fees.*

- *While a business lawyer has no ethical obligation to render legal advice until asked to do so, he may volunteer legal advice without being asked.*

- *The rules prohibiting lawyers from soliciting clients have been relaxed somewhat in recent years, as courts and bar associations have grown generally more comfortable with the idea that lawyering is a service business and should not be treated differently than other service businesses.*

- *A lawyer may give a client not only legal advice, but also moral, economic, social, or political advice where it is relevant to the client's situation.*

- *When dealing on behalf of a client with a third person, a lawyer must not knowingly make a false statement of law or material fact.*

- *While a lawyer has no duty to inform a third person of relevant facts, he must not misrepresent the facts.*

- *A business lawyer never, ever, ever talks to a businessperson on the opposite side of the table unless the opposing party's lawyer is present (in person or on the telephone), or the opposing party's lawyer has consented to his client's communicating directly with the lawyer.*

- *In most states it is a criminal misdemeanor, if not a felony, to practice law without being admitted to the bar of that state.*

- *A lawyer in one state can give advice on the law of another state (or country) if he is diligent and thorough in his work; he will, however, be held to the same standard of competence and due care as a lawyer admitted to practice in the other state (or country).*

- *In-house lawyers have special ethical problems, some of which have not been settled in the courts; a current issue is whether in-house counsel may sue his employer for wrongful termination using information that his employer deems confidential and part of the attorney-client relationship.*

CHAPTER TWENTY-ONE

ONE HUNDRED BASIC BOOKS FOR THE LAWYER REPRESENTING THE SMALL BUSINESS

Elisabeth Tavss Ohman

ONE HUNDRED BASIC BOOKS

The following books were specifically selected to meet the needs and the budget of the small business lawyer. The list contains what we believe to be the most current and practical sources covering the basics of corporate law and related fields.

1. *Accounting for Business Lawyers: Teaching Materials.* 4th edition. Ted J. Fiflis. 838 pages. 1991. $42.95. West Publishing Co. New York, N.Y.

2. *Anatomy of a Merger: Strategies and Techniques for Negotiating Corporate Acquisitions.* James C. Freund. 559 pages. 1975. $70.00. Law Journal Seminars-Press. New York, N.Y.

3. *Annual Meetings of Shareholders: A Guidebook.* 2nd edition. 131 pages. 1986. $90.00. American Society of Corporate Secretaries. New York, N.Y.

4. *Antitrust Adviser.* 3rd Revised Edition. Carla A. Hills. 600 pages. 1985. $95.00. Shepard's/McGraw-Hill, Inc. Colorado Springs, Colorado.

5. *Antitrust Compliance Manual: A Guide for Counsel, Management, and Public Officials.* Walker B. Comegys. Hardcover Text Edition. 209 pages. 1986. $60.00. Practising Law Institute. New York, N.Y.

6. *The Arthur Young Business Plan Guide.* Eric Siegel, Loren Schultz, Brian Ford and David Carney. 184 pages. 1990. $24.95. John Wiley & Sons. New York, N.Y.

7. *Assisting Insiders with Federal Securities Law Compliance: A Guide For the Corporate Secretary.* 30 pages. 1985. $36.00. American Society for Corporate Secretaries. New York, N.Y.

8. *Bankruptcy Law Manual.* Benjamin Weintraub. 1986. $115.00. Warren Gorham & Lamont. Boston, Mass.

9. *Bankruptcy Practice and Strategy.* Alan N. Resnick. 1987. $155.00. Warren Gorham & Lamont. Boston, Mass.

10. *Basic Corporate Practice.* 2nd Edition. George Seward and John Nauss. 500 pages. 1977. $20.00. American Law Institute. Philadelphia, Pa.

11. *Blueprint for Franchising a Business*. Steven Raab and Gregory Matusky. 275 pages. 1987. $29.95. John Wiley & Sons. New York, N.Y.

12. *Business Acquisitions*. 2nd edition, 3 volumes. John W. Herz and Charles K. Baller. 3041 pages. 1981. $175.00. Practising Law Institute. New York, N.Y.

13. *Business Information for Today's Practicing Lawyer*. Adolf J. Levy. 631 pages. 1984. $40.00. Practising Law Institute. New York, N.Y.

14. *The Business Lawyers' Handbook*. Clifford R. Ennico. 1992. $39.95. Clark Boardman Callaghan, New York, N.Y.

15. *Business Workouts Manual*. Donald Lee Rome. 1985. $105.00. Warren Gorham & Lamont. Boston, Mass.

16. *Choice of Entity: Legal Considerations of Selection*. Glen Davis, Michael Kushner and Patrick Rockelli. Corporate Practice Series No. 50. 1986. $95.00. Bureau of National Affairs. Washington, D.C.

17. *O'Neal's Close Corporations: Law and Practice*. 3rd edition, 2 volumes. F. O'Neal and R. Thompson. 1971. $185.00. Clark Boardman Callaghan. Wilmette, Ill.

18. *Commercial Loan Documentation*. 3rd edition. William C. Hillman. 426 pages. 1990. $85.00. Practising Law Institute. New York, N.Y.

19. *Complete Guide to Buying and Selling a Business*. Arnold S. Goldstein. 273 pages. 1983. $24.95. John Wiley & Sons. New York, N.Y.

20. *Legal Capital: Being a Concise Practical Exposition with Illustrative Examples*. 3rd edition. Bayless Manning. 213 pages. 1990. $14.95. Foundation Press. Westbury, N.Y.

21. *Corporate Bond Financing*. Ray Garrett and Thomas Arthur. Corporate Practice Series No. 13. 1979. $95.00. Bureau of National Affairs. Washington, D.C.

ONE HUNDRED BASIC BOOKS

22. *Corporate and Tax Aspects of Closely Held Corporations.* 2nd edition. William Painter. 625 pages. 1981. $95.00. Little Brown & Co. Boston, Mass.

23. *Corporate Officer's and Director's Desk Book with Model Documents, Agreements, and Forms.* William E. Read. 557 pages. 1980. $65.00. Prentice-Hall. Englewood Cliffs, N.J.

24. *Creating the Successful Business Plan for New Ventures.* LaRue Hosmer and Roger Guiles. 192 pages. 1987. $28.50. McGraw-Hill Book Co. Hightstown, N.J.

25. *Creditors' Rights in Bankruptcy.* 2nd edition. Patrick A. Murphy. 1988. $95.00. Shepard's/McGraw-Hill Book Co. Hightstown, N.J.

26. *Delaware General Corporation Law Annotated, Franchise Tax Law, and Uniform Limited Partnership Act.* Yearly. 1991. $12.40. Prentice-Hall Legal and Financial Services. Paramus, N.J.

27. *The Delaware General Corporation Law: A Commentary and Analysis.* 2nd edition, 2 volumes. Ernest C. Folk. 1988. $195.00. Little Brown & Co. Boston, Mass.

28. *The Developing Labor Law: The Board, the Courts, and the National Labor Relations Act.* 2nd edition, 2 volumes. Charles J. Morris. 2133 pages. 1983. $180.00. Bureau of National Affairs, Inc. Washington, D.C.

29. *Dictionary of Finance and Investment Terms.* 3rd edition. John Downes and Jordon Elliot Goodman. 537 pages. 1991. $9.95. Barron's Educational Service. Hauppauge, N.Y.

30. *Drafting Corporate Documents for the Close Corporation: Course Materials.* B. Alter, L. Beane, E. Lach and J. Rosengarten. 1990. $25.00. New York State Bar Association. Albany, N.Y.

31. *Drafting of Partnership Agreements.* Marlin M. Volz and Arthur L. Berger. 199 pages. 1976 and supplement. $69.00. American Law Institute. Philadelphia, Pa.

32. *Employer's Guide to Labor Relations.* James W. Hunt. 162 pages. 1979. $12.00. Bureau of National Affairs, Inc. Washington, D.C.

33. *Employment Discrimination Law*. 2nd edition. Barbara Schlei and Paul Grossman. 1720 pages. 1983. $95.00. (Paper Text Edition. $35.00). Bureau of National Affairs, Inc. Washington, D.C.

34. *Encyclopedia of Corporate Meetings, Minutes, and Resolutions*. 3rd edition, 2 volumes. William Sardell. 1300 pages. 1986. $99.95. Prentice-Hall. Englewood Cliffs, N.J.

35. *Equipment Leasing—Leveraged Leasing*. 3rd edition, 2 volumes. Bruce Fritch and Albert F. Reisman. 1988. $140.00. Practising Law Institute. New York, N.Y.

36. *The Essentials of Corporation Law*. 2nd edition. Leona Beane. 352 pages. 1987. $23.95. Kendall/Hunt Publishing Co. Dubuque, Iowa.

37. *The Essentials of Partnership Law*. Leona Beane. 200 pages. 1982. $18.95. Kendall/Hunt Publishing Co. Dubuque, Iowa.

38. *Estate Planning for the Small Business Owner*. John C. Howell. 176 pages. 1980. $6.95. Prentice-Hall. Englewood Cliffs, N.J.

39. *Ethics Compliance for Business Lawyers*. Brooke Wunnicke. 447 pages. 1987. $85.00. John Wiley & Sons. New York, N.Y.

40. *Federal Regulation of Personnel and Human Resource Management*. 2nd edition. James Ledvinka. 343 pages. 1991. Text Edition. $14.50. PWS-Kent Publishing Co. Boston, Mass.

41. *Financial Accounting: An Introduction to Concepts, Methods, and Uses*. 6th edition. S. Davidson, C. Stickney and R. Weil. 838 pages. 1991. $50.75. Harcourt Brace Jovanovich. San Diego, Cal.

42. *Forming and Advising Businesses—Corporations and Partnerships: Course Materials*. 328 pages. 1989. $25.00. New York State Bar Association. Albany, N.Y.

43. *Franchising: A Planning and Sales Compliance Guide*. Norman D. Axelrad, Lewis G. Rudnick, Dennis E. Wieczorek and Pamela J. Mills. 272 pages. 1987. $35.00. Commerce Clearing House, Inc. Chicago, Ill.

ONE HUNDRED BASIC BOOKS 535

44. *Fundamentals of Federal Income Taxation of Corporations and Shareholders.* Boris Bittker and James Eustice. 1983 and current supplement. $37.00. Student Edition. ($12.75, Study Guide). Warren Gorham & Lamont. Boston, Mass.

45. *Fundamentals of Financial Management.* 8th edition. J. Van Horne. 732 pages. 1991. $56.00. Prentice-Hall. Englewood Cliffs, N.J.

46. *Fundamentals of Securities Regulation.* 2nd edition. Louis Loss. 1175 pages. 1988. $125.00. Little Brown & Co. Boston, Mass.

47. *A Guide to Modern Business and Commercial Law.* Bernard M. Kaplan. 1344 pages. 1985. $65.00. Commerce Clearing House, Inc. Chicago, Ill.

48. *Guidebook to New York Taxes.* 360 pages. 1991 edition (published annually). $6.00. Commerce Clearing House, Inc. Chicago, Ill.

49. *Handbook for Corporate Directors.* Edward Mattar. 640 pages. 1987. $51.95. McGraw-Hill. Hightstown, N.J.

50. *Handbook of Financial Markets and Institutions.* 6th edition. Edward I. Altman. 1174 pages. 1987. $95.00. John Wiley & Sons. New York, N.Y.

51. *Handbook of Modern Finance.* 2nd edition. Dennis Logue. 1990. $105.00. Warren Gorham & Lamont. Boston, Mass.

52. *Hazardous Wastes, Superfund, & Toxic Substances: ALI-ABA Course of Study Material.* American Law Institute-American Bar Association Committee on Continuing Legal Education. 594 pages. 1987. $50.00. ALI-ABA. Philadelphia, Pa.

53. *How to Incorporate: A Handbook for Entrepreneurs and Professionals.* Michael R. Diamond and Julie L. Williams. 256 pages. 1987. $34.95. John Wiley & Sons. New York, N.Y.

54. *1991 Immigration Procedures Handbook: A How-to Guide for Legal and Business Professionals.* A. Fragomen, A.J. Del Rey, and S.C. Bell. 1991. $105.00. Clark Boardman Callaghan. New York, N.Y.

55. *Incorporating a Small Business.* Allan J. Parker. 250 pages. 1987. $50.00. Practising Law Institute. New York, N.Y.

56. *Israels on Corporate Practice.* 4th edition. A. Hoffman. 803 pages. 1983. $75.00. Practising Law Institute. New York, N.Y.

57. *How to Put Together a Real Estate Syndicate or Joint Venture.* Daniel S. Berman. 288 pages. 1984. $37.50. Prentice-Hall. Englewood Cliffs, N.J.

58. *The Law of Corporate Groups: Procedural Problems in the Law of Parent and Subsidiary Corporations.* Phillip I. Blumberg. 527 pages. 1983 and supplement. $105.00. Little Brown & Co. Boston, Mass.

59. *The Law of Corporate Officers and Directors: Indemnification and Insurance.* Joseph W. Bishop, Jr. 1982. $100.00. Clark Boardman Callaghan. Wilmette, Ill.

60. *Law of Environmental Protection.* Sheldon M. Novick, Donald W. Stever, and Margaret G. Mellon. Environmental Law Institute. 2 volumes. 1987. $195.00. Clark Boardman Callaghan. New York, N.Y.

61. *The Law of Hazardous Waste: Management, Cleanup, Liability, and Litigation.* Susan M. Cooke. 3 volumes. 1987. $320.00. Matthew Bender & Co. New York, N.Y.

62. *Laws of Corporations and Other Business Enterprises.* 3rd edition. Harry Henn and John Alexander. 1371 pages. 1983. $70.00. West Publishing Co. Mineola, N.Y.

63. *The Lawyer's Basic Corporate Practice Manual.* 3rd edition. Richard E. Deer. 320 pages. 1984. $92.00. American Law Institute. Philadelphia, Pa.

64. *A Lawyer's Basic Guide to Secured Transactions.* Donald Baker. 342 pages. 1983. $60.00. American Law Institute. Philadelphia, Pa.

65. *The Lawyer's Code of Professional Responsibility.* 83 pages. 1990. $4.00. New York State Bar Association. Albany, N.Y.

66. *Liability of Corporate Officers and Directors.* 4th edition. William E. Knepper. 950 pages. 1988. $90.00. Michie Company. Charlottesville, Va.

67. *Materials on Accounting for Lawyers*. David Herwitz. 612 pages. 1980. $24.00. Foundation Press. Mineola, N.Y.

68. *Meetings of the Board of Directors and its Committees: A Guidebook*. 180 pages. 1985. $60.00. American Society of Corporate Secretaries. New York, N.Y.

69. *The Mergers and Acquisitions Handbook*. Milton L. Rock. 544 pages. 1987. $73.50. McGraw-Hill. Hightstown, N.J.

70. *Modern Corporation Checklists*. 3rd edition. William Sardell. 1990. $117.00. Warren Gorham & Lamont. Boston, Mass.

71. *The Money Market*. 3rd edition. Marcia Stigum. 1252 pages. 1990. $70.00. Dow-Jones Irwin. Homewood, Ill.

72. *New York Close Corporations*. 2 volumes. Robert A. Kessler. 1983. $95.00. William S. Hein Company. Buffalo, N.Y.

73. *The New York Corporation: Legal Aspects of Organization and Operation*. H. Henn and J. Alexander. Corporate Practice Series No. 2. 1978. $92.00. Bureau of National Affairs. Washington, D.C.

74. *New York Laws Affecting Corporations*. 1991 edition (published annually). $33.90. Prentice-Hall Corporation Service. Englewood Cliffs, N.J.

75. *Forming and Advising the New York Not-For-Profit Organization*. 353 pages. 1989. $25.00. New York State Bar Association. Albany, N.Y.

76. *New York Uniform Commercial Code Annotated*. 1991 edition. $30.00. Matthew Bender & Co. New York, N.Y.

77. *New York Securities Law: Practice and Policy*. Catherine J. Douglass and Ellen Lieberman. $24.95. New York State Bar Association. Albany, N.Y.

78. *Oppression of Minority Shareholders*. 1975 and current supplement, 2 volumes. F. O'Neal. 2000 pages. $185.00. Clark Boardman Callaghan. Wilmette, Ill.

79. *The Partnership Book: How to Write Your Own Small Business Partnership Agreement*. 4th edition. D. Clifford and R. Warner. 1991. $24.95. Nolo Press. Berkeley, Ca.

80. *The Partnership Handbook*. Raymond W. Merritt and Martin Helpern. 961 pages. 1986. $70.00. New York State Bar Association. Albany, N.Y.

81. *The Practical Lawyer's Manual of Business Forms and Checklists*. 230 pages. 1984. $11.00. American Law Institute-American Bar Association Committee on Continuing Professional Education. ALI-ABA. Philadelphia, Pa.

82. *The Professional Skills of the Small Business Lawyer*. Harry J. Haynsworth. 255 pages. 1984. $82.00. American Law Institute-American Bar Association Committee on Continuing Professional Education. ALI-ABA. Philadelphia, Pa.

83. *Resource Materials: Partnerships*. 9th edition. 928 pages. 1990. $175.00. American Law Institute. Philadelphia, Pa.

84. *The S Corporation Handbook*. Peter M. Fass and Barbara S. Gerrard. 583 pages. 1991. $90.00. Clark Boardman Callaghan. New York, N.Y.

85. *The S Corporation Manual: A Special Tax Break for Small Business Corporations*. Peter L. Faber. 1990. $89.00. MacMillan. Englewood Cliffs, N.J.

86. *Securities Law Handbook*. Harold S. Bloomenthal. 1991. $95.00. Clark Boardman Callaghan. New York, N.Y.

87. *Start-Up Companies: Planning, Financing and Operating the Successful Business*. Richard D. Harroch. 1200 pages. 1985. $125.00. Law Journal Seminars-Press. New York, N.Y.

88. *Starting and Managing the Small Business*. Arthur M. Kuriloff and John M. Hemphill. 2nd edition. 663 pages. 1988. $42.85. McGraw-Hill. Hightstown, N.J.

89. *Strategies for Creditors in Bankruptcy Proceedings*. Lynn M. Lopucki. 752 pages. 1985. $95.00. Little Brown & Co. Boston, Mass.

ONE HUNDRED BASIC BOOKS

90. *Structuring Commercial Loan Agreements.* 2nd edition. Sandra Stern. 1990. $105.00. Warren Gorham & Lamont. Boston, Mass.

91. *A Student's Guide to Accounting for Lawyers.* D. Lipsky and D. Lipton. 300 pages. 1985. $22.95. Matthew Bender & Co. New York, N.Y.

92. *Term Loan Handbook.* John J. McCann. 300 pages. 1983. $55.00. Harcourt Brace Jovanovich. New York, N.Y.

93. *The Valuation of Privately Held Businesses: State-of-the-Art Techniques for Buyers, Sellers, and their Advisors.* Irving Blackman. 360 pages. 1986. $55.00. Probus Publishing Co. Chicago, Ill.

94. *Venture Capital and Public Offering Negotiation.* Michael Halloran. 900 pages. 1983. $160.00. Prentice-Hall Law & Business. Clifton, N.J.

95. *Venture Capital and Small Business Financings.* Robert J. Haft. Volumes 2, 2A, 2B, 2C. 1984. $395.00. Clark Boardman Callaghan. New York, N.Y.

96. *The Venture Magazine Complete Guide to Venture Capital.* C. Richardson. 261 pages. 1987. $12.95. New American Library. New York, N.Y.

97. *Venture Capital Handbook.* David J. Gladstone. 350 pages. 1988. $43.95. Prentice-Hall. Englewood Cliffs, N.J.

98. *West's Federal Taxation: Corporations, Partnerships, Estates and Trusts.* W. Hoffman and W. Raabe. Annual Edition. 1992. $57.50. ($14.50, Self-Study Guide). West Publishing Co. Mineola, N.Y.

99. *What Constitutes Doing Business by a Corporation in States Foreign to the State of its Creation.* 145 pages. 1981. $7.50. CT Corporation System. New York, N.Y.

100. *Where To Find Business Information: A Worldwide Guide for Everyone Who Needs the Answers to Business Questions.* 2nd Edition. David M. Brownstone and Gordon Carruth. 632 pages. 1982. $84.50. John Wiley & Sons. New York, N.Y.

FORMS AND MATERIALS

FORMS AND MATERIALS

TABLE OF CONTENTS

		Page
Form One:	Comparison of Forms of Business Organization.	547
Form Two:	Certificate of Assumed or Fictitious Name	551
Form Three:	Agreement to Form a Corporation (Pre-Incorporation Agreement) . . .	553
Form Four:	Application for Reservation of Corporation Name	561
	a. New York Secretary of State Guidelines for Corporate Names	563
Form Five:	Certificate of Incorporation and Accompanying Form of Notarization	567
Form Six:	Checklist of Provisions to Consider for Inclusion in Certificate of Incorporation	571
Form Seven:	Sample By-laws	573
Form Eight:	Checklist of Provisions Valid Only if Included in By-laws or Certificate of Incorporation	589
Form Nine:	Statement of Incorporator in Lieu of Organization Meeting	591
Form Ten:	Minutes of Organization Meeting of Board of Directors	593

Form Eleven:	Waiver of Notice of First Board of Directors Meeting	597
Form Twelve:	Subscription Agreement..........	599
Form Thirteen:	Material for Election of Subchapter S Status	613
Form Fourteen:	Preferred Stock Certificate of Designation	629
Form Fifteen:	Shareholders Agreement	647
Form Sixteen:	Stock Transfer Restriction Agreement (Buy-Sell Agreement)	659
Form Seventeen:	Voting Agreement	665
Form Eighteen:	Voting Trust Agreement	671
Form Nineteen:	Stock Escrow Agreement........	677
Form Twenty:	Employment Agreement (Short Form).......................	681
Form Twenty-One:	Employment Agreement (Long Form).......................	689
Form Twenty-Two:	Incentive and Nonqualified Stock Option Plan	703
Form Twenty-Three:	Materials on Limitation of Directors' Liability and Indemnification of Directors and Officers	713
Form Twenty-Four:	Consulting Agreement	719
Form Twenty-Five:	Confidentiality, Trade Secret and Invention Agreement	725
Form Twenty-Six:	Agreement for Appointment of Independent Domestic Sales Representative	733
Form Twenty-Seven:	Unanimous Written Consent (Board of Directors).................	745

Form Twenty-Eight:	Unanimous Written Consent (Stockholders)	749
Form Twenty-Nine:	Forms for Annual Meeting of Shareholders	751
	— Shareholder Ballot (Noncumulative Voting)	751
	— Shareholder Ballot (Cumulative Voting)	753
	— Shareholder's Proxy	755
	— Agenda for Annual Meeting of Shareholders	757
Form Thirty:	Officer and Director Questionnaire for Proxy Statements and Annual Reports	761
Form Thirty-One:	Certificate of Incumbency (Secretary's Certificate)	773
Form Thirty-Two:	Merger Materials	777
	— Agreement and Plan of Merger	777
	— Unanimous Written Consent (Board of Directors)	807
	— Unanimous Written Consent (Stockholders)	810
	— Notice to Shareholders of Merger	811
	— Certificate of Merger	813
Form Thirty-Three:	Checklist for Stock or Asset Acquisition	815
Form Thirty-Four:	Agreement for Purchase of Stock	821
Form Thirty-Five:	Agreement for Purchase of Assets	841
	a. Form of Opinion of Seller's Counsel	873
	b. Bulk Sales Affidavit	877
Form Thirty-Six:	Agreement of Recapitalization	879

Form Thirty-Seven:	Warrant Agreement	883
Form Thirty-Eight:	Stock Option Agreement	901
Form Thirty-Nine:	Stock Redemption Agreement	905
Form Forty:	Certificate of Amendment of the Certificate of Incorporation	915
Form Forty-One:	Certificate of Change	917
Form Forty-Two:	Materials to Dissolve and Liquidate the Closely Held New York Corporation	919
	a. Resolutions Adopted on Unanimous Written Consent of Shareholders	920
	b. Certificate of Dissolution	922
	c. Notice to Creditors and Claimants	924
	d. Internal Revenue Service Form 966	925
	e. Information and Instruction for Termination of Business Corporations (New York State Department of Taxation and Finance, Publication 110)	926
	f. Sample Petition for Judicial Dissolution Under BCL § 1104-a	954

FORM ONE

COMPARISON OF FORMS OF BUSINESS ORGANIZATION

	Proprietorship	Partnership	Limited Partnership	Corporation
Ease and cost of creation	Proprietorship is automatically created when there is one owner and no other form is selected.	Partnership is automatically created when there are two or more owners and no other form is selected.	Limited partnership is created by complying with state statute authorizing limited partnership form. Detailed documents must be filed with appropriate public officials. Publication required in New York.	Corporation is created by complying with state statute authorizing corporate form. Detailed documents must be filed with appropriate public officials.
Ease and cost of operation	Proprietorship operates under few legal restraints.	Partnership operates under few legal restraints. No requirement for written agreement, but it is useful to have one.	Limited partnership operates under more restrictions than partnership.	Operations are subject to substantial legal formality. For example, corporate minutes must be kept; meetings and elections must be held; franchise, share transfer, and other taxes must be paid; a registered office and agent must be maintained; and if the corporation does business

	Proprietorship	Partnership	Limited Partnership	Corporation
Extent of liability	Proprietor has unlimited personal liability for all business debts and obligations. Insurance can play an important role.	Partners have unlimited personal liability for all business debts and obligations. One partner can sign for the others.	General partners have unlimited personal liabilities for all business debts and obligations; limited partners' liability is limited to their investment in the business unless they participate in management and control.	in another state, it must qualify there as a foreign corporation. Corporate shareholders are liable only to the extent of their investment in the business, and may also participate in management if they are officers or directors of the corporation.
Management and control	Proprietor has exclusive right to manage the business.	Absent contrary agreement, all partners have equal voice in management. This can be cumbersome in large partnerships. No role for outside experts; the owners are the managers.	Control is vested in one or more general partners; limited partners may take advantage of management "safe harbors."	Centralized management is created when shareholders elect directors who appoint officers to manage business. Allows owners to retain "outside" managers.

FORMS AND MATERIALS 549

	Proprietorship	Partnership	Limited Partnership	Corporation
Continuity of existence	Proprietorship ceases when the proprietor dies or abandons the business.	Partnership is dissolved by death or withdrawal of a partner and a variety of other events, but continuity may be provided by agreement.	Partnership is dissolved by death or withdrawal of a partner and a variety of other events, but continuity may be provided by agreement.	A corporation, as a legal entity, possesses perpetual existence unless terminated in a manner prescribed by law.
Transferability of interest	Proprietor's interest is freely transferable.	Absent contrary agreement, partner may not transfer entire interest without consent of other partners. But, agreement can make them transferable. There may not be a market for partnership interests, however.	Transferability is similar to a partnership, but the partnership agreement may allow an assignee to become a full limited partner.	Ownership interests in a corporation, evidenced by shares of stock, may generally be freely sold, assigned, or otherwise transferred. Transferability may be restricted by agreement in close corporations.
Access to capital	Credit is available to the extent of the value of assets committed to business and the personal assets of the proprietor.	Credit is available to extent of value of assets committed to business and the personal assets of the partners. New equity investment requires	Limited partnership may attract additional equity by selling additional limited partnership interests without diluting control of general partners.	In a small corporation, credit availability is generally similar to a partnership. As a corporation grows in size, substantial corporate assets, a public market for

	Proprietorship	Partnership	Limited Partnership	Corporation
		admitting new partners which dilutes control.		its shares, free transferability of its securities, and predictable limited liability of investors facilitate corporate expansion through issuance of debt or equity securities without diluting control.
Income tax considerations	Proprietor's business income or loss combined with other income or loss and taxed on the proprietor's individual return.	Partnership pays no tax, but files an information return indicating each partner's proportionate share of profit or loss. Respective shares of income or loss are then included on each partner's individual return.	Tax treatment is similar to general partnership.	Corporation is an entity for tax purposes, leading to "double taxation." Its income is taxed to the corporation on a corporation tax return and again to the shareholders on their individual returns when later distributed as dividends. S Corporation status can alleviate double taxation problem.

FORM TWO

New York State
DEPARTMENT OF STATE
CORPORATIONS AND STATE RECORDS DIVISION
162 Washington Avenue
Albany, NY 12231

CORPORATION — CERTIFICATE OF ASSUMED NAME
(Pursuant to Section 130 General Business Law)

FEES: The Filing fee payable to the Secretary of State is $25.00 plus a $25.00 fee for each county listed in which business will be transacted under assumed name.

1. Corporation name ....
2. Law corporation formed under: ☐ Business ☐ Not-for-Profit ☐ Education ☐ Insurance

   ☐ Other (specify) ....

3. Assumed name ....

4. Principal place of business in New York State*
   No. and Street _____
   City _____ State _____ Zip Code _____ County _____

   * ☐ If none, check box and insert principal out-of-state address above.

5. Counties in which business will be conducted under assumed name.
   ☐ All counties
   ☐ If not all, circle which counties below

Albany	Chenango	Essex	Jefferson	New York City	Oneida	Putnam	Schuyler	Ulster
Allegany	Clinton	Franklin	Lewis	Bronx	Onondaga	Rensselaer	Seneca	Warren
Broome	Columbia	Fulton	Livingston	Kings	Ontario	Rockland	Steuben	Washington
Cattaraugus	Cortland	Genesee	Madison	New York	Orange	St. Lawrence	Suffolk	Wayne
Cayuga	Delaware	Greene	Monroe	Queens	Orleans	Saratoga	Sullivan	Westchester
Chautauqua	Dutchess	Hamilton	Montgomery	Richmond	Oswego	Schenectady	Tioga	Wyoming
Chemung	Erie	Herkimer	Nassau	Niagara	Otsego	Schoharie	Tompkins	Yates

6. The addresses of each location within New York State where business is or will be conducted under assumed name — list on reverse side. If no business locations in New York State, check box ☐

   Corporation officer signature ....
   Type name and office ....

ACKNOWLEDGMENT (Must be completed)

State of .... County of .... ss.:
On .... 19...... before me personally came ....
to me known, who being by me duly sworn, did depose and say that he/she is the ....
of ...., the corporation described in the foregoing certificate, and acknowledged that he/she executed the same by order of the Board of Directors of such corporation.

....

Filer's name ....
For Department of State use only
Date filed ....

Filer's address ....
No. and Street _____ City _____ State _____ Zip Code

7. Addresses or business locations:

No. and Street		No. and Street	
City	State	City	State
Zip Code	County	Zip Code	County
No. and Street		No. and Street	
City	State	City	State
Zip Code	County	Zip Code	County
No. and Street		No. and Street	
City	State	City	State
Zip Code	County	Zip Code	County
No. and Street		No. and Street	
City	State	City	State
Zip Code	County	Zip Code	County
No. and Street		No. and Street	
City	State	City	State
Zip Code	County	Zip Code	County
No. and Street		No. and Street	
City	State	City	State
Zip Code	County	Zip Code	County

Use continuation sheet if necessary
Do not use space below.

FORM THREE

AGREEMENT TO FORM A CORPORATION
(PRE-INCORPORATION AGREEMENT)

AGREEMENT, dated as of this ____ day of ____, 19____ between _____, a ____ corporation located at _____, _____ (herein called "Company A"), and _____, a _____ corporation with its registered office located at ____, ____ (herein called "Company B").

WITNESSETH:

WHEREAS, Company A and Company B (herein collectively called the "Stockholders") desire to form a corporation to engage from time to time in ventures in the ____ industry of mutual interest to both corporations;

NOW, THEREFORE, the parties hereto hereby agree as follows:

1. Formation of Corporation

Company A and Company B shall forthwith cause a corporation to be formed pursuant to the laws of the State of ____, to be known as [New Company] (herein called "Newco"). Promptly after the incorporation of Newco, the parties shall also cause Newco to become qualified to do business in the State of ____.

2. Articles of Incorporation; By-laws

The Articles of Incorporation and the By-laws of Newco shall be substantially the same as the forms thereof annexed hereto and made a part hereof as Exhibits A and B, respectively.

3. Capitalization and Issuance of Shares

(a) *Capitalization*. The capital stock of Newco shall consist of ____ shares of Common Stock, par value $____ (U.S.) per share, subdivided into two classes, each consisting of 100 shares and being designated, respectively, "Class A Common Stock" and "Class B Common Stock." The two classes of Common Stock shall be equal in all respects, including, without limitation, voting powers, rights in respect of dividends and rights upon liquidation or dissolution, except that the two classes shall have separate voting rights with respect to the election of Newco's directors as described in Paragraph 4 below.

(b) *Issuance of Shares*. Within ten days after the incorporation of Newco, a closing shall take place at _____, at which closing Newco shall issue and sell to each of the Stockholders and each of the Stockholders shall purchase from Newco the number of shares of Common Stock set forth opposite the name of such Stockholder below, for the aggregate purchase price set forth after the name of such Stockholder:

Stockholder	Shares	Aggregate Purchase Price
Company A	____ of Class A Common Stock	$____
Company B	____ of Class B Common Stock	$____

The Certificates evidencing the Common Stock shall be registered in the name of the respective Stockholder and duly executed on behalf of Newco. Payment of the purchase price for the Common Stock shall be made by each Stockholder by the delivery to Newco at such closing of a certified or bank check, payable to the order of Newco, in the respective amount set forth above.

(c) *Use of Proceeds*. Newco shall use the proceeds from the sale of its Common Stock to pay for the costs and expenses incurred in connection with its incorporation and the preparation of this Agreement. The balance of such proceeds shall be used to defray operating expenses of Newco during the initial period of its operation, as determined from time to time by the Board of Directors.

4. Management of Newco

(a) *Board of Directors*. The Board of Directors shall consist of six members, three elected only by the holders of the Class A Common Stock ("Class A Directors") and three elected only by the holders of the Class B Common Stock ("Class B Directors"). The Articles of Incorporation shall provide that a quorum of the Board shall be deemed to exist only if at least one Class A Director and one Class B Director are present, and that no action may be taken by the Board at any meeting at which a quorum is present unless both (i) a majority of directors present have voted in favor of such action and (ii) at least one Class A Director and one Class B Director shall have voted in favor of such action. The initial Class A Directors and Class B Directors shall be as follows:

Class A Directors	Class B Directors

(b) *Officers*. At the first meeting of the Board of Directors of Newco, which shall take place on the date of the closing described in Paragraph 3(b) hereof, the Class A Directors shall have the right to elect the Chairman of the Board and the Class B Directors shall have the right to elect the President. On each anniversary of such first meeting, an organizational meeting of the Board of Directors shall be called at which the Class A Directors shall have the right to elect a person to the office to which the Class B Directors had, at the previous organizational meeting of the Board, the right to elect their designee, and the Class B Directors shall have the right to elect a person to the office to which the Class A Directors had, at the previous organizational meeting, the right to elect their designee. Vice Presidents, a Secretary, a Treasurer and one or more Assistant Treasurers and Assistant Secretaries may be elected from time to time by the Board of Directors of Newco. The compensation of the officers and directors of Newco shall be established by the Board of Directors from time to time.

5. Corporate Financial Matters

(a) *Loans*. From time to time, upon the request of the Board of Directors of Newco, Company A and Company B shall lend to Newco such amounts as may be so requested. Of such amounts requested, Company A shall lend 50 percent and Company B shall lend 50 percent. At the time any such amount is requested to be loaned, neither Company A nor Company B shall have any obligation to make any such loan unless the other party shall simultaneously make the requested loan. Any loans made at the same time in accordance with the foregoing by both Company A and Company B shall be on the same terms and conditions, bear interest at the same rate and be repaid at the same time to Company A and Company B in the same percentage of the respective amounts so loaned. Repayments shall be applied against the oldest loans existing at the time.

(b) *Guarantees*. In the event that, from time to time, either Company A or Company B guarantees any of the obligations of Newco, Newco shall pay such Stockholder a guarantee fee, payable monthly, calculated at the rate of ____% per annum on the average amount of the loans guaranteed by such Stockholder outstanding during such month.

(c) *Fiscal Year*. The fiscal year of Newco shall commence on ____ and end on ____.

(d) *Dividends*. Each year, promptly after the delivery to the Board of Directors of the annual certified financial statements of Newco, a meeting of the Board of Directors shall be called and duly held. At such meeting the Board of Directors shall, to the extent legally permissible, declare a dividend with respect to the Common Stock in an amount not less than ____ percent of the net income after taxes of Newco as shown on such annual financial statements. Such dividend shall be payable in one installment within 30 days from the receipt of such annual financial statements.

6. Transfers of Stock

(a) No Stockholder shall sell, dispose of, encumber or otherwise transfer shares of Common Stock except as herein provided.

(b) At any time and upon notice to Newco and the other Stockholder, a Stockholder ("Transferor") may cause Newco to purchase all the shares of Common Stock it then owns at the price provided in subpara-

FORMS AND MATERIALS 557

graph (c) hereof and in the manner provided in subparagraph (d) below; *provided, however,* that should the other Stockholder elect, upon receipt of such notice, to dissolve Newco, he shall notify Newco and the Transferor of such election not later than fifteen days after the giving of notice by the Transferor, and thereafter, Newco shall be promptly dissolved pursuant to the laws of the State of [state of incorporation].

(c) The purchase price to be paid to the Transferor for its shares of Common Stock shall be as follows:

(i) in the event the Transferor's notice is given prior to the completion of the first fiscal year of Newco, the purchase price per share shall equal $____;

(ii) in the event the Transferor's notice is given on or before the completion of the fifth fiscal year of Newco but after the first fiscal year, the purchase price per share shall equal the Book Value per share as of the end of the fiscal year immediately preceding the date of such notice less the amount or value of all dividends and distributions with respect to the Common Stock declared after the end of such fiscal year and payable to Stockholders of record as of a date before the closing of such purchase; and

(iii) in the event the Transferor's notice is given after the completion of the fifth fiscal year of Newco, the purchase price per share shall equal the greater of (x) the average net income per share of Newco for the preceding two fiscal years as shown on the certified financial statements of Newco multiplied by 5 or (y) the book value per share of Newco at the end of the fiscal year immediately preceding the date for the giving of the Transferor's notice less the amount or value of all dividends and distributions with respect to the Common Stock declared after the end of such fiscal year and payable to Stockholders of record as of a date before the closing of such purchase.

(d) The closing of the purchase of the Transferor's shares hereunder shall occur no later than 30 days after the giving of the Transferor's notice, unless the Board of Directors has not yet received the annual financial statements of Newco for the fiscal year immediately preceding the date of the Transferor's notice in which case the closing shall occur on or before 30 days after the date of such receipt. The closing shall take place at ____. At the closing, Newco shall pay the Transferor an amount equal to the purchase price per share times the number of shares then owned by the Transferor by certified check. The Transferor shall deliver to Newco certificates evidencing all the shares of Common Stock owned by it, free and clear of any encumbrances, duly endorsed in blank, with all requisite transfer tax stamps annexed thereto together with the registrations and releases of those directors elected by the Transferor and those officers elected by such directors.

(e) "Book Value" for purposes of this Agreement shall be determined solely by the independent certified public accountants of Newco in accordance with generally accepted accounting principles as applied in the United States and shall mean the Stockholders' equity per share appearing in the annual financial statements of Newco as prepared by such independent certified public accountants of Newco, *less* the value per share given in such financial statements to any intangibles, including, without limitation, goodwill, organizational expenses, patents, trademarks, copyrights, trade names, trade secrets and leaseholds (other than leasehold improvements). The terms "net income" and "net income after taxes" shall mean the amounts for such items set forth in such annual financial statements. All determinations by such accountants shall be binding upon the Stockholders.

7. Stockholder Representations

Each Stockholder represents to the other that:

(a) It is a corporation duly organized, validly existing and in good standing under the laws of the jurisdiction in which it is incorporated and has all requisite corporate power and authority to enter into this Agreement and to consummate the transactions contemplated hereby.

(b) Neither the execution nor delivery of this Agreement, nor the carrying out of the transactions contemplated hereby, will result in any violation of any contract or instrument to which such Stockholder is a party or by which it is bound.

FORMS AND MATERIALS 559

8. Notices

Any communication required or permitted hereunder shall be in writing and deemed effectively given, upon delivery, when delivered personally, or on the third business day after mailing, if mailed registered mail, postage prepaid, and properly addressed to the party to be notified at the following address:

(a) To Company A:

(b) To Company B:

9. Execution of Counterparts

This Agreement may be simultaneously executed in any number of counterparts and such counterparts shall together constitute one and the same instrument.

10. Amendment

This Agreement shall not be modified, changed, altered, terminated or cancelled except by an instrument in writing, executed by all of the parties hereto.

11. Share Certificate Legend

All certificates for shares issued to the Stockholders shall be endorsed with the following legend:

"Ownership and transfer of the shares represented by this Certificate are subject to an agreement among Newco and the Stockholders thereof, dated as of _____, 19_____, a copy of which is on file with the Secretary of Newco."

12. Company to Become a Party

The Stockholders will cause Newco to become a party to this Agreement upon its incorporation.

13. Law to Govern

This Agreement shall be governed by, construed and enforced in accordance with the laws of the State of New York.

IN WITNESS WHEREOF, the parties hereto have duly executed this Agreement as of the day hereinbefore written.

                        COMPANY A

                        By_____

                        COMPANY B

                        By_____

FORM FOUR

APPLICATION FOR RESERVATION OF NAME UNDER SECTION 303 OF THE BUSINESS CORPORATION LAW

THE NAME AND ADDRESS OF THE APPLICANT ARE:

_____

_____

_____

THE NAME TO BE RESERVED IS:_____

THE RESERVATION IS INTENDED FOR:

(Check one)   ( )   a new domestic corporation

                       ( )   a foreign corporation intending to apply for authority to do business in New York*

                       ( )   a change of name of an existing domestic or an authorized foreign corporation*

                       ( )   a foreign corporation intending to apply for authority to do business in New York whose corporate name is not available for use in New York*

                       ( )   an authorized foreign corporation intending to change its fictitious name under which it does business in this state*

---

* The foreign corporation must be the applicant.

_____

( ) an authorized foreign corporation which has changed its corporate name in its jurisdiction, such new corporate name not being available for use in New York*

[Signature of applicant, his attorney or agent] (If attorney or agent, so specify)

By:_____

---
* The foreign corporation must be the applicant.

FORM FOUR(a)

NEW YORK SECRETARY OF STATE GUIDELINES FOR CORPORATE NAMES

PART 147
AVAILABILITY OF NAMES

Section 147.1 Standards—conflict of names. A proposed corporation name shall be rejected as not being distinguishable from the name of an existing domestic or foreign corporation, a fictitious name or a reserved name if the only significant difference between the proposed name and the existing or reserved name is one or more of the following:

(a) a change in tense, reference to singular as opposed to plural, hyphenation of words, or the addition or omission of prepositions or contractions;

(b) the spelling of a word, including abbreviations, that has the same meaning in both spellings, or the reversal of words or phrases;

(c) the inclusion or omission of a letter or letters, number or numbers, whether in arabic, roman numeral form or spelled out, other than any series thereof which may be viewed to represent the distinctive word of the name;

(d) the addition or deletion of the word *company*;

(e) a change in the word indicating corporate status.

147.2 Distinguishability. For the purposes of determining availability of name, a name shall not be considered distinguishing when the only difference(s) from the existing word(s) is/are a change in tense, a change in phonetic spelling, an abbreviation versus a spelling out, or any other deviation from or derivative of the same base word(s).

147.3 Reconsideration procedure. An applicant may request reconsideration of any rejection of a proposed name, upon written request addressed to the Secretary, attention the Director of the Division of Corporations and State Records, at 162 Washington Avenue, Albany, N.Y. 12231. The applicant shall attach to his request a copy of the written determination made rejecting the name, and shall include a statement of the reasons upon which the applicant seeks approval of the name. The applicant may include materials in support of the request for approval.

147.4 Applicability. The provisions of this Part shall be applicable to business and not-for-profit corporations, including foreign corporations seeking authority to do business or engage in activities in this State.

PART 148

FICTITIOUS NAMES

Section 148.1 Statement of fictitious name. Every foreign corporation qualifying to do business in this State shall include a statement in its application for authority, or amendment thereto: "The fictitious name under which the corporation shall conduct its business or activities in New York is ....," or words to such effect.

148.2 Filing an assumed name certificate. A foreign corporation authorized to do business or conduct activities in this State, under a fictitious name, may file a certificate of assumed name pursuant to section 130 of the General Business Law. In the certificate of assumed name, the corporation shall set forth its true corporate name and its fictitious name under which it conducts its business or activities in this State.

148.3 Discontinuance of a fictitious name. When a foreign corporation is authorized to do business or conduct activities under a fictitious name and files a certificate of amendment changing its true corporate name to a name which is available in New York, it must discontinue use of the fictitious name in New York State. The certificate of amendment must contain a statement: "The fictitious name of ...., under which the corporation has conducted its business or activities, is discontinued," or similar words to that effect, combined with a statement deleting the appropriate paragraph or section from the original application for authority or original application as amended.

PART 149

EXAMINATION OF CERTIFICATES

Section 149.1 Pre-examination of draft documents. When an attorney is uncertain as to the correct form of a certificate or its contents and desires assistance to avoid rejection, he may submit a draft to the Department of State for pre-examination. An attorney in the Corporations Bureau will examine such a draft after the conclusion of his regular duties and advise the correspondent as to its acceptability for filing or the reasons why certificate in the form presented could not be filed.

149.2 Correction of executed documents prohibited. Attorneys in the division examining executed documents offered for filing cannot under law make any alterations or add omissions no matter how obvious the intent might have been or insignificant the change might be. Such documents will be returned with a statement of the reasons therefor.

149.3 Clarity of documents. Documents offered for filing must be clear executed copies and must not contain numerous deletions or marginal notations. Any document executed or altered by pencil will not be filed.

FORM FIVE

CERTIFICATE OF INCORPORATION OF [CORPORATION] UNDER SECTION 402 OF THE BUSINESS CORPORATION LAW

I, [NAME OF INCORPORATOR], being of the age of eighteen years or over, for the purpose of forming a corporation pursuant to Section 402 of the Business Corporation Law of New York, do hereby certify:

1. The name of the corporation is [NAME OF CORPORATION].

2. The purposes for which it is formed are:

To purchase, receive, take by grant, gift, devise, bequest or otherwise, lease or otherwise acquire, own, hold, improve, employ, use and otherwise deal in and with real or personal property, or any interest therein, wherever situated; and

To have and to exercise all rights and powers that are now or may hereafter be granted to a corporation by law.

The foregoing shall be construed as objects, purposes and powers, and the enumeration thereof shall not be held to limit or restrict in any manner the powers now or hereafter conferred on this corporation by the laws of the State of New York. The objects and powers specified herein shall, except as otherwise expressed, be in no way limited or restricted by reference to or inference from the terms of any other clause or paragraph of these articles. The objects, purposes, and powers specified in each of the clauses or paragraphs of this Certificate of Incorporation shall be regarded as independent objects, purposes, or powers.

3. The office of the corporation is to be located in the City of ____, County of ____, State of New York.

4. The aggregate number of shares of stock which the corporation shall have the authority to issue is ____ (____) shares of Common Stock, each of which shall have a par value of ____ Dollars ($____) per share.

5. The Secretary of State is designated as the agent of the corporation upon whom process against the corporation may be served. The post office address to which the Secretary of State shall mail a copy of any process against the corporation served upon him is: _____
_____.

6. The name and address of the registered agent which is to be the agent of the corporation upon whom process against it may be served are: _____
_____

IN WITNESS WHEREOF, I have made and signed this certificate this ____ day of ____, 19____, and I affirm the statements contained herein as true under penalties of perjury.

_____
[Name and Home or Business Address of Incorporator]

FORM OF NOTARIZATION

STATE OF _____)
                   : ss.:
COUNTY OF ___)

    On this ____ day of ____, 19____, before me personally came [NAME OF INCORPORATOR], to me personally known, who, being by me duly sworn, did depose and say that (s)he resides at [HOME ADDRESS OF INCORPORATOR]; that (s)he is the individual who executed the within instrument; and that (s)he signed [his] [her] name thereto.

                                                                _____
                                                                        Notary Public

FORM SIX

CHECKLIST OF PROVISIONS TO CONSIDER FOR INCLUSION IN CERTIFICATE OF INCORPORATION*

The certificate of incorporation may include any provision which is not inconsistent with New York law. The following provisions are valid only if they are included in the certificate of incorporation. (See Form Eight for provisions regarding corporate management that may be included in either the certificate of incorporation or the by-laws.)

BCL Section

202(a)	limiting corporate power
501(a), 502(a), 512(a), 519	authorizing more than one class of stock, or series of stock with different rights and preferences, including redeemable securities and convertible securities
402(b)	limiting liability of directors
504(d)	reserving to shareholders the right to fix consideration for shares without par value
505	limiting or defining the issuance of rights and options to purchase shares
510	restrictions on dividends

* SOURCE: *Fall 1991 Practical Skills: Forming and Advising Businesses* (NYSBA), "Forming and Managing the Closely Held Business Corporation," Suzanne M. Warshavsky, Esq., Warshavsky, Hoffman & Cohen, P.C.

515	requiring cancellation of reacquired shares
518(c)	conferring stockholder rights upon holders of corporate debt
612 and 613	provisions concerning shareholder voting rights
615	permitting written consent in lieu of meeting by less than all the shareholders, or denying right to act by written consent
616	super majority for shareholder quorum or vote
617 and 703(a)	authorizing class voting
618	cumulative voting
620(b)	provisions removing management from directors
622	denial or change of preemptive rights
709	super majority for quorum or vote of directors
713(d)	additional restrictions on transactions between the corporation and its directors
715(b)	election of officers by shareholders instead of by directors
911	requiring shareholder consent to mortgage or pledge of corporate property
912(d)	elections regarding applicability of take-over statute
1002	shareholder right to require dissolution at will or upon the happening of stated events
1104	limiting right of shareholders to require dissolution in case of deadlock

FORM SEVEN

SAMPLE BY-LAWS

ARTICLE I

OFFICES

Section 1. The office of the Corporation shall be located in the City of ____, in the County of _____, in the State of New York.

Section 2. The Corporation may also have offices at such other places both within and without the State of New York as the board of directors may from time to time determine or the business of the Corporation may require.

ARTICLE II

ANNUAL MEETINGS OF SHAREHOLDERS

Section 1. All meetings of shareholders for the election of directors shall be held in such City, County and State and at such time and place as may be fixed from time to time by the board of directors and set forth in the notice of such meeting.

Section 2. Annual meetings of shareholders shall be held on the third Friday in ____ of each year if not a legal holiday, and if a legal holiday, then on the next business day following at which they shall elect by a plurality vote a board of directors, and transact such other business as may properly be brought before the meeting.

Section 3. Written or printed notice of the annual meeting stating the place, date and hour of the meeting shall be delivered not less than ten nor more than fifty days before the date of the meeting, either personally or by mail, by or at the direction of the president, the secretary, or the officer or persons calling the meeting, to each shareholder of record entitled to vote at such meeting.

ARTICLE III

SPECIAL MEETINGS OF SHAREHOLDERS

Section 1. Special meetings of shareholders may be held at such time and place within or without the State of New York as shall be stated in the notice of the meeting or in a duly executed waiver of notice thereof.

Section 2. Special meetings of shareholders, for any purpose or purposes, unless otherwise prescribed by statute or by the certificate of incorporation, may be called by the president, the board of directors, or the holders of not less than a majority of all the shares entitled to vote at the meeting.

Section 3. Written or printed notice of a special meeting stating the place, date and hour of the meeting and the purpose or purposes for which the meeting is called shall be delivered not less than ten nor more than fifty days before the date of the meeting, either personally or by mail, by, or at the direction of, the president, the board or, if the special meeting is called by holders of not less than a majority of all the shares entitled to vote at the special meeting, the secretary, to each shareholder of record entitled to vote at such meeting. The notice should also indicate that it is being issued by, or at the direction of, the person calling the meeting.

Section 4. The business transacted at any special meeting of shareholders shall be limited to the purposes stated in the notice.

ARTICLE IV

QUORUM AND VOTING OF STOCK

Section 1. The holders of a majority of the shares of stock issued and outstanding and entitled to vote, represented in person or by proxy, shall constitute a quorum at all meetings of the shareholders for the transac-

FORMS AND MATERIALS

tion of business except as otherwise provided by statute or by the certificate of incorporation. If, however, such quorum shall not be present or represented at any meeting of the shareholders, the shareholders present in person or represented by proxy shall have power to adjourn the meeting from time to time, without notice other than announcement at the meeting, until a quorum shall be present or represented. At such adjourned meeting at which a quorum shall be present or represented, any business may be transacted which might have been transacted at the meeting as originally notified.

Section 2. If a quorum is present, the affirmative vote of a majority of the shares of stock represented at the meeting shall be the act of the shareholders, unless the vote of a greater or lesser number of shares of stock is required by law or the certificate of incorporation.

Section 3. Each outstanding share of stock having voting power shall be entitled to one vote on each matter submitted to vote at a meeting of shareholders. A shareholder may vote either in person or by proxy executed in writing by the shareholder or by his duly authorized attorney-in-fact.

Section 4. The board of directors in advance of any shareholders' meeting may appoint one or more inspectors to act at the meeting or any adjournment thereof. If inspectors are not so appointed, the person presiding at a shareholders' meeting may, and, on the request of any shareholder entitled to vote thereat, shall, appoint one or more inspectors. In case any person appointed as inspector fails to appear or act, the vacancy may be filled by the board in advance of the meeting or at the meeting by the person presiding thereat. Each inspector, before entering upon the discharge of his duties, shall take and sign an oath faithfully to execute the duties of inspector at such meeting with strict impartiality and according to the best of his ability.

Section 5. Whenever shareholders are required or permitted to take any action by vote, such action may be taken without a meeting on written consent, setting forth the action so taken, signed by the holders of all outstanding shares entitled to vote thereon.

ARTICLE V
DIRECTORS

Section 1. The number of directors shall be ____ (____), which number may be increased or decreased by amendment of these by-laws. Each director shall be at least eighteen years of age. The directors need not be residents of the State of New York nor shareholders of the Corporation. The directors, other than the first board of directors, shall be elected at the annual meeting of the shareholders, except as hereinafter provided, and each director elected shall serve until the next succeeding annual meeting or until his successor shall have been elected and qualified. The first board of directors shall hold office until the first meeting of shareholders.

Section 2. Any or all of the directors may be removed, with or without cause, at any time by the vote of the shareholders at a special meeting called for that purpose.

Any director may be removed for cause by the action of the directors at a special meeting called for that purpose.

Section 3. Unless otherwise provided in the certificate of incorporation, newly created directorships resulting from an increase in the board of directors and all vacancies occurring in the board of directors, including vacancies caused by removal without cause, may be filled by the affirmative vote of a majority of the board of directors; however, if the number of directors then in office is less than a quorum, then such newly created directorships and vacancies may be filled by a vote of a majority of the directors then in office. A director elected to fill a vacancy shall hold office until the next meeting of shareholders at which election of directors is the regular order of business, and until his successor shall have been elected and qualified. A director elected to fill a newly created directorship shall serve until the next succeeding annual meeting of shareholders and until his successor shall have been elected and qualified.

Section 4. The business affairs of the Corporation shall be managed by its board of directors, which may exercise all such powers of the

Corporation and do all such lawful acts and things as are not by statute or by the certificate of incorporation or by these by-laws directed or required to be exercised or done by the shareholders.

Section 5. The directors may keep the books of the Corporation, except such as are required by law to be kept within the State of New York, at such place or places as they may from time to time determine.

Section 6. The board of directors, by the affirmative vote of a majority of the directors then in office, and irrespective of any personal interest of any of its members, shall have authority to establish reasonable compensation of all directors for services to the Corporation as directors, officers or otherwise.

ARTICLE VI

MEETINGS OF THE BOARD OF DIRECTORS

Section 1. Meetings of the board of directors, regular or special, may be held either within or without the State of New York.

Section 2. The first meeting of each newly elected board of directors shall be held at such time and place as shall be fixed by the vote of the shareholders at the annual meeting and no notice of such meeting shall be necessary to the newly elected directors in order legally to constitute the meeting, provided a quorum shall be present, or it may convene at such place and time as shall be fixed by the consent in writing of all the directors.

Section 3. Regular meetings of the board of directors may be held upon such notice, or without notice, and at such time and at such place as shall from time to time be determined by the board of directors.

Section 4. Special meetings of the board of directors may be called by the chairman of the board of directors or by the president or by any two directors at any time. Notice of any special meeting shall be mailed to each director addressed to him at his residence or usual place of business at least two days before the day on which the meeting is to be held, or if sent to him at such place by telegraph or cable, or delivered personally or by telephone, not later than the day before the day on which the meeting is to be held.

Section 5. Notice of a meeting need not be given to any director who submits a signed waiver of notice whether before or after the meeting, or who attends the meeting without protesting, prior thereto or at its commencement, the lack of notice. Neither the business to be transacted at, nor the purpose of, any regular or special meeting of the board of directors need be specified in the notice or waiver of notice of such meeting.

Section 6. A majority of the directors shall constitute a quorum for the transaction of business unless a greater or lesser number is required by law or by the certificate of incorporation. The vote of a majority of the directors present at any meeting at which a quorum is present shall be the act of the board of directors, unless the vote of a greater number is required by law or by the certificate of incorporation. If a quorum shall not be present at any meeting of directors, the directors present may adjourn the meeting from time to time, without notice other than announcement at the meeting, until a quorum shall be present.

Section 7. Unless the certificate of incorporation provides otherwise, any action required or permitted to be taken at a meeting of the directors or a committee thereof may be taken without a meeting if a consent in writing to the adoption of a resolution authorizing the action so taken shall be signed by all of the directors entitled to vote with respect to the subject matter thereof.

Section 8. Unless otherwise restricted by the certificate of incorporation or these by-laws, members of the board of directors, or any committee designated by the board of directors, may participate in a meeting of the board of directors, or any committee, by means of conference telephone or similar communications equipment by means of which all persons participating in the meeting can hear each other, and such participation in a meeting shall constitute presence in person at the meeting.

ARTICLE VII

EXECUTIVE COMMITTEE

Section 1. The board of directors, by resolution adopted by a majority of the entire board, may designate, from among its members, an executive committee and other committees, each consisting of three or more directors, and each of which, to the extent provided in the resolution, shall have all the authority of the board, except as otherwise required by law. Vacancies in the membership of the committee shall be filled by the board of directors at a regular or special meeting of the board of directors.

Section 2. Any member of a committee may resign at any time. Such resignation shall be made in writing and shall take effect at the time specified therein, or, if no time be specified, at the time of its receipt by the president or secretary. The acceptance of a resignation shall not be necessary to make it effective unless so specified therein.

Section 3. A majority of the members of a committee shall constitute a quorum. The act of a majority of the members of a committee present at any meeting at which a quorum is present shall be the act of such committee. The members of a committee shall act only as a committee, and the individual members thereof shall have no powers as such.

Section 4. Each committee shall keep a record of its acts and proceedings, and shall report the same to the board of directors when and as required by the board of directors.

Section 5. A committee may hold its meetings at the principal office of the Corporation, or at any other place which a majority of the committee may at any time agree upon. Each committee may make such rules as it may deem expedient for the regulation and carrying on of its meetings and proceedings. Unless otherwise ordered by the executive committee, any notice of a meeting of such committee may be given by the secretary or by the chairman of the committee and shall be sufficiently given if mailed to each member at his residence or usual place of business at least two days before the day on which the meeting is to be held or if sent to him at such place by telegraph or cable, or delivered personally or by telephone, not later than 24 hours prior to the time at which the meeting is to be held.

Section 6. The members of any committee shall be entitled to such compensation as may be allowed them by resolution of the board of directors.

ARTICLE VIII

NOTICES

Section 1. Whenever, by law or by the provisions of the certificate of incorporation or of these by-laws, notice is required to be given to any director or shareholder, it shall not be construed to mean personal notice, but such notice may be given in writing, by mail, addressed to such director or shareholder, at his address as it appears on the records of the Corporation, with postage thereon prepaid, and such notice shall be deemed to be given at the time when the same shall be deposited in the United States mail. Notice to directors may also be given by telegram.

Section 2. Whenever any notice of a meeting is required to be given by law or by the provisions of the certificate of incorporation or these by-laws, a waiver thereof in writing signed by the person or persons entitled to such notice, whether before or after the time stated therein, shall be deemed equivalent to the giving of such notice.

ARTICLE IX

OFFICERS

Section 1. The officers of the Corporation shall be chosen by the board of directors and shall be a president, a vice president, a secretary and a treasurer, and such other officers, as may be appointed in accordance with the provisions of Section 3 of this Article IX. The board of directors in its discretion may also elect a chairman of the board of directors. The board of directors may also choose one or more additional vice presidents, and one or more assistant secretaries and assistant treasurers.

Section 2. The board of directors at its first meeting after each annual meeting of shareholders shall choose a president, a vice president, a secretary and a treasurer, none of whom need be a member of the board.

Any two or more offices may be held by the same person, except the offices of president and secretary. When all the issued and outstanding stock of the Corporation is owned by one person, such person may hold all or any combination of offices.

Section 3. The board of directors may appoint such other officers and agents as it shall deem necessary who shall hold their offices for such terms and shall exercise such powers and perform such duties as shall be determined from time to time by the board of directors.

Section 4. The salaries of all officers and agents of the Corporation shall be fixed by the board of directors.

Section 5. The officers of the Corporation shall hold office until their successors are chosen and qualify. Any officer elected or appointed by the board of directors may be removed at any time by the affirmative vote of a majority of the board of directors. Any vacancy occurring in any office of the Corporation shall be filled by the board of directors.

CHAIRMAN OF THE BOARD OF DIRECTORS

Section 6. The chairman of the board of directors shall be a director and shall preside at all meetings of the board of directors at which he shall be present and shall have such power and perform such duties as may from time to time be assigned to him by the board of directors.

THE PRESIDENT

Section 7. The president shall be the chief executive officer of the Corporation, shall preside at all meetings of the shareholders and, in the absence of the chairman of the board of directors, shall have general and active management of the business of the Corporation and shall see that all orders and resolutions of the board of directors are carried into effect.

He shall have the power to call special meetings of the stockholders or of the board of directors or of the executive committee at any time.

Section 8. He shall execute bonds, mortgages and other contracts requiring a seal under the seal of the Corporation, except where required or permitted by law to be otherwise signed and executed and except where the signing and execution thereof shall be expressly delegated by the board of directors to some other officer or agent of the Corporation.

THE VICE PRESIDENTS

Section 9. The vice president or, if there shall be more than one, the vice presidents in the order determined by the board of directors shall, in the absence or disability of the president, perform the duties and exercise the powers of the president and shall perform such other duties and have such other powers as the board of directors may from time to time prescribe.

THE SECRETARY AND ASSISTANT SECRETARIES

Section 10. The secretary shall attend all meetings of the board of directors and all meetings of the shareholders and record all the proceedings of the meetings of the Corporation and of the board of directors in a book to be kept for that purpose and shall perform like duties for the standing committees when required. He shall give, or cause to be given, notice of all meetings of the shareholders and special meetings of the board of directors, and shall perform such other duties as may be prescribed by the board of directors or the president, under whose supervision he shall be. He shall have custody of the corporate seal of the Corporation, if any, and he shall have authority to affix the same to any instrument requiring it and, when so affixed, it may be attested by his signature. The board of directors may give general authority to any other officer to affix the seal of the Corporation and to attest the affixing by his signature.

Section 11. The assistant secretary or, if there be more than one, the assistant secretaries in the order determined by the board of directors shall, in the absence or disability of the secretary, perform the duties and exercise the powers of the secretary and shall perform such other duties and have such other powers as the board of directors may from time to time prescribe.

THE TREASURER AND ASSISTANT TREASURERS

Section 12. The treasurer shall have the custody of the corporate funds and securities and shall keep full and accurate accounts of receipts and disbursements in books belonging to the Corporation and shall deposit all moneys and other valuable effects in the name and to the credit of the Corporation in such depositories as may be designated by the board of directors.

Section 13. He shall disburse the funds of the Corporation as may be ordered by the board of directors, taking proper vouchers for such disbursements, and shall render to the president and the board of directors at its regular meetings, or when the board of directors so requires, an account of all his transactions as treasurer and of the financial condition of the Corporation.

Section 14. If required by the board of directors, he shall give the Corporation a bond in such sum and with such surety or sureties as shall be satisfactory to the board of directors for the faithful performance of the duties of his office and for the restoration to the Corporation, in case of his death, resignation, retirement or removal from office, of all books, papers, vouchers, money and other property of whatever kind in his possession or under his control belonging to the Corporation.

Section 15. The assistant treasurer or, if there shall be more than one, the assistant treasurers in the order determined by the board of directors shall, in the absence or disability of the treasurer, perform the duties and exercise the powers of the treasurer and shall perform such other duties and have such other powers as the board of directors may from time to time prescribe.

ARTICLE X
CERTIFICATES FOR SHARES

Section 1. The shares of the Corporation shall be represented by certificates signed by the chairman or the president or a vice president and the secretary or an assistant secretary or the treasurer or an assistant treasurer of the Corporation and may be sealed with the seal of the Corporation or a facsimile thereof.

When the Corporation is authorized to issue more than one class of shares, there shall be set forth upon the face or back of the certificate, or the certificate shall have a statement, that the Corporation will furnish to any shareholder upon request and without charge, a full statement of the designation, relative rights, preferences and limitations of the shares of each class of stock which the Corporation is authorized to issue.

Section 2. The signatures of the officers of the Corporation upon a certificate may be facsimiles if the certificate is countersigned by a transfer agent or registered by a registrar other than the Corporation itself or an employee of the Corporation. In case any officer who has signed or whose facsimile signature has been placed upon a certificate shall have ceased to be such officer before such certificate is issued, it may be issued by the Corporation with the same effect as if he were such officer at the date of issue.

LOST CERTIFICATES

Section 3. The board of directors may direct a new certificate to be issued in place of any certificate theretofore issued by the Corporation alleged to have been lost or destroyed. When authorizing such issue of a new certificate, the board of directors, in its discretion and as a condition precedent to the issuance thereof, may prescribe such terms and conditions as it deems expedient, and may require such indemnities as it deems adequate, to protect the Corporation from any claim that may be made against it with respect to any such certificate alleged to have been lost or destroyed.

TRANSFER OF SHARES

Section 4. Upon surrender to the Corporation or the transfer agent of the Corporation of a certificate representing shares duly endorsed or accompanied by proper evidence of succession, assignment or authority to transfer, a new certificate shall be issued to the person entitled thereto, and the old certificate cancelled and the transaction recorded upon the books of the Corporation.

The board of directors may make other and further rules and regulations concerning the transfer and registration of certificates for stock and may appoint a transfer agent or registrar or both and may require all certificates of stock to bear the signature of either or both.

FIXING RECORD DATE

Section 5. For the purpose of determining shareholders entitled to notice of or to vote at any meeting of shareholders or any adjournment thereof, or to express consent to or dissent from any proposal without a meeting, or for the purpose of determining shareholders entitled to receive payment of any dividend or the allotment of any rights, or for the purpose of any other action, the board of directors may fix, in advance, a date as the record date for any such determination of shareholders. Such date shall not be more than fifty nor less than ten days before the date of any meeting nor more than fifty days prior to any other action. When a determination of shareholders of record entitled to notice of or to vote at any meeting of shareholders has been made as provided in this section, such determination shall apply to any adjournment thereof, unless the board fixes a new record date for the adjourned meeting.

REGISTERED SHAREHOLDERS

Section 6. The Corporation shall be entitled to recognize the exclusive right of a person registered on its books as the owner of shares to receive dividends, and to vote as such owner, and to hold liable for calls and assessments a person registered on its books as the owner of shares, and shall not be bound to recognize any equitable or other claim to or interest in such share or shares on the part of any other person, whether or not it shall have express or other notice thereof, except as otherwise provided by the laws of the State of New York.

LIST OF SHAREHOLDERS

Section 7. A list of shareholders as of the record date, certified by the corporate officer responsible for its preparation or by a transfer agent, shall be produced at any meeting upon the request thereat or prior thereto of any shareholder. If the right to vote at any meeting is challenged, the inspectors of election, or person presiding thereat, shall require such list of shareholders to be produced as evidence of the right of the persons challenged to vote at such meeting and all persons who appear from such list to be shareholders entitled to vote thereat may vote at such meeting.

ARTICLE XI

GENERAL PROVISIONS
DIVIDENDS

Section 1. Subject to the provisions of the certificate of incorporation relating thereto, if any, and to the laws of the State of New York, dividends may be declared by the board of directors at any regular or special meeting. Dividends may be paid in cash, in shares of the capital stock or in the Corporation's bonds or its property, including the shares or bonds of other corporations, subject to the laws of the State of New York and to the provisions of the certificate of incorporation.

Section 2. Before payment of any dividend, there may be set aside out of any funds of the Corporation available for dividends such sum or sums as the directors from time to time, in their absolute discretion, think proper as a reserve fund to meet contingencies, or for equalizing dividends, or for repairing or maintaining any property of the Corporation, or for such other purpose as the directors shall think conducive to the interest of the Corporation, and the directors may modify or abolish any such reserve in the manner in which it was created.

CHECKS

Section 3. All checks or demands for money and notes of the Corporation shall be signed by such officer or officers or such other person or persons as the board of directors may from time to time designate.

FISCAL YEAR

Section 4. The fiscal year of the Corporation shall be fixed by resolution of the board of directors.

ARTICLE XII

AMENDMENTS

Section 1. These by-laws may be amended or repealed or new by-laws may be adopted at any regular or special meeting of shareholders at which a quorum is present or represented, by the vote of the holders of shares entitled to vote in the election of any directors, provided notice of the proposed alteration, amendment or repeal be contained in the notice of such meeting. These by-laws may also be amended or repealed or new by-laws may be adopted by the affirmative vote of a majority of the board of directors at any regular or special meeting of the board. If any by-law regulating an impending election of directors is adopted, amended or repealed by the board, there shall be set forth in the notice of the next meeting of shareholders for the election of directors the by-law so adopted, amended or repealed, together with a precise statement of the changes made. By-laws adopted by the board of directors may be amended or repealed by the shareholders.

FORM EIGHT

CHECKLIST OF PROVISIONS VALID ONLY IF INCLUDED IN BY-LAWS OR CERTIFICATE OF INCORPORATION—NEW YORK

BCL Section	
*601(a)	Right of directors to adopt or amend by-laws
602(c)	Authorization of any person to call special meetings
608(b)	Fixing quorum of shareholders at less than a majority
701	Qualifications for directors
**702(b)	Authorizing directors to fix number of Board
*704	Classification of directors
*705(b)	Authorization of directors to fill vacancies on Board on account of removal of directors without cause
*706(a)	Authorizing Board to remove a director for cause (subject to certain exceptions)

* Not valid unless in charter or provision of by-laws adopted by shareholders.

** Not valid unless in by-laws adopted by shareholders.

706(b)	Authorizing shareholders to remove directors without cause
707	Fixing quorum of Board at less than a majority
708(c)	Authorizing Board action by telephone conference calls
710	Time and place of Board meetings
712(a)	Committees of Board
713(e)	Limiting authority of Board to fix compensation of directors
715(c)	Fixing terms of officers
721, 725	Provisions regarding indemnification

FORM NINE

STATEMENT OF INCORPORATOR IN LIEU OF ORGANIZATION MEETING OF [CORPORATION]

The certificate of incorporation of this corporation having been filed in the Department of State of the State of New York, the undersigned, being the incorporator named in said certificate, does hereby state that the following actions were taken on this day for the purpose of organizing this corporation:

1. By-laws for the regulation of the affairs of the corporation were adopted by the undersigned incorporator and were ordered inserted in the minute book immediately following the copy of the certificate of incorporation and before this instrument.

2. The following persons were unanimously elected as directors to hold office until the first annual meeting of stockholders or until their respective successors are elected and qualified:

[NAMES OF DIRECTORS]

Dated: _____

[Name of Incorporator]

FORM TEN

MINUTES OF ORGANIZATION MEETING OF BOARD OF DIRECTORS OF [CORPORATION]

The first meeting of the board of directors of [NAME OF CORPORATION] was called and held at ____, New York on the ____ day of ____, 19____ at ____.

PRESENT:

There were present:

[NAMES OF DIRECTORS]

being all the directors.

_____ was chosen temporary chairman and ____ was chosen temporary secretary of the meeting.

The secretary presented and read a waiver of notice of the meeting, signed by all the directors, which was ordered filed with the minutes of the meeting.

The minutes of the incorporator were read and approved.

The chairman stated that the first business to come before the meeting was the election of officers.

The following persons were thereupon nominated to the offices set forth opposite their respective names, to serve until the next annual meeting and until their successors are chosen and shall qualify:

President - _____

Secretary - _____

All the directors present having voted, the chairman announced that the aforesaid persons had been unanimously elected as said officers respectively.

The president and the secretary thereupon entered upon the discharge of the duties of their respective offices.

Upon motion, duly made, seconded and carried, it was

RESOLVED, that the form of stock certificate presented and read be and it is hereby approved and adopted, and the secretary is instructed to insert a specimen thereof in the minute book.

Upon motion, duly made, seconded and carried, it was

RESOLVED, that the seal, an impression of which is hereto affixed, be and it is hereby adopted as the corporate seal of the corporation.

The secretary was authorized and directed to procure the proper corporate books.

Upon motion, duly made, seconded and carried, it was

RESOLVED, that the president be and he hereby is authorized to open a bank account on behalf of this corporation in a bank selected by the president.

RESOLVED, that until otherwise ordered said bank be and it hereby is authorized to make payments from the funds on deposit with it upon and according to the check of this corporation, signed by its president.

Upon motion, duly made, seconded and carried, it was

RESOLVED, that an office of the corporation be established and maintained at ____, in the City of ____, in the County of _____, in the State of New York, and that meetings of the board of directors from time to time may be held either at such office in the City of ____ or elsewhere, as the board of directors shall from time to time order.

Upon motion, duly made, seconded and carried, it was

FORMS AND MATERIALS

RESOLVED, that the president and secretary be and they each are authorized to execute and file, or cause to be filed, with the New York State Tax Commission a certificate pursuant to Section 275-a of the New York Tax Law.

The president stated that the corporation had received a subscription to _____ shares of the common stock of this corporation having a par value of _____ Dollars ($_____) per share.

The president stated further that the subscriber had tendered to the corporation the sum of _____ Dollars ($_____) in full payment at par for the common stock subscribed.

Upon motion, duly made, seconded and carried, the president and the secretary were authorized to issue to the said subscriber or its nominee certificates representing fully paid and nonassessable common stock of this corporation to the amount of the subscription.

Upon motion, duly made, seconded and carried, it was

RESOLVED, that for the purpose of authorizing the corporation to do business in any state, territory or dependency of the United States or any foreign country in which it is necessary or expedient for this corporation to transact business, the officers of this corporation are hereby authorized to appoint and substitute all necessary agents or attorneys for service of process, to designate and change the location of all necessary statutory offices and, under the corporate seal, to make and file all necessary certificates, reports, powers of attorney and other instruments as may be required by the laws of such state, territory, dependency or country to authorize the corporation to transact business therein, and whenever it is expedient for the corporation to cease doing business therein and withdraw therefrom, to revoke any appointment of agent or attorney for service of process and to file such certificates, reports, revocation of appointment or surrender of authority as may be necessary to terminate the authority of the corporation to do business in any such state, territory, dependency or country.

Upon motion, duly made, seconded and carried, it was

RESOLVED, that the fiscal year of the corporation shall begin the first day of ____ in each year.

Upon motion, duly made, seconded and carried, it was

RESOLVED, that the treasurer be and he hereby is authorized to pay all fees and expenses incident to and necessary for the organization of the corporation.

Upon motion, duly made, seconded and carried, the meeting thereupon adjourned.

[Name of Secretary elected at meeting]

FORM ELEVEN

WAIVER OF NOTICE OF FIRST MEETING OF THE BOARD OF DIRECTORS OF [CORPORATION]

    We, the undersigned, being all the directors of [NAME OF CORPORATION], do hereby call and waive notice of the time, place and purpose of the first meeting of the board of directors of said corporation.

    We call and designate the ____ day of ____, 19____, at ____, ____.M., as the time and _____, New York as the place of said meeting, the purpose thereof being to elect officers, authorize the issue of the capital stock, complete the organization of said corporation and transact such other business as may be necessary or advisable.

Dated: _____

                                            _____
                                            [NAME OF DIRECTOR]

                                            _____
                                            [NAME OF DIRECTOR]

                                            _____
                                            [NAME OF DIRECTOR]

FORM TWELVE

SUBSCRIPTION AGREEMENT

This SUBSCRIPTION AGREEMENT (the "Agreement") is entered into as of ____, 19____, between ____ (the "Company"), a New York corporation and wholly-owned subsidiary of ____ ("____"), and ____ ("Purchaser") (together, the "Parties").

WITNESSETH:

WHEREAS, Purchaser desires to subscribe for and purchase, and the Company desires to sell to Purchaser, the total number of shares of the Common Stock of the Company set forth on Schedule I hereto (the "Stock") at a price of $____ per share (the "Per Share Price") for a total purchase price in the amount set forth on Schedule I (the "Purchase Price"); and

WHEREAS, this Agreement is one of several agreements ("Other Purchasers' Agreements") being entered into between the Company and the key employees of the Company, set forth on Schedule I hereto (collectively, the "Other Purchasers"), each of which agreements is substantially identical except as to the number of shares of Common Stock covered thereby. The Purchaser and the Other Purchasers are sometimes collectively referred to therein as the "Management Investors";

NOW, THEREFORE, in order to implement the foregoing and in consideration of the mutual agreements contained herein and for other good and valuable consideration, the receipt and adequacy of which is hereby acknowledged, the Parties agree as follows:

I. Subscription for and Purchase of Stock

1.01. *Purchase of Stock*. Subject to the terms and conditions hereinafter set forth, Purchaser hereby subscribes for and agrees to purchase, and the Company hereby agrees to sell to Purchaser, on ____, 19____ (the "Purchase Date"), the Stock at a purchase price per share equal to the Per Share Price.

1.02. *Closing of Purchase of Stock.*

(a) The Purchaser shall deliver to the Company on the proposed Purchase Date the Purchase Price payable in immediately available funds by wire transfer to the Company's account at [Bank] or by a certified bank check or checks payable to the order of the Company in the amount set forth on Schedule I attached hereto.

(b) On the Purchase Date, in consideration of receipt of the Purchase Price as aforesaid, the Company will deliver to Purchaser certificates, registered in Purchaser's name, for such Stock.

II. Purchaser's Representations; Restriction on Transfer

2.01. *General Restriction on Transfer.* Except for Transfers otherwise permitted by this Agreement, Purchaser agrees that he will not transfer any shares of the Acquired Securities at any time. No Transfer of any Acquired Securities in violation of this Agreement shall be made or recorded on the books of the Company, and any such Transfer shall be void and of no effect.

2.02. *Not for Resale.* The Purchaser hereby represents and warrants that he is acquiring the Stock and will acquire any Common Stock acquired from Other Purchasers as permitted in the Other Purchasers' Agreements (collectively, with the Stock, the "Acquired Securities") for investment for his own account and not with a view to, or for resale in connection with, the distribution or other disposition thereof. Purchaser agrees and acknowledges that he will not, directly or indirectly, voluntarily or involuntarily, offer, transfer, sell, assign, pledge, hypothecate or otherwise dispose of (hereinafter, a "Transfer") any of the Acquired Securities unless such Transfer complies with the provisions of this Agreement and (i) the Transfer is pursuant to an effective registration statement under the Securities Act of 1933, as amended, and the rules and regulations in effect thereunder (the "Act"), or (ii) counsel for Purchaser (which counsel shall be reasonably acceptable to the Company) shall have furnished the Company with an opinion, reasonably satisfactory in form and substance to the Company, to the effect that no such registration is required because of the availability of an exemption from registration under the Act.

2.03. *Certain Permitted Transfers.*

(a) Notwithstanding the general prohibition on Transfers contained in Sections 2.01 and 2.02 hereof, the Company acknowledges and agrees that any of the following Transfers are deemed to be in compliance with the Act and this Agreement, and no opinion of counsel is required in connection therewith:

(i) a Transfer made by Purchaser to the Company or a proposed transferee pursuant to Article II or III or Section 6.02 hereof, as the case may be;

(ii) a Transfer upon the death of Purchaser to his executors, administrators, testamentary trustee, legatees or beneficiaries (the "Purchaser's Estate") or a Transfer to the executors, administrators, testamentary trustees, legatees or beneficiaries of a person who has become a holder of the Acquired Securities in accordance with the terms of this Agreement; provided, however, that no such Transfer shall be given effect on the books of the Company unless prior to such Transfer the transferee shall deliver to the Company a valid written undertaking to become bound by the terms of this Agreement;

(iii) a Transfer made after the Purchase Date in compliance with the Act to a trust, the beneficiaries of which include only Purchaser, his spouse, his lineal descendants or the descendants of any ancestor of Purchaser or his spouse (a "Purchaser's Trust"); provided, however, that no such Transfer shall be of any force or effect or shall be given effect on the books of the Company unless prior to such Transfer the transferee shall deliver to the Company a valid written undertaking to become bound by the terms of this Agreement; and

(iv) a pledge or hypothecation by Purchaser of the Acquired Securities or his interest therein to a bank or other financial institution to secure a loan by such bank or financial institution to Purchaser for the purchase of the Acquired Securities, or the refinancing of any indebtedness incurred to purchase the Acquired Securities; provided that (i) the Company receives written notice of the identity of such bank or financial institution and the terms of such pledge or hypothecation at least 15 days prior to the effective date thereof; (ii) the Company approves of such bank or financial institution and such terms, such approval, in each case, not to be unreasonably withheld; (iii) such bank or financial institution accepts, in a writing delivered to the Company prior to the effective date of such pledge or hypothecation, the Acquired Securities or interest therein subject to all of the terms and conditions of this Agreement and provided, further, that such bank or financial institution shall agree that prior to any foreclosure of the interests in the Acquired Securities or its acceptance of Acquired Securities in satisfaction of its debt, it shall give the Company 15 days' prior written notice and shall permit the Company, within such prior 15-day period, to acquire the Acquired Securities at the Per Share Price.

(b) In addition, notwithstanding the general prohibition on Transfers, Purchaser may transfer Acquired Securities at any time, or from time to time, to the Other Purchasers (i) if the Transfer is pursuant to an effective registration statement under the Act or counsel for Purchaser (which counsel shall be reasonably acceptable to the Company) shall have furnished the Company with an opinion reasonably satisfactory in form and substance to the Company to the effect that no such registration is required because of the availability of an exemption from registration under the Act; and (ii) such Other Purchasers accept in a writing, delivered to the Company prior to the effective date of such Transfer, the Acquired Securities subject to all of the terms and conditions of this Agreement in respect of Purchaser.

(c) Any transferee of Acquired Securities described in Section 2.03(a)(ii), (iii) or (b) hereof is herein called a "Permitted Transferee" in respect of Purchaser transferring Acquired Securities thereto.

(d) From and after the earlier of the date on which the Company (i) shall have filed a registration statement pursuant to the requirements of Section 12 of the Securities Exchange Act of 1934, as amended (the

"Exchange Act"), in respect of the Common Stock or (ii) engaged in a primary or secondary offering of shares of Common Stock pursuant to an effective registration under the Act (either of which events being herein called the "Public Offering"), Purchaser may at any time sell any or all of his Acquired Securities in a Rule 144 Transaction (as hereinafter defined); provided, however, that (A) prior to the fifth anniversary (the "Fifth Anniversary") of the closing of the Acquisition no such sale shall be effected without the consent of the Company unless Purchaser's employment with the Company has been terminated by Purchaser as a result of a Substantial Breach, as defined in Section 3.03 hereof and (B) each such sale shall be made in compliance with Section 2.04 hereof.

2.04. *Rule 144 Sales.* If any of the Acquired Securities are to be disposed of in accordance with Rule 144 ("Rule 144 Transaction") under the Act or otherwise, Purchaser shall promptly notify the Company of such intended disposition and shall deliver to the Company at or prior to the time of such disposition such documentation as the Company may reasonably request in connection with such sale and, in the case of a disposition pursuant to Rule 144, shall deliver to the Company an executed copy of any notice on Form 144 required to be filed with the Securities and Exchange Commission.

2.05. *Legend.* Each certificate or instrument representing Acquired Securities shall bear the following legend:

"THE SECURITIES REPRESENTED BY THIS CERTIFICATE OR INSTRUMENT MAY NOT BE TRANSFERRED, SOLD, ASSIGNED, PLEDGED, HYPOTHECATED OR OTHERWISE DISPOSED OF UNLESS SUCH TRANSFER, SALE OR ASSIGNMENT, PLEDGE, HYPOTHECATION OR OTHER DISPOSITION COMPLIES WITH THE PROVISIONS OF A SUBSCRIPTION AGREEMENT DATED AS OF ____, 19____ (A COPY OF EACH OF WHICH IS ON FILE WITH THE SECRETARY OF THE COMPANY)."

III. Puts and Calls of Common Stock

3.01. *Option to Put.* In the event of:

(a) the death, disability (as hereinafter defined) or Retirement (as hereinafter defined) of Purchaser;

(b) the death of Purchaser's spouse (if Purchaser predeceases his spouse);

(c) the termination by Purchaser of his employment with the Company as a result of a Substantial Breach (as hereinafter defined);

(d) the termination by Purchaser of Purchaser's employment with the Company after the Fifth Anniversary; or

(e) the termination by the Company of Purchaser's employment with the Company for Cause after the later of the Fifth Anniversary or the Public Offering;

then, Purchaser shall have the option (as hereinafter described) to cause the Company to purchase the number of shares of Acquired Securities designated by him in the notice described in Section 3.04 hereof at a price equal to his Cost Per Share.

3.02. *Option to Call.*

(a) In the event of:

(i) the termination by the Company of Purchaser's employment with the Company for Cause on or before the later of the Fifth Anniversary or the Public Offering; or

(ii) the termination by Purchaser for any reason (other than a termination by Purchaser as a result of death, disability, Retirement or a Substantial Breach) of Purchaser's employment with the Company on or before the Fifth Anniversary;

the Company shall have the option (as hereinafter described) to cause Purchaser to sell to the Company the number of shares of Acquired Securities designated by it in the notice described in Section 3.04(a) hereof at a per share price equal to the lesser of (x) his Cost Per Share or (y) the Book Value Per Share (as hereinafter defined).

FORMS AND MATERIALS 605

(b) In case of:

(i) the death of Purchaser or his spouse, whichever occurs later, or the death of Purchaser who is not married at the time of his death, in each case prior to the Public Offering Date; or

(ii) termination of Purchaser's employment with the Company for Cause before the Public Offering but after the Fifth Anniversary;

the Company shall have the option (as hereinafter described) to cause Purchaser or his spouse, as the case may be, to sell to the Company the number of Acquired Securities designated by it in the notice described in Section 3.04(a) hereof at a price equal to the greater of (i) his Cost Per Share or (ii) the Book Value Per Share; provided that no Acquired Securities of a Purchaser or his Permitted Transferees shall be purchased pursuant to this Section 3.02(b) unless all such securities of the Purchaser and his Permitted Transferees are purchased by the Company, as the case may be.

3.03. *Certain Definitions*. For purposes of this Agreement, the following definitions shall apply:

"Permanent Disability" shall be the time when, and only when, Purchaser is permanently disabled in accordance with the disability policy of the Company, as in effect from time to time.

"Retirement" shall mean the voluntary termination of employment by Purchaser after he attains age 62 or two years after the closing of the Acquisition, whichever is later.

"Termination for Cause" shall mean termination of Purchaser's employment with the Company by the Board of Directors because of (a) any act or omission which constitutes a material breach by Purchaser of his obligations or agreements under this Agreement or his employment agreement (if any) with the Company or the failure or refusal of Purchaser to satisfactorily perform any duties reasonably required of him, after notification by the Board of such breach, failure or refusal and failure of Purchaser to correct such breach, failure or refusal within ten business days of such notification (other than by reason of the incapacity of Purchaser due to physical or mental illness) or (b) the commission by

Purchaser of a felony, or the perpetration by Purchaser of common law fraud against any of the Company or any affiliate or subsidiary.

"Substantial Breach" shall (a) in the case of a Purchaser having a written employment agreement with the Company, have the meaning ascribed thereto therein and (b) in all other cases, mean a reduction by the Company in Purchaser's base salary as compared to the base salary on the closing of the Acquisition, but shall not include a Termination for Cause. Termination of employment by the Company (other than upon death or disability) under circumstances not constituting a Termination for Cause shall be deemed a Substantial Breach.

"Cost Per Share" shall mean $____, together with simple interest thereon computed at the rate of ____ percent per annum from the closing of the Acquisition to the date of purchase of the shares in respect of which the computation is being made, less all cash dividends received on such shares.

"Book Value Per Share" shall mean (a) the stockholders' equity per share of Common Stock of the Company, excluding amounts attributable to shares of the Company's capital stock other than its Common Stock (assuming that all currently outstanding convertible securities of the Company are fully converted into Common Stock), as of the Calculation Date (as hereinafter defined), determined in accordance with generally accepted accounting principles applied on a basis consistent with prior periods. In determining the Book Value Per Share, appropriate adjustments shall be made for any future issuance (to the extent dilutive) of rights to acquire any securities convertible into Common Stock and any stock dividends, splits, combinations, recapitalizations or any other adjustments in the number of shares of Common Stock. The Calculation Date shall mean the last day of the month preceding the month in which an event giving rise to a put or call occurs. The computation of Book Value Per Share shall be based on the unaudited financial statements of the Company as of the Calculation Date.

3.04. *Procedure for Exercising Put/Call.*

(a) Notice.

(i) If Purchaser elects to exercise the option in Section 3.01 hereof, then, within 60 business days after the date of an event specified in Section 3.01 hereof, he shall send to the Company a notice stating that he is exercising his right to sell, and cause the Company to purchase, any or all of his Acquired Securities pursuant to Section 3.01 hereof.

(ii) If the Company elects to exercise any option in Section 3.02 hereof, then, within 60 business days of an event specified in Section 3.02 hereof, the Company shall send Purchaser or his spouse, as the case may be, a notice to such effect.

(iii) All such notices shall set forth the number of Acquired Securities to be sold or purchased and the date for delivery of and payment therefor, which date shall not be more than 30 business days from the date of delivery of the notice of exercise.

(b) Deliveries.

On the dates specified in the applicable notice, Purchaser and his spouse, if applicable, shall be required to deliver certificates for the Acquired Securities to be purchased and sold, duly endorsed or accompanied by written instruments of transfer in form satisfactory to the Company, duly executed by Purchaser or his spouse, as the case may be, free and clear of any liens. In exchange therefor, the Company shall pay the applicable aggregate purchase price therefor by a check or checks payable to or upon the order of Purchaser, in immediately available funds on the date of such purchase.

IV. The Company's Representations and Warranties

4.01. *The Company's Representations and Warranties.* The Company represents and warrants to Purchaser that: (a) this Agreement has been duly authorized, executed and delivered by the Company; (b) the Stock, when issued and delivered in accordance with the terms hereof, will be duly and validly issued, fully paid and nonassessable; and (c) Exhibit A hereto sets forth the capitalization of the Company on the closing of the Acquisition and the consideration received by the Company for the sale of its capital stock described therein.

V. "Piggyback" Registration Rights

5.01. *Purchaser's Right to Request Registration.* If the Company in connection with any Public Offering initiated by the Company plans to register any shares of Common Stock, the Company will promptly notify Purchaser in writing (a "Notice") of such proposed registration (a "Proposed Registration"). If within ten business days of the receipt by Purchaser of such Notice the Company receives from Purchaser a written request (a "Request") to register shares of Acquired Securities (which Request will be irrevocable unless otherwise mutually agreed to in writing by Purchaser and the Company), shares of Acquired Securities will be so registered as provided in this Article V. Anything in this Agreement to the contrary notwithstanding, any Acquired Securities registered pursuant to this Article V shall not be subject to the provisions of Articles II, III and IV or Sections 6.01 and 6.02 hereof, once sold pursuant to such registration statement.

5.02. *Number of Acquired Securities to be Registered.* The number of Acquired Securities which will be registered pursuant to a Request will be the maximum number of shares the managing underwriter in respect of such offering reasonably concludes Purchaser and the Other Purchasers and their Permitted Transferees may sell without reducing the price of the securities to be sold therein or the number of securities which the Company or other holders of securities thereof desire to sell therein (pro rata based upon the aggregate number of shares of Acquired Securities Purchaser and all Other Purchasers have requested be registered) and all Other Purchasers to register.

5.03. *Terms of Registration.* Acquired Securities will be registered by the Company and offered to the public pursuant to this Article V on the same terms and subject to the same conditions applicable to the registration in a Proposed Registration of shares of Common Stock held by all Other Purchasers, and Purchaser shall not be required to pay the costs of the registration, other than its pro rata share of the underwriter's discounts or commissions.

5.04. *Other Agreements*. Each Purchaser including Acquired Securities in a registration shall execute and deliver such other agreements and instruments as are reasonably and customarily required by the managing underwriter (or the Company if there is not an underwritten offering) of selling shareholders in a public offering.

VI. Miscellaneous

6.01. *Purchaser's Employment by Company*. Nothing contained in this Agreement (a) obligates the Company or any subsidiary of the Company to employ Purchaser in any capacity whatsoever, or (b) prohibits or restricts the Company (or any such subsidiary) from terminating the employment, if any, of Purchaser at any time or for any reason whatsoever, with or without cause. Purchaser and the Company have executed a separate agreement concerning Purchaser's employment by the Company.

6.02. *State Securities Laws*. The Company hereby agrees to comply with all state securities or "blue sky" laws which might be applicable to the sale of the Stock.

6.03. *Binding Effect*. The provisions of this Agreement shall be binding upon and inure to the benefit of the Parties hereto and their respective heirs, legal representatives, successors and assigns. A Permitted Transferee shall be deemed a Purchaser hereunder for purposes of obtaining the benefits or enforcing the rights of Purchaser hereunder and shall be deemed the Purchaser who transferred Acquired Securities thereto for purposes of the computations in Section 5.02 hereof; provided, however, that (a) no transferee (including, without limitation, a Permitted Transferee), except a transferee that is an Other Purchaser, shall derive any rights under this Agreement unless the Company receives a valid undertaking and becomes bound by the terms of this Agreement; (b) that so long as Purchaser owns any Acquired Securities, such Purchaser shall exercise all rights in Sections 3.01 and 6.04 and Article V on behalf of all his Permitted Transferees, and thereafter only Permitted Transferees holding a majority of the Acquired Securities held by all Permitted Transferees of such Purchaser shall exercise such rights on behalf of such Permitted Transferees; and (c) the Company's rights herein against Purchaser shall extend equally to his Permitted Transferees at the same time such rights apply to Purchaser.

6.04. *Amendment*. This Agreement may be amended only by a written instrument signed by the Parties hereto which specifically states that it is amending this Agreement.

6.05. *Applicable Law*. The laws of the State of New York shall govern the interpretation, validity and performance of the terms of this Agreement, regardless of the law that might be applied under principles of conflicts of law.

6.06. *Notices*.

(a) All notices and other communications provided for herein shall be in writing and shall be deemed to have been duly given if delivered personally or sent by registered or certified mail, return receipt requested, postage prepaid, to the Party to whom they are directed:

If to the Company:

If to Purchaser:

or at such other address as either Party shall have specified by notice in writing to the other.

(b) Purchaser hereby irrevocably appoints _____ as his agent for all notices hereunder; irrevocably appoints the Company as his agent for service of process in connection with any litigation brought hereunder; and irrevocably consents to the jurisdiction of the courts of New York in respect of any such litigation.

6.07. *Time and Place of Purchases by and Sales to the Company*. Except as otherwise provided herein, the closing of each purchase and sale of shares of Acquired Securities pursuant to this Agreement shall take place at the principal office of the Company.

6.08. *Remedies for Violations*. The shares of Common Stock cannot be readily purchased or sold on the open market and for this reason, among others, the Parties will be irreparably damaged in the event that

FORMS AND MATERIALS

this Agreement is not followed by the Parties. In the event of any controversy concerning the right or obligation to purchase or sell such shares, such right or obligation shall be enforceable in a court of equity by decree of specific performance.

6.09. *Rights to Negotiate Purchase Price.* Nothing in this Agreement shall be deemed to restrict or prohibit the Company from purchasing shares of Stock from Purchaser, at any time, upon such terms and conditions, and for such price, as may be mutually agreed upon between the Parties, whether or not at the time of such purchase circumstances exist which specifically grant the Company the right to purchase, or Purchaser the right to sell, shares of Stock under the terms of this Agreement.

6.10. *Purchase by Custodian or Trustee of Individual Retirement Account.* References herein to Purchaser shall be deemed to include the custodian or trustee of an Individual Retirement Account ("IRA") established for Purchaser's benefit and the Company agrees (i) to accept payment (which may take the form of a promissory note or notes for the amount of the Purchase Price executed by said custodian or trustee of the IRA and payable in not more than six months from the date thereof with interest at a rate not to exceed ten percent per annum) and (ii) notwithstanding the provisions of Section 1.02(b) hereof in consideration of the receipt of said note or notes, to deliver to said custodian or trustee of the IRA certificates for the Stock registered in the name of said custodian or trustee, upon the written direction of said custodian or trustee.

6.11. *Headings.* The headings herein are for convenience of reference only, do not constitute a part of this Agreement, and shall not be deemed to limit, expand or otherwise affect any of the provisions hereof.

IN WITNESS WHEREOF, the parties hereto have executed this Agreement as of the date first above written.

[COMPANY]

By: _____

[PURCHASER]

_____

FORM THIRTEEN

MATERIAL FOR ELECTION OF SUBCHAPTER S STATUS

FORMS AND MATERIALS 615

Department of the Treasury
Internal Revenue Service

Instructions for Form 2553
(Revised December 1990)
Election by a Small Business Corporation

(Section references are to the Internal Revenue Code unless otherwise noted.)

Paperwork Reduction Act Notice.—We ask for the information on this form to carry out the Internal Revenue laws of the United States. You are required to give us the information. We need it to ensure that you are complying with these laws and to allow us to figure and collect the right amount of tax.

The time needed to complete and file this form will vary depending on individual circumstances. The estimated average time is:

Recordkeeping	6 hrs., 28 min.
Learning about the law or the form	3 hrs., 16 min.
Preparing, copying, assembling, and sending the form to IRS	3 hrs., 31 min.

If you have comments concerning the accuracy of these time estimates or suggestions for making this form more simple, we would be happy to hear from you. You can write to both the **Internal Revenue Service**, Washington, DC 20224, Attention: IRS Reports Clearance Officer, T:FP, and the **Office of Management and Budget**, Paperwork Reduction Project (1545-0146), Washington, DC 20503. **DO NOT** send the tax form to either of these offices. Instead, see the instructions below for information on where to file.

the other corporation has not begun business and has no gross income;

(b) a bank or thrift institution;

(c) an insurance company subject to tax under the special rules of Subchapter L of the Code;

(d) a corporation that has elected to be treated as a possessions corporation under section 936; or

(e) a domestic international sales corporation (DISC) or former DISC.

See section 1361(b)(2) for details.

7. It has a permitted tax year as required by section 1378 or makes a section 444 election to have a tax year other than a permitted tax year. Section 1378 defines a permitted tax year as a tax year ending December 31, or any other tax year for which the corporation establishes a business purpose to the satisfaction of the IRS. See Part II for details on requesting a fiscal tax year based on a business purpose or on making a section 444 election.

8. Each shareholder consents as explained in the instructions for Column K.

See sections 1361, 1362, and 1378 for additional information on the above tests.

C. Where To File.—File this election with the Internal Revenue Service Center listed below.

Illinois, Iowa, Minnesota, Missouri, Wisconsin	Kansas City, MO 64999
Alabama, Arkansas, Louisiana, Mississippi, North Carolina, Tennessee	Memphis, TN 37501
Delaware, District of Columbia, Maryland, Pennsylvania, Virginia	Philadelphia, PA 19255

D. When To Make the Election.—Complete Form 2553 and file it either:

(1) at any time during that portion of the first tax year the election is to take effect which occurs before the 16th day of the third month of that tax year (if the tax year has 2½ months or less, and the election is made not later than 2 months and 15 days after the first day of the tax year, it shall be treated as timely made during such year), or (2) in the tax year before the first tax year it is to take effect. An election made by a small business corporation after the 15th day of the third month but before the end of the tax year is treated as made for the next year. For example, if a calendar tax year corporation makes the election in April 1991, it is effective for the corporation's 1992 calendar tax year. See section 1362(b) for more information.

E. Acceptance or Non-Acceptance of Election.—The Service Center will notify you if your election is accepted and when it will take effect. You will also be notified if

General Instructions

A. Purpose.—To elect to be treated as an "S Corporation," a corporation must file Form 2553. The election permits the income of the S corporation to be taxed to the shareholders of the corporation rather than to the corporation itself, except as provided in Subchapter S of the Code. For more information, see **Publication 589,** Tax Information on S Corporations.

B. Who May Elect.—Your corporation may make the election to be treated as an S corporation only if it meets all of the following tests:

1. It is a domestic corporation.

2. It has no more than 35 shareholders. A husband and wife (and their estates) are treated as one shareholder for this requirement. All other persons are treated as separate shareholders.

3. It has only individuals, estates, or certain trusts as shareholders. See the instructions for Part III regarding qualified subchapter S trusts.

4. It has no nonresident alien shareholders.

5. It has only one class of stock. See sections 1361(c)(4) and (5) for additional details.

6. It is not one of the following ineligible corporations:

(a) a corporation that owns 80% or more of the stock of another corporation, unless

If the corporation's principal business, office, or agency is located in	Use the following Internal Revenue Service Center address
New Jersey, New York (New York City and counties of Nassau, Rockland, Suffolk, and Westchester)	Holtsville, NY 00501
New York (all other counties), Connecticut, Maine, Massachusetts, New Hampshire, Rhode Island, Vermont	Andover, MA 05501
Florida, Georgia, South Carolina	Atlanta, GA 39901
Indiana, Kentucky, Michigan, Ohio, West Virginia	Cincinnati, OH 45999
Kansas, New Mexico, Oklahoma, Texas	Austin, TX 73301
Alaska, Arizona, California (counties of Alpine, Amador, Butte, Calaveras, Colusa, Contra Costa, Del Norte, El Dorado, Glenn, Humboldt, Lake, Lassen, Marin, Mendocino, Modoc, Napa, Nevada, Placer, Plumas, Sacramento, San Joaquin, Shasta, Sierra, Siskiyou, Solano, Sonoma, Sutter, Tehama, Trinity, Yolo, and Yuba), Colorado, Idaho, Montana, Nebraska, Nevada, North Dakota, Oregon, South Dakota, Utah, Washington, Wyoming	Ogden, UT 84201
California (all other counties), Hawaii	Fresno, CA 93888

your election is not accepted. You should generally receive a determination on your election within 60 days after you have filed Form 2553. If the Q1 box in Part II is checked on page 2, the corporation will receive a ruling letter from IRS in Washington, DC, which approves or denies the selected tax year. When Item Q1 is checked, it will generally take an additional 90 days for the Form 2553 to be accepted.

Do not file Form 1120S until you are notified that your election is accepted. If you are now required to file **Form 1120,** U.S. Corporation Income Tax Return, or any other applicable tax return, continue filing it until your election takes effect.

Care should be exercised to ensure that the election is received by the Internal Revenue Service. If you are not notified of acceptance or nonacceptance of your election within 3 months of date of filing (date mailed), or within 6 months if Part II, Item Q1, is checked, you should take follow-up action by corresponding with the Service Center where the election was filed. If filing of Form 2553 is questioned by IRS, an acceptable proof of filing is: (1) certified receipt (timely filed); (2) Form 2553 with accepted stamp; (3) Form 2553 with stamped IRS received date; or (4) IRS letter stating that Form 2553 had been accepted.

F. End of Election.—Once the election is made, it stays in effect for all years until it is terminated. During the 5 years after the

FORMS AND MATERIALS

election is terminated under section 1362(d), the corporation can make another election on Form 2553 only with IRS consent.

Specific Instructions

Part I

Part I must be completed by all corporations.

Name and Address of Corporation.—Enter the true corporate name as set forth in the corporate charter or other legal document creating it. If the corporation's mailing address is the same as someone else's, such as a shareholder's, please enter this person's name below the name of the corporation. Include the suite, room, or other unit number after the street address. If the Post Office does not deliver to the street address and the corporation has a P.O. box, show the P.O. box number instead of the street address. If the corporation has changed its name or address since applying for its EIN (filing Form SS-4), be sure to check the box in item F of Part I.

A. Employer Identification Number.—If you have applied for an employer identification number (EIN) but have not received it, enter "applied for." If the corporation does not have an EIN, you should apply for one on Form SS-4, Application for Employer Identification Number, available from most IRS and Social Security Administration offices.

C. Effective Date of Election.—Enter the beginning effective date (month, day, year) of the tax year that you have requested for the S corporation. Generally, this will be the beginning date of the tax year for which the ending effective date is required to be shown in item I, Part I. For a new

An election made during the first 2½ months of the tax year is considered made for the following tax year if one or more of the persons who held stock in the corporation during such tax year and before the election was made did not consent to the election. See section 1362(b)(2).

If a husband and wife have a community interest in the stock or in the income from it, both must consent. Each tenant in common, joint tenant, and tenant by the entirety also must consent.

A minor's consent is made by the minor or the legal representative of the minor, or by a natural or adoptive parent of the minor if no legal representative has been appointed. The consent of an estate is made by an executor or administrator.

Continuation sheet or separate consent statement.—If you need a continuation sheet or use a separate consent statement, attach it to Form 2553. The separate consent statement must contain the name, address, and employer identification number of the corporation and the shareholder information requested in columns J through N of Part I.

If you want, you may combine all the shareholders' consents in one statement.

Column L.—Enter the number of shares of stock each shareholder owns and the dates the stock was acquired. If the election is made during the corporation's first tax year for which it is effective, do not list the shares of stock for those shareholders who sold or transferred all of their stock before the election was made. However, these shareholders must still consent to the election for it to be effective for the tax year.

Column M.—Enter the social security number of each shareholder who is an-

Revenue Procedure 87-32, 1987-2 C.B. 396. A corporation that does not have a 47-month period of gross receipts cannot establish a natural business year under section 4.01(1).

Box Q1.—For examples of an acceptable business purpose for requesting a fiscal tax year, see Revenue Ruling 87-57, 1987-2 C.B. 117.

In addition to a statement showing the business purpose for the requested fiscal year, you must attach the other information necessary to meet the ruling request requirements of Revenue Procedure 90-1, 1990-1 C.B. 356 (updated annually). Also attach a statement that shows separately the amount of gross receipts from sales or services (and inventory costs, if applicable) for each of the 36 months preceding the effective date of the election to be an S corporation. If the corporation has been in existence for fewer than 36 months, submit figures for the period of existence.

If you check box Q1, you must also pay a user fee of $200 (subject to change). Do not pay the fee when filing Form 2553. The Service Center will send Form 2553 to the IRS in Washington, DC, who, in turn, will notify the corporation that the fee is due. See Revenue Procedure 90-17, 1990-1 C.B. 479.

Box Q2.—If the corporation makes a back-up section 444 election for which it is qualified, then the election must be exercised in the event the business purpose request is not approved. Under certain circumstances, the tax year requested under the back-up section 444 election may be different than the tax year requested under business purpose. See **Form 8716**, Election To Have a Tax Year Other Than a corporation (first year the corporation exists) it will generally be the date required to be shown in item H, Part I. The tax year of a new corporation starts on the date that it has shareholders, acquires assets, or begins doing business, whichever happens first. If the effective date for item C for a newly formed corporation is later than the date in item H, the corporation should file Form 1120 or Form 1120-A, for the tax period between these dates.

Column K. Shareholders' Consent Statement.—Each shareholder who owns (or is deemed to own) stock at the time the election is made must consent to the election. If the election is made during the corporation's first tax year for which it is effective, any person who held stock at any time during the portion of that year which occurs before the time the election is made, must consent to the election although the person may have sold or transferred his or her stock before the election is made. Each shareholder consents by signing and dating in column K or signing and dating a separate consent statement described below. If stock is owned by a trust that is a qualified shareholder, the deemed owner of the trust must consent. See section 1361(c)(2) for details regarding qualified trusts that may be shareholders and rules on determining who is the deemed owner of the trust.

individual. Enter the employer identification number of each shareholder that is an estate or a qualified trust.

Column N.—Enter the month and day that each shareholder's tax year ends. If a shareholder is changing his or her tax year, enter the tax year the shareholder is changing to, and attach an explanation indicating the present tax year and the basis for the change (e.g., automatic revenue procedure or letter ruling request).

If the election is made during the corporation's first tax year for which it is effective, you do not have to enter the tax year of any shareholder who sold or transferred all of his or her stock before the election was made.

Signature.—Form 2553 must be signed by the president, treasurer, assistant treasurer, chief accounting officer, or other corporate officer (such as tax officer) authorized to sign.

Part II

Complete Part II if you selected a tax year ending on any date other than December 31 (other than a 52-53-week tax year ending with reference to the month of December).

Box P1.—Attach a statement showing separately for each month the amount of gross receipts for the most recent 47 months as required by section 4.03(3) of Required Tax Year, for details on making a back-up section 444 election.

Boxes Q2 and R2.—If the corporation is not qualified to make the section 444 election after making the item Q2 back-up section 444 election or indicating its intention to make the election in item R1, and therefore it later files a calendar year return, it should write "Section 444 Election Not Made" in the top left corner of the 1st calendar year Form 1120S it files.

Part III

Certain Qualified Subchapter S Trusts (QSSTs) may make the QSST election required by section 1361(d)(2) in Part III. Part III may be used to make the QSST election only if corporate stock has been transferred to the trust on or before the date on which the corporation makes its election to be an S corporation. However, a statement can be used in lieu of Part III to make the election.

Note: *Part III may be used only in conjunction with making the Part I election (i.e., Form 2553 cannot be filed with only Part III completed).*

The deemed owner of the QSST must also consent to the S corporation election in column K, page 1, of Form 2553. See section 1361(c)(2).

*U.S. Government Printing Office: 1992 — 619-071/40536

FORMS AND MATERIALS

Form 2553 — Election by a Small Business Corporation
(Rev. December 1990)
(Under section 1362 of the Internal Revenue Code)
Department of the Treasury
Internal Revenue Service
▶ For Paperwork Reduction Act Notice, see page 1 of instructions.
▶ See separate instructions.

OMB No. 1545-0146
Expires 11-30-93

Notes:
1. This election, to be treated as an "S corporation," can be accepted only if all the tests in General Instruction B are met; all signatures in Parts I and III are originals (no photocopies); and the exact name and address of the corporation and other required form information are provided.
2. Do not file Form 1120S until you are notified that your election is accepted. See General Instruction E.

Part I Election Information

Please Type or Print

Name of corporation (see instructions)

A Employer identification number (see instructions)

Number, street, and room or suite no. (If a P.O. box, see instructions.)

B Name and telephone number (including area code) of corporate officer or legal representative who may be called for information

City or town, state, and ZIP code

C Election is to be effective for tax year beginning (month, day, year) ▶

D Is the corporation the outgrowth or continuation of any form of predecessor? . . ☐ Yes ☐ No
If "Yes," state name of predecessor, type of organization, and period of its existence ▶

E Date of incorporation

F Check here ▶ ☐ if the corporation has changed its name or address since applying for the employer identification number shown in item A above.

G State of incorporation

H If this election takes effect for the first tax year the corporation exists, enter month, day, and year of the earliest of the following: (1) date the corporation first had shareholders, (2) date the corporation first had assets, or (3) date the corporation began doing business. ▶

I Selected tax year: Annual return will be filed for tax year ending (month and day) ▶
If the tax year ends on any date other than December 31, except for an automatic 52-53-week tax year ending with reference to the month of December, you **must** complete Part II on the back. If the date you enter is the ending date of an automatic 52-53-week tax year, write "52-53-week year" to the right of the date. See Temporary Regulations section 1.441-2T(e)(3).

J Name of each shareholder, person having a community property interest in the corporation's stock, and each tenant in common, joint tenant, and tenant by the entirety. (A husband and wife (and their estates) are counted as one shareholder in determining the number of shareholders without regard to the manner in which the stock is owned.)

K Shareholders' Consent Statement.
We, the undersigned shareholders, consent to the corporation's election to be treated as an "S corporation" under section 1362(a). (Shareholders sign and date below.)*

Signature | Date

L Stock owned
Number of shares | Dates acquired

M Social security number or employer identification number (see instructions)

N Shareholder's tax year ends (month and day)

*For this election to be valid, the consent of each shareholder, person having a community property interest in the corporation's stock, and each tenant in common, joint tenant, and tenant by the entirety must either appear above or be attached to this form. (See instructions for Column K if continuation sheet or a separate consent statement is needed.)

Under penalties of perjury, I declare that I have examined this election, including accompanying schedules and statements, and to the best of my knowledge and belief, it is true, correct, and complete.

Signature of officer ▶ _____ Title ▶ _____ Date ▶ _____

See Parts II and III on back.

Form **2553** (Rev. 12-90)

FORMS AND MATERIALS

Form 2553 (Rev. 12-90) Page 2

Part II Selection of Fiscal Tax Year (All corporations using this Part must complete item O and one of items P, Q, or R.)

O Check the applicable box below to indicate whether the corporation is:

1. ☐ A new corporation adopting the tax year entered in item I, Part I.
2. ☐ An existing corporation retaining the tax year entered in item I, Part I.
3. ☐ An existing corporation changing to the tax year entered in item I, Part I.

P Complete item P if the corporation is using the expeditious approval provisions of Revenue Procedure 87-32, 1987-2 C.B. 396, to request: (1) a natural business year (as defined in section 4.01(1) of Rev. Proc. 87-32), or (2) a year that satisfies the ownership tax year test in section 4.01(2) of Rev. Proc. 87-32. Check the applicable box below to indicate the representation the corporation is making as required under section 4 of Rev. Proc. 87-32.

1. **Natural Business Year** ▶ ☐ I represent that the corporation is retaining or changing to a tax year that coincides with its natural business year as defined in section 4.01(1) of Rev. Proc. 87-32 and as verified by its satisfaction of the requirements of section 4.02(1) of Rev. Proc. 87-32. In addition, if the corporation is changing to a natural business year as defined in section 4.01(1), I further represent that such tax year results in less deferral of income to the owners than the corporation's present tax year. I also represent that the corporation is not described in section 3.01(2) of Rev. Proc. 87-32. (See instructions for additional information that must be attached.)

2. **Ownership Tax Year** ▶ ☐ I represent that shareholders holding more than half of the shares of the stock (as of the first day of the tax year to which the request relates) of the corporation have the same tax year or are concurrently changing to the tax year that the corporation adopts, retains, or changes to per item I, Part I. I also represent that the corporation is not described in section 3.01(2) of Rev. Proc. 87-32.

Note: *If you do not use item P and the corporation wants a fiscal tax year, complete either item Q or R below. Item Q is used to request a fiscal tax year based on a business purpose and to make a back-up section 444 election. Item R is used to make a regular section 444 election.*

Q **Business Purpose**—To request a fiscal tax year based on a business purpose, you must check box Q1 and pay a user fee. See instructions for details. You may also check box Q2 and/or box Q3.

1. Check here ▶ ☐ if the fiscal year entered in item I, Part I, is requested under the provisions of section 6.03 of Rev. Proc. 87-32. Attach to Form 2553 a statement showing the business purpose for the requested fiscal year. See instructions for additional information that must be attached.

2. Check here ▶ ☐ to show that the corporation intends to make a back-up section 444 election in the event the corporation's business purpose request is not approved by the IRS. (See instructions for more information.)

3. Check here ▶ ☐ to show that the corporation agrees to adopt or change to a tax year ending December 31 if necessary for the IRS to accept this election for S corporation status in the event: (1) the corporation's business purpose request is not approved and the corporation makes a back-up section 444 election, but is ultimately not qualified to make a section 444 election, or (2) the corporation's business purpose request is not approved and the corporation did not make a back-up section 444 election.

R   Section 444 Election—To make a section 444 election, you must check box R1 and you may also check box R2.

1. Check here ▶ ☐ to show the corporation will make, if qualified, a section 444 election to have the fiscal tax year shown in item I, Part I. To make the election, you must complete **Form 8716**, Election To Have a Tax Year Other Than a Required Tax Year, and either attach it to Form 2553 or file it separately.

2. Check here ▶ ☐ to show that the corporation agrees to adopt or change to a tax year ending December 31 if necessary for the IRS to accept this election for S corporation status in the event the corporation is ultimately not qualified to make a section 444 election.

Part III   Qualifed Subchapter S Trust (QSST) Election Under Section 1361(d)(2)**

Income beneficiary's name and address	Social security number

Trust's name and address	Employer identification number

Date on which stock of the corporation was transferred to the trust (month, day, year) ▶

In order for the trust named above to be a QSST and thus a qualifying shareholder of the S corporation for which this Form 2553 is filed, I hereby make the election under section 1361(d)(2). Under penalties of perjury, I certify that the trust meets the definition requirements of section 1361(d)(3) and that all other information provided in Part III is true, correct, and complete.

Signature of income beneficiary or signature and title of legal representative or other qualified person making the election	Date

** Use of Part III to make the QSST election may be made only if stock of the corporation has been transferred to the trust on or before the date on which the corporation makes its election to be an S corporation. The QSST election must be made and filed separately if stock of the corporation is transferred to the trust after the date on which the corporation makes the S election.

☆ U.S. GPO: 1992-312-669/60012

FORMS AND MATERIALS

New York State Department of Taxation and Finance

CT-6-I (8/89) Instructions for Form CT-6
Election by a Federal S Corporation to be Treated as a New York State S Corporation

General Information

Shareholders of a federal S corporation may elect under section 660(a) of the Tax Law to be taxed as a New York State S Corporation under the personal income tax (Article 22) and to exempt the corporation from corporation franchise tax (Article 9-A).

An S corporation which elects S status for New York State must file Form CT-3-S on or before the fifteenth day of the third month following the end of each tax year. If the New York State S corporation fails to file Form CT-3-S on time or fails to include the required information, it must pay a penalty of $50 per shareholder per month or fraction of a month the failure continues, for up to five months. Any individual who was a shareholder during any part of the year and is subject to the New York State personal income tax will be included.

Filing Fee

Corporations electing S status for New York State must pay a filing fee (section 658(c)(2) of Article 22). For periods beginning on or after January 1, 1989, the filing fee is $325. The filing fee of $325 is reduced for short periods of nine months or less.

- All of the corporation's shareholders must consent to the election.

When to Make the Election

- Use Form CT-6 to make an election to treat the corporation as a New York State S corporation. To be effective for the tax year, the election must be made at one of the following times:

- At any time during the preceding tax year.

- On or before the fifteenth day of the third month of the tax year to which the election will apply. However, this election will not be effective until the following tax year if, during the tax year but before the date of election:

a) the corporation did not qualify as a federal S corporation, under section 1361(b) of the Internal Revenue Code on one or more days, or

b) one or more of the shareholders who held stock before the date of election did not consent to the corporation being an S corporation.

- If the corporation is organized within New York State and anticipates being a New York State S Corporation for its first tax year, it must file Form CT-6 on or before

623

Foreign S Corporations

In addition, if the New York State S corporation is incorporated in another state, it is subject to the two fees imposed by Article 9, section 181:

- a license fee on foreign corporations doing business in New York State (section 181.1) (Report of License Fee Form CT-240)

- an annual maintenance fee of $300 on foreign corporations authorized by the Secretary of State to do business in New York State (section 181.2). The maintenance fee may be applied as a credit against the filing fee. This fee is reduced for short periods of nine months or less.

Who May Elect

To elect to treat the corporation as a New York State S corporation, you must meet the following requirements:

- The corporation must be a federal S corporation. If your federal election is pending, file your New York election and indicate that your federal election is pending. When you receive federal approval, forward a copy to the Tax Department at the address at the end of these instructions.

- The corporation must be a general business corporation taxable under Article 9-A of the New York State Tax Law. A corporation cannot make a New York State S election if taxable under Articles 9, 13, 13-A, 32 or 33 of the Tax Law.

the fifteenth day of the third month following the effective date of its certificate of incorporation.

- If the corporation is organized outside New York State, begins to do business in New York State, and anticipates being a New York State S Corporation for its first tax year, it must file Form CT-6 on or before the fifteenth day of the third month following the date it began doing business in New York State.

It is your responsibility to mail the election on time. The date of the U.S. postmark will be considered the date of delivery. If sent by registered or certified mail, the date of registration or certification will be considered the date of delivery.

Approval or Disapproval of Election

You will be notified whether your election is approved or disapproved, and if approved, when it will take effect. Until then, do not file Form CT-3-S. If you are now required to file Form CT-3 or CT-4, continue filing it until your election takes effect.

If you do not receive confirmation or denial of your election before your return is due, you should write to the Registration Section. See address and special instructions at the end of these instructions.

Years for Which Election is Effective

The election will be effective for the entire corporate tax year for which it is made and for all succeeding tax years until terminated.

FORMS AND MATERIALS 625

CT-6-I (8/89) (back)

When Termination Occurs

An election to treat the corporation as a New York State S corporation will cease to be effective:

- On the day the federal election to be treated as an S corporation ceases;
- When shareholders owning a majority of the shares revoke the election (see "Revocation of Election" below); or
- On the day an individual who refuses to consent to the S corporation treatment becomes a new shareholder.

Revocation of Election

Shareholders who collectively own more than 50% of the outstanding shares of the S corporation stock may revoke the New York State S corporation status by filing a written statement with the Commissioner of Taxation and Finance. The statement must contain:

- Name, address and ID number of corporation;
- The total number of shares of stock (including nonvoting stock) that is outstanding at the time revocation is made and the number held by each revoking shareholder;
- Name, address, social security number and signature of each revoking shareholder;
- A statement that the corporation is revoking its election to be treated as an S corporation under section 660(c)(2) of the New York State Tax Law; and
- The date on which the revocation is to be effective.

stock that have been issued to shareholders and have not been reacquired by the corporation. It should equal the total shares owned by all shareholders, as reported in column C.

Column A — Enter the name and address of each shareholder.

Column B — Enter the social security number of each shareholder.

Column C — Enter the number of shares of stock each shareholder owns and the dates the stock was acquired. Do not list the shares of stock for those shareholders who sold or transferred all of their stock before the election was made but who still must consent to the election for it to be effective for the tax year. For more information, see instructions for Column D below.

Column D — Each shareholder at the time the election is made must consent to the election by signing in column D or by signing a separate consent statement, described below.

If the election is made during the corporation's first tax year to be effective for that year, any former shareholder who held stock at any time on or before the fifteenth day of the third month of the electing year must also consent to the election. If the former shareholder does not consent, the election will not be effective until the following tax year.

If a husband and wife have a community interest in the stock or the income from it, both must consent. Each tenant in common, joint tenant, and tenant by the entirety must also consent.

626 CORPORATE PRACTICE HANDBOOK

This statement should be signed by an officer authorized to sign the S corporation return. It should be sent to the address shown at the end of these instructions.

The revocation is effective:

- On the first day of the tax year, if the revocation is made on or before the fifteenth day of the third month of the tax year;
- On the first day of the following tax year if the revocation is made after the fifteenth day of the third month of the tax year; or
- On the date specified, if the revocation specifies a date on or after the date the revocation is made.

Specific Instructions

Enter the name of the corporation as it appears in the records of the New York State Department of State.

Enter the trade name that appears on the Trade Name Certificate filed with the New York State Department of State.

Enter the number of shares issued and outstanding (from federal Form 2553) — The number of shares entered in this box should be the number of shares of

A minor's consent is made by the minor or the legal guardian. If no legal guardian has been appointed, the natural guardian makes the consent (even if a custodian holds the minor's stock under a law patterned after the Uniform Gifts to Minors Act).

Continuation Sheet or Separate Consent Statement — If you need a continuation sheet or use a separate consent statement, attach it to Form CT-6. The separate consent statement must contain the name, address, and employer identification number of the corporation and the shareholder information requested in columns A through D.

If you wish, you may combine all the shareholders' consents in one statement.

Where to File

Mail Form CT-6 to:
NYS Tax Department
Corporation Tax Registration
Building 8, Room 409
W. A. Harriman Campus
Albany, New York 12227

If you do not receive confirmation or denial of your election within 3 months of the date filed (date mailed), you should write to the address shown above.

Privacy Notification

Our authority to require this personal information, including identifying numbers (social security numbers, etc.) is found in sections 211, 213-a and 1096, Article 9-A in general of the Tax Law and Parts 6 and 7 of the Business Corporation Franchise Tax Regulations.

We will use this information primarily to determine New York State corporation tax liabilities under Article 9-A of the Tax Law. We will also use it for tax administration and as necessary under Tax Law section 211 and for any other purpose authorized by law, and when the taxpayer gives written authorization to this department for another department, person, agency or entity to have access, limited or otherwise, to information contained in the return.

Your failure to provide the required information may result in civil penalties under sections 217 and 1085 of the Tax Law and Part 9 of the Business Corporation Franchise Tax Regulations and/or criminal penalties under Article 37 of the Tax Law.

Our authority to maintain this information is found in section 211(7) of the Tax Law. This information will be maintained by the Director, Data Management Services Bureau, NYS Tax Department, Building 8, Room 905, W. A. Harriman Campus, Albany, NY 12227; telephone (from New York State only) 1 800 CALL TAX (1 800 225-5829); from outside New York State, call (518) 438-8581.

FORMS AND MATERIALS

New York State Department of Taxation and Finance

CT-6 (8/90) Election by a Federal S Corporation to be Treated as a New York S Corporation

Employer identification number	File number	Business group code number from federal return	Date received

Name of corporation		Principal business activity	

Trade name		Telephone number	

Number and street		State of incorporation/date	

City or town	State	ZIP code	Date began business in New York State	

Number of shareholders who are nonresidents of New York State	Authorized to do business in NYS? Yes ☐ No ☐	Number of shares issued and outstanding (from federal Form 2553)	

The federal election to treat the corporation as an S corporation is effective for the tax year beginning _____, 19___

Check box if federal election is pending ☐

This election is to be effective for the tax year beginning _____, 19___

If your tax year is not a calendar year, indicate the month and day your tax year ends _____

Shareholders' Unanimous Consent and Individual Affirmation By signing below each shareholder of the above corporation elects to include all amounts required by Tax Law, Article 22, Section 660, in computing his or her New York taxable income and certifies that the personal information given below is to the best of his or her knowledge and belief true, correct and complete.

A Name and address of each shareholder (include ZIP code)	B Social security number	C Stock owned		D Shareholder's signature * For this election to be valid, all shareholders must signify consent by signing below.
		Number of shares	Date acquired	

627

* **(See instructions for column D if continuation sheet or a separate consent statement is needed.)**
I certify that this election and all attachments are to the best of my knowledge and belief true, correct, and complete.

Date	Signature of elected officer or authorized person	Official title
Date	Signature of individual or name of firm preparing this election	Preparer's address

CT-6

FORM FOURTEEN

[NAME OF CORPORATION] CERTIFICATE OF THE DESIGNATION, POWERS, PREFERENCES AND RIGHTS OF THE $___ CUMULATIVE REDEEMABLE PREFERRED STOCK PAR VALUE $___ PER SHARE

Pursuant to Section 501 of the Business Corporation Law of the State of New York

The following resolutions were duly adopted by the Board of Directors of ___ Corporation, a New York corporation (the "Corporation"), pursuant to the provisions of Section 501 of the Business Corporation Law of the State of New York, on ___, 19___ (the "Preferred Stock Resolution Date"), at a meeting of the Board of Directors at which there was at all times present and acting a quorum of the Board of Directors of the Corporation:

WHEREAS, the Board of Directors of the Corporation is authorized, within the limitations and restrictions stated in the Certificate of Incorporation, to fix by resolution or resolutions the designation of each series of Preferred Stock (as hereinafter defined) and the powers, preferences and relative participating, optional or other special rights, and qualifications, limitations or restrictions thereof, including, without limiting the generality of the foregoing, such provisions as may be desired concerning voting, redemption, dividends, dissolution or the distribution of assets, conversion or exchange, and such other subjects or matters as may be fixed by resolution or resolutions of the Board of Directors under the Business Corporation Law of New York; and

WHEREAS, it is the desire of the Board of Directors of the Corporation, pursuant to its authority as aforesaid, to authorize and fix the terms of a series of such Preferred Stock and the number of shares constituting such series;

NOW, THEREFORE, BE IT RESOLVED:

1. Designation and Number of Shares. The designation of said series of Preferred Stock, par value $\_\_\_\_ per share (the "Series Preferred Stock"), authorized by this resolution shall be "$____ Cumulative Redeemable Preferred Stock" (the "Preferred Stock"). The number of shares of Preferred Stock authorized hereby shall be ____ and no more.

2. Rank. The Preferred Stock shall, with respect to dividend rights and rights on liquidation, winding up and dissolution, rank (a) junior to any other series of the Series Preferred Stock established by the Board of Directors, the terms of which shall specifically provide that such series shall rank prior to the Preferred Stock (any such other securities being referred to herein collectively as the "Senior Securities"), (b) on a parity with any other series of the Series Preferred Stock established by the Board of Directors, the terms of which shall specifically provide that such series shall rank on a parity with the Preferred Stock (the Preferred Stock and any such other securities being referred to herein collectively as the "Parity Securities"), and (c) prior to any other equity securities of the Corporation, including the Common Stock, par value $.____ per share, of the Corporation (the "Common Stock") (all of such equity securities of the Corporation to which the Preferred Stock ranks prior, including the Common Stock, being referred to herein collectively as the "Junior Securities").

3. Dividends.

(a) The holders of the shares of Preferred Stock shall be entitled to receive, when and as declared by the Board of Directors, out of funds legally available for the payment of dividends, cumulative dividends at the annual rate of $____ per share in equal quarterly payments com-

FORMS AND MATERIALS 631

mencing ____, 19____, in preference to dividends on the Junior Securities. Such dividends shall be paid to the holders of record at the close of business on the date specified by the Board of Directors of the Corporation at the time such dividend is declared; provided, however, that such date shall not be more than 60 days nor less than 10 days prior to the respective dividend payment date. Each of such quarterly dividends (whether payable in cash or in stock) shall be fully cumulative and shall accrue (whether or not declared), without interest, from the first day of the quarter in which such dividend may be payable as herein provided. Any dividend payments due with respect to the Preferred Stock on any dividend payment date during the first ____ quarterly periods after the first dividend payment date may be made, in the sole discretion of the Corporation, in cash or by issuing additional fully paid and nonassessable shares of Preferred Stock at the rate of ____ of one share for each $____ of such quarterly dividend not paid in cash; provided, however, that in lieu of issuing fractional additional shares in payment of such dividends, the Corporation shall pay to the person otherwise entitled to such fractional share cash in the amount of $[amount of liquidation preference] multiplied by the amount of such fraction. The issuance of such additional shares or the issuance of such additional shares together with the payment of cash in lieu of the issuance of any fractional additional shares shall constitute full payment of such dividend.

(b) All dividends paid with respect to shares of the Preferred Stock pursuant to paragraph (3)(a) shall be paid pro rata to the holders entitled thereto.

(c) In the event the Corporation elects to pay the holders of Preferred Stock cash in lieu of the issuance of fractional additional shares, the Corporation may aggregate such fractional additional shares into whole shares of Preferred Stock and issue and sell such whole shares of Preferred Stock.

(d) Notwithstanding anything contained herein to the contrary, no cash dividends on shares of the Preferred Stock (other than the payment of cash in lieu of the issuance of fractional additional shares), the Parity Securities or the Junior Securities shall be declared by the Board of Directors or paid or set apart for payment by the Corporation at any time that the terms or provisions of any indenture or agreement of the Corporation, including any agreement relating to its indebtedness, specifically prohibit such declaration, payment or setting apart for payment or at any time that such declaration, payment or setting apart for payment would constitute (after notice or lapse of time or otherwise) a breach of or a default under any such indenture or agreement; provided, however, that nothing herein contained shall in any way or under any circumstances be construed or deemed to require the Board of Directors to declare or the Corporation to pay or set apart for payment any cash dividends or shares of the Preferred Stock at any time, whether permitted by any of such agreements or not.

(e) (i) If at any time the Corporation shall have failed to pay full dividends which have accrued (whether or not declared) on any Senior Securities, no cash dividend (other than the payment of cash in lieu of the issuance of fractional additional shares) shall be declared by the Board of Directors or paid or set apart for payment by the Corporation on shares of the Preferred Stock or any other Parity Securities unless, prior to or concurrently with such declaration, payment or setting apart for payment, all accrued and unpaid dividends on all outstanding shares of such other prior series of the Series Preferred Stock shall have been or be declared and paid or set apart for payment, without interest. No full dividends shall be declared or paid or set apart for payment on any Parity Securities for any period unless full cumulative dividends have been or contemporaneously are declared and paid or declared and a sum sufficient for the payment thereof set apart for such payment on the Preferred Stock for all dividend payment periods terminating on or prior to the date of payment of such full cumulative dividends. If any dividends are not paid in full, as aforesaid, upon the shares of the Preferred Stock and any other Parity Securities, all dividends declared upon shares of the Preferred Stock and any other Parity Securities shall be declared pro rata so that the amount of dividends declared per share on the Preferred Stock and such other Parity Securities shall in all cases bear to each other the same ratio that accrued dividends per share on the Preferred Stock and such other Parity Securities bear to each other. No interest, or sum of money in lieu of interest, shall be payable in respect

FORMS AND MATERIALS

of any dividend payment or payments on the Preferred Stock or any other Parity Securities which may be in arrears.

(ii) The Corporation shall not declare, pay or set apart for payment any dividend on any of the Preferred Stock or make any payment on account of, or set apart for payment money for a sinking or other similar fund for the purchase, redemption or other retirement of any of the Preferred Stock or any warrants, rights, calls or options exercisable for or convertible into any of the Preferred Stock, or make any distribution in respect thereof, either directly or indirectly, and whether in cash, obligations or shares of the Corporation, or other property (other than distributions or dividends in shares of Preferred Stock (including the payment of cash in lieu of the issuance of fractional shares of Preferred Stock) to the holders thereof), and shall not permit any corporation or other entity directly or indirectly controlled by the Corporation to purchase or redeem any of the Preferred Stock or any warrants, rights, calls or options exercisable for or convertible into any of the Preferred Stock, unless prior to or concurrently with such declaration, payment, setting apart for payment, purchase or distribution, as the case may be, all accrued and unpaid dividends on shares of any Senior Securities shall have been or be duly paid in full and all redemption payments which have become due with respect to such Senior Securities shall have been or be duly discharged.

Any dividend not paid pursuant to paragraph (3)(a) hereof or this paragraph (3)(e) shall be fully cumulative and shall accrue (whether or not declared), without interest, as set forth in paragraph (3)(a) hereof.

(f) (i) Holders of shares of the Preferred Stock shall be entitled to receive the dividends provided for in paragraph (3)(a) hereof in preference to and in priority over any dividends upon any of the Junior Securities.

(ii) The Corporation shall not declare, pay or set apart for payment any dividend on any of the Junior Securities or make any payment on account of, or set apart for payment money for a sinking or other similar fund for, the purchase, redemption or other retirement of any of the Junior Securities or any warrants, rights, calls or options exercisable for or convertible into any of the Junior Securities or make any distribution in respect thereof, either directly or indirectly, and whether in cash, obligations or shares of the Corporation, or other property (other than distributions or dividends in Junior Securities to the holders of Junior Securities), and shall not permit any corporation or other entity directly or indirectly controlled by the Corporation to purchase or redeem any of the Junior Securities or any warrants, rights, calls or options exercisable for or convertible into any of the Junior Securities (A) so long as the Corporation has the option to pay Preferred Stock dividends in additional shares of Preferred Stock, or (B) thereafter, if upon giving effect thereto the aggregate amount expended for all such purposes immediately prior to the first dividend payment date shall exceed the sum of (w) 50 percent of the aggregate Consolidated Net Income of the Corporation (as hereinafter defined), accrued on a cumulative basis immediately prior to the first dividend payment date, plus (x) the aggregate net proceeds, including cash and the fair market value of property other than cash, received by the Corporation from the issue or sale, immediately prior to the first dividend payment date, of Junior Securities, less (y) all dividends on the Preferred Stock immediately prior to the first dividend payment date (whether (i) paid in cash or additional shares of Preferred Stock or (ii) accrued and unpaid) and less (z) $2,000,000; provided, however, that in no event shall any such declaration, payment, setting apart for payment, purchase, redemption or distribution be made unless, prior to or concurrently therewith, all accrued and unpaid dividends on shares of the Preferred Stock not paid on the dates provided for in paragraph (3)(a) hereof (including if not paid pursuant to the terms and conditions of paragraph (3)(a), paragraph (3)(d) or paragraph (3)(e) hereof) shall have been or be paid. For purposes of determining the "amount expended" for such purposes, property other than cash shall be valued at the fair market value of such property. For purposes of this paragraph, the "fair market value" of any property other than cash shall be determined by the Board of Directors of the Corporation. For purposes of this paragraph, the "Consolidated Net Income" of the Corporation shall mean the amount of consolidated net income, including gains on sales of assets (less 100 percent of the

FORMS AND MATERIALS

consolidated net losses), of the Corporation and its consolidated Subsidiaries, as determined in accordance with generally accepted accounting principles; and a "Subsidiary" is any corporation or other entity of which at least a majority of the capital stock having ordinary power for the election of directors is owned by the Corporation directly or through one or more Subsidiaries.

(g) Subject to the foregoing provisions of this Section (3) and the provisions of paragraph (5)(e), the Board of Directors may declare, and the Corporation may pay or set apart for payment, dividends and other distributions on any of the Junior Securities, and may purchase or otherwise redeem any of the Junior Securities or any warrants, rights or options exercisable for or convertible into any of the Junior Securities, and the holders of the shares of the Preferred Stock shall not be entitled to share therein.

4. Liquidation Preference.

(a) In the event of any voluntary or involuntary liquidation, dissolution or winding up of the affairs of the Corporation, the holders of shares of Preferred Stock then outstanding shall be entitled to be paid out of the assets of the Corporation available for distribution to its stockholders an amount in cash equal to $____ for each share outstanding, plus an amount in cash equal to all accrued but unpaid dividends thereon to the date fixed for liquidation, dissolution or winding up, before any payment shall be made or any assets distributed to the holders of any of the Junior Securities; provided, however, that the holders of outstanding shares of the Preferred Stock shall not be entitled to receive such liquidation payment until the liquidation payments on all outstanding shares of Senior Securities, if any, shall have been paid in full. If the assets of the Corporation are not sufficient to pay in full the liquidation payments payable to the holders of outstanding shares of the Preferred Stock or any other Parity Securities, then the holders of all such shares shall share ratably in such distribution of assets in accordance with the amount which would be payable on such distribution if the amounts to which the holders of outstanding shares of Preferred Stock and the holders of outstanding shares of such other Parity Securities are entitled were paid in full.

(b) The liquidation payment with respect to each fractional share of the Preferred Stock outstanding or accrued but unpaid shall be equal to a ratably proportionate amount of the liquidation payment with respect to each outstanding share of Preferred Stock.

(c) For the purposes of this Section (4), neither the voluntary sale, conveyance, lease, exchange or transfer (for cash, shares of stock, securities or other consideration) of all or substantially all the property or assets of the Corporation nor the consolidation or merger of the Corporation with one or more other corporations shall be deemed to be a liquidation, dissolution or winding up, voluntary or involuntary, unless such voluntary sale, conveyance, lease, exchange or transfer shall be in connection with a dissolution or winding up of the business of the Corporation.

5. Redemption.

(a) From and after the Preferred Stock Resolution Date, the Corporation at its option may redeem, to the extent funds are legally available therefor, the Preferred Stock, at any time in whole or from time to time in part, at the following per share redemption prices, together with an amount equal to accrued and unpaid dividends thereon to the date fixed for redemption, without interest, if redeemed during the twelve-month period ending on the anniversary of the Preferred Stock Resolution Date indicated:

Anniversary	**Redemption Price**
First	$
Second	
Third	
Fourth	
Fifth	
Sixth and thereafter	

The Corporation shall not optionally redeem the Preferred Stock or any other Parity Securities, in whole or in part, without redeeming, on a pro rata basis, shares of all outstanding series of Parity Securities (including the Preferred Stock) in accordance with the relative amounts which the holders of such Parity Securities would be entitled to receive upon liquidation, if paid in full, pursuant to paragraph (4)(a).

(b) Commencing on the first dividend payment date after the eleventh anniversary of the Preferred Stock Resolution Date and on each anniversary of the Preferred Stock Resolution Date thereafter, so long as any shares of the Preferred Stock shall be outstanding and to the extent the Corporation shall have funds legally available for such payment, the Corporation shall set aside, in trust, as and for a sinking fund for the Preferred Stock, a sum sufficient to redeem and shall redeem the number of shares of Preferred Stock equal to the quotient obtained by dividing (i) the product of (x) 20% of the sum of the Aggregate Preferred Stock Liquidation Value multiplied by (y) a fraction, the numerator of which is the Preferred Stock Liquidation Value as of such redemption date, in the case of the first such redemption, or as of the time immediately after the immediately preceding redemption date, in the case of each subsequent redemption, and the denominator of which is the Preferred Stock Liquidation Value as of such redemption date, in the case of the first such redemption, or as of the time immediately after the immediately preceding redemption date, in the case of each subsequent redemption, by (ii) $[amount of liquidation preference]. For purposes of the foregoing, "Aggregate Preferred Stock Liquidation Value" means (i) the total number of shares of Preferred Stock outstanding on the eleventh anniversary of the first dividend payment date, multiplied by (ii) $[amount of liquidation preference]; "Preferred Stock Liquidation Value," as of any redemption date, means (i) the total number of shares of Preferred Stock outstanding on such redemption date, in the case of the first such redemption, or as of the time immediately after the immediately preceding redemption date, in the case of each subsequent redemption, multiplied by (ii) $[amount of liquidation preference]. The Corporation may reduce the number of shares of Preferred Stock to be redeemed pursuant to this paragraph (5)(b) by subtracting the number of shares of Preferred Stock that the Corporation has (x) redeemed other than pursuant to this paragraph (5)(b) or (y) purchased or otherwise acquired other than pursuant to Section (6). The Corporation may so subtract the same share of Preferred Stock only once.

(c) Shares of Preferred Stock which have been issued and reacquired in any manner, including shares purchased or redeemed or exchanged, shall (upon compliance with any applicable provisions of the laws of the State of New York) have the status of authorized and unissued shares of the class of Series Preferred Stock, undesignated as to series, and may be redesignated and reissued as part of any series of the Series Preferred Stock, par value $.____ per share, of the Corporation; provided, however, that no such issued and reacquired shares of Preferred Stock shall be reissued or sold as Preferred Stock unless reissued as a stock dividend on shares of Preferred Stock.

(d) Notwithstanding the foregoing provisions of this Section (5), unless the full cumulative dividends on all outstanding shares of Preferred Stock shall have been paid or contemporaneously are declared and paid for all past dividend periods, none of the shares of Preferred Stock shall be redeemed unless all outstanding shares of Preferred Stock are simultaneously redeemed, and the Corporation shall not purchase or otherwise acquire (except pursuant to Section (6) hereof) any shares of Preferred Stock; provided, however, that the foregoing shall not prevent the purchase or acquisition of shares of Preferred Stock pursuant to a purchase or exchange offer made on the same terms to holders of all outstanding shares of Preferred Stock.

(e) If the Corporation shall fail to discharge its sinking fund obligation pursuant to paragraph (5)(b), such sinking fund obligation shall be discharged as soon as the Corporation is able to discharge such obligation. If and so long as any sinking fund obligation with respect to the Preferred Stock shall not be fully discharged, the Corporation shall not (i) discharge any sinking fund obligation in respect of any Parity Securities or (ii) declare or pay any dividend or make any distributions on, or, directly or indirectly, purchase, redeem or satisfy any sinking fund obligation in respect of, the Junior Securities or any warrants, rights or options exercisable for or convertible into any of the Junior Securities.

FORMS AND MATERIALS 639

(f) No redemption shall be made pursuant to paragraph (5)(a) or (5)(b), and no sum shall be set aside for any such redemption unless, at the time thereof, (i) all accrued dividends payable on any Senior Securities, if any, then outstanding, (ii) all mandatory redemptions of any such Senior Securities, if any, then required and (iii) all optional redemptions of any such Senior Securities, if any, previously declared, shall in each case have been paid in full.

(g) No redemption shall be made pursuant to paragraph (5)(a) or (5)(b) and no sum shall be set aside for any such redemption at any time that the terms or provisions of any indenture or agreement of the Corporation, including any agreement relating to its indebtedness, specifically prohibits such redemption or setting aside for redemption or that such redemption or setting aside for redemption would constitute (after notice or lapse of time or otherwise) a breach of or a default under any such indenture or agreement.

6. Procedure for Redemption.

(a) In the event that fewer than all the outstanding shares of Preferred Stock are to be redeemed, the number of shares to be redeemed shall be determined by the Board of Directors and the shares to be redeemed shall be determined by lot or pro rata as may be determined by the Board of Directors, except that in any redemption of fewer than all outstanding shares of the Preferred Stock the Corporation may redeem all shares held by any holders of a number of shares not to exceed 100 as may be determined by the Corporation.

(b) In the event the Corporation shall redeem shares of Preferred Stock, notice of such redemption shall be given by first class mail, postage prepaid, mailed not less than 30 days nor more than 60 days prior to the redemption date, to each holder of record of the shares to be redeemed at such holder's address as the same appears on the stock register of the Corporation; provided, however, that no failure to mail such notice nor any defect therein shall affect the validity of the proceeding for the redemption of any shares of Preferred Stock to be redeemed except as to the holder to whom the Corporation has failed to mail said notice or except as to the holder whose notice was defective.

Each such notice shall state: (i) the redemption date; (ii) the number of shares of Preferred Stock to be redeemed and, if less than all the shares held by such holder are to be redeemed from such holder, the number of shares to be redeemed from such holder; (iii) the redemption price; (iv) the place or places where certificates for such shares are to be surrendered for payment of the redemption price; and (v) that dividends on the shares to be redeemed will cease to accrue on such redemption date.

(c) Notice having been mailed as aforesaid, from and after the redemption date (unless, in the case of redemptions, default shall be made by the Corporation in providing money for the payment of the redemption price of the shares called for redemption) dividends on the shares of Preferred Stock so called for redemption shall cease to accrue, and said shares shall no longer be deemed to be outstanding and shall have the status of authorized but unissued shares of Series Preferred Stock, unclassified as to series, and shall not be reissued as shares of Preferred Stock (unless reissued as a stock dividend on Preferred Stock), and all rights of the holders thereof as stockholders of the Corporation with respect to said shares (except the right to receive from the Corporation the redemption price) shall cease. Upon surrender in accordance with said notice of the certificates for any shares so redeemed (properly endorsed or assigned for transfer, if the Board of Directors of the Corporation shall so require and the notice shall so state), such shares shall be redeemed by the Corporation at the redemption price aforesaid. In case fewer than all the shares represented by any such certificate are redeemed, a new certificate shall be issued representing the unredeemed shares without cost to the holder thereof.

7. Voting Rights. The holders of record of shares of Preferred Stock shall not be entitled to any voting rights except as hereinafter provided in this Section (7) or as otherwise provided by law.

(a) If and whenever at any time or times either (i) dividends payable on the Preferred Stock shall have been in arrears and unpaid in an aggregate amount equal to or exceeding the amount of dividends payable thereon for six (6) quarterly periods or (ii) the Corporation shall have failed to make any mandatory redemption as required in respect of

FORMS AND MATERIALS 641

the Preferred Stock, then the number of directors constituting the Board of Directors shall, without further action, be increased by one-third (but not less than two directors) and the holders of Preferred Stock shall have the exclusive right, voting separately as a class, to elect the directors of the Corporation to fill such newly created directorships, the remaining directors to be elected by the other class or classes of stock entitled to vote therefor, at each meeting of stockholders held for the purpose of electing directors.

(b) Whenever such voting right shall have vested, such right may be exercised initially either at a special meeting of the holders of the Preferred Stock, called as hereinafter provided, or at any annual meeting of stockholders held for the purpose of electing directors, and thereafter at such annual meetings or by the written consent of the holders of the Preferred Stock entitled to vote thereon pursuant to Section 615 of the New York Business Corporation Law. Such voting right shall continue until such time as (i) all cumulative dividends accumulated on the Preferred Stock shall have been paid in full, and (ii) all sinking fund obligations with respect to the Preferred Stock which have matured have been met, at which time such voting right of the holders of the Preferred Stock shall terminate, subject to revesting in the event of each and every subsequent event of the character indicated above.

(c) At any time when such voting right shall have vested in the holders of the Preferred Stock, and if such right shall not already have been initially exercised, a proper officer of the Corporation shall, upon the written request of any holder of record of Preferred Stock then outstanding, addressed to the Secretary of the Corporation, call a special meeting of holders of the Preferred Stock having such voting right and of any other class or classes of stock having voting power with respect thereto for the purpose of electing directors. Such meeting shall be held at the earliest practicable date upon the notice required for annual meetings of stockholders at the place for holding annual meetings of stockholders of the Corporation or, if none, at a place designated by the Secretary of the Corporation. If such meeting shall not be called by the proper officer of the Corporation within 30 days after the personal service of such written request upon the Secretary of the Corporation, or within 30 days after mailing the same within the United States, by registered mail, addressed to the Secretary of the Corporation at its principal office (such mailing to be evidenced by the registry receipt issued by the postal authorities), then the holders of record of 10 percent of the shares of the Preferred Stock then outstanding which would be entitled to vote at such meeting may designate in writing a holder of Preferred Stock to call such meeting at the expense of the Corporation, and such meeting may be called by such person so designated upon the notice required for annual meetings of stockholders and shall be held at the same place as is elsewhere provided in this paragraph (7)(c). Any holder of the Preferred Stock which would be entitled to vote at such meeting shall have access to the stock books of the Corporation for the purpose of causing a meeting of stockholders to be called pursuant to the provisions of this paragraph (7)(c). Notwithstanding the provisions of this paragraph (7)(c), however, no such special meeting shall be called during a period within 90 days immediately preceding the date fixed for the next annual meeting of stockholders.

(d) At any meeting held for the purpose of electing directors at which the holders of Preferred Stock shall have the right to elect directors as provided herein, the presence in person or by proxy of the holders of 33-1/3 percent of the then outstanding shares of Preferred Stock shall be required and be sufficient to constitute a quorum of such class for the election of directors by such class. At any such meeting or adjournment thereof (i) the absence of a quorum of the holders of the Preferred Stock shall not prevent the election of directors other than those to be elected by the holders of the Preferred Stock, and the absence of a quorum or quorums of the holders of capital stock entitled to elect such other directors shall not prevent the election of directors to be elected by the holders of the Preferred Stock and (ii) in the absence of a quorum of the holders of any class of stock entitled to vote for the election of directors, a majority of the holders present in person or by proxy of such class shall have the power to adjourn the meeting for the election of directors which the holders of such class are entitled to elect, from time to time, without notice (except as required by law) other than announcement at the meeting, until a quorum shall be present.

(e) The term of office of all directors elected by the holders of the Preferred Stock pursuant to paragraph (7)(a) in office at any time when the aforesaid voting rights are vested in the holders of the Preferred Stock shall terminate upon the election of their successors at any meeting of stockholders for the purpose of electing directors. Upon any termination of the aforesaid voting rights, the term of office of all directors elected by the holders of the Preferred Stock pursuant to paragraph (7)(a) shall thereupon terminate, and upon such termination the number of directors constituting the Board of Directors shall, without further action, be reduced by the number of directors by which the number of directors constituting the Board of Directors shall have been increased pursuant to paragraph (7)(a), subject always to the increase of the number of directors pursuant to paragraph (7)(a) in case of the future right of the holders of Preferred Stock to elect directors.

(f) In exercising the voting rights set forth in this Section (7), each share of Preferred Stock shall have one vote per share and each fractional share of Preferred Stock shall be entitled to a vote equal to the fraction of a whole share of Preferred Stock represented by such fractional share.

(g) So long as any shares of Preferred Stock are outstanding, the Corporation shall not, without the affirmative vote of the holders of at least two-thirds of the then outstanding shares of Preferred Stock voting separately as a class, change by amendment to the Corporation's Certificate of Incorporation or otherwise the terms or provisions of the Preferred Stock so as to adversely affect the powers, special rights and preferences of the holders thereof.

(h) No consent of holders of the Preferred Stock shall be required for (i) the creation, authorization or issuance of any indebtedness of any kind of the Corporation, (ii) the creation, authorization or issuance of any other class of stock of the Corporation senior, pari passu or subordinate as to dividends and upon liquidation to the Preferred Stock or (iii) any increase or decrease in the amount of authorized Common Stock or Series Preferred Stock or any increase, decrease or change in the par value thereof, and none of the foregoing shall be deemed to affect adversely the powers, special rights or preferences of holders of Preferred Stock.

8. Restrictions on Mergers. Except for the Merger, the Corporation may not consolidate with or merge with or into another corporation unless (a) the Corporation is the successor corporation or the person formed by such consolidation or merger is organized in the United States or any state, municipality or other governmental division thereof; (b) immediately after giving effect to such transaction, the consolidated net worth of the successor corporation and its subsidiaries, as determined on a pro forma basis after giving effect to such consolidation or merger and after deduction of the aggregate liquidation preference of the Preferred Stock then outstanding, is at least equal to the consolidated net worth of the Corporation and its Subsidiaries immediately prior to such transaction after deduction of such aggregate liquidation preference of the Preferred Stock; and (c) immediately after giving effect to such transaction, the Pro Forma Consolidated Net Income of the successor corporation and its subsidiaries shall be at least equal to Annualized Preferred Stock Dividends. In the event of any such transaction, if (a) the terms of the Preferred Stock are changed in any manner which is materially adverse to the holders or (b) the powers, special rights and preferences of any securities (the "Replacement Securities") into which the Preferred Stock is converted in such transaction are not substantially the same as the rights and preferences of the Preferred Stock provided for herein, then such transaction shall be subject to the affirmative vote of the holders of at least two-thirds of the outstanding shares of Preferred Stock voting separately as a class. For purposes of this Section (8), (a) "Pro Forma Consolidated Net Income" of the successor corporation in such merger or consolidation and its subsidiaries shall mean, as of any date, the consolidated net income of the successor corporation and its subsidiaries, before deducting dividends on the Preferred Stock, for the most recent four successive fiscal quarters ended on or before such date for which financial information is available immediately prior to the effective date of such transaction, determined in accordance with generally accepted accounting principles and on a pro forma basis giving effect to such consolidation or merger; and (b) "Annualized Preferred Stock Dividends" shall mean (x) $[amount of dividend], multiplied by (y) the number of shares of Preferred Stock outstanding immediately prior to such consolidation or merger.

9. Amendment of Resolution. The Board of Directors of the Corporation reserves the right by subsequent amendment of this resolution from time to time to decrease the number of shares which constitute the Preferred Stock (but not below the number of shares thereof then outstanding) and in other respects to amend this resolution within the limitations provided by law, this resolution and the Certificate of Incorporation of the Corporation.

IN WITNESS WHEREOF, _____ Corporation has caused this certificate to be signed by its Chairman of the Board and Chief Executive Officer and attested by its Secretary this ____ day of ____, 19____.

                        [NAME OF CORPORATION]

                        By:_____

ATTEST:

_____
Secretary

FORM FIFTEEN

SHAREHOLDERS AGREEMENT

This SHAREHOLDERS AGREEMENT, dated ____, 19____, is entered into by and among ____ ("Shareholder A"), ____ ("Shareholder B") and ____ ("Shareholder C") (each individually a "Shareholder" and collectively the "Shareholders"), who are all of the shareholders of ____, a New York corporation (the "Corporation"). The Shareholders agree as follows:

1. Share Ownership. Each Shareholder owns ____ shares of the Common Stock, $____ par value per share, of the Corporation, representing 33 1/3 percent of the total issued and outstanding shares of the Corporation (the "Shares").

2. Legended Certificates. Each certificate representing Shares currently owned by a Shareholder shall be stamped or otherwise imprinted with a legend in substantially the following form:

THE SHARES OF [CORPORATION] REPRESENTED BY THIS CERTIFICATE ARE SUBJECT TO THE TERMS AND, RESTRICTIONS SET FORTH IN A SHAREHOLDERS AGREEMENT, DATED AS OF ____, 19____, AMONG [SHAREHOLDER A], [SHAREHOLDER B] AND [SHAREHOLDER C]. THESE SHARES MAY NOT BE SOLD OR OTHERWISE TRANSFERRED EXCEPT AS SET FORTH IN SAID AGREEMENT.

3. Subsidiaries. Except as provided in Section 5, the Corporation owns and will own all of the outstanding stock of two other corporations: _____, a New York corporation ("Subsidiary A"), and _____, a New York corporation ("Subsidiary B"); (Subsidiary A and Subsidiary B each individually a "Subsidiary" and collectively the "Subsidiaries").

4. Issuance and Sale of Shares of the Corporation. Additional Shares of the Corporation, any other equity security of the Corporation or any security convertible into or exchangeable for any equity security of the Corporation may be issued only with the unanimous written consent of all three Shareholders. During the period beginning on the date hereof and ending ____ years after the date hereof, no Shareholder may sell, give or otherwise transfer in any way whatsoever any Shares of the Corporation or Subsidiaries without the express written consent of the other Shareholders, which consent may be withheld for any reason. At any time after the expiration of such ____-year period, any proposed transfer by a Shareholder (the "Transferring Shareholder") may only be made upon written notice to the other Shareholders of the terms of the proposed transfer, including the number of Shares proposed to be transferred, the consideration for such Shares, the method and timing of the transfer and the identity of the proposed transferee, which notice shall include a written copy of the proposed offer from the prospective transferee. Such notice shall constitute an irrevocable offer by the Transferring Shareholder to sell all, but not less than all, of the Shares specified in the notice to the other Shareholders on a pro rata basis and on the same terms as are contained in such notice. In the event that one of the other Shareholders chooses not to accept the Transferring Shareholder's offer, the remaining Shareholder must elect to purchase all or none of the Shares being offered by the Transferring Shareholder. The other Shareholders shall have sixty (60) days from the date notice is given to accept or reject such offer. The acceptance or rejection by the other Shareholders of such irrevocable offer shall not constitute the exclusive remedy of such other Shareholders in the event that the Transferring Shareholder shall convey Shares contrary to the terms and provisions of this Section 4.

5. Distribution of Equity Ownership in Subsidiaries. Any sale or distribution of equity interests in either Subsidiary shall require the unanimous written consent of the Shareholders.

6. Shareholder Entitlements. The Shareholders shall enjoy equal rights and shall be entitled to equal compensation, including perquisites, under this Agreement. Any interference or attempt to interfere by two

FORMS AND MATERIALS 649

Shareholders with the rights of a third Shareholder under this Agreement, including but not limited to failing to elect a Shareholder as director of the Corporation and the Subsidiaries and failing to grant a Shareholder compensation (including salary, benefits and perquisites) equal to that received by the other two Shareholders, shall constitute the firing (the "Firing") of that third Shareholder (the "Fired Shareholder") and shall entitle him to sell his Shares back to the Company in the following manner: the Fired Shareholder shall give notice to the Corporation of his intention to sell his Shares to the Corporation pursuant to this Section 6, which notice shall specifically set forth the events and/or acts which constitute the Firing. The Corporation shall cause to be conducted an audit of the Corporation within a reasonable time following the date of such notice (the "Notice Date"). Such audit shall determine the Fired Shareholder's Net Income (as defined in Section 7 hereof) as of the Notice Date. Within two weeks of completion of the audit the Fired Shareholder shall sell to the Corporation, and the Corporation shall buy, the Fired Shareholder's Shares for a purchase price equal to [____] times the Fired Shareholder's Net Income. The purchase price shall be paid in the following manner: ____ percent of the purchase price shall be paid on the date the Fired Shareholder tenders his Shares (the "Tender Date") and ____ percent of the purchase price shall be paid on each succeeding one-year anniversary of the Tender Date until the purchase price is fully paid. In the event that, as of the Notice Date, the Corporation's assets include real property or any interest in real property, and so long as the Corporation, in its sole discretion, shall continue to hold such real property or such interest in real property, the Fired Shareholder shall be entitled to (a) one-third of the net income, if any, generated by such real property or interest in real property; and (b) upon sale, if any, of any such real property or interest in real property, one-third of the net income, if any, from such sale.

7. Shareholder Net Income. Under this Agreement, a Shareholder's Net Income shall equal an amount, the numerator of which shall be the aggregate average yearly income of the Subsidiaries based upon the eight fiscal quarters preceding a Notice Date (as that term is defined in Sections 6 and 16) or, in the case of the death of a Shareholder, the date of the death, less all expenses of the Subsidiaries other than salaries, benefits and perquisites of the Shareholders, and the denominator of which shall be three. Any calculation of Shareholder Net Income pursuant to this Agreement shall be according to generally accepted accounting principles.

8. Voluntary Departure of a Shareholder. Any Shareholder who wishes to terminate his employment with the Corporation shall give the Corporation notice of his intention to sell his Shares, and the Corporation shall purchase such Shareholder's Shares in accordance with the provisions of Section 16 hereof.

9. Death or Disability of a Shareholder.

(a) *Death*: Within a reasonable time after the death of a Shareholder, the Corporation shall cause to be conducted an audit of the Corporation, which audit shall determine the deceased Shareholder's Net Income. Within two weeks of completion of such audit, the deceased Shareholder's estate shall sell, and the Corporation shall purchase, the deceased Shareholder's Shares. The purchase price shall be ____ times the Shareholder's Net Income as determined by the audit, and shall be paid to the Shareholder's estate in the following manner: the Corporation shall pay to the estate at the time of such purchase one-third of the deceased Shareholder's Net Income. Of the remaining amount, one-half shall be paid to the estate one calendar year after the completion of the audit and the other one-half shall be paid to the estate two calendar years after the completion of the audit. In the event that, as of the date of the Shareholder's death, the Corporation's assets include real property or any interest in real property, and so long as the Corporation, in its sole discretion, shall continue to hold such real property or such interest in real property, the deceased Shareholder's estate shall be entitled to (a) one-third of the net income, if any, generated by such real property or interest in real property; and (b) upon sale, if any, of any such real property or interest in real property, one-third of the net income, if any, from such sale.

(b) *Disablement*: Upon the permanent disablement of a Shareholder such that his ability to contribute significantly to the Corporation and/or

Subsidiaries is substantially impaired, or if a Shareholder is temporarily disabled and it is expected that he will remain disabled as described above for more than ____ years, he shall resign from the Corporation, and he shall sell to the Corporation, and the Corporation shall purchase, his Shares in the manner provided in Section 16. If a Shareholder is temporarily disabled and it is expected that he will remain disabled as described above for more than ____ months, but less than ____ years, for the period of his disablement his salary shall be reduced to one-half of that received by the other Shareholders but his benefits and perquisites shall not be reduced in relation to those received by the other Shareholders. Upon a Shareholder's death, permanent disablement or temporary disablement which is expected to continue for more than three years, in addition to the above, said Shareholder or his estate shall receive a sum of $____ per annum from the Corporation for each of ____ consecutive years immediately following his disablement or death. Payments will be made in equal bimonthly installments.

10. Key Man Insurance. Within fifteen (15) days after the execution of this Agreement, the Corporation shall obtain a life and disability insurance policy on each of Shareholder A, Shareholder B and Shareholder C, each in the face amount of $____, and shall maintain the same until such time as Shareholder A, Shareholder B or Shareholder C, as the case may be, shall have ceased to own any Shares of the Corporation. The Shareholders may, from time to time, cause the amounts of such policies to be increased in equal amounts. Upon the death or disability of any Shareholder, the proceeds from his life and disability insurance policy shall be the property of the Corporation and shall not be included as an asset of the Corporation for purposes of the audit described in Sections 6, 9 and 16.

11. Board of Directors of the Corporation. The Corporation shall be governed by a Board of Directors, which shall consist of Shareholder A, Shareholder B and Shareholder C, as long as each continues to be a Shareholder. In the event that a director ceases to be a Shareholder, the Board of Directors shall consist of the remaining Shareholders.

12. Control of Subsidiaries. Each Subsidiary will be controlled by a Board of Directors comprised of all three Shareholders and any other persons whom the Shareholders shall unanimously elect. The Board of Directors of each Subsidiary will select a chief executive officer or officers for that Subsidiary who will be responsible to the Board of Directors of that Subsidiary for its operations. The corporate objectives, policies and strategies of each Subsidiary will be determined by its Board of Directors and be carried out by its chief executive officer.

13. Other Activities. No Shareholder may undertake or otherwise engage in any of the business activities in which the Corporation or Subsidiaries are normally involved or plan to be involved in any manner that is separate and apart from the activities of the Corporation and Subsidiaries without the express permission of all the other Shareholders. However, business undertaken prior to the signing of this Agreement may be completed by any Shareholder so involved in a manner separate and apart from the Corporation and Subsidiaries' activities.

14. Allocation of Time to the Corporation and Subsidiaries. Every Shareholder shall devote his full time, attention and energies to the business of the Corporation and Subsidiaries and shall not, so long as he remains a Shareholder, be engaged in any other business activity, whether or not such business activity is pursued for gain, profit or other pecuniary advantage, except as otherwise permitted in Sections 13 and 15. Any Shareholder who violates this provision and continues to so act after written notice from the other Shareholders may have his salary withheld and, in the event of such withholding, shall forfeit said salary from the time of such written notice until he ceases to so act. If such behavior continues for more than ____ months from said written notice, the other Shareholders by unanimous decision may require him to sell his Shares to the Corporation in the manner provided in Section 16, less $____, which sum he shall forfeit.

15. Other Permitted Activities. In the application of the provisions contained in Section 14 hereof, activities which will strengthen the credentials of the Shareholder, and thereby the Corporation and Subsidiaries, will be treated more liberally. However, even in such circumstances, at least a majority of the Shareholder's business time must be devoted to the business of the Corporation and Subsidiaries. The type of activities to be treated more liberally would include, but are not limited to, a membership on a Board of Trustees or Board of Directors or a comparable position with a charitable, corporate, governmental, religious or similar entity.

16. Purchase of a Shareholder's Shares by the Corporation. If the Corporation purchases the Shares of any Shareholder pursuant to Section 8, 9(b) or 14 hereof or for any reason except the death or Firing of a Shareholder, payment for such Shares shall be made in the following manner: the Corporation shall give written notice to a Shareholder (the "Selling Shareholder") of its intention to purchase such Shareholder's Shares pursuant to this Agreement. The Corporation shall cause to be conducted an audit of the Corporation within a reasonable time following the date of such notice (the "Notice Date"). Such audit shall determine the Selling Shareholder's Net Income as of the Notice Date. The Selling Shareholder shall sell to the Corporation, and the Corporation shall buy, his Shares within two weeks after completion of the audit.

In the case of a permanently or temporarily disabled Shareholder, the purchase price shall be ____ times the Shareholder's Net Income, one-third of which shall be paid on the date the Selling Shareholder tenders his Shares to the Corporation pursuant to this Section 16 (the "Tender Date"), one-third of which shall be paid to the Shareholder one calendar year after the Tender Date and the final one-third of which shall be paid to the Selling Shareholder two calendar years after the Tender Date.

In all other cases the purchase price shall be the Shareholder's Net Income, one-fifth of which shall be paid on the Tender Date and one-fifth of which shall be paid on each succeeding anniversary of the Tender Date, until the purchase price is fully paid.

In the event that, as of the Notice Date, the Corporation's assets include real property or any interest in real property, and so long as the Corporation, in its sole discretion, shall continue to hold such real property or such interest in real property, the Selling Shareholder shall be entitled to (a) one-third of the net income, if any, generated by such real property or interest in real property; and (b) upon sale, if any, of such real property or interest in real property, one-third of the net income, if any, from such sale.

17. Solicitation Not Permitted. So long as a Shareholder continues to own Shares, he shall not (a) offer employment to any person who is an employee or prospective employee of the Corporation or Subsidiaries (other than on behalf of the Corporation or a Subsidiary); or (b) solicit any securities brokerage or investment advisory business (other than for the Corporation or a Subsidiary) from any client or customer of the Corporation or Subsidiaries. In the event that any Shareholder (the "Departing Shareholder") ceases to be a Shareholder, then the Departing Shareholder agrees that, for a period of ____ months from the date he sells his Shares, he will not, directly or indirectly, as a sole proprietor, member of a partnership or stockholder, investor, officer or director of a corporation or as an employee, agent, associate or consultant of any person, firm or corporation other than the Corporation or its Subsidiaries, (y) offer employment to any person who is an employee or prospective employee of the Corporation or Subsidiaries upon the date of the sale of his Shares or who was an employee at any time during the one-year period preceding such event; or (z) solicit business of the type engaged in by the Corporation or the Subsidiaries (other than for the Corporation or Subsidiaries) from any person who is a client or prospective client of the Corporation or Subsidiaries upon the date of the sale of his Shares or who has been a client of the Corporation or Subsidiaries at any time during the one-year period preceding such sale.

18. Liquidated Damages and Injunctive Relief. Inasmuch as any damages arising from the breach of Section 17 hereof would be difficult to determine, any Shareholder or Departing Shareholder who violates Section 17 agrees to be liable in the following manner:

(a) Any Shareholder or Departing Shareholder who violates Section 17(a) or 17(y), as the case may be, shall be liable in an amount equal to ____ times the yearly salary or salaries of the employee or employees who were subject to the solicitation which resulted in the violation of Section 17(a) or 17(y). In the event that an employee is a prospective

FORMS AND MATERIALS 655

employee, the amount of damages shall be ____ times the yearly salary for the position for which the prospective employee was being considered.

(b) Any Shareholder or Departing Shareholder who violates Section 17(b) or 17(z), as the case may be, shall be liable in an amount equal to ____ times the average fees paid or due and owing to the Corporation or the Subsidiaries by the customer annually over the two years preceding the violation of Section 17(b) or 17(z). In the event that a solicited customer has been a customer for less than two years, damages shall be in an amount equal to ____ times the total amount of fees the solicited customer would have paid had he remained a customer for two years, based upon the average size of the customer's advisory account (if the customer was an investment advisory client) during the period he was a customer and/or based upon the customer's average monthly brokerage fees (if the customer was a brokerage client) during the period he was a customer. In the event that the solicitation is of a prospective customer, damages shall be in an amount equal to $____.

19. Attorneys' Fees. In the event of any breach by any Shareholder or Departing Shareholder of the provisions of Section 17 hereof which leads to a settlement or an injunction, an award of damages or other judgment against the Shareholder or Departing Shareholder, the Shareholder or Departing Shareholder hereby agrees to pay all costs and expenses of every kind, including reasonable attorneys' fees, incurred by the remaining Shareholders and the Corporation or Subsidiaries in connection with obtaining such settlement or injunction, award of damages or other judgment.

20. Arbitration. Any and all disputes, controversies and claims arising out of or relating to this Agreement, or with respect to the construction of this Agreement, or concerning the respective rights or obligations hereunder of the parties hereto and their respective permitted successors and assigns shall be determined by arbitration in New York, New York, in accordance with and pursuant to the then existing rules of the American Arbitration Association. The arbitration award shall be final and binding upon the parties and judgment thereon may be entered in any court of the State of New York and federal courts in said state, the jurisdiction of which courts is hereby consented to by the parties for such purposes. The service of any notice, process, motion or other document in connection with an arbitration award hereunder may be effectuated either by personal service upon a party or by certified or registered mail.

21. Survival of Agreement. Any Shareholder who, for any reason, ceases to own Shares shall thereafter have no voting or other rights regarding the operation and control of the Corporation and the Subsidiaries or regarding decisions to be made by the Shareholders pursuant to this Agreement, but shall otherwise continue to be bound by the terms of this Agreement.

22. Entire Agreement. This document sets forth the entire Agreement between the parties. There are no verbal or other written agreements that are part of this Agreement.

23. Termination. This Agreement may be terminated by the unanimous written consent of all the Shareholders owning Shares on the date of termination. This Agreement may be terminated by the written consent of two Shareholders but in such event, for a period of ____ months following the termination, the two Shareholders who consented to the termination (the "Consenting Shareholders") shall not, together, as members of the same partnership, as stockholders, investors, officers or directors of the same corporation or as employees, agents, associates or consultants of or to the same person or company, engage in business of the type engaged in by the Corporation or the Subsidiaries.

24. Successors and Assigns. This Agreement shall be binding on any and all successors and assigns of the Shareholders.

25. Retention of Attorney. Each of the parties signing below certifies that he has thoroughly read and fully understands all the provisions herein and that he has shown this contract to an attorney who has represented him and acted as his advisor in the signing of this Agreement.

26. Governing Law. This Agreement shall be governed by and construed in accordance with the laws of the State of New York.

We, the undersigned, hereby agree to all the provisions of this Agreement this ____ day of ____, 19____.

_____
[Shareholder A]

_____
[Shareholder B]

_____
[Shareholder C]

FORM SIXTEEN

STOCK TRANSFER RESTRICTION AGREEMENT

(Buy-Sell Agreement)

This STOCK TRANSFER RESTRICTION AGREEMENT is entered into as of ____, 19____, by and between ____ ("Shareholder") and ____, a New York corporation (the "Company"), in connection with and in consideration of the acquisition by Shareholder of ____ shares of Common Stock, par value $____, of the Company (the "Stock"), and shall apply to all shares of the Stock now or hereafter issued to Shareholder, unless by separate written agreement signed by the Company certain of Shareholder's shares are excepted from this Agreement.

NOW, THEREFORE, the parties agree as follows:

1. Definitions.

1.1 *Purchase Value* means the fair market value of shares of the Stock as established at least annually by the Company's Board of Directors. As of this date, said Purchase Value is $____ per share.

1.2 *Termination Date* means the date fixed by the Board of Directors of the Company as the date that Shareholder's affiliation with the Company (as an employee, director or consultant) ceases, whether such cessation was voluntary or involuntary or resulted from death, termination or otherwise.

1.3 *Vested; Unvested.*

(a) All of Shareholder's shares of the Stock shall be "Unvested" until they become "Vested" as hereinafter defined.

(b) Shareholder's shares of the Stock shall become "Vested" on a monthly basis, commencing on the first day of the first full calendar month after the date such shares are issued to Shareholder, which issuance shall be the date that Shareholder pays for the shares or the date shown on the share certificate evidencing the shares, whichever is earlier. Said monthly vesting shall be over a period of forty-eight (48) months as follows:

(i) At the end of each of the first twelve (12) full calendar months after issuance of the shares, 1/120th of such shares shall become Vested.

(ii) At the end of each of the next twelve (12) full calendar months, 1/60th of such shares shall become Vested.

(iii) At the end of each of the next twelve (12) full calendar months, 1/40th of such shares shall become Vested.

(iv) At the end of each of the next twelve (12) full calendar months, 1/30th of such shares shall become Vested, at which time all of such shares shall become fully Vested.

(c) Any fractional shares resulting from the foregoing calculations shall be Unvested.

(d) Upon Shareholder's leave of absence from employment with the Company, Shareholder's Unvested shares of the Stock shall cease vesting, and Shareholder's Unvested shares of the Stock shall not recommence vesting according to the vesting schedule until, and only at such time as, Shareholder's leave of absence ceases and Shareholder returns to full-time employment with the Company.

2. Restriction on Transfer. Shareholder shall not sell, transfer, assign, pledge, donate or in any other way encumber or alienate any shares of the Stock or any interest therein, except in conformance with the provisions of this Agreement. Any attempted transfer without compliance with this Agreement shall be null and void.

3. The Company's Option to Repurchase Unvested Shares.

3.1 *Option*. Upon the Termination Date, the Company shall have the option to purchase all or any part of Shareholder's Unvested shares of the Stock at a purchase price (the "Purchase Price") equal to the Pur-

FORMS AND MATERIALS 661

chase Value which was applicable at the date of issuance of such shares to Shareholder, plus simple interest on said Purchase Value at the rate of ____ percent per annum commencing on the date of issuance until the date the Company gives written notice to Shareholder of the Company's election to exercise this option. The Purchase Price shall be payable in cash or, at the option of the Company, by a promissory note bearing interest at ____ percent per annum, payable in ____ equal monthly installments of combined principal and interest.

3.2 *Exercise*. This option shall be exercised, if at all, by the Company's giving to Shareholder a written notice of exercise within ____ days following the Termination Date. Upon Shareholder's receiving said notice of exercise, Shareholder shall promptly deliver to the Company the certificate(s) evidencing the Unvested shares of the Stock being purchased, which certificate(s) shall be duly endorsed by Shareholder and delivered to the Company free and clear of all liens or other encumbrances. Promptly upon receiving said share certificate(s), the Company shall pay Shareholder the Purchase Price. Notwithstanding any delays in the delivery of the share certificate(s), for all purposes of voting and dividends, and other beneficial stock ownership purposes, the Company shall be treated as the owner of the shares from and after the date of the Company's delivery of its notice of exercise of option to purchase such shares. If the Company does not exercise its option to purchase Unvested shares as specified above, said shares shall thereafter become Vested, but shall remain subject to the remaining provisions of this Agreement.

3.3 *Stock Change*. Upon any stock split, stock dividend or other recapitalization or reorganization of the Company, the Purchase Value and number of shares subject to this Agreement shall be adjusted accordingly.

4. The Company's First Refusal.

4.1 *Notice to the Company*. If at any time Shareholder desires to sell any shares of the Stock, Shareholder shall give notice (the "Notice") to the Secretary of the Company containing:

(a) A statement signed by Shareholder notifying the Company that he desires to sell and has a bona fide offer to purchase such shares.

(b) A statement signed by the intended purchaser containing (i) his full name and address; (ii) the number of shares to be purchased; (iii) the price per share; (iv) all other terms under which the purchase is intended to be made; (v) a representation that the offer, under the terms specified, is bona fide and that such intended purchaser has the financial and other capabilities necessary to complete the transaction as proposed; and (vi) an agreement that at the time of purchase of said shares he will provide the Company with adequate proof that said shares are acquired at the same price and upon the same terms as set forth in said statement.

4.2 *Option.* The Company shall have an option exercisable within ten (10) days of receipt of the Notice by the Secretary to purchase said Vested shares of the Stock at the same price and upon the same terms as set forth in the Notice and to purchase said Unvested shares of the Stock at the price and on the terms specified in Section 3 above. In the event that part or all of the purchase consideration specified in the Notice to the Company is other than money, the Company's Board of Directors shall determine the fair market value in monetary terms of such other consideration and may pay the Shareholder such amount in cash. The Company may, instead of purchasing the shares itself, designate one or more nominees to purchase such shares. Said option shall be for the purchase of all, but not less than all, of the shares specified in the Notice. The Company shall exercise this option by delivering written notice of exercise within said ten (10) days and thereafter promptly completing the purchase transaction. In the event that the Company does not exercise said option, then Shareholder may, subject to the receipt by the Company of an opinion of counsel to the Company that such transfer and the resulting ownership by the intended purchaser does not violate any state or federal securities laws or regulations, sell the shares at any time within six (6) months to the intended purchaser on the terms set forth in the Notice, provided that such intended purchaser executes and becomes a party to this Agreement and thereby agrees to receive and hold all such shares of the Stock subject to all of the provisions and restrictions contained herein (except Section 3 above). Share-

FORMS AND MATERIALS 663

holder may not sell said shares to any other person, or at any different price, or on any different terms, without first complying with the provisions of Section 4.1 and this Section 4.2.

4.3 *Gift Exception*. The Company shall have no right of first refusal in the event that Shareholder makes a gift of Vested shares of Stock to or for the benefit of Shareholder's immediate family, provided, that Shareholder obtains the prior written approval of the Company, which approval shall not be unreasonably withheld. Any such approval for a gift transfer shall be subject to the transferee's executing and becoming a party to this Agreement (except Section 3 above).

5. Legend. All certificates representing shares subject to this Agreement shall bear a legend referencing the existence of the restrictions contained in this Agreement.

6. Reservation of Right. The Company reserves the right at any time and for any reason to grant waivers as to some or all of the provisions of this Agreement, which waivers shall be effective only as authorized by the Company's Board of Directors or its authorized officer, and which waivers shall be applicable only to the shares of the Stock of Shareholder and only to the extent expressly set forth in the written waivers. Shareholder acknowledges that the Company reserves the right at the discretion of the Company's Board of Directors to enter into different stock transfer restriction agreements with other shareholders, or to have no stock transfer restriction agreements with other shareholders.

7. Securities Law. Shareholder represents that all shares of the Stock covered by this Agreement are acquired for Shareholder's own investment purposes and not with a view to distribution or resale. All shares covered by this Agreement are subject to any restrictions which may be imposed under applicable state or federal securities laws, rules and regulations.

8. Entirety. This Agreement contains the entire agreement of the parties with respect to its subject matter.

9. No Employment Guarantee. Neither this Agreement nor any subsequent issuance of shares or options for shares in any way implies a guarantee of Shareholder's continued employment by the Company.

10. Attorneys' Fees. In the event of any proceedings to enforce or interpret the provisions of this Agreement, the party prevailing in such proceedings shall be entitled to recover from the other party all reasonable attorneys' fees and related legal costs and expenses.

11. Successors. This Agreement shall be binding upon and inure to the benefit of the respective parties, the successors and assigns of the Company, and the heirs, legatees and personal representatives of Shareholder.

12. Governing Law. This Agreement shall be governed by and construed in accordance with the laws of the State of New York.

IN WITNESS WHEREOF, the parties hereto have executed this Agreement as of the date first set forth above.

                                COMPANY

                                By:_____

                                SHAREHOLDER

                                By:_____

FORM SEVENTEEN

FORM OF VOTING AGREEMENT*

AGREEMENT entered into as of this ____ day of ____, 19____, by and among _____ ("Shareholder A") and _____ ("Shareholder B") (individually referred to as the "Shareholder" and collectively as the "Shareholders").

WHEREAS, each Shareholder owns the number of shares of issued and outstanding voting common stock of _____, a New York corporation (the "Corporation"), set opposite their respective signatures hereto;

WHEREAS, the Shareholders desire to maintain the continuity and stability of the policy and management of the Corporation; and

WHEREAS, the Shareholders believe it to be in their best interests and the best interests of the Corporation that the shares of the Shareholders now owned or hereafter acquired (the "Shares") be voted in accordance with the terms and conditions.

NOW, THEREFORE, in consideration of the foregoing, and of the mutual promises and covenants contained herein, it is hereby agreed as follows:

A. Voting

1. *General.* The Shareholders hereby agree to pool the voting of their Shares, and to vote or consent with respect to all of their Shares as a block or unit in all votes, in person or by proxy at any and all meetings of the shareholders of the Corporation, for whatever purpose called or

---

* SOURCE: *Fall 1991 Practical Skills: Forming and Advising Businesses* (NYSBA), "Shareholder Agreements and Voting Agreements," Annabelle I. Forrestel, Esq., Phillips, Lytle, Hitchcock, Blaine & Huber.

held, and in any and all proceedings, whether at a meeting of the shareholders or otherwise, wherein the vote or written consent of the shareholders may be required or authorized by law. Without limiting the generality of the foregoing, with respect to the following matters the Shareholders shall vote their Shares as follows:

(a) *Vote for Directors.*

(i) *Election.* So long as the board of directors of the Corporation shall consist of five directors, the Shares shall be voted for two persons nominated by Shareholder A and two persons nominated by Shareholder B. Votes for the remaining director position shall be cast for such nominee as the Shareholders are able to agree upon from time to time. If the Shareholders fail to agree upon the nominee for the remaining director position, then such nominee shall be ____ or ____ as agreed upon by the Shareholders. If the Shareholders fail to agree upon which of such designated persons shall be the nominee for the remaining director position, ____ shall be such nominee in odd-numbered calendar years, and ____ shall be such nominee in even-numbered calendar years. The Shares shall be voted for the designated person so nominated whether or not an election is held. If the board of directors is reduced or expanded to an even number of directors, the Shareholders shall each be entitled to nominate one-half of the directors, and their Shares shall be voted for the persons so nominated. If the board of directors is reduced or expanded to an odd number of directors, the Shareholders shall each be entitled to nominate one-half of the next lowest even number of the directors, and their Shares shall be voted for the persons so nominated. The procedure set forth above for electing the remaining director shall apply.

(ii) *Replacement.* If any director so elected should die, resign, be removed or become incapacitated or otherwise refuse to act in his or her capacity as director, the Shareholder who nominated such director shall be entitled to nominate a person as a replacement director and the other Shareholder agrees to fully cooperate and to vote for the nominee so selected.

(b) *Vote on Other Issues*. In the event of a vote of the shareholders involving authorization of (i) any amendment to the Corporation's Certificate of Incorporation; (ii) any amendment to the Corporation's By-laws; (iii) merger, consolidation or binding share exchange; (iv) sale or other disposition of all or substantially all of the assets of the Corporation; (v) bankruptcy; (vi) dissolution; or (vii) any other matter submitted to a vote of the shareholders, the Shareholders agree to pool their Shares and to vote them as a block or unit. A vote on any particular issue shall be made in the manner that the Shareholders may then agree upon. If the Shareholders are unable to agree, the Shares shall nonetheless be voted as a block or unit in accordance with the procedures set forth in Section B below.

B. Arbitration. If the Shareholders are unable to agree on any matter subject to a vote of the Shareholders, the dispute and the manner of voting the Shares shall be submitted to such independent third party as the Shareholders are then able to agree upon. If the Shareholders are unable to agree upon an independent third party, then the dispute and the manner of voting the Shares shall be settled by the appointment of an independent third party arbitrator in accordance with the rules of the American Arbitration Association.

C. Proxy. In order to facilitate the resolution of any dispute referred to in Section B hereof, the Shareholders do hereby grant, pursuant to Section 609(f)(5) of the New York Business Corporation Law, to _____ or to such other person as may be designated by the arbitrator chosen by the methods set forth in Section B hereof, an irrevocable proxy to vote the Shares in his or her sole discretion. This irrevocable proxy shall take effect only upon the occurrence of a dispute regarding the manner of voting the Shares and shall only apply to such dispute as may be submitted to an arbitrator from time to time.

D. Provisions to Survive Death or Incapacity of any Shareholder. In the event of the death, incapacity or incompetency of any Shareholder, the provisions of this Agreement will be binding on the estate, committee or personal representative of such Shareholder and such estate, committee or personal representative shall act on behalf of such Shareholder in accordance with the provisions hereof. Notwithstanding the above, the provisions of this Agreement are subject to a Shareholders Agreement dated ____ by and between the Shareholders (the "Shareholders Agreement"), and the provisions of such Shareholders Agreement to the extent applicable shall govern.

E. Transfer of Shares. Shares may be transferred only in accordance with the terms and conditions of the Shareholders Agreement. Upon a transfer of Shares to a person who is not a Shareholder, the Shares shall remain subject to, and be voted in accordance with, the terms of this Agreement.

F. Termination of Shareholder Status. A Shareholder shall no longer be treated as a Shareholder hereunder when he ceases to own any Shares.

G. Endorsement of Share Certificates. Certificates for Shares of the Corporation subject to this Agreement shall be endorsed as follows:

> Any assignment, transfer, pledge, or other disposition of the shares represented by this certificate, and any subsequent disposition thereof, is restricted by, and subject to, the By-laws of the Corporation and the terms and provisions of a Voting Agreement dated as of the ____ day of ____, 199___, copies of which are on file with the Secretary of the Corporation.

H. Termination. This Agreement shall terminate upon the happening of the earliest of any of the following events:

1. Reduction in the number of Shareholders to one;

2. The written agreement of all of the Shareholders;

3. The expiration of the term of this Agreement or any renewal thereof and the failure of some or all of the remaining Shareholders to have agreed to renew this Agreement;

4. The merger or consolidation of the Corporation with or into another entity or a binding share exchange between the Corporation and another entity, if the Corporation is not the surviving corporation and the Shareholders own less than the number of outstanding shares of such

surviving corporation that is needed to confer upon the Shareholders 51 percent of the outstanding voting power of such surviving corporation.

I. Term. This Agreement shall become effective upon the date hereof and continue in effect for a period of ____ (____) years from the date hereof.

J. Renewal. This Agreement may be renewed for successive ____- year periods or such other term as may be permitted by law, provided that the Shareholders desiring to extend and renew this Agreement give their written consent to such renewal prior to the expiration of this Agreement.

K. Amendment. This Agreement may be amended by the written agreement of all of the parties hereto.

L. Benefit. This Agreement shall be for the benefit of the parties hereto and shall be binding on the parties hereto, their heirs, legal representatives, successors, assigns and transferees.

M. Governing Law. This Agreement shall be governed, construed and enforced in accordance with the laws of the State of New York.

IN WITNESS WHEREOF, the Shareholders have executed this Agreement as of the date and year first written above.

Number of Shares	*Shareholders*
————	————————————
————	————————————

FORM EIGHTEEN

FORM OF VOTING TRUST AGREEMENT*

AGREEMENT entered into as of this ____ day of ____, 199____, by and among _____ ("Shareholder A") and _____ ("Shareholder B"), and any other shareholders of _____, a New York corporation, who may hereafter become parties hereto, and _____ (the "Trustee"). Shareholder A, Shareholder B and such other shareholders who may become parties hereto are sometimes referred to herein individually as the "Shareholder," but collectively as the "Shareholders."

WHEREAS, each Shareholder now owns the number of shares of the issued and outstanding voting common stock ("Shares") of ____, a New York corporation (the "Corporation") set opposite his or her signature hereto; and

WHEREAS, the Shareholders desire to secure the continuity and stability of the policy and management of the Corporation; and

WHEREAS, the Shareholders believe that securing the continuity of voting control of the Corporation is in their best interests and in the best interests of the Corporation;

NOW, THEREFORE, in consideration of the foregoing, and of the mutual promises and covenants herein contained, it is hereby agreed as follows:

---

* SOURCE: *Fall 1991 Practical Skills: Forming and Advising Businesses* (NYSBA), "Shareholder Agreements and Voting Agreements," Annabelle I. Forrestel, Esq., Phillips, Lytle, Hitchcock, Blaine & Huber.

1. Appointment of the Trustee. The Shareholders appoint _____ as Trustee under this Agreement and shall transfer the Shares of the Corporation to the Trustee upon the terms and conditions of this Agreement.

2. Transfer of Shares to the Trustee. The Shareholders, simultaneously with the execution of this Agreement, will duly assign and deliver all of their respective certificates representing their Shares with all appropriate stock transfer tax stamps duly affixed thereto to the Trustee, who will cause the Shares represented thereby to be transferred to it as the Trustee on the share records of the Corporation.

3. Trust Certificates. The Trustee will issue and deliver to each Shareholder a voting trust certificate ("Voting Trust Certificate") for the number of Shares transferred by such Shareholder to the Trustee, in substantially the form attached hereto as Exhibit A.

4. Voting Trust. The voting trust hereby declared and created will continue for a term of ten (10) years from the date of this Agreement. At any time within six (6) months prior to the expiration of the original term or any renewal term of this Agreement, some or all of the Shareholders may extend the term of this Agreement for one or more additional periods of ten (10) years. Throughout the term of this Agreement, the Trustee will have the exclusive right to vote the Shares transferred hereunder or to give written consents in lieu of voting thereon, subject to any limitation on the right to vote contained in the Certificate of Incorporation of the Corporation or other certificate filed pursuant to applicable law, in person or by proxy at any and all meetings of the shareholders of the Corporation, for whatever purpose called or held, and in any and all proceedings, whether at a meeting of the shareholders or otherwise, wherein the vote or written consent of the shareholders may be required or authorized by law.

5. Dividends and Other Distributions. The Trustee shall distribute all dividends and other distributions declared and paid on the Shares transferred hereunder to the registered holders of Voting Trust Certificates in proportion to their respective interests therein as shown on the books of the Trustee.

6. Records. The Trustee shall keep at the office of the Corporation the correct and complete books and records of account of all of the business and transactions of the voting trust, and a record of any and all persons holding Voting Trust Certificates as provided for in Section 3 hereof containing the names, alphabetically arranged, of all persons who are holders of the Voting Trust Certificates, showing their places of residence, the number and class of shares represented by the Voting Trust Certificate held by them respectively, and the date when they respectively become the owners thereof. The Trustee shall make such books and records available for inspection by the holders of the Voting Trust Certificates in accordance with the New York Business Corporation Law. In addition, the Trustee shall keep a copy of this Agreement at the office of the Corporation.

7. Transfer at Termination. At the expiration of the term of the voting trust hereby created, the Trustee shall, upon surrender of the Voting Trust Certificates, cause to be delivered to the holders thereof certificates for shares of the common stock of the Corporation equivalent in amount to the Shares represented by the Voting Trust Certificates so surrendered.

8. Duty of the Trustee. The Trustee will use his or her best judgment in voting upon the Shares held by the Trustee, but the Trustee assumes no responsibility for the consequences of any vote cast, or consent given by the Trustee, in good faith, and in the absence of gross negligence.

9. Death, Resignation or Incapacity of the Trustee. Upon death, resignation or incapacity of the Trustee, ____ shall become the successor Trustee and shall possess all rights, title and powers of the original Trustee during the remainder of the term of this Agreement.

10. Amendment. This Agreement may be amended by the written agreement of all of the parties hereto.

11. Benefit. This Agreement shall be for the benefit of the parties hereto and shall be binding on the parties hereto, their heirs, legal representatives, successors, assigns and transferees.

12. Governing Law. This Agreement shall be governed, construed and enforced in accordance with the laws of the State of New York.

IN WITNESS WHEREOF, the parties have executed this Agreement as of the date and year first written above.

_____
                                                  Trustee

Number of Shares   *Shareholders*

_____   _____

_____   _____

EXHIBIT A

Voting Trust Certificate

No. _____ _____ Shares

    The undersigned, the voting trustee of the shares of _____ (the "Corporation"), under a Voting Trust Agreement dated ____, 199____ (the "Agreement"), having received certain shares of the common stock of the Corporation (the "Shares") pursuant to the Agreement and which Agreement the holder hereof (the "Certificate Holder") by accepting this Certificate ratifies, adopts, and assents to, hereby certifies that the Certificate Holder will be entitled to receive a certificate for ____ Shares on the expiration of the Agreement, and during the period of the Agreement will be entitled to receive payments equal to the dividends or any other distributions that may be collected by the Trustee upon a like number of such Shares held by the Trustee under the terms of the Agreement.

    This Certificate is transferable only on the share records of the Trustee by the registered Certificate Holder in person or by the Certificate Holder's duly authorized attorney, and the Certificate Holder by accepting this Certificate consents that the Trustee may treat the Certificate Holder as the true owner for all purposes, except the delivery of certificates for Shares, which delivery shall not be made without surrender hereof.

    IN WITNESS WHEREOF, the Trustee has caused this Certificate to be executed this ____ day of ____, 19____.

                                                        Trustee

FORM NINETEEN

STOCK ESCROW AGREEMENT

STOCK ESCROW AGREEMENT ("Agreement") made as of the ____th day of ____, 19____, by and among ____ of ____, New York ("Secured Party"), _____ of ____, New York ("Stockholder") and _____ of ____, New York ("Escrow Agent").

1. Escrow Shares. Stockholder hereby delivers and deposits with the Escrow Agent Certificate No. ____ representing ____ (____) shares of the issued and outstanding common stock of _____ ("Corporation") now owned of record by Escrow Agent but beneficially owned by the Stockholder, in proper form for transfer. The common stock referred to in paragraph 1 of this Agreement shall be hereinafter referred to as the "Escrow Shares."

2. Promissory Note. Such Escrow Shares shall be held by the Escrow Agent in order to secure the payment of a certain promissory note of the Corporation, dated ____, made payable to Secured Party (hereinafter referred to as the "Note"), a copy of which is attached hereto as Exhibit A.

3. Escrow Term. The term of this escrow arrangement (the "Escrow Term") is from the date hereof until all sums, including, but not limited to, the interest and principal due under the Note are paid in full.

4. Rights to Escrow Shares. During the Escrow Term, subject to this Agreement, all rights to and interest in the Escrow Shares, including, but not limited to, voting and dividend rights, shall be retained by the Stockholder. The Stockholder shall not sell, assign, pledge or otherwise transfer any right to or interest in the Escrow Shares, including, but not limited to, dividend and voting rights during the term of this Agreement, unless all sums, including, but not limited to, the entire principal and all interest under the Note, shall have been paid in full.

5. Termination of Escrow. In the event that all sums, including, but not limited to, the entire principal and all interest under the Note, have been paid in full, Secured Party shall forthwith give notice of said full payment to Escrow Agent, with a copy of said notice to the Stockholder. Upon receipt of said notice by the Escrow Agent, this Escrow shall terminate and the Escrow Agent shall forthwith transfer the Escrow Shares from escrow to the Stockholder.

6. Default. In the event that, at any time during the Escrow Term, Stockholder shall be in default on the Note (after expiration of any grace period provided in the Note), Secured Party may give stockholder written notice of said default, with a copy of said written notice to the Escrow Agent. If the default has not been corrected and remedied within the ten-day period following giving of such notice, Secured Party shall so notify the Escrow Agent, who shall transfer ownership of the Escrow Shares to Secured Party after ten (10) days from receipt of said notice from Secured Party unless the Escrow Agent receives written notice within said ten-day period from Secured Party that the default has been corrected and remedied. In the event said default is corrected and remedied, Secured Party shall give written notice to such effect to the Escrow Agent, and the Escrow Agent shall retain the Escrow Shares in escrow as security for future payments under the Note in accordance with the terms of this Agreement. If the default was corrected and remedied by payment of the entire unpaid principal balance and the interest and all other amounts due on the Note, the Escrow Agent shall transfer the Escrow Shares from escrow to the Stockholder and this Escrow shall thereupon terminate. Escrow Agent shall make the above transfers in reliance upon said notices and shall not question their execution or validity, the effectiveness of their provisions or the truth or accuracy of any information contained therein.

7. Resignation of Escrow Agent, Successors. The Escrow Agent may resign as escrow agent by giving notice of such resignation to the parties hereto, and in the event of such resignation he may appoint as successor escrow agent a bank or trust company, or he may appoint one or more responsible individuals acceptable to all the parties hereto as

FORMS AND MATERIALS

successor escrow agent, and any such successor or successors shall have the same rights and duties as if originally named herein.

8. Court Order. Notwithstanding anything herein contained to the contrary, upon the receipt by the Escrow Agent of a certified judgment, decree or order of a court which directs the Escrow Agent to take any action, the Escrow Agent shall take such action.

9. Duties of Escrow Agent. The duties and responsibilities of the Escrow Agent shall be limited to those specifically set forth in this Agreement and the performance of such action as, in the judgment of the Escrow Agent, shall be reasonable, necessary or appropriate to carry out Escrow Agent's duties specified in this Agreement.

10. Liability of Escrow Agent. The Escrow Agent shall not be liable for any act which the Escrow Agent may do or omit to do hereunder while acting in good faith and in the exercise of his own judgment. Any act done or omitted by him pursuant to the advice of independent legal counsel shall be conclusive evidence of such good faith. The Escrow Agent may act in reliance upon any instrument or signature which he believes to be genuine and may assume that any person purporting to give notice or advice or instructions in connection with the provisions hereof has been duly authorized to do so. The Escrow Agent is authorized to disregard any directions, instructions, notices, communications, or information from any source whatsoever, excepting only a statement executed by Secured Party or a duly authorized agent of Secured Party or a judgment, order or decree of any court. In any case in which the Escrow Agent obeys or otherwise complies with any such directive, statement, judgment, order or decree, the Escrow Agent shall not be liable to any person by reason of such obedience or compliance, notwithstanding that such directive, statement, judgment, order or decree may be subsequently withdrawn, rescinded, reversed, modified, annulled, set aside or vacated, or, in the case of a judgment, order or decree, found to have been entered without jurisdiction.

11. Termination. This Agreement shall not be terminated, revoked, rescinded or modified in any respect without the prior written approval of all of the parties hereto.

12. Indemnity. Secured Party, Stockholder and Corporation hereby jointly and severally agree to indemnify and hold harmless the Escrow Agent against any and all losses, claims, damages, liabilities and expenses, including reasonable costs of investigation and reasonable counsel fees and disbursements, which may be imposed upon him or incurred by him hereunder or in the performance of his duties hereunder, including any litigation arising from this Escrow Agreement or involving the subject matter hereof or the Escrow Shares deposited hereunder.

13. Termination of Duties. The Escrow Agent's duties hereunder shall cease upon the disbursement of the Escrow Shares as provided in paragraph 5 against a written receipt therefor.

14. Notices. All notices or other communication required or permitted to be given under this Escrow Agreement shall be in writing and shall be deemed to have been given if received by certified mail, return receipt requested, to the address first set forth above.

15. Binding Effect. This Escrow Agreement shall bind and inure to the benefit of the parties and their respective successors and assigns and their respective subsidiaries, parents or affiliates.

16. Applicable Law. This Escrow Agreement shall be governed and carried out in accordance with the laws of the State of New York.

IN WITNESS WHEREOF, the parties hereto have cause this Escrow Agreement to be executed and signed as of the day and year first above written.

By: _____   _____
    Its President

FORM TWENTY

EMPLOYMENT AGREEMENT

(Short Form)

This EMPLOYMENT AGREEMENT (this "Agreement"), dated as of ____, 19____, is entered into by and between ____, a New York corporation ("Employer") and ____ ("Employee").

WHEREAS, Employer deems Employee's services and experiences useful and necessary; and

WHEREAS, Employee is willing to provide his services and experiences as an employee of Employer on the terms and conditions set forth herein.

NOW, THEREFORE, in consideration of the foregoing, the parties agree as follows:

1. Employment. Employer hereby engages Employee, and Employee hereby accepts such engagement, upon the terms and conditions set forth herein.

2. Duties. Employee is engaged in the position of ____. Employee shall perform faithfully and diligently the duties customarily performed by persons in the position for which Employee is engaged and such other duties as the Board of Directors of Employer shall designate to Employee from time to time. Employee shall devote Employee's full business time and efforts to the rendition of such services and to the performance of such duties as are set forth herein, and shall at all times be in compliance with, and ensure that Employer is in compliance with, any and all laws, rules and regulations applicable to Employer or its business.

3. Compensation.

3.1 *Base Salary.* During the term of this Agreement, as compensation for the proper and satisfactory performance of all duties to be performed by Employee hereunder, Employer shall pay to Employee a base salary of $____ per month, payable in equal semi-monthly installments of $____ each (annualized at $____ per year), payable in arrears on the first and fifteenth day of each month, less required deductions for state and federal withholding tax, Social Security and other employee taxes.

[OPTIONAL: 3.2 *Bonus Compensation and Stock Plan.* Employee may receive bonus in the form of a stock option, stock, or cash, the amount and timing of which shall be determined in the sole discretion of the Board of Directors of Employer.]

4. Fringe Benefits.

[OPTIONAL: 4.1 *Automobile.* Employer shall provide Employee with an automobile for use in the business of Employer. Employer, in the discretion of the Board, shall either purchase or make lease payments or installment payments on any such automobile and shall pay all operating expenses thereof.]

[OPTIONAL: 4.2 *Vacation and Sick Leave.* Employee shall be entitled to an aggregate of ____ week(s) of paid vacation per year, and ____ day(s) of paid sick leave per year, during the term hereof, prorated for any portion of a year to the date of termination. The timing and duration of any vacation shall be subject to the prior written approval of Employer, in its discretion.]

4.3 *[Other] Fringe Benefits.* Employee shall be entitled to such [other] fringe benefits as Employer may in its discretion determine. Such fringe benefits may include, but not be limited to, health and disability insurance coverage, attendance at conventions or trade meetings and a business development expense allowance.

4.4 *No Accumulation.* The fringe benefits described in this paragraph accrue on an annual basis, and Employee shall not be entitled to accumulate unused vacation, sick leave, or other fringe benefits from year to year, without the prior written consent of Employer. Further, Employee

FORMS AND MATERIALS 683

shall not be entitled to receive payments in lieu of any compensation or payment for or in lieu of said fringe benefits prorated to the date of termination of this Agreement.

4.5 *Payment of Compensation upon Termination.* Upon termination for cause, Employee shall be entitled to the compensation set forth as "base salary" herein, prorated to the effective date of such termination as full compensation for any and all claims of Employee under this Agreement.

5. Term. The term of this Agreement shall be for a period of ____ year(s), commencing on ____, unless sooner terminated in accordance with the provisions hereof.

6. Termination.

6.1 *Termination without Cause.* Either party may terminate this Agreement without cause upon not less than ____ days' prior written notice delivered to the other. The death of Employee shall automatically terminate this Agreement.

6.2 *Termination with Cause.* Employer shall have the right to terminate this Agreement, in its sole discretion, upon the occurrence of any one of the following events:

(a) Employee fails to perform faithfully, diligently and expeditiously the duties of Employee's employment under this Agreement, and a reasonable period of time (which shall, in no event, exceed thirty (30) days from issuance of written notice by Employer to Employee thereof specifying in reasonable detail the nature of the default) passes without cure. Performance by Employee shall be determined by Employer in its discretion, applying standards customarily applied in industry; or

(b) Employee is disabled, mentally or physically or both, for three or more consecutive months (as used in this Paragraph 6, "disabled" shall be shown by the inability of Employee to diligently and expeditiously perform Employee's ordinary functions and duties on a full-time basis in accordance with the provisions of this Agreement); or

(c) Employee engages in any conduct which, in the sole discretion of Employer, is unethical, illegal or which otherwise brings notoriety to Employer or has an adverse effect on the name or public image of Employer; or

(d) Employee is declared of unsound mind by an order of court, commits a felony or fraudulently or intentionally commits an act which is, in the sole discretion of Employer, directly detrimental to Employer.

7. Confidentiality.

7.1 *Acknowledgment of Proprietary Interest.* Employee recognizes the proprietary interest of Employer in any Trade Secrets of Employer. As used herein, the term "Trade Secrets" includes all of Employer's confidential or proprietary information, including without limitation any confidential information of Employer encompassed in any reports, investigations, experiments, research or developmental work, experimental work, work in progress, drawings, designs, plans, proposals, codes, marketing and sales programs, financial projections, cost summaries, pricing formulas and all concepts or ideas, materials or information related to the business, products or sales of the Employer or the Employer's customers which has not previously been released to the public at large by duly authorized representatives of the Employer, whether or not such information would be enforceable as a trade secret, or the copying of such information which would be enjoined or restrained by a court as constituting unfair competition. Employee acknowledges and agrees that any and all Trade Secrets of Employer, learned by Employee during the course of the engagement by Employer or otherwise, whether developed by Employee alone or in conjunction with others or otherwise, shall be and is the property of Employer.

7.2 *Covenant not to Divulge Trade Secrets.* Employee acknowledges and agrees that Employer is entitled to prevent the disclosure of Trade Secrets of Employer. As a portion of the consideration for the employment of Employee and for the compensation being paid to Employee by Employer, Employee agrees at all times during the term of the employment by Employer and thereafter to hold in strictest confidence, and not to disclose or allow to be disclosed to any person, firm or corporation, other than to persons engaged by Employer to further the business of Employer, and not to use except in the pursuit of the business of Employer, Trade Secrets of Employer, without the prior written consent of Employer, including Trade Secrets developed by Employee.

7.3 *Return of Materials at Termination.* In the event of any termination of Employee's employment, with or without cause, Employee will promptly deliver to Employer all materials, property, documents, data and other information belonging to Employer or pertaining to Trade Secrets. Employee shall not take any materials, property, documents or other information, or any reproduction or excerpt thereof, belonging to Employer or containing or pertaining to any Trade Secrets.

7.4 *Remedies upon Breach.* In the event of any breach of this Agreement by Employee, Employer shall be entitled, if it so elects, to institute and prosecute proceedings in any court of competent jurisdiction, either at law or in equity, to enjoin Employee from violating any of the terms of this Agreement, to enforce the specific performance by Employee of any of the terms of this Agreement and to obtain damages, or any of the foregoing, but nothing herein contained shall be construed to prevent such remedy or combination of remedies as Employer may elect to invoke. The failure of Employer promptly to institute legal action upon any breach of this Agreement shall not constitute a waiver of that or any other breach hereof.

8. Covenant not to Compete.

(a) During the term hereof, Employee shall not (i) solicit any person or entity who or which was a client of Employer at the time of such solicitation or immediately prior thereto, (ii) act as officer, director, employee, consultant, shareholder, lender or agent of a company which has or acquires such a client, (iii) perform any services, directly or indirectly, for any such client for the benefit of any other company or (iv) receive any fees from or relating to services rendered to such client.

(b) In the event any court decides that the provisions of Section 8(a), or any part thereof, are not enforceable, Employer shall petition that court to determine to what extent such provision, or part thereof, must be modified in order to be considered enforceable and, for purposes of the case in which the issue arose and thereafter in the territorial jurisdiction of that court, such provision or part thereof shall be interpreted as that court or panel so determines.

9. Insurance. Employer may, at its election and for its benefit, insure Employee against accidental loss or death and Employer shall be entitled to any and all insurance proceeds in the event of any such accidental loss or death. Employee shall submit to such physical examination and supply such information as may be required in connection therewith.

10. Governing Law. This Agreement shall be interpreted, construed, governed and enforced according to the laws of the State of New York.

11. Attorneys' Fees. In the event of any litigation concerning any controversy, claim or dispute between the parties hereto, arising out of or relating to this Agreement or the breach hereof, or the interpretation hereof, the prevailing party shall be entitled to recover from the losing party reasonable expenses, attorneys' fees and costs incurred therein or in the enforcement or collection of any judgment or award rendered therein. The "prevailing party" means the party determined by the court to have most nearly prevailed, even if such party did not prevail in all matters, not necessarily the one in whose favor a judgment is rendered. Further, in the event of any default by a party under this Agreement, such defaulting party shall pay all the expenses and attorneys' fees incurred by the other party in connection with such default, whether or not any litigation is commenced.

12. Amendments. No amendment or modification of the terms or conditions of this Agreement shall be valid unless in writing and signed by the parties hereto.

13. Successors and Assigns. The rights and obligations of Employer under this Agreement shall inure to the benefit of and shall be binding upon the successors and assigns of Employer. Employee shall not be entitled to assign any of Employee's rights or obligations under this Agreement.

14. Entire Agreement. This Agreement constitutes the entire agreement between the parties with respect to the employment of Employee.

IN WITNESS WHEREOF, the parties have executed this Agreement as of the date set forth above.

EMPLOYER:

By:_____

EMPLOYEE:

By:_____

FORM TWENTY-ONE

EMPLOYMENT AGREEMENT

(Long Form)

This AGREEMENT, dated as of ____, 19____, is entered into by and between ____, a New York corporation (the "Company") and ____ (the "Executive").

WITNESSETH:

WHEREAS, on the date hereof, the Company will acquire (the "Acquisition") substantially all the assets, and assume certain of the liabilities of ____; and

WHEREAS, the Executive, as owner of shares of Common Stock of the Company, may be substantially benefited by the Acquisition; and

WHEREAS, it is of the utmost importance to the Company that it continue to have the benefit of the Executive's services, experience and loyalty, and the Executive has indicated his willingness to provide his services, experience and loyalty on the terms and conditions set forth herein;

NOW, THEREFORE, in consideration of the premises and the mutual covenants herein contained, the parties hereto agree as follows:

1. Employment and Duties.

(a) *General.* The Company hereby employs the Executive and the Executive agrees upon the terms and conditions herein set forth to serve as President and Chief Executive Officer of the Company, and in such capacity, the Executive agrees to perform the duties delineated in the by-laws of the Company, together with such additional duties, commensurate with the Executive's position as President and Chief Executive

Officer, as may be assigned to the Executive from time to time by the Board of Directors (the "Board") of the Company. Notwithstanding the foregoing, the Executive's position and title may be changed by the Board; provided that the Executive shall at all times be an executive of the Company. If elected or appointed, the Executive shall also serve as a director or officer of any of the Company's subsidiaries or affiliated companies and, if elected, will serve as a member of the Board or committees of the Board, without further compensation. The principal location of the Executive's employment shall be in ____, although the Executive understands and agrees that he may be required to travel from time to time for business reasons.

(b) *Exclusive Services.* Throughout the Period (as defined in paragraph 2 below), the Executive shall, except as may from time to time be otherwise agreed in writing by the Company, devote his full-time working hours to his duties hereunder, shall faithfully serve the Company, shall in all respects conform to and comply with the lawful and reasonable directions and instructions given to him by the Chief Executive Officer of the Company and the Board, and shall use his best efforts to promote and serve the interests of the Company.

(c) *No Other Employment.* Throughout the Period, the Executive shall not, directly or indirectly, render services to any other person or organization for which he receives compensation without the consent of the Board or otherwise engage in activities which would interfere significantly with the faithful performance of his duties hereunder. The Executive may perform inconsequential services without direct compensation therefor in connection with the management of personal investments; provided that such activity does not contravene the provisions of subparagraph 1(b) or paragraph 5 hereof.

2. Term of Employment. The Company shall retain the Executive and the Executive shall serve in the employ of the Company for a period of ____ years commencing as of the closing of the Acquisition and extending through and including the last day of ____, 19____ following such closing (the "Period"). Notwithstanding the foregoing, the term of this Agreement may, at the option of the Company and with the approval

FORMS AND MATERIALS 691

of the Executive, be extended from time to time in a written memorandum signed by the Company and the Executive. This Agreement shall be of no force and effect in the event the Acquisition is not consummated.

3. Compensation and Other Benefits. Subject to the provisions of this Agreement, the Company shall pay and provide the following compensation and other benefits to the Executive during the Period as compensation for services rendered hereunder:

(a) *Base Salary.* The Company shall pay to the Executive an annual base salary (the "Base Salary") at the rate of $____ per annum, payable in accordance with the payroll practices of the Company. The Company shall be entitled to deduct or withhold all taxes and charges which the Company may be required to deduct or withhold therefrom. The Base Salary will be reviewed not less than annually by the Board and may be increased, but not decreased below the amount of the Base Salary set forth in the first sentence of this subparagraph (a), as adjusted annually for changes in the U.S. City Average Consumer Price Index for all urban consumers (CPI-U (1967 = 100)), as published by the U.S. Department of Labor, Bureau of Labor Statistics, after the closing of the Acquisition.

(b) *Employee Benefit Plans.* At all times during the Period, the Executive shall be provided the opportunity to participate in pension and welfare plans, programs and benefits (the "Plans") offered generally to all executives of the Company.

(c) *Fringe Benefits.* The Executive shall be entitled to ____ weeks of vacation annually and the use of an automobile, subject to and in accordance with the policies of the Company.

4. Termination of Employment.

(a) *Termination for Cause; Resignation without Substantial Breach.*

(i) If, prior to the expiration of the Period, the Executive's employment is terminated by the Company for Cause, as defined in subparagraph 4(a)(ii), or if the Executive resigns from his employment hereunder, other than by reason of a Substantial Breach, as defined in subparagraph 4(b)(ii), the Executive shall be entitled to payment of the pro rata portion of the Executive's Base Salary under subparagraph 3(a) through and including the date of termination or resignation at the rate in effect on the date of the written notice of termination or resignation delivered in accordance with subparagraph 4(a)(iii) hereof. The Executive shall not be eligible to receive Base Salary or to participate in any Plans under subparagraph 3(b), with respect to future periods after the date of such termination or resignation, except for the right to receive vested benefits under any Plan in accordance with the terms of such Plan.

(ii) Termination for "Cause" shall mean termination of the Executive's employment with the Company by the Board because of (A) any act or omission which constitutes a material breach by the Executive of his obligations or agreements under this Agreement or the failure or refusal of the Executive to satisfactorily perform any duties reasonably required hereunder, after notification by the Board of such breach, failure or refusal and failure of the Executive to correct such breach, failure or refusal within ten business days of such notification (other than by reason of the incapacity of the Executive due to physical or mental illness) or (B) the commission by the Executive of a felony, or the perpetration by the Executive of common law fraud against any of the Company or any affiliate or subsidiary thereof.

(iii) The date of termination of employment by the Company under this paragraph 4(a) shall be the later of the date, if any, set forth in the written notice of termination delivered by the Company to the Executive or the date of receipt by the Executive of written notice of termination. The date of resignation under this paragraph 4(a) shall be ten business days after receipt by the Company of written notice of resignation.

(b) *Termination without Cause; Resignation after Substantial Breach.*

(i) Subject to the provisions of subparagraph 4(b)(iii), if, prior to the expiration of the Period, the Executive's employment is terminated by the Company without Cause, as defined in subparagraph 4(a)(ii), or if the Executive resigns from his employment hereunder following a Substantial Breach, as defined in subparagraph 4(b)(ii) (such Substantial

Breach having not been corrected by the Company within ten business days of receipt of written notice from the Executive of the occurrence of such Substantial Breach, which notice shall specifically set forth the nature of the Substantial Breach that is the reason for such resignation), the Executive shall be entitled to payment of (A) the pro rata portion of the Executive's Base Salary through and including the date of termination or resignation at the rate in effect on the date of the written notice of termination or resignation delivered in accordance with subparagraph 4(b)(iv) hereof and (B) any amounts to which the Executive is entitled as of such date of termination or resignation under any Plan. In addition, the Executive shall be entitled (C) to the payment of Severance Benefits, as such term is defined below in this subparagraph, and (D) subject to the provisions of subparagraphs 4(c) and 4(d) hereof, to coverage for the Executive and the Executive's immediate family under any life, health, disability or accident insurance plan (the "Welfare Plans") maintained by the Company, or to comparable benefits, through the period beginning with the date of termination or resignation and ending with the last day of the Period. "Severance Benefits" shall mean an amount equal to the excess of (x) the sum of (I) the product of (1) the Base Salary, determined as of the date of termination or resignation, as the case may be, multiplied by (2) a fraction, the numerator of which is the number of calendar months (or portions thereof) remaining in the Period after the date of termination or resignation and the denominator of which is 12, and (II) the amount of any bonus awarded (but not received) during the year preceding the date of termination (or in the year of termination if a bonus in respect of such year had been awarded prior to the date of termination) over (y) any amounts which the Executive receives in connection with any employment (including self-employment) commencing one year after the date of such termination but before ____, 19___. The Executive shall collect such amounts promptly in good faith and in accordance with customary commercial practice. Subject to the provisions of paragraph 5 hereof, the Executive shall use his best efforts to obtain such employment, the Executive shall provide the Company with any evidence of such amounts received in connection with such employment which the Company shall request, and the Executive shall cooperate with the Company in determining such amounts.

(ii) "Substantial Breach" shall mean (A) the assignment to the Executive of any position or duties or principal office materially inconsistent with the provisions of paragraph 1 hereof; (B) a reduction by the Company in the Base Salary; or (C) the failure by the Company to allow the Executive to participate in the Plans in accordance with subparagraph 3(b); provided, however, that the term "Substantial Breach" shall not (x) include an immaterial breach by the Company of any provisions of this Agreement, including clause (A) or (C) above, which does not result in substantial detriment to the Executive, or (y) a termination for Cause.

(iii) If, following a termination of employment without Cause or a resignation following a Substantial Breach, the Executive materially breaches the provisions of paragraph 5 hereof such that the Company has or is likely to suffer substantial detriment, the Executive shall not be eligible, as of the date of such breach, for the payment of Severance Benefits, and all obligations and agreements of the Company to pay Severance Benefits shall thereupon cease.

(iv) The date of termination of employment by the Company under this subparagraph 4(b) shall be the later of the date specified in a written notice of termination to the Executive or the date on which such notice is given to the Executive. The date of resignation under this subparagraph 4(b) shall be ten business days after receipt by the Company of written notice or resignation; provided that the Substantial Breach specified in such notice shall not have been corrected by the Company during such ten-business-day period.

(v) Severance Benefits shall be paid at the time compensation would otherwise have been paid in accordance with the payroll policy of the Company in effect immediately preceding the date of termination of the Executive's employment or the Executive's resignation under subparagraph 4(b).

(c) *Death.* If the Executive dies prior to the expiration of the Period, his beneficiary or estate shall be entitled to receive a pro rata portion up to the date of death of the cash compensation payable to the Executive (Base Salary, at the rate paid to the Executive pursuant to subparagraph 3(a) at the date of death plus any bonus or other accrued compensation). In addition, the Executive's immediate family shall be entitled to participate in the Welfare Plans for a period of 180 days following the date of death.

(d) *Disability.* If the Executive becomes Permanently Disabled, as defined below in this subparagraph 4(d), prior to the expiration of the Period, the Company shall be entitled to terminate his employment. In the event of such termination, the Executive shall be entitled to receive a pro rata portion of the Base Salary, at the rate paid to the Executive at the date of such termination for a period of 180 days following such date and such amounts, if any, as are payable to the Executive under any applicable insurance policies. In addition, the Executive and the Executive's immediate family shall be entitled to participate in the Welfare Plans for a period of 180 days following such date of termination of employment. For the purposes of this subparagraph 4(d), the Executive shall be deemed "Permanently Disabled" when, and only when, he is deemed permanently disabled in accordance with the disability policy of the Company as in effect from time to time.

(e) *Retirement.* If the Executive's employment is terminated upon his Retirement, as defined below in this subparagraph 4(e), the Executive shall be entitled to receive Base Salary, bonus and benefits in accordance with paragraph 3 for and in connection with the period through and including the date of such termination of employment. The Executive shall have no right under this Agreement or otherwise to receive any other compensation, or to participate in employee benefit programs with respect to future periods after such termination of employment with respect to the year of such termination and later years. "Retirement" shall mean the voluntary termination of employment by the Executive after the Executive attains age 62 or two years after the closing of the Acquisition, whichever is later.

5. Secrecy and Noncompetition.

(a) *No Competing Employment.* For so long as the Executive is employed by the Company and continuing for two years after the termination of such employment or resignation therefrom (such period being referred to hereinafter as the "Restricted Period"), the Executive shall not, unless he receives after the closing of the Acquisition the prior written consent of the Company, directly or indirectly, (i) own an interest in, manage, operate, join, control, lend money or render financial or other assistance to or participate in or be connected with, as an officer, employee, partner, stockholder, consultant or otherwise, any individual, partnership, firm, corporation or other business organization or entity that, at such time, competes with the Company in, or is engaged in, or (ii) otherwise enter into, the business of [business of the Company] anywhere in the United States or Europe (a "Competitor"); provided, however, that nothing herein shall be deemed to restrict the Executive from owning an interest in a publicly traded Competitor, which interest does not exceed ____ percent of the outstanding capital stock of a Competitor.

(b) *Consultation.* The Executive agrees that during the Restricted Period the Executive shall be available to the Company for consultation for up to ____ days per year at such times and locations as are agreed by both the Executive and the Company. In consideration for the Executive's consulting and advisory services, the Company agrees to make payments to the Executive twice monthly at the rate of $____ per day for each day of actual service as a consultant for the balance of the Restricted Period following the Executive's termination of employment with the Company; provided that the Executive continues to comply with the provisions of this paragraph 5. In addition, the Company will reimburse the Executive for any reasonable out-of-pocket expenses incurred by the Executive in connection with the Executive's consulting and advisory services following presentation to the Company of reasonable documentation evidencing such expenses. The rate of the Executive's compensation pursuant to this subparagraph 5(b) shall be reviewed annually and may be increased, but not decreased, by the Board. Upon two weeks' prior written notice to the Executive, the Company may elect to discontinue payments pursuant to this subparagraph 5(b); and provided that the Executive has not failed to comply with the provisions of this subparagraph 5(b), the Executive shall not be bound by the covenants set forth in subparagraph 5(a) hereof, effective two weeks after receipt of such notice by the Executive.

(c) *No Interference.* During the Restricted Period, the Executive shall not, whether for his own account or for the account of any other individual, partnership, firm, corporation or other business organization (other than the Company), intentionally solicit, endeavor to entice away from the Company, or otherwise interfere with the relationship of the Company with, any person who is employed by or otherwise engaged to perform services for the Company (including, but not limited to, any independent sales representatives or organizations) or any person or entity who is, or was within the then most recent twelve-month period, a customer or client of the Company.

(d) *Secrecy.* The Executive recognizes that the services to be performed by him hereunder are special, unique and extraordinary in that, by reason of his employment hereunder and his past employment with the Company, he may acquire or has acquired confidential information and trade secrets concerning the operation of the Company's predecessors, or any of its affiliates or subsidiaries, the use or disclosure of which could cause the Company, or any of its affiliates or subsidiaries, substantial loss and damages which could not be readily calculated and for which no remedy at law would be adequate. Accordingly, the Executive covenants and agrees with the Company that he will not at any time, except in performance of the Executive's obligations to the Company hereunder or with the prior written consent of the Board, directly or indirectly, disclose any secret or confidential information that he may learn or has learned by reason of his association with the Company, or any predecessors. The term "confidential information" includes, without limitation, information not in the public domain and not previously disclosed to the public or to the trade by the Company's management with respect to the Company's affiliates' or subsidiaries' products, facilities and methods, trade secrets and other intellectual property, systems, procedures, manuals, confidential reports, product price lists, customer lists, financial information (including the revenues, costs or profits associated with any of the Company's products), business plans, prospects or opportunities. The Executive understands and agrees that the rights and obligations set forth in this subparagraph 5(d) are perpetual and, in any case, shall extend beyond the Restricted Period and the Executive's employment hereunder.

(e) *Exclusive Property.* The Executive confirms that all confidential information is and shall remain the exclusive property of the Company. All business records, papers and documents kept or made by the Executive relating to the business of the Company shall be and remain the property of the Company. Upon the termination of his employment with the Company or upon the request of the Company at any time, the Executive shall promptly deliver to the Company, and shall not, without the consent of the Company, which shall not be unreasonably withheld, retain copies of any written materials prepared by or for the Company not previously made available to the public, or records and documents made by the Executive or coming into his possession and not in the public domain concerning the business or affairs of the Company or any predecessors to its business, or any of its affiliates or subsidiaries. The Executive understands and agrees that the rights and obligations set forth in this subparagraph 5(e) are perpetual and, in any case, shall extend beyond the Restricted Period and the Executive's employment hereunder.

(f) *Inventions.* The Executive hereby sells, transfers and assigns to the Company or to any person, or entity designated by the Company, all of the entire right, title and interest of the Executive in and to all inventions, ideas, disclosures and improvements, whether patented or unpatented, and copyrightable material, made or conceived by the Executive, solely or jointly, or in whole or in part, during his employment (including employment prior to the date hereof) by the Company which are not generally known to the public or recognized as standard practice and which (i) relate to methods, apparatus, designs, products, processes or devices sold, leased, used or under construction or development by the Company or any subsidiary and (ii) arise (wholly or partly) from the efforts of the Executive during the term hereof (an "Invention"). The

FORMS AND MATERIALS

Executive shall communicate promptly and disclose to the Company, in such form as the Company requests, all information, details and data pertaining to any such Inventions; and, whether during the term hereof or thereafter, the Executive shall execute and deliver to the Company such formal transfers and assignments and such other papers and documents as reasonably may be required of the Executive to permit the Company or any person or entity designated by the Company to file and prosecute the patent applications and, as to copyrightable material, to obtain copyright thereon. Any invention by the Executive within six months following the termination of this Agreement shall be deemed to fall within the provisions of this paragraph unless the Executive bears the burden of proof of showing that the Invention was first conceived and made following such termination.

(g) *Injunctive Relief.* Without intending to limit the remedies available to the Company, the Executive acknowledges that a breach of any of the covenants contained in this paragraph 5 may result in material irreparable injury to the Company or its affiliates or subsidiaries for which there is no adequate remedy at law, that it will not be possible to measure damages for such injuries precisely and that, in the event of such a breach or threat thereof, the Company shall be entitled to obtain a temporary restraining order and/or a preliminary or permanent injunction restraining the Executive from engaging in activities prohibited by this paragraph 5 or such other relief as may be required specifically to enforce any of the covenants in this paragraph 5. The Executive hereby agrees and consents that such injunctive relief may be sought *ex parte* in any state or federal court of record in the State of New York, or in the state and county in which such violation may occur, or in any other court having jurisdiction, at the election of the Company. The Executive agrees to and hereby does submit to *in personam* jurisdiction before each and every such court for that purpose.

(h) *Extension of Restricted Period.* In addition to the remedies the Company may seek and obtain pursuant to subparagraph (g) of this paragraph 5, the Restricted Period shall be extended by any and all periods during which the Executive shall be found by a court possessing personal jurisdiction over him to have been in violation of the covenants contained in this paragraph 5.

6. Nonassignability; Binding Agreement.

(a) *By the Executive.* Neither this Agreement nor any right, duty, obligation or interest hereunder shall be assignable or delegable by the Executive without the Company's prior written consent; provided, however, that nothing in this paragraph shall preclude the Executive from designating any of his beneficiaries to receive any benefits payable hereunder upon his death, or his executors, administrators, or other legal representatives, from assigning any rights hereunder to the person or persons entitled thereto.

(b) *By the Company.* This Agreement and all of the Company's rights and obligations hereunder may be assigned, delegated or transferred by it to any business entity which at any time by merger, consolidation or otherwise acquires all or substantially all of the assets of the Company or to which the Company transfers all or substantially all of its assets. Upon such assignment, delegation or transfer, any such affiliate, subsidiary or business entity shall be deemed to be substituted for all purposes as the Company hereunder.

(c) *Binding Effect.* This Agreement shall be binding upon and inure to the benefit of the parties hereto, any successors to or assigns of the Company and the Executive's heirs and the personal representatives of the Executive's estate.

7. Severability. If the final determination of a court of competent jurisdiction declares, after the expiration of the time within which judicial review (if permitted) of such determination may be perfected, that any term or provision hereof is invalid or unenforceable, (a) the remaining terms and provisions hereof shall be unimpaired and (b) the invalid or unenforceable term or provision shall be deemed replaced by a term or provision that is valid and enforceable and that comes closest to expressing the intention of the invalid or unenforceable term or provision.

8. Amendment; Waiver. This Agreement may not be modified, amended or waived in any manner except by an instrument in writing signed by both parties hereto; provided, however, that any such modification, amendment or waiver on the part of the Company shall have been previously approved by the Board. The waiver by either party of compliance with any provision of this Agreement by the other party shall not operate or be construed as a waiver of any other provision of this Agreement, or of any subsequent breach by such party of a provision of this Agreement.

9. Governing Law. All matters affecting this Agreement, including the validity thereof, are to be governed by, interpreted and construed in accordance with the laws of the State of New York.

10. Notices. Any notice hereunder by either party to the other shall be given in writing by personal delivery or certified mail, return receipt requested. If addressed to the Executive, the notice shall be delivered or mailed to the Executive at the address specified under the Executive's signature hereto, or if addressed to the Company, the notice shall be delivered or mailed to the Company at its executive offices to the attention of the Board of Directors of the Company. A notice shall be deemed given, if by personal delivery, on the date of such delivery or, if by certified mail, on the date shown on the applicable return receipt.

11. Supersedes Previous Agreements. This Agreement supersedes all prior or contemporaneous negotiations, commitments, agreements and writings with respect to the subject matter hereof, all such other negotiations, commitments, agreements and writings will have no further force or effect, and the parties to any such other negotiation, commitment, agreement or writing will have no further rights or obligations thereunder.

12. Counterparts. This Agreement may be executed by either of the parties hereto in counterparts, each of which shall be deemed to be an original, but all such counterparts shall together constitute one and the same instrument.

13. Headings. The headings of paragraphs herein are included solely for convenience of reference and shall not control the meaning or interpretation of any of the provisions of this Agreement.

IN WITNESS WHEREOF, the Company has caused this Agreement to be signed by its officer pursuant to the authority of its Board, and the Executive has executed this Agreement as of the day and year first written above.

[COMPANY]

By: _____

[EXECUTIVE]

By: _____

FORM TWENTY-TWO

INCENTIVE AND NONQUALIFIED STOCK OPTION PLAN

ARTICLE I

PURPOSE

This [date] STOCK OPTION PLAN (the "Plan") is intended as an incentive to improve the performance and encourage the continued employment of eligible employees of ____ (the "Company") participating in the Plan, by means of increasing their proprietary interest in the Company's long-term success through stock ownership and by affording them the opportunity for additional compensation related to the value of the Company's stock.

The word "Company," when used in the Plan with reference to employment, shall include subsidiaries of the Company. The word "subsidiary," when used in the Plan, shall mean any subsidiary of the Company within the meaning of Section 425(f) of the Internal Revenue Code of 1986, as it may be amended from time to time (the "Code").

It is intended that certain options granted under the Plan will qualify as "incentive stock options" under Section 422A of the Code.

ARTICLE II

ADMINISTRATION

The Plan shall be administered by a Stock Option Committee (the "Committee") appointed by the Board of Directors of the Company (the "Board") from among its members and shall consist of not less than three members thereof who are (and shall remain Committee members only so long as they remain) "disinterested persons" as defined in Rule 16b-3 under the Securities Exchange Act of 1934 (the "Exchange Act").

Subject to the provisions of the Plan, the Committee shall have sole authority, in its absolute discretion, (a) to determine which of the eligible employees of the Company and its subsidiaries shall be granted options; (b) to authorize the granting of both incentive stock options and nonqualified stock options; (c) to determine the times when options shall be granted and the number of shares to be subject to options; (d) to determine the option price of the shares subject to each option, which price shall be not less than the minimum specified in Article V hereof; (e) to determine the time or times when each option becomes exercisable, the duration of the exercise period and any other restrictions on the exercise of options issued hereunder; (f) to prescribe the form or forms of the option agreements under the Plan (which forms shall be consistent with the terms of the Plan but need not be identical and may contain such terms as the Committee may deem appropriate to carry out the purposes of the Plan); (g) to adopt, amend and rescind such rules and regulations as, in its opinion, may be advisable in the administration of the Plan; and (h) to construe and interpret the Plan, the rules and regulations and the option agreements under the Plan and to make all other determinations deemed necessary or advisable for the administration of the Plan. All decisions, determinations and interpretations of the Committee shall be final and binding on all optionees.

ARTICLE III

STOCK

The stock to be subject to options granted under the Plan shall be shares of authorized but unissued Common Stock of the Company or previously issued shares of Common Stock reacquired by the Company and held in its treasury (the "Stock"). Under the Plan, the total number of shares of Stock which may be purchased pursuant to options granted hereunder shall not exceed, in the aggregate, _____ shares, except as such number of shares shall be adjusted in accordance with the provisions of Article X hereof.

The number of shares of Stock available for grant of options under the Plan shall be decreased by the sum of the number of shares with respect to which options have been issued and are then outstanding and the number of shares issued upon exercise of options. In the event that any outstanding option under the Plan for any reason expires, is terminated or is cancelled prior to the end of the period during which options may be granted, the shares of Stock called for by the unexercised portion of such option may again be subject to an option under the Plan.

ARTICLE IV

ELIGIBILITY OF PARTICIPANTS

Subject to Article VII hereof, officers and other key employees of the Company or of its subsidiaries (excluding any person who is a member of the Committee) shall be eligible to participate in the Plan.

ARTICLE V

OPTION PRICE

The option price of each option granted under the Plan shall be determined by the Committee; provided, however, that in the case of each incentive stock option granted under the Plan, the option price shall be not less than the fair market value of the Stock at the time the option was granted. In no event shall the option price of any option be less than the par value per share of Stock on the date an option is granted.

If the Company's Common Stock is quoted on the National Association of Securities Dealers Automated Quotation System ("NASDAQ"), the fair market value shall be deemed to be the mean between the last quoted bid and asked prices on NASDAQ on the date immediately preceding the date on which the option is granted, or if not quoted on that day, then on the last preceding date on which such stock is quoted. If the Company's Common Stock is listed on one or more national securities exchanges, the fair market value shall be deemed to be the mean between the highest and lowest sale prices reported on the principal national securities exchange on which such stock is listed and traded on the date immediately preceding the date on which the option is granted, or, if there is no such sale on that date, then on the last preceding date on which such a sale was reported. If the Company's Common Stock is not quoted on NASDAQ or listed on an exchange, or representative quotes are not otherwise available, the fair market value of the Stock shall mean the amount determined by the Committee to be the fair market value based upon a good faith attempt to value the Stock accurately and computed in accordance with applicable regulations of the Internal Revenue Service.

ARTICLE VI
EXERCISE AND TERMS OF OPTIONS

The Committee shall determine the dates after which options may be exercised, in whole or in part. If an option is exercisable in installments, installments or portions thereof which are exercisable and not exercised shall remain exercisable.

Any other provision of the Plan notwithstanding and subject to Article VII hereof, no option which is not an incentive stock option shall be exercised after the date ten years and one month from the date of grant of such option, and no option which is an incentive stock option shall be exercised after the date which is ten years from the date of grant of such option (in each case, a "Termination Date").

Stock options granted hereunder to employees may provide that if prior to the Termination Date an optionee shall cease to be employed by the Company or a subsidiary thereof for any reason (including death or disability), the option will remain exercisable by the optionee or, in the event of his death, by the person or persons to whom the optionee's rights under the option would pass by will or the applicable laws of descent and distribution for a period not extending beyond three years after the date of cessation of employment, but in no event later than the Termination Date, to the extent it was exercisable at the time of cessation of employment. Notwithstanding the foregoing, stock options granted hereunder shall provide that no option shall be exercisable after the optionee's cessation of employment unless at the time of exercise the By-laws of the Company do not limit the ownership of Common Stock of the Company to selected persons, including employees of the Company.

ARTICLE VII

SPECIAL PROVISIONS APPLICABLE TO INCENTIVE STOCK OPTIONS ONLY

With respect to incentive stock options, the aggregate fair market value (determined at the time the option is granted) of the Stock with respect to which incentive stock options may be exercisable for the first time by an optionee during any calendar year (under the Plan and any other stock option plan of the Company and any parent or subsidiary thereof) shall not exceed $100,000.

No incentive stock option may be granted to an individual who, at the time the option is granted, owns directly, or indirectly within the meaning of Section 425(d) of the Code, stock possessing more than 10 percent of the total combined voting power of all classes of stock of the Company or of any parent or subsidiary thereof, unless such option (i) has an option price of at least 110 percent of the fair market value of the Stock on the date of the grant of such option; and (ii) such option cannot be exercised more than five years after the date it is granted.

ARTICLE VIII

PAYMENT FOR SHARES

Payment for shares of Stock acquired pursuant to an option granted hereunder shall be made in full, upon exercise of the option, by certified or bank cashier's check payable to the order of the Company, by the surrender to the Company of shares of its Common Stock or by any combination thereof. The form of payment shall be at the election of the optionee. The Company in its discretion, and subject to any reasonable procedures required by its registrars and transfer agents, may credit or apply shares of Common Stock held by the optionee and identified to the Company toward payment of the applicable option exercise price without actual surrender of the certificate representing such shares and may cause to be issued to the optionee certificates for shares representing the balance of the shares to be issued upon exercise of the option. The Company may, in its discretion, require that an optionee pay to the Company, at the time of exercise, such amount as the Company deems necessary to satisfy its obligation to withhold federal, state, or local income or other taxes incurred by reason of the exercise or the transfer of shares thereupon.

ARTICLE IX

NONTRANSFERABILITY OF OPTION RIGHTS AND SARS

No option shall be transferable, except by will or the laws of descent and distribution. During the lifetime of the optionee, the option shall be exercisable only by the optionee.

ARTICLE X

ADJUSTMENT FOR RECAPITALIZATION, MERGER, ETC.

The aggregate number of shares of Stock which may be purchased or acquired pursuant to options granted hereunder, the number of shares of Stock covered by each outstanding option and the price per share thereof in each such option shall be appropriately adjusted for any increase or decrease in the number of outstanding shares of Stock resulting from a stock split or other subdivision or consolidation of shares of Stock or for other capital adjustments or payments of stock dividends or distributions or other increases or decreases in the outstanding shares of Stock effected without receipt of consideration by the Company. Any adjustment shall be conclusively determined by the Committee.

If the Company shall be the surviving corporation in any merger or reorganization or other business combination, any option granted hereunder shall cover the securities or other property to which a holder of the number of shares of Stock covered by the unexercised portion of the option would have been entitled pursuant to the terms of the merger. Upon any merger or reorganization or other business combination in which the Company shall not be the surviving corporation, or a dissolution or liquidation of the Company, or a sale of all or substantially all of its assets, the Company shall pay to each optionee in cash, in exchange for the cancellation of any outstanding options of the optionee hereunder, an amount equal to the difference between the fair market value (on the date of the applicable corporate transaction) of the Stock subject to the unexercised portion of the option and the exercise price of such portion of the option. Notwithstanding the foregoing, in the event of such merger or other business combination or a sale of all or substantially all of the Company's assets, the surviving or resulting corporation, as the case may be, or any parent or acquiring corporation thereof may grant substitute options to purchase its shares on such terms and conditions, both as to the number of shares and otherwise, which shall substantially preserve, in the good faith judgment of the Committee, the rights and benefits of any option then outstanding hereunder.

Stock option agreements under the Plan may provide that upon stockholder approval of a merger, reorganization or other business combination, whether or not the Company is the surviving corporation, or a dissolution or liquidation of the Company or a sale of all or substantially all of its assets, all unmatured installments of the stock option shall vest and become immediately exercisable in full.

The foregoing adjustments and the manner of application of the foregoing provisions, including the issuance of any substitute options, shall be determined by the Committee in its sole discretion. Any such adjustment may provide for the elimination of any fractional share which might otherwise become subject to an option.

ARTICLE XI

NO OBLIGATION TO EXERCISE OPTION

Granting of an option shall impose no obligation on the recipient to exercise such option.

ARTICLE XII
USE OF PROCEEDS

The proceeds received from the sale of Stock pursuant to the Plan shall be used for general corporate purposes.

ARTICLE XIII
RIGHTS AS A STOCKHOLDER

An optionee or a transferee of an option shall have no rights as a stockholder with respect to any share covered by his option until such person shall have become the holder of record of such share, and such person shall not be entitled to any dividends or distributions or other rights in respect of such share for which the record date is prior to the date on which such person shall have become the holder of record thereof, except as otherwise provided in Article X.

ARTICLE XIV
EMPLOYMENT RIGHTS

Nothing in the Plan or in any option granted hereunder shall confer on any optionee any right to continue in the employ of the Company or any of its subsidiaries, or to interfere in any way with the right of the Company or any of its subsidiaries to terminate the optionee's employment at any time.

ARTICLE XV
COMPLIANCE WITH THE LAW

The Company is relieved from any liability for the nonissuance or nontransfer or any delay in the issuance or transfer of any shares of Stock subject to options under the Plan which results from the inability of the Company to obtain, or any delay in obtaining, from any regulatory body having jurisdiction, all requisite authority to issue or transfer any such shares if counsel for the Company deems such authority necessary for lawful issuance or transfer thereof. Appropriate legends may be placed on the stock certificates evidencing shares issued upon exercise of options to reflect any transfer restrictions.

ARTICLE XVI
CANCELLATION OF OPTIONS

The Committee, in its discretion, may, with the consent of any optionee, cancel any outstanding option hereunder.

ARTICLE XVII
EFFECTIVE DATE; EXPIRATION DATE OF PLAN

The Plan shall become effective upon adoption by the Company's Board of Directors. The expiration date of the Plan, after which no option may be granted hereunder, shall be the tenth anniversary of the adoption of the Plan by the Board of Directors.

ARTICLE XVIII
AMENDMENT OR DISCONTINUANCE OF PLAN

The Board may, without the consent of the optionees under the Plan, at any time terminate the Plan entirely and at any time or from time to time amend or modify the Plan; provided, however, that no such action shall adversely affect options theretofore granted hereunder without the optionee's consent.

FORM TWENTY-THREE

MATERIALS ON LIMITATION OF DIRECTORS' LIABILITY AND INDEMNIFICATION OF DIRECTORS AND OFFICERS:

SAMPLE CERTIFICATE OF INCORPORATION PROVISIONS

ARTICLE ____: To the fullest extent that the Business Corporation Law of the State of New York, as the same exists or may hereafter be amended, permits elimination or limitation of the liability of directors, a director of the Corporation shall not be personally liable to the Corporation or any of its shareholders for any breach of duty in his or her capacity as a director. Any repeal or modification of the foregoing sentence by the stockholders of the Corporation shall not adversely affect any right or protection of a director of the Corporation existing at the time of such repeal or modification.

ARTICLE ____: The directors and officers of the Corporation shall be entitled to such rights of indemnification and advancement of expenses, including attorneys' fees, in the defense of any action or threatened action in which a director or officer is or may be made a party as the Board of Directors may by resolution prescribe.

INDEMNIFICATION AGREEMENT

This INDEMNIFICATION AGREEMENT is made as of the _____ day of _____, 19____, by and among _____, a New York corporation (the "Company"), and the undersigned ("Agent").

WHEREAS, the Agent is currently serving as a Director and Officer of the Company and certain of its subsidiaries and the Company wishes the Agent to continue in such capacity. The Agent is willing, under certain circumstances, to continue in such capacity; and

WHEREAS, in addition to the indemnification to which the Agent is entitled pursuant to the Certificate of Incorporation of the Company, and as additional consideration for the Agent's service, the Company has, in the past, furnished at its expense directors' and officers' liability insurance protecting the Agent in connection with such service; and

WHEREAS, in order to induce the Agent to continue to serve as a Director and Officer for the Company and in consideration for his continued service, the Company hereby agrees to indemnify the Agent as follows:

NOW, THEREFORE, in consideration of the foregoing, the parties agree as follows:

1. The Company will pay on behalf of the Agent, and his executors, administrators or assigns, any amount which he is or becomes legally obligated to pay because of any claim or claims made against him because of any act or omission or neglect or breach of duty, including any actual or alleged error or misstatement or misleading statement, which he commits or suffers while acting in his capacity as a Director and Officer of the Company and/or its subsidiaries and solely because of his being a Director and/or Officer. The payments which the Company will be obligated to make hereunder shall include, inter alia, damages, judgments, settlements and costs, costs of investigation (excluding salaries of officers or employees of the Company) and costs of defense of legal actions, claims or proceedings and appeals therefrom, and costs of attachment or similar bonds; provided, however, that the Company

shall not be obligated to pay fines or other obligations or fees imposed by law or otherwise which it is prohibited by applicable law from paying as indemnity or for any other reason.

2. If a claim under this Agreement is not paid by the Company, or on its behalf, within ninety (90) days after a written claim has been received by the Company or any subsidiary which the Agent serves as Director or Officer, the claimant may at any time thereafter bring suit against the Company to recover the unpaid amount of the claim and if successful in whole or in part, the claimant shall be entitled to be paid also the expense of prosecuting such claim.

3. In the event of payment under this Agreement, the Company shall be subrogated to the extent of such payment to all of the rights of recovery of the Agent, who shall execute all papers required and shall do everything that may be necessary to secure such rights, including the execution of such documents necessary to enable the Company effectively to bring suit to enforce such rights.

4. The Company shall not be liable under this Agreement to make any payment in connection with any claim made against the Agent:

(a) for which payment is actually made to the Agent under a valid and collectible insurance policy, except in respect of any excess beyond the amount of payment under such insurance;

(b) for which the Agent is entitled to indemnity and/or payment by reason of having given notice of any circumstance which might give rise to a claim under any policy of insurance, the terms of which have expired prior to the effective date of this Agreement;

(c) for which the Agent is indemnified by the Company otherwise than pursuant to this Agreement;

(d) based upon or attributable to the Agent gaining in fact any personal profit or advantage to which he was not legally entitled;

(e) for an accounting of profits made from the purchase or sale by the Agent of securities of the Company within the meaning of Section 16(b) of the Securities Exchange Act of 1934 and amendments thereto or similar provisions of any state statutory law or common law; or

(f) brought about or contributed to by the dishonesty of the Agent seeking payment hereunder; however, notwithstanding the foregoing, the Agent shall be protected under this Agreement as to any claims upon which suit may be brought against him by reason of any alleged dishonesty on his part, unless a judgment or other final adjudication thereof adverse to the Agent shall establish that he committed (i) acts of active and deliberate dishonesty or (ii) acts with actual dishonest purpose and intent, which acts were material to the cause of action so adjudicated.

5. No costs, charges or expenses for which indemnity shall be sought hereunder shall be incurred without the Company's consent, which consent shall not be unreasonably withheld.

6. The Agent, as a condition precedent to his right to be indemnified under this Agreement, shall give to the Company notice in writing as soon as practicable of any claim made against him for which indemnity will or could be sought under this Agreement. Notice to the Company shall be directed to ____ or such other address as the Company shall designate in writing to the Agent; notice shall be deemed received if sent by prepaid mail properly addressed, the date of such notice being the date postmarked. In addition, the Agent shall give the Company such information and cooperation as it may reasonably require and as shall be within the Agent's power.

7. Costs and expenses (including attorneys' fees) incurred by the Agent in defending or investigating any action, suit, proceeding or investigation shall be paid by the Company in advance of the final disposition of such matter, upon receipt of a written undertaking by or on behalf of the Agent to repay any such amounts if it is ultimately determined that the Agent is not entitled to indemnification under the terms of this Agreement. Notwithstanding the foregoing or any other provision of this Agreement, no advance shall be made by the Company if a determination is reasonably and promptly made by the Board of Directors by a majority vote of a quorum of disinterested directors, or (if such a quorum is not obtainable or, even if obtainable, a quorum of disinterested directors so directs) by independent legal counsel, that, based upon the facts known to the Board or counsel at the time such

determination is made, (a) the Agent acted in bad faith or in a manner that he or she did not believe to be in or not opposed to the best interest of the Company, or (b) with respect to any criminal proceeding, the Agent believed or had reasonable cause to believe his conduct was unlawful, or (c) the Agent deliberately breached his duty to the Company or its stockholders.

8. In the event that the indemnification provided for herein is held by a court of competent jurisdiction to be unavailable to the Agent in whole or in part, the Company shall contribute to the payment of the Agent's liabilities in an amount that is just and equitable in the circumstances, taking into account, among other things, payments by other directors and officers of the Company or its subsidiaries for their respective liabilities in consequence of the event or events which gave rise to the Agent's liability. The Company and the Agent agree that, in the absence of personal enrichment, acts of intentional fraud or dishonesty or criminal conduct on the part of the Agent, it would not be just and equitable for the Agent to contribute to the payment of Losses arising out of any action, suit, proceeding or investigation in an amount greater than, (i) in a case where the Agent is a director of the Company, but not an officer of the Company, the amount of fees paid to the Agent for serving as a director during the twelve (12) months preceding the commencement of such action, suit, proceeding or investigation; or (ii) in a case where the Agent is a director of the Company and is an officer of the Company, the amount set forth in clause (i) plus 5 percent of the aggregate cash compensation paid to the Agent for service in such office(s) during the twelve (12) months preceding the commencement of such action, suit, proceeding or investigation; or (iii) in a case where the Agent is only an officer of the Company, 5 percent of the aggregate cash compensation paid to the Agent for service in such office(s) during the twelve (12) months preceding the commencement of such action, suit, proceeding or investigation.

9. This Agreement may be executed in any number of counterparts, all of which taken together shall constitute one document.

10. Nothing herein shall be deemed to diminish or otherwise restrict the Agent's right to indemnification under any provision of the Certificate of Incorporation or By-laws of the Company or under New York law.

11. This Agreement shall be governed by and construed in accordance with New York law.

12. This Agreement shall be binding upon all successors and assigns of the Company (including any transferee of all or substantially all of its assets and any successor by merger or operation of law) and shall inure to the benefit of the heirs, personal representatives and estate of Agent.

13. If any provision or provisions of this Agreement shall be held to be invalid, illegal or unenforceable for any reason whatsoever, (i) the validity, legality and enforceability of the remaining provisions of this Agreement (including, without limitation, all portions of any paragraphs of this Agreement containing any such provision held to be invalid, illegal or unenforceable, that are not by themselves invalid, illegal or unenforceable) shall not in any way be affected or impaired thereby, and (ii) to the fullest extent possible, the provisions of this Agreement (including, without limitation, all portions of any paragraph of this Agreement containing any such provision held to be invalid, illegal or unenforceable, that are not themselves invalid, illegal or unenforceable) shall be construed so as to give effect to the intent of the parties that the Company provide protection to the Agent to the fullest enforceable extent.

IN WITNESS WHEREOF, the parties hereto have caused this Agreement to be duly executed and signed as of the day and year first above written.

[COMPANY]

By: _____

[DIRECTOR/OFFICER]

_____

FORM TWENTY-FOUR

CONSULTING AGREEMENT

This CONSULTING AGREEMENT (the "Agreement") is entered into as of ____, 19____, by and between ____, a New York corporation ("Company") and ____ ("Consultant").

WHEREAS, Company deems it useful and in the best interests of Company to have the benefit of Consultant's services and experience as a consultant; and

WHEREAS, Consultant has indicated his willingness to provide his services and experience as a consultant on the terms and conditions set forth herein.

NOW, THEREFORE, in consideration of the foregoing, the parties hereby agree as follows:

1. Engagement. Company hereby retains the consulting services of Consultant, and Consultant hereby agrees to do and perform consulting services, upon the terms and conditions set forth herein.

2. Duties; Extent of Service. During the Consulting Term (as hereinafter defined), Consultant shall perform and discharge well and faithfully the duties which may be assigned to him from time to time by the Company in connection with the conduct of its business, up to ____ hours per week, and Consultant shall be available by telephone or in person at reasonable times to executive officers of the Company.

3. Compensation. For services rendered pursuant to this Agreement, the Company shall pay Consultant a fee of $____, payable in equal biweekly installments from the date hereof and throughout the Consulting Term unless sooner terminated pursuant to the terms herein.

4. Term. The term of this Agreement (the "Consulting Term") shall commence on ____, 19____, and shall continue until ____, 19____, at which time this Agreement shall terminate, unless sooner terminated in accordance with the provisions hereof.

5. Termination for Cause. The nondefaulting party shall have the right to terminate this Agreement upon the occurrence of any of the following events, and the expiration of any applicable period of cure: (a) the failure of Company to make any payment within ten (10) days after the date when payment is due; (b) the failure of Consultant to perform the assignment to the reasonable satisfaction of Company; (c) the failure of a party to comply with any other term or condition of this Agreement within ten (10) days after written notice specifying the nature of such default, without cure; and (d) any attempt by Consultant to assign or otherwise transfer Consultant's rights hereunder.

6. Termination Without Cause. Either party may terminate this Agreement without cause upon not less than ____ days' prior written notice delivered to the other. The death of Consultant shall automatically terminate this Agreement.

7. Independent Contractor. The parties expressly intend and agree that Consultant is acting as an independent contractor and not as an employee of Company. Consultant retains sole and absolute discretion, control, and judgment in the manner and means of carrying out the assignment. Consultant understands and agrees that it shall not be entitled to any of the rights and privileges established for Company's employees (if any), including but not limited to the following: retirement benefits, medical insurance coverage, life insurance coverage, disability insurance coverage, severance pay benefits, paid vacation and sick pay, overtime pay, or any of them. Consultant understands and agrees that Company will not pay or withhold from the compensation paid to Consultant pursuant to this Agreement any sums customarily paid or withheld for or on behalf of employees for income tax, unemployment insurance, social security, workers' compensation or any other withholding tax, insurance, or payment pursuant to any law or governmental requirement, and all such payments as may be required by law are the sole responsibility of Consultant. Consultant agrees to hold Company harmless against, and indemnify Company for, any of such payments of liabilities for which Company may become liable with respect to such matters. This Agreement shall not be construed as a partnership agreement. Company shall have no responsibility for any of Consultant's debts, liabilities or other obligations, or for the intentional, reckless, negligent or unlawful acts or omissions of Consultant or Consultant's employees or agents.

8. Confidentiality.

(a) Consultant recognizes the proprietary interest of Company in any Trade Secrets of Company. As used herein, the term "Trade Secrets" includes all of Company's confidential or proprietary information, including without limitation any confidential information of Company encompassed in any reports, investigations, experiments, research or developmental work, experimental work, work in progress, drawings, designs, plans, proposals, codes, marketing and sales programs, financial projections, cost summaries, pricing formulae, and all concepts or ideas, materials or information related to the business, products, or operation of Company or Company's customers which has not previously been released to the public at large by duly authorized representatives of Company, whether or not such information would be enforceable as a trade secret or the copying of which would be enjoined or restrained by a court as constituting unfair competition. Consultant acknowledges and agrees that any and all Trade Secrets of Company, learned by Consultant during the Consulting Term or otherwise, whether developed by Consultant alone or in conjunction with others or otherwise, shall be and are the sole property of Company.

(b) Consultant acknowledges and agrees that Company is entitled to prevent the disclosure of Trade Secrets of Company. As a portion of the consideration for the appointment of Consultant and for the compensation being paid to Consultant by Company, Consultant agrees at all times during the Consulting Term and thereafter to hold in strictest confidence, and not to disclose or allow to be disclosed to any person, firm, or corporation, other than to persons engaged by Company to further the business of Company, and not to use except in the pursuit of the business of Company, Trade Secrets of Company, without the prior written consent of Company, including Trade Secrets developed by Consultant.

9. Return of Materials at Termination. At the conclusion of the Consulting Term or at such sooner time as the Agreement shall terminate, Consultant will promptly deliver to Company originals and copies of all materials, property, documents, data, and other information belonging to Company or pertaining to Trade Secrets. Consultant shall not take any materials, property, documents or other information, or any reproduction or excerpt thereof, belonging to Company or containing or pertaining to any Trade Secrets.

10. Remedies Upon Breach. In the event of any breach of this Agreement by Consultant, Company shall be entitled, if it so elects, to institute and prosecute proceedings in any court of competent jurisdiction, either in law or in equity, to enjoin Consultant from violating any of the terms of this Agreement, to enforce the specific performance by Consultant of any of the terms of this Agreement, and to obtain damages, or any of the above, but nothing herein contained shall be construed to prevent such remedy or combination of remedies as Company may, in its discretion, choose to invoke. The failure of Company to promptly institute legal action upon any breach of this Agreement shall not constitute a waiver of that or any other breach hereof.

11. Governing Law. This Agreement shall be interpreted, construed, governed and enforced according to the laws of the State of New York.

12. Attorneys' Fees. In the event of any litigation concerning any controversy, claim or dispute between the parties hereto arising out of or relating to this Agreement or the breach hereof, or the interpretation hereof, the prevailing party shall be entitled to recover from the losing party reasonable expenses, attorneys' fees, and costs incurred therein or in the enforcement or collection of any judgment or award rendered therein. The "prevailing party" means the party determined by the court to have most nearly prevailed, even if such party did not prevail in all matters, not necessarily the one in whose favor a judgment is rendered. In the event of any default by a party under this Agreement, such defaulting party shall pay all the expenses and attorneys' fees incurred by the other party in connection with such default, whether or not any litigation is commenced.

13. Amendments. No amendment or modification of the terms or conditions of this Agreement shall be valid unless in writing and signed by the parties hereto.

14. Successors and Assigns. The rights and obligations of Company under this Agreement shall inure to the benefit of and shall be binding upon the successors and assigns of Company. Consultant shall not be entitled to assign any of Consultant's rights or obligations under this Agreement.

15. Entire Agreement. This Agreement constitutes the entire agreement between the parties with respect to the appointment of Consultant.

IN WITNESS WHEREOF, the parties have executed this Agreement as of the date first set forth above.

By: _____
[COMPANY]

_____
[CONSULTANT]

FORM TWENTY-FIVE

CONFIDENTIALITY, TRADE SECRET AND INVENTION AGREEMENT

This CONFIDENTIALITY, TRADE SECRET AND INVENTION AGREEMENT (this "Agreement") is made as of ____, 19____, between ____, a New York corporation (hereinafter referred to as "Company"), and ____ (hereinafter referred to as "Employee").

WHEREAS, Employee is engaged by Company to perform certain services, and in connection with such duties has access to certain confidential information and trade secrets of Company, and may in the course of his employment with Company discover or conceive an invention, and

WHEREAS, Company and Employee desire to define the rights and obligations between the parties with respect to the subject matter hereto.

NOW, THEREFORE, for and in consideration of the covenants herein contained, the parties hereto agree as follows:

1. Definitions. As used herein, the following terms shall have the meanings set forth below:

1.1 *Invention.* "Invention" includes, but is not limited to, any invention, discovery, know-how, idea, trade secret, technique, formula, machine, method, process, use, apparatus, product, device, composition, code, design, program, confidential information, proprietary information, or configuration of any kind, which is discovered, conceived, developed, made or produced by Employee (alone or in conjunction with others) during the duration of Employee's employment agreement with Company, and which:

a. relates in any manner to the actual or anticipated business of Company, including actual or anticipated research or development; or

b. results from or is suggested by work performed by Employee for or on behalf of Company; or

c. results from the use of equipment, supplies, facilities, information, time or resources of Company. The term "Invention" shall also include any improvements to an invention. The term "Invention" shall not be limited to the definition of a patentable or copyrightable invention as contained in the United States patent or copyright laws.

1.2 *Trade Secret*. The term "Trade Secret" includes all of Company's confidential or proprietary information, including without limitation any information encompassed in all Inventions, and any reports, investigations, experiments, research or developmental work, experimental work, work in progress, drawings, designs, plans, proposals, codes, marketing and sales programs, financial projections, cost summaries, pricing formulae, and all concepts or ideas, materials or information related to the business, products or sales of Company or Company's customers that have not previously been released to the public at large by duly authorized representatives of Company, whether or not such information would be enforceable as a trade secret or the copying of which would be enjoined or restrained by a court as constituting unfair competition.

2. Inventions.

2.1 *Disclosure*. Employee shall disclose promptly to Company each Invention, whether or not reduced to practice, which is conceived or learned by Employee (either alone or jointly with others) during the term of his employment with Company. Further, Employee shall disclose in confidence to Company all patent applications filed by or on behalf of Employee during the term of his employment and for a period of ____ years thereafter.

2.2 *Company Property; Assignment*. Employee acknowledges and agrees that all Inventions shall be the sole property of Company, including without limitation all domestic and foreign patent rights, rights of registration or other protection under the copyright laws, or other rights, pertaining to the Inventions. Employee hereby assigns all of his right, title and interest in any such Inventions to Company.

2.3 *Exclusion Notice.* The assignment by Employee of Inventions under this Agreement does not apply to any Inventions for which all of the following are applicable:

a. no equipment, supplies, facility, or trade secret information of Company were used and the Invention or idea was developed entirely on Employee's own time, and

b. the Invention or idea does not relate to the business of Company, and

c. the Invention or idea does not relate to Company's actual or demonstrably anticipated research or development, and

d. the Invention or idea does not result from any work performed by Employee for Company.

2.4 *Patents and Copyrights; Attorney-in-Fact.* Employee agrees to assist Company in any way Company deems necessary or appropriate (at Company's expense) from time to time to apply for, obtain and enforce patents on, and to apply for, obtain and enforce copyright protection and registration of, the Inventions in any and all countries. To that end, Employee shall (at Company's request), without limitation, testify in any suit or other proceeding involving any of the Inventions, execute all documents which Company reasonably determines to be necessary or convenient for use in applying for and obtaining patents or copyright protection and registration thereon and enforcing same, and execute all necessary assignments thereof to Company or parties designated by it. Employee's obligation to assist Company in obtaining and enforcing patents or copyright protection and registration for the Inventions shall continue beyond the termination of his employment, but Company shall compensate Employee at a reasonable rate after such termination for the time actually spent by Employee at Company's request on such assistance. Employee hereby irrevocably appoints Company, and its duly authorized officers and agents, as Employee's agent and attorney-in-fact to act for and on behalf of Employee in filing all patent applications, applications for copyright protection and registration amendments, renewals, and all other appropriate documents in any way related to the Inventions.

2.5 *Prior Inventions*. This Agreement shall not embrace or include any Inventions owned or controlled by Employee, either alone or in conjunction with others, prior to the time of employment of Employee by Company. Employee has set forth on [if desired, include Appendix listing prior Inventions] attached hereto a complete list of all Inventions, if any, patented or unpatented, copyrighted or not copyrighted, including numbers of all patents and patent applications filed thereon, and applications for copyright protection and registration filed thereon, and a brief description of all unpatented Inventions which Employee has made prior to his employment by Company and which are to be excluded from the scope of this Agreement. Any patentable improvements made on the listed Inventions after the commencement of the employment of Employee by Company shall be within the scope of this Agreement. In the event Employee does not list any such Inventions on Exhibit A or fails to attach an Exhibit A, there shall conclusively be deemed to be no Inventions to be excluded from the scope of this Agreement.

2.6 *Time of Invention; Presumption*. For the purposes of this Agreement, an Invention is deemed to have been made during the term of Employee's employment if the Invention was conceived or first actually reduced to practice during the term of such employment, and Employee agrees that any disclosures of an Invention or any patent application made within one year after termination of his employment shall be presumed to relate to an Invention which was made during the term of Employee's employment unless Employee provides satisfactory and compelling evidence to the contrary.

3. Confidentiality.

3.1 *Acknowledgment of Proprietary Interest*. Employee recognizes the proprietary interest of Company in any Trade Secrets of Company. Employee acknowledges and agrees that any and all Trade Secrets of Company, whether developed by Employee alone or in conjunction with others or otherwise, shall be and are the property of Company.

3.2 *Covenant Not to Divulge Trade Secrets*. Employee acknowledges and agrees that Company is entitled to prevent the disclosure of Trade

Secrets of Company. As a portion of the consideration for the employment of Employee and for the compensation being paid to Employee by Company, Employee agrees at all times during the term of his employment with Company and thereafter to hold in strictest confidence, and not to disclose or allow to be disclosed to any person, firm, or corporation, other than to persons engaged by Company to further the business of Company, and not to use, except in the pursuit of the business of Company, Trade Secrets, including Trade Secrets developed by Employee, without the prior written consent of Company.

3.3 *Confidential Information of Others*. Employee represents and warrants that he does not have in his possession any confidential information or documents belonging to others, and that he will not use, disclose to Company or induce Company to use any such information or documents during his employment. Employee represents that his employment will not require him to violate any obligation to or confidence with any other party.

3.4 *Return of Materials at Termination*. In the event of any termination of his employment, with or without cause and whatever the reason, Employee will promptly deliver to Company all documents, data, and other information pertaining to Inventions and Trade Secrets; and Employee shall not take with him any documents, or other information, or any reproduction or excerpt thereof, containing or pertaining to any Trade Secrets or Inventions.

3.5 *Remedies Upon Breach*. In the event of any breach of this Agreement by Employee, Company shall be entitled, if it so elects, to institute and prosecute proceedings in any court of competent jurisdiction, either in law or in equity, to enjoin Employee from violating any of the terms of this Agreement, to enforce the specific performance by Employee of any of the terms of this Agreement, and to obtain damages, or any of them, but nothing herein contained shall be construed to prevent such remedy or combination of remedies as Company may elect to invoke. The failure of Company to promptly institute legal action upon any breach of this Agreement shall not constitute a waiver of that or any other breach hereof.

4. Covenant Not to Compete. Employee agrees that, during his employment and for a period of ____ years thereafter, he will not directly or indirectly compete with Company in any way, and that he will not act as an officer, director, employee, consultant, shareholder, lender, or agent of any entity which is engaged in any business of the same nature as, or in competition with, the business in which Company is now engaged or in which Company becomes engaged during the term of his employment.

5. General Provisions.

5.1 *Entire Agreement*. This Agreement represents the entire agreement between Employee and Company with respect to the subject matter hereof, superseding all previous oral or written communications, representations, understandings or agreements relating to this subject. This Agreement may be modified only by a duly authorized and executed writing signed by the parties hereto.

5.2 *Successors and Assigns*. The rights and remedies of Company under this Agreement shall inure to the benefit of the successors, assigns and transferees of Company. Employee shall have no right to assign, transfer or otherwise dispose of his right, title and interest in and to any part of this Agreement or to assign the burdens hereof, without the prior written consent of Company.

5.3 *Attorneys' Fees*. In the event of any litigation concerning any controversy, claim or dispute between the parties hereto, arising out of or relating to this Agreement or the breach hereof, or the interpretation hereof, the prevailing party shall be entitled to recover from the losing party reasonable expenses, attorneys' fees, and costs incurred therein or in the enforcement or collection of any judgment or award rendered therein. The "prevailing party" means the party determined by the court to have most nearly prevailed, even if such party did not prevail in all matters, not necessarily the one in whose favor a judgment is rendered. Further, in the event of any default by a party under this Agreement, such defaulting party shall pay all the expenses and attorneys' fees incurred by the other party in connection with such default, whether or not any litigation is commenced.

FORMS AND MATERIALS

5.4 *Governing Law*. This Agreement shall be governed by and construed in accordance with the laws of the State of New York.

IN WITNESS WHEREOF, the parties hereto have executed this Agreement as of the date set forth above.

COMPANY: EMPLOYEE:

_____   _____
                                            (Signature)

By:_____   _____
                                            (Typed or Printed Name)

FORM TWENTY-SIX

AGREEMENT FOR APPOINTMENT OF INDEPENDENT DOMESTIC SALES REPRESENTATIVE

This APPOINTMENT OF INDEPENDENT REPRESENTATIVE (the "Agreement") is made as of the ____ day of ____, 19____, by and between ____, a New York corporation ("Manufacturer"), and ____ ("Representative").

The parties agree as follows:

1. Definitions. As used herein, the following terms have the indicated meanings:

1.1 *Representative*. "Representative" shall mean Representative and all its sales personnel, if any.

1.2 *Product*. "Product" shall mean any product manufactured, produced, or otherwise marketed by Manufacturer.

1.3 *Product Territory*. "Product Territory" shall mean the geographical area in which Representative is entitled to market and sell a given Product, as evidenced by the then-current Schedule, more particularly described in Section 2.2.

1.4 *Purchase Order*. "Purchase Order" shall mean a written order for the purchase of a Product or Products from Manufacturer and shall be Manufacturer's form of purchase order or such other form as is satisfactory to Manufacturer.

1.5 *Customer*. "Customer" shall mean any persons or entity located in the Product Territory who shall have placed or may reasonably be expected to place a Purchase Order for the purchase of any Product.

1.6 *Net Billings.* "Net Billings" shall mean the amounts due and owing pursuant to invoices arising out of Purchase Orders, less the following: (a) replacement of damaged, lost or stolen Product; (b) service charges for labor, parts or repair; (c) parts sales; (d) freight, handling, and shipping charges; (e) excise taxes, sales taxes, use and other personal property taxes; (f) restocking fees charged for returned goods; and (g) finance charges on overdue invoices.

2. Appointment and Authority.

2.1 *Appointment.* Manufacturer hereby appoints Representative, and Representative hereby accepts such appointment, as an independent sales representative for certain Manufacturer's Products upon the terms and conditions hereinafter set forth.

2.2 *Schedules.* Each Product which Representative is entitled to market and sell, the Product Territory within which each such Product shall be marketed and sold, and the commission payable to Representative on the sale of each such Product shall be set forth in a separate schedule in the form attached hereto as Exhibit A. Each such schedule shall be attached to this Agreement and sequentially numbered, commencing with Schedule A-1 (the "Schedules"). In the event Representative's right to market and sell a Product is terminated, or the terms and conditions with respect thereto are modified, the relevant Schedule shall be modified accordingly by Manufacturer.

2.3 *Marketing Authority.* Unless the prior written consent of Manufacturer is obtained, Representative shall not accept or submit Purchase Orders (a) for a Product not listed on the then-current Schedule; (b) from any person or entity with a place of business outside the Product Territory for such Product; or (c) from any person or entity with a place of business within the applicable Product Territory, whom Representative knows intends to ship to an ultimate user with a place of business outside said Product Territory, including, without limitation, a transaction or transactions in which Representative desires to enter into a sharing of commission with one or more representatives. Unless such consent is first obtained, Representative shall not be entitled to any commission on such Purchase Orders even if accepted by Manufacturer.

2.4 *Exclusivity and Reservation.* Representative shall have the exclusive right during the term hereof to market and sell each Product within its Product Territory as is designated on the then-current Schedule.

3. Operations.

3.1 *Sales.* Representative's sales of Products shall be at the price set forth on Manufacturer's then-current price list. Representative shall submit to Manufacturer for acceptance a Purchase Order for each sale identifying, at a minimum, the Product, the price per Product and the quantity to be purchased.

3.2 *Acceptance of Sales.* Manufacturer shall have the absolute right, in its sole discretion, to refuse to accept any Purchase Order submitted by Representative, and Representative shall not be entitled to any commission on any Purchase Order not accepted.

3.3 *Payment.* All payments by Customers for Products shall be made directly to Manufacturer, and Representative shall so advise all Customers to whom sales are made. Payments shall be made in accordance with the terms and conditions of the applicable Purchase Order.

3.4 *Prices, Terms and Sales Policy.* Prices, discounts, terms, and sales policy with respect to the sale of Products shall be under the exclusive control of Manufacturer, and may be modified at any time and from time to time in Manufacturer's sole discretion. Changes in price for Products shall become effective on the stated effective date of the change. All sales by Representative shall comply with prices in effect at the time of placement of such Purchase Order. Representative shall, promptly upon receipt of same, communicate to sales management of Manufacturer any and all requests by customers for discount pricing, and shall communicate to any such customer that discounts off the then-current list price must be approved by management of Manufacturer. Upon, and only upon, authorization from Manufacturer, Representative shall sell such Products at the authorized price(s).

4. Duties of Representative.

4.1 *Best Efforts*. Representative shall use its best efforts to promote demand for and the sale of each Product designated on the then-current Schedule within the Product's respective Product Territory, and shall maintain adequate facilities and personnel for such purpose.

4.2 *Exclusive Dealings*. Representative shall not, directly or indirectly, act as distributor, independent agent, sales representative, employee, or other sales personnel of any person or entity engaged in the manufacture, marketing or sale of any products which, in the sole discretion of Manufacturer, compete with or are of a like nature to any one or more Products designated on the then-current Schedule.

4.3 *Customer Relations*. Representative hereby acknowledges that prompt, courteous and professional service to all Customers and the fostering and maintenance of good relations with Customers is of paramount importance to Manufacturer and this Agreement, and Representative hereby agrees to use its best efforts to so serve Customers and promote such relations with Customers. Representative shall call upon Customers regularly, provide assistance and information to Customers as requested by Customers or Manufacturer, serve as liaison between Customers and Manufacturer, and comply with such policies and procedures as Manufacturer may from time to time communicate to Representative.

4.4 *Representative's Expertise*. Representative shall take all necessary steps to ensure that it and all of its sales personnel are fully familiar with the Products, Manufacturer's then-current price list, and applicable Manufacturer's policies and procedures.

4.5 *Customer Training*. If applicable to the particular Product sold, upon initial installation and from time to time as thereafter requested by Customers or Manufacturer, Representative shall provide Customers within its Product Territory with training in the proper use of Products.

4.6 *Delinquent Accounts*. Representative shall, when requested by Manufacturer, call upon Customers with delinquent accounts within its Product Territory, and use its best efforts to procure payment thereon.

4.7 *Sales Meetings and Conventions*. Representative shall attend such sales meetings for, among other things, the training and education of Representative's sales personnel, as Manufacturer may request; provided, however, that Representative shall not be required to attend more than ____ such meetings per year nor spend more than ____ working days per year attending such meetings. Representative shall attend such conventions as Representative deems necessary to meet its best efforts obligation hereunder. All expenses, including transportation, lodging and meal expenses, incurred by Representative in attending such sales meetings shall be borne by Representative.

4.8 *Regular Reports*. Representative shall deliver to Manufacturer on a regular basis, but not less than ____, written reports setting forth all matters of common interest to the parties, including information on new or improved competing products, business activities of competitors, and proposals for improvement of Manufacturer's Products.

4.9 *Other Sales*. Representative shall promptly report to Manufacturer any inquiry or order for Products received from any person or entity with a place of business outside Representative's Product Territory or Territories.

4.10 *Satisfaction*. Representative shall perform all its duties and obligations hereunder to the reasonable satisfaction of Manufacturer.

5. Duties of Manufacturer.

5.1 *Materials*. Manufacturer shall supply Representative with Manufacturer's current catalogues, literature, price lists and applicable policies and procedures, if any. Manufacturer shall also provide Representative with such information and training aids as Manufacturer deems reasonably necessary to enable Representative to carry out its responsibilities under this Agreement. All the foregoing materials shall be supplied at Manufacturer's expense and shall remain the property of Manufacturer. Upon termination of this Agreement, said material shall be returned to Manufacturer at Representative's expense promptly, but not more than seven (7) days from the effective date of termination.

5.2 *Sales and Technical Assistance*. Manufacturer, at its expense, shall provide periodic sales and technical assistance to Representative and its sales personnel to assist them in effective marketing of Products, education of Customers and relations with Customers, and may accompany Representative or its personnel from time to time on calls to Customers. All other expenses of sales and promotion shall be borne by Representative unless said expenses shall have been approved in writing by Manufacturer.

5.3 *Demonstration Models*. Manufacturer shall provide demonstration models of Products to Representative, in such quantity and model mix as Manufacturer, in its sole discretion, deems reasonably necessary to enable Representative to promote the demand for and sale of Products in their respective Product Territory or Territories. Said demonstration models shall remain the property of Manufacturer, and upon termination of this Agreement shall be returned to Manufacturer in good repair at Representative's expense. Representative shall bear the expense of any repairs which the demonstration models may require. If any demonstration model is lost, stolen or damaged beyond repair, Representative shall pay Manufacturer the full current list price therefor.

5.4 *Warranty and Other Representations*. Manufacturer shall be entitled to give to Customers such warranty or warranties as Manufacturer deems appropriate. Representative shall have no right to make any representations or warranties, or otherwise cause the Customers, or any of them, to believe that any warranty, except as is provided in writing by Manufacturer, is applicable to any Product. Representative hereby agrees to indemnify and hold Manufacturer harmless from any expenses which Manufacturer may incur arising out of or resulting from any warranty or representation by Representative other than a warranty in conformity with Manufacturer's then-current express warranty. Unless the prior written consent of Manufacturer is first obtained, Representative shall not, in connection with the sale of Products, use any advertising, promotional material or other literature other than that provided by Manufacturer, nor shall Representative make any representations or warranties other than those contained in such materials and literature as Manufacturer may provide.

5.5 *Indemnification*. Manufacturer shall indemnify and hold Representative harmless from and against any and all liabilities, losses, damages, injuries, costs, expenses, causes of action, claims, demands, assessments and similar matters, including, without limitation, reasonable attorneys' fees resulting from or arising out of the manufacture, delivery, and performance of the Products, including, without limitation, claims for Product liability and patent and trademark or trade name infringement, but excluding any claim arising from or in connection with any act or omission by Representative or any officer, agent or employee of Representative.

6. Commissions and Payment.

6.1 *Commission*. Representative shall be entitled to commissions, in accordance with the commission rates set forth on the then-current Schedule, upon Net Billings pursuant to Purchase Orders within the applicable Product Territory which Representative has submitted and Manufacturer has accepted.

6.2 *Payment of Commissions*. Not less frequently than ____ during the term hereof, Manufacturer shall issue Representative a check for the amount of commissions payable to Representative on billings for Purchase Orders filled by Manufacturer ____ (____) or more days prior to such payment date for which Representative has not theretofore received commissions. In the event payment is not received by Manufacturer from Customer on billings for which Representative shall have received commissions, upon the expiration of ____ (____) days from the date of the applicable invoice, Manufacturer shall be entitled to a credit against the next-to-come-due commission payment in an amount equal to such previously paid commission.

6.3 *Commissions After Termination*. Commissions upon Purchase Orders accepted from the Product Territory during the term of this Agreement shall continue to be paid notwithstanding the termination of this Agreement.

7. Relationship of Parties.

7.1 *Independent Contractor*. The parties expressly intend and agree that Representative is acting as an independent contractor and not as an employee of Manufacturer. Representative retains sole and absolute discretion, control, and judgment in the manner and means of carrying out Representative's selling and marketing activities, except as set forth herein. Representative understands and agrees that it shall not be entitled to any of the rights and privileges established for Manufacturer's employees (if any), including, but not limited to, the following: retirement benefits, medical insurance coverage, life insurance coverage, disability insurance coverage, severance pay benefits, paid vacation and sick pay, overtime pay, or any of them. Representative understands and agrees that Manufacturer will not pay or withhold from the compensation paid to Representative pursuant to this Agreement any sums customarily paid or withheld for or on behalf of employees for income tax, employment insurance, social security, workers' compensation or any other withholding tax, insurance, or payment pursuant to any law or governmental requirement, and all such payments as may be required by law are the sole responsibility of Representative. Representative agrees to hold Manufacturer harmless against and indemnify Manufacturer for any of such payments or liabilities for which Manufacturer may become liable with respect to such matters. This Agreement shall not be construed as a partnership agreement, and Manufacturer shall have no responsibility for any of Representative's debts, liabilities or other obligations, or for the intentional, reckless or negligent acts or omissions of Representative or Representative's employees or agents.

7.2 *Authority*. Without the prior written approval of Manufacturer, Representative shall not: (a) pledge the credit of Manufacturer; (b) collect any monies from Customers; (c) execute or vary the terms of any agreement on behalf of Manufacturer; or (d) represent that Representative has the authority to do any of the foregoing.

7.3 *Loyalty*. Representative shall not, during the term of this Agreement, sell, lease, promote or manufacture goods or merchandise of a nature or class similar to Products, either on Representative's account or on behalf of any other person, company, or firm whatsoever, without the prior written consent of Manufacturer.

7.4 *Indemnification*. Representative shall indemnify and hold Manufacturer harmless from and against any and all liabilities, losses, damages, injuries, costs, expenses, causes of action, claims, demands, assessments, and similar matters, including, without limitation, reasonable attorneys' fees resulting from or arising out of the failure of Representative to fully and completely conform and comply with each and all of the covenants, agreements, terms and conditions to be performed and complied with by Representative under this Agreement.

8. Term and Termination.

8.1 *Term*. The term of this Agreement shall be for an initial period of ____ (____) year(s) commencing on the date first written above, and shall be automatically renewed for successive terms of ____ (____) year(s) each, unless either party notifies the other in writing of its intention not to renew not less than thirty (30) days prior to the expiration of the initial or any renewal term.

8.2 *Termination for Cause*. Either party shall have the right to terminate this Agreement upon the occurrence of any of the following, and the expiration of any applicable period of cure: (a) the failure to make any payment due and owing hereunder within ____ (____) days after written notice of such default; (b) the failure of a party to comply with any other term or condition of this Agreement, and the expiration of ____ (____) days after written notice thereof, specifying the nature of such default, without cure; (c) the attempt by Representative to assign this Agreement, or any rights or obligations hereunder, without the prior written consent of Manufacturer; (d) the occurrence of a change in the control or management of Representative which is unacceptable to Manufacturer in its sole discretion; (e) Representative ceases to do business as a going concern; (f) Representative becomes subject to the insolvency, receivership or bankruptcy laws of any jurisdiction; and (g) there occurs any willful misconduct, wrongful act, neglect or bad faith on the part of Representative or any of its officers, agents or employees.

8.3 *Termination Without Cause*. Either party shall have the right to terminate this Agreement upon ____ (____) days' prior written notice; provided, that if Manufacturer shall desire to market and sell Products directly to Customers within Representative's Product Territory, then Manufacturer shall be required to provide not less than ____ (____) days' prior written notice of termination before the effective date of such termination.

9. Proprietary Interests of Manufacturer.

9.1 *Trademarks and Trade Names.* Nothing contained herein shall be construed to authorize Representative (a) to use any trademark or trade name of Manufacturer as a style or name, or as part of the style or name, of any firm, partnership, or corporation other than Manufacturer; (b) to apply the same to any goods other than the Products; or (c) at any time after the expiration or sooner termination of this Agreement, to apply the same to goods or to any other use whatsoever. Representative shall not use any name, mark, or style to identify Products other than the trademark or trade name used by Manufacturer, without the prior written consent of Manufacturer.

9.2 *Proprietary Interest.* Representative recognizes the proprietary interest of Manufacturer in technical data, marketing and confidential business information provided by Manufacturer to, or otherwise discovered by, Representative from time to time. Representative acknowledges and agrees that such information constitutes trade secrets of Manufacturer. Representative acknowledges and agrees that any and all such information shall be and is the property of Manufacturer. Representative hereby waives any and all right, title or interest in and to such information and agrees, upon termination of this Agreement, to promptly return all copies of such information to Manufacturer, at Representative's expense.

9.3 *Confidentiality.* Representative acknowledges and agrees that Manufacturer is entitled to prevent its competitors from obtaining and utilizing its trade secrets. Representative agrees to hold Manufacturer's trade secrets in strictest confidence and not to disclose them or allow them to be disclosed, directly or indirectly, to any other person or entity, other than to persons engaged by Representative for the purpose of performance hereunder, without Manufacturer's prior written consent. Representative acknowledges its fiduciary obligations to Manufacturer and the confidential nature of its relationship with Manufacturer and of any confidential proprietary information or trade secrets which Representative may obtain during the term of this Agreement. Representative shall not, either during the term of this Agreement or at any time after the expiration or sooner termination of this Agreement, or during any extension hereof, disclose to anyone, other than persons engaged by it for the purpose of performing hereunder, any confidential or proprietary information or trade secrets of Manufacturer obtained by Representative. Representative also agrees to place upon any persons to whom said information is disclosed for the purpose of performance hereunder a legal obligation to treat such information as strictly confidential.

10. General Provisions.

10.1 *No Waiver*. Failure by either party hereto to enforce at any time any term or condition under this Agreement shall not be a waiver of that party's right thereafter to enforce each and every term and condition of this Agreement.

10.2 *Assignment*. The rights conferred upon Representative hereunder are personal and may not be transferred or assigned without the prior written consent of Manufacturer, and any assignment in violation of this section shall be void.

10.3 *Notice*. Any communication under this Agreement shall be given by prepaid, certified mail, return receipt requested, or prepaid telegram or personally delivered at the addresses first set forth on the signature page hereof, or such addresses as either party shall furnish to the other in writing. If the communication is mailed, delivery shall be deemed complete three (3) days after the communication is placed in the United States mail; otherwise delivery shall be deemed complete on the date actually delivered.

10.4 *Modification*. No modification in the terms of this Agreement shall be binding on either party unless in writing and executed by the duly authorized representatives of each party.

10.5 *Paragraph Headings.* The headings of the several paragraphs of this Agreement are inserted solely for convenience of reference and are not a part of and are not intended to govern, limit or aid in the construction of any term or provision hereof.

10.6 *Number and Gender.* All words used herein in the singular number shall include the plural, and the present tense shall include the future, and the neuter gender shall include the masculine and feminine.

10.7 *Entire Agreement.* This Agreement and the documents referenced herein constitute the entire agreement between the parties in connection with the subject matter hereof and shall supersede all prior agreements, whether oral or written, whether explicit or implicit, which have been entered into prior to the execution hereof.

10.8 *Governing Law.* This Agreement shall be governed by and construed in accordance with the laws of the State of New York.

IN WITNESS WHEREOF, the parties hereto have caused this Agreement to be executed by their duly authorized representatives as of the date first above written.

MANUFACTURER	REPRESENTATIVE
By:_____	By:_____
Title:_____	Title:_____
Address:	Address:
_____	_____
_____	_____

FORM TWENTY-SEVEN

UNANIMOUS WRITTEN CONSENT
OF
THE BOARD OF DIRECTORS
OF
[CORPORATION]

We, the undersigned, being all the directors of _____ (the "Corporation"), a corporation organized and existing under the laws of the State of New York, do hereby consent, pursuant to Section 708 of the New York Business Corporation Law, to the adoption of the following resolutions by the directors of the Corporation and that such action be taken without a meeting pursuant to said Section 708, which consent may be executed in any number of counterparts:

WHEREAS, it is necessary to (i) elect officers of the Corporation; (ii) adopt a form of Stock Certificate; (iii) authorize the issuance of Common Stock; (iv) designate a principal office for the Corporation; and (v) authorize the opening of a bank account.

NOW, THEREFORE, BE IT RESOLVED, that the following individuals be, and hereby are, elected to serve as corporate officers (the "Officers") of the Corporation until their successors are chosen and qualified in accordance with the By-laws:

[LIST OFFICERS]

and be it

FURTHER RESOLVED, that the term of office of any of the above elected Officers shall expire upon the termination of employment by reason of retirement, resignation or other separation; and be it

FURTHER RESOLVED, that the form of stock certificate for fully paid and nonassessable shares of Common Stock, $____ par value, of the Corporation ("Common Stock"), reviewed by the undersigned be, and hereby is, adopted as the certificate to represent fully paid and nonassessable shares of Common Stock and that the Secretary of the Corporation cause a specimen copy of such certificate (or photocopy thereof) to be inserted in the minute book of the Corporation as Exhibit A to this Unanimous Written Consent; and

WHEREAS, [Shareholder]'s subscription for ____ shares of Common Stock at $____ per share be, and it hereby is, accepted; and

WHEREAS, in the judgment of this Board, said property is necessary for the business of the Corporation and is of a value at least equal to the aggregate par value of the stock demanded therefor;

NOW, THEREFORE, BE IT RESOLVED, that the offer of said [Shareholder] to transfer to the Corporation the consideration hereinbefore described, which said property the Board of Directors does hereby adjudge and declare to be necessary for the business of the Corporation, be and it is hereby accepted; and be it

FURTHER RESOLVED, that the President and Secretary of the Corporation be, and they hereby are, authorized and directed to execute and deliver, in the name and on behalf of the Corporation, such agreement or agreements as may be necessary for the acquisition of said property in accordance with said offer and that the Officers of the Corporation be, and they hereby are, further authorized and directed to issue to said [Shareholder] or his nominees, a certificate representing ____ shares of fully paid and nonassessable Common Stock, such shares to be issued pursuant to this resolution, upon transfer of said consideration to the Corporation; and be it

FURTHER RESOLVED, that the principal office of the Corporation be, and hereby is, located at _____; and be it

FURTHER RESOLVED, that the Treasurer be, and hereby is, authorized to decide upon the opening of bank and brokerage accounts and the establishment of other traditional banking and brokerage relationships with any bank or brokerage firm or similar institution on behalf of the

FORMS AND MATERIALS

Corporation and is hereby duly authorized to open and maintain, transfer, modify, and close bank and brokerage accounts in the name of and on behalf of the Corporation, and to place such restrictions on withdrawals and loans from such accounts as shall be within the policy of the Corporation and to enter into such other forms of banking and brokerage transactions, including entering into loans and obtaining letters of credit, as they may deem necessary or desirable for the successful and continued operation of the business of the Corporation; that, subject to such decision, any document may be executed which is necessary from time to time to effectuate any of the foregoing actions regarding any such account with any such bank, broker or similar institution; and be it

FURTHER RESOLVED, that the Treasurer be, and hereby is, authorized and directed to pay any such additional fees and expenses, to reimburse any persons for expenses incurred by them in connection with the organization of the Corporation, and to procure and pay for the proper corporate books; and be it

FURTHER RESOLVED, that for the purpose of authorizing the Corporation to do business in any state, territory or dependency of the United States or any foreign country in which it is necessary or expedient for the Corporation to transact business, the proper Officers of the Corporation be, and hereby are, authorized to appoint and substitute all necessary agents or attorneys for service of process, to designate and change the location of all necessary statutory offices and to make and file all necessary certificates, reports, powers of attorney and other instruments as may be required by the laws of such state, territory, dependency or country to authorize the Corporation to transact business therein and whenever it is expedient for the Corporation to cease doing business therein and withdraw therefrom, to revoke any appointment of agent or attorney for service of process, and to file such certificates, reports, revocation of appointments, or surrender of authority as may be necessary to terminate the authority of the Corporation to do business in any such state, territory, dependency or country; and be it

FURTHER RESOLVED, that the proper Officers of the Corporation be, and each of them severally hereby is, empowered, authorized and directed to take such actions as they may deem necessary or convenient to carry out the intent of any and all of the foregoing resolutions in accordance therewith; and be it

FURTHER RESOLVED, that the execution by such Officers of any such paper or document or the doing by them of any act in connection with the foregoing matters shall conclusively establish their authority therefor from the Corporation and the approval and ratification by the Corporation of the papers and documents so executed and the action so taken; and be it

FURTHER RESOLVED, that any and all actions heretofore or hereafter taken by such Officer or Officers of the Corporation within the terms of the foregoing resolutions be, and hereby are, ratified and confirmed as the act and deed of the Corporation.

IN WITNESS WHEREOF, the undersigned hereby execute this consent as of the ____ day of ____, 19____.

_____

_____

_____

FORM TWENTY-EIGHT

UNANIMOUS WRITTEN CONSENT OF THE STOCKHOLDERS OF XYZ CORP.

We, the undersigned, being all of the Stockholders of XYZ Corp., a New York corporation (the "Corporation"), do hereby adopt the following resolutions pursuant to Section 615 of the Business Corporation Law of the State of New York:

(INSERT TEXT OF RESOLUTIONS)

FURTHER RESOLVED, that the proper Officers of the Corporation be, and each of them severally hereby is, empowered, authorized and directed to take such actions as they may deem necessary or convenient to carry out the intent of any and all of the foregoing resolutions in accordance therewith; and be it

FURTHER RESOLVED, that the execution by such Officers of any such paper or document or the doing by them of any act in connection with the foregoing matters shall conclusively establish their authority therefor from the Corporation and the approval and ratification by the Corporation of the papers and documents so executed and the action so taken; and be it

FURTHER RESOLVED, that any and all actions heretofore or hereafter taken by such Officer or Officers of the Corporation within the terms of the foregoing resolutions be, and hereby are, ratified and confirmed as the act and deed of the Corporation.

IN WITNESS WHEREOF, the undersigned hereby execute this consent as of the _____ day of _____, 19____.

STOCKHOLDERS:

_____

_____

_____

_____

FORM TWENTY-NINE

FORMS FOR ANNUAL MEETING OF SHAREHOLDERS:

SHAREHOLDER BALLOT (NONCUMULATIVE VOTING) ANNUAL MEETING OF SHAREHOLDERS OF _____

_____
(Date)

The undersigned hereby votes all shares of common stock standing in the name of the undersigned for the matters set forth below:

1. Election of Directors:

    ____   ALL MANAGEMENT NOMINEES

    ____   _____

    ____   _____

    ____   _____

    ____   _____

    ____   _____

    ____   _____

    ____   _____

Instructions: Place a check mark opposite the name of each candidate for whom you are voting, or opposite "Management Nominees" if you wish to vote for all Management Nominees. Otherwise, vote for ____ [number of Directors to be elected] Directors. You cannot cumulate votes.

2. FOR ____ AGAINST ____ ABSTAIN ____ the amendment of the Corporation's Certificate of Incorporation [to add certain provisions].

3. FOR ____ AGAINST ____ ABSTAIN ____ ratification of the selection of ____ as independent auditors for the fiscal year ending ____.

SHAREHOLDER

_____
Signature

_____
Print Name

_____
Number of Shares

SHAREHOLDER BALLOT (CUMULATIVE VOTING) ANNUAL MEETING OF SHAREHOLDERS OF _____

(Date)

The undersigned hereby votes all shares of common stock standing in the name of the undersigned for the matters set forth below:

1. Election of Directors:

____ Cast votes equally for nominees checked

MANAGEMENT NOMINEES		VOTES
_____	____	_____
_____	____	_____
_____	____	_____
_____	____	_____
_____	____	_____

Instructions: You are entitled to a number of votes equal to the number of Directors to be elected (____) multiplied by the number of shares for which you are entitled to vote. You may divide such votes between any or all of the candidates in any manner you see fit or may cast all of such votes for one Director. If you wish to cumulate your votes equally for all management nominees, you should check the line at the top of the slate. If you wish to cumulate your votes equally for fewer than all of the nominees, you should check the lines opposite the names for whom you are voting. If you wish to cumulate unequally, write the number of votes cast beside the name of each nominee for whom you vote.

2. FOR ____ AGAINST ____ ABSTAIN ____ the amendment of the Corporation's Certificate of Incorporation [to add certain provisions].

3. FOR ____ AGAINST ____ ABSTAIN ____ ratification of the selection of ____ as independent auditors for the fiscal year ending ____.

SHAREHOLDER

_____
Signature

_____
Print Name

_____
Number of Shares

SHAREHOLDER'S PROXY

This proxy is solicited on behalf of the Board of Directors of _____, Inc. (the "Corporation") for its annual meeting of shareholders scheduled for ____, 19____.

The undersigned hereby appoints ____ as proxy, with full power of substitution and all powers the undersigned would have if personally present. The undersigned hereby authorizes said proxy to represent and to vote, as specified below, all shares of the Corporation held of record by the undersigned on the designated record date at the annual meeting of shareholders of the Corporation to be held at ____ a.m. on ____, 19____, at ____, New York, and at any adjournment thereof.

This proxy will be voted as specified below and in favor of any proposal where no choice is specified.

1. Election of Directors.

____a. Vote for all nominees (except as marked to the contrary), consisting of

_____

_____

_____

_____

and

_____

____b. Withhold authority to vote for all nominees.

2. Ratify Selection of Auditors.

_____a.   Vote for ratification of the Board's selection of _____ as the independent certified public accountants to audit the Corporation's financial statements for the fiscal year ending _____, 19_____.

_____b.   Vote against such ratification.

_____c.   Abstain from voting for such ratification.

3. Approval of Incentive Stock Option Plan.

_____a.   Vote to approve [the amendment of the Certificate of Incorporation] as approved and recommended by the Board.

_____b.   Vote against said [amendment].

_____c.   Abstain from voting with respect to said [amendment].

4. Other. The proxy shall have discretionary authority to vote upon such other business as may properly come before the meeting of shareholders.

DATED: _____

_____
(Shareholder to sign name exactly as the stock is registered, as indicated below.)

Please sign, date and return this proxy in the enclosed self-addressed, stamped envelope. You may subsequently submit a new proxy changing this proxy; and you may also attend the meeting in person, revoke this proxy and vote your shares personally.

AGENDA FOR ANNUAL MEETING OF SHAREHOLDERS OF _____
_____, 199__

1. Call to Order. The Chairman calls the Meeting to order at ____:____ ____.m. Welcomes shareholders to Meeting.

2. Officials. The Chairman announces that the Inspector of Elections shall be ____, who is ____, and that the Secretary of the Meeting shall be ____, Secretary of the Company.

3. Notice of Meeting. The Chairman asks the Secretary if due notice of the Meeting has been given and the Secretary responds affirmatively.

4. Quorum. The Chairman asks the Inspector of Elections if a quorum is present, and the Inspector responds that at least ____ percent (____%) of all the shares of the Company are represented by proxy and that a quorum is present. The Chairman declares that a quorum exists and that the Meeting is competent to conduct business.

5. Introductions. The Chairman introduces the President, the Chief Executive Officer, and members of the Board.

6. Agenda. The Chairman states that the Meeting will consider each of the items specified in the notice of the Meeting in the order they were presented, and then entertain other business should any be presented.

7. Election of Directors. The Chairman announces that pursuant to the notice of the Meeting, the first matter for consideration is the election of a board of directors to hold office for the ensuing year and until their successors are elected and qualified. The Chairman states that the Board of Directors has nominated the following persons to stand for election as directors:

_____

_____

_____

_____

_____

_____

_____

_____

a. The Chairman states that nominations need no second.

b. The Chairman announces that the Board of Directors has already received proxies for approximately ____ percent (____%) of the shares of the Company, which is sufficient to elect each of the board nominees. The Chairman asks whether any shareholder who has not submitted a proxy would like to vote or if any shareholder who has submitted a proxy would like to change his/her vote and vote by ballot rather than proxy, or if any shareholder who has not previously submitted a proxy wishes to submit one now. If any one shareholder gives notice prior to the voting that he/she intends to cumulate his/her votes, the Chairman announces that cumulative voting is appropriate, and the cumulative voting ballots are distributed. If not, regular ballots are distributed.

c. If any shareholder wishes to vote by ballot, ballots are distributed and collected by the Inspector of Elections.

d. Upon collection of the ballots and proxies, if necessary, the Inspector of Elections reports all nominees have been elected.

FORMS AND MATERIALS

8. Other Business (e.g., Employee Stock Option Plan). The Chairman then states that the next matter for consideration as specified in the notice of the Meeting is the approval of the Company's 199____ Employee Stock Option Plan. The Chairman states that the Board of Directors has proxies for approximately ____ percent (____%) of the shares voting in favor of the approval of the Employee Stock Option Plan, enough to approve the proposal. The Chairman states that he/she will entertain the following motion from the shareholders of the Company:

"*BE IT RESOLVED*, that the Company's 199____ Employee Stock Option Plan, as adopted and approved by the Board of Directors of the Company, and as described in the proxy statement, be and hereby is approved, ratified and confirmed by the shareholders."

a. Motion made by Management Representative.

b. Motion seconded by another Management Representative.

c. The Chairman asks whether any shareholder present who has not submitted a proxy wants one to vote on this issue. If there are any affirmative responses, proxies are distributed.

d. Proxies are collected by the Inspector of Elections, who announces the motion passes.

9. Auditors. The Chairman then states that the next matter for consideration as specified in the notice of the Meeting is the approval of the selection of ____ as independent certified public accountants for the Company for the fiscal year ending ____, 199____. The Chairman states that the Board of Directors has already received proxies for approximately ____ percent (____%) of the shares voting in favor of the approval of the selection of ____, which is enough to approve the proposal. The Chairman states that he/she will entertain the following motion:

"*BE IT RESOLVED*, that the selection of ____, certified public accountants, as the independent certified public accountants for the Company for the fiscal period ending ____, 199____, is hereby ratified, confirmed and approved."

a. Motion made by Management Representative.

b. Motion seconded by another Management Representative.

c. The Chairman states that representatives from ___ will be happy to entertain any questions.

d. The Chairman asks whether any shareholder present who has not submitted a proxy wants one to vote on this issue. If there are any affirmative responses, proxies are distributed.

e. Proxies are collected by the Inspector of Elections, who announces the motion passes.

10. Adjournment. The Chairman states that there is no further business and that he/she will entertain a motion to adjourn.

a. Motion to adjourn made by Management Representative.

b. Motion seconded by Management Representative.

c. Chairman calls for voice vote and adjourns Meeting.

FORM THIRTY

OFFICER AND DIRECTOR QUESTIONNAIRE FOR PROXY STATEMENTS AND ANNUAL REPORTS ON FORM 10-K

DEFINITIONS

(Please read carefully before completing Questionnaire)

For purposes of this Questionnaire, the following terms have the following meanings:

1. "*Affiliate*" means a Person who directly, or through one or more intermediaries, controls, is controlled by or is under common control with another Person. An Affiliate of a Person includes members of his family and trusts for his or their benefit.

2. "*Beneficial Owner*," "*Beneficial Ownership*," "*Beneficially Owns or Owned*" or "*Beneficial Interest*" refers to any security with respect to which a Person, directly or indirectly, has or *shares* (for example, as joint tenant, co-trustee or co-executor) voting power or investment power or any security with respect to which a Person has the right to acquire Beneficial Ownership at any time within 60 days, for instance, through the exercise of any option, warrant or right or through the conversion of a security or pursuant to the power to revoke a trust, discretionary account or similar arrangement. Voting power includes the power to direct the voting of a security as well as to vote the security directly, and investment power includes the power to direct the disposition of a security as well as to dispose of the security directly.

3. "*Common Stock*" means the common stock, par value $\_\_\_$ per share, of the Company.

4. "*Preferred Stock*" means the preferred stock, par value $____ per share, of the Company.

5. "*Company*" means ____ Corporation and/or any subsidiary thereof.

6. "*Material*" or "*Materially*," with respect to any subject, refers to the kind of information an average, prudent investor would require or desire in order to be reasonably informed before purchasing, selling or voting shares of stock.

7. "*Person*" means an individual as well as any corporation, association, trust, unincorporated organization or other entity.

8. "*Principal Shareholder*" means any Person who owns of record or Beneficially Owns more than 5 percent of the outstanding stock.

PLEASE ANSWER EACH QUESTION CAREFULLY. IF THE ANSWER IS "NO" OR "NONE," PLEASE SO STATE. IF THE INFORMATION REQUESTED IS THE SAME AS STATED IN THE ATTACHED COPY OF LAST YEAR'S PROXY STATEMENT, PLEASE STATE "SAME."

[NOTE: OBTAIN INFORMATION FOR PAST FISCAL YEAR UNLESS NOTED OTHERWISE.]

A. Personal Information

1. Please set forth below your name, business address and age.

NAME	BUSINESS ADDRESS	AGE

2. Do you have any "family relationship" with any other director or officer of the Company or anyone nominated to fill such a position? "Family relationship" for this purpose means any relationship by blood, marriage or adoption not more remote than first cousin. If your answer is "Yes," please identify the Person or Persons to whom you are related and specify the relationship(s).

Answer:

B. Occupations and Directorships

1. State your present principal occupation or employment position with, and any other occupations or employment positions you held at any time since [insert date to obtain information for past five years] with the Company or any other Person. Include the name and principal business of any corporation or other organization in which such occupations and employment were carried on, a brief description of your responsibilities in undertaking such occupations and employment and the dates involved. The description should provide adequate disclosure as to your prior business experience, including, if appropriate, such specific information as the size of any operations you have supervised.

Answer:

2. List any directorships (other than with the Company) which you have held after [insert date to obtain information for past five years] in companies which file periodic reports with the Securities and Exchange Commission.

Dates during which you served as a Director	Company

C. Arrangements Regarding Positions with the Company

Is there any arrangement or understanding between you and any other Person(s) with respect to your being selected or nominated for election as a director or appointed as an officer of the Company? If your answer is "Yes," please name such Person or Persons and briefly describe such arrangement or understanding.

Answer:

D. Compensation

1. Please state the basis upon which you received salary, fees, commissions, bonuses or other cash compensation (other than the reimbursement of out-of-pocket expenses) from the Company or any other Person between ____ and ____ for services in any capacity to the Company and whether any other cash compensation has been set aside or accrued on your behalf by the Company or any other Person during such period. *You may omit items such as salary in respect of which the Company withholds amounts for federal income tax purposes.*

Answer:

2. Describe briefly any Personal Benefits which you received from the Company since ____.

"*Personal Benefits*" means, for present purposes, all benefits you received from the Company, either directly or through third parties, and all benefits furnished by the Company to other Persons which indirectly benefited you (other than cash compensation with respect to which the Company withheld amounts for federal income tax purposes, stock options and benefits arising from interests in pension or profit-sharing plans and other forms of deferred compensation) which are not directly related to your performance of services for the Company.

For example, payments by the Company for, or provision by the Company of, any of the following items are considered to be Personal Benefits:

(a) repairs and improvements to your home;

(b) housing and other living expenses (including domestic service) provided at your principal or vacation residence;

(c) your personal use of property of the Company, such as automobiles, planes, yachts, apartments, hunting lodges or vacation houses, whether or not the Company has incurred additional cost in permitting your use of such facility;

FORMS AND MATERIALS

(d) your personal travel expenses;

(e) your personal entertainment and related expenses; and

(f) your legal, accounting and other professional fees for matters unrelated to the business of the Company.

In addition, your personal use of the Company's staff may also constitute Personal Benefits to you. You need not, however, list such benefits as parking spaces and meals at the Company's facilities; office space and furnishings at the Company's offices; or expense accounts to the extent that you use them only for the Company's business. Please note that the Personal Benefits to be listed below will not necessarily be limited to those items which you have reported, or plan to report, on your income tax return. Moreover, all such Personal Benefits should be described whether or not Material in amount. You need not value Personal Benefits provided that you adequately describe them to permit their identification in the Company's records.

Answer:

3. Please describe any compensation plans or arrangements involving payments to you in excess of $60,000 which will result from your resignation or retirement or any other termination of your employment with the Company or from a change in control of the Company or a change in your responsibilities following a change in control of the Company.

Answer:

E. Security Ownership

1. Please set forth below the aggregate number of shares of each class of stock beneficially owned directly or indirectly as of the close of business on ____, by you or any Affiliate of yours, including, without limitation, any puts or calls.

Answer:

_____ shares of Common Stock.

_____ shares of Preferred Stock.

2. Please indicate in the following tables the number of shares of Common Stock and the number of shares of Preferred Stock with respect to which you or any Affiliate of yours has or shares either voting power or investment power as of the close of business on _____:

	NUMBER OF SHARES	
COMMON STOCK	YOU	AFFILIATE
(a) Sole Voting Power	_____	_____
(b) Sole Investment Power	_____	_____
(c) Shared Voting Power	_____	_____
(d) Shared Investment Power	_____	_____

	NUMBER OF SHARES	
PREFERRED STOCK	YOU	AFFILIATE
(a) Sole Voting Power	_____	_____
(b) Sole Investment Power	_____	_____
(c) Shared Voting Power	_____	_____
(d) Shared Investment Power	_____	_____

3. Please explain the nature of the Beneficial Ownership of any shares set forth in Question 2 (other than shares owned directly and of record by you), including the name of any Affiliate of yours who Beneficially Owns such shares, the relationship of such Affiliate to you and the

FORMS AND MATERIALS 767

number and class of shares Beneficially Owned by such Affiliate. You should also indicate whether you disclaim Beneficial Ownership of any shares set forth in Question 2.

Answer:

4. Are you aware of any Person, or any group consisting of two or more Persons acting as a partnership or syndicate (or otherwise in concert) for the purpose of acquiring, holding, voting or disposing of stock, which has Beneficial Ownership of more than 5 percent of the outstanding stock of the Company? If so, please give the name(s) and address(es) of such Person(s) and a brief description of any agreement among them.

Answer:

5. Please state whether you are aware of any change in control of the Company since _____ or of any arrangements which could result in such a change of control at a subsequent date. If so, please describe.

Answer:

F. Business Relationships

For purposes of this Part F, no information need be furnished with respect to (a) remuneration for your services to the Company as an employee, provided that the Company withheld amounts from such remuneration for federal income tax purposes, (b) Personal Benefits as defined in Part D(2) hereof and (c) benefits received from the Company in your capacity as a shareholder as long as such benefits were shared proportionately by all holders of stock.

1. Since _____, did you or any other director, officer, nominee for election as a director, Principal Shareholder or any of their Affiliates, to your knowledge, have any Material interest, direct or indirect, in any

transaction involving more than $60,000 to which the Company was a party? If your answer is "Yes," please name the interested Person, indicate the Person's relationship to the Company, identify and describe the transaction, give the amount of the transaction, explain the Person's interest in the transaction, and, where practicable, state the approximate amount of the Person's interest in the transaction.

Answer:

2. Do you, any other present director, officer, nominee for election as a director, Principal Shareholder or any of their Affiliates, to your knowledge, have any Material interest, direct or indirect, in any proposed transaction involving more than $60,000 to which the Company is to be a party? If your answer is "Yes," please name the interested Person, indicate the Person's relationship to the Company, identify and describe the proposed transaction, give the amount of the proposed transaction, explain the Person's interest in the proposed transaction and, where practicable, state the approximate amount of the Person's interest in the proposed transaction.

Answer:

3. Please state whether, to your knowledge, any Person of which you are, or have been at any time since ____, a director, officer or owner of more than 10 percent of the equity interest:

(a) has made payments to the Company for property or services during the period from ____ through ____ in an amount exceeding $____ or 5 percent of the Person's consolidated gross revenues for ____;

(b) proposes or is likely to make such payments during the period from ____ through December 31, ____;

FORMS AND MATERIALS 769

(c) has received payments from the Company for property or services during the period from _____ through _____ in an amount exceeding $_____ or 5 percent of such Person's consolidated gross revenues for such year;

(d) is likely to receive such payments during the period from _____ through _____;

(e) was owed by the Company on _____ an amount exceeding $_____; or

(f) has had any other relationship with the Company that is similar in nature and scope to those listed above. If your answer is "Yes," please identify the Person, indicate your relationship to the Person, describe the transaction, state the amount of business involved and discuss any relationship between the Person and the Company.

Answer:

4. Are you, or have you been at any time since _____, a member of or counsel to a law firm that the Company has retained during _____ or proposes to retain in _____? If your answer is "Yes," please state the fees the Company has paid to the law firm during _____.

Answer:

5. Are you, or have you been at any time since _____, a partner or executive officer of any investment banking firm that the Company has had during _____, or proposes to have during _____, to provide services other than participating in an underwriter syndicate? If your answer is "Yes," please state the fees the Company has paid to the investment banking firm during _____.

Answer:

6. Briefly describe all transactions (other than those already described in this Part F) since ____ between the Company and third parties, the primary purpose of which was to furnish compensation to any director or officer of the Company.

Answer:

G. Indebtedness to the Company

(1) Were you or any other director, officer or nominee for election as a director, or (2) was any member of the immediate family of a Person specified in (1), or (3) was any corporation or organization (other than the Company) of which a Person specified in (1) is an officer or partner or beneficial owner of 10 percent or more of any class of stock, or (4) was any trust or estate in which a Person specified in (1) has a substantial beneficial interest or for which a Person specified in (1) serves as a trustee or in a similar capacity indebted to the Company in an amount in excess of $60,000 at any time since ____?

If your answer is "Yes," please state the name of the debtor, the debtor's relationship to the Company, the largest amount of each such indebtedness outstanding at any time since that date, the nature thereof and of the transaction in which it was incurred, the amount outstanding as of this date and the rate of interest paid or charged thereon.

Answer:

H. Legal Proceedings

1. Please indicate if any of the following events have occurred since [5 years ago] and, if so, describe each:

(a) the filing of a petition under the Federal Bankruptcy Act or any state insolvency law by or against, or the appointment of a receiver, fiscal agent or similar officer with respect to the business or property of, you or any partnership or corporation in which you were a general partner or officer within two (2) years prior to the time of such filing;

(b) your conviction in a criminal proceeding or your having been named as the subject of a pending criminal proceeding (other than traffic violations or other minor offenses); or

(c) the issuance of any order, judgment or decree (not subsequently reversed, suspended or vacated) limiting in any way your engaging in any type of business practice (or associating with any Person engaged in any type of business practice) or any activity in connection with the purchase or sale of any security.

Answer:

2. At any time within the last five (5) years were you found by a court or the Securities and Exchange Commission to have violated any federal or state securities law? If so, please describe the violation and the sanction.

Answer:

3. Are you or, to your knowledge, any of your Affiliates or any other director or officer of the Company or any of their Affiliates a party in any litigation to which the Company is also a party? If so, please explain.

Answer:

———

I HAVE SUPPLIED THE FOREGOING INFORMATION TO THE COMPANY FOR USE IN THE PREPARATION OF ITS PROXY STATEMENT FOR THE ____ ANNUAL MEETING OF SHAREHOLDERS AND THE COMPANY'S ____ ANNUAL REPORT ON FORM 10-K. I AGREE TO ADVISE THE COMPANY PROMPTLY

OF ANY CHANGES IN THE ABOVE INFORMATION WHICH MAY OCCUR PRIOR TO THE DATE OF SUCH MEETING.

Dated: _____, ____

_____
(Signature)

FORM THIRTY-ONE

CERTIFICATE OF INCUMBENCY OF THE XYZ CO., INC.

(SECRETARY'S CERTIFICATE)

I, the undersigned, am the duly qualified and serving _____ of the XYZ Co., Inc. (the "Company") and DO HEREBY CERTIFY that:

1. The following named persons have been, except as otherwise indicated, since at least January 1, 199___, and presently are, on and as of the date of this certificate, the officers of the Company holding the respective offices indicated below, and the signature of each person indicated below is a true and correct specimen of such person's signature:

Name	Office	Signature
_____	_____	_____
_____	_____	_____
_____	_____	_____
_____	_____	_____

2. The Company has been duly incorporated, is validly existing and is in good standing as a corporation under the laws of the State of New York, with power and authority to own its properties and conduct its business, and is lawfully qualified to do business in each jurisdiction where the ownership of its property requires such qualification. Annexed hereto as Exhibit I, and certified to by the Secretary of State of the

State of New York, is a true, correct and complete copy of the Certificate of Incorporation of the Company, together with all amendments thereto, as the same is in full force and effect on and as of the date of this certificate.

3. Annexed hereto as Exhibit II, and certified to by the Secretary of State of the State of ____, is a true, correct and complete copy of the Certificate of Authority evidencing the qualification of the Company as a foreign corporation authorized to do business in the State of ____, together with all amendments thereto, as the same is in full force and effect on and as of the date of this certificate.

4. Annexed hereto as Exhibit III is a true, correct and complete copy of the By-laws of the Company, together with all amendments thereto, as the same are in full force and effect on and as of the date of this certificate.

5. Annexed hereto as Exhibits IV and V, respectively, are certificates of the Secretaries of State of the State of New York and the State of ____, respectively, relating to the good standing and tax status of the Company in such jurisdictions.

6. A meeting of the Board of Directors of the Company was duly held on ____, 199____, and at such meeting there were presented to the Board of Directors of the Company copies of the document mentioned in paragraph 7 of this certificate, which document was marked by the Secretary of the Company to indicate that it was so presented to the meeting and was filed with the permanent records of the Company.

7. The form and substance of a certain proposed Agreement, dated as of ____, 199____, between the Company, as borrower, and _____, pursuant to which the Company will ____ (the "Agreement"), was duly approved by, and authorized to be executed and delivered on behalf of, the Company.

8. Attached hereto as Exhibit VI is a true and correct copy of resolutions duly adopted by the Board of Directors of the Company at such meeting, at which a quorum was present and acting throughout; such

resolutions have been recorded in the minute books of the Company and have not been modified, repealed or rescinded and are in full force and effect.

9. No event of default specified in Article ____ of the Agreement and no event, which with notice or the passage or lapse of time or both would become such an event of default, has occurred and is continuing.

10. The representations and warranties of the Company in Article ____ of the Agreement are true and correct on and as of the date hereof with the same force and effect as though such representations and warranties were made on and as of the date hereof.

11. The Company has complied with all of the agreements and satisfied all the conditions on its part to be performed or satisfied by the terms of the Agreement at or prior to the Closing Date (as defined in the Agreement).

12. Annexed hereto as Exhibit VII is a true, correct and complete copy of a schedule showing compliance by the Company with the financial covenants set forth in Section ____ of the Agreement on and as of the Closing Date, based on the consolidated financial statements of the Company for the ____-month period ending on _____, 199____, which are the most recent such statements available.

IN WITNESS WHEREOF, I have hereunto set my hand on _____, 199____.

THE XYZ CO., INC.

[Name]
[Title]

I, the undersigned, the duly qualified and serving ____ of the XYZ Co., Inc., the corporation mentioned in the within Certificate, do hereby certify that _____, the officer of the Company who executed the within Certificate, is, and has been at all times since January 1, 199____, a duly qualified and acting officer of the Company, duly elected or appointed to the office of _____, and that his signature set forth in paragraph 1 of the within Certificate is a true and correct specimen of his signature.

_____   Dated: _____, 199____
[Name]

FORM THIRTY-TWO

MERGER MATERIALS: AGREEMENT AND PLAN OF MERGER

This AGREEMENT AND PLAN OF MERGER (this "Agreement"), dated as of ____, 199____, among ____ Corporation (the "Purchaser"), ____ Corporation, a New York corporation and a wholly owned subsidiary of the Purchaser ("Sub"), and ____ Corporation, a New York corporation (the "Company").

ARTICLE I

THE OFFER

1.01 *The Offer*. As promptly as practicable (but in no event later than five business days after the public announcement of the execution hereof), the Purchaser shall cause Sub to commence an offer to purchase for cash (the "Offer") any and all of the Company's issued and outstanding shares of common stock, par value $.____ per share (the "Shares"), at a price of $____ per Share, net to the seller in cash. The obligation of Sub to commence the Offer and to accept for payment and to pay for any Shares tendered shall be subject only to the conditions set forth in Annex A hereto. The Company agrees that no Shares held by the Company or any Subsidiary (as defined in Section 4.01) will be tendered into the Offer.

1.02 *Company Actions*. The Company hereby consents to the Offer and represents that (a) its Board of Directors (at a meeting duly called and held) has unanimously (i) determined that each of the Offer and the Merger (as hereinafter defined) is fair to and in the best interests of the shareholders of the Company, (ii) resolved to recommend acceptance of the Offer and approval and adoption of this Agreement by the shareholders of the Company and (iii) approved the Purchaser or Sub or any of their affiliates purchasing the Shares pursuant to the Offer and becoming an "Interested Shareholder" of the Company pursuant to the Offer as such term is defined in Section 912 of the New York Business Corporation Law (the "NYBCL") and (b) [Investment Bank] has advised the Company's Board of Directors that the $____ per Share cash consideration to be received by the Company's shareholders is fair to such shareholders from a financial point of view. The Company hereby agrees to prepare promptly and, after review by the Purchaser, to file with the Securities and Exchange Commission (the "SEC"), contemporaneously with the commencement of the Offer, a Solicitation/Recommendation Statement on Schedule 14D-9 (the "Schedule 14D-9") containing such recommendations. In connection with the Offer, the Company will promptly furnish Sub with mailing labels, security position listings and any available listing or computer file containing the names and addresses of the recordholders of the Shares as of a recent date, and shall furnish Sub with such additional information and assistance as Sub or its agents may reasonably request in connection with communicating the Offer to the shareholders of the Company.

ARTICLE II

THE MERGER

2.01 *The Merger*. Upon the terms and subject to the satisfaction or waiver, if permissible, of the conditions set forth in Article VII hereof, and in accordance with the NYBCL, Sub shall be merged with and into the Company (the "Merger"). The Merger will occur at a closing (the "Closing") which will occur as promptly as practicable following the latest to occur of (a) the date by which shareholders of the Company shall have adopted the Merger Agreement, if such adoption is required; or (b) the date of expiration or termination of any waiting period, including extensions thereof, which may be applicable to the Merger under the provisions of the Hart-Scott-Rodino Antitrust Improvements

Act of 1976, as amended, and the rules and regulations promulgated thereunder (the "HSR Act"). The Closing shall take place at such time and at such place as the parties hereto may agree in writing. The date on which the Closing occurs is hereinafter referred to as the "Closing Date." Following the Merger, the Company shall continue as the surviving corporation (the "Surviving Corporation") and the separate corporate existence of Sub shall cease. Notwithstanding this Section 2.01, the Purchaser may elect, with the consent of the Company (which consent shall not be unreasonably withheld), that instead of merging Sub into the Company as hereinabove provided, to merge the Company into Sub or another direct or indirect wholly owned subsidiary of the Purchaser. In such event, the parties agree to execute an appropriate amendment to this Agreement in order to reflect the foregoing and to provide that Sub or such other subsidiary of the Purchaser shall be the Surviving Corporation and will continue under the name "____."

2.02 *Effective Time*. The Merger shall be consummated by the delivery to the Department of State of the State of New York (the "Department") of a certificate of merger (the "New York Certificate") in such form as is required by, and signed and verified in accordance with, the relevant provisions of the NYBCL and the filing by the Department of the certificate of merger (the time of the filing being the "Effective Time"). Within 20 days after the New York Certificate is filed (but not prior to the Effective Time), the Surviving Corporation shall cause a copy of the New York Certificate, certified by the Department, to be filed pursuant to Section 904(b) of the NYBCL.

2.03 *Effects of the Merger*. The Merger shall have the effects set forth in Section 906 of the NYBCL. As of the Effective Time, the Company shall be a subsidiary of the Purchaser.

2.04 *Certificate of Incorporation and By-laws*. The Certificate of Incorporation and By-laws of Sub, in each case as in effect at the Effective Time, shall be the Certificate of Incorporation and By-laws of the Surviving Corporation, provided that, at the Effective Time, the first item of the Certificate of Incorporation shall read as follows:

"FIRST: The name of the Corporation is ____."

2.05 *Directors and Officers.* At the Effective Time, the Board of Directors of the Surviving Corporation shall be comprised of the directors of Sub and the current chief executive officer and chief financial officer of the Company, and the officers of the Company shall be the initial officers of the Surviving Corporation.

2.06 *Conversion of Shares.* Each Share issued and outstanding immediately prior to the Effective Time (other than Shares held by the Purchaser or any subsidiary of the Purchaser, the Company or any of its subsidiaries, which shall be cancelled, and Dissenting Shares (as hereinafter defined)) shall, by virtue of the Merger and without any action on the part of the holder thereof, be converted into the right to receive $____ in cash (the "Merger Consideration"), payable to the holder thereof, without interest thereon.

2.07 *Conversion of Sub Common Stock.* Each share of common stock, par value $.____ per share, of Sub issued and outstanding immediately prior to the Effective Time shall, by virtue of the Merger and without any action on the part of the holder thereof, be converted into and become 200 validly issued, fully paid and nonassessable shares of common stock of the Surviving Corporation.

2.08 *Shareholders Meeting.* If required by applicable law in order to consummate the Merger, the Company, acting through its Board of Directors, shall, in accordance with applicable law:

(a) duly call, give notice of, convene and hold a special meeting (the "Special Meeting") of its shareholders as soon as practicable following the expiration or termination of the Offer for the purpose of considering and taking action upon this Agreement;

(b) include in the Proxy Statement (as herein defined) the recommendation of its Board of Directors that shareholders of the Company vote in favor of the approval and adoption of this Agreement; and

(c) use its best lawful efforts (i) to obtain and furnish the information required to be included by it in the Proxy Statement and, after consultation with the Purchaser, to respond promptly to any comments made by the SEC with respect to the Proxy Statement and any preliminary version thereof and cause the Proxy Statement to be mailed to its shareholders at the earliest practicable time following the expiration or termination of the Offer and (ii) to obtain the necessary approval of the Merger by its shareholders. The Purchaser agrees that, at the Special Meeting, all of the Shares then owned by the Purchaser and any subsidiary of the Purchaser will be voted in favor of the Merger.

2.09 *Merger Without Meeting of Shareholders*. Notwithstanding the foregoing, in the event that the Purchaser, Sub, or any other direct or indirect subsidiary of the Purchaser shall acquire at least 90 percent of the outstanding Shares, the parties hereto agree, at the request of the Purchaser or Sub, to take all necessary and appropriate action to cause the Merger to become effective, as soon as practicable after the expiration of the Offer, without a meeting of shareholders of the Company, in accordance with Sections 905 and 907 of the NYBCL.

ARTICLE III
DISSENTING SHARES; EXCHANGE OF SHARES

3.01 *Dissenting Shares*. Notwithstanding anything in this Agreement to the contrary, Shares which are issued and outstanding immediately prior to the Effective Time and which are held by shareholders who do not vote such Shares in favor of the Merger and who comply with all of the relevant provisions of Sections 623 and 910 of the NYBCL (the "Dissenting Shares") shall not be converted into or be exchangeable for the right to receive the Merger Consideration, unless and until such holders fail to perfect or effectively withdraw or lose their rights to appraisal and payment under the NYBCL. If any such holder fails to perfect or effectively withdraw or loses such right, his Shares shall thereupon be deemed to have been converted into and to have become exchangeable for, at the Effective Time, the right to receive the Merger Consideration without any interest thereon.

3.02 *Exchange of Shares*.

(a) Prior to the Effective Time, the Purchaser shall designate a bank or trust company to act as Exchange Agent in the Merger (the "Exchange Agent"), reasonably satisfactory to the Company. After the Effective Time, the Purchaser will take all steps necessary to enable and cause the Surviving Corporation to provide the Exchange Agent with the funds necessary to make the payments contemplated by Section 2.06.

(b) Promptly after the Effective Time, the Surviving Corporation shall cause the Exchange Agent to mail to each recordholder, as of the Effective Time, a certificate or certificates which immediately prior to the Effective Time represented outstanding Shares (each a "Certificate"), a form letter of transmittal (which shall specify that delivery shall be effected, and risk of loss and title to a Certificate shall pass, only upon proper delivery of a Certificate to the Exchange Agent) and instructions for use in effecting the surrender of the Certificate or payment therefor. Upon surrender to the Exchange Agent of a Certificate, together with such letter of transmittal duly executed, the holder of such Certificate shall be entitled to receive in exchange therefor an amount equal to the product of the number of Shares represented by such Certificate multiplied by the amount of the Merger Consideration, and such Certificate shall then be cancelled. No interest will be paid or accrued on the cash payable upon the surrender of the Certificate. If payment is to be made to a person other than the person in whose name the Certificate surrendered is registered, it shall be a condition of payment that the Certificate so surrendered shall be properly endorsed or otherwise in proper form for transfer and that the person requesting such payment shall pay transfer or other taxes required by reason of the payment to a person other than the registered holder of the Certificate surrendered, or establish to the satisfaction of the Surviving Corporation that such tax has been paid or is not applicable. One hundred and eighty (180) days following the Effective Time, the Purchaser shall be entitled to require the Surviving Corporation or the Exchange Agent to deliver to it any funds (including any interest received with respect thereto) which it has made available to the Surviving Corporation or the Exchange Agent and which have not been disbursed to holders of Certificates, and, thereafter, such holders shall be entitled to look to the Surviving Corporation (subject to abandoned property, escheat or other similar laws) only as general creditors thereof with respect to the cash payable upon due surrender of their Certificates. The Surviving Corporation shall pay all charges and expenses, including those of the Exchange Agent, in connection with the exchange of cash for Shares. Until surrendered in accordance with the provisions of this Section 3.02, each Certificate (other than Certificates representing Shares held by the Purchaser or any subsidiary of the Purchaser or the Company or any Subsidiary (as hereinafter defined) and Dissenting Shares) shall represent for all purposes the right to receive the Merger Consideration in cash multiplied by the number of Shares evidenced by such Certificate, without any interest thereon.

(c) From and after the Effective Time, there shall be no transfers on the stock transfer books of the Surviving Corporation of the Shares which were outstanding immediately prior to the Effective Time. If, after the Effective Time, Certificates are presented to the Surviving Corporation, they shall be cancelled and exchanged for cash as provided in this Article III.

ARTICLE IV

REPRESENTATIONS AND WARRANTIES OF THE COMPANY

The Company represents and warrants to the Purchaser and Sub as follows:

4.01 *Organization.* Each of the Company and the Subsidiaries (as hereinafter defined) is a corporation duly organized, validly existing and in good standing under the laws of the jurisdiction of its incorporation, and each has all requisite corporate power and authority to own, lease and operate its properties and to carry on its business as now being conducted, except where the failure to be so existing and in good standing or to have such power and authority would not, in the aggregate, have a material adverse effect on the business, financial condition, operations, prospects, properties, assets or liabilities (the "Business") of the Company and the Subsidiaries taken as a whole. Each of the Company and the Subsidiaries is duly qualified or licensed and in good standing to do business in each jurisdiction in which the property owned, leased or operated by it or the nature of the business conducted by it makes such qualification necessary, except in such jurisdictions where the failure to be so duly qualified or licensed and in good standing, in the aggregate, would not have a material adverse effect on the Business of the Company and the Subsidiaries taken as a whole. The Company has heretofore delivered to the Purchaser accurate and complete copies of the Certificate of Incorporation and By-laws of the Company as currently in effect. All issued and outstanding shares of each of the Subsidiaries are owned directly or indirectly by the Company free and clear of any charges, liens, encumbrances or security interests with respect thereto. As used in this Agreement, the term "Subsidiary" shall mean any corporation or other legal entity of which the Company or any of its subsidiaries owns, directly or indirectly, 50 percent of the stock or other equity interest entitled to vote on the election of directors.

4.02 *Capitalization*. The authorized capital stock of the Company consists of ____ Shares. As of the date hereof, there are ____ Shares issued and outstanding. As of the date hereof, ____ Shares are held by the Company in its treasury and no Shares are held by any of the Subsidiaries. As of the Effective Time, there will not be, and, as of the date hereof, except for the obligation of the Company to issue (a) no more than ____ Shares pursuant to options ("Options") and stock appreciation rights ("SARs") currently outstanding under the Company's existing 19____ Stock Option Plan and 19____ Stock Option Plan (collectively, the "Stock Option Plans"), (b) ____ Shares pursuant to a rights dividend (the "Rights") announced by the Company on ____, 19____ and (c) ____ Shares pursuant to a Stock Option Agreement between the Purchaser and the Company entered into on the date hereof (the "Option Agreement"), there are no existing options, warrants, calls, subscriptions, or other rights or other agreements or commitments obligating the Company or any of the Subsidiaries to issue, transfer or sell any shares of capital stock of the Company or the Subsidiaries. All issued and outstanding Shares are validly issued, fully paid, nonassessable and free and clear of any preemptive rights with respect thereto.

4.03 *Authority Relative to this Agreement*. The Company has full corporate power and authority to execute and deliver this Agreement and to consummate the transactions contemplated hereby. The execution and delivery of this Agreement and the consummation of the transactions contemplated hereby have been duly and validly authorized by the Board of Directors of the Company, and no other corporate proceedings on the part of the Company are necessary to authorize this Agreement or to consummate the transactions so contemplated (other than the adoption of this Agreement by the holders of the Shares if and to the extent required by applicable law). This Agreement has been duly and validly executed and delivered by the Company, and, assuming this Agreement constitutes a valid and binding obligation of each of the Purchaser and Sub, this Agreement constitutes a valid and binding agreement of the Company, enforceable against the Company in accordance with its terms, except that (a) such enforcement may be subject to bankruptcy, insolvency, reorganization, moratorium or other similar laws now or hereafter in effect relating to creditors' rights and (b) the remedy of specific performance and injunctive and other forms of equitable relief may be subject to equitable defenses and to the discretion of the court before which any proceeding therefor may be brought.

4.04 *Absence of Certain Changes.* Since ____, 19____, and as of the date on which the Purchaser first purchases Shares under the Offer, there has not, and there will not have been, occurred or arisen any material adverse change in or effect on the Business of the Company and the Subsidiaries taken as a whole, except for changes resulting from the Offer and the Merger.

4.05 *Reports.* Since ____, 19____, the Company has filed all required forms, reports and documents with the SEC required to be filed by it pursuant to the Securities Act of 1933, as amended, and the rules and regulations promulgated thereunder (the "Securities Act") and the Securities Exchange Act of 1934, as amended, and the rules and regulations promulgated thereunder (the "Exchange Act"), all of which have complied in all material respects with all applicable requirements of the Securities Act and the Exchange Act. None of such forms, reports or documents, including, without limitation, any financial statements or schedules included therein, at the time filed, contained any untrue statement of a material fact or omitted to state a material fact required to be stated therein or necessary in order to make the statements therein, in light of the circumstances under which they were made, not misleading.

The consolidated balance sheets and the related consolidated statements of earnings, stockholders' equity and changes in financial position (including the related notes thereto) of the Company and the Subsidiaries included in the financial statements contained in the Company's Annual Report on Form 10-K for the year ended ____, 19____, and in the Company's Quarterly Report on Form 10-Q for the quarter ended ____, 19____, present fairly the consolidated financial position of the Company and the Subsidiaries as of their respective dates, and the results of consolidated operations and changes in consolidated financial position for the periods presented therein, all in conformity with generally accepted accounting principles applied on a consistent basis, except as otherwise noted therein, and subject in the case of quarterly financial statements to normal year-end audit adjustments, except that the quarterly financial statements do not contain all of the footnote disclosures required by generally accepted accounting principles.

4.06 *Offer Documents; Proxy Statements; Other Information.* If a Proxy Statement is required for the consummation of the Merger under applicable law, the Proxy Statement will comply in all material respects with the Exchange Act, except that no representation is made by the Company with respect to information supplied in writing by the Purchaser or any affiliate of the Purchaser (other than the Company or any of the Subsidiaries) specifically for inclusion in the Proxy Statement. The Proxy Statement will not, at the time the Proxy Statement is filed with the SEC or is mailed or at the time of the Special Meeting or the Effective Time, contain any untrue statement of a material fact or omit to state any material fact required to be stated therein or necessary to make the statements therein, in light of the circumstances under which they were made, not misleading, provided that no representation or warranty is being made with respect to any information, with respect to the Purchaser and its affiliates, supplied in writing by the Purchaser to the Company specifically for inclusion in the Proxy Statement. None of the information relating to the Company and its affiliates, supplied in writing by the Company specifically for inclusion in the Offer to Purchase and Letter of Transmittal relating to the Offer, including any amendments or supplements thereto, or any schedules required to be filed with the SEC in connection therewith (the "Offer Documents") will, at the respective times the Offer Documents or any amendments or supplements thereto or any such schedules are filed with the SEC, contain any untrue statement of a material fact or omit to state any material fact required to be stated therein or necessary in order to make the statements therein, in light of the circumstances under which they were made, not misleading. The Schedule 14D-9 will comply in all material respects with the Exchange Act. The letter to shareholders, notice of meeting, proxy statement and form of proxy, or the information statement, as the case may be, to be distributed to shareholders in connection with the Merger, or any schedules required to be filed with the SEC in connection therewith are collectively referred to herein as the "Proxy Statement."

4.07 *Consents and Approvals; No Violation.* Neither the execution and delivery of this Agreement by the Company nor the consummation of the transactions contemplated hereby will (a) conflict with or result in any breach of any provision of the respective Certificates of Incorporation or By-laws (or other similar governing documents) of the Company or any of the Subsidiaries; (b) require any consent, approval, authorization or permit of, or filing with or notification to, any governmental or regulatory authority, except (i) in connection with the HSR Act, (ii) pursuant to the Exchange Act, (iii) filing a certificate of merger pursuant to the NYBCL or (iv) filing a registration statement and Schedule 14D-9 if required under the New York Security Takeover Disclosure Act; (c) except as disclosed in writing by the Company prior to the execution of this Agreement, result in a default (or give rise to any right of termination, cancellation or acceleration) under any of the terms, conditions or provisions of any note, license, agreement or other instrument or obligation to which the Company or any of the Subsidiaries is a party or by which the Company, any of the Subsidiaries or any of their respective assets may be bound, other than such defaults (or rights of termination, cancellation or acceleration) which individually or in the aggregate do not have a material adverse effect on the Business of the Company and the Subsidiaries taken as a whole; or (d) violate any order, writ, injunction, decree, statute, rule or regulation applicable to the Company, any of the Subsidiaries or any of their respective assets, other than such violations which individually or in the aggregate do not have a material adverse effect on the Business of the Company and the Subsidiaries taken as a whole.

4.08 *Disclosure*. No representation or warranty by the Company in this Agreement and no statement contained in any document, certificate or other writing furnished by the Company to the Purchaser or Sub, contains any untrue statement of a material fact or omits to state a material fact required to be stated therein or necessary in order to make the statements therein, in light of the circumstances under which they were made, not misleading.

4.09 *Brokers and Finders*. Neither the Company nor any of its officers, directors or employees nor any of the Subsidiaries nor any of their officers, directors or employees has employed any broker or finder or incurred any liability for any brokerage fees, commissions or finder's fees in connection with the transactions contemplated by this Agreement, except for the fees and expenses of [Investment Bank] pursuant to a letter agreement dated ____, 19____, a copy of which has previously been delivered to the Purchaser.

ARTICLE V

REPRESENTATIONS AND WARRANTIES OF THE PURCHASER AND SUB

The Purchaser and Sub represent and warrant to the Company as follows:

5.01 *Organization*. Each of the Purchaser and Sub is a corporation duly organized, validly existing and in good standing under the laws of the jurisdiction of its incorporation, and each has all requisite corporate power and authority to own, lease and operate its properties and to carry on its business as now being conducted, except where the failure to be so existing and in good standing or to have such power and authority would not, in the aggregate, have a material adverse effect on the business, operations or financial condition of the Purchaser and Sub taken as a whole. Each of the Purchaser and Sub is duly qualified or licensed and is in good standing to do business in each jurisdiction in which the property owned, leased or operated by it or the nature of the business conducted by it makes such qualification necessary, except in such jurisdictions where the failure to be so duly qualified or licensed and in good standing, in the aggregate, would not have a material adverse effect on the business, operations or financial condition of the Purchaser and Sub taken as a whole.

5.02 *Authority Relative to this Agreement.* Each of the Purchaser and Sub has full corporate power and authority to execute and deliver this Agreement and to consummate the transactions contemplated hereby. The execution and delivery of this Agreement and the consummation of the transactions contemplated hereby have been duly and validly authorized by the respective Boards of Directors of the Purchaser and Sub and the Purchaser as the sole shareholder of Sub, and no other corporate proceedings on the part of the Purchaser or Sub are necessary to authorize this Agreement or commence the Offer or consummate the transactions so contemplated by this Agreement (including the Offer). This Agreement has been duly and validly executed and delivered by each of the Purchaser and Sub and, assuming this Agreement constitutes a valid and binding obligation of the Company, this Agreement constitutes a valid and binding agreement of each of the Purchaser and Sub, enforceable against each of the Purchaser and Sub in accordance with its terms, except that (a) such enforcement may be subject to bankruptcy, insolvency, reorganization, moratorium or other similar laws now or hereafter in effect relating to creditors' rights, and (b) the remedy of specific performance and injunctive and other forms of equitable relief may be subject to equitable defenses and to the discretion of the court before which any proceeding therefor may be brought.

5.03 *Offer Documents; Proxy Statement.* The Offer Documents and the Offer will comply in all material respects with the Exchange Act, except that no representation is made by the Purchaser with respect to information supplied in writing by the Company specifically for inclusion in the Offer Documents. The Offer Documents will not, at the time of the filing of the Offer Documents with the SEC, at the time that they are published or given and at the time Shares are purchased pursuant to the Offer, contain any untrue statement of a material fact or omit to state any material fact required to be stated therein or necessary to make the statements therein, in light of the circumstances under which they were made, not misleading, provided that no representation or warranty is being made with respect to any information, with respect to the Company and its affiliates, supplied in writing by the Company specifically for inclusion in the Offer Documents. None of the information relating to the Purchaser and its affiliates, supplied in writing by the Purchaser specifically for inclusion in the Proxy Statement, will, at the time the Proxy Statement is mailed, or, at the time of the Special Meeting or at the Effective Time, contain any untrue statement of a material fact or omit to state any material fact required to be stated therein or necessary in order to make the statements therein, in light of the circumstances under which they were made, not misleading.

5.04 *Consents and Approvals; No Violation.* Neither the execution and delivery of this Agreement by the Purchaser and Sub nor the consummation of the transactions contemplated hereby will (a) conflict with or result in any breach of any provision of the respective Certificate of Incorporation or By-laws (or other similar governing documents) of the Purchaser or Sub; (b) require any consent, approval, authorization or permit of, or filing with or notification to, any governmental or regulatory authority, except (i) in connection with the HSR Act, (ii) pursuant to the Exchange Act, (iii) filing a certificate of merger pursuant to the NYBCL or (iv) filing a registration statement and Schedule 14D-9 if required under the New York Security Takeover Disclosure Act; (c) except as disclosed in writing by the Purchaser prior to the execution of this Agreement, result in a default (or give rise to any right of termination, cancellation or acceleration) under any of the terms, conditions or provisions of any note, license, agreement or other instrument or obligation to which the Purchaser or Sub is a party or by which the Purchaser or Sub or any of their respective assets may be bound, other than such defaults (or rights of termination, cancellation or acceleration) which individually or in the aggregate do not have a material adverse effect on the business, operations or financial condition of the Purchaser and Sub taken as a whole; or (d) violate any order, writ, injunction, decree, statute, rule or regulation applicable to the Purchaser or Sub or any of their respective assets, other than such violations which individually or in the aggregate do not have a material adverse effect on the business, operations or financial condition of the Purchaser and Sub taken as a whole.

5.05 *Financing*. The Purchaser has commitments from financial institutions and working capital which in the aggregate are sufficient to provide the Purchaser with the funds necessary to consummate the Offer and the Merger and the other transactions contemplated hereby.

ARTICLE VI

COVENANTS

6.01 *Conduct of Business of the Company*. Except as contemplated by this Agreement, during the period from the date of this Agreement to the Effective Time, each of the Company and the Subsidiaries will conduct its operations only in the ordinary and usual course of business and consistent with past practice and will use its best efforts to preserve intact its present business organization, keep available the services of its present officers and employees and preserve its relationships with customers, suppliers and others having business dealings with it to the end that its goodwill and ongoing business shall not be impaired at the Effective Time. Without limiting the generality of the foregoing, and except as otherwise expressly provided in this Agreement, the Option Agreement or disclosed in writing to the Purchaser prior to the execution hereof, neither the Company nor any of the Subsidiaries will, prior to the Effective Time, without the prior written consent of the Purchaser, (a) issue, sell or pledge, or authorize or propose the issuance, sale or pledge of (i) any shares of capital stock of any class (including the Shares), or securities convertible into any such shares, or any rights (other than the issuance of the Rights), warrants or options to acquire any such shares or other convertible securities, or upon the exercise, in accordance with the present terms thereof, of Options outstanding on the date hereof, or (ii) any other securities in respect of, in lieu of or in substitution for Shares outstanding on the date hereof; (b) purchase or otherwise acquire, or propose to purchase or otherwise acquire, any outstanding Shares; (c) declare or pay any dividend or distribution on any shares of its capital stock (other than the issuance and redemption of the Rights for a price not in excess of $.05 per Right) other than a regular quarterly dividend in the amount of $.____; (d) authorize, recommend, propose or announce an intention to authorize, recommend or propose, or enter into an agreement in principle or an agreement with respect to, any merger, consolidation or business combination (other than the Merger), any acquisition of a material amount of assets or securities, any disposition of a material amount of assets or securities or any material change in its capitalization, or any entry into a material contract or any release or relinquishment of any material contract rights, not in the ordinary course of business; (e) propose or adopt any amendments to its Certificate of Incorporation or By-laws; (f) adopt, amend or accelerate in any respect any agreement or plan for the benefit of employees; (g) incur, assume or prepay any long-term debt or, except in the ordinary course of business under existing lines of credit, incur or assume any short-term debt; (h) except as permitted by existing credit facilities, make any loans, advances or capital contributions to, or investments in, any other person (other than the Subsidiaries); (i) except as permitted by existing credit facilities, assume, guarantee, endorse or otherwise become liable or responsible (whether directly, contingently or otherwise) for the obligations of any other person (other than the Subsidiaries); or (j) agree in writing or otherwise to take any of the foregoing actions or any action which would make any representation or warranty in this Agreement untrue or incorrect, including as of the date hereof and as of the Effective Time, as if made as of such time.

6.02 *No Solicitation.* Neither the Company nor any of the Subsidiaries, officers, directors, employees, agents or representatives (including, without limitation, investment bankers, attorneys and accountants) or any of the officers, directors, employees, agents or representatives of any of the Subsidiaries shall, directly or indirectly, initiate contact with, solicit or encourage (including by way of furnishing information) any inquiries or proposals by or enter into any discussions or negotiations with any corporation, partnership, person or other entity or group concerning any possible proposal (an "Acquisition Proposal") regarding a sale of the Company's capital stock or a merger, consolidation, sale of all or a substantial portion of the Company's assets or sale of any major assets of the Company or any similar transaction; and the Company will notify the Purchaser immediately if any discussions or negotiations are sought to be initiated, or any such information is requested, with respect to an Acquisition Proposal or potential Acquisition Proposal or if any Acquisition Proposal is received or indicated to be forthcoming.

6.03 *Access to Information.*

(a) From the date of this Agreement, the Company will give the Purchaser and its authorized representative full access to the offices and other facilities and to the books and records of the Company and the Subsidiaries, will permit the Purchaser to make such inspections as it may require and will cause its officers and the Subsidiaries to furnish the Purchaser with such financial and operating data and other information with respect to the business and properties of the Company and the Subsidiaries as the Purchaser may from time to time request.

(b) The Purchaser will, and will cause its employees and agents and Sub to, hold in strict confidence, unless compelled to disclose by judicial or administrative process or, in the opinion of its counsel, by other requirements of law, all Confidential Information (as hereinafter defined) and will not disclose the same to any person. If this Agreement is terminated, the Purchaser will promptly return to the Company or destroy all documents (including all copies thereof) received by the Purchaser containing such Confidential Information. For purposes hereof, "Confidential Information" shall mean all information of any kind concerning the Company, except information (i) ascertainable or obtained from public or published information, (ii) received from a third party not known to the Purchaser to be under an obligation to the Company to keep such information confidential, (iii) which is or becomes known to the public (other than through a breach of this Agreement), (iv) which was in the Purchaser's possession prior to disclosure thereof to the Purchaser in connection with the Merger or (v) which was independently developed by the Purchaser.

6.04 *Best Lawful Efforts.* Subject to the terms and conditions herein provided, each of the parties hereto agrees to use its best lawful efforts to take, or cause to be taken, all action and to do, or cause to be done as promptly as practicable, all things necessary, proper or advisable under applicable laws and regulations to consummate and make effective the transactions contemplated by this Agreement. If at any time after the Effective Time any further action is necessary or desirable to carry out the purposes of this Agreement, the proper officers and directors of each party to this Agreement shall take all such necessary action.

6.05 *Consents.* Each of the Purchaser and the Company will use its best lawful efforts to obtain as promptly as practicable such consents of third parties to agreements which would otherwise be violated by any provisions hereof and to make such filings with governmental authorities necessary to consummate the transactions contemplated by this Agreement.

6.06 *Public Announcements.* The Purchaser and the Company will consult with each other before issuing any press release or otherwise making any public statements with respect to the Offer or the Merger and shall not issue any press release or make any such public statement prior to such consultation, except as may be required by law.

6.07 *Options.* Prior to the Effective Time, the Company shall (a) offer to each holder of an outstanding Option and SAR, granted prior to the date hereof under the Company's Stock Option Plans, an amount in cash in cancellation of such Option or SAR equal to the excess of $____ over the per Share exercise price of such Option multiplied by the number of Shares subject to such Option, (b) use its best efforts to secure the agreement of each such holder to accept such cash payment in cancellation of such Options and SARs and (c) subject to the conditions of this Agreement, terminate the Stock Option Plans. After the date of this Agreement, the Company shall not issue any Shares pursuant to any employee benefit plan other than pursuant to the exercise of currently

FORMS AND MATERIALS

outstanding Options. The Company will take all such actions as are necessary to ensure that neither the Company nor any of the Subsidiaries is or will be bound by any Options or SARs, warrants, rights or agreements which would entitle any person, other than the Purchaser or its affiliates, to own any capital stock of the Surviving Corporation or to receive any payment in respect thereof.

6.08 *HSR Act*. The Company and the Purchaser shall, as soon as practicable, file Notification and Report Forms under the HSR Act with the Federal Trade Commission (the "FTC") and the Antitrust Division of the Department of Justice (the "Antitrust Division") and shall use best efforts to respond as promptly as practicable to all inquiries received from the FTC or the Antitrust Division for additional information or documentation.

6.09 *Redemption of Rights*. The Company will redeem the Rights as promptly as practicable, but in no event later than the earlier of (a) the purchase of Shares by the Purchaser pursuant to the Offer or (b) the closing of the purchase of Shares pursuant to the Stock Option, for a redemption price not in excess of $.____ per Right.

6.10 *Future Benefit Programs*. At the Effective Time, the Purchaser, Sub and any other direct or indirect wholly owned subsidiary of the Purchaser participating in the Merger, as applicable, shall cause the Surviving Corporation to continue to employ all individuals of each of the Company and the Subsidiaries so employed by such company (the "Employees") on terms and conditions which are at least as favorable in the aggregate as the terms and conditions applicable to each Employee immediately prior to the Closing Date. The foregoing is not intended to obligate the Purchaser, Sub or any such subsidiary to continue the employment of any Employee after the Closing Date or for any specific period.

Without limiting the generality of the foregoing, but subject to the last sentence of the preceding paragraph, for a period of at least two years from the Closing Date, the Purchaser, Sub or any such subsidiary shall cause the Surviving Corporation to (a) pay after the Effective Time a package of base and incentive compensation, other than employee stock options, at least as favorable in the aggregate to each of the Employees as exists immediately prior to the Effective Time, and (b) continue without modification, except as herein otherwise required, sponsorship of all other employee pension and welfare benefit plans of the Company and each Subsidiary (including all qualified and nonqualified pension, excess benefit, benefit equalization and other retirement plans, group life insurance, severance policies, group health care plans and disability programs) on an overall basis at least as favorable in the aggregate as in effect prior to the Effective Time. Nothing herein shall be intended to limit the ability of the Purchaser or the Surviving Corporation to terminate any employee pension, welfare or other benefit plan.

6.11 *Indemnification.*

(a) The Purchaser agrees that for not less than ____ years after the Closing Date it shall cause to be maintained in full force and effect all applicable provisions in the By-laws of the Company in respect of the rights of the Company's officers and directors to indemnity from the Company.

(b) The Purchaser will use its best efforts to seek to obtain and maintain in effect for not less than ____ years after the Closing Date directors' and officers' insurance policies covering the current and all former directors and officers of the Company with respect to acts or failures to act prior to the Closing Date, on terms and conditions no less advantageous to such directors and officers as shall exist from time to time with respect to the comparable insurance covering the Company's existing members of its Board of Directors, provided that such insurance is available on commercially reasonable terms.

ARTICLE VII

CONDITIONS TO CONSUMMATION OF THE MERGER

7.01 *Conditions to Each Party's Obligation to Effect the Merger.* The respective obligations of each party to effect the Merger are subject to the satisfaction or waiver, where permissible, on or prior to the Closing Date of the following conditions:

(a) This Agreement shall have been adopted by the affirmative vote of the shareholders of the Company by the requisite vote in accordance with applicable law, if such vote is required by applicable law;

(b) Any waiting period applicable to the consummation of the Merger under the HSR Act shall have expired or been terminated; and

(c) There shall not be in effect (i) any judgment, decree or order issued by any federal or state court or administrative body of competent jurisdiction, or (ii) any statute, rule or regulation enacted or promulgated by any federal or state legislative, administrative or regulatory body of competent jurisdiction, that in either of case (i) or (ii) prohibits the consummation of the Merger or makes such consummation illegal.

7.02 *Conditions to Obligations of the Purchaser and Sub to Effect the Merger.* The obligations of the Purchaser and Sub to effect the Merger are further subject to the conditions that (a) the representations and warranties of the Company contained in this Agreement are true and correct in all material respects as of the Closing Date (except for changes permitted by this Agreement); (b) the Company shall have performed in all material respects all its covenants contained in this Agreement; and (c) the Purchaser shall have accepted for payment and paid for Shares tendered pursuant to the Offer or purchased Shares pursuant to the Option Agreement, provided that this condition will be deemed satisfied if the Purchaser fails to accept for payment and to pay for any Shares pursuant to the Offer in violation of the terms thereof.

7.03 *Conditions to Obligation of the Company to Effect the Merger.* The obligation of the Company to effect the Merger is further subject to the conditions that (a) the representations and warranties of the Purchaser and Sub contained in this Agreement are true and correct in all material respects as of the Closing Date (except for changes permitted by this Agreement); and (b) the Purchaser and Sub shall have performed in all material respects all their covenants contained in this Agreement.

ARTICLE VIII
TERMINATION; AMENDMENTS; WAIVER

8.01 *Termination.* This Agreement may be terminated and the Merger contemplated hereby may be abandoned at any time notwithstanding approval thereof by the shareholders of the Company, but prior to the Effective Time,

(a) by the consent of the Company, the Purchaser and Sub;

(b) by the Purchaser or the Company if, without fault of the terminating party, the Effective Time shall not have occurred on or before ____, 19___;

(c) by the Purchaser or the Company if any court of competent jurisdiction in the United States or other governmental body in the United States shall have issued an order (other than a temporary restraining order), decree or ruling or taken any other action restraining, enjoining or otherwise prohibiting the Merger and such order, decree, ruling or other action shall have become final and nonappealable; or

(d) by the Purchaser or the Company, if the Offer terminates or expires in accordance with its terms without the Purchaser having purchased any Shares thereunder and there shall not have been a purchase of Shares by the Purchaser or Sub within thirty days thereafter, provided that the Purchaser may not terminate this Agreement pursuant to this Section 8.01(d) if the Purchaser has failed to purchase Shares in the Offer in violation of the terms thereof.

8.02 *Effect of Termination.* In the event of the termination and abandonment of this Agreement pursuant to Section 8.01 hereof, this Agreement shall forthwith become void and have no effect, without any liability on the part of any party or its directors, officers or stockholders, other than the provisions of Sections 9.08 and 6.03(b), which shall survive. Nothing contained in this Section 8.02 shall relieve any party from liability for any breach of this Agreement.

8.03 *Amendment.* This Agreement may be amended by the Company, the Purchaser and Sub at any time before or after adoption of this

Agreement by the shareholders of the Company but, after any such approval, no amendment shall be made which decreases the Merger Consideration per Share or which adversely affects the rights of the Company's shareholders hereunder without the approval of such shareholders. This Agreement may not be amended except by an instrument in writing signed on behalf of all the parties.

8.04 *Extension; Waiver*. At any time prior to the Effective Time, the parties hereto may (a) extend the time for the performance of any of the obligations or other acts of any other applicable party hereto, (b) waive any inaccuracies in the representations and warranties contained herein by any other applicable party or in any document, certificate or writing delivered pursuant hereto by any other applicable party or (c) subject to Section 8.03, waive compliance with any of the agreements of any other applicable party or with any conditions to its own obligations. Any agreement on the part of any other applicable party to any such extension or waiver shall be valid only if set forth in an instrument in writing signed on behalf of such party.

ARTICLE IX

MISCELLANEOUS

9.01 *Survival of Representations, Warranties and Agreements*. The representations, warranties and agreements made in this Agreement shall not survive beyond the Effective Time, except those agreements set forth in Sections 3.02, 6.10 and 6.11 hereof.

9.02 *Entire Agreement; Assignment*. This Agreement and the Option Agreement (a) constitute the entire agreement among the parties with respect to the subject matter hereof and supersede all other prior agreements and understandings, both written and oral, among the parties or any of them with respect to the subject matter hereof, and (b) shall not be assigned by operation of law or otherwise, provided that the Purchaser or Sub may assign its respective rights and obligations to any direct or indirect subsidiary of the Purchaser, but no such assignment shall relieve the Purchaser of its obligations hereunder. It is understood and agreed that either the Purchaser, Sub or any other subsidiary of the

Purchaser may commence the Offer or purchase Shares thereunder and that the right of assignment provided by clause (b) of the preceding sentence shall specifically include the right to assign to a direct or indirect subsidiary of the Purchaser the right and obligation of Sub to be merged into the Company pursuant to the terms of this Agreement, in which case the Certificate of Incorporation and By-laws of such direct or indirect subsidiary of the Purchaser shall become the Certificate of Incorporation and By-laws of the Surviving Corporation, provided that the first item of the Certificate of Incorporation shall be restated as set forth in Section 2.04 of this Agreement.

9.03 *Validity*. The invalidity or unenforceability of any provision of this Agreement shall not affect the validity or enforceability of any other provisions of this Agreement, each of which shall remain in full force and effect.

9.04 *Notices*. All notices, requests, claims, demands and other communications hereunder shall be in writing and shall be deemed to have been duly given when delivered in person, by cable, telegram or telex, or by registered or certified mail (postage prepaid, return receipt requested) to the respective parties as follows:

If to the Purchaser or Sub:

If to the Company:

or to such other address as the person to whom notice is given may have previously furnished to the others in writing in the manner set forth above (provided that notice of any change of address shall be effective only upon receipt thereof).

9.05 *Governing Law*. This Agreement shall be governed by and construed in accordance with the laws of the State of New York, regardless of the laws that might otherwise govern under applicable principles of conflicts of laws thereof.

9.06 *Descriptive Headings*. The descriptive headings herein are inserted for convenience of reference only and are not intended to be part of or to affect the meaning or interpretation of this Agreement.

9.07 *Counterparts*. This Agreement may be executed in two or more counterparts, each of which shall be deemed to be an original, but all of which shall constitute one and the same agreement.

9.08 *Expenses*. All costs and expenses incurred in connection with the transactions contemplated by this Agreement shall be paid by the party incurring such expenses.

9.09 *Parties in Interest*. This Agreement shall be binding upon and inure solely to the benefit of each party hereto and, except as set forth in Section 6.11 hereof, nothing in this Agreement, express or implied, is intended to confer upon any other person any rights or remedies of any nature whatsoever under or by reason of this Agreement.

IN WITNESS WHEREOF, each of the parties has caused this Agreement to be executed on its behalf by its officers thereunto duly authorized, all as of the day and year first above written.

	PURCHASER
Attest:	By:_____
	Title:_____
———————	
	SUB
Attest:	By:_____
	Title:_____
———————	
	COMPANY
Attest:	By:_____
	Title:_____
———————	

ANNEX A
TO
MERGER AGREEMENT

Conditions of the Offer. Notwithstanding any other provision of the Offer, the Purchaser (or Sub, if Sub is making the Offer) shall not be required to accept for payment, purchase or pay for any Shares tendered until the expiration of the applicable waiting period under the HSR Act and may terminate or amend the Offer and may postpone the purchase of, and payment for, Shares if, at any time on or after [date of Merger Agreement], and prior to the time of payment for any such Shares (whether or not any such Shares have theretofore been accepted for payment or paid for pursuant to the Offer), any of the following events shall occur and remain in effect:

1. Any change shall have occurred or been threatened in the business, properties, assets, liabilities, condition (financial or otherwise), operations, prospects or results of operations of the Company or any of the Subsidiaries which is or is likely to be materially adverse to the Company and the Subsidiaries taken as a whole, or the Purchaser shall have become aware of any fact which is or is likely to be materially adverse with respect to the value of the Company and the Subsidiaries taken as a whole or the value of the Shares to the Purchaser; or

2. There shall have occurred (a) any general suspension of trading in, or limitation on prices for, securities on The New York Stock Exchange, Inc.; (b) a declaration of a banking moratorium or any suspension of payments in respect of banks in the United States; (c) a commencement of a war, armed hostilities or other national or international calamity directly or indirectly involving the United States; (d) any limitation (whether or not mandatory) by any governmental authority on, or any other event which affects, the extension of credit by banks or other financial institutions; or (e) in the case of any of the foregoing existing at the time or the commencement of the Offer, a material acceleration or worsening thereof; or

FORMS AND MATERIALS 803

3. The Company or any Subsidiary shall have (a) issued, distributed or sold, or authorized, proposed or announced the issuance, distribution or sale of (i) any shares of capital stock of any class (including, without limitation, the Shares other than Shares issued pursuant to the Stock Split), or securities convertible into any such shares of capital stock, or any rights, warrants or options to acquire any such shares or convertible securities, other than (1) the Rights, (2) Shares issued or sold upon the exercise or conversion (in accordance with the present terms thereof) of employee stock options outstanding on [date of Merger Agreement] or (3) Shares issued pursuant to the Stock Option; or (ii) any other securities (other than the Rights) in respect of, in lieu of, or in substitution for Shares outstanding on [date of Merger Agreement]; (b) purchased or otherwise acquired, or proposed or offered to purchase or otherwise acquire, any outstanding Shares or other securities (other than the redemption of the Rights for a price not in excess of $.____ per Right); (c) declared or paid any dividend or distribution on any Shares (other than the Rights and regular quarterly dividends not in excess of $.____ per Share) or issued, authorized, recommended or proposed the issuance of any other distribution in respect of the Shares (other than the issuance and redemption of the Rights for a price not in excess of $.____ per Right), whether payable in cash, securities or other property or altered or proposed to alter any material term of any outstanding security; (d) authorized, recommended, proposed or publicly announced its intention to enter into or effect, other than as permitted by the Merger Agreement, (i) any merger, consolidation, liquidation, dissolution, business combination, acquisition of assets or securities, disposition of assets or securities or any agreement contemplating any of the foregoing or any comparable events other than in the ordinary course of business, (ii) any material change in its capitalization or (iii) any release or relinquishment of any material contract rights or any comparable event not in the ordinary course of business; (e) taken any action to implement any such transaction previously authorized, recommended, proposed or publicly announced; (f) authorized, recommended, proposed or announced its intention to authorize, recommend or propose any transaction which could materially and adversely affect the value of the Shares; or (g) proposed, adopted or authorized any amendment to its Certificate

of Incorporation or By-laws or similar organizational documents or the Purchaser shall have learned that the Company or any of the Subsidiaries shall have proposed or adopted any such amendment which shall not have been previously disclosed; or

4. A tender or exchange offer for any shares of capital stock of the Company shall have been made or publicly proposed to be made by another person (including the Company and the Subsidiaries), or it shall have been publicly disclosed or the Purchaser shall have learned that (a) any person (including the Company and the Subsidiaries), entity or "group" (as that term is used in Section 13(d)(3) of the Exchange Act) shall have acquired, or proposed to acquire, more than 10 percent of any class or series of capital stock of the Company (including the Shares), other than acquisitions for bona fide arbitrage purposes and other than acquisitions by any person, entity or group which has publicly disclosed such ownership in a Schedule 13D or 13G (or an amendment thereto) on file with the Commission on or prior to [date of Merger Agreement]; (b) any such person, entity or group which publicly disclosed such ownership to such date shall have acquired or proposed to acquire more than 1 percent of any class or series of capital stock of the Company (including the Shares) or shall have been granted any option or right to acquire more than 1 percent of any class or series of capital stock of the Company (including the Shares), other than acquisitions for bona fide arbitrage purposes; (c) any new group shall have been formed which beneficially owns more than 10 percent of any class or series of capital stock of the Company (including the Shares); (d) any person, entity or group shall have entered into a definitive agreement or an agreement in principle with the Company with respect to a tender offer or exchange offer for any shares of capital stock of the Company or a merger, consolidation or other business combination with or involving the Company; or (e) any person shall have filed a Notification and Report Form under the HSR Act or made a public announcement reflecting an intent to acquire the Company or assets or securities of the Company; or

5. There shall have been any action taken, or any statute, rule, regulation, judgment, order or injunction proposed, sought, promulgated,

FORMS AND MATERIALS

enacted, entered, enforced or deemed applicable to the Offer, by any state, federal or foreign government or governmental authority or by any court, domestic or foreign, that (a) makes the acceptance for payment of, the payment for, or the purchase of, some or all of the Shares illegal or otherwise restricts or prohibits consummation of the Offer; (b) results in the delay in or restricts the ability of the Purchaser, or renders the Purchaser unable, to accept for payment, pay for or purchase some or all of the Shares, other than pursuant to the HSR Act; (c) requires the divestiture by the Purchaser or the Company or any of their respective subsidiaries or affiliates of all or any material portion of the business, assets or property of any of them or any Shares, or imposes any limitation on the ability of any of them to conduct their business and own such assets, properties and Shares; (d) imposes material limitations on the ability of the Purchaser to acquire or hold or to exercise effectively all rights of ownership of the Shares, including the right to vote any Shares purchased by it on all matters properly presented to the shareholders of the Company; (e) imposes any limitations on the ability of the Purchaser or any of its subsidiaries or affiliates effectively to control in any material respect the business or operations of the Company, the Purchaser or any of their respective subsidiaries or affiliates; or (f) otherwise materially and adversely affects the Purchaser or the Company or any of their respective subsidiaries or affiliates; or

6. There shall be instituted or pending any action or proceeding by or before any court or governmental, administrative or regulatory agency or any other person or tribunal, domestic or foreign, challenging the making of the Offer, the acquisition by the Purchaser of any Shares, or otherwise directly or indirectly relating to the Offer or otherwise materially and adversely affecting the Company, the Purchaser or any of their respective subsidiaries or affiliates or the value of the Shares; or

7. Any representation or warranty made by the Company in the Merger Agreement shall be untrue or incorrect in any material respect or there shall have been a material breach by the Company of any of its covenants contained in the Merger Agreement or the Merger Agreement shall have been terminated in accordance with its terms; or

8. The Company's Board of Directors shall have modified or amended in any respect its recommendation of the Offer or shall have resolved to do so; or

9. The Company shall have failed to redeem the Rights at a redemption price not to exceed $.____ per Right no later than the earlier of (a) the time the Purchaser proposes to purchase Shares pursuant to the Offer or (b) the closing of the purchase of Shares pursuant to the Stock Option.

The foregoing conditions are for the sole benefit of the Purchaser and may be asserted by the Purchaser regardless of the circumstances giving rise to any such conditions (including any action or inaction by the Purchaser) or may be waived by the Purchaser in whole or in part at any time and from time to time in the sole discretion of the Purchaser. The failure by the Purchaser at any time to exercise any of the foregoing rights shall not be deemed a waiver of any such right, and each such right shall be deemed an ongoing right which may be asserted at any time and from time to time.

UNANIMOUS WRITTEN CONSENT OF THE BOARD OF DIRECTORS OF [COMPANY]

We, the undersigned, being all the directors of ____ (the "Company"), a corporation organized and existing under the laws of the State of New York, do hereby consent, pursuant to Section 708(b) of the New York Business Corporation Law, to the adoption of the following resolutions by the directors of this Company and that such action be taken without a meeting pursuant to said Section 708(b), which consent may be executed in any number of counterparts:

NOW, THEREFORE, BE IT RESOLVED, that the terms and conditions contained in the Merger Agreement between the Company and ____, a New York corporation (the "Merger Agreement"), in substantially the form attached hereto as Exhibit A, are deemed to be fair and equitable to and in the best interests of the stockholders of the Company and the Company; and be it

FURTHER RESOLVED, that the Merger Agreement be, and it hereby is, approved by the Board of Directors, and that the Chairman of the Board of Directors, the President or any Vice President of the Company be, and each of them hereby is, authorized and empowered to execute and deliver the Merger Agreement in the name and on behalf of the Company in substantially the form presented to the Board of Directors, with blanks therein, if any, filled in and with such amendments, additions, modifications or corrections thereto as the officer executing and delivering the Merger Agreement may approve in accordance with the terms thereof, such approval to be evidenced conclusively by his execution and delivery thereof; and be it

FURTHER RESOLVED, that the Chairman of the Board of Directors, the President or any Vice President of the Company be, and each of them hereby is, authorized and empowered to waive or modify any term or condition of the Merger Agreement, to amend the Merger Agreement on behalf and in the name of the Company, and/or to terminate the Merger Agreement in accordance with the terms thereof; and be it

FURTHER RESOLVED, that the Chairman of the Board of Directors, the President or any Vice President of the Company be, and each of them hereby is, authorized to execute and file on behalf of the Company any request, report, schedule or application (and any amendments or supplements thereto) with the Securities and Exchange Commission which may be required from time to time under the Securities Act of 1933 or the Securities Exchange Act of 1934, each as amended from time to time, and the rules and regulations promulgated thereunder, such request, report, schedule or application (or amendment or supplement thereto) to be in form and substance satisfactory to counsel for the Company; and be it

FURTHER RESOLVED, that the appropriate officers and representatives of the Company be, and each of them hereby is, authorized, empowered and directed to take any and all actions and to prepare, execute and deliver any and all documents, contracts, agreements, instruments or certificates on behalf of the Company necessary to effectuate the merger, including, but not limited to, the preparation of a certificate of merger to be filed with the Secretary of State of the State of New York and the preparation of all documents or certificates necessary to obtain required regulatory approvals; and be it

FURTHER RESOLVED, that the Merger Agreement shall be submitted to the stockholders of the Company for their approval; and be it

FURTHER RESOLVED, that the appropriate officers and representatives of the Company be, and each of them hereby is, authorized and directed on behalf of the Company to take such further action as may be necessary, appropriate or desirable to implement and to effectuate the merger and in order to give effect to and carry out the foregoing resolutions; and be it

FURTHER RESOLVED, that the execution by such officers or representatives of any such paper or document or the doing by them of any act in connection with the foregoing shall conclusively establish their

FORMS AND MATERIALS

authority therefor from the Company and the approval and ratification by the Company of the papers and documents so executed and the action so taken; and be it

FURTHER RESOLVED, that any and all actions heretofore or hereafter taken by any of such officers or representatives of the Company within the terms of the foregoing resolutions be, and they hereby are, ratified and confirmed as the act and deed of the Company; and be it

FURTHER RESOLVED, that the Secretary or any Assistant Secretary of the Company is hereby authorized and directed to certify under the seal of this Company the adoption of the foregoing preambles and resolutions, and any person to whom such certified resolutions are delivered shall be entitled to rely upon such certification until written notice of modification or rescission has been furnished to and received by such person.

IN WITNESS WHEREOF, the undersigned hereby execute this unanimous consent as of the _____ day of _____, 19_____.

UNANIMOUS WRITTEN CONSENT OF STOCKHOLDERS OF [COMPANY]

The undersigned, consisting of the holders of all issued and outstanding shares of the Common Stock, par value $____, of ____, a New York corporation (the "Company"), do hereby consent, pursuant to Section 615(b) of the New York Business Corporation Law, to the adoption of the following resolution and that such action be taken without a meeting pursuant to said Section 615(b):

RESOLVED, that the Merger Agreement in substantially the form attached hereto, dated ____, 19____, between the Company and ____, pursuant to which the Company will merge with and into ____, is hereby approved.

IN WITNESS WHEREOF, the undersigned have executed this consent this ____ day of ____, 19____.

_____

_____

_____

_____

_____

NOTICE TO SHAREHOLDERS OF MERGER

To Our Stockholders: ____, 19____

I am pleased to inform you that on ____, 19____, the Company entered into an Agreement and Plan of Merger (the "Agreement") providing for the acquisition of the Company by [Purchaser]. As required by the Agreement, [Purchaser] has commenced today a cash tender offer for any and all shares of the Company at $____ per share. The Agreement contemplates that each share of the Company's stock not acquired by [Purchaser] in the offer will be exchanged for $____ per share in cash upon the merger of a wholly owned subsidiary of [Purchaser] with the Company.

Your Board of Directors has unanimously approved [Purchaser]'s offer and the merger and unanimously recommends that stockholders of the Company accept the offer.

In arriving at its decision, the Board considered a number of factors, including the opinion of [Investment Bank], financial advisor to the Company, that [Purchaser]'s offer was fair to the Company's stockholders from a financial point of view.

Enclosed with this letter is a copy of the Company's Solicitation/Recommendation Statement on Schedule 14D-9 (without exhibits), which contains detailed information regarding the factors considered by the Board in its deliberations and certain other information regarding [Purchaser]'s tender offer and the merger. Also enclosed is [Purchaser]'s Offer to Purchase and related materials, including a Letter of Transmittal, to be used for tendering stock certificates. These documents, which together make up [Purchaser]'s tender offer, set forth in detail the terms and conditions of the offer and provide instructions on how to tender shares.

On behalf of the Board of Directors
of [Company]

_____
Chairman of the Board
President and Chief Executive Officer

CERTIFICATE OF MERGER OF [PURCHASER SUBSIDIARY] INTO [COMPANY]

Pursuant to Section 904 of the Business Corporation Law:

We, the undersigned, being respectively the President and Secretary of [Company] and the President and Assistant Secretary of [Purchaser Subsidiary], certify that:

1. The name of each constituent corporation is as follows: [Company] and [Purchaser Subsidiary]. The name of the surviving corporation is ____.

2. [Company] has ____ shares of common stock, par value $.____ per share, outstanding, all of which are entitled to vote. [Purchaser Subsidiary] has ____ shares of common stock, par value $.____ per share, outstanding, all of which are entitled to vote.

3. The effective date of the merger is ____, 19____.

4. [Company] was incorporated on, and its Certificate of Incorporation was filed by the Department of State on ____, 19____. [Purchaser Subsidiary] was incorporated on ____, and its Certificate of Incorporation was filed by the Department of State on ____, 19____.

5. The merger was authorized at a meeting of the shareholders of [Company] by vote of the holders of two-thirds of all outstanding shares entitled to vote thereon and by the consent in writing of the sole shareholder of [Purchaser Subsidiary].

IN WITNESS WHEREOF, we have made and subscribed this Certificate and affirm the same as true and correct under the penalties of perjury this ____ day of ____, 19____.

[COMPANY]   [PURCHASER SUBSIDIARY]

_____, President   _____, President

_____, Secretary   _____, Secretary

FORM THIRTY-THREE

CHECKLIST FOR STOCK OR ASSET ACQUISITION

Copies of the following items are requested to be produced for _____ (hereinafter referred to as the "Company").

A. Overview of Business

1. If applicable, registration statements filed with the SEC and/or any offering circulars.

2. If applicable, applications filed with any national securities exchanges.

3. If applicable, proxy statements and letters to shareholders.

4. Private placement memoranda.

5. Copy of Company minute books for Company and all subsidiaries and all predecessor corporations. Please include all documents relative to any reorganization and all charter documents and by-laws.

6. Classes and series of capital stock, showing for each the number of shares authorized, issued and outstanding, par value (if any), rights of shareholders and copies of all stock certificates, including those of subsidiaries.

7. Names of directors and their affiliation with Company.

8. Names, addresses and phone numbers of Company's independent accountants and name of partner in charge of account.

9. Names, addresses and phone numbers of any brokers connected with the sale of the Company and a copy of any such broker contracts.

10. States and countries where Company sells products/services.

11. List of subsidiaries.

B. Assets

1. Copy of any appraisals of machinery and equipment.

2. Copies of all lease/rental agreements for personal property.

3. Schedule of owned real property, including location, description of any encumbrances on the property, copy of recent title insurance policies or commitments, copies of deeds and any recent surveys.

4. Copies of any appraisals for real property.

5. Schedule of leases for real property, including location and copy of lease.

6. Location of material assets not located on Company's premises (e.g., tools, dies, blueprints).

7. Schedule of all U.S. and foreign patents, trademarks, trade names, copyrights, brand names, trade secrets or other proprietary information (including inventions, processes, know-how and formulas), including name of record owner, description of any registrations or applications for registration, licensing agreements or other agreements pursuant to which Company uses the property or permits the use of the property by others, royalties received or incurred, and any infringement action or challenges to ownership pending or threatened.

C. Labor Matters

1. Description of composition of work force, including union affiliation and wage and benefit packages, including (a) copies of any labor contracts; (b) description of pending or threatened grievance proceedings, disputes or labor litigation; (c) description of charges of any unfair labor practices, EEOC violations or labor law violations; and (d) work stoppages.

2. Details of any violations, citations or allegations regarding the failure to comply with any environmental regulations of OSHA or similar employee health and safety laws and regulations.

3. All side agreements, local understandings having a current impact.

4. All settlement agreements having a current impact.

5. All arbitration awards and grievance resolutions having a current impact.

6. Ten (10) years' strike history and related documents.

7. Documentation regarding organizational attempts for the past five (5) years.

8. All NLRB documentation for the past five (5) years.

9. All Department of Labor documentation for the past five (5) years.

10. All personnel policies.

11. All employee handbooks.

12. All affirmative action plans with current status reports.

13. All audit reports of OFCCP.

14. All compliance agreements, letters of commitment or conciliation agreements entered into with any agencies.

D. Products

1. Copies of all brochures and catalogs used in the sale of products by Company.

2. Copies of all warranties of products given with sale.

3. A description of product liability considerations, including Company's historical experience, details of any product liability insurance carried (including amounts of coverage and term), and details of any products liability litigation.

4. Approvals, authorizations or certifications obtained from industry associations or underwriters laboratories and any requisite consents to transfer the same.

E. Credit Agreements

1. Loan agreements.

2. Term agreements.

3. Bonds, notes and debentures.

4. Guaranties, contracts of indemnity or suretyship.

5. Revolving credit agreements.

6. Lines of credit.

7. Mortgages, pledge agreements, deeds of trust, title retention agreements.

8. Grants by the Company of security interest in its property or security interest held by the Company in the property of others.

9. Security agreements.

10. Financing statements, continuation statements, fixture filings.

11. Letters of credit.

12. Lease purchase agreements.

13. List of receivables from related parties.

14. Any other material financing arrangements.

F. Employee Benefit Plans and Employment Agreements

1. Pension or profit-sharing plans, including IRS determination letters, IRS Form 5616 and most recent IRS Form 1500.

2. Deferred compensation plans.

3. Stock option plans and bonus plans.

4. Incentive compensation plans.

5. Life insurance plans.

6. Medical and disability plans.

7. Other plans, agreements or arrangements.

8. Employment, noncompetition and consulting agreements.

9. Confidentiality agreements.

10. Severance agreements or arrangements.

11. Employee benefit booklets, including summary plan descriptions for plans (pension and welfare).

12. The two (2) most recent actuarial reports and accountant's reports on all plans.

13. List of assets of each plan at most current available market value.

G. Insurance

Schedule of insurance indicating type of risk, amount of coverage, insurer, insurance broker, deductibles, premium and term.

H. Other Contracts, Agreements and Arrangements

1. Franchise agreements (Company as franchisee or franchisor).
2. License agreements.
3. Joint venture/partnership agreements.
4. Agency agreements.
5. Performance bonds.
6. Customs bonds.
7. Powers of attorney.
8. Agreements restricting the conduct of the Company or its business.
9. Letters of intent.
10. Dealer agreements.
11. Agreements with foreign and domestic sales agents and sales representatives.
12. Consulting agreements.
13. Service agreements.
14. Installment sales agreements, conditional sales agreements.
15. Forms of purchase orders and sales orders.
16. Consignment agreements.
17. Contracts with advertising/public relations agencies.
18. Research and development contracts.
19. Contracts with federal/state/local government or agencies.

20. Shareholder voting agreements or arrangements.

21. Copies of letters received by auditors for the most recent fiscal year.

22. All side agreements, local understandings having a current impact.

23. Any other material agreements.

I. Litigation

1. Pending or threatened lawsuits.

2. Pending or threatened investigations or proceedings before governmental or regulatory entities.

3. Pending or threatened arbitration proceedings.

4. Consent decrees, judgments, orders, injunctions to which Company is subject.

J. Government Compliance

Permits, authorizations, registrations, licenses or qualifications necessary for the conduct of the Company's business (including qualifications to transact business as a foreign corporation in various states).

FORM THIRTY-FOUR

AGREEMENT FOR PURCHASE OF STOCK

AGREEMENT FOR PURCHASE OF STOCK, dated as of ____, 19____, by and between [Purchasers], [Insiders] and [Company].

In consideration of the mutual covenants and agreements hereinafter set forth, the parties hereto covenant and agree as follows:

A. Issuance, Sale and Purchase of Shares of Stock

1. Upon the terms and subject to the conditions set forth in this Agreement, the Company shall cause to be issued from its authorized but unissued share capital and sold to the Purchasers, and the Purchasers shall purchase from the Company, an aggregate of ____ shares of Common Stock of the Company, par value $____ per share (the "Issued Shares"), in the following manner: (a) in full and complete payment for ____ of the Issued Shares to be acquired by First Purchaser, the Broker (as hereinafter defined) shall pay to the Company a per-share purchase price of approximately $____ for an aggregate purchase price of $____ to be paid to the Company by the Broker. Said purchase price shall be linked to the rate of exchange between the English pound sterling and the United States dollar, and shall be increased or decreased, as the case may be, by multiplying said purchase price by a fraction, the numerator of which is such rate of exchange on the day preceding the Closing (as hereinafter defined) and the denominator of which is $____; (b) in full and complete payment for ____ of the Issued Shares to be acquired by him, [Name of Second Purchaser] shall pay to the Company a per-share price of approximately $____ for an aggregate purchase price of $____, by transferring to the Company all of the outstanding shares of [Name of corporation in which Second

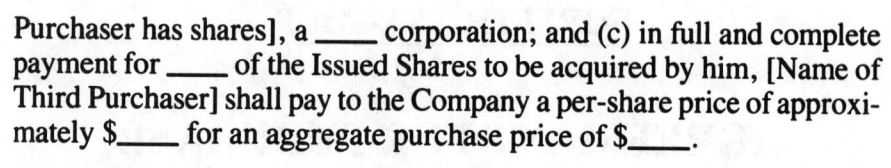

Purchaser has shares], a _____ corporation; and (c) in full and complete payment for _____ of the Issued Shares to be acquired by him, [Name of Third Purchaser] shall pay to the Company a per-share price of approximately $_____ for an aggregate purchase price of $_____.

2. Upon the terms and subject to the conditions set forth in this Agreement, [Names of "Insiders"] shall sell to [Name of Fourth Purchaser], and [Name of Fourth Purchaser] shall purchase from them, _____ shares of Common Stock of the Company, par value $_____ per share (the "Acquired Shares"). In full and complete payment for the Acquired Shares and the other obligations of the Insiders hereunder, [Name of Fourth Purchaser] shall pay to the Insiders a per-share purchase price of approximately $_____ for an aggregate purchase price of $_____, subject to and in accordance with the terms of this Agreement.

3. The Issued Shares to be acquired by [Name of First Purchaser] pursuant to paragraph (1)(a) above shall be acquired in the following manner: such Issued Shares shall be subscribed for and purchased by _____, a [Name of State] broker-dealer (the "Broker"), and shall be sold by the Broker to [Name of First Purchaser] (the share certificates therefor to be registered in the name of _____).

4. Upon the terms and subject to the conditions set forth in this Agreement, the Company shall cause to be issued from its authorized but unissued share capital and sold to [Name of Fifth Purchaser], or an affiliate designated by [Name of Fifth Purchaser] shall purchase from the Company, an aggregate of _____ shares of Common Stock of the Company, par value $_____ per share (the "[Name of Fifth Purchaser] Shares"), at a per-share purchase price of approximately $_____ for an aggregate purchase price of $_____ to be paid to the Company by [Name of Fifth Purchaser] or his affiliate at the Closing.

B. Representations and Warranties Concerning the Company

The Company and the Insiders each represent and warrant to the Purchasers that:

1. *Organization, Good Standing, Power, etc.* The Company (a) is and has been throughout its corporate existence a corporation duly

incorporated, validly existing and in good standing under the laws of the State of New York; (b) is and has been throughout its corporate existence duly qualified to do business and in good standing in each United States jurisdiction in which the nature of the business conducted by it and the property owned by it makes such qualification necessary; and (c) has all requisite corporate power and authority to execute, deliver and perform this Agreement and consummate the transactions contemplated hereby.

2. *Trading in Shares.* At the Closing (as defined herein), the outstanding shares of the Company shall be listed and traded on the ____ Stock Exchange (the "Exchange"), and the Company has been in the past and is currently in full compliance with all rules and regulations of the Exchange.

3. *Articles of Incorporation and By-laws.* The Company's Articles of Incorporation and By-laws, certified copies of which are attached hereto as Exhibits A and B, respectively, are in full force and effect, have not been subsequently amended and the Company is not in violation of any of the provisions thereof.

4. *Capitalization, Directors and Officers.* The authorized capital stock of the Company consists as of the date hereof, and will consist on the Closing, of ____ shares of Common Stock, par value $____ per share, of which ____ shares are presently issued and outstanding. All shares issued and outstanding have been duly authorized, validly issued and are fully paid and nonassessable.

The Board of Directors of the Company consists as of the date hereof, and will consist on the Closing, of Messrs. ____. The officers of the Company serving as of the date hereof, and who will continue to serve until the Closing, are ____, President; ____, Vice President; and ____, Secretary/Treasurer. The Company has no other directors or officers and will have no other directors or officers upon the Closing.

5. *Outstanding Rights to Purchase Securities.* The Company has not issued or granted any options, warrants or other rights to purchase or to

convert any security or obligation into any shares of its capital stock, nor has the Company agreed to issue or sell any shares of its capital stock, except as provided herein.

6. *Authorization of Acquired Shares and Issued Shares.* The Acquired Shares have been validly issued and are fully paid and nonassessable. The number of shares required for issuance of the Issued Shares are duly authorized and reserved for issuance and, when issued, paid for and delivered as contemplated by this Agreement, will be validly issued, fully paid and nonassessable.

7. *Investments in Others.* The Company is not, directly or indirectly, a shareholder of, has no equity investments in and does not control any corporation, partnership or other entity, and the Company does not conduct any part of its business obligations through any subsidiaries or through any other entity in which it has an equity investment or which it directly or indirectly controls.

8. *Agreements Relating to Capital Stock.* There are no agreements among any of the Company's shareholders with respect to the voting of 5 percent or more of the Company's outstanding shares on any matter. The Company is not a party to any agreement nor has it taken any action involving any limitations on the voting rights of its outstanding shares or any rights to acquire its shares, except as referred to herein.

9. *Authorization of Agreement.* This Agreement has been duly and validly authorized, executed and delivered by the Company and constitutes the valid and binding obligation of the Company.

10. *Effect of Agreement.* The execution, delivery and performance of this Agreement by the Company and consummation of the transactions contemplated hereby in the manner contemplated herein will not (a) violate any provisions of law, statute, rule or regulation to which the Company is subject; (b) violate any judgment, order, writ, injunction or decree of any court applicable to the Company; (c) have any adverse effect on the Company's compliance with any laws, statutes, rules, regulations, orders, decrees, licenses, permits or authorizations; or (d) result in the breach of or conflict with any item, covenant, condition or provision of, require the modification or termination of, constitute a

default under or result in the creation or imposition of any material lien, pledge, mortgage, claim, charge or encumbrance upon any of the properties or assets of the Company pursuant to any corporate charter, by-law, commitment, contract or other agreement or instrument to which the Company is a party or by which any of its assets or properties is or may be bound or affected or from which the Company derives any benefit.

11. *Government and Other Consents.* No consent, authorization, license, permit, registration or approval of, or exemption or other action by, any governmental or public body, commission or authority is required in connection with (a) the execution, delivery and performance by the Company of this Agreement, (b) the issuance, sale and delivery of the Issued Shares and (c) the sale and delivery of the Acquired Shares.

12. *Financial Statements.* Audited balance sheets, statements of income and retained earnings and changes in financial position for the period ending ____, 19____, together with the related reports of independent certified public accountants (the "Financial Statements") are attached hereto as Exhibit C. The Financial Statements (a) are in accordance with all books, records and accounts of the Company; (b) are true, correct and complete in accordance with generally accepted accounting principles; and (c) have been prepared in conformity with generally accepted accounting principles applied on a consistent basis. The Financial Statements fairly present the financial position of the Company on the above dates, reflect all liabilities, contingent or other, of the Company and fairly present the results of operations and changes in financial position of the Company for the periods covered therein.

13. *Title to Properties; Liens.* The Company has good and marketable title to all the properties and assets reflected in the Financial Statements, in each case subject to no mortgage, pledge, lien, charge or encumbrance.

14. *Tax Matters.* The Company has prepared and filed with the appropriate United States, state and local governmental agencies all tax returns and reports required to be filed by it, and each such return or

report is true, complete and correct in all material respects. The Company has paid all taxes shown on such tax returns to be payable or which have become due pursuant to any assessment, deficiency, "30-day letter" or similar notice received by it. The Internal Revenue Service has not audited the tax returns of the Company for any year and no deficiencies have therefore been proposed; no waivers of the statute of limitations granted by the Company are now outstanding and there are no agreements providing for the extension of time with respect to the assessment of any tax deficiency; the Company has paid over to the proper taxing and other authorities all income and other taxes and other amounts required to be withheld and so paid with respect to salaries and earnings of the directors, officers and employees of the Company and of others receiving compensation from the Company; and the Company has made adequate provision on the Financial Statements for all accrued and unpaid domestic and foreign taxes, whether or not disputed, for all periods to and including the date of the Financial Statements.

15. *Material Contracts.* There are no contracts or agreements to which the Company is a party which are (a) for the future purchase or sale of products, materials, merchandise, inventories, supplies, services or equipment; (b) continuing over a period (including any periods covered by an option to renew by any party) of more than one year from its date; (c) for any lease of property; (d) for capital improvements or expenditures; (e) for the borrowing of money or for a line of credit; (f) with the Insiders or any current or former shareholder, director or officer of the Company (or any spouse, relative or controlled entity of any of the foregoing), except as provided herein; (g) with respect to security interests, liens, pledges, charges, encumbrances, options, rights of first refusal, mortgages, indentures or security agreements entered into; (h) not made in the ordinary course of business; (i) pursuant to its right to compete with any corporation, business trust, firm, partnership, joint venture, entity or organization, in the conduct of any business, restrained or restricted for any reason or in any way; (j) with any labor union or organization representing employees; (k) for any bonus, pension, profit sharing, retirement, severance, termination pay, stock purchase, incentive or deferred compensation, stock option, med-

ical, hospitalization, accident insurance or similar plan or practice, formal or informal, in effect with respect to its directors, officers, employees or others; or (l) for the employment of any person. The Company has complied with all obligations required to be performed by it to date under all prior contracts, and no event has occurred which would constitute a breach or default by any party thereto, would cause acceleration by any party thereto, would permit termination by any party thereto, or would cause the creation of any lien, encumbrance or security interest in or upon any of the Company's assets.

16. *Compliance with Laws.* The Company has complied and is complying with all applicable laws or statutes, rules, regulations, orders or decrees promulgated by any national, state or local government or any department, bureau, board, agency or instrumentality thereof relating to the ownership and operation of its properties and business and the issuance, sale and trading of its shares; there are no such laws, statutes, rules, regulations, orders or decrees outstanding which require extraordinary actions or expenditures by or on behalf of the Company other than those required of corporations of like character, business and/or location; the Company has not received any notice of alleged violation of any such law, statute, rule, regulation, order or decree; and all filings, licenses, permits, approvals, applications and authorizations required by law in connection with the operations of the Company and the issuance, sale and trading of its shares have been made or obtained and are in full force and effect, and no revocation or material limitation of any thereof is pending or threatened.

17. *Litigation.* There is no action, suit or arbitration, claim, proceeding, investigation or inquiry pending before any federal, state, municipal, foreign or other court or governmental or administrative body or agency, or any private arbitration tribunal, or threatened against or relating to the Company or any of its properties or business. There is not in existence at present any order, judgment or decree of any court or other tribunal or any agency enjoining or requiring the Company to take action of any kind or to which the Company, its business, properties or assets are subject or bound.

18. *Minute Books.* The minute books of the Company accurately reflect all material corporate action of its shareholders and Board of Directors.

19. *Accuracy of Financial Records and Accounts.* The financial records and accounts of the Company are complete and correct in all material respects and accurately reflect in all material respects the nature, extent and purpose of the assets, liabilities, receipts, disbursements and transactions recorded therein.

20. *No Material Change.* Since the last period covered by the Financial Statements, (a) there has been no change in the business, financial condition, operations or affairs of the Company and (b) there has been no declaration or payment of any dividend or other distribution by the Company in respect of, or any direct or indirect retirement, redemption, purchase or other acquisition of, any shares of capital stock of the Company. Since the last period covered by the Financial Statements, the Company has not (i) incurred any obligation or liability, absolute or contingent, liquidated or unliquidated, choate or inchoate; (ii) discharged, satisfied or paid any claim, absolute or contingent, liquidated or unliquidated, choate or inchoate, other than liabilities shown in the Financial Statements and liabilities incurred since such date in the ordinary course of business, or waived any material rights; (iii) mortgaged or pledged or subjected any of its assets, tangible or intangible, to any security interest, liens, pledges, charges, encumbrances, options, rights of first refusal, mortgages, indentures or security agreements; (iv) sold, assigned, leased or transferred any of its assets or property or cancelled any claims; (v) entered into or made any amendment of or terminated any contract, license or lease; (vi) amended its Articles of Incorporation or By-laws; (vii) effected any change in its accounting practices, procedures or methods; (viii) made any expenditures or commitments; or (ix) changed in any material way its business policies or practices.

21. *Disclosures.* The Purchasers have been informed of all matters concerning or relating to the Company or its affairs, assets and business which are or could be deemed material to making an informed judgment as to whether to enter into this Agreement.

22. *Survival of Representations and Warranties.* These representations and warranties (a) shall be deemed made again at and as of the Closing and (b) shall survive the Closing, except for any action specifically required to be taken prior thereto in fulfillment of this Agreement.

The Insiders waive all rights and claims against the Company for breach by the Company of any of its aforesaid representations and warranties.

C. Conduct of Business Prior to Closing

The Company and the Insiders covenant and agree that from the date of this Agreement until the Closing, except with respect to transactions with the Purchasers as contemplated by this Agreement, the Company:

1. will not incur or agree to incur any new liability or obligation, absolute or contingent;

2. will not incur or agree to incur any indebtedness for borrowed money or otherwise or pay, redeem or otherwise discharge any other indebtedness for borrowed money;

3. will not permit or allow any of its assets to be subject to any lien, pledge, mortgage, claim, charge or encumbrance whatsoever;

4. will not authorize any additional capital expenditures;

5. will not declare, set aside or pay any dividend on, or make any other distribution in respect of, or issue, purchase or otherwise acquire, any shares or other securities of the Company;

6. will not amend its Articles of Incorporation or By-laws;

7. will not make any investment in any corporation, firm, joint venture or persons;

8. will not make (a) any loan or advance to any person or entity, including any officer, director, employee or shareholder of the Company, (b) any guarantee of any obligation or liability of any person or entity or (c) any new or extended indemnification of any person or entity;

9. will permit the Purchasers and their attorneys, engineers, accountants, financial advisers and other representatives to have full access to all of the Company's properties, records and documents, will furnish to the Purchasers such additional financial and other information with respect to its businesses, properties and affairs (including operating and financial reports) as the Purchasers may from time to time request and will authorize the Company's attorneys and accountants to discuss freely the affairs of the Company with the Purchasers and their attorneys;

10. will not waive or release any claim or right of value or cancel any debt or claim held by the Company or sell, assign, transfer, distribute or otherwise dispose of any properties or assets;

11. will not make any change in any method of accounting or accounting practice;

12. will not do or permit any act or omission to act which will cause a breach of any material provision of any material contract or commitment to which the Company is a party;

13. will not enter into any transaction of merger or consolidation or enter into or participate in the establishment of any joint venture, partnership, firm, corporation, company or other business organization;

14. will prepare and file all tax returns and amendments required to be filed after the date hereof;

15. will diligently pursue and defend all actions, suits, claims and proceedings in which the Company may become involved; and

16. will not do or permit any act or omission to act which may prevent its shares from becoming listed on the Exchange.

D. Closing

1. The closing under this Agreement (the "Closing") shall take place within fifteen (15) days after the Registration Statement (as hereinafter defined) has been declared effective by the Securities and Exchange

FORMS AND MATERIALS

Commission (the "SEC"), at the offices of [Name and Address of Company's Attorney] or at such other time and place as may be mutually agreed upon by the parties hereto.

2. At the Closing, the Company and the Insiders shall deliver to the Purchasers the following documents:

(a) Minutes of a meeting of the Board of Directors of the Company in the form set forth in Exhibit D to this Agreement;

(b) Four share certificates of the Company, one in the name of [Name of First Purchaser], for ____ shares of Common Stock (for a share certificate for such amount of shares in the name of the Broker) duly endorsed to [Name of First Purchaser], one for ____ shares of Common Stock in the name of [Name of Second Purchaser], one for ____ shares of Common Stock in the name of [Name of Third Purchaser] and one for ____ shares of Common Stock in the name of [Name of Fourth Purchaser];

(c) An opinion of ____, counsel to the Company, or such other counsel acceptable to the Purchasers, addressed to counsel for the Purchasers and to the Transfer Agent (as hereinafter defined), dated as of the Closing and satisfactory to counsel for the Purchasers, that:

(i) the Issued Shares have been validly issued to the Broker and [Names of the First, Second and Third Purchasers] and are fully paid and nonassessable;

(ii) this Agreement has been duly and validly authorized, executed and delivered by the Company and constitutes a valid and binding obligation of the Company;

(iii) the Acquired Shares have been validly issued, are fully paid and nonassessable and have been validly transferred by the Insiders to [Name of Fourth Purchaser]; and

(iv) the Company files reports with the SEC, has filed all required reports with the SEC and its shares of Common Stock are duly listed on the ____ Stock Exchange;

(d) A confirmation from ____, the Transfer Agent of the Company (the "Transfer Agent"), that the Issued Shares and Acquired Shares have been registered in the stockholder lists of the Company in the manner appearing in paragraph 2(b) above;

(e) The resignations of Messrs. ____ as directors and officers of the Company;

(f) A Certificate of Good Standing of the Company issued by the Office of the [Name of State] Secretary of State and a Certificate of Good Standing of the Company by the Exchange, in either case issued not more than four weeks prior to the Closing;

(g) A confirmation from the independent public accountants of the Company, dated as of the Closing, addressed to counsel for the Purchasers and satisfactory to counsel for the Purchasers, that after reasonable inquiry, such accountants are not aware of any material changes in the assets or liabilities of the Company since the last period covered by the Financial Statements;

(h) A certified check payable to the Company in the amount of $____ equal to the balance of the Company's current assets appearing in the Financial Statements (Exhibit C); and

(i) Any other documents required by the Purchasers in order to complete and perfect the transactions contemplated by this Agreement.

3. At the Closing, the Purchasers shall deliver to the Company the following: (a) a certified check drawn by the Broker and payable to the Company in the amount of $____, adjusted in accordance with the provisions of Section A.1(a) herein, in full payment of the Broker's consideration for the ____ Issued Shares to be acquired by [Name of First Purchaser]; (b) share certificates representing all of the outstanding shares of [stock exchanged for stock of the Company], duly endorsed by [Name of Second Purchaser] to the Company; (c) a check drawn by [Name of Third Purchaser] in the amount of $____; and (d) a check payable to the Insiders in the amount provided in Section B.2 herein, in full payment of [Name of Fourth Purchaser]'s consideration for the Acquired Shares.

4. At the Closing, the Company shall deliver to [Name of Fifth Purchaser] a share certificate of the Company in the name of [Name of Fifth Purchaser] or his designated affiliate for the [Name of Fifth Purchaser] Shares, and [Name of Fifth Purchaser] shall deliver to the Company a certified check drawn by [Name of Fifth Purchaser] or said affiliate in the amount of $____, in full payment of [Name of Fifth Purchaser]'s consideration for the [Name of Fifth Purchaser] Shares.

5. This Agreement and the documents and checks referred to in clauses 1, 2, 3 and 4 above will be deposited in escrow with Messrs. ____ as Escrow Agent (the "Escrow Agent"). The Escrow Agent shall take such action as it deems necessary, including, without limitation, release to the Transfer Agent of certain of the said documents, to arrange for the registration by the Transfer Agent of the Issued Shares and Acquired Shares in the names of the [Names of First, Second, Third and Fourth Purchasers] or their nominees and the issuance by the Transfer Agent of share certificates therefor. Upon receipt by the Escrow Agent of said share certificates, the Escrow Agent shall release said documents, checks and share certificates to the appropriate parties.

6. If for any reason the Closing shall not take place on or before ____, 19____, all obligations of the Purchasers may be terminated by the Purchasers without any further liability to them.

E. Conditions of Purchasers' Obligations

The obligations of [Names of First, Second, Third and Fourth Purchasers] to purchase the Issued Shares and Acquired Shares as contemplated in this Agreement are subject to the accuracy, as of the Closing (other than as a result of the transactions contemplated by this Agreement), of the representations and warranties made to the [Names of First, Second, Third and Fourth Purchasers] by the Company and the Insiders in this Agreement and to the satisfaction of all of the following conditions:

1. *Conditions Precedent to Closing.*

(a) Upon completion of the Closing, the Purchasers shall together own (directly or through their affiliates) at least ____ percent of the issued and outstanding shares of the Company;

(b) The Insiders and the Company shall have supplied the Purchasers with all such certificates, resolutions, documents and further opinions with respect to the transactions contemplated by this Agreement as the Purchasers may have requested;

(c) No changes shall have occurred in any U.S. or foreign law, rule, regulation or court ruling which, in the Purchasers' opinion, prohibits, impedes or adversely affects in any way the Purchasers' participation in the transactions contemplated in this Agreement;

(d) Shares of the Company shall be listed for trading on the Exchange;

(e) A registration statement on Form 10-K relating to the listing of shares of the Company on the Exchange (the "Registration Statement") shall have been filed with and declared effective by the SEC; and

(f) The Purchasers shall have obtained an opinion of their auditors, Messrs. ____, that the transfer of the shares of [stock exchanged for shares of Company] to the Company, as contemplated in Section A.1(b) herein, shall qualify as a tax-free exchange of shares under the Internal Revenue Code of 1954, as amended.

If for any reason the above conditions have not been satisfied as aforesaid, all obligations of the Purchasers may be terminated by the Purchasers without any further liability to them.

2. *Conditions Subsequent to Closing.*

If the shareholders of the Company (excluding the shares owned or controlled by the Insiders and the Purchasers) fail to ratify this Agreement at the upcoming Special Meeting of Shareholders of the Company to be called for this purpose, the Purchasers may, at their sole discretion, within ten (10) days after said Meeting, cause this Agreement to be cancelled and declared null and void. In such case, the Company and the Insiders agree forthwith to cause the Company to return to the [Names of First, Second and Third Purchasers], in exchange for the Issued Shares, all amounts and the shares of [stock exchanged for shares of Company] received from [Names of First, Second and Third Purchasers] therefor, and to cause the Insiders forthwith to return to [Name of Fourth Purchaser] in exchange for the Acquired Shares, all amounts received from [Name of Fourth Purchaser] therefor.

F. Indemnification and Rescission

1. The Insiders hereby undertake and agree, jointly and severally, for the four-year period following the Closing, to indemnify and hold the Purchasers harmless from and against and in respect of (a) any damage or loss to the Purchasers resulting from the inaccuracy on the date hereof or on the Closing of any of the representations and warranties contained herein, (b) any liability (absolute or contingent) which is not shown on the Financial Statements which should be shown thereon in accordance with generally accepted accounting principles, (c) any obligation or liability arising from the failure of the Company to discharge any duty or perform any obligation required of it or because of any default by the Company under any agreement, lease, contract, commitment, instrument or obligation to which it is a party, in any case arising from or based on actions or failures to act by the Company occurring on or before the Closing, or (d) any liability arising from violations by the Company of any federal, state or local law, ordinance, regulation, rule or order on or before the Closing.

2. The Company and the Insiders hereby grant each of the Purchasers the right to rescind their purchase of the Issued Shares and Acquired Shares, and the Company and the Insiders undertake to repay to each of the Purchasers sums paid by said Purchasers (or the Broker) to them for said purchase, together with interest thereon at the rate paid by the [Name of Bank] for 12-month Certificates of Deposit on the date of rescission, and to return the shares of [stock exchanged for shares of Company] to [Name of Second Purchaser] in the event of any breach of any representations or warranties of the Company appearing in this Agreement. Said right of rescission shall remain in full force and effect

for a period of one year after the date of Closing, and shall be in addition to any other rights or remedies available to the Purchasers against the Company or the Insiders.

G. Consulting Agreement

Within 15 days after the Closing, the Company will enter into a Consulting Agreement with an affiliate of [Name of Fifth Purchaser] in the form appearing in Exhibit F hereto.

H. Confidentiality

The Insiders hereby acknowledge and agree that this Agreement is confidential and that its terms and contents shall not be disclosed to any person other than through a press release of the Company, in form and substance satisfactory to and approved in advance by counsel to the Purchasers.

I. Payment of Expenses

Each of the parties hereto shall pay all expenses and disbursements incurred by it, its officers, employees, attorneys, accountants, financial advisers and other agents and representatives in connection with this Agreement and the performance of its obligations hereunder. Notwithstanding the foregoing, all expenses incurred in connection with the listing of the shares of the Company on the Exchange, including, without limitation, the preparation and filing of the Registration Statement and all documents required by the SEC, shall be borne by the Insiders.

J. Notices

Any notices required or permitted to, or served upon, any party hereto pursuant to this Agreement shall be sufficiently given or served if sent to such party by registered airmail and by telex, addressed to it at its address and telex call number, as set forth below, or to such other address or call number as it shall designate by written notice given to the other parties addressed as follows:

1. if to the Insiders, to:

   [Names and Addresses]

2. if to the Company, to:

   [Names and Addresses]

   with a copy to

   [Name and Address of Company's Attorney]

3. if to the Purchasers, to:

   [Names and Addresses]

K. Table of Contents; Section and Other Headings

The table of contents, section and other headings herein contained are for convenience only and shall not be construed as part of this Agreement.

L. Counterparts

This Agreement may be executed in any number of counterparts and each counterpart shall constitute an original instrument, but all such separate counterparts shall constitute only one and the same instrument.

M. Entire Agreement

This Agreement constitutes the entire agreement between the parties hereto and supersedes all prior agreements, understandings and arrangements, oral or written, between the parties hereto with respect to the subject matter hereof.

N. Amendments and Waivers

This Agreement may not be modified or amended except by an instrument or instruments in writing signed by the party against whom enforcement of any such modification or amendment is sought. Any party hereto may, by an instrument in writing, waive compliance by the other parties with any term or provision of this Agreement to be performed or complied with by such other parties hereto. The waiver by any party hereto of a breach of any term or provision of this Agreement shall not be construed as a waiver of any subsequent breach.

O. Assignment

This Agreement is personal in nature and none of the parties hereto shall, without the written consent of the others, assign or transfer its rights or obligations hereunder to another company or person, except as herein expressly provided or permitted and except that the Purchasers may transfer all or any portion of their rights or obligations hereunder to any of their affiliates without such prior written consent. Subject to the foregoing provisions of this Section 15, this Agreement shall be binding upon and inure to the benefit of the parties hereto and their respective successors and assigns.

P. Governing Law

This Agreement shall be governed by and construed in accordance with the laws of New York, and all disputes arising hereunder shall be adjudicated solely before the courts of New York to whose jurisdiction the parties hereto consent.

IN WITNESS WHEREOF, the parties hereto have duly executed this Agreement and caused the same to be delivered on their behalf as of the date first above written.

[Name of Company]

[Name of Purchaser]

By: [Name of Authorized Officer]

[Name of Purchaser]

[Name of Insider]

[Name of Purchaser]

FORMS AND MATERIALS

_____   _____
         [Name of Insider]   [Name of Purchaser]

_____   _____
         [Name of Insider]   [Name of Purchaser]

FORM THIRTY-FIVE

AGREEMENT FOR PURCHASE OF ASSETS

AGREEMENT, dated as of ____, 19____, among ____, a New York corporation ("Buyer"), ____, a ____ corporation ("Seller") and [Name of Parent or Other Entity Controlling the Seller] ("Parent").

WITNESSETH:

WHEREAS, Seller desires to sell, and Buyer desires to purchase, all of the assets of Seller, including the assets more particularly described herein, all upon the terms and subject to the conditions herein set forth;

NOW, THEREFORE, in consideration of the premises and the mutual agreements herein set forth, the Seller, Buyer and the Parent hereby agree as follows:

A. Definitions

As used herein the following terms shall, unless the context clearly indicates otherwise, have the following meanings:

1. "*Assorted Tools*" shall mean all hand tools and machine tools in which the Seller has on the Purchase Date any right, title and interest, including, without limitation, the hand tools and machine tools listed on Exhibit A annexed hereto.

2. "*Assumed Contracts*" shall mean the Business Space Lease, Sales Contracts, Purchase Orders and such other contracts and agreements listed on Exhibit B hereto.

3. "*Business Space*" shall mean the office, warehousing and manufacturing space presently occupied by Seller and located at ____, a lease with respect to which is annexed hereto as Exhibit C.

4. *"Business Space Lease"* shall mean the lease between the Seller and [Name of Lessor] with respect to the Business Space annexed hereto as Exhibit C.

5. *"Closing Date"* or *"Closing"* shall mean 10:00 A.M. Eastern Standard Time on such date as shall be mutually agreed to by the parties hereto, provided, that such date shall not be later than ____, 19____.

6. *"Inventory"* shall mean all of the raw materials, work-in-process and finished goods and other inventory and all other supplies used in the operation of its business in which the Seller shall have any right, title and interest on the Purchase Date (a list of which has previously been provided by Seller to Buyer), together with any rights of the Seller to the warranties received from its suppliers with respect to such inventory and any related claims, credits, rights of recovery and set-off with respect thereto.

7. *"Machinery and Equipment"* shall mean all of the machinery, equipment, furniture, fixtures and improvements, spare parts, supplies and motor vehicles used by the Seller in connection with the operation of its business and located on the Business Space or elsewhere on the Purchase Date and all of the replacement parts for any of the foregoing, in which the Seller has on the Purchase Date any right, title or interest, and the Tools and Dies, the Punch Presses and the Assorted Tools, together with any rights of the Seller to the warranties and licenses, if any, received from manufacturers and sellers of the aforesaid items and any related claims, credits and rights of recovery with respect to such Machinery and Equipment.

8. *"Patents and Trademarks"* shall mean all of the inventions, patent applications, patents, trademarks, trademark registrations and applications, copyrights, know-how, formulae, trade secrets and trade names in which Seller has on the Purchase Date any right, title or interest, including, without limitation, the patents, trademarks and copyrights listed on Exhibit D annexed hereto.

FORMS AND MATERIALS 843

9. *"Punch Presses"* shall mean all of the punch presses in which the Seller has on the Purchase Date any right, title and interest, including, without limitation, the punch presses listed on Exhibit E annexed hereto.

10. *"Purchase Date"* shall mean ____, 19____.

11. *"Purchase Orders"* shall mean those purchase orders and purchase commitments of Seller outstanding on the Purchase Date which are listed in Exhibit F annexed hereto, and such purchase orders and purchase commitments of Seller outstanding on the Purchase Date not so listed which do not in the aggregate exceed $1,000.

12. *"Purchased Property"* shall mean collectively the Machinery and Equipment, Punch Presses, Tools and Dies, Assorted Tools, Inventory, Patents and Trademarks, the Business Space Lease and all of the tangible and intangible property of every kind and description, including, without limitation, all of the assets, receivables, cash, contract rights, name and goodwill, properties, real and personal, engineering data, drawings, cuts, plates, stationery, office supplies and forms, catalogues, manuals, customer lists and data, and all of the tangible and intangible assets (including patent and trademark rights) assigned, transferred or sold to Seller or the Parent by [Name of Seller] or the Trustee in Bankruptcy thereof, and other rights and interests, in which the Seller has on the Purchase Date any right, title or interest or which are used in connection with the business of the Seller on the Purchase Date, it being understood that the business of the Seller includes, without limitation, the following: (a) the ____ division of Seller which manufactures and distributes hardware for the electronics and defense industries, including, without limitation, component chips, printed circuit board holders and bus bars; (b) the ____ division of Seller which is involved in the business of re-inking its machine rolls, supplying spare parts for and providing other services to users of its machines; and (c) the ____ division of Seller which manufactures and distributes a proprietary annular power saw and accessory equipment.

13. *"Tools and Dies"* shall mean all of the tools and dies in which the Seller has on the Purchase Date any right, title and interest, including,

without limitation, all tools and dies used in connection with the manufacture of chips and bus bars and including, without limitation, the tools and dies listed on Exhibit G annexed hereto.

14. *"Sales Contracts"* shall mean those unfilled sales contracts, customer orders and commitments between Seller and its customers listed in Exhibit H annexed hereto, and such sales contracts, customer orders and commitments unfilled as of the Purchase Date and not so listed which do not in the aggregate exceed $____.

B. Balance Sheet

All references in this Agreement to the balance sheet of Seller or to the balance sheet of Seller as included in Exhibit K annexed hereto shall mean the balance sheet of Seller as at ____, 19____, included in such Exhibit K.

C. Purchase and Sale of the Purchased Property

1. *Purchase.* Subject to the terms and conditions herein set forth, on the Closing Date Seller shall sell (and the Parent shall cause Seller to sell) and Buyer shall purchase all of the Purchased Property as of the Purchase Date, free and clear of all mortgages, liens, charges, encumbrances or defects of any nature whatsoever, except as described on Exhibit I annexed hereto.

2. *Sale at Closing Date.* The sale, transfer, assignment and delivery by Seller of the Purchased Property to Buyer, as herein provided, shall be effected on the Closing Date by full warranty deeds, bills of sale, endorsements, assignments and such other instruments of transfer and conveyance satisfactory in form and substance to counsel for Buyer. To the extent that any sales or other similar taxes may be imposed by reason of such sale, transfer, assignment and delivery of the Purchased Property, Seller shall pay any excess of such taxes over $____.

3. *Subsequent Documentation.* Seller shall, at any time and from time to time after the Closing Date, upon the request of Buyer and at the expense of Seller, do, execute, acknowledge and deliver or will cause to

be done, executed, acknowledged and delivered all such further acts, deeds, assignments, transfers, conveyances and assurances as may be reasonably required for the better assigning, transferring, granting, conveying, assuring and confirming to Buyer, or to its successors and assigns, or for aiding and assisting in collecting and reducing to possession any or all of the Purchased Property to be purchased by Buyer as provided herein.

4. *Assignment of Contracts.* On the Closing Date, the Seller shall assign to Buyer, and Buyer shall assume, as of the Purchase Date all of the Assumed Contracts by means of an Assignment and Assumption Agreement in the form of Exhibit J annexed hereto and made a part hereof. To the extent that the assignment of any Assumed Contract shall require the consent of the party thereto, this Agreement shall not constitute an agreement to assign the same if an attempted assignment would constitute a breach thereof. The Seller will use its best efforts to obtain the consent of the other parties to such contracts for the assignment thereof to the Buyer. If such consent is not obtained in respect of any such Assumed Contract, the Seller will cooperate with the Buyer in any reasonable arrangement requested by the Buyer to provide for the Buyer the benefits under any such Assumed Contract, including enforcement, at the cost of and for the benefit of the Buyer, of any and all rights of the Seller against the other party thereto with respect to such Assumed Contract.

5. *Assumption of Liabilities.* At the Closing the Buyer shall assume and agree to pay, perform or discharge, subject to the provisions of Paragraph 3(d) above, the obligations of Seller under the Assumed Contracts accruing from and after the Purchase Date, all sales contracts, customer orders, customer commitments, purchase orders, purchase commitments and liabilities of Seller arising in the ordinary course of business between the Purchase Date and Closing Date, and all liabilities of Seller disclosed on the balance sheet of Seller included as part of Exhibit K annexed hereto, except for the amount of $____ of "income taxes to parent company" reflected on such balance sheet. Except as specifically provided in the foregoing sentence, the Buyer shall not assume or agree to pay, perform or discharge, nor shall the Buyer be

responsible, directly or indirectly, for any debts, obligations, contracts or liabilities of the Seller wherever or however incurred, including, without limitation, all federal, state and local tax liabilities for all periods ended on or prior to ____, 19____.

6. *Collection of Receivables.* Seller agrees that Buyer shall have the right and authority to collect, for the account of Buyer, all receivables and other items which shall be transferred to Buyer as provided herein, and to endorse with the name of Seller any checks received on account of any such receivables or other items. Seller agrees that it will transfer and deliver to Buyer or its designee any cash or other property that Seller may receive in respect of such receivables or other items. A list of all receivables of Seller as of the Purchase Date broken down by name of customer, date incurred and amount is contained in Exhibit L annexed hereto.

7. *Conduct of Business.* All operations of the Seller between the Purchase Date and the date hereof have been, and all operations of the Seller between the date hereof and the Closing Date shall be, conducted in the ordinary course of business consistent with its prior business practice by the Seller for the account and benefit, and at the expense, of the Buyer as if this Agreement had been consummated on the Purchase Date, provided that if for any reason the Closing shall not occur hereunder, the Buyer shall have no rights or liabilities with respect to such operations, and in such event the business of Seller from and after the Purchase Date shall be conducted at the expense and for the account and benefit of the Seller. For purposes of the foregoing sentence, all income received or receivable from and after the Purchase Date, and all expenses incurred, accrued or paid in the ordinary course of business from and after the Purchase Date shall, as to such income, be the property of, and as to such expenses, be the obligations of, the Buyer if the Closing hereunder shall occur or of the Seller if the Closing hereunder shall not occur. The Seller has not taken from and after the Purchase Date, and shall not take from and after the date hereof through the Closing Date, any action in connection with the conduct of the business of Seller other than in the ordinary course of business without the written consent of Buyer, and, except as approved by the Buyer, has not from and after the

FORMS AND MATERIALS 847

Purchase Date sold, leased, disposed of or encumbered or entered into any commitment to sell, lease, dispose of or encumber and shall not from and after the date hereof through the Closing Date, sell, lease, dispose of or encumber or enter into any commitment to sell, lease, dispose of or encumber, any item of Purchased Property, except items of finished goods Inventory sold only in the ordinary course of business. Without limiting the generality of the foregoing, the Seller has not from and after the Purchase Date and shall not from and after the date hereof through the Closing Date, without the consent of the Buyer:

(a) changed or change the type of business conducted by it;

(b) hired or hire any additional employees except for ____;

(c) terminated or terminate any employee;

(d) changed or change any salary of any employee, except for: ____ (increased from $____ to $____ per annum as of ____, 19____), ____ (increased from $____ per week to $____ per week as of ____, 19____) and ____ (increased from $____ to $____ per annum as of ____, 19____);

(e) made or make any general or uniform increase in the rate of pay of its employees or entered or enter into any collective bargaining agreements pertaining to its employees;

(f) entered or enter into any commitment, contract or lease with respect to the purchase, lease or sale of capital assets;

(g) failed or fail to repair, maintain or replace all its equipment in accordance with practices and procedures theretofore followed and failed or fail to maintain its equipment and the Business Space in its present operating condition; and

(h) paid or pay or included or include in any expenses for which Buyer shall be liable for the period between the Purchase Date and the Closing Date any expenses incurred by Seller for the purpose of consummating this Agreement and the transactions contemplated hereby, including, but not limited to, any expenses for attorneys' or accountants' fees, except for expenses accrued on the balance sheet of Seller included as part of Exhibit K.

D. Payment of Purchase Price

The purchase price for the Purchased Property shall be $____. Subject to the terms and conditions herein set forth, the Buyer will pay the purchase price as follows:

1. on the Closing Date Buyer shall deliver to Seller a certified or bank check payable to the order of Seller, in the amount of $____; and

2. on the Closing Date, Buyer shall deliver to Seller the Note (the "Note") of the Buyer in the principal amount of $____ in the form annexed hereto as Exhibit M.

E. Closing

The Closing under this Agreement shall take place at the offices of [Name and Address of Buyer's Attorney] on the Closing Date.

F. Representations and Warranties of Seller and Parent

The Seller and the Parent, as a material inducement to Buyer to execute and deliver this Agreement, jointly and severally represent and warrant to Buyer as follows:

1. *Organization and Standing.* Seller is a corporation duly organized, validly existing and in good standing under the laws of the State of ____, is qualified to do business as a foreign corporation and is in good standing in all states wherein the character of the property owned or the nature of the business transacted by Seller makes qualification by Seller as a foreign corporation necessary. The Parent is a corporation duly organized, validly existing and in good standing under the laws of the State of ____.

2. *Authority.* Seller and the Parent have full corporate authority to operate their respective businesses as conducted on the date hereof and to execute and perform in accordance with this Agreement, and this Agreement constitutes a valid and binding obligation of Seller and the Parent enforceable in accordance with its terms, and each document of transfer contemplated by this Agreement when executed and delivered

by Seller in accordance with the provisions hereof shall be valid and legally binding upon Seller in accordance with its terms. This Agreement and all transactions contemplated hereby have been duly authorized by all requisite corporate action by Seller and the Parent.

3. *Conflicting Agreements; No Liens.* Neither the execution nor delivery of this Agreement nor fulfillment nor compliance with the terms and conditions hereof will constitute a breach by Seller or the Parent of their respective certificates of incorporation or by-laws or result in a breach of the terms, conditions or provisions of, or constitute a default under or result in a violation of any agreement, contract, instrument, order, judgment or decree to which Seller or the Parent is a party or by which any of them is bound except for items specified on Exhibit N, or result in a violation by Seller or the Parent of any existing law or statute or any material rule or regulation of any jurisdiction or of any order, decree, writ or injunction of any court or governmental department, bureau, board, agency or instrumentality or result in the creation or imposition of any lien, charge, restriction, security interest or encumbrance of any nature whatsoever on the Purchased Property, except as listed on Exhibit I annexed hereto.

4. *Consents.* Except for items specified on Exhibit N, no consent from or other approval of any governmental entity or other person is necessary in connection with the execution of this Agreement or the consummation by Seller or the Parent of the transactions contemplated hereby or the continuation of the business of Seller by Buyer in the manner previously conducted by Seller.

5. *Real Property; Leaseholds.* No real property is owned or held under lease by Seller or is used in connection with or, to the knowledge of Seller or the Parent, necessary for the business of Seller as such business is now conducted except for the Business Space. Seller is the owner and holder of all leasehold estates purported to be granted by the Business Space Lease and Seller has not been notified of any default under or termination of such lease.

6. *Title to Purchased Property.* Seller owns all of the right, title and interest in and to all of the Purchased Property and shall own such

property on the Closing Date free and clear of all mortgages, liens, charges, encumbrances or title defects of any nature whatsoever except as specified on Exhibit I annexed hereto.

7. *Inventory.* The Inventory is merchantable and fit for intended use and is free of any material defects in workmanship. The finished goods Inventory is of a type, quantity and quality usable and salable in the ordinary course of business of the Seller. This subparagraph 7 shall not be applicable with respect to Inventory which is not valued or which is written down or reserved against (to the extent of such write-down or reserve) on the balance sheet included as part of Exhibit K. This subparagraph 7 shall not be applicable with respect to the ____ division of Seller and the second sentence of this subparagraph 7 shall not be applicable with respect to the ____ division of Seller.

8. *Compensation Due Employees.* Except as shown in Paragraph C.7 hereof, Exhibit O annexed hereto and made a part hereof is a true and complete list showing the names and job descriptions of all persons employed by Seller or employed in connection with the business of Seller together with a statement as to the full amount of compensation paid or payable to, or on behalf of, each person for services rendered during the period from ____, 19____, through ____, 19____, and the current aggregate base compensation rate for each such person. The Seller or the Parent does not have any outstanding liability other than amounts included in the $____ of accrued expenses on the balance sheet included as part of Exhibit K annexed hereto with respect to such employees for payment of wages, vacation pay (whether accrued or otherwise), salaries, bonuses, reimbursable employee business expenses, pensions, contributions under any employee benefit plans or any other compensation, current or deferred, under any labor or employment contracts, whether oral or written, based upon or accruing with respect to those services of such employees performed prior to the date hereof except for (a) any payment due at the rate specified for an employee listed on Exhibit O with respect to any period after the Purchase Date, (b) amounts accrued with respect to vacation pay for periods after the Purchase Date, and (c) amounts accrued with respect to periods after the Purchase Date for any pension plan or insurance policy listed on Exhibit

U. Seller or the Parent has not, because of past practices or previous commitments with respect to such employees, established any rights on the part of such employees to receive additional compensation with respect to any period after the Purchase Date, except for commissions as described on Exhibit O annexed hereto. Any outstanding liabilities or amounts payable with respect to such employees or rights to receive additional compensation of the types described in the preceding two sentences (other than amounts included in such $____ or described in clauses (a), (b) and (c) above) shall be paid by the Parent.

9. *Union Agreements and Employment Agreements.* Seller or the Parent is not a party to any union, collective bargaining or similar agreements covering any employees employed in the conduct of the business of Seller, nor does Seller have any employment agreements with any employees that are not terminable at will on 30 days' notice at the election of Seller, without extra payment of penalty. The Seller does not have any policy arrangement of any kind with any of its employees regarding the payment of termination pay, irrespective of the reason or cause of termination, other than the payment of two weeks' pay in the case of layoff. There are no pending or threatened labor disputes between the Seller or the Parent and any of the employees employed in the conduct of the business of Seller, and Seller has not received any claim affecting labor relations or threat of strike or other interruptions of work. No union has attempted, is attempting or has threatened to unionize the employees employed in the conduct of the business of Seller.

10. *Contracts and Agreements.* Seller has performed all of its obligations under the Assumed Contracts required to have been performed by it on or prior to the date hereof, and Seller has not received any notice of default, nor is Seller in default, nor does any condition exist which with notice or lapse of time, or both, would render Seller in default under any Assumed Contract. The assignment of the Assumed Contracts does not require the consent of the other party thereto except as specified in Exhibit N annexed hereto.

11. *Insurance.* Exhibit P annexed hereto lists and describes all insurance policies now in force with respect to the Purchased Property and the business of Seller. Copies of all such policies have previously been

delivered to Buyer. The Seller will continue in full force and effect through the Closing Date all of such policies of insurance. The Seller has not been refused any insurance with respect to the Purchased Property during the last three years.

12. *Licenses, Permits and Consents.* There are no licenses and permits currently required by the Seller for the operation of the business of the Seller. Seller is not aware of any circumstances relating to Buyer's proposed use of the Purchased Property which would require Buyer to obtain any licenses or permits except for permits relating to its ____ division.

13. *Litigation.* Except as described on Exhibit Q annexed hereto, there are no actions, suits, proceedings or investigations pending or, to the knowledge of the Seller or the Parent, threatened against or involving Seller or brought by Seller or affecting any of the Purchased Property at law or in equity or admiralty or before or by any federal, state, municipal or other governmental department, commission, board, agency or instrumentality, domestic or foreign, nor has any such action, suit, proceeding or investigation been pending during the 24-month period preceding the date hereof; and Seller is not operating its business under or subject to, or in default with respect to, any order, writ, injunction or decree of any court or federal, state, municipal or governmental department, commission, board, agency or instrumentality, domestic or foreign.

14. *Compliance with Laws.* To the best of its knowledge, Seller has complied with and is operating its business in compliance with all laws, regulations and orders applicable to the business conducted by it, and the present uses by the Seller of the Purchased Property do not violate any such laws, regulations and orders. Seller has no knowledge of any material present or future expenditures that will be required with respect to any of Seller's facilities to achieve compliance with any present statute, law or regulation, including those relating to the environment or occupational health and safety.

15. *Pension Plans.* Except for plans specified on Exhibit U, there are no profit-sharing, pension plans or other plans of indirect or deferred

compensation or employee benefit plans for any of Seller's employees or employees engaged in the conduct of Seller's business except for an option granted to ____ under the Parent's Non-Qualified Stock Option Plan. The Parent agrees that so long as he continues to be employed by Buyer, such employment shall be treated as employment by Seller for purposes of options held by him, which are vested or which will become vested in the future under the Parent's Non-Qualified Stock Option Plan.

16. *Disclosure.* No representation or warranty by the Seller contained in this Agreement, and no statement contained in any certificate or other instrument furnished or to be furnished to Buyer pursuant hereto, or in connection with the transactions contemplated hereby, contains or will contain any untrue statement of a material fact, or omits or will omit to state any material fact which is necessary in order to make the statements contained therein not misleading.

17. *Subsidiaries.* There are no wholly or partly owned subsidiaries of Seller or other entities in which Seller has a proprietary interest. Each division or type of major subdivision of Seller's operations and business is disclosed in items (a) through (c) of Paragraph A.12.

18. *Bank Accounts.* Exhibit R annexed hereto specifies accurately and completely each and every bank account, banking arrangement and safe deposit box used in connection with the business or operations of Seller at the Purchase Date, specifying the bank or type of account or other arrangement and the balance or amount of funds in such account or deposit box or subject to such arrangement.

19. *Purchase Order and Commitments of Seller.* Exhibit F annexed hereto lists all unfilled purchase orders and purchase commitments of Seller outstanding as of the Purchase Date, all of which were made in the usual and ordinary course of business; to the best of Seller's knowledge, the suppliers under said orders and commitments are not in default, pursuant to the terms of said orders and commitments, as to product quality and time of delivery as of said date except as set forth in Exhibit F.

20. *Customer Orders and Commitments.* Exhibit H annexed hereto lists all unfilled customer orders and commitments pertaining to Seller's business, received by Seller and on hand as of the Purchase Date; none of the orders of the ten largest customers listed on Exhibit H has been cancelled nor has cancellation thereof been threatened except as shown on Exhibit T annexed hereto. Buyer shall be entitled to receive on the Closing Date all advances or prepayments received by Seller from such customers under the provisions of such orders or otherwise for products to be delivered by Buyer (or by Seller for the account of Buyer) after the Purchase Date.

21. *Medical, Hospitalization, Life Insurance, etc.* The Seller has set forth in Exhibit U annexed hereto a list of all medical, health, hospitalization and life insurance plans, programs and policies in effect pertaining to any of the employees of Seller.

22. *Necessary Property.* Seller is selling Buyer all machinery and equipment and other assets required by Buyer to manufacture the product lines and continue the business of Seller in the same manner as heretofore conducted by Seller. Seller has the full right to produce, manufacture, sell and distribute such products produced, manufactured, sold and distributed by it without incurring any liability for license fees, royalties or other compensation, or for any claims of infringement of patent or trademark rights. All of the business described in items (a) through (c) of Paragraph A.12 hereof is conducted by Seller and not by the Parent itself or any other subsidiary, division or entity of the Parent.

23. *Patents and Trademarks.* Seller owns no patents, trademarks, inventions, patent rights, trade secrets, formulae, trade names or copyrights nor has Seller applied for any patents or trademark registrations except those listed on Exhibit D hereto, which are to be assigned to Buyer at the Closing without additional consideration and which are not subject to any royalty or license arrangements whatsoever, except as related to the Agreement between Seller and ____. If Seller hereafter learns of the existence of any additional patents, patent rights, trademarks, trade secrets, inventions, trade names or copyrights intended to

be sold hereunder, Seller shall promptly assign the same to Buyer. Except as shown on Exhibit D, Seller or the Parent has not received any notice or claim of infringement of any patent, invention, rights, trademarks, trade names or copyrights of others with reference to the processes, methods, formulae or procedures used by Seller in the operation of its business, and Seller or the Parent has no actual knowledge not generally available in the trade of any new products, inventions, procedures or methods of manufacturing developed by any of Seller's competitors or any other information concerning same which could reasonably be expected to supersede or make obsolete the products of Seller or the procedures or methods of manufacturing used by Seller or the significant suppliers of Seller.

24. *Contracts, Agreements and Commitments.* There are no material contracts, agreements or other commitments, written or oral, not listed herein or in the Exhibits hereto, to which Seller is a party, or by which it is bound or which pertain in any way to Seller's business.

25. *Liabilities.* Seller has as of the Purchase Date and shall have on the Closing Date no liabilities of any kind whatsoever, contingent or otherwise, except liabilities under the Assumed Contracts, such liabilities which are disclosed on the balance sheet of the Seller annexed hereto as Exhibit K, liabilities relating to the litigation described on Exhibit Q hereto and liabilities incurred in the ordinary course of business between the Purchase Date and Closing Date.

26. *Capital Stock.* All of the issued and outstanding capital stock of Seller is owned, beneficially and of record, by the Parent. No options, warrants or other rights to subscribe to or purchase any shares of capital stock of Seller exist.

27. *Conduct of Business Since Purchase Date.* During the period between the Purchase Date and the date hereof, Seller has not taken any action with respect to the conduct of Seller's business other than in the ordinary course of business, and there has been no material adverse change in the assets or liabilities or in the condition, financial or otherwise, or business, properties, earnings or net worth of Seller.

G. Representations and Warranties of Buyer

The Buyer represents and warrants to the Seller as follows:

1. *Organization and Standing.* Buyer is a corporation duly organized, validly existing and in good standing under the laws of the State of New York.

2. *Corporate Authority.* Buyer has full corporate authority to execute, deliver and perform this Agreement, the Note and all of the documents required to be executed by Buyer hereunder, and this Agreement and the Note will constitute valid and binding obligations of Buyer; this Agreement and the Note and all transactions contemplated hereby have been duly authorized by all requisite corporate action.

3. *Conflicting Agreements.* Neither the execution or delivery of this Agreement or the Note nor fulfillment of or compliance with the terms and conditions hereof or thereof will constitute a breach by Buyer of its certificate of incorporation or by-laws or result in a breach of the terms, conditions or provisions of or constitute a default under or result in a violation of any agreement, contract or instrument to which Buyer is a party or by which it is bound or result in a violation by Buyer of any existing law or statute or any rule or regulation of any jurisdiction or of any order, decree, writ or injunction of any court or governmental department, bureau, board, agency or instrumentality.

4. *Consents.* No consent from or other approval of any governmental entity or other person is necessary in connection with the execution of this Agreement or the consummation by Buyer of the transactions contemplated hereby or the continuation of the business of Seller by Buyer in the manner previously conducted by Seller.

5. *Insurance.* Buyer shall maintain reasonable insurance with respect to its assets including product liability insurance.

6. *Disclosure.* No representation or warranty of Buyer contained in this Agreement, and no statement contained in any certificate or other instrument furnished or to be furnished to Buyer pursuant hereto, or in connection with the transactions contemplated hereby, contains or will

contain any untrue statement of a material fact, or omits or will omit to state any material fact which is necessary in order to make the statements contained therein not misleading.

7. *Capital Stock.* All of the issued and outstanding capital stock of Buyer is owned beneficially and of record by ____. No options, warrants or other rights to subscribe to or purchase any shares of capital stock of Buyer exist.

H. Covenants of Seller and the Parent

1. *Interference.* Seller shall not interfere with, disrupt or attempt to disrupt the relationship, contractual or otherwise, between the Buyer and any supplier or customer of the Seller, which was such on or prior to the Closing Date, or any supplier or customer of Buyer.

2. *Investigation.* From and after the date hereof through the Closing Date, the Seller will afford to the officers and representatives of the Buyer, free access to the Business Space and Seller's books and records relating to its business during normal business hours in order that the Buyer may have full opportunity to make such investigation as it shall desire with respect to the condition of the Purchased Property and the business of Seller.

3. *Working Papers.* Seller shall cause Messrs. ____ to preserve for at least two years after the Closing Date their working papers relating to their audit of Seller's financial statements for the period ended ____, 19____, and their working papers relating to Seller in connection with their audit of the Parent's financial statements for the period ended ____, 19____. Seller shall cause Messrs. ____, during such period, to grant the auditors of Buyer reasonable access to and the opportunity to make copies of such papers at Buyer's expense during normal business hours. If after such two-year period ____ wishes to dispose of such papers, it shall turn them over to Buyer.

4. *Customers; Employees.* Seller shall use its best efforts through the Closing Date to preserve the customers and suppliers of its business. In addition, Seller will use its best efforts through the Closing Date to keep available Seller's present employees now employed for employment by

the Buyer, without making any increase after the date hereof in the compensation, current or deferred, payable to such employees without the prior consent of Buyer, and Seller will cooperate fully with Buyer so that Buyer may, in its discretion, retain some or all of such employees. Seller shall not hire any employees during the period between the date hereof and the Closing Date without the consent of Buyer.

5. *Names*. Seller and the Parent shall, from and after the Closing Date, cease to use the words ____ or any variations thereof or any other trademarks, trade names or copyrights listed on Exhibit D.

6. *Books and Records*. Seller shall preserve its books, records, files and correspondence relating to its business conducted prior to the Closing Date and Buyer shall have reasonable access to them and to make copies thereof. Seller shall turn over to Buyer such books, records, files and correspondence when Seller wishes to dispose of them.

7. *Dividends and Distributions; Liabilities to Parent*. During the period from the Purchase Date through the date hereof Seller has not made, and during the period from the date hereof through the Closing Date Seller shall not make, any dividend payments to its stockholders, any distributions of assets of any kind on its stock or any redemption or retirement of any of its stock. Except as specified in Exhibit V, during the period from the Purchase Date through the date hereof Seller has not, and during the period from the date hereof through the Closing Date Seller shall not, incur any liability to the Parent except for the $____ of "income taxes to parent company" reflected on the balance sheet included as part of Exhibit K annexed hereto, which $____ liability the Parent hereby agrees to pay.

8. *Computer Accounts*. The Parent at its expense shall maintain on its computer system for ninety (90) days after the Closing the general ledger, computer-based accounts of the business of Seller purchased by Buyer hereunder.

9. *Covenant Not to Compete*. From and after the Closing Date for a period of five (5) years, Seller, the Parent and any of their subsidiaries and any business in which either of them owns directly or indirectly more than 20 percent of the equity interest thereof shall not compete

with Buyer or its subsidiaries in any business of the type carried on by Seller prior to the Closing Date in any area in which Buyer or its subsidiaries are engaged in business. The term "compete," as used herein, means to engage in competition, directly or indirectly (including, without limitation, soliciting or selling to any customer with which Buyer has or Seller had any direct or indirect business contacts), either as a proprietor, partner, employee, agent, consultant, stockholder or in any capacity or manner whatsoever. The parties hereby acknowledge that remedies at law for violations of this paragraph are inadequate and that only injunctive relief is an adequate remedy for such violations. The provisions of this paragraph are severable; if any provision of this paragraph or application thereof to any circumstance is held invalid, such invalidity shall not affect other provisions or applications of this paragraph which can be given effect without the invalid provisions or application.

10. *Accounts Receivable*. The Parent shall buy for cash at face value from Buyer on the first anniversary of the Closing Date the amount of receivables, net of bad debt reserve, reflected on the balance sheet included as part of Exhibit K annexed hereto, which is not collected in full by Buyer within one year after the Closing Date.

I. Covenants of Buyer

From the Closing Date until payment in full of the Note, Buyer agrees that unless Seller shall otherwise consent in writing:

1. Within 30 days of the Closing the Buyer shall cause the Parent to be released from all liabilities under its guarantees of the Seller's indebtedness to banks referred to in this Agreement.

2. Buyer shall not pay any dividends (other than dividends payable solely in shares of any class of its stock) on any shares of its stock if the Note is in default. If the Note is not in default, Buyer shall not pay any such dividends unless at the time of such payment after giving effect to such payment the debt/equity ratio of Buyer is equal to or less than one to one.

3. Unless at the time of any payment referred to in this sentence, after giving effect to such payment, the debt/equity ratio of Buyer is equal to or less than one to one, (a) Buyer shall not use the cash flow derived from the assets purchased hereunder to make any payment of a material amount for matters or expenses unrelated to the business or expansion plans of Buyer of corporations in which it owns directly or indirectly a majority interest; (b) the aggregate of any payments derived from such cash flow made by Buyer to its affiliates in connection with such business or expansion plans shall be reasonable; (c) the financial statements referred to in the Note annexed hereto as Exhibit M shall be accompanied by a statement of the aggregate amount of any such payments to affiliates; and (d) Seller shall have the right to make reasonable requests to examine at reasonable times records or information pertaining to such payments.

4. For purposes of calculating the debt/equity ratio with respect to Paragraphs 9.2 and 9.3 above, (a) the debt/equity ratio shall refer to the debt/equity ratio on an equity accounting basis of Buyer, and (b) "debt" shall mean the difference between (i) the sum of long-term debt and other indebtedness or borrowed money and (ii) the excess of current assets over current liabilities.

5. On the Closing Date, Buyer shall have $____ of equity.

J. Conditions Precedent of Buyer

The obligations of the Buyer hereunder are subject to the conditions that on or prior to the Closing Date:

1. *Representations and Warranties True at Closing.* The representations and warranties of the Seller contained in this Agreement or in any certificate or document delivered pursuant to the provisions hereof or in connection with the transactions contemplated hereby shall be true on and as of the Closing Date as though such representations and warranties were made at and as of such date, except if such representations and warranties were made as of a specified date and such representations and warranties shall be true as of such date.

2. *Seller's Compliance with Agreement.* The Seller shall have performed and complied with all agreements and conditions required by this Agreement to be performed or complied with by it prior to or at the Closing of this Agreement.

3. *Resolutions and Seller's Certificate.* The Seller shall have delivered to the Buyer copies of the resolutions of the Board of Directors of the Seller authorizing the transactions contemplated herein, with such resolutions to be certified to be true and correct by its Secretary or Assistant Secretary, together with a certificate of an officer of the Seller, dated the Closing Date, certifying in such detail as the Buyer may request to the fulfillment of the conditions specified in subparagraphs 1 and 2 above.

4. *Opinion of Seller's Counsel.* Seller shall have delivered to Buyer an opinion of Messrs. ____, dated the Closing Date, to the effect that:

(a) Seller is a corporation duly organized, validly existing and in good standing under the laws of the State of ____, has the legal and corporate power to own or lease and operate the Purchased Property and carry on the business of Seller as and where such assets are now owned or leased and operated and such business is now conducted, and has the legal and corporate power and authority to make, execute, deliver and perform this Agreement; the Parent is a corporation duly organized, validly existing and in good standing under the laws of the State of ____ and has the legal and corporate power and authority to make, execute, deliver and perform this Agreement;

(b) All corporate and other proceedings required to be taken by the Seller and the Parent to authorize them to execute and carry out this Agreement and the transactions contemplated herein have been duly and properly taken, and this Agreement has been duly and validly executed and delivered and constitutes the valid and binding obligation of the Seller and the Parent enforceable in accordance with its terms;

(c) The instruments of conveyance delivered by Seller to Buyer at the Closing have been duly authorized and validly executed and delivered and constitute valid and binding obligations of the Seller enforceable in accordance with their respective terms; and

(d) The execution and delivery of this Agreement, and the performance by the Seller and the Parent of their respective obligations hereunder will not conflict with or violate any provision of the Certificate of Incorporation or By-laws of Seller or the Parent or conflict with or violate any provisions of, or result in a default or acceleration of any obligation under, any mortgage, lease, contract, agreement, indenture, or other instrument or undertaking, of which such counsel has knowledge, or any order, decree or judgment, of which such counsel has knowledge, to which the Seller or the Parent is a party or by which the Seller or the Parent or the property of either of them is bound or, to the best of such counsel's knowledge, result in the creation or imposition of any lien, charge, restriction or security interest on the Purchased Property except to the extent contemplated by this Agreement.

5. *Injunction.* On the Closing Date, there shall be no effective injunction, writ, preliminary restraining order or any order of any nature issued by a court of competent jurisdiction directing that the transactions provided for herein or any of them not be consummated as herein provided.

6. *Approval of Proceedings.* All actions, proceedings, instruments and documents required to carry out this Agreement, or incidental thereto, and all other related legal matters shall have been approved by Messrs. ____, counsel for the Buyer.

7. *Casualty.* The Purchased Property or any substantial portion thereof shall not have been adversely affected in any material way as a result of any fire, accident, flood or other casualty or act of God or the public enemy, nor shall any substantial portion of the Purchased Property have been stolen, taken by eminent domain or been subject to condemnation. If the Closing occurs hereunder despite such casualty as a result of the waiver of this condition by Buyer, the Seller shall assign or pay over to the Buyer the proceeds of any insurance or any condemnation proceeds with respect to any casualty involving the Purchased Property which occurs after the date hereof.

8. *Adverse Change*. There shall have been between the Purchase Date and the Closing Date no material adverse change in the assets or liabilities, or in the condition, financial or otherwise, or in the business, properties, earnings or net worth of Seller.

9. *Consent*. Buyer shall have received a copy of the consent of _____ and ____ Bank to this Agreement and the transactions contemplated hereby.

10. *Employment Agreement*. Buyer shall have entered into an employment agreement with _____.

11. *Dismissal of Action*. The action entitled ____ and counterclaims in such action and the other actions and counterclaims referred to in Exhibit W attached hereto shall have been dismissed with prejudice and settled pursuant to Exhibit W attached hereto.

12. *Audited Financial Statements*. Seller shall have delivered to Buyer a signed opinion of Seller's auditors reporting on an examination of the financial statements of Seller for the years ended ____, 19____ and ____, 19____, identical to the opinion included as part of Exhibit K annexed hereto. Such opinion shall have reported on the balance sheets of Seller as at such dates and the related statements of income, stockholders' equity and changes in financial position of Seller for the years then ended, including the notes thereto, which shall be identical to the financial statements included as part of Exhibit K annexed hereto.

13. Seller shall have assigned the Business Space Lease to Buyer and shall have obtained the necessary approval of any party thereto.

K. Conditions Precedent of Seller

The obligations of the Seller hereunder are subject to the conditions that on or prior to the Closing Date:

1. *Representations and Warranties True at Closing*. The representations and warranties of the Buyer contained in this Agreement or in any certificate or document delivered pursuant to the provisions hereof or in connection with the transactions contemplated hereby shall be true on

and as of the Closing Date as though such representations and warranties were made at and as of such date, except as otherwise contemplated herein.

2. *Buyer's Compliance with Agreement*. The Buyer shall have performed and complied with all agreements and conditions required by this Agreement to be performed or complied with by it prior to or at the Closing.

3. *Resolutions and Buyer's Certificate*. The Buyer shall have delivered to the Seller copies of the resolutions of the Board of Directors of the Buyer authorizing the transactions contemplated herein, with such resolutions to be certified to be true and correct by its Secretary or Assistant Secretary, together with a certificate of an officer of the Buyer, dated the Closing Date, certifying in such detail as the Seller may request to the fulfillment of the conditions specified in subparagraphs 1 and 2 above.

4. *Opinion of Buyer's Counsel*. Buyer shall have delivered to Seller at the Closing an opinion of Messrs. ____, dated the Closing Date, to the effect that:

(a) Buyer is a corporation duly organized, validly existing and in good standing under the laws of the State of New York;

(b) Buyer has full power and authority to enter into this Agreement and to purchase the Purchased Property from Seller;

(c) All corporate action required to be taken by the Buyer to authorize it to carry out this Agreement and the transactions contemplated herein has been duly and properly taken; and

(d) The execution and delivery of this Agreement and the performance by the Buyer of its obligations hereunder will not conflict with or violate any provision of the Buyer's Certificate of Incorporation or its By-laws or conflict with or violate any provisions of, or result in a default or acceleration of any obligation under, any mortgage, lease, contract, agreement, indenture or other instrument or undertaking, of

FORMS AND MATERIALS 865

which such counsel has knowledge, or any order, decree or judgment, of which such counsel has knowledge, to which the Buyer is a party or by which it or its property is bound.

5. *Injunction*. On the Closing Date, there shall be no effective injunction, writ, preliminary restraining order or any order of any nature issued by a court of competent jurisdiction directing that the transactions provided for herein or any of them not be consummated as herein provided.

6. *Approval of Proceedings*. All actions, proceedings, instruments and documents required to carry out this Agreement, or incidental thereto, and all other related legal matters shall have been approved by Messrs. ____, counsel for Seller.

L. Indemnification

1. The Seller and the Parent jointly and severally shall indemnify and hold Buyer harmless from and against and in respect of any and all liabilities, losses, damages, claims, costs and expenses, including, but not limited to, attorneys' fees, arising out of or due to:

(a) a breach of any representation, warranty, covenant or agreement of the Seller or the Parent contained in this Agreement or in any statement or certificate furnished to Buyer pursuant hereto or in connection with the transactions contemplated hereby;

(b) any claim by customers of Buyer or the ultimate users with respect to the finished goods Inventory assigned to Buyer on the Closing Date based upon defects or alleged defects therein; except that as to Inventory which is not valued or which is written down or reserved against (to the extent of such write-down or reserve) on the balance sheet of Seller included as part of Exhibit K annexed hereto, indemnification may not be had hereunder for any claims by any such user or customer for a refund or credit of the price paid for such goods;

(c) any liabilities of Seller which are not expressly assumed by Buyer under the terms of this Agreement; or

(d) the action captioned ____, and any counterclaims in such action, and any other actions or counterclaims referred to in Exhibit W or other actions or counterclaims brought by ____, ____ or any affiliate of either of them relating to or arising out of the same or similar facts as that of such actions or counterclaims and any and all actions, suits, proceedings, demands, assessments or judgments, costs and expenses incidental to any of the foregoing, provided, that with respect to item (a) above, indemnification may be had pursuant to this Paragraph L(d) only if a claim is made by Buyer in respect thereof prior to the second anniversary of the Closing Date.

2. Buyer shall indemnify and hold harmless the Seller from and against and in respect of any and all liabilities, losses, damages, claims, costs and expenses, including, but not limited to, attorneys' fees, arising out of or due to a breach of any representation, warranty or covenant of Buyer contained in this Agreement, and any and all actions, suits, proceedings, demands, assessments or judgments, costs and expenses incidental to any of the foregoing, provided, that such indemnification may be had hereunder only if a claim is made by Seller in respect thereof prior to the second anniversary of the Closing Date.

3. (a) Promptly after the receipt by any party hereto of notice under this Paragraph L of (x) any claim or (y) the commencement of any action or proceeding, such party (the "Aggrieved Party") will, if a claim with respect thereto is to be made against any party obligated to provide indemnification pursuant to this Paragraph L (the "Indemnifying Party"), give such Indemnifying Party written notice of such claim or the commencement of such action or proceeding and shall permit the Indemnifying Party to assume the defense of any such claim or any litigation resulting from such claim. Failure by the Indemnifying Party to notify the Aggrieved Party of its election to defend any such action within a reasonable time, but in no event more than fifteen (15) days after notice thereof shall have been given to the Indemnifying Party, shall be deemed a waiver by the Indemnifying Party of its right to defend such action.

(b) If the Indemnifying Party assumes the defense of any such claim or litigation resulting therefrom, the obligations of the Indemnifying Party as to such claim or litigation shall be limited to taking all steps

FORMS AND MATERIALS

necessary in the defense or settlement of such claim or litigation and to holding the Aggrieved Party harmless from and against any and all losses, damages and liabilities caused by or arising out of any settlement approved by the Indemnifying Party or any judgment in connection with such claim or litigation. The Aggrieved Party may participate, at its expense, in the defense of such claim or litigation provided that the Indemnifying Party shall direct and control the defense of such claim or litigation. The Indemnifying Party shall not, in the defense of such claim or litigation, consent to entry of any judgment, except with the written consent of the Aggrieved Party, or enter into any settlement, except with the written consent of the Aggrieved Party, which does not include as an unconditional term thereof the giving by the claimant or the plaintiff to the Aggrieved Party of a release from all liability in respect of such claim or litigation.

(c) If the Indemnifying Party shall not assume the defense of any such claim or litigation, the Aggrieved Party may defend against such claim or litigation in such manner as it may deem appropriate and, unless the Indemnifying Party shall deposit with the Aggrieved Party a sum equivalent to the total amount demanded in such claim or litigation, or shall deliver to the Aggrieved Party a surety bond or an irrevocable letter of credit in form and substance reasonably satisfactory to the Aggrieved Party, the Aggrieved Party may settle such claim or litigation on such terms as it may deem appropriate, and the Indemnifying Party shall promptly reimburse the Aggrieved Party for the amount of all expenses, legal or otherwise, incurred by the Aggrieved Party in connection with the defense against or settlement of such claim or litigation. If no settlement of such claim or litigation is made, the Indemnifying Party shall promptly reimburse the Aggrieved Party for the amount of any judgment rendered with respect to such claim or in such litigation and of all expenses, legal or otherwise, incurred by the Aggrieved Party in the defense against such claim or litigation.

M. Guaranty

The Parent hereby unconditionally guarantees to the Buyer the prompt, full and faithful performance of the obligations of Seller to be performed under this Agreement and all agreements ancillary thereto, as if the Parent were the primary obligor hereunder and thereunder. The Buyer may proceed against the Parent under this Guaranty independently of and without recourse to any action against the Seller, provided, that the Parent shall have any and all rights of defense, set-off and counterclaim which are available to Seller.

The Parent's maximum liability under this Agreement shall be $____, except that if its total liability under this Agreement (without giving effect to such maximum) exceeds $____ and the Parent is liable under this Agreement (without giving effect to such maximum) for a breach of warranty under Paragraph F(3) hereof, or for the indemnification under Paragraph L hereof with respect to a breach of a warranty under Paragraph F(3) hereof, the Parent's maximum liability shall be the sum of (1) $____ and (2) the amount of all liabilities for all such breaches or all such indemnifications not included in the $____ referred to in clause (1) above.

N. Brokerage

The Seller, Buyer and the Parent represent and warrant to each other that all negotiations relative to this Agreement and the transactions contemplated hereby have been carried on by the Seller and the Parent directly with the Buyer and without the intervention of any broker, finder or other third party.

O. Notices

All notices, requests, demands and other communications hereunder shall be in writing and shall be deemed to have been duly given upon delivery, if delivered in person, or on the third business day after mailing, if mailed, by registered mail, postage prepaid, return receipt requested:

1. To Seller:

    [ADDRESS]

With a copy to:

[ADDRESS OF SELLER'S ATTORNEY]

2. To Buyer:

[ADDRESS]

With a copy to:

[ADDRESS OF BUYER'S ATTORNEY]

or to such other address or to such other person as Seller or Buyer shall have last designated by notice to the other party.

P. Entire Agreement; Modification

This Agreement contains the entire agreement between the parties hereto with respect to the transactions contemplated herein, and no representation, promise, inducement or statement of intention relating to the transactions contemplated by this Agreement has been made by any party which is not set forth in this Agreement. This Agreement shall not be modified or amended except by an instrument in writing signed by or on behalf of the parties hereto.

Q. Nature and Survival of Representations

All statements contained in any certificate or other instrument delivered by or on behalf of the Buyer or Seller pursuant to this Agreement or in connection with the transactions contemplated hereby shall be deemed representations and warranties respectively by the Buyer and Seller hereunder. All representations and warranties and agreements made by the parties hereto in this Agreement or pursuant hereto shall survive the Closing hereunder and any investigation at any time made by or on behalf of any party hereto.

R. Bulk Sales Law

Buyer waives compliance by Seller with the bulk sales law of the State of ____ and any state or jurisdiction in which Seller (1) was doing business, (2) had property located or (3) had existing creditors on the Closing Date.

S. Specific Performance

Without limiting or waiving in any respect any rights or remedies of any party given under this Agreement, or now or hereafter existing at law or in equity or by statute, any party, upon its fulfillment of the conditions precedent to the other party's obligations as provided in this Agreement, shall be entitled to specific performance of the obligations to be performed by the other party in accordance with the provisions of this Agreement.

T. Compliance with Closing Conditions

The parties hereto shall use their best efforts to comply with the respective closing conditions to be performed on their part.

U. Termination

Buyer and Seller may, at any time prior to the Closing Date, mutually consent to the termination of this Agreement. If the Closing hereunder is not held, or an action or proceeding for specific performance as provided above is not commenced on or before ____, 19__, this Agreement shall be terminated as of that date and neither Buyer nor Seller shall have any further obligation thereunder.

V. Parties

Nothing contained in this Agreement is intended or shall be construed to give any person or corporation, other than the parties hereto and their respective successors, any legal or equitable right, remedy or claim under or in respect of this Agreement or any provision herein contained; this Agreement being intended to be and being for the sole and exclusive benefit of the parties hereto and their respective successors and for the benefit of no other person or corporation.

W. New York Law to Govern

This Agreement shall be governed by and construed and enforced in accordance with the laws of the State of New York.

X. Assignment

This Agreement shall not be assignable by either party hereto.

Y. Counterparts

This Agreement may be executed simultaneously in any number of counterparts, each of which shall be deemed an original but all of which together shall constitute one and the same instrument.

Z. Paragraph Headings

The paragraph headings in this Agreement are for convenience of reference only and shall not be deemed to alter or affect any provision thereof. Reference to numbered "paragraphs," "subparagraphs," and "Exhibits" refers to paragraphs and subparagraphs of this Agreement and Exhibits annexed hereto.

AA. Taxes

1. Buyer shall deliver to Seller at the Closing a check in the amount of $____. It is agreed that upon payment of such amount, Seller hereby assumes, and releases Buyer from all liability with respect to, any and all federal, state and local tax liability of Seller (a) relating to the period between the Purchase Date through and including the Closing Date, including, without limitation, all liability for income taxes and (b) for sales taxes in excess of $____ relating to the sale of assets hereunder.

Said payment shall not be subject to any later adjustment by either party.

2. Buyer shall be liable for all federal, state and local taxes of any kind for any period commencing from and after the Closing Date. Seller shall be liable for, and hold Buyer harmless with respect to, all federal, state and local taxes of any kind for all periods ended on or prior to the Purchase Date.

IN WITNESS WHEREOF, Seller and Buyer have caused this Agreement to be executed as of the day and year first written above.

[NAME OF SELLER]

By:_____

[NAME OF BUYER]

By:_____

[NAME OF PARENT]

By:_____

FORM THIRTY-FIVE(a)

FORM OF OPINION
OF SELLER'S COUNSEL

_____,19____

Gentlemen:

This opinion letter is furnished to you pursuant to Section J(4) of the Agreement for Purchase of Assets, dated as of ____, 19____ (the "Agreement") by and between [Seller], a ____ corporation, [Parent of Seller], a ____ corporation, and ____, a New York corporation (the "Buyer"). Unless otherwise defined herein, the terms used herein shall be defined the same as those in the Agreement.

We have acted as special counsel to the Seller in connection with the transactions contemplated by the Agreement and, in connection therewith, have participated in the preparation of the Agreement and certain documents referred to therein and have attended the Closing. As a basis for our opinions as hereinafter expressed, we have examined such corporate records and documents, such certificates of public officials and officers of the Seller and its Parent, and such other documents and questions of law, and have made such other investigation and have taken such other actions as we deem necessary.

Based upon the foregoing and the assumptions hereinafter set forth, and subject to the further limitations, qualifications and exceptions hereinafter set forth, we are of the opinion that:

1. Seller is a corporation duly organized, validly existing and in good standing under the laws of the State of ____; has the legal and corporate power to own or lease and operate the Purchased Property and carry on the business of Seller as and where such assets are now owned or leased and operated and such business is now conducted, and has the legal and corporate power and authority to make, execute, deliver and perform the Agreement; the Parent is a corporation duly organized, validly

existing and in good standing under the laws of the State of ____ and has the legal and corporate power and authority to make, execute, deliver and perform the Agreement;

2. All corporate and other proceedings required to be taken by the Seller and the Parent to authorize them to execute and carry out the Agreement and the transactions contemplated herein have been duly and properly taken, and the Agreement has been duly and validly executed and delivered and constitutes the valid and binding obligation of the Seller and the Parent enforceable in accordance with its terms;

3. The instruments of conveyance delivered by Seller to Buyer at the Closing have been duly authorized and validly executed and delivered and constitute valid and binding obligations of the Seller enforceable in accordance with their respective terms; and

4. The execution and delivery of the Agreement, and the performance by the Seller and the Parent of their respective obligations hereunder will not conflict with or violate any provision of the Certificate of Incorporation or By-laws of Seller or the Parent or conflict with or violate any provisions of, or result in a default or acceleration of any obligation under, any mortgage, lease, contract, agreement, indenture, or other instrument or undertaking, of which such counsel has knowledge, or any order, decree or judgment, of which such counsel has knowledge, to which the Seller or the Parent is a party or by which the Seller or the Parent or the property of either of them is bound or, to the best of such counsel's knowledge, result in the creation or imposition of any lien, charge, restriction or security interest on the Purchased Property except to the extent contemplated by this Agreement.

The foregoing opinions are based, in part, upon the assumptions and are subject to the further limitations, qualifications, and exceptions set forth below:

(a) The opinions expressed in paragraph 3 above are subject to the qualifications that:

  (i) the validity, binding effect and enforceability of the obligations contained in the Agreement may be limited or affected by bankruptcy, insolvency, reorganization, moratorium, foreclosure, receivership, redemption, or similar laws affecting the rights of creditors generally; and

(ii) the enforceability of any obligation contained in the Agreement is subject to the principles of equity which may limit the availability of certain equitable remedies such as specific performance, regardless of whether such enforceability is considered in a proceeding in equity or at law.

(b) In rendering all of the opinions set forth above, we have assumed the genuineness, completeness and authenticity of all documents submitted to us as originals and the conformity with genuine, complete and authentic originals of all documents submitted to us as copies.

(c) Except as otherwise set forth herein, as to matters of fact relevant to this opinion letter, we have not made any independent investigation, but have relied solely upon the representations and warranties made by the Seller and the Seller's Parent in the Agreement and upon the certificates of officers of the Seller.

This opinion letter is limited in its use solely to reliance by you in consummating the transactions contemplated by the Agreement. No other person or entity may rely or claim reliance upon this opinion letter, and it is not to be quoted in whole or in part or otherwise referred to or furnished to any other person or entity without the prior written consent of this firm.

Sincerely,

[SELLER'S COUNSEL]

By:_____

FORM THIRTY-FIVE(b)

BULK SALES AFFIDAVIT

The undersigned, being duly sworn, deposes and states as follows:

1. I am over the age of eighteen (18) years.

2. I believe in the obligation of an oath.

3. I am the ____ of ____ (the "Seller"), a New York corporation with offices at ____, New York.

4. Attached hereto is a list of all creditors of the undersigned who will be paid in full by the undersigned on or before ____, 19____.

5. This Affidavit is being given to ____ (the "Buyer") to induce Buyer to enter into a certain ____ Agreement with Seller, dated ____, 19____.

6. The undersigned hereby agrees to indemnify and hold the Buyer harmless in respect of any breach of this Affidavit or any failure to pay such creditors as aforesaid. The foregoing indemnity includes all costs, including reasonable attorneys' fees.

By:_____

Subscribed and sworn to this ____ day of ____, 19____.

_____
Notary Public

FORM THIRTY-SIX

AGREEMENT OF RECAPITALIZATION

This Agreement of Recapitalization, made this ____ day of ____, 19____, by and among ____, residing at ____, ____, New York ("A"), ____, residing at ____, ____, New York ("B"), ____, residing at ____, ____, New York ("C"), and XYZ CORPORATION, a New York corporation, with a principal office at ____, New York, New York ____ ("Corporation") (A, B and C are sometimes hereinafter individually referred to as a "Shareholder" and collectively referred to as the "Shareholders").

WITNESSETH:

WHEREAS, the Shareholders own all of the issued and outstanding common shares, no par value, of the Corporation ("Shares"); and

WHEREAS, the Shareholders desire to modify the capital structure of the Corporation to facilitate the retirement of B from the active operations of the Corporation;

NOW, THEREFORE, in consideration of the mutual promises contained herein and for other good and valuable consideration, receipt of which is hereby acknowledged, the parties hereto agree as follows:

1. *Present Capitalization.* The current authorized capitalization of the Corporation is Two Hundred (200) shares of no par value voting common stock, One Hundred (100) of which are issued, fully paid and outstanding in the hands of the following shareholders:

Name of Shareholder	Number of Common Shares
A	34
B	33
C	33

2. *Purpose of the Recapitalization.* The purpose of the recapitalization of the Corporation's current capital structure is to provide a mechanism by which B may retire from the active day-to-day operations of the Corporation and to segregate the present value of B's common shares. Further, the purpose is to segregate the element of present value, future value and voting control of the Corporation so that they may be disposed of as elements in any manner that the Shareholders so choose. It is expected that the recapitalization will increase the Corporation's flexibility in business planning.

3. *Certificate of Amendment.* The Shareholders agree to vote to amend the Certificate of Incorporation of the Corporation to provide that the capital structure of the Corporation be modified to provide that the Two Hundred (200) shares currently authorized be modified into One Hundred (100) shares of common stock, no par value, and One Hundred (100) shares of nonvoting 9 percent cumulative preferred stock, with a par value of ____ per share, provided, however, that of said 9 percent dividend only a total dividend of 4 percent shall be cumulative in the event that dividends are not declared or paid in any calendar year.

4. *Terms of Exchange.* One Hundred (100) shares of preferred stock shall be issued to B in exchange for all of his shares of common stock in the Corporation. No other Shareholder shall receive preferred stock pursuant to the terms of the plan. Each remaining outstanding common share shall be exchanged for three common shares.

5. *Dividends.* Before any dividends may be declared on common stock in any fiscal year, the holders of the preferred stock shall be entitled to receive, as and when declared, out of any surplus or net profits, a 9 percent preferred dividend on par value per share per annum, of which a 4 percent dividend shall be cumulative if not declared

in any year. After the aforementioned dividends on the preferred stock shall have been paid or declared and set apart, in any year, the board of directors may declare and pay from any remaining surplus, dividends to the holders of the common stock.

6. *Voting Rights.* The holders of the common stock shall have and possess the exclusive right to vote at every shareholders meeting and the holders of the preferred stock shall not be entitled to vote at any such shareholders meeting.

7. *Liquidation.* In the event of any liquidation or dissolution or winding up of the Corporation or its business, either voluntarily or involuntarily, the holders of the preferred stock shall be entitled to be paid, before any of the assets of the Corporation are distributed among or paid over to the holders of the common stock, an amount equal to the par value of such preferred stock. After the holders of the preferred stock shall have received the amount of the par value thereof, any remaining assets and/or surplus funds of the Corporation shall be distributed among and paid over pro rata to the holders of the common stock.

8. *Amendment of the Certificate of Incorporation.* The certificate of incorporation of the Corporation shall be amended so as to be consistent with the terms contained in this plan and agreement of recapitalization. The amendment shall be substantially in the form annexed hereto as Exhibit A.

9. *Authorization of Necessary Acts.* The directors and officers of the Corporation shall carry out and consummate the plan and shall have the power to adopt all resolutions, execute all documents and file all papers and take all other actions they deem necessary or desirable for the purposes of effecting the Plan.

10. *Miscellaneous.*

(a) This agreement shall bind the heirs, successors, and assigns of the parties hereto.

(b) This agreement shall be interpreted under the laws of the State of New York.

(c) If any of the provisions of this agreement are held invalid, such invalidity shall not affect the other provisions hereof which can be given effect without the invalid provision, and the provisions of this agreement are intended to be and shall be deemed severable.

(d) Any and all notices, requests, demands or communications hereunder shall be in writing and shall be deemed given if delivered personally or sent by certified or registered mail, return receipt requested, postage prepaid, to each of the parties at the respective addresses set forth first above or to such addresses as may from time to time be designated by and of them in writing by notice similarly given to all parties in accordance with this paragraph.

(e) A waiver by any party of any breach of this agreement or failure to exercise any right hereunder shall not be deemed to be a waiver of any other breach or right. The failure of any party to take any action by reason of any such breach or to exercise any such right shall not deprive such party of the right to take action at any time while such breach or condition giving rise to such right continues.

_____
[Name of A]

_____
[Name of B]

_____
[Name of C]

[Name of Corporation]

By: _____
     [Name and Title]

FORM THIRTY-SEVEN

WARRANT AGREEMENT

This WARRANT AGREEMENT (the "Agreement"), dated as of ____, 19____, is made by and between ____, a New York corporation (the "Company") and ____ (the "Warrantholder").

In consideration of the payment of $____, and other good and valuable consideration, the sufficiency and receipt of which is hereby acknowledged, the Company hereby agrees to issue a Stock Purchase Warrant, as hereinafter described (the "Warrant"), to purchase up to an aggregate of ____ shares (the "Shares") of Common Stock, par value $____ per share, of the Company (the "Common Stock"). The Warrant and the Common Stock of the Company are subject to the provisions of that certain Shareholders Agreement, dated as of ____, 19____ (the "Shareholders Agreement"), by and among [insert names of shareholders of the Company].

In consideration of the foregoing and for the purpose of defining the terms and provisions of the Warrant and the respective rights and obligations thereunder, the Company and the Warrantholder, for value received, hereby further agree as follows:

Section 1. Transferability and Form of Warrant

1.1 *Registration*. The Warrant shall be numbered and shall be registered on the books of the Company when issued.

1.2 *Transfer*. Upon compliance with the provisions of the Shareholders Agreement, the Warrant shall be transferable only on the books of the Company maintained at its principal office in ____, New York, or wherever its principal executive offices may then be located, upon delivery thereof duly endorsed by the Warrantholder or by its duly authorized attorney or representative, or accompanied by proper evidence of succession, assignment or authority to transfer; provided, that such transferee has agreed to be bound by the terms and provisions of the Shareholders Agreement pursuant to a written instrument in form and substance reasonably satisfactory to the Company. Upon any registration of transfer, the Company shall execute and deliver a new Warrant to the person entitled thereto.

1.3 *Form of Warrant.* The text of the Warrant and the form of election to purchase Shares shall be substantially as set forth in Annex A attached hereto. The price per Share and the number of Shares issuable upon exercise of the Warrant are subject to adjustment upon the occurrence of certain events, all as hereinafter provided. The Warrant shall be executed on behalf of the Company by its Chairman of the Board and Chief Executive Officer, or by its Chief Operating Officer.

A Warrant bearing the signature of an individual who was at any time the proper officer of the Company shall bind the Company, notwithstanding that such individual shall have ceased to hold such office prior to the delivery of such Warrant or did not hold such office on the date of this Agreement.

The Warrant shall be dated as of the date of signature thereof by the Company either upon initial issuance or upon division, exchange, substitution or transfer.

1.4 *Legend on Warrant Shares.* The Warrant and each certificate for Shares initially issued upon exercise of the Warrant, unless at the time of exercise such Shares are registered under the Securities Act of 1933, as amended (the "Securities Act"), shall bear the following legend:

> No sale, transfer, pledge or other disposition of this Warrant or the Shares purchasable hereunder shall be made except pursuant to registration under the Securities Act of 1933, as amended, and registration or qualification under state securities laws or pursuant to an opinion of counsel satisfactory to the issuer that such registration is not required. Sale, transfer, pledge and other disposition of this Warrant and such Shares is also restricted by that certain Warrant Agreement, dated ____, 19____, and

FORMS AND MATERIALS

by that certain Shareholders Agreement, dated as of ____, 19____, by and among [list names of shareholders of the Company], copies of which are available from the Issuer.

Any certificate issued at any time in exchange or substitution for any certificate bearing such legend (except a new certificate issued upon completion of a public distribution pursuant to a registration statement under the Securities Act of the securities represented thereby) shall also bear the above legend unless, in the case of the first sentence of such legend, the Company receives the opinion of ____, counsel for the Company ("Company Counsel"), that registration or qualification of the securities represented thereby under the laws referred to therein is not required.

Section 2. Exchange of Warrant Certificate. Any Warrant certificate may be exchanged for another certificate or certificates of like tenor entitling the Warrantholder to purchase a like aggregate number of Shares as the certificate or certificates surrendered then entitle such Warrantholder to purchase. Any Warrantholder desiring to exchange a Warrant certificate shall make such request in writing delivered to the Company, and shall surrender, properly endorsed, the certificate evidencing the Warrant to be so exchanged. Thereupon, the Company shall execute and deliver to the person entitled thereto a new Warrant certificate as so requested.

Section 3. Term of Warrants; Exercise of Warrants. Subject to the terms of this Agreement, the Warrantholder shall have the right, upon compliance with applicable federal and state securities laws, at any time during the period commencing at 9:00 a.m., New York time, on ____, 19____ (the "Exercisability Date"), and ending at 5:00 p.m., New York time, on ____, 19____ (the "Termination Date"), to purchase from the Company up to the number of Shares which the Warrantholder may at the time be entitled to purchase pursuant to this Agreement, upon surrender to the Company, at its principal office in ____, New York, or wherever its principal executive offices may then be located, of the certificate evidencing the Warrant to be exercised, together with the purchase form on the reverse thereof duly filled in and signed, and upon payment to the Company of the Warrant Price (as defined in and determined in accordance with the provisions of Sections 7 and 8 hereof) for the number of Shares with respect to which such Warrant is then exercised. Payment of the aggregate Warrant Price shall be made in cash or by cashier's check.

Subject to the terms of this Agreement, upon such surrender of the Warrant and payment of such Warrant Price as aforesaid, the Company shall issue and cause to be delivered to or, subject to the Shareholders Agreement and receipt by the Company of an opinion of Company Counsel that registration or qualification under any federal, state or other securities law is not required in connection therewith, upon the written order of the Warrantholder and in such name or names as the Warrantholder may designate, a certificate or certificates for the number of duly authorized, fully paid and nonassessable whole Shares so purchased upon the exercise of the Warrant, together with cash, as provided in Section 9 hereof, with respect to any fractional Shares otherwise issuable upon such surrender. Such certificate or certificates shall be deemed to have been issued and any person so designated to be named therein shall be deemed to have become a holder of such Shares as of the close of business on the date of the surrender of the Warrant, payment of the Warrant Price and receipt by the Company of an opinion of Company Counsel, as aforesaid, notwithstanding that the certificates representing such Shares shall not actually have been delivered or that the stock and warrant transfer books of the Company shall then be closed. The Warrant shall be exercisable, at the election of the Warrantholder, either in full or from time to time in part and, in the event that any certificate evidencing the Warrant (or any portion thereof) is exercised prior to that Termination Date with respect to less than all of the Shares specified therein at any time prior to the Termination Date, a new certificate of like tenor evidencing the remaining Warrant shall be issued by the Company.

Section 4. Payment of Taxes. The Company shall pay all documentary stamp taxes, if any, attributable to the initial issuance of the Shares; *provided, however*, that the Company shall not be required to pay any tax or taxes which may be payable (a) with respect to any secondary transfer of the Warrant or the Shares or (b) as a result of the issuance of the Shares to any person other than the Warrantholder, and the Company shall not be required to issue or deliver any certificate for any Shares unless and until the person requesting the issuance thereof shall have paid to the Company the amount of such tax or shall have produced evidence that such tax has been paid to the appropriate taxing authority.

Section 5. Mutilated or Missing Warrant. In case the certificate or certificates evidencing the Warrant shall be mutilated, lost, stolen or destroyed, the Company shall, at the request of the Warrantholder, issue and deliver in exchange and substitution for and upon cancellation of the mutilated certificate or certificates, or in lieu of and substitution for the certificate or certificates lost, stolen or destroyed, a new Warrant certificate or certificates of like tenor and representing an equivalent right or interest, but only upon receipt of evidence satisfactory to the Company of such loss, theft or destruction of such Warrant and of a bond of indemnity, if requested, also satisfactory to the Company in form and amount, and issued at the applicant's cost. Applicants for such substitute Warrant certificate shall also comply with such other reasonable regulations and pay such other reasonable charges as the Company may prescribe.

Section 6. Reservation of Shares of Capital Stock. The Company has reserved, and shall at all times so long as any Warrant remains outstanding, keep reserved, out of its authorized and unissued capital stock, such number of shares of Common Stock as shall be subject to purchase under the Warrant. Every transfer agent for the Common Stock and other securities of the Company issuable upon the exercise of the Warrant shall be irrevocably authorized and directed at all times to reserve such number of authorized shares and other securities as shall be requisite for such purpose. The Company shall keep a copy of this Agreement on file with every transfer agent for securities of the Company issuable upon the exercise of the Warrant. The Company shall supply such transfer agent with duly executed stock and other certificates for such purpose and shall provide or otherwise make available any cash which may be payable as provided in Section 9 hereof.

Section 7. Warrant Price. The price per Share (the "Warrant Price") at which Shares shall be purchasable upon the exercise of the Warrant shall be $____, subject to adjustment pursuant to Section 8 hereof.

Section 8. Adjustment of Warrant Price and Number of Shares. The number and kind of securities purchasable upon the exercise of the Warrant and the Warrant Price shall be subject to adjustment from time to time after the date hereof upon the happening of certain events, as follows:

8.1 *Adjustments*. The number of Shares purchasable upon the exercise of the Warrant and the Warrant Price shall be subject to adjustment as follows:

(a) In case the Company shall after the date of this Agreement (i) pay a dividend on the Common Stock in shares of the Common Stock, (ii) subdivide its outstanding Common Stock, (iii) combine its outstanding Common Stock into a smaller number of shares of Common Stock, or (iv) issue by reclassification of its Common Stock of the Company, the number of Shares purchasable upon exercise of the Warrant immediately prior thereto shall be adjusted so that the Warrantholder shall be entitled to receive, upon exercise of the Warrant after such time, the kind and number of Shares or other securities of the Company which it would have owned or would have been entitled to receive after the happening of any of the events described above had the Warrant been exercised immediately prior to the happening of such event or any record date with respect thereto. Any adjustment made pursuant to this paragraph (a) shall become effective immediately after the effective date of such event and such adjustment shall be retroactive to the record date, if any, for such event.

(b) Except in respect of transactions described in paragraph (a) above, in the event that, after the date hereof, the Company shall sell or issue Common Stock or rights, options, warrants or convertible securities, or rights, options or warrants to purchase convertible securities containing the right to subscribe for or purchase shares of Common Stock (collectively, "Rights"), and the sale or issuance price per Share

FORMS AND MATERIALS 889

of Common Stock (or in the case of any Rights the sum of (x) the consideration paid or payable for any such Right entitling the holder thereof to acquire one share of Common Stock and (y) such additional consideration paid or payable upon exercise or conversion of any such Right to acquire one share of Common Stock) is less than the Current Market Price (as defined in Section 8.6), then the number of Shares purchasable upon exercise of the Warrant shall equal the product of (A) the number of Shares issuable upon exercise of the Warrant immediately prior to the first public announcement (or consummation of such transaction if the Common Stock is not then publicly traded) of such transaction (or the record date for determination of shareholders entitled to receive (or purchase) such Rights in the case of a distribution or issuance thereof in respect of the Common Stock) multiplied by (B) a fraction (not to be less than one) with a numerator equal to the product of the number of shares of Common Stock outstanding after giving effect to such sale or issuance (and assuming, in the case of Rights that such Rights had been fully exercised or converted, as the case may be) and the Current Market Price determined immediately before such public announcement date, consummation date or record date, as the case may be, and a denominator equal to the sum of (i) the number of shares of Common Stock outstanding immediately before such public announcement date, consummation date or record date, as the case may be, multiplied by the Current Market Price determined immediately before such public announcement date, consummation date or record date, as the case may be, and (ii) the aggregate consideration received by the Company for the shares of Common Stock to be so issued or sold or to be purchased or subscribed for upon exercise of such Rights. For the purposes of such adjustments, the Common Stock which the holders of any such Rights shall be entitled to subscribe for or purchase shall be deemed to be issued and outstanding as of the date of such public announcement date, consummation date or record date, as the case may be, and the consideration received by the Company therefor shall be deemed to be the consideration received by the Company for such Rights, plus any underwriting discounts or selling commissions paid by the Company, plus the consideration or premiums stated in such Rights to be paid for the Common Stock covered thereby. In case the Company shall sell or issue Common Stock or Rights for a consideration consisting, in whole or in part, of property other than cash or its equivalent, then in determining the "consideration received by the Company" for purposes of this paragraph (b), the Board of Directors of the Company shall determine the fair value of said property, and such determination, if reasonable and based upon the Board of Directors' good-faith business judgment, shall be binding upon the Warrantholder.

(c) In case the Company shall distribute to all holders of its Common Stock evidences of its indebtedness (including, without limitation, convertible securities referred to in paragraph (b) above) or assets (excluding cash dividends or distributions, in each case out of earnings after the date hereof, and dividends payable in shares of Capital Stock), then in each case the number of Shares thereafter purchasable upon the exercise of the Warrant shall be that number which is equal to the product of (x) the number of Shares theretofore purchasable upon exercise of the Warrant multiplied by (y) a fraction, of which the numerator shall be the then Current Market Price on the record date for the determination of shareholders entitled to receive such distribution, and of which the denominator shall be such Current Market Price on such date minus the then fair value of the portion of the assets or evidences of indebtedness so distributed, allocable to one share of Common Stock. The Board of Directors of the Company shall determine the "fair value of the portion of the assets or evidences of indebtedness so distributed allocable to one share of Common Stock" and such determination, if reasonable and based upon the Board of Directors' good-faith business judgment, shall be binding upon the Warrantholder. Such adjustment shall be made whenever any such distribution is made and shall become effective on the date of distribution retroactive to the record date for the determination of shareholders entitled to receive such distribution.

(d) No adjustment in the number of Shares purchasable hereunder shall be required unless such adjustment would require an increase or decrease of at least 1 percent in the number of Shares then purchasable upon the exercise of the Warrant; *provided, however,* that any adjust-

FORMS AND MATERIALS

ments which by reason of this paragraph (d) are not required to be made immediately shall be carried forward and taken into account in any subsequent adjustment.

(e) Whenever the number of Shares purchasable upon the exercise of the Warrant is adjusted as herein provided, the Warrant Price payable upon exercise of the Warrant shall be adjusted by multiplying such Warrant Price immediately prior to such adjustment by a fraction, of which the numerator shall be the number of Shares purchasable upon the exercise of the Warrant immediately prior to such adjustment, and of which the denominator shall be the number of Shares so purchasable immediately thereafter.

(f) Whenever the number of Shares purchasable upon the exercise of the Warrant or the Warrant Price is adjusted as herein provided, the Company shall cause to be promptly mailed to the Warrantholder by first class mail, postage prepaid, notice of such adjustment or adjustments and a certificate of a firm of independent public accountants selected by the Board of Directors of the Company (who may be the regular accountants employed by the Company) setting forth the number of Shares purchasable upon the exercise of the Warrant and the Warrant Price after such adjustment, a brief statement of the facts requiring such adjustment and the computation by which such adjustment was made.

(g) For the purpose of this Subsection 8.1, the term "Common Stock" shall mean (i) the class of stock designated as the Common Stock of the Company at the date of this Agreement and (ii) where appropriate, any other security purchasable upon the exercise of the Warrant as provided for herein upon the happening of certain events. In the event that at any time, as a result of an adjustment made pursuant to this Section 8, the Warrantholder shall become entitled to purchase any shares of the Company other than Common Stock, thereafter the number of such other shares so purchasable upon exercise of the Warrant and the Warrant Price of such shares shall be subject to adjustment from time to time in a manner and on terms as nearly equivalent as practicable to the provisions with respect to the Shares contained in this Section 8.

(h) Upon the expiration of any rights, options, warrants or conversion privileges, if such shall not have been exercised, the number of Shares purchasable upon exercise of the Warrant and the Warrant Price, to the extent the Warrant has not then been exercised, shall, upon such expiration, be readjusted and shall thereafter be such as they would have been had they been originally adjusted (or had the original adjustment not been required, as the case may be) on the basis of (A) the fact that the only shares of Common Stock so issued were the shares of Common Stock, if any, actually issued or sold upon the exercise of such rights, options, warrants or conversion rights and (B) such shares of Common Stock, if any, were issued or sold for the consideration actually received by the Company upon such exercise plus the consideration, if any, actually received by the Company (including, for purposes hereof, any underwriting discounts or selling commissions paid by the Company) for the issuance, sale or grant of all such rights, options, warrants or conversion rights whether or not exercised; *provided, however*, that no such readjustment shall have the effect of increasing the Warrant Price by an amount in excess of the amount of the adjustment initially made with respect to the issuance, sale or grant of such rights, options, warrants or conversion rights.

8.2 *No Adjustment in Certain Cases.* No adjustments shall be made in connection with the issuance of Common Stock upon any exercise of the Warrant.

8.3 *Preservation of Purchase Rights Upon Reclassification, Consolidation, etc.* In case of any consolidation or merger of the Company with or into another corporation or any reclassification of the Common Stock of the Company (other than a reclassification referred to in Subsection (a) of Section 8.1) as a result of which the holders of the Company's Common Stock become holders of other shares or securities of the Company or of another corporation or entity, or such holders receive cash or other assets, or in case of any sale or conveyance to another corporation or other entity of the property, assets or business of the Company as an entirety or substantially as an entirety, in any such case, with an effective date after the date of this Agreement, the Company or such successor or purchasing corporation or entity, as the case may be,

FORMS AND MATERIALS

shall execute with the Warrantholder an agreement that the Warrantholder shall have the right thereafter upon payment of the Warrant Price in effect immediately prior to such action to purchase upon exercise of the Warrant the kind and amount of shares and/or other securities and property which he would have owned or have been entitled to receive after the happening of such consolidation, merger, sale or conveyance had the Warrant been exercised immediately prior to such action.

The agreements referred to in this Subsection 8.3 shall provide for adjustments and registration rights, which shall be as nearly equivalent as may reasonably be practicable to the adjustments and registration rights provided for in this Section 8 and referred to in Section 11. The provisions of this Subsection 8.3 shall similarly apply to successive consolidations, mergers, sales or conveyances.

8.4 *Statement on Warrants.* Irrespective of any adjustments in the Warrant Price or the number or kind of Shares purchasable upon the exercise of the Warrant, the Warrant certificate or certificates theretofore or thereafter issued may continue to express the same price and number and kind of Shares as are stated in the Warrant initially issuable pursuant to this Agreement.

8.5 *Definition of Current Market Price.* For purposes of this Agreement, the term "Current Market Price" shall mean (a) if the Common Stock is not publicly traded, the Warrant Price determined as of the date in question, (b) if the Common Stock is traded in the over-the-counter market and not in the NASDAQ National Market System or on any national securities exchange, the average of the daily mean of the per-share closing bid and asked prices of the Common Stock on the 30 consecutive trading days immediately preceding the date in question, as reported by NASDAQ or an equivalent generally accepted reporting service, or (c) if the Common Stock is traded in the NASDAQ National Market System or on a national securities exchange, the average for the 30 consecutive trading days immediately preceding the date in question of the daily per-share closing prices of the Common Stock in the NASDAQ National Market System or on the principal stock exchange on which the Common Stock is listed, as the case may be. If the Common Stock is traded as provided in clauses (b) or (c) of the preceding sentence, it shall be deemed to be "publicly traded" for the purposes hereof. The closing price referred to in clause (c) above shall be the last reported sales price or, in case no such reported sale takes place on such day, the average of the reported closing bid and asked prices, in either case in the NASDAQ National Market System or on the national securities exchange on which the Common Stock is then listed.

Section 9. Fractional Interests. The Company shall not be required to issue fractional Shares on the exercise of the Warrant from and after the time the Common Stock is publicly traded. If any fraction of a Share would, except for the provisions of this Section 9, be issuable on the exercise of the Warrant (or specified portions thereof), the Company shall pay an amount in cash equal to the then Current Market Price multiplied by such fraction.

Section 10. No Rights as Shareholder; Notices to Warrantholder. Nothing contained in this Agreement or in any of the Warrants shall be construed as conferring upon the Warrantholder or its transferees any rights as a Shareholder of the Company, including the right to vote, receive dividends, consent or receive notices as a Shareholder with respect to any meeting of shareholders for the election of directors of the Company or any other matter (except that the Warrantholder and its transferees have the rights referred to in Section 11 hereof to the extent they exercise their Warrants). If, however, at any time prior to the Termination Date and prior to the exercise of this Warrant, any of the following events shall occur:

(a) any action which would require an adjustment pursuant to Subsection 8.1 or 8.3; or

(b) a dissolution, liquidation or winding up of the Company (other than in connection with a consolidation, merger or sale of its property, assets and business as an entirety) shall be proposed;

then in any one or more of said events, the Company shall give notice in writing of such event to the Warrantholder as provided in Section 12 hereof at least 20 days prior to the date fixed as a record date or the date of closing the transfer books for the determination of the shareholders entitled to any relevant dividend, distribution, subscription rights or other rights or for the determination of shareholders entitled to vote on such proposed dissolution, liquidation or winding up, but failure to mail or receive such notice or any defect therein or in the mailing thereof shall not affect the validity of any such action taken. Such notice shall specify such record date or the date of closing the transfer books, as the case may be.

Section 11. Notices. Any notice pursuant to this Agreement by the Company or by the Warrantholder shall be in writing and shall be deemed to have been duly given if delivered or mailed by certified mail five days after mailing, return receipt requested:

If to the Warrantholder:

If to the Company:

Each party hereto may from time to time change the address to which notices to it are to be delivered or mailed hereunder by notice in accordance herewith to the other party.

Section 12. Successors. All the covenants and provisions of this Agreement by or for the benefit of the Company or the Warrantholder shall bind and inure to the benefit of their respective successors and permitted assigns hereunder and under the Shareholders Agreement.

Section 13. Applicable Law. This Agreement shall be deemed to be a contract made under the laws of the State of New York and for all purposes shall be construed in accordance with the internal laws of said state.

Section 14. Benefits of this Agreement. Nothing in this Agreement shall be construed to give to any person or corporation other than the Company and the Warrantholder any legal or equitable right, remedy or claim under this Agreement, and this Agreement shall be for the sole and exclusive benefit of the Company and the Warrantholder.

IN WITNESS WHEREOF, the parties have caused this Agreement to be duly executed, all as of the day and year first above written.

[COMPANY]

By: _____

[WARRANTHOLDER]

By: _____

EXHIBIT A

WARRANT NO. _____

NO SALE, TRANSFER, PLEDGE OR OTHER DISPOSITION OF THIS WARRANT OR THE SHARES PURCHASABLE HEREUNDER SHALL BE MADE EXCEPT PURSUANT TO REGISTRATION UNDER THE SECURITIES ACT OF 1933, AS AMENDED, AND REGISTRATION OR QUALIFICATION UNDER STATE SECURITIES LAWS OR PURSUANT TO AN OPINION OF COUNSEL SATISFACTORY TO THE ISSUER THAT REGISTRATION IS NOT REQUIRED. SALE, TRANSFER, PLEDGE AND OTHER DISPOSITION OF THIS WARRANT AND SUCH SHARES IS ALSO RESTRICTED BY THAT CERTAIN WARRANT AGREEMENT, DATED ____, 19___, AND BY THAT CERTAIN SHAREHOLDERS AGREEMENT, DATED AS OF ____, 19___, BY AND AMONG [SHAREHOLDERS OF THE COMPANY], COPIES OF WHICH ARE AVAILABLE FROM THE ISSUER.

WARRANT TO PURCHASE UP TO ____ SHARES OF COMMON STOCK OF [COMPANY]

Exercisable commencing ____, 19___;
Void after ____, 19___.

THIS CERTIFIES that, for value received, [Warrantholder], or registered assigns, is entitled, subject to the terms and conditions set forth in this Warrant, to purchase from [Company], a New York corporation (the "Company"), up to ____ shares of Common Stock, $____ par value, of the Company, at any time commencing 9:00 a.m., New York City time, on ____, 19___, and continuing up to 5:00 p.m., New York City time, on ____, 19___, at $____ per Share, such number of Shares and price per Share being subject to adjustment from time to time as set forth in the Warrant Agreement referred to below. This Warrant is issued pursuant to a Warrant Agreement between the Warrantholder and the Company, dated as of ____, 19___ (the "Warrant Agreement"), and is subject to all the terms thereof, including the limitations on transferability set forth therein and in the Shareholders Agreement referred to therein.

Subject to the conditions set forth herein and in the Warrant Agreement, this Warrant may be exercised by the holder hereof, in whole or in part (but not, in certain circumstances, as to a fractional share), by the presentation and surrender of this Warrant with the form of Election to Purchase duly executed and upon delivery of an opinion of legal counsel as provided in the Warrant Agreement, at the principal office of the Company (or at such other address as the Company may designate by notice in writing to the holder hereof at the address of such holder appearing on the books of the Company), and upon payment to the Company of the purchase price in cash or by cashier's check. Certificates for the Shares so purchased shall be delivered or mailed to the holder promptly after this Warrant shall have been so exercised, and, unless this Warrant has expired or has been exercised in full, a new Warrant identical in form but representing the number of Shares with respect to which this Warrant shall not have been exercised shall also be issued to the holder hereof.

Nothing contained herein shall be construed to confer upon the holder of this Warrant, as such, any of the rights of a Shareholder of the Company.

The Company may treat the registered holder(s) hereof as the absolute owner of this Warrant for the purpose of any exercise hereof and for all other purposes, and the Company shall not be affected by any notice to the contrary.

Dated: _____, 19____

[COMPANY]

By_____

[COMPANY]
ELECTION TO PURCHASE

[COMPANY]
[Company Address]

The undersigned hereby irrevocably elects to exercise the right of purchase represented by the within Warrant for, and to purchase thereunder, _____ Shares provided for therein, and requests that certificates for the Shares be issued in the name of:*

_____

(Please Print Name, Address and Social Security Number)

and, if said number of Shares shall not be all of the Shares purchasable under the Warrant, that a new Warrant certificate for the balance of the Shares purchasable under the within Warrant be registered in the name of the undersigned Warrantholder or his Assignee* as below indicated and delivered to the address stated below:

Dated: _____, 19___

Name of Warrantholder or

  Assignee (Please Print): _____

Address: _____

Signature:** _____

Signature Guaranteed: _____
                              Signature of Guarantor

(To be signed only upon assignment of Warrant)*

---

  * The Warrant and the Warrant Agreement contain restrictions on sale, assignment or transfer of this Warrant.

** Note: The signature of this assignment must correspond with the name as it appears upon the face of the within Warrant certificate in every particular, without alteration or enlargement or any change whatever.

FOR VALUE RECEIVED, the undersigned hereby sells, assigns and transfers unto

_____

_____

(Name and Address of Assignee must be Printed or Typewritten)

the within Warrant, hereby irrevocably constituting and appointing _____ Attorney to transfer said Warrant on the books of the Company, with full power of substitution in the premises.

Dated: _____, 19___

           _____

Signature Guaranteed: Signature of Registered Holder**

_____   _____

              Signature of Guarantor

_____

** Note: The signature of this assignment must correspond with the name as it appears upon the face of the within Warrant certificate in every particular, without alteration or enlargement or any change whatever.

_____

FORM THIRTY-EIGHT

STOCK OPTION AGREEMENT

This STOCK OPTION AGREEMENT (the "Agreement") is entered into as of _____, 19___, by and between _____, a New York corporation (the "Company") and ____ ("Optionee").

NOW, THEREFORE, the parties agree as follows:

1. Grant. In consideration of the payment of $____, and other good and valuable consideration, the sufficiency and receipt of which is hereby acknowledged, the Company hereby grants to Optionee the exclusive, irrevocable option (the "Option") to purchase from the Company up to ____ shares of the Company's Common Stock ("Common Stock") for cash at a price of $____ per share on the terms and conditions hereinafter set forth.

2. Term. The Option will expire and be of no further force or effect at midnight on ____, 19___.

3. Exercise. The Option may be exercised at any time prior to its expiration, or from time to time prior to its expiration, by delivering to the Company at its principal place of business written notice of exercise specifying the number of shares which are being purchased pursuant to the terms hereof, accompanied by the purchase price of such shares in cash or certified or cashier's check. The Option shall be surrendered to the Company at the time of the exercise of the last shares purchasable hereunder. In the event and each time that this Option is exercised with respect to less than the maximum number (a "Partial Exercise") of the shares purchasable hereunder, this Option shall be returned to the Company and the Company shall issue to Optionee a Stock Option Agreement in substantially the same form as this Stock Option Agreement, which Stock Option Agreement shall provide for the grant of an Option to purchase that number of shares of Common Stock purchasable hereunder immediately prior to such Partial Exercise less the number of shares of Common Stock purchased as a result of such Partial Exercise.

4. Stock Transfer Restriction. In the event that Optionee exercises this Option for all or any number of shares of Common Stock purchasable hereunder, the Optionee shall, prior to or contemporaneously with such exercise, execute a counterpart of the [Stock Transfer Restriction Agreement] and Optionee hereby agrees that upon such exercise, Optionee will execute and be bound by such Agreement. Optionee shall be bound by the terms and provisions of such [Stock Transfer Restriction Agreement] with respect to all shares of Common Stock owned by Optionee whether acquired by any exercise hereunder or otherwise.

5. Securities Laws or Regulations. Neither the Option nor the shares of Common Stock of the Company are registered under the Securities Act of 1933, and the shares of Common Stock issued upon exercise hereof will not be so registered. Optionee represents that Optionee is acquiring the Option, and, upon exercise of the Option, will purchase shares for Optionee's own account, in both cases without any intention of making or engaging in a distribution thereof or any interest therein in violation of the Securities Act of 1933; and Optionee acknowledges that this Option is being granted and said shares will be sold and issued in express reliance on the foregoing investment representation by the Optionee. Optionee agrees to execute such documents as the Company may in its discretion or the discretion of its counsel deem necessary in order that the Company not be in violation of any applicable securities laws or regulations applicable to the Option of the shares of Common Stock purchasable under this Option.

6. Information. Upon written request by Optionee, the Company shall furnish to Optionee such information regarding the Company and its operation as shall be reasonably necessary to enable Optionee to make a decision as to whether or not to exercise the Option, *provided,* *however*, that in no event shall the Company be required to furnish information which constitutes trade secrets or other proprietary information or the furnishing of which would be unduly burdensome, financially or otherwise, to the Company.

7. Anti-Dilution. In the event of any stock split, reverse stock split, stock dividend or other recapitalization of the Company, the number of shares purchasable hereunder as to which the Option has not been theretofore exercised shall be adjusted so that on exercise of the Option thereafter Optionee shall receive the same number and kind of shares which Optionee would have received had the exercise occurred prior to such event, and the purchase price per share shall be adjusted in inverse ratio to the change in the number of shares as to which the Option then becomes exercisable in order that the total amount payable on exercise of the Option shall remain unchanged.

8. No Shareholder's Rights. Optionee shall have no voting rights or other rights as a shareholder of the Company with respect to the shares covered by the Option, until such time as Optionee has exercised the Option and purchased the shares purchasable hereunder.

9. Death. If Optionee shall die prior to the expiration of the Option, to the extent that the Option remains unexercised as to all or any portion of the shares subject to it, it shall terminate and be of no further force or effect to the extent unexercised.

10. Entirety; Successors. This Agreement represents the entire agreement between the parties with respect to its subject matter herein.

11. Assignment. Optionee may not assign, transfer, lien or otherwise encumber this Option, any shares of Common Stock purchasable hereunder or any interests thereunder.

IN WITNESS WHEREOF, the parties have executed this Stock Option as of the date first set forth above.

[COMPANY]　　　　　　　　[OPTIONEE]

By:_____　　_____

FORM THIRTY-NINE

STOCK REDEMPTION AGREEMENT*

AGREEMENT made this ____ day of ____, 19____, among JOHN DOE and RICHARD ROE (together referred to as "Stockholders" and singularly referred to as "Stockholder") and ____, INC. ("Corporation"), a domestic corporation having its principal office and place of business at _____, ____, New York ____.

RECITALS

WHEREAS, JOHN DOE owns fifty (50) shares of the capital stock of the Corporation and RICHARD ROE owns fifty (50) shares of the capital stock of the Corporation and together the Stockholders own all of the issued and outstanding shares of the capital stock of the Corporation; and

WHEREAS, it is in the best interest of the Corporation to maintain and preserve the continuity of harmonious management of its affairs and to avoid transfers of its stock to persons not active or fully familiar with the problems of its management or prohibited under the laws of the State of New York; and

WHEREAS, it would be inimical to the best interest of the Corporation for a dispute to arise in respect of the disposition of ownership of any of its stock or the creation of rights in creditors of Stockholders, corporate creditors or other persons who are not beneficially active or who are otherwise legally disqualified for any reason from owning stock in the Corporation or participating in the management of the corporate business.

---

* Source: NYSBA Seminar, "Drafting Corporate Documents for the Close Corporation," November 14, 1986, Albany.

NOW, THEREFORE, in consideration of the premises, and the promises, covenants and agreements made, the mutual benefits to be derived from this Agreement, and other valuable consideration, receipt of which is acknowledged, the parties agree and understand as follows:

ARTICLE I
CERTAIN DEFINITIONS

When used in this Agreement:

1.1 "Termination Date" shall mean the date upon which the Stockholder's employment is terminated for any reason whatsoever.

1.2 "Offer Date" shall mean the date upon which the Stockholder or his legal representative shall offer for sale the Stockholder's shares of capital stock of the Corporation.

1.3 "Closing Date" shall mean the date upon which the stock shall be transferred and the purchase price paid therefor which must occur, if at all, not later than six (6) months from the Termination Date, unless otherwise agreed to by the parties.

1.4 "Disability" shall mean disablement from any ailment or other physical cause whatsoever which prevents any Stockholder from actively participating in the affairs of the Corporation for a continuous period of twelve (12) months. In the event of any dispute as to whether a Stockholder is or is not disabled, the dispute shall be determined exclusively by a physician to be selected by the Corporation, and his determination shall be conclusive and binding.

1.5 "Stock" shall mean the capital stock of the Corporation.

ARTICLE II
RESTRICTION ON TRANSFER

2.1 *Restriction*. Each Stockholder agrees that for so long as this Agreement shall continue in full force and effect, he shall not transfer, sell, convey, assign, encumber or otherwise dispose of all or any portion of his Stock without the prior written consent of the other Stockholder, except where the transfer is expressly required by this Agreement.

2.2 *Endorsement*. Upon the execution of this Agreement, each Stockholder's certificates of Stock shall be surrendered to the Corporation and endorsed as follows:

This certificate is transferable only upon compliance with the provisions of an Agreement dated 1986, among John Doe and Richard Roe and the Corporation, a copy of which is on file in the offices of the Corporation.

After endorsement, the certificates shall be returned to each Stockholder, who shall, subject to the terms of this Agreement, be entitled to exercise all rights of ownership of the Stock. All stock issued to the Stockholders following the date of this Agreement shall be subject to this Agreement and shall bear the same endorsement.

ARTICLE III

REDEMPTION AND SALE

3.1 *Redemption*. Each Stockholder is currently employed by the Corporation. Upon the termination of his employment for any reason whatsoever (including, without limitation, his death or Disability), the Stockholder (or his legal representative) shall offer for sale to the Corporation all of the Stock then owned by him. This offer shall be made within sixty (60) days from the Termination Date or, if later, sixty (60) days from the date of the appointment of his legal representative in the event of death or, if necessary, the appointment of his legal representative in the event of his Disability.

3.2 *Death or Disability*. If a Stockholder's employment terminates by reason of his death or Disability, the Corporation shall accept the offer to purchase all of the Stockholder's Stock within sixty (60) days of the Offer Date, except as otherwise authorized by this Agreement.

3.3 *Other Termination*. If a Stockholder's employment terminates for any reason other than death or Disability, the Corporation shall have the option to accept the offer to purchase all and not less than all of the Stockholder's Stock within sixty (60) days of the Offer Date, except as otherwise authorized by this Agreement.

3.4 *Purchase Price.* The purchase price ("Purchase Price") for each share of Stock shall be the higher of:

(a) the price fixed by the latest certificate in writing signed by the Stockholders and the Corporation, annexed as Exhibit A; or

(b) the price determined under the formula specified in Exhibit B.

3.5 *Payment.* At its option, the Corporation shall pay the total Purchase Price:

(a) in cash in one lump sum; or

(b) if the Corporation shall be entitled to receive the proceeds of life insurance on the life of the decedent Stockholder by virtue of his death at that time, then:

(i) cash up to the proceeds of the life insurance received by the Corporation less the smaller of (x) Fifty Thousand Dollars ($50,000) or (y) the amount of the life insurance proceeds; and

(ii) the balance of the Purchase Price shall be paid by the Corporation by executing and delivering its promissory note for that balance substantially in the form of the Note annexed as Exhibit C; or

(c) if the Corporation shall not be entitled to receive the proceeds of life insurance on the life of the decedent Stockholder by virtue of his death at that time, then:

(i) cash in the sum of Ten Thousand Dollars ($10,000); and

(ii) the balance of the Purchase Price shall be paid by the Corporation by executing and delivering its promissory note for that balance substantially in the form of the Note annexed as Exhibit C.

3.6 *Insufficient Surplus.* If at the time the Corporation is required to make payment of the total Purchase Price, its surplus is insufficient for that purpose, then (a) the entire available surplus shall be used to purchase part of the Stockholder's Stock, and (b) the Corporation and the remaining Stockholder shall promptly take all required action to reduce the capital of the Corporation or to take such other steps as may be appropriate or necessary in order to enable the Corporation to purchase the Stock, including, but not limited to, an up-to-date appraisal of the assets of the Corporation. If the Corporation shall, nevertheless, be unable or unwilling to accept the offer to purchase all of the Stock, then the selling Stockholder (or his legal representative) shall offer and the other Stockholder shall have the option, within thirty (30) days of that offer date, to accept the offer to purchase all, but not less than all, of the unpurchased and unredeemed Stock, at the same price per share and upon the same terms and conditions available to the Corporation under this Agreement.

If the Stock shall not be purchased by the Corporation or the other Stockholder, the selling Stockholder may offer for sale the Stock to anyone ("Offeree"), provided, however:

(a) the Stock shall be offered at a price not less than or upon terms more favorable to the Offeree than those upon which it was offered to the Corporation and the other Stockholder. If so, the selling Stockholder shall offer the Stock for sale to the Corporation at the more favorable terms. The Corporation shall have ten (10) days to accept that offer. If the Corporation is unable or unwilling to accept that offer, the selling Stockholder shall offer the Stock for sale to the other Stockholder at the more favorable terms. The other Stockholder shall have ten (10) days to accept that offer; and

(b) the Stock shall be transferred to the Offeree not later than one hundred twenty (120) days from the last offer to the other Stockholder.

3.7 *Closing*. At the closing:

(a) the selling Stockholder (or his legal representative) shall deliver the certificates representing the shares owned by him or his legal representative, duly endorsed, to the purchaser. All shares of Stock acquired by any Stockholder shall be subject to the terms and conditions of this Agreement; and

(b) the purchaser shall execute and deliver the cash and promissory note provided for under this Agreement.

ARTICLE IV

TERMINATION

4.1 *Events of Termination*. This Agreement shall terminate upon the occurrence of any of the following events:

(a) The bankruptcy, receivership or dissolution of the Corporation;

(b) The written agreement of all of the parties to this Agreement;

(c) The death of the Stockholders simultaneously or within a period of thirty (30) days;

(d) The termination of employment of the Stockholders within a period of thirty (30) days;

(e) The transfer of Stock by a Stockholder to any person other than a party (or his legal representative) to this Agreement, under the terms of paragraph 3.6 of this Agreement;

(f) Whenever either Stockholder ceases to be a party to this Agreement;

(g) The date three (3) years from the date of this Agreement.

ARTICLE V

MISCELLANEOUS

5.1 *Entire Agreement*. This Agreement sets forth the entire agreement of the parties and supersedes all prior agreements, arrangements, communications, representations and warranties, either oral or written, by any officer, employee or representative of any party.

5.2 *Notice*. Any notice, request, instruction or document to be given by either party to the other shall be in writing and delivered personally or mailed, first class registered or certified mail, postage prepaid, as follows:

If to the Corporation, addressed to:

If to John Doe, addressed to:

If to Richard Roe, addressed to:

Any party shall have the right to give notice to the other parties changing the address stated above. The notice shall be effective on the date personally delivered or mailed.

5.3 *Benefit*. This Agreement shall be binding upon and inure to the benefit of the parties and their respective successors and assigns, provided that any permitted assignment of either party's obligations or liabilities shall not relieve that party of any of its liabilities or obligations under this Agreement.

5.4 *Insurance*. If an insured Stockholder disposes of all of this Stock under this Agreement (other than by reason of his death) or this Agreement terminates (other than by reason of his death), the insured Stockholder shall have the right to purchase from the Corporation the policies of life insurance owned by the Corporation on his life at a price equal to the cash surrender value plus the unearned premiums determined as of the date of transfer of those policies. The insured Stockholders must exercise this right and pay the purchase price for the insurance policies within thirty (30) days from the earlier of the date he disposes of his Stock or this Agreement terminates. The Corporation will deliver the insurance policies and execute all necessary instruments of transfer upon receipt of the purchase price.

5.5 *Titles*. The titles of Articles and Sections in this Agreement are for convenience of reference and shall not be deemed to modify or affect the interpretation of this Agreement.

5.6 *Modification*. Neither this Agreement nor any of its provisions shall be modified, changed, discharged, or terminated except by an instrument in writing signed by the party against whom the enforcement of any modification, change, discharge or termination is sought.

5.7 *Additional Actions*. In connection with the transactions contemplated by this Agreement, the parties agree to execute any additional documents and papers and to perform and do any additional acts and things as may be reasonably necessary and proper to effectuate and carry out the transactions contemplated by this Agreement.

5.8 *Waiver*. No delay or omission on the part of any party in exercising any right shall operate as a waiver of that right or any other right. A waiver on any one occasion shall not be construed as a bar to or waiver of any right on any future occasion.

5.9 *Law*. This Agreement shall be governed by, construed and interpreted according to the laws of the State of New York.

5.10 *Arbitration*. Any controversy or claim arising out of or relating to this Agreement shall be settled by arbitration in accordance with the rules, then pertaining, of the American Arbitration Association, and judgment upon the award rendered may be entered in any court having jurisdiction thereof.

5.11 *Counterparts*. This Agreement may be executed in several counterparts, each of which shall be determined to be an original, and such counterparts shall, together, constitute and be one and the same instrument.

5.12 *Prior Agreements*. This Agreement supersedes all prior agreements among the parties with respect to the redemption and purchase of the Stock of the Corporation.

IN WITNESS OF THE FOREGOING, the parties have executed this Agreement as of the day and year specified.

_____, INC. _____
                                                 JOHN DOE

By:_____ _____
                                                 RICHARD ROE

EXHIBIT A

CERTIFICATE OF PURCHASE PRICE

The Stockholders and Corporation agree that the Purchase Price per share of the Stock owned by each Stockholder for purposes of paragraph 3.4 of the Agreement shall be $_____$.

Dated:

_____, INC.

By:_____

_____
JOHN DOE

_____
RICHARD ROE

EXHIBIT B

FORMULA FOR PURCHASE PRICE

The price per share of the Stock shall be computed under the terms of the following formula:

Dated:

_____, INC.

By:_____

_____
JOHN DOE

_____
RICHARD ROE

FORM FORTY

CERTIFICATE OF AMENDMENT OF THE CERTIFICATE OF INCORPORATION OF [CORPORATION]

Under Section 805(a) of the Business Corporation Law

The undersigned, being a duly elected officer of ____, does hereby certify that:

FIRST: The name of the Corporation is _____.

SECOND: The Certificate of Incorporation was filed by the Department of State of the State of New York on ____, 19____.

THIRD: Article ____ of said Certificate of Incorporation is hereby amended to read as follows: [insert full text of provision being amended].

FOURTH: The amendment to the Certificate of Incorporation set forth herein was authorized by unanimous written consent of the Board of Directors followed by the affirmative vote of the holders of a majority of all outstanding shares entitled to vote thereon.

IN WITNESS WHEREOF, this Certificate of Amendment has been subscribed to this ____ day of ____, 19____, by the undersigned, who affirms that the statements made herein are true, under the penalties of perjury.

_____
[Officer]

FORM FORTY-ONE

CERTIFICATE OF CHANGE OF
_____*

Under Section 805-A of the Business Corporation Law

The undersigned, desiring to change the Certificate of Incorporation of ____, for the purpose of changing the _____, do hereby certify that:

FIRST: The name of the corporation is _____, and the corporation was formed under [said name] [under the name _____].

SECOND: The Certificate of Incorporation was filed with the Department of State of the State of New York on _____.

THIRD: The Certificate of Incorporation is changed to change the _____.

FOURTH: The change of the Certificate of Incorporation was authorized by unanimous written consent of the Board of Directors.

IN WITNESS WHEREOF, this Certificate has been subscribed to this ____ day of ____, 19____, by the undersigned, who affirm that the statements made herein are true, under the penalties of perjury.

_____, President

_____, Secretary

---

* Source: NYSBA seminar, "Drafting Corporate Documents for the Close Corporation," November 14, 1986, Albany.

FORM FORTY-TWO

MATERIALS TO DISSOLVE AND LIQUIDATE THE CLOSELY HELD NEW YORK CORPORATION*

A. Resolutions Adopted on Unanimous Written Consent of Shareholders

B. Certificate of Dissolution of the Corporation

C. Notice to Creditors and Claimants

D. Internal Revenue Service Form 966—Corporate Dissolution or Liquidation

E. Information and Instruction for Termination of Business Corporations (New York State Department of Taxation and Finance, Publication 110)

F. Sample Petition for Judicial Dissolution Under BCL § 1104-a

---

* SOURCE: *Fall 1991 Practical Skills: Forming and Advising Businesses* (NYSBA), "Dissolution and Liquidation Documents," Anthony D. Mancinelli, Esq. and Daniel J. Scully, Esq., Magavern & Magavern. (Note: Sections A through E are new.)

A. RESOLUTIONS ADOPTED ON UNANIMOUS WRITTEN CONSENT OF SHAREHOLDERS OF _____
Adopted: _____, 199__

The undersigned, being the holders of all outstanding shares entitled to vote of ____, do hereby adopt the following resolutions and consent to the action to be taken thereby upon written unanimous consent without a meeting pursuant to Section 615(b) of the New York Business Corporation Law and the By-laws of this Corporation.

1. *Voluntary Dissolution of the Corporation.* Approval of filing for the Corporation's dissolution by adoption of the following resolution:

> *RESOLVED*, that the shareholders have assessed the present financial condition of the Corporation, upon the recommendation of the Board of Directors, and it is deemed that it is in the best interests of the Shareholders of this Corporation that its business be terminated, that the Corporation be dissolved, and that the assets be distributed pursuant to Article 10 of the New York Business Corporation Law,* and it is

> *RESOLVED*, that the President and Secretary are hereby authorized to execute and deliver the proper Certificate of Dissolution to the Department of State, and to obtain the necessary consent for such dissolution from the New York State Tax Commission, and it is

---

* *Treatment to Shareholders of a C Corporation*: Section 331(a) treats a shareholder as having exchanged stock for the amount received in liquidation. This exchange treatment normally provides capital gains treatment on the difference between the amount realized and the shareholder's adjusted basis in stock, § 1001. The shareholders' basis in the assets distributed is generally fair market value, § 334(a).

RESOLVED, that the officers are authorized to take any and all other steps prescribed by law to complete the dissolution and wind up the affairs of the corporation in a proper manner.**

_____
Shareholder

_____
Shareholder

_____
Shareholder

** *Treatment to the C Corporation*: Prior to the enactment of the Tax Reform Act of 1986, *old* § 336 codified the general utilities doctrine (i.e., that a distributing corporation was nontaxable on a distribution of appreciated property). Under current § 336(a), a liquidating corporation generally will be taxed on a distribution of property as if the property had been sold to shareholders at fair market value. In addition, § 336(a) recognizes losses, but under § 336(d)(1), a liquidating corporation cannot recognize a loss or a distribution to a "related person" if the distributed property is "disqualified property" or is not pro rata. A "related person" is defined by § 267.

B. CERTIFICATE OF DISSOLUTION OF THE CORPORATION (UNDER SECTION 1003 OF THE NEW YORK BUSINESS CORPORATION LAW)

The undersigned, _____ and _____, being [the holders of all outstanding shares entitled to vote on dissolution of the corporation,] [respectively, the president and the secretary of _____,] or [the subscribers for shares or the incorporators (if no shares were issued),] do hereby certify and set forth:

1. The name of the Corporation is _____. The name under which the Corporation was formed is _____.

2. The Certificate of Incorporation of this Corporation was filed by the Department of State of the State of New York on the ___ day of ___, 19___.

3. The names and addresses of each of this Corporation's officers and directors are:

Officers

Name	Office	Address

Directors

Name	Address

4. This Corporation hereby elects to terminate business operations, dissolve and distribute assets.

5. This Corporation's dissolution was authorized by

(a) written consent of the shareholders, BCL § 615(b);

(b) at a meeting of shareholders and with such voting quorum as specified in the Certificate of Incorporation, BCL § 616;

(c) voting as a class as provided in the Certificate of Incorporation and on share certificates, BCL § 617;

(d) two-thirds (2/3) vote of all outstanding shares entitled to vote at a meeting of the shareholders, BCL § 1001;

(e) upon such event or at the will of any shareholder as specified in the Certificate of Incorporation and on share certificates, BCL § 1002;

(f) the written consent of a majority in interest of subscribers for shares whose subscriptions have been accepted or their successors in interest, or the incorporators, or a majority of incorporators (if no subscriptions were accepted), BCL § 615(c).

IN WITNESS WHEREOF, we have signed this Certificate of Dissolution on the ____ day of ____, 19____, and hereby affirm the statements contained herein are true, under the penalties of perjury.

_____

_____

_____

C. NOTICE TO CREDITORS AND CLAIMANTS OF

_____

Pursuant to BCL § 1007, notice is hereby given to all creditors and claimants of ____, which was dissolved by the New York Department of State on ____, 1990, to present their claims against the corporation in writing and in detail to the office of the Corporation at ____, City of ____, New York 14220, on or before [not less than six months after first publication of such notice] ____, 19____. A failure to file by the creditors and claimants will forever bar such claims against the property, directors or shareholders of the Corporation.*

Dated: _____, 19____.

_____
                              Corporation

---

* BCL § 1007 requires notice be given to all creditors and claimants of the Corporation's dissolution. This notice must be published in a newspaper of general circulation at least once a week for two successive weeks in the county in which the office of the Corporation was located as of the date of dissolution. On or before such publication, a copy of this notice must be mailed to all known creditors, or creditors able to be known through due diligence, at their last known address. Such notice is not a recognition of any claim or a waiver of defenses or counterclaims against such claimant.

D. INTERNAL REVENUE SERVICE FORM 966

Form 966
(Rev. April 1990)
Department of the Treasury
Internal Revenue Service

Corporate Dissolution or Liquidation
(Required under Section 6043(a) of the Internal Revenue Code)

OMB No. 1545-0041
Expires 4-30-93

Please type or print

Name of corporation	Employer identification number
Number and street (or P.O. box number if mail is not delivered to street address)	Check type of return ☐ 1120 ☐ 1120L ☐ 1120-IC-DISC ☐ 1120S ☐ Other ▶
City or town, state, and ZIP code	

1 Date incorporated	2 Place incorporated	3 Type of liquidation ☐ Complete ☐ Partial
4 Internal Revenue Service Center where last income tax return was filed and tax year covered	Service Center	Tax year ending Month Year

5 Date of adoption of resolution or plan of dissolution, or complete or partial liquidation

6 Tax year of final return . . . .
Was final return filed with a parent corporation (consolidated return)? . . ☐ Yes ☐ No
If "Yes," enter:
Name of parent corporation ▶ ....
Employer identification number ▶ ....
IRS Center where consolidated return was filed ▶

	Common	Preferred
7 Total number of shares outstanding at time of adoption of plan or liquidation		

8 Dates of any amendments to plan of dissolution . . . .

9 Section of the Code under which the corporation is to be dissolved or liquidated . . . .

10 If this return concerns an amendment or supplement to a resolution or plan for which a return was filed, give the date filed . . . .

Attach a certified copy of the resolution or plan, together with all amendments or supplements not previously filed.

Under penalties of perjury, I declare that I have examined this return, including accompanying schedules and statements, and to the best of my knowledge and belief it is true, correct, and complete.

▶ Signature of officer _____ Title _____ Date _____

Instructions

Paperwork Reduction Act Notice.—We ask for this information to carry out the Internal Revenue laws of the United States. We need it to ensure that taxpayers are complying with these laws and to allow us to figure and collect the right amount of tax. You are required to give us this information.

The time needed to complete and file this form will vary depending on individual circumstances. The estimated average time is:

Recordkeeping . . . . 5 hrs., 1 min.
Learning about the law or the form . . . . 6 min.
Preparing and sending the form to IRS . . . . . 11 min.

If you have comments concerning the accuracy of these time estimates or suggestions for making the form more simple, we would be happy to hear from you. You can write to both the Internal Revenue Service, Washington, DC 20224, Attention: IRS Reports Clearance Officer, T:FP; and the Office of Management and Budget, Paperwork Reduction Project (1545-0041), Washington, DC 20503.

Who Must File.—A corporation files Form 966 if it is to be dissolved or if any of its stock is to be liquidated. Exempt organizations are not required to file Form 966. These organizations should see the instructions for Form 990 or 990-PF

When To File.—File Form 966 within 30 days after the resolution or plan is adopted to dissolve the corporation or liquidate any of its stock. If the resolution or plan is amended or supplemented after Form 966 is filed, file an additional Form 966 within 30 days after the amendment or supplement is adopted. The additional form will be sufficient if you show the date the earlier form was filed and attach a certified copy of the amendment or supplement and all other information required by Form 966 and not given in the earlier form.

Where To File.—File Form 966 with the Internal Revenue Service Center where the corporation is required to file its income tax return.

Distribution of Property.—A corporation must recognize gain or loss on the distribution of its assets in the complete liquidation of its stock. For purposes of determining gain or loss, the distributed assets are valued at fair market value. Exceptions to this rule apply to liquidation of a subsidiary and to a distribution that is made pursuant to a plan of reorganization.

Signature.—The return must be signed and dated by the president, vice president, treasurer, assistant treasurer, chief accounting officer, or any other corporate officer (such as tax officer) authorized to sign. A receiver, trustee, or assignee must sign and date any return required to be filed on behalf of a corporation.

Form **966** (Rev. 4-90)

E. INFORMATION AND INSTRUCTION FOR TERMINATION AND INSTRUCTIONS FOR TERMINATION OF BUSINESS CORPORATIONS (NEW YORK STATE DEPARTMENT OF TAXATION AND FINANCE, PUBLICATION 110)*

TABLE OF CONTENTS

Part I

Voluntary Dissolution—New York Corporation	929
Certificate of Dissolution	929
Filing Fee	930
Franchise Tax Reports and Taxes	930
Consent of the Tax Commissioner	932
Summary	932

Part II

Surrender of Authority—Foreign Corporation	933
Certificate of Surrender	933
Filing Fee	934
Statement Indicating the Date Taxable New York Business Activities Ceased	934
Franchise Tax Reports and Maintenance Fees	935
Consent of the Tax Commissioner to the Surrender of Authority	935
Summary	936

---

* Has not been updated since February 1987 for any legislative revisions.

FORMS AND MATERIALS

Part III

Mergers and Consolidations. 937
    Certificate of Merger or Consolidation 938
    Filing Fee 939
    Franchise Tax Reports 939
    Consent of the Tax Commissioner to Merger or
        Consolidation 939
    Summary 940

Part IV

Disposition of Assets—New York Corporation 941
    Certificate of Incorporation (New Domestic
        Corporation) 942
    Filing Fee 942
    Franchise Tax Reports 942
    Consent of the Tax Commissioner 942
    Summary 943

Part V

Termination of Existence—Foreign Corporations 943
    Certificate of Termination. 944
    Filing Fee 944

Part VI

Liquidation Under Internal Revenue Code. 945

Part VII

Dissolution by Proclamation for Delinquent Taxes 945

Part VIII

Annulment of Authority by Proclamation for
    Delinquent Taxes and/or Fees. 946

Part IX

Sales Tax Consequences of Changes in
    Corporate Structure 947
    Bulk Sales Transactions 947

* * * * * *

The terms "New York corporation" and "domestic corporation" have been used interchangeably in this publication.

"Domestic corporation" means a corporation incorporated under the laws of New York State.

"Foreign corporation" means a corporation incorporated under the laws of another state, territory or country.

PART I
VOLUNTARY DISSOLUTION—NEW YORK CORPORATION

A New York business corporation (domestic corporation) that no longer wants to exercise its franchise can be dissolved by the Secretary of State, with the consent of the State Tax Commissioner.

The next few pages describe in detail the requirements and forms necessary for the voluntary dissolution of a New York business corporation.

Forms and fees required:

1. Certificate of Dissolution*
2. Filing fee of $20
3. Franchise report(s) and tax(es)
4. Consent of the Tax Commissioner

A. Certificate of Dissolution

The corporation must prepare a "Certificate of dissolution of [name of corporation] under Section 1003 of the Business Corporation Law." It must be signed and verified.

This form must contain

1. the present name of the corporation. If the corporation has changed its name, also include the name as shown on the original Certificate of Incorporation. The name must be exact, including uppercase and lowercase letters, punctuation, abbreviations, etc.;
2. the exact date the corporation's Certificate of Incorporation was filed by the Department of State;
3. the name and address of each of the corporation's officers and directors;

---

* Printed Certificate of Dissolution forms may be obtained from legal form suppliers. However, it is not necessary to use a printed form.

4. a statement that the corporation elects to dissolve;

5. an explanation of the manner in which the dissolution was authorized; and

6. the signature of the president and secretary or one of the alternatives prescribed by Section 104(d) of the Business Corporation Law.

The Certificate of Dissolution *WILL NOT BE ACCEPTED* by the Department of State unless it is accurate and complete. The most common errors made in the Certificate of Dissolution are incorrect name, incorrect date of incorporation and improper signatures.

B. Filing Fee

A certified check, cashier's check, attorney's check or money order in the amount of $20 (twenty dollars), made payable to the Department of State, must accompany the Certificate of Dissolution.

C. Franchise Tax Reports and Taxes

A New York business corporation is required to file franchise tax reports and pay all franchise taxes for each fiscal or calendar period (or part of a fiscal or calendar period) of the corporation's existence.

The Tax Commissioner will not give its consent to the termination of a corporation until all reports are filed and all taxes paid.

A New York corporation is required to pay a tax for the privilege of having a charter, even though no business is conducted. The most frequent filing omissions are the initial report, beginning with the exact date of incorporation, and the cessation report, covering the period from the last report filed to the dissolution date. The cessation report may not cover more than 12 calendar months.

FORMS AND MATERIALS

EXAMPLE

A corporation is incorporated by the Secretary of State on December 30, 1982, and files its franchise tax reports based upon a calendar year. It has requested to be dissolved as of July 31, 1985.

	Period Ended	Report Due
1st period (initial report)	12/31/82	3/15/83
2nd period	12/31/83	3/15/84
3rd period	12/31/84	3/15/85
4th period (cessation report)	7/31/85	7/31/85

If final figures for the last period are not available, an estimated report may be filed. All taxes due, including the amount of the estimated tax for the last period, must be paid. When an estimated report is filed, the "final" report must be filed within 30 days after the Certificate of Dissolution is filed by the Secretary of State. A reasonable extension of time for filing the final report may be granted.

A record indicating whether any delinquent reports or taxes are due may be obtained by writing the Dissolution Unit (see address and phone number listed below).

To avoid any delay in processing the Certificate of Dissolution, send the cessation report, any delinquent reports due and a check for the tax, interest and additional charges to the Dissolution Unit with the Certificate of Dissolution. *DO NOT SEND THESE REPORTS SEPARATELY TO THE TAX DEPARTMENT.*

Forms and checks listed in paragraphs 1, 2 and 3 should be mailed to:

> Dissolution Unit
> Corporation Tax
> State Campus
> Albany, NY 12227

> Telephone: (518) 457-3777

D. Consent of the Tax Commissioner

The Tax Commissioner must consent to the dissolution of a New York business corporation.

The New York State Tax Department must receive the Certificate of Dissolution prepared by the corporation before the last day of the corporation's final period. In addition, the corporation must have filed franchise tax reports and paid all franchise taxes for each fiscal or calendar period (or any part of a fiscal or calendar period) of the corporation's existence, including the final or cessation period. The Tax Commissioner *will not* give consent to a corporation owing reports or taxes.

The consent will be supplied by the Corporation Tax Dissolution Unit within 60 days of the last day of the corporation's final fiscal year.

Delay caused by the failure of the corporation to provide the proper forms, fees, reports or tax payments described in the preceding paragraphs may prevent the Tax Commissioner from issuing the consent to the dissolution within this 60-day period. If this occurs, the corporation will be required to file a tax report and pay the franchise tax due for the additional period the corporation remains in existence.

The Dissolution Unit will forward to the Secretary of State the Certificate of Dissolution, the $20 filing fee and the Tax Commissioner's consent to the dissolution.

The legal date of dissolution is the actual date the Secretary of State files the Certificate of Dissolution.

E. Summary

1. Mail all forms and checks listed in items a through c below to:

     Dissolution Unit
     Corporation Tax
     State Campus
     Albany, NY 12227

    a. A Certificate of Dissolution prepared by the corporation, which must be filed prior to the last day of the corporation's final period.

FORMS AND MATERIALS

    b. A filing fee of $20 made payable to the Department of State.

    c. A cessation report with payment for tax due and any delinquent franchise tax reports and payment for taxes, penalty and interest that may be due.

2. Upon receipt of the Certificate of Dissolution, all franchise tax reports due and all payments due, the Dissolution Unit will provide the Tax Commissioner's consent to the dissolution.

3. The Certificate of Dissolution, filing fee and the Tax Commissioner's consent will be forwarded to the Department of State.

4. The Secretary of State will review the forms forwarded by the Tax Department and if the documents are acceptable to the Department of State, the Certificate of Dissolution will be filed and a filing receipt mailed to the filer of the certificate.

PART II
SURRENDER OF AUTHORITY—FOREIGN CORPORATION
(Business Corporation Law—Section 1310)

A foreign corporation which no longer conducts business activities in New York and no longer requires authority to do business in New York may surrender authority to do business in this state.

Forms and fees required:

1. Certificate of Surrender of Authority
2. Filing fee of $60
3. A statement indicating the date the corporation's taxable business activities ceased in New York
4. Franchise tax report(s) and maintenance fee
5. Consent of the Tax Commissioner

A. Certificate of Surrender

The corporation must prepare a "Certificate of Surrender of Authority of [name of corporation] under Section 1310 of the Business Corporation Law." It must be signed and verified by an officer of or attorney-in-fact for the foreign corporation or by a trustee, receiver or other liquidator of the corporation.

This form must contain

1. the corporate title as it appears in the records of the Department of State. The name must be exact, including uppercase and lowercase letters, punctuation, abbreviations, etc.;
2. the jurisdiction of its incorporation;
3. the exact date the corporation was authorized to do business in this state;
4. a statement that the corporation surrenders its authority to do business in this state;
5. a statement revoking the authority of a registered agent if the corporation has one;
6. the Consent of the Corporation so that process against it in any action or special proceeding based upon any liability or obligation incurred by it within this state before the filing of the Certificate of Surrender may be served on the Secretary of State after it is filed as stated in paragraph (b) of Section 306 (Service of Process); and
7. the post office address to which the Secretary of State can mail a copy of any process against the corporation served upon the Secretary of State.

B. Filing Fee

A certified check, cashier's check, attorney's check or money order in the amount of $60 (sixty dollars), made payable to the Department of State, must accompany the Certificate of Surrender of Authority.

C. Statement Indicating the Date Taxable New York Business Activities Ceased

A statement must be submitted to the Tax Department indicating the date on which all taxable New York business activities ceased.

FORMS AND MATERIALS

D. Franchise Tax Reports and Maintenance Fees

The Tax Commissioner will not consent to the Surrender of Authority until all maintenance fees and franchise taxes are paid and reports are filed.

Every corporation organized outside New York and authorized to do business in New York State must pay an annual maintenance fee. The fee may be claimed as a credit against a franchise tax due under Article 9 and 9-A (Tax Law Article 9, Section 181.2).

In addition to the fee, every corporation doing business in New York is required to file franchise tax reports for each fiscal or calendar period (or part of a fiscal or calendar period) that the corporation is active in New York State. When final figures for the last franchise tax report are not available, an estimated report may be filed. All taxes due, including the amount estimated for the final period, must be paid.

If an estimated report is filed, the final report must be filed within a reasonable time after the Surrender of Authority is filed by the Secretary of State.

A record indicating whether any delinquent reports, franchise taxes, or maintenance fees are due may be obtained upon request from the Dissolution Unit.

To avoid any delay in processing the Certificate of Surrender, send any delinquent report due and the cessation report, along with checks for fees and/or franchise taxes, interest and additional charges to the Dissolution Unit with the Certificate of Surrender of Authority. *DO NOT SEND THESE REPORTS SEPARATELY TO THE TAX DEPARTMENT.*

E. Consent of the Tax Commissioner to the Surrender of Authority

The Tax Commissioner must consent to the Surrender of Authority of an authorized foreign corporation.

To obtain the Tax Commissioner's consent, the Certificate of Surrender of Authority prepared by the corporation must be received by the Tax Department *PRIOR* to the last day of the corporation's final period.

In addition, the corporation must have filed franchise tax reports and paid franchise taxes and maintenance fees for each fiscal or calendar period, or any part of a fiscal or calendar period, that the corporation is authorized to do business, including the final period. The Tax Commissioner's consent *WILL NOT BE GRANTED* to a corporation owing reports, taxes or fees.

A delay caused by the failure of the corporation to provide the proper forms, fees, reports or tax payments described in the preceding paragraphs may prevent the Tax Commissioner from issuing the consent to the Surrender of Authority promptly. If this happens, the corporation will be required to file reports and fees for the additional period the corporation remains authorized.

The Dissolution Unit will forward to the Secretary of State the Certificate of Surrender of Authority, the $60 filing fee and the Tax Commissioner's consent to the Surrender of Authority.

The legal date of the surrender is the actual date the Secretary of State files the Surrender of Authority.

F. Summary

1. Mail all forms and checks listed in items a through d below to:

    Dissolution Unit
    Corporation Tax
    State Campus
    Albany, NY 12227

    a. Certificate of Surrender of Authority prepared by the corporation (must be filed with the Tax Department prior to the last day of the corporation's final period).

    b. Filing fee of $60 made payable to the Department of State.

    c. Statement to the Tax Department indicating the date the corporation ceased all taxable business activities in New York State.

    d. Cessation report plus tax or fee due and any delinquent franchise tax reports and/or taxes and fees, additional charges and interest that may be due.

FORMS AND MATERIALS

2. Upon receipt of the certificate and any reports, fees and taxes that may be due, the Dissolution Unit will provide the Tax Commissioner's consent to the Surrender of Authority.

3. The Certificate of Surrender of Authority, the Department of State's filing fee and the Tax Commissioner's consent will be forwarded to the Department of State by the Dissolution Unit.

4. The documents will be reviewed by the Secretary of State and if the forms are acceptable to the Department of State, the Certificate of Surrender of Authority will be filed.

PART III
MERGERS AND CONSOLIDATIONS
(Business Corporation Law—Sections 904, 905 and 907)

Sections 904 and 905 provide for the merger or consolidation of domestic corporations and the merger of any domestic corporation owning at least 95 percent of another domestic corporation.

Domestic corporations merging or consolidating under these sections should file a Certificate of Merger with the Department of State. The Secretary of State will notify the Tax Department of all completed mergers and consolidations.

Section 907(c) and (d) provides for the merger or consolidation of a domestic and a foreign corporation in which the domestic corporation is the survivor. This section permits the merger or consolidation to be processed in the same manner as the joining of two domestic corporations. The Certificate of Merger should be sent to the Department of State.

The consent of the Tax Commissioner is not required in these mergers and consolidations. However, merged or consolidated domestic and foreign corporations that are subject to franchise taxes must file franchise tax reports and pay taxes to the date of merger or consolidation.

Section 907(e) provides for the merger or consolidation of a domestic and a foreign corporation in which the survivor is the foreign corporation. The Tax Commissioner must give its consent to the merger or consolidation.

Forms and fees required:

1. Certificate of Merger or Consolidation
2. Filing fee of $60
3. Franchise tax reports
4. Letter of guarantee from the surviving corporation if estimated tax report is filed
5. Consent of the Tax Commissioner, where required

A. Certificate of Merger or Consolidation

The certificate must be prepared by the corporation in accordance with Section 907 of the Business Corporation Law.

This form must contain

1. the title of the certificate, which should appear as follows: Certificate of Merger (or Consolidation) of [name of merged corporation] into [name of surviving corporation] under Section 907 of the Business Corporation Law;
2. the plan of merger or consolidation, including the names of each constituent corporation, and, if changed, the name under which it was formed and the name of the surviving corporation;
3. the designation and number of outstanding shares of each constituent corporation;
4. the effective date of the merger or consolidation if other than the date of filing of the certificate by the Department of State; and

FORMS AND MATERIALS

5. the manner in which the merger or consolidation was authorized with respect to each constituent domestic corporation and that the merger is permitted by the laws of the jurisdiction of each constituent foreign corporation.

More detailed information about the required contents of the Certificate of Merger or Consolidation may be obtained from the Secretary of State.

B. Filing Fee

A certified check, cashier's check, attorney's check or money order in the amount of $60 (sixty dollars), made payable to the Department of State, must accompany the Certificate of Merger or Consolidation.

C. Franchise Tax Reports

The Tax Commissioner will not give its consent to the merger or consolidation until all tax reports are filed and all taxes are paid for each corporation. A domestic corporation is required to file franchise tax reports and pay all franchise taxes for each fiscal or calendar period (or part of a fiscal or calendar period) of a corporation's existence.

Every corporation doing business in New York is required to file franchise tax reports for each fiscal or calendar period (or part of a fiscal or calendar period) that the corporation is active in New York State.

For additional details refer to Part I, Voluntary Dissolution, item C, and Part II, Surrender of Authority, item D.

To avoid any delays in processing the Certificate of Merger or Consolidation, send any delinquent reports due, the cessation report and checks for tax, fees, interest and additional charges to the Dissolution Unit, together with the $60 filing fee and Certificate of Merger or Consolidation.

D. Consent of the Tax Commissioner to Merger or Consolidation

The consent of the Tax Commissioner to the merger or consolidation will be supplied by the Dissolution Unit. To qualify for the consent of the Tax Commissioner, domestic corporations and foreign corporations which have been subject to tax in New York are required to file franchise tax reports and pay all franchise taxes for each fiscal or calendar period (or part of a fiscal or calendar period) from the date of incorporation or date the foreign corporation became taxable to the date of the merger or consolidation. In addition, the foreign corporations must file and pay any maintenance fees due.

A delay caused by the failure of the corporation to provide the proper forms, fees, reports and tax payments described in the preceding paragraphs may prevent the Tax Commissioner from issuing its consent to the merger or consolidation. Should this happen, the domestic corporation will be required to file a tax report and pay the franchise tax due for the additional period the corporation remains in existence.

The foreign corporation that is the survivor of a Section 907 merger or consolidation is responsible for all franchise tax reports due after the merger or consolidation. The Tax Department recommends the surviving corporation be authorized by the Secretary of State. In the event the surviving corporation does not intend to function in New York State, the Tax Department requires

1. a statement that the corporation does not maintain a business office, have officers or employees, have property or conduct any business in New York and is thereby exempt from filing an annual franchise tax report and from paying an annual franchise tax;

    OR

2. Corporation Tax Form CT-245, *Activities Report of Foreign Corporations Disclaiming Tax Liability.*

E. Summary

1. Mail all forms and checks listed in items a through c below to:

    Dissolution Unit
    Corporation Tax
    State Campus
    Albany, NY 12227

FORMS AND MATERIALS

    a. Certificate of Merger or Consolidation prepared by corporation.

    b. Filing fee of $60 made payable to the Department of State. Cashier's check, money order or attorney's check will be accepted in lieu of a certified check.

    c. Franchise tax reports, any taxes, additional charges and interest that may be due.

2. Upon receipt by the Dissolution Unit of the certificate and franchise tax reports that may be due, the Dissolution Unit will provide the Tax Commissioner's consent to the merger or consolidation.

3. The Certificate of Merger or Consolidation, filing fee and the Tax Commissioner's consent will be forwarded by the Dissolution Unit to the Department of State.

4. The documents will be reviewed by the Secretary of State and if the forms are acceptable to the Department of State, the merger or consolidation will be filed.

PART IV
DISPOSITION OF ASSETS—NEW YORK CORPORATION
(Business Corporation Law—Section 909(d))

A transaction by a domestic corporation involving a sale, lease, exchange or other disposition of all or substantially all assets of the corporation (including its name) to a new corporation must be authorized by the Secretary of State and requires the consent of the Tax Commissioner. Thirty (30) days after filing the Certificate of Incorporation of the new corporation, the existing corporation will be automatically dissolved unless it has changed its name before the end of that 30-day period. The adjustment and the conclusion of the affairs of such a dissolved corporation shall proceed in accordance with the provisions of Article 10 of the Business Corporation Law (nonjudicial dissolution).

Forms and fees required:

    1. Certificate of Incorporation (new domestic corporation)

2. Filing fee of $100 plus organization tax on authorized shares
3. Franchise tax reports
4. Consent of the Tax Commissioner

A. Certificate of Incorporation (New Domestic Corporation)

Detailed information concerning what is required to be included in the Certificate of Incorporation can be obtained from the Department of State and the Business Corporation Law, Article 4 and Section 909.

The completed Certificate of Incorporation must be sent to the Dissolution Unit of the Tax Department.

The Certificate of Incorporation will not be accepted by the Secretary of State without the consent of the Tax Commissioner to the dissolution of the old corporation.

B. Filing Fee

A certified check, cashier's check, attorney's check or money order payable to the Department of State in the amount of $100 plus organization tax on authorized shares must accompany the Certificate of Incorporation.

C. Franchise Tax Reports

The Tax Commissioner will not give its consent to the termination by disposition of assets until all franchise tax reports are filed and all taxes paid.

Please refer to Part I, Voluntary Dissolution, item C, for additional information.

D. Consent of the Tax Commissioner

The consent of the Tax Commissioner to the termination will be supplied by the Dissolution Unit.

To qualify for the consent, the corporation which is to be dissolved must file franchise tax reports and pay all franchise taxes for each fiscal or calendar period (or part of a fiscal or calendar period) from the date of incorporation to the date of termination.

If all requirements are not met and if the Certificate of Incorporation is not accurate, the filing of the certificate may be delayed, resulting in additional taxes.

E. Summary

1. Mail all the forms and checks listed in items a through c below to:

    Dissolution Unit
    Corporation Tax
    State Campus
    Albany, NY 12227

    a. Certificate of Incorporation.

    b. Filing fee of $100 plus organization tax on authorized shares.

    c. Franchise tax reports.

2. Upon receipt of the certificate, the filing fees and any franchise tax reports that may be due, the Dissolution Unit will provide the Tax Commissioner's consent to the termination and forward the proper forms to the Department of State.

3. The documents will be reviewed by the Secretary of State and if the forms are acceptable, the Certificate of Incorporation for the new corporation will be filed. The existing corporation will be automatically terminated 30 days after the incorporation of the new corporation.

PART V
TERMINATION OF EXISTENCE—
FOREIGN CORPORATIONS
(Business Corporation Law—Section 1311)

Section 1311 of the Business Corporation Law provides for the termination or Surrender of Authority of a foreign corporation authorized to do business in New York which has been terminated in the state of its incorporation by dissolution, merger or consolidation with another foreign corporation.

Forms and fees required:

1. Certificate of Termination
2. Filing fee of $60

A. Certificate of Termination

This certificate, issued by the Secretary of State or an equivalent official of the state or country of incorporation, attests to the termination, dissolution, merger or consolidation of the corporation.

B. Filing Fee

Payment in the amount of $60 (sixty dollars) must accompany the certificate, order or decree. The check must be made payable to the Department of State and must be certified.

Mail the certificate, order or decree and the certified check to:

> Department of State
> 162 Washington Avenue
> Albany, NY 12231

The filing of such a certificate, order or decree by the New York Secretary of State shall have the same effect as the filing of the Certificate of Surrender of Authority under Section 1310 of the Business Corporation Law.

The Secretary of State will notify the Tax Commissioner of the termination.

It is not necessary for the Tax Commissioner to consent to the Surrender of Authority. However, the Tax Commissioner does require the corporation to file tax reports and pay all taxes due for each fiscal or calendar period that the corporation is active in New York State. Any unpaid tax is a lien until paid.

PART VI
LIQUIDATION UNDER INTERNAL REVENUE CODE
(IRC Sections 332, 333, 334 and 337)

A domestic corporation liquidating all corporate assets under Sections 332, 333, 334 and 337 of the Internal Revenue Code which no longer wishes to retain its charter may be voluntarily dissolved. Refer to Part I of this form for the details of a voluntary dissolution.

New York business corporations choosing to retain their charter will continue to be subject to franchise taxes for each fiscal or calendar period of their existence.

Foreign corporations liquidating all corporate assets are not generally subject to tax after the liquidation.

Foreign corporations which have been authorized by the Secretary of State may choose to surrender authority to do business. Refer to Part II of this form for details.

PART VII
DISSOLUTION BY PROCLAMATION
(New York Tax Law Article 9, Section 203-a
Business Corporation Law—Section 1009—
"Dissolution of a Corporation for
Delinquent Taxes")

A domestic corporation which has failed to file required franchise tax reports or pay franchise taxes due for two consecutive years may be dissolved by the Secretary of State upon recommendation by the State Tax Commissioner. A corporation is *not* automatically dissolved after two or more years of delinquency. The dissolution by proclamation procedure is *not* a substitute for voluntary dissolution and will result in substantial penalties against the corporation.

Once dissolved, the corporation loses the benefits of incorporation and may no longer legally use its corporate name. Any assets of the corporation remain subject to tax liens. Taxes, additional charges of up to 47 1/2 percent and interest continue to accrue. The interest rate should be determined in accordance with Part 603 of the Tax Regulations.

If assets are transferred at the time of or prior to dissolution to an officer, stockholder, partnership or unincorporated business, all accrued taxes, additional charges and interest may be assessed and collected from the transferee.

On or before the last day of March, June, September or December in each calendar year, the Tax Commissioner sends to the Department of State a certified list of domestic stock corporations recommended for dissolution by proclamation. The Secretary of State makes a proclamation under his seal of office declaring such corporations dissolved and their charters forfeited. The original proclamation is filed in the office of the Secretary of State. A copy is published in the *New York State Register* no later than three months following receipt of the list. Upon publication of the proclamation, each corporation named is deemed dissolved without further legal proceedings.

PART VIII
ANNULMENT OF AUTHORITY BY PROCLAMATION
(New York Tax Law, Article 9, Section 203-b—
"Annulment of Authority to do Business for
Delinquent Taxes and/or Fees")

A foreign corporation authorized to do business in New York State which has failed to file the required franchise tax reports or to pay franchise taxes and/or maintenance fees for two consecutive years may have its authority annulled by the Secretary of State upon recommendation by the State Tax Commissioner.

A foreign corporation subject to tax under Article 9-A, Section 209.1, would continue to be liable for franchise reports and franchise taxes even though its authority was annulled.

On or before the last day of March, June, September or December in each calendar year, the Tax Commissioner sends to the Department of State a certified list of authorized foreign corporations recommended for annulment of authority to do business by proclamation. The Secretary of State makes a proclamation under his seal of office declaring the authority of a corporation to do business in this state annulled. The original proclamation is filed in the office of the Secretary of State. A copy is published in the *New York State Register* no later than three months following receipt of the list. Upon publication of the proclamation, each corporation named shall be deemed to have had its authority annulled without further legal proceeding.

PART IX
SALES TAX CONSEQUENCES OF CHANGES IN CORPORATE STRUCTURE

If your corporation does business in New York State and its corporate status is terminated in any manner, including voluntary dissolution, you should be aware of the sales tax consequences for corporations registered as sales tax vendors.

If your corporation disposes of any of its assets, or if its corporate status is terminated, refer to the "Bulk Sales Transactions" section that follows to determine whether these transactions require bulk sale notification.

If your corporation is dissolved or ceases to do business but does not dispose of its assets, it must still surrender its Certificate of Authority and pay any outstanding sales tax liability, as well as the sales tax on inventory or other taxable assets purchased tax-free. Failure to surrender a Certificate of Authority is a misdemeanor.

A. Bulk Sales Transactions

Every vendor who (other than in the ordinary course of business) intends to sell, transfer or assign in bulk all or any part of this business or business assets, including furniture, fixtures, equipment, merchandise inventory, land and buildings must give each prospective purchaser a copy of Form TP-153D, Notice to Prospective Purchasers of Business and Business Assets. This notice may be obtained from the New York State Department of Taxation and Finance, Taxpayer Assistance Bureau, W.A. Harriman Campus, Albany, NY 12227.

The purchaser of a business or business assets must notify the Tax Commissioner of the purchase by filing a Notification of Sale, Transfer or Assignment in Bulk (Form AU-196.10) at least ten days before taking possession of or paying for the business assets, whichever comes first.

As of September 1, 1985, anyone required to file a Certificate of Registration who takes possession of or pays for business assets in a bulk sale transaction without filing the certificate may be subject to a penalty of up to $200 plus any other penalties imposed by the Tax Law.

If you are going to be involved in a bulk sale transaction as either a seller or buyer, you should request the additional information contained in Regulation Part 537 and TSB-M-83(6)S.

F. SAMPLE PETITION FOR JUDICIAL DISSOLUTION UNDER BCL § 1104-a

SUPREME COURT OF THE STATE OF NEW YORK
COUNTY OF BONZO
------------------X

In the Matter of the Application of   Index No.
JOHN DOE AND WILLIAM DOE,

    Petitioners,

VERIFIED PETITION FOR
DISSOLUTION
For the Judicial Dissolution of

FLIBBERTIGIBBET FACSIMILE CORP.

    Pursuant to Section 1104-a of the
    Business Corporation Law.

------------------X

The petition of JOHN DOE and WILLIAM DOE, pursuant to Section 1104-a of the Business Corporation Law, respectfully shows to this Court and alleges:

1. FLIBBERTIGIBBET FACSIMILE CORP. (the "Corporation") is a domestic corporation duly organized and existing under and by virtue of the laws of the State of New York, having its principal place of business at 100 Main Street, in the County of Bonzo, State of New York.

2. The Corporation commenced doing business in the year 1945 and was and is engaged in the business of manufacturing and selling metal filing cabinets under the trade name "METAL FILES."

3. The Corporation is authorized to issue 5,000 shares of common stock and there are and have been issued 2,500 shares of its common stock which are owned and held by various persons.

4. The petitioners, JOHN DOE and WILLIAM DOE, are holders of more than 20 percent of the issued and outstanding common stock of the Corporation as follows:

JOHN DOE holds:	500 shares
WILLIAM DOE holds:	500 shares

Your petitioners hold and control approximately 40 percent of the common stock of the Corporation.

5. The Corporation is not registered as an investment company under the Federal Investment Company Act of 1940, as amended, and no shares thereof are listed on a national securities exchange or regularly quoted on an over-the-counter market.

6. Petitioners, pursuant to Section 1104-a of the Business Corporation Law of the State of New York, demand that the Corporation be dissolved for the reasons hereinafter set forth.

7. The Corporation was formed by JAMES DOE, petitioners' father, who died on ____, 19____. JOHN DOE, now 55 years old, was employed by the Corporation since it was formed and worked for it continuously until 19____; WILLIAM DOE, who is 47 years old, worked for it continuously from 19____ until 19____, when they were both discharged as hereinafter set forth.

The said JAMES DOE was the holder of 750 shares of the common stock in 19____, which constituted 30 percent of the capital stock of the Corporation; his wife, MARY DOE, the petitioners' mother, owned 250 shares or 10 percent; JAMES DOE, JR., the petitioners' brother, owned 250 shares, or 10 percent thereof; PAUL DOE, the petitioners' brother, owned 25 shares or 1 percent; the petitioners' sister, ALMERINDA "BABY" DOE, owned 50 shares or 2 percent, and other nonfamily members owned 175 shares, approximately 7 percent of the capital stock of the Corporation.

On or about ____, 19____, the Corporation entered into an agreement with JAMES DOE, a copy of which is attached hereto as Exhibit A, wherein and whereby it was agreed that the Corporation would purchase from his estate upon his death all of the shares of the common stock owned by JAMES DOE in the Corporation at the time of his death. The purchase price was to be based on one and one-half times the net worth of the Corporation divided by the number of the outstanding shares multiplied by the number of shares that he owned at the time of his death. The intention of this agreement was to ensure that upon their father's death, the petitioners would become the major stockholders of the Corporation since the corporate redemption of their father's stock would constitute your petitioners as the owners of the majority of the outstanding stock of the Corporation.

In _____ of 19____, their father, who had dominated and run the Corporation as he saw fit, suffered a paralyzing stroke. At the time, their father was the President and Petitioner JOHN DOE was the Treasurer and WILLIAM DOE was Secretary of the Corporation. We also were the sole directors of the Corporation. After their father had the stroke, the family decided to sell the business and actively sought a potential purchaser. At the time and for several years prior thereto, JOHN DOE earned an annual salary of $118,000, WILLIAM DOE earned a salary of $67,000 and their brother, JAMES DOE, JR., who was acting as a salesman, earned $38,000 per year.

For various reasons, the transaction with the purchaser of the business was not consummated, and this triggered a lawsuit with the purchaser that was waged over a four-year period and nearly wrecked the Corporation financially. Ultimately, the purchaser's action for specific performance was dismissed by the Trial Court and the judgment was affirmed by the Appellate Division, Second Department on ____, 19____.

When the litigation by the purchaser was commenced in 1973, your petitioners were in full charge of the Corporation and ran it on a daily basis. The expense of the litigation together with union problems with other employees, which had resulted in the plant being closed for six months, severely drained our income and left the Corporation in dire financial straits.

In order to protect the Corporation and keep it solvent, your petitioners agreed to temporarily reduce their salaries from the amounts above stated to $52,000 each until the Corporation could afford to pay us the previously earned salary. Their brother, JAMES DOE, JR., who performed no work and no services, was permitted to draw the same salary, which resulted in a $14,000 increase to him while we took a substantial reduction.

Your petitioners slaved long and arduous hours and scrimped and saved in order to restore the Corporation to financial health and put it back on a successful basis. As a result of our prodigious labors, your petitioners succeeded in putting the Corporation into the black and built sales up to more than $3,000,000 per year.

During all that time, their brother, JAMES DOE, JR., who was not performing any work and refused to do any work, was scheming with their brother, PAUL, and sister, ALMERINDA, to gain control of the Corporation. The latter two had absolutely no connection with the business of the Corporation at all; they did not perform any work for the Corporation.

Ultimately, their brother, JAMES DOE, JR., with the aid of PAUL and ALMERINDA, managed to maneuver their parents to give over their proxies so that JAMES DOE, JR., could gain control of the Corporation. He annoyed, harassed, cajoled, bullied and threatened their parents until he succeeded in forcing them to execute proxies in his favor.

In _____, 19____, a stockholders meeting was called by JAMES DOE, JR., PAUL and ALMERINDA for the election of directors. Based upon the proxies that had been executed by JAMES DOE, SR., and MARY DOE, JAMES DOE, JR., PAUL and ALMERINDA were elected directors. They then proceeded to elect JAMES DOE, JR., as President, PAUL DOE as Vice-President and ALMERINDA DOE as

Secretary. The election of directors was confirmed by this court on _____, 19____, and affirmed by the Appellate Division, Second Department on _____, 19____.

Virtually simultaneously with the takeover of the Corporation by JAMES DOE, JR., your petitioners were discharged by the Corporation and their employment terminated. Since that time, neither petitioner has been employed by the Corporation.

Subsequently, the new directors cancelled the agreement with JAMES DOE, SR., which provided for the redemption of his capital stock at the time of his death.

8. Since _____, 19____, your petitioners have not been employed by the Corporation, have had no voice in the management and operation of the Corporation, have not been consulted by the officers and the directors concerning any aspect of the business of the Corporation, have been denied access to and an examination of the books and records of the Corporation, have been barred from the premises of the Corporation under the threat of bodily harm, and have been completely frozen out of the business of the Corporation despite their substantial equity therein and their lifelong devotion to the business and affairs of the Corporation.

9. As a result thereof, the Corporation has been deprived and denied the services of the petitioners and of qualified and effective management of the Corporation and has been irreparably harmed and damaged by the hostility toward the petitioners by the Corporation's officers and directors, who have sacrificed the welfare of the Corporation and its stockholders for their own personal gain and self-aggrandizement.

10. It was the reasonable expectation of the petitioners and the other stockholders-members of their family, including their father, JAMES DOE, SR., that petitioners would be key employees of the Corporation, have a voice in the management and operation of the business of the Corporation, that upon the death of their father they would become the majority stockholders of this family-run Corporation and that they would derive substantial salaries as a result of their successful operation of the business, as well as from the dividends on their capital stock.

11. That relying upon the said reasonable expectations, the petitioners devoted their entire working lives to the business of the Corporation and were successful, good, efficient, devoted and loyal officers, directors and employees under whose control the Corporation prospered and made large profits. Notwithstanding the foregoing, in _____, 19____, your petitioners were improperly and unjustly discharged by the Corporation, severed from the business and removed as officers and directors, and as signatories of the corporate bank account, denied access to information concerning the operation of the Corporation and barred from access to the premises of the Corporation.

12. The action of the Corporation, its officers and directors toward the petitioners constitutes a freeze-out from the business and affairs of the Corporation, and the directors and those in control of the Corporation have been and are guilty of oppressive, harsh and wrongful actions toward the petitioners.

13. Liquidation of the Corporation is the only feasible means whereby the petitioners may reasonably expect to obtain a fair return on their investment.

14. Liquidation is reasonably necessary for the protection of the rights and interests of the petitioners.

15. Judicial dissolution is, therefore, warranted and required pursuant to Section 1104-a of the Business Corporation Law.

16. In the interim, an immediate appointment of a receiver is essential and mandated in order to prevent further oppressive, harsh and wrongful conduct by the Corporation, its officers and directors against the petitioners.

17. No previous application for the relief sought herein has been made to any other Court of Justice thereof.

WHEREFORE, Petitioners JOHN DOE and WILLIAM DOE respectfully request that the instant order to show cause be signed, that the **FLIBBERTIGIBBET FACSIMILE CORP.**, its officers and directors and stockholders show cause before this Court why it should not be dissolved and liquidated pursuant to the applicable provisions of Section 1104-a of the Business Corporation Law of the State of New York.

New York, New York

Dated: _____, 19____

_____
JOHN DOE

_____
WILLIAM DOE

STATE OF NEW YORK)
                         : ss.:
COUNTY OF BONZO)

JOHN DOE, being duly sworn, deposes and says:

That deponent is one of the two petitioners in the within action; that deponent has read the foregoing petition and knows the contents thereof; that the same is true to deponent's own knowledge, except as to the matters therein stated to be alleged on information and belief, and that as to those matters deponent believes it to be true.

JOHN DOE

Sworn to before me this
30th day of November, 1982

STATE OF NEW YORK)
                         : ss.:
COUNTY OF BONZO)

WILLIAM DOE, being duly sworn, deposes and says:

That deponent is one of the two petitioners in the within action; that deponent has read the foregoing petition and knows the contents thereof; that the same is true to deponent's own knowledge, except as to the matters therein stated to be alleged on information and belief, and that as to those matters deponent believes it to be true.

WILLIAM DOE

TABLE OF AUTHORITIES

CASES

Federal

Alexander v. Commissioner 411
American Bantam Car Co. v. Commissioner 111
Arkansas Best Corp. and Subsidiaries v.
    Commissioner............................. 149

Balla v. Gambro............................. 524
Bardahl Mfg. Corp. 406
Bart v. Commissioner......................... 149
Beneficial Corp. v. Commissioner 148
Brown v. Commissioner....................... 79
Buckley v. Valeo 27

Commissioner v. Donald E. Clark 302
Consolidated Edison Co. v. Public Service
    Commission 27
Corn Products Refining Co. v. Commissioner 149

DuPont v. United States....................... 69

Establishment Tomis, In v. Shearson Hayden
    Stone................................... 24
Essex Universal Corp. v. Yates.................. 258

Feldman v. Commissioner 63
First National Bank of Boston v. Bellotti 22, 27
Florida Machinery & Foundry Co. v. Fahs 111
Frentz v. Commissioner 63

Gardner v. Snyder 24
Grabowski Trust............................ 225
Grauman v. Commissioner 149

Haber v. Commissioner 78
Halley Bros. Const. Corp. v. Commissioner 54
Hardman v. Commissioner 152
Hauptman v. Director of Internal Revenue 63
Heller, Walter E. & Co. v. Video Innovations, Inc. .. 24
Hooper v. Commissioner 61

IBM v. Murray.............................. 525
Imler, Joseph W. 227

Lane-Wells Co............................... 403
LDS, Inc. v. Commissioner 152
Leib, Alden M. 467
Leve v. Commissioner 62
Lewis v. S.L.&E., Inc........................ 171

Millar v. Commissioner 78
Murphy Logging Co. v. United States 153

TABLE OF AUTHORITIES

Nash v. United States 114

Ober v. Commissioner 63

Paparo, Jack 225
Paramount Publix Corp., In re 167
Pearlman v. Feldman 258
Pepper v. Litton 23, 203
Perry v. Commissioner 78
Pike v. Commissioner 78
Plantation Patterns, Inc. v. Commissioner 153

Raich, Peter 112
Roesel v. Commissioner 76
Rothenberg v. Lincoln Farm Camp, Inc. 169

Schwartz v. Romnes 26
S.E.C. v. Liberty Banking Corp. 23
S.E.C. v. Texas Gulf Sulphur Co. 179
Segel v. Commissioner 152
Selfe v. United States 79
Shaffer v. Heitner 21
Shapero v. Kentucky Bar Ass'n 518
Speca v. Commissioner 76

United States v. Donruss Co. 405

Virginia State Board of Pharmacy v. Virginia Citizens
  Consumer Council, Inc. 22

Wilgard Realty Co. v. Commissioner 111

Zaretsky v. Commissioner 63
Zuckman v. United States 34

State

Delaware
Smith v. Van Gorkom 181,186

New York
Abberger v. Kulp 161
Adler v. Svingsos 207
Allen v. Biltmore Tissue 209
Alpert v. 28 William St. Corp. 203

Bartle v. Home Owners Co-op, Inc. 23
Beacher v. Gregg 258

Clark v. Dodge 207
Costello v. New York State Dep't of Taxation and Finance 429,430

D&W Central Station Alarm Co., Inc. v. Copymasters, Inc. 429
Diamond v. Oreamuno 180

Farega Realty Corp, In re 435
Farm Stores, Inc. v. School Feeing Corp. 24

TABLE OF AUTHORITIES 961

Gallagher v. Lambert 213
Goldenberg v. Bartel Broadcasting Corp. 166
Greenbaum v. American Metal Climax, Inc. 169
Gunzberg v. Art-Lloyd Metal Products Corp. 434

Imperatore, In re 435
Ingle v. Glamore Motor Sales 213

Kemp & Beatley, In re 434
Kreitner v. Burgweger 171

Lewis v. Jones 436
Litwin v. Allen 171
Lorisa Capital Corp. v. Gallo 430

Manson v. Curtis 207
Marian v. Mariani 171
Mayerson v. 3701 Tenants Corp. 169
McQuade v. Stoneham 207

Petraglia v. Whirlwind Music Distributors, Inc. 435
Powers v. Schlicht Heat Co. 166
Prentice Corp. v. Martin 430

Rafe v. Hindin 209
Raskin v. Walter Karl, Inc. 434
Rye Psychiatric Hospital Center v. Schoenholtz 190

Sasso v. Vachris 17

Sterling Industries, Inc. v. Ball Bearing Pen Corp. . . . 165

Taines v. Gene Barry One Hour Photo Process, Inc. . . 434
Triggs v. Triggs 207

Walkovszky v. Carlton 23
We're Associates Co. v. Cohen, Stracher & Bloom P.C. 24
Westview Hills, Inc. v. Lizau Realty Corp. 165
Wiedy's Furniture Clearance Center Co., In re 435

Zetlin v. Hanson Holding 258
Zion v. Kurtz 207

Texas

Griggs v. Capital Machine Works, Inc. 248

STATUTES

Federal

Bankruptcy Code (Title 11, United States Code) 259,265
Employee Retirement Income Security Act of 1974 ("ERISA") (Title 29, United States Code) 238,262,438, 490
Fair Labor Standards Act (Title 29, United States Code) 262
Federal Election Campaign Act (Title 2, United States Code) 26

TABLE OF AUTHORITIES

Hart-Scott-Rodino Antitrust Improvements Act
(Title 15, United States Code) 249

Internal Revenue Code of 1986 (Title 26, United States Code)

Section	1	36
	11	36
	11(b)	403, 418
	47(a)	68
	47(b)	68
	55	419
	55-59	36
	56(a)	419
	56(g)	419
	57(a)	419
	58	419
	61(a)	70
	63(a)	37
	83	108
	83(a)	109
	83(b)	108
	108(a)	70
	108(b)	70
	108(d)	70
	108(e)	70
	162	37
	163	298
	163(e)	151
	163(f)	151, 466

165	460
165(g)	79,148
165(j)	151
166(a)	149
166(d)	79
170	39,219,220, 488,491,501, 502,505
170(a)	39,491
170(b)	40
170(e)	40
172	38,67,151
172(b)	305
216(b)	146
243	39
243(a)	37
248	38
263(c)	219
265(a)	151
267	220,454
267(a)	69,148,151
267(b)	69
269	305
269A	403,407,408, 410,412
279	151,298
280G	467
291	69

291(a)	40
301	217,218
301(b)	222
301(c)	146,218,222
302	217,218,224, 227,297
302(a)	77
302(b)	225,226,227, 228,229,230, 231,232,233
302(e)	227
303	224,225,227, 228,229,230, 232,233
303(a)	77,228
303(b)	228,229
304	218,230,232
304(c)	232
305	222
306	218,230,231, 232,303,304
306(a)	231
306(b)	232
307	223
307(a)	230
311	222
312	219
312(b)	222
312(d)	223

312(m)	151
312(n)	229
316	217,218
316(a)	146
317	217,218,224
317(a)	76
318	69,224,225, 226,232,233
331	67,447,457
332	447,459,460
334	447,460
334(a)	458
336	447,453,455
336(a)	452
336(b)	453
336(d)	454,455
337	453
338	83,298,299, 300,447,452, 459,460,461
338(h)	299
341	416,458
341(d)	417,418
341(e)	418
346	227
351	42,107,108, 109,110,111, 113,114,454, 517

TABLE OF AUTHORITIES

351(a)	107
351(b)	107
351(d)	108
354	70,289,290, 293,295,296
355	70,231,284, 293,294,295, 296
356	70,288,289, 293,294,296
356(a)	302
357	107,111,112, 113
357(b)	111,112
357(c)	111,112,113
358(a)	108
358(d)	113
362(a)	108
367	286
368	231,232,284, 285,286,297
368(a)	283,287,288, 289,291,292, 293,294,295, 296,297,302, 451
368(c)	110,289,295
381	67,305,307
381(c)	305,307

382	291,305,306, 307,308
383	305,307
384	305,308
385	153
401(a)	491
414(a)	245
415(a)-(e)	56
416(g)	56
416(i)	56
444	71,72
444(a)-(d)	72
453	298,300,451
453(h)	447,458
465	44,75,409, 412
465(b)	411
465(c)	410,411
469	44,411,412
469(a)	75
469(c)	75
469(e)	75
469(h)	75,413
531	449
531-537	405
532(a)	405,450
533(a)	405
535(b)	406

TABLE OF AUTHORITIES

535(c)	450
537	406
541	450
542(a)	402
542(c)	404
542(d)	404
543(a)	402
543(b)	402
544	403
545	404, 450
547	405
564	404
565	404
581	54
585(a)	54
593	54
593(a)	54
616(a)	219
617	219
704(b)	43
752	43
904(f)	70
936(a)	55
936(d)	55
992(a)	55

1014	228
1014(a)	285
1031	475,478
1059	38
1211	39
1212	39
1221(1)	148
1239(b)	458
1244	75,79,148,150, 151,471
1245	40,297
1245(b)	113
1250	40
1250(d)	113
1274	147
1361(a)	52
1361(b)	52,53,54,55, 56,59
1361(c)	53,55,57,58, 59,61
1361(d)	58,59,80
1362(a)	52,59,61
1362(b)	64
1362(c)	62
1362(d)	66,67,79,80, 81
1362(e)	83
1362(f)	82

TABLE OF AUTHORITIES

1362(g)	63
1363(a)	64
1363(b)	69
1363(c)	71
1363(d)	66, 70
1363(e)	70
1366	79
1366(a)	73
1366(b)	73
1366(c)	74
1366(d)	74, 82
1366(e)	76
1366(f)	75
1366(g)	71
1367	77, 79
1367(a)	74, 75, 78
1367(b)	74, 78, 79
1368	78
1368(b)	76
1368(c)	77
1368(e)	68, 77, 78
1371(b)	42, 73
1371(d)	68
1371(e)	83
1372	70

1373	70
1374	75,455,456
1374(a)	64
1374(b)	66
1374(c)	64,66
1374(d)	64,65,66,68
1375	75
1375(b)	68
1375(c)	65,68
1375(d)	68
1377(a)	74
1377(b)	82
1378	71
1504(a)	53,299
1551	407
1561	407
1563	454
1564	407
4701	151,466
4971	467
4972	467
4973	467
4974	467
4975	467
4976	467
4979	467
4980	467

TABLE OF AUTHORITIES 973

4999	467
6041	147
6049	147
6241	71, 73
6242	73
6245	71
6601	407
6659	499
6660	499
6662	499, 500, 501
6664	500
6901	247
7519	72
7701	33
7701(a)	55
7872	147
Revenue Act of 1987 (Title 26, United States Code)	49, 308
Revenue Reconciliation Act of 1989 (Title 26, United States Code)	420
Robinson-Patman Act (Title 15, United States Code)	328
Securities Act of 1933 (Title 15, United States Code)	313, 327, 330
Securities Exchange Act of 1934 (Tile 15, United States Code)	88, 172, 258
Section 12	162
12(b)	313
12(g)	313

16(a)	173,177
16(b)	177,178
16(c)	178
Subchapter S Revision Act of 1982 (Title 26, United States Code)	49
Tax Reform Act of 1984 (Title 26, United States Code)	491
Tax Reform Act of 1986 (Title 26, United States Code)	49,229,230, 299,300,305, 447,453,488
Tax Reform Act of 1989 (Tilte 26, United States Code)	499

New York State

Abandoned Property Law
Section	500-504	442
Business Corporation Law		117
Section	102(a)(1)	118,139
	102(a)(6)	138
	102(a)(10)	22,92
	102(a)(14)	124
	104	87,92
	107	101
	201(a)	25
	202	22,94,424
	202(a)	26,101
	203	25,94

TABLE OF AUTHORITIES

301	87,91
302	88
303	21,90
304	93
305	93
401	19,92
402	16,19,25,92, 93,94,96,251, 252,396
402(a)	25
402(b)	185
403	21
404	98
404(a)	158,159
405-407	93
501	117,118
501(c)	118
502	119
502(d)	119
503(a)	120
503(b)	120
503(d)	121
504	100,121,124, 139
504(a)	122,139
504(b)	122
504(c)	123
504(d)	123

504(e)	124
540(f)	122
504(g)	140
504(h)	123
504(i)	121,123,125
505	125
505(a)	124
505(a)(2)	126
505(d)	19,124
505(e)	121,125,388
505(f)	121,125
505(g)	125,126
505(h)	125
506(b)	127
506(c)	127
507	127
508	388
508(a)	127,128
508(c)	128
508(e)	129
508(f)	128
509(a)	129
509(b)	130
509(c)	130
509(d)	130
510	19,130,197, 198

TABLE OF AUTHORITIES

511	131
511(a)	122
511(c)	132
511(f)	132, 133
511(g)	132, 133
512	133
512(c)	133
513	136, 210
513(a)	134, 136
513(e)	135
514	134, 136
515	136, 137
515(c)	137
516	127, 137
516(a)	394
516(b)	138
517	138
517(a)	138
517(a)(2)	138
517(a)(4)	138
517(a)(5)	137, 138
518	139
518(a)	139
518(c)	139, 390
519	139

519(e)	140
520	131,137,389
601	196
601(a)	96
601(c)	96
602	97
602(a)	189
602(b)	189
602(c)	190
603	97,190
604	192
605	190,249
606	190
607	192
608	190
609	191,192
609(b)	20
609(f)	211
609(h)	388
610	193
611	193
612	94
612(a)	194
613	94
614	94
615	20,195

TABLE OF AUTHORITIES

616	94,190,191, 249
616(c)	194,388
617	94
618	94,194
619	195
620	158,208
620(a)	192,208,211
620(b)	95,208
620(f)	208
620(g)	388
621	211
621(a)	211
621(d)	212
622	94,198
622(e)	198
623	20,135,199,200, 201,250,257, 398,434
623(g)	200
623(j)	201
623(k)	200,201,204
624	100,197
624(a)	386
624(b)	389
624(e)	389
624(g)	100
626	202

626(e)	202
627	202
628(a)	123,438
628(b)	124
630	17,20,438
630(a)	438,440
701	158,159,206
702	159,160
702(b)	160
703(a)	159
703(b)	160
704	99,159
705(c)	160
706	196
706(a)	161,195
706(c)	161
707	162
708	94,98
708(c)	163
709	94
709(a)	162
709(b)	162
709(c)	162,388
710	162
711(c)	162
712	20,164
712(a)	163

713	388,395
713(a)	171
713(b)	171
713(c)	171
714	172
715	166,169
715(c)	167
715(d)	167
715(e)	166
715(h)	170
716(b)	167
717	169,170,185
718	389
719	185
719(a)	172
720	185
721	181,182,183, 184
721 to 726	20
722	183
722(a)	182,183
722(b)	182
722(c)	183
723	184
723(a)	183

723(b)	183
723(c)	183
724	184
725(d)	182
801	395,424
801(b)	396,424
802	137
802(b)	394
803	196
803(a)	397
803(b)	396,397
804	397
805	397
805-A	397,398
806(b)	204,257,397,398
807	396
807(a)	397
807(b)	398
808	398
901	250,256
901(a)	251
902	254,256
903	20,197,256
903(a)	251,252

TABLE OF AUTHORITIES

903(b)	252
904	252,256
904(a)	252
904(b)	253,255
905	253,256,257
905(a)	253
905(b)	253
905(c)	253
905(d)	253
906(a)	253
906(b)	253
907	254,256
907(b)	254
907(c)	257
907(d)	254
907(e)	254
907(f)	254
907(g)	254
907(h)	255
909	20,197,199, 255
909(a)	255
909(b)	255
909(d)	255,256,427
909(e)	255,256,427

909(f)	255
910	257
910(a)	204
912	250
913	256,257
913(e)	256
913(f)	256
913(g)	256
1001	20,424,426
1002	424
1002(a)	424
1002(b)	424
1002(c)	388,424
1003	256,426,427
1004	427
1005(a)	439,440,441
1005(c)	442
1006	439
1007	439
1007(a)	439
1007(b)	439
1007(c)	440
1007(d)	440
1008	439
1101	428
1101(a)	428
1102	394,436

TABLE OF AUTHORITIES

1103	431
1103(a)	431, 432
1103(b)	431
1104	432
1104(a)	432
1104(b)	433
1104(c)	433
1104-a	433, 434, 435, 436
1105	436
1106(a)	437
1106(c)	437
1107	437
1109	437
1111(a)	437
1111(b)	433, 437
1111(c)	438
1111(d)	438
1115	437
1116	437
1118(a)	434
1118(b)	434
1301	18
1312	18
1317-1320	18

Civil Practice Law and Rules
    Section   503(c) 22
                    3020-3023 436

Election Law
    Section   14-116 26

General Associations Law
    Section   2 14
                    7-a 15

General Business Law
    Section   130 3,4
                    130(3) 4
                    130(8) 4
                    130(9) 4
                    132 3

General Obligations Law
    Section   5-701(10) 242

Judiciary Law
    Appendix 509, 526

Partnership Law
    Section   82 4
                    90 et seq. 6
                    90 to 115-c 11
                    91 7
                    91(b) 7
                    94 7
                    95 7
                    99 7

TABLE OF AUTHORITIES

	108	7
	109	8
	115-a	7
	120	9
	120-1	9
	120-101 to 121-1300	9
	121-102	10
	121-110	11
	121-201	10
	121-201(c)	10
	121-303	13
	121-303(a)	13
	121-303(d)	13
	121-501	12
	121-902(d)	10
	121-1002	13
	121-1003	13
	121-1101 to 121-1104	13
	121-1201	11
	121-1202	11
Penal Law		
Section	175	388
Tax Law		
Article	9	478
	9-A	469

	11	476
	12	476
	28	472
	31	477
	31-B	248, 474
Section	186-a	478
	203-a	387, 428, 430
	208 et seq.	469
	209(8)	50
	250 et seq.	476
	270 et seq.	476
	275-a	102
	612	50
	632(a)(2)	50
	660	50
	1101 et seq.	472
	1141	247
	1141(c)	246
	1400 et seq.	477
	1441 et seq.	474

Uniform Commercial Code

Section	6-104	246
	8-204	81, 209
	8-408	129

TABLE OF AUTHORITIES

ADMINISTRATIVE MATERIALS

Federal

Internal Revenue Service
    Announcement 86-128, 1986-51 I.R.B. 27 66,456
    Form   88-60, 1988-15 I.R.B. 47 456
              966 461
              1096 461
              1099-DIV 461
              2553 61,62,469
              8283 492
              SS-4 102
Private Letter Ruling   7716014 81
                              7748034 81
                              9009010 58
                              9010042 57
                              9015024 58
                              9017025 58
                              9018045 60
                              9044003 60
Revenue Procedure
              76-22, 1976-1 C.B. 562 ... 109
              77-37, 1977-2 C.B. 568 ... 286
              79-24 240
              87-32, 1987-28 I.R.B. 14. . 72
              89-12 44

Revenue Ruling	59-60, 1959-1 C.B. 237...	240,487,490, 491,492,494, 495,505,506
	59-84, 1959-1 C.B. 71....	303
	63-234, 1963-2 C.B. 148..	289
	67-274, 1967-2 C.B. 141..	291
	67-448, 1967-2 C.B. 144..	290
	68-55, 1968-1 C.B. 140...	108
	73-478, 1973-2 C.B. 310..	60
	73-496, 1973-2 C.B. 312..	54
	75-261, 1975-2 C.B. 350..	62
	77-37, 1977-2 C.B. 568...	291
	77-220, 1977-1 C.B. 263..	56
	77-287	490
	77-479, 1977-2 C.B. 119..	303
	80-236, 1980-2 C.B. 240..	78
	83-120	240,490
	86-141, 1986-2 C.B. 151..	65
	89-12, 1989-1 C.B. 319...	34
	89-55, 1989-1 C.B	59

Technical Information Release No. 113
(Nov. 26, 1958) 55

Securities and Exchange Commission

Form	3	175,176,177
	4	173,174,176, 177,314
	5	175,176,177
	8-K	313

TABLE OF AUTHORITIES

	10	313
	10-K	177,313
	10-Q	177,313
Regulation	S-K	329,390
Rule	144	144
Schedule	13D	314
	13G	314

Treasury Department

Regulation	1.355-1	294
	1.351-1(a)	109,110
	1.351-1(b)	111
	1.368-1(c)	286
	1.368-1(d)	286
	1.368-2(e)	296
	1.368-3	287
	1.537-2(b)	450
	1.1361-1A(d)(Proposed)	53,54
	1.1361-1A(e)(Proposed)	55,60
	1.1361-1A(f)(Proposed)	56,57
	1.1361-1A(h)(Proposed)	57
	1.1361-1A(i)(Proposed)	58,59,80
	1.444-1T(Temporary)	72
	1.7872-4(d)(Proposed)	147
	18.1362-1(a)(Temporary)	61
	18.1362-2(a)(Temporary)	61

18.1362-2(b)(Temporary)	61,62
18.1362-2(c)(Temporary)	62
18.1362-3(Temporary)	79
18.1377-1(Temporary)	74
301.6241-1T(Temporary)	71
301.6245-1T(Temporary)	71

New York State

Tax Commission—Rules

New York Code of Rules and Regulations Vol. 20

1-11	472
400-404	477
440-447	476
502	479
525-541	474
575	478
590	475

Tax Commission—Forms

Form	CT-6	469
	MT610.1	102
	ST-150	474

Tax Commission—Publications

Publication 880	473

New York City

New York City Administrative Code

Section	11-601 et seq.	50,479

TABLE OF AUTHORITIES

11-701 et seq.	480
11-1101 et seq.	482
11-2001 et seq.	480
11-2101 et seq.	481
11-2601 et seq.	482

OTHER

American Bar Association

Code of Professional Responsibility 509,510,511, 514,518,519, 520,521,522, 526,527

Disciplinary Rule	2-104	518
	2-107	520
	3-101	522
	4-101	511
	6-101	510,511,520
	7-104	521
Ethical Consideration		
	6-2	511
	6-3	520
	7-3	519
	7-8	511,519
	7-9	519
	9-2	511

Model Rules of Professional Conduct 509,510,511, 512,513,514,

Rule	1.1	....	515,519,520, 521,522,524, 526,527 510
	1.3	....	511
	1.4	....	511
	1.5(e)	....	520
	1.6	....	511,512
	1.13	....	513,515
	1.13(b)	....	514
	1.13(c)	....	513
	1.13(e)	....	513
	2.1	....	518,519
	2.3	....	519
	4.1	....	521
	4.2	....	521,522
	5.5	....	522
	7.3	....	518,519

Bittker, B. and Eustice, J. *Federal Income Taxation of Corporations and Shareholders* 145,401

Commerce Clearing House, Inc., *Guidebook to New York Taxes* 465

Craig, *The ACE Adjustment to AMSI: An Update*, 68 Taxes 206 (1990) 420

Germain, *Techniques of Drafting Acquisition Agreements* (NYSBA Course Materials, 1984) ... 270

Haynsworth, *The Professional Skills of the Small Business Lawyer* 516,523

TABLE OF AUTHORITIES

Kury, *Acquisition Checklist*, 36 Bus. Law 207 (1981)..................................... 263

Lipper, *Venture's Guide to Investing in Private Companies* 517

Mason & Horne, *The Passive Activity Loss Rules and Closely Held Corporations*, 26 The Tax Adviser 280 (1990) 414

New York State Department of Taxation and Finance, Publication 110.......................... 427

Plumb, W., *The Federal Income Tax Significance of Corporate Debt: A Critical Analysis and a Proposal*, 26 Tax. L. Rev. 369 (1971) 152

O. Tilevitz, *"Condopping" a Co-op*, 69 Taxes 558 (1991)..................................... 146